Reviews of the first edition

"Nothing is passed over ... Unreservedly recommended."

Jazz Journal International

"An excellent guide, brimming with richness and variety that will be of immense value to experienced blues collectors, as well as students of popular music, popular culture and American studies. A thorough index and brief bibliography complete this superb reader/reference. It is an informative survey that is apt to become a standard for many years to come."

Come-all-ye

"Thoroughly recommended to anybody and everybody who has an interest in the blues."

British Blues Review

"Essential for the beginning blues collector, the long-time record fiend can still find much to enjoy here."

Tempo

D1373473

THE NEW BLACKWELL GUIDE TO
Recorded Blues

EDITED BY

John Cowley and Paul Oliver

Copyright © Blackwell Publishers Ltd 1996

First published 1996

Morse Mus. Ref
ML
156.4
B6
B6
1996

2 4 6 8 10 9 7 5 3 1

Blackwell Publishers Ltd
108 Cowley Road
Oxford OX4 1JF
UK

Blackwell Publishers Inc.
238 Main Street
Cambridge, Massachusetts 02142
USA

All rights reserved. Except for the quotation of short passages for the purposes of criticism and review, no part of this publication may be reproduced, stored in a retrieval system, or transmitted, in any form or by any means, electronic, mechanical, photocopying, recording or otherwise, without the prior permission of the publisher.

Except in the United States of America, this book is sold subject to the condition that it shall not, by way of trade or otherwise, be lent, resold, hired out, or otherwise circulated without the publisher's prior consent in any form of binding or cover other than that in which it is published and without a similar condition including this condition being imposed on the subsequent purchaser.

British Library Cataloging in Publication Data

A CIP catalogue record for this book is available from the British Library.

Library of Congress Cataloging-in-Publication Data

The new Blackwell guide to recorded blues/edited by John Cowley and Paul Oliver.
p. cm.
Rev. ed. of: The Blackwell guide to recorded blues.
ISBN 0-631-20163-7.—ISBN 0-631-19639-0
1. Blues (Music)—Discography. 2. Blues (Music)—History and criticism. I. Cowley, John, 1947–. II. Oliver, Paul, 1927–
III. Blackwell guide to recorded blues.
ML156.4.B6B6 1996
016.781643'0266—dc20 96–12140
CIP
MN

Typeset in Times on 10/12 pt by Acorn Bookwork
Printed in Great Britain by Hartnolls Ltd, Bodmin, Cornwall

This book is printed on acid-free paper

APR 15 1996
00011

Contents

Contributors

BRUCE BASTIN is the Managing Director of Interstate Music Ltd and has issued many records of blues and jazz on several labels. He is the author of numerous articles and of the books *Crying for the Carolinas* (1971) and the award-winning *Red River Blues: the blues tradition in the Southeast* (1986).

JOHN BROVEN is a former editor of *Blues Unlimited* and *Juke Blues* and currently works for Ace Records. In addition to publishing articles, he is the author of *Walking to New Orleans: the story of New Orleans rhythm and blues* (1974) and *South to Louisiana: the music of the Cajun bayous* (1983).

NORM COHEN is the author of *Long Steel Rail: the railroad in American folk song* (1981) and *Traditional Anglo-American Folk Music: an annotated discography of published recordings* (1994), editor of an abridged edition of Vance Randolph's *Ozark Folksongs* (1982). He has been recordings review editor for the *Journal of American Folklore* and *Western Folklore*, and was editor of the *JEMF Quarterly*.

JOHN COWLEY has worked in publishing and for the Civil Service. He is the author of *Carnival, Canboulay and Calypso: traditions in the making* (1966) and a contributor to *Black Music in Britain* (1990), *Songs about Work*, and *Nothing but the blues* (1993). His articles have been published in such journals as *Blues & Rhythm*, the *Journal of Folklore Research, Musical Traditions*, and *Popular Music*.

DAVID EVANS is Professor of Music at the University of Memphis, where he directs a doctorate program on Southern Regional Music Studies. He writes for scholarly and popular journals, and is author of *Tommy Johnson* (1971) and *Big Road Blues: tradition and creativity in the folk blues* (1982). He produces High Water Records.

PAUL GARON is a partner in Beasley Books, Chicago. Formerly a consulting editor of the journal *Living Blues*, he is the author of *The Devil's Son-in-Law: the story of Peetie Wheatstraw and his songs* (1971), *Blues and the Poetic Spirit* (1975, 1979) and, with his wife Beth, *Woman with Guitar: Memphis Minnie's blues* (1992).

BOB GROOM was the editor of *Blues World* from 1965 to 1974 and is a contributor to the major journals on blues. The author of *The Blues Revival* (1971), Groom is currently researching a book on the theme of war and conflict in African-American music.

MICHAEL HARALAMBOS began his working life in Liverpool, playing blues and soul music. His research in anthropology at the University of Minnesota formed the basis for his book *Right On: from blues to soul in black America* (1974, 1994). He has since written sociological textbooks and formed a publishing company.

MARK HARRIS is an architect living in London. He was founder and editor of Scotland's only blues magazine *Pickin' the Blues* (1982–84) and is now review editor for *Juke Blues*.

DAPHNE DUVAL HARRISON is a Professor and Chair of the Department of African-American Studies at the University of Maryland, Baltimore County. She has published articles on black women and jazz, and is the author of *Black Pearls: blues queens of the 1920s* (1988).

PAUL OLIVER writes and lectures on vernacular architecture. His books on African-American music include *Blues Fell this Morning* (1960, 1990), *Conversation with the Blues* (1964), *The Story of the Blues* (1969), *Savannah Syncopators* (1970), *Songsters and Saints* (1984), and *Blues off the Record* (1984). He also edited *Black Music in Britain* (1990).

DAVE PENNY is on the editorial board of *Blues and Rhythm* and is responsible for discographies in that magazine. Specializing in post-war blues and jazz, he contributes to British and American journals devoted to these subjects.

MIKE ROWE became editor of *Blues Unlimited* in 1975, having been a contributor since 1963. He is author of *Chicago Breakdown* (1973, 1981), a history of blues in Chicago, and is researching a book on Sippie Wallace.

DICK SHURMAN has been active as a record producer, journalist, collector, and disc jockey in the USA and around the world for more than 25 years. Based in Chicago, he is an administrator of a library computer network. He is a frequent contributor to blues publications.

Abbreviations

(used in discographical lists for countries of origin)

Au	Austria
Belg	Belgium
Dan	Denmark
Fr	France
Ger	Germany
Jap	Japan
Neth	Netherlands
Swe	Sweden
UK	United Kingdom

PRINCIPAL BLUES LOCATIONS
SOUTH-WEST AND WEST COAST
Reno
NEVADA
Oakland
San Francisco
UTAH
COLORADO
Fresno
KANSAS
CALIFORNIA
Las Vegas
Bakersfield
OKLAHOMA
Oklah City
Los Angeles
ARIZONA
Albuquerque
San Diego
Phoenix
NEW MEXICO
Wichita Falls
Red Riv
El Paso
Fort Worth
Rio Grande
TEXAS
Waco
Austin
San Antonio
Houst
Richmon
MEXICO
PACIFIC OCEAN

PRINCIPAL BLUES LOCATIONS
EASTERN UNITED STATES AND MISSISSIPPI VALLEY
0 100 200 300 400 500
Scale in miles
WISCONSIN
Port Washington
Milwaukee
Mississippi River
Lake Michigan
MICHIGAN
Detroit
Lake Erie
NEW YORK
Rochester
PENNSYLVANIA
Philadelphia
New York
Pittsburgh
Cleveland
Chicago
Gary
ILLINOIS
INDIANA
OHIO
Columbus
Cincinnati
Indianapolis
Baltimore
Washington D.C.
MARYLAND
East St Louis
St Louis
Kansas City
WEST VIRGINIA
Richmond
Lynchburg
VIRGINIA
Louisville
KENTUCKY
MISSOURI
Durham
Raleigh
NORTH CAROLINA
Nashville
Knoxville
TENNESSEE
Charlotte
Brownsville
Jackson
Memphis
ARKANSAS
Little Rock
Helena
Chattanooga
SOUTH CAROLINA
ATLANTIC OCEAN
Clarksdale
MISSISSIPPI (Delta)
Birmingham
Atlanta
Pine Bluff
Texarkana
Yazoo City
ALABAMA
GEORGIA
Macon
Statesboro
Charleston
Sea Islands
Savannah
Sea Islands
Shreveport
Jackson
Montgomery
LOUISIANA
Natchez
Mobile
Tallahassee
Jacksonville
Lake Charles
Baton Rouge
Hattesburg
Crowley
Galveston
New Orleans
FLORIDA
Gulf of Mexico

PAUL OLIVER AND JOHN COWLEY

Introduction

As editor of the original editions of *The Blackwell Guide to Blues Records* and *The Blackwell Guide to Recorded Blues* I welcome this opportunity to add a personal word of appreciation to all the contributors, some of whom have joined us for this revision. Through the exchange of lists and discs we have debated at length the merits of every recommended item.

When a new edition to cover compact discs was proposed by Blackwell I was very enthusiastic, but other commitments prevented me from devoting the time to editing that I had been able to spare previously. John Cowley's attention to detail and extensive files, coupled with his publishing experience, were well known to me. They made him the ideal co-editor and I was delighted when he accepted the invitation to share the editorial direction of this exacting work. As it turned out, his was by far the greatest burden. It is due to John's assiduous research and patient editing that this new edition is the dependable work that you will find it to be.

All the team have enjoyed selecting these CDs and we are sure that you will obtain equal pleasure from listening to them and building your collection.

PAUL OLIVER

If the major influence on popular music in the first half of the 20th century was jazz in its various manifestations, including swing, since the 1950s the greatest influence has been blues. This might be reason enough for listening to blues recordings, but this music, which is as varied in style as jazz, has attracted a large following. Today, any specialist dealer in blues records will list some 3,000 or so CDs; the number currently available throughout the world is likely half as many again, probably more. In over 30 years of issues of long-playing records devoted to the subject, many thousands of records have been deleted from the catalogs, some to be reissued, some to become rare collectors' items. This trend has continued with the compact disc. Most established collectors find this vast amount of recorded blues difficult to comprehend, let alone purchase, and they soon "specialize" in a

"Negro" boy playing phonograph, Louisiana, 1939 (*Russell Lee/FSA/Library of Congress*)

particular aspect of the music. For the newcomer to the blues the abundance of issues is even more confusing.

The New Blackwell Guide to Recorded Blues has been compiled to meet an obvious need: a clear indication of the best examples of blues records in each of a number of broad categories. To do this a team of American and British writers has been brought together, each of whom has a reputation for expertise in a particular branch of the music and a record of publication in the form of books, articles, discographies, or reviews. It is the team's intention to make the book as useful as possible to both new and experienced blues collectors and to students of popular music, popular culture, and American studies.

A number of decisions had to be made in order that the book should fulfill its function as a *Guide*, and these may require a few words of explanation. As with the first edition, one of the greatest difficulties, provoking the largest exchange of correspondence, was whether or not to include white blues singers. As the *Guide* is developed largely along historical and stylistic lines, it was decided that coverage should be given to early white vernacular American music that was influenced by and existed alongside similar black traditions. Chapter 9 has been added accordingly. From the mid-1960s blues has been emulated by white players, sometimes performing together with black musicians. This, however, is a very complicated development with world-wide implications, and requirements of space and time have precluded attention here.

Another problem arose from consideration of the aspects to be covered in each of the chapters. As noted above, blues may be subdivided into a number of categories. Some of these have been widely employed, even if they are far from precise. Mississippi blues, "Classic" blues, boogie woogie, R&B (rhythm and blues), for example. Broadly, these follow the areas identified in *The New Grove Gospel, Blues and Jazz*, though contributors have sometimes chosen to define them further and this is reflected in the chapter titles.

Some of the differences in categories have been the result of external influences on the music itself, such as changes in the recording industry and the introduction of electric instruments, or fieldwork arising from research in blues history. Many styles of blues have existed in parallel, but there is a general historical sequence, which the *Guide* follows, commencing with kinds of music prevalent at the beginning of the century and continuing to the present. There is more than one way to slice a cake, and the team is aware of the risk that some aspects of the subject might be given more or less attention than is their due. But, by way of frequent mutual advice it is hoped that any imbalances have been minimized.

By far the greatest problem confronting the contributors has been selection. While every writer could draft a list of a few hundred items, limiting these to numbers that would not overwhelm the reader and thus defeat the purpose of the *Guide* proved difficult. A newcomer to the field, a collector with a specialized interest desiring to acquire a broader knowledge, or a librarian wishing to stock a representative collection of blues could be expected to invest in a hundred or so CDs. Contributors have therefore selected ten records which they consider to be essential to their category, making a total of 140 Essential Records. To supplement these, in each chapter a further 30 Basic Records are listed to provide fuller coverage for the listener who wishes to go deeper into the subject. Certain issues are packaged in sets of two, three, or even four CDs, and cannot be obtained separately. Two- and three-CD sets rate as one entry in the lists. Generally, sets of four or more CDs are classed as two entries and have been selected on grounds of the singular availability of essential recordings. Such entries have been kept to a minimum and their inclusion is a reflection of the CD era. A purchaser of the entire collection of Essential and Basic Records would be the possessor of some 560 discs.

Availability of records is always difficult for the collector. Many of the best releases may be issued only in the Netherlands, Austria, or Japan; records may not be repressed when stocks are low, or may be withdrawn from the lists as the result of contractual arrangements. There are, however, specialist dealers in the United States and most Western countries who publish frequent catalogs of records that may be purchased by mail order. These usually include foreign releases and, not infrequently, bargain purchases. All items incorporated in the Essential Records lists were available in 1995. A small number (i.e. up to 20 percent, or not more than six in any one list) of records deleted from current catalogs have been admitted in the Basic Records lists, with preference given to the most likely to be reissued. Issues listed are assumed to be of United States origin unless they are followed by an abbreviation indicating another source. Exact equivalent releases from other countries are given where known.

Many of the CDs recommended are "anthologies" or "collections". The terms have been borrowed from literature and poetry, but in blues they are used synonymously. A "blues anthology" is a varied collection of recordings by different artists. It is generally selective as being the "best" of its kind, though the criteria for selection are seldom made explicit. Some collections are selected from the catalog of a particular recording company, or group of companies, and are in their copyright as a result of past recording activity or deals with other "labels" (as the issues of a recording company are often termed). Some may be leased from a parent company to a lessee company, while others may not be officially leased. These latter are often termed "bootleg" issues, which means that they have been used without permission, though their age and the uncertainties of ownership means that they may not be violating any known rights.

Another group of anthologies, legitimate or bootleg, comprises those that have been compiled with a specific purpose, or within deliberate constraints. They may demonstrate the virtuosity of specific instrumentalists – guitarists, pianists, or harmonica players for example. Or they illustrate the recordings of a particular "school" or group of musicians, or are representative of a period, such as the early 1950s. Another group may serve as "samplers" demonstrating the range of music available within the catalog of one company.

The rarity of many 78rpm originals from which performances have been copied means that some items that are musically good have been reissued with poor surface noise. When better copies have been discovered, these sometimes appear on subsequent compilations. Productions that include all known titles by an artist, arranged chronologically in recording session order, have recently become the norm for some types of releases.

It is apparent that anthologies are compiled with a number of intentions not necessarily evident to the new collector. There is also considerable overlap of chosen artists, and often of the specific recordings that they made.

When recommending the anthologies that we consider to be important for both the new and experienced collector we have drawn on all the types of collections, and attempted to avoid duplication of specific recordings as far as possible. However, it should be understood that some duplication is unavoidable.

The majority of recorded blues, on original 78rpm, microgroove and CD releases, are issued under the name of a single artist. Usually this is a singer, who may be self-accompanied on guitar or piano, or backed up by one or two instrumentalist, or sometimes a big band. The reasons for this are varied: as in many fields of artistic endeavor the "cult of the personality" places special emphasis on the creative individual. But there are also commercial interests in recording, where the companies wish to "build up" the desirability of their records, and of their blues artists. There is also an emphasis on individual expression intrinsic to blues, both in content and in performance style, which performers may cultivate.

When 78s were issued with only two titles on each record it was possible to contrast the paired recordings. But sometimes the personal mannerisms of specific blues singers or musicians become familiar through repetition. This can annoy some listeners; for others it is part of the attraction of the blues which makes the creative work of each performer distinct. Some collectors specialize in the recordings of a limited number of artists whose songs they particularly enjoy. A few of these may be quite obscure, but often there are singers who are greatly respected by their peers and who also have considerable appeal for contemporary listeners, or who are regarded as typifying or otherwise representing a regional or musical style. All this means that certain names become very familiar and appear frequently on CD reissues, while other performers of great interest and quality become overlooked in the process.

Some blues singers in the 78rpm era recorded prolifically, and reissues reflect this with several CDs documenting their work. In general, artists who recorded after the introduction of the LP were encouraged to record sufficient titles for one long-playing record; this trend has continued with the CD. In compiling their lists contributors have maintained a balance between anthologies or collections, and single artist or group releases.

The criteria for inclusion or exclusion of a record have been many. In the first place that choice has been made by a writer with special interest in the chapter theme, and this personal knowledge and taste is evident in every case. While recordings that are considered to be of high, even outstanding, musical quality have been chosen, they have also been selected as being representative of a particular facet of the subject. Whereas a number of records within a narrow compass could be listed, breadth has been considered as more important, resulting in the enlarging of the field and the number of performers. In several cases the same singer appears in more than one list; generally this is so that earlier and later aspects of their work may be illustrated, though sometimes it is simply an indication of their importance, or even their longevity as a recording artist.

Perhaps the most noticeable disparity between the Essential Records and the Basic Records is the respective lengths of the descriptive texts. Obviously, many readers will not be very familiar with the subject, or with some aspects of it and this is recognized in the extended essays in which the Essential Records are discussed. The essays take the form of discursive commentaries which explain the importance of the CDs and the artists, evaluate the performances, place them in context, and often give their historical background. Other features such as the absence of surface noise, the quality of the notes or booklets, the use of illustrative material such as photographs or ephemera, and the accuracy of discographical data, may also be taken into consideration, though inadequate packaging or the lack of notes has never been a reason for exclusion. The same criteria apply to the choice of Basic Records, but only brief notes are appended, summarizing content, relevance and points of special interest.

Essential information is entered: names of artists, titles of recordings, record labels and numbers, together with their country of origin, are followed by the list of individual items. As a general rule, these reflect the details (often discrepant with those given on the original recording) as cited on the relevant CD, LP, or cassette; in the interest of clarity, minor adjustments have occasionally been made or editorial comments added. Excepting alternative recordings in the same compilation, discographical details have been omitted—recording dates, full lists of personnel, matrix and take numbers, and original issue numbers. This information is available in published discographies, which are cited in our list of Recommended Reading; the instruments played by blues artists whose records have been listed or who are mentioned in the text are given in the Index.

Collectors of blues share characteristics in common with collectors in many other fields. Among these is a tendency to specialize: some try to obtain every record made by a single artist, while others seek all the issues of a particular label. Some collectors have a preference for a period, a region, or a style, and though their quarry becomes increasingly rare and expensive, they may try and obtain through purchase, "auctions" and trading, the original issues (often on 78rpm discs) of the recordings. Early 45rpm issues and 10- or 12-inch long-playing records ($33\frac{1}{3}$ rpm) are also eagerly sought. We are assuming that the collector who uses this volume as a *Guide* will be seeking and enjoying blues as music and song only, at least at first. We also assume that the preferred form of reproduction is through CDs.

Unfortunately, by no means all the records that the authors believe to be the most important are available on CD; in many cases they may have been issued or reissued from 78rpm only on LP. Rather than omit these we have recommended some long-playing discs, hoping that the reader may be able to obtain them and also perhaps to encourage recording companies to release them on CD. Similarly, certain significant recordings are available currently only on cassette and these are listed using the same criteria. Such items do not represent more than 10 percent of the Basic Records in each chapter, and none are listed among the Essentials.

With the wealth of vernacular and popular music currently available on CD, as work progressed on this revision we thought it might be helpful to place the music in a broad-based context. Accordingly, we have added an introductory chapter that looks at the subject in a different perspective to the rest of the *Guide*. This provides a sampling of related recordings.

JOHN COWLEY AND PAUL OLIVER

I Recorded Blues: Considerations and Contexts

(i) Precursors and Parallel Traditions

Like any other music, blues does not, and did not, exist in a social or musical vacuum. It did not spring up suddenly, without precursors or anticipations, and it did not arise without reference to, or reflecting, the lives and milieu of those who first created it. It is helpful for anyone who is coming new to the blues to have a sense of its history.

So what came before the blues? Though all the musical and social currents that helped shape the blues have not been traced with certainty, a number are evident. The problem is that as the recording of blues did not take place until the 1920s, when the music was perhaps a quarter of a century old, we have little recorded evidence of its precedents. One form of black song that was significant from the 1880s was performance in close harmony. The technique paralleled and perhaps was cross-influenced by "barbershop quartet" singing in the white communities, though black vocal quartets and quintettes drew from a distinctive repertoire. Among the earliest to be recorded are reissued on **The Earliest Negro Vocal Groups: Volume 2** which covers the period from 1893 until 1922, when blues by women singers had recently become the fashion among black purchasers. As the anthology demonstrates, the earliest quartette recordings were generally religious in character. Secular themes, however, were present in the repertoire and, once blues became popular on record they were soon taken up by groups such as the Excelsior Quartette. Their sessions of 1922 include very early versions of familiar blues lyrics such as *Kitchen Mechanic* and *Jelly Roll Blues*.

Early 19th-century observers had noted that the singing of slaves on Southern plantations usually took a leader and chorus form, with little singing in parts or in harmony. Though the process of change is undocumented, close harmony may have arisen in part from Jubilee Singing, or the presentation of spirituals, "anthems" and plantation songs on the concert stage, which was a feature of the popularization of African-American culture after the Civil War.

The tours of the Fisk Jubilee Singers, the Hampton Jubilee Singers and other vocal ensembles were intended to raise financial and moral support for the emergent black universities. Such choirs and vocal groups travelled to Europe and beyond, while early recordings stimulated local initiatives as far away as South Africa. Blues and Jazz were not the only direction that black music might have taken in the Reconstruction period and its aftermath. The achievements of blues and jazz and, at the same time, their relationship to other African-American music forms are more clearly recognized when heard in the context of traditions that preceded and paralleled their development. Of these, Carnival in the West Indies and one of its offspring, Trinidad calypso bear close comparison. **Trinidad Loves to Play Carnival** documents the later stages of music and song traditions whose origin can be traced to 17th-century Caribbean plantations. *Kalendas* sung in French creole (patois) became the songs of Trinidadian stick-fighting bands whose defiance of authority led to their being vigorously controlled by the early 1910s. Nonetheless, Jules Sims' recording of *Bagai Sala Que Pocheray Moin* made in 1914, gives a strong indication of the rhythmic complexity of its African roots. Calypso was heavily indebted to this music; a song form with staggered rhythms and verse structures often boastful or taunting in content when singers, accompanied by bands playing bamboo or string instruments, challenged each other as in *Don't Break It I Say* by King Radio, The Tiger and The Lion. Calypsonians often took on "power names" and this collection includes representative examples of the aggressive, witty and heroic calypsos of The Black Price, The Atilla [*sic*], The Growler and The Executor, among others for whom competitive singing parallels the substitution of cricket matches for stick-fighting. In the 1930s Calypsonians became popular in New York, but there were other African and Caribbean musics of the late 19th and early 20th centuries whose growth and maturation was concurrent with the blues. Some of these are exemplified in the Basic Records.

In the United States, a close contemporary of blues in its formative years was ragtime, a piano music which may have arisen from imitations of rural and minstrel banjo playing. A distinct genre which has been the subject of several scholarly studies, it was regarded as a composed form by its principal exponents. Ragtime is characterized by a succession of "strains", some of which are repeated in a sequence within the total composition. Ragtime performances have a steady pulse with a quick release of the keys, and particular use of syncopation, or accented off-beats. Best known of the ragtime composers was Scott Joplin, born in Texas though a leading figure in the "school" of ragtime performers centered on Sedalia, Missouri. Published in 1897, Joplin's *Maple Leaf Rag* was a remarkable success and initiated a score of years of ragtime musical publications. Late in life, around 1910, he cut piano rolls of this and several more of his rags, some of which appear on **Original Ragtime Classics From The Original Piano Rolls.**

Ragtime swept through the States at the turn of the century, with local "schools" emerging. Among the most significant was the "stride" style of such pianists associated with Harlem, New York, as Eubie Blake, James P. Johnson, and Thomas "Fats" Waller, who cut piano rolls in the early 1920s. Meanwhile, in New Orleans, Jelly Roll Morton was one of the jazz pianists who had assimilated ragtime, adapting and improvising on its themes. Representative examples of rags by these artists are included on the CD. Many of the ragtime pianists also played blues and comparisons may be made between Eubie Blake's *Fare Thee Honey Blues*, Morton's *Tom Cat Blues* and *Mr. Freddie Blues* played in Chicago by the youthful Jimmy Blythe. Blythe was typical of the saloon players who explored the bass figures that anticipated boogie woogie. By this time ragtime had been long popular in Europe and was even adopted indirectly by African vocal groups.

Essential Records

1 **The Earliest Negro Vocal Groups: Volume 2 (1893–1992)**
Various Artists
Document DOCD 5288 (Au)
Unique Quartette, *Mamma's Black Baby Boy*; The Standard Quartette, *Every Day'll Be Sunday Bye And Bye*; Dinwiddie Colored Quartette, *My Way Is Cloudy*; Afro-American Folk Song Singers, *Swing Along/The Rain Song*; The Right Quinttete, *Exhortation/Rain Song*; Lieut. Jim Europe's Singing Serenaders, *Exhortation (Jubilee Shout)/Little David Play On Your Harp/ Ev'rybody Dat Talks 'Bout Heaven Ain't Goin' There/Roll Jordan Roll*; Lieut. Jim Europe's Four Harmony Kings, *Swing Low, Sweet Chariot/One More Ribber To Cross*; Excelsior Quartette, *Kitchen Mechanic Blues* (70568)/*Roll Them Bones/If Hearts Win Tonight, You Lose/Good-Bye, My Coney Island Baby/Jelly Roll Blues* (7827)/*Kitchen Mechanic Blues* (7828)/*Nobody Knows The Trouble I See/Going Up To Live With God (Golden Slipper)/Walk in Jerusalem Just Like John/I Am The King Of The Sea/Good Lord I Done Done/ Sinners Crying, Come Here Lord/Coney Island Babe/Jelly Roll Blues* (BS 2060)

2 **Trinidad Loves To Play Carnival: Carnival, Calenda and Calypso From Trinidad 1914–1939**
Various Artists
Matchbox "Calypso Series" MBCD 302-2 (UK)
Jules Sims, *Native Trindad Kalenda [Bagai Sala Que Pocheray Moin]*; King Radio, *Texilia*; King Radio, The Tiger, The Lion, *Don't Break It I Say*; The Atilla, *La Reine Maribone*—Calypso Patois; The Lion, *Ancient Carnival*; The

Atilla, *Fire Brigade*—Kalendar/*Man Man Biscoe*; The Black Prince, *The Bamboo Band*; The Caresser, *Clear The Way When The Bamboo Play*; Lord Invader, *Ten Thousand To Bar Me One*; The Growler, *In The Morning*; The Lion, *Man, Man, Man Peter*; Wilmoth Houdini, *Constantine*; Keskidee Trio, *Sa Gomes' Emporiums*; Lord Executor, *The Bells*; Carnival's Vagabonds, *We Want Sa Gomes*; The Lion, *Sa Gomes' Emporiums*; Wilmoth Houdini, *Good Night Ladies And Gents*—Paseo/*Executor Doomed To Die*; King Radio, The Tiger, The Lion, *War*; The Atilla, The Lion, The Executor, The Caresser, *War*; The Executor, *They Say I Reign Too Long*; The Caresser, *Carnival Is We Bachanal*; Lord Beginner, *After The Bacanal*; The Growler, *Trinidad Loves To Play Carnival*

3 **Original Ragtime Classics From The Original Piano Rolls**
Various Artists
Charly Classic Jazz CDCD 1086 (UK)
Scott Joplin, *Maple Leaf Rag/Something Doing/Weeping Willow Rag/Ole Miss Rag/Magnetic Rag*; Eubie Blake, *Charleston Rag/It's Right Here For You/Fare Thee Honey Blues*; Jelly Roll Morton, *Shreveport Stomp/Tom Cat Blues*; James P. Johnson, *Steeplechase Rag/Twilight Rag*; Fats Waller, *Got To Cool My Doggies Now/Nobody But My Baby (Is Gettin' My Love)*; Jimmy Blythe, *Mr. Freddie Blues/Regal Stomp*

(ii) Blues in History

Barrelhouse-style playing was occasionally evident in the gospel music of the Sanctified churches, as on *God's Got A Crown* by Arizona Dranes, a spirited blind young woman pianist from Texas. It is included in a sampler **The Beauty Of The Blues**. The basis for improvisation when playing for dancing, barrelhouse was an influence on the evolution of piano blues. It continued after ragtime virtually stopped being published once blues compositions became popular during World War I. The sampler concludes with a majestic version of *St. Louis Blues*, which was written in 1915 by W.C. Handy and was one of the first composed blues to be published. It includes a tango passage, evidence of his awareness of contemporary music genres from other parts of the African-American World. The singer was the great "Classic" blues singer Bessie Smith, accompanied by the brilliant New Orleans trumpet player Louis Armstrong and a harmonium. She also sang *Nobody's Business If I Do* which had been collected "in the field" early in the century. Her expressive delivery and capacity to exert every ounce of meaning from her songs made Bessie Smith an ideal artist for the stage. On black vaudeville and traveling companies she shared the boards with artists like Coot Grant and Wesley "Kid Sox" Wilson who (as Hunter and Jenkins) perform wry duets and exchanges.

This collection also contains lively dance songs like Buddy Woods' *Don't Sell It*, accomplished folk blues such as Memphis Minnie's *I*

Hate To See You Go, effortless guitar playing by Lonnie Johnson and the white jazz musician Eddie Lang on *Hot Fingers*, and even an item by Amédée Breaux—a white Louisiana Cajun—*Vas Y carrement*. There are memorable examples of traditional 12-bar blues including the opening title, Robert Johnson's *Traveling Riverside Blues*. In this as in other tracks the listener may be drawn to the passionate expression of the blues as well as the quality of musicianship. Often the initial appeal of the music is aesthetic, a response to the unconventional but highly emotive syntheses of voice, instrument, and poetic content.

Whereas the collection demonstrates by contrast both the variety and beauty of the blues, the relationship of the singers in time, place, or function is confusing. To assist in a fuller understanding of the background to this music **The Story Of The Blues** was compiled, being originally intended to accompany an historical study of the blues under the same title.

One question that is asked by all who are interested in the subject is: "If blues was primarily the music of black Americans in its formative years, how much did it owe to slavery, and to Africa?" The problem of lack of contemporary recorded evidence is even greater here than with the precursors of blues in the United States. The inclusion of *Yarum Praise Songs* by Ghanaian griots, or praise singers' performing in a village in the 1960s, however, points to musical and tonal relationships between the blues, and string music and vocal quality in West African savannah music.

An introductory section gives examples of proto-blues songsters like Mississippi John Hurt and Blind Willie McTell. Through recordings by the seminal figures of Charley Patton, Blind Lemon Jefferson and Peg Leg Howell, among others, it also shows how blues developed with different rhythmic foundations and vocal or instrumental coloration in the Mississippi valley, Texas and the South-west, and in south-eastern states such as Georgia. Most of these singers and their contemporaries also performed music for dances and entertainment at country suppers. Barbecue Bob from Georgia, the Mississippi Jook Band and the Memphis Jug Band all amused the crowds with vocal exchanges and novelty instruments, while on the stages of tent shows or theatre circuits, singers like Lillian Glinn or Butterbeans and Susie aroused their audiences with their power and humor.

On record at any rate, some of these forms were held in suspension during the Depression years. Urban blues, however, which reflected the spirit of the times, as in Leroy Carr's melancholy piano blues, or made direct reference to social conditions, like Peetie Wheatstraw's *Good Whiskey*, or Casey Bill's ironic *W.P.A. Blues*, cemented a bond between singers and their audiences. Later in the 1930s the down-home blues of a Robert Johnson or a Bukka White were evidence of continuing rural traditions. Further west in Kansas City, blues shouter Joe Turner and pianist Pete Johnson were on the threshold of the boogie-woogie "craze" by 1938, while during World War II there was a forceful renewal of the blues with the increasing popularity of Chicago musicians like Big Bill Broonzy and Sonny Boy Williamson who led small groups. They prepared the way for the last creative phases of blues as singers like Elmore James and Johnny Shines electrified the Mississippi traditions in northern clubs. Compressed though such a survey must be, it provides an historical framework for detailed elaboration and qualifications, which is broadly followed in the chapter sequence of this *Guide*.

Our understanding of blues, especially in its formative stages and early history, is inevitably conditioned by what is available on records. This places considerable importance on phonograph discs. Though enjoyment of blues on record does not depend on textual information about the singers and their records, the authors know from their own experience and that of a great many other collectors that there is much pleasure to be gained from knowing more about the circumstances in which the records were made. Over a span of several decades some "discographers" (those who study and list information on record issues) have specialized in blues, gospel, and other forms of black secular and sacred music. Generally, they will list the name of the artist (singer or musician) as it appears on record. This will include nicknames and pseudonyms, as well as variants in spelling. A great many performers are accompanied by associates, and these are also identified. Sometimes this is speculative, for recording companies may have kept inadequate files, or would not disclose them; or the files have been lost. So discographers have to deduce some of the information they supply, or simply enter "unknown" where a musician remains anonymous.

From this information we learn how singers relate to each other, with whom they worked and recorded, and who were perhaps influenced by them; we discover how local traditions can be identified, and learn more about conventional and improvised instruments that have been used. We also learn a great deal about the activities of those folklorists who have recorded blues and related music "in the field". Most commercially recorded blues have been issued and their catalog numbers are given in the discographies. For the 78rpm era, so are the matrix numbers which list the supposed *order* of recording, which is generally not the same as the sequence in which they were released. These also reveal missing items and, occasionally, these rare previously unissued items have been recovered from the companies, or have been traced elsewhere and made available.

It may seem that all the work on discography has been completed but this is not the case; collectors find they have bits of information which helps fill out the picture, and some actively hunt for old (if sometimes worn) 78rpm records which may add to our knowledge. There have been remarkable finds often a lifetime after the records were made; some so recent in fact, their discovery has followed release of "complete" sets on CD. **"Too Late, Too Late": Volume 2** is a collection (one of several) which includes previously unknown or unheard sides, as well as "alternate" (alternative) "takes", or versions of the same item recorded at an identical session.

One of several such collections, **Volume 2** has recordings which anticipate blues discs by 15 years or more, including *Pour [Poor] Mourner, Turkey In The Straw* and *Way Down Yonder In The Cornfield*, black songs which date from before the Civil War. Previously unreissued, the Booker Orchestra's *Salty Dog* is one of a precious few recordings made of black string band music at its rip-roaring best. Exceptionally rare recordings, of which only sole copies are known to exist, include *"Toby" Woman Blues* by Gene Campbell and *Ground Hog Blues* No. 2 by fellow Texas guitarist Ramblin' Thomas. Other rarities and alternative takes by such singers as Moses Mason, Kansas Joe McCoy with Memphis Minnie, Josh White, Bo Carter and Lonnie Johnson enrich our knowledge of these artists, though some collectors may be more excited by good copies of Ma Rainey's *Traveling Blues* and *I'm Goin' Home* by Charley Patton. Such discoveries add to our appreciation and understanding of the currents which contributed to the mainstream of the blues. By comparing alternative takes of recordings we also learn more about the creative process of blues singers.

4 **The Beauty Of The Blues: Roots N' Blues Sampler**
Various Artists
Columbia CK 47465/468768-2 (UK)
Robert Johnson, *Traveling Riverside Blues*; Blind Sammie [Blind Willie McTell], *Southern Can Is Mine*; Amédée Breaux, *Vas Y Carrément [Step It Fast]*; Buddy Woods With The Wampus Cats, *Don't Sell It (Don't Give It Away)*; Willie 'Long Time' Smith, *Homeless Blues*; Big Three Trio, *Signifying Monkey*, Lonnie Johnson; *No More Troubles Now*; Big Bill Broonzy, *Horny Frog* Hunter & Jenkins [Coot Grant & Socks Wilson], *Lollypop*; Lonnie Johnson & Eddie Lang, *Hot Fingers*; Blind Boy Fuller, *You've Got Something There*; Memphis Minnie, *I Hate To See The Sun Go Down*; Arizona Dranes, *God's Got A Crown*; Bessie Smith, *Tain't Nobody's Bizness If I Do*; Big Joe [McCoy] & His Washboard Band, *If You Take Me Back*; Bill McKinley [Jazz Gillum], *Is That A Monkey You Got*?; Bessie Smith, *St. Louis Blues*

5 **The Story Of The Blues: A Documentary History of the Blues Compiled by Paul Oliver**
Various Artists
Columbia 468992-2 (UK)—*2 CD set*
DISC ONE—THE ORIGINS OF THE BLUES: Fra-Fra Tribesmen, *Yarum Praise Songs*; Mississippi John Hurt, *Stack O' Lee Blues*; Blind Willie McTell, *Travelin' Blues*; Charley Patton, *Stone Pony Blues*; Blind Lemon Jefferson, *Black Snake Moan*; Leadbelly, *Pig Meat Papa*; Texas Alaxander, *Broken Yo-Yo*; Peg Leg Howell, *Broke And Hungry Blues*; BLUES AND ENTERTAINMENT: Barbecue Bob & Laughing Charlie [Lincoln], *It Won't Be Long Now*; Henry Williams & Eddie Anthony, *Georgia Crawl*; Mississippi Jook Band, *Dangerous Woman*; Memphis Jug Band, *Gator Wobble*; Bessie Smith, *In The House Blues*; Lillian Glinn, *Shake It Down*; Bertha "Chippie" Hill, *Pratt City Blues*; Butterbeans & Susie, *What It Takes To Bring You Back (Mama Keeps It All The Time)*

DISC TWO—THE THIRTIES, URBAN AND RURAL BLUES: Leroy Carr [& Scrapper Blackwell], *Midnight Hour Blues*; Faber Smith [& Jimmy Yancey], *East St. Louis Blues*; Peetie Wheatstraw, *Good Whiskey Blues*; Casey Bill Weldon [& Black Bob], *W.P.A. Blues*; Bo Carter, *Sorry Feeling Blues*; Robert Johnson, *Little Queen Of Spades*; Bukka White, *Parchman Farm Blues*; Memphis Minnie, *Me And My Chauffeur Blues*; WORLD WAR II AND AFTER: Blind Boy Fuller [& Sonny Terry], *I Want Some Of Your Pie*; Brownie McGhee, *Million Lonesome Women*; [Big] Joe Williams [& Sonny Boy Williamson], *Wild Cow Moan*; Big Bill Broonzy, *All By Myself*; Joe Turner [& Pete Johnson], *Roll 'Em Pete*; Otis Spann, *Bloody Murder*; Elmore James, *Sunnyland*; Johnny Shines, *I Don't Know*

6 **"Too Late, Too Late": Volume 2—More Newly Discovered Titles & Alternate Takes (1897–1935)**
Various Artists
Document DOCD 5216 (Au)
Cousins & De Moss, *Pour [Poor] Mourner*; Jim Jackson, *Jim Jackson's Affinity* [Negro Vaudeville Sketch]; Unknown, *Turkey In The Straw* [Negro Shout]; Male Quartette, *Way Down Yonder In The Cornfield*; Blind Blake, *West Coast Blues* (alternate take)/*Come On Boys Let's Do That Messin' Around* (take 1); Booker Orchestra, *Salty Dog*; Brantley & Williams, *Big Fat Mamma*; Rev. Moses Mason, *John The Baptist* (take 1)/*Go Wash In The Beautiful Stream* (take 2); Ma Rainey, *Traveling Blues* (take 2); Charley Patton, *Lord I'm Discouraged*/*I'm Goin' Home*; Gene Campbell, *"Toby" Woman Blues*/*Turned Out Blues*; Lonnie Johnson, *Jelly Killed Old Sam*/*The Faults Of All Women And Men*; Kansas Joe [McCoy], *I'm Going Crazy*/*Dresser Drawer Blues*; Ramblin' Thomas, *Ground Hog Blues* No. 2/*Little Old Mamma Blues*; Joshua White, *Broad Players Blues*/*Big House Blues*; Bo Carter, *Backache Blues* (82610)/*Nobody Knows My Baby*; Kokomo Arnold, *Policy Wheel Blues* (alternate take)

(iii) Jazz and Blues

Traditionally, New Orleans has been regarded as the birthplace of jazz. And though the number of blues singers known to have played and sung in New Orleans before World War II is rather less than in several other cities in the South, such as Memphis or Atlanta, a few recorded with jazz orchestras in their home city. The jazz musicians, playing in particular lead trumpet or clarinet, developed techniques which imitated the sound quality of the blues singers' voice—wailing, croaking, rasping, or "talking," with the aid of mutes and unconventional lip pressure. The combination of singers and jazz musicians playing blues is heard to singular effect on the New Orleans collection **Sizzling The Blues** made on location between 1927 and 1929.

Though Genevieve Davis was not of the first rank of blues singers, she had a sharpness of tone and directness of delivery which was associated with singers from up-river in St Louis. She was given solid backing by Louis Dumaine's Jazzola Eight, who provided a straight cornet lead, but clarinetist Willie Humphrey and trombonist Earl Humphrey wove effectively around the vocal on *I Haven't Got A Dollar To Pay The House Rent Man.* Supplementary vocals were provided by Leonard Mitchell, banjo player with the band, while pianist Morris Rouse played forcefully, backed by percussion. The band was trimmed to a quartet to provide the accompaniment to the husky voiced Ann Cook, a notorious prostitute from "the District," who sang the autobiographical *Mama Cookie.* Other tracks in this collection do not include vocals, but the playing of both black and white New Orleans musicians demonstrates how blues permeated much jazz expression, notably on Sharkey Bonano's solo modeled on King Oliver's in *Dippermouth Blues* and the fluent clarinet work of Sidney Arodin on several titles. Arodin also played on the excellent titles with trumpet player Lee Collins and tenor saxophonist David Jones with their Astoria Hot Eight.

Many jazz musicians who left New Orleans for Chicago and New York, or who traveled with the road shows and toured the theater circuits, were soon accompanying blues singers. Gertrude "Ma" Rainey, Ida Cox, and Victoria Spivey were just a few of the numerous "Classic" singers whose recordings were enriched by the orchestras of Fletcher Henderson or Louis Armstrong, while "house bands" like Lovie Austin's Blues Serenaders would be fired by the blues playing of a Tommy Ladnier. However, the technology scarcely existed for the recording of live events, made while bands were working a club or dance dates.

There is no doubt that, throughout its history, blues has been influential on other musical genres. Of these, arguably the most important and the earliest was jazz. How well and with what depth of feeling and expression a jazz musician can play the blues has always been a criterion of quality in this music in its various forms. Whether blues preceded jazz, whether it was assimilated by it, or whether it was inherent in the music is a matter of debate. While the two musics have developed independently and alongside each other, there has been a measure of crossover, with blues singers sometimes singing a few titles with jazz groups, and jazz bands or units from them accompanying blues singers in road shows or on record.

Both jazz and blues performers entertained in a variety of settings, dependent on particular audiences, and represent a diversity of black musical traditions developed for disparate functions. For the blues singers who performed with small jazz units, these were tent shows and burlesque theaters, or more sophisticated venues. Other—generally string-based musicians—might participate in medicine shows, entertain at rural dances, or play on street corners.

In the United States, markets were both compartmentalized and racially segregated from the beginning of the boom for "race records" (as they were called originally). This "boom" is recognized to have begun with Mamie Smith's recording of Perry Bradford's *Crazy Blues*, which she cut for OKeh Records in 1920. This marketing trend continued until after World War II, but began to change in the late 1930s as African-American musical culture became better known to a wider audience. Two key moments in this process were the "From Spirituals To Swing" concerts held at Carnegie Hall in New York in 1938 and 1939. Organized by John Hammond, an enthusiastic journalist, promoter, and record producer, it was the first of these events that sparked the popularity of boogie woogie (with performances by Albert Ammons, Meade Lux Lewis, and Pete Johnson) and introduced other aspects of black secular and sacred music to a white audience.

Hammond privately recorded each concert, or concert performer, but it was not until many years later that these recordings were released on LP and subsequently on the Music Memoria CD: **From Spirituals To Swing**.

The title of Hammond's concerts indicates the breadth of repertoire represented at these events. In addition to the music of the Boogie Woogie Trio (Ammons, Lewis, and Johnson), blues was represented by many performers who are now well known. These include Sonny Terry (vocal/harmonica), Big Bill Broonzy (vocal/guitar), and three famous vocalists—Ida Cox, Helen Humes, and Big Joe Turner. There was gospel music from Mitchell's Christian Singers and the Golden Gate Quartet, plus instrumental blues from jazz-based units and a representative sample of contemporary swing. In all, the high quality of the musicianship and live settings mark this collection as an epitome of the time and a representative sample of the extent of black musical traditions in the era before World War II.

7 **Sizzling The Blues; Recorded In New Orleans 1927–1929**
Various Artists
Frog DGF 5 (UK)
Genevieve Davis, *I Haven't Got A Dollar To Pay The House Rent Man* (take 1)/*I Haven't Got A Dollar To Pay The House Rent Man* (take 2)/*I've Got That Something* (take 1) [duet with Leonard Mitchell]/*I've Got That Something* (take 2) [duet with Leonard Mitchell]; Louis Dumaine's Jazzola Eight, *Pretty Audrey/ To-Wa-Bac-A-Wa/Franklin Street Blues* [Leonard Mitchell, vocal]/*Red Onion Drag*; Ann Cook, *Mama Cookie* (take 1)/*Mama Cookie* (take 2)/*He's The Sweetest Black Man in Town*; Johnny Miller's New Orleans Frollickers, *Panama/Dippermouth Blues*; Monk Hazel & His Bienville Roof Orchestra, *Sizzling The Blues/High Society/Git-Wit-It/Ideas* [Monk Hazel, scat vocal]; Jones & Collins Astoria Hot Eight, *Astoria Strut/Duet Stomp* [Al Morgan, scat vocal]/*Damp Weather* (take 1)/*Damp Weather* (take 2)/*Tip Easy Blues* (take 1)/ *Tip Easy Blues* (take 2)

8 **From Spirituals To Swing**
Various Artists
Music Memoria 34007 (Fr)—*2 CD set*
DISC ONE (December 23, 1938): Pete Johnson, Meade Lux Lewis, Albert Ammons, *Cavalcade Of Boogie*; Joe Turner, Pete Johnson, *It's All Right Baby*; Mitchell's Christian Singers, *What More Can My Jesus Do?/My [Poor] Mother Died A-Shouting*; Sonny Terry, *Mountain Blues*; Sonny Terry, Bull City Red, *New John Henry*; James P. Johnson, *Mule Walk/Carolina Shout*; New Orleans Feetwarmers, *Weary Blues/I Wish I Could Shimmy Like My Sister Kate*; Big Bill Broonzy, *Done Got Wise/Louise, Louise*; Count Basie Trio, *I Ain't Got Nobody*; Members of the Basie Band, *Don't Be That Way/Mortgage Stomp*; Helen Humes, *Blues With Helen*; Count Basie Band, *One O' Clock Jump/Blues With Lips/Rhythm Man*

DISC TWO (December 24, 1939): Golden Gate Quartet, *Gospel Train/I'm On My Way*; Ida Cox, *'Fore Day Creep/Low Down Dirty Shame*; Kansas City Six, *Paging The Devil/Good Morning Blues/Way Down Yonder In New Orleans*; Benny Goodman Sextet, *I Got Rhythm/Flying Home/Memories Of You/ Stomping At The Savoy/Honeysuckle Rose*; Jam Session, *Lady Be Good*

(iv) Continuing Traditions

While World War II is a turning-point, convenient in historical terms (and coinciding with a union ban on recording, by the American Federation of Musicians), continuities and changes in the history of blues are far less precise. One form of troubadour singing, that paralleled and sometimes crossed over into blues, was that of the Christian evangelist. Usually a singer-guitarist (male or female) might perform on a street corner or in the confines of particular churches, doing the rounds from service to service across the United States. A dichotomy between secular and sacred, often assumed by black musicians, was never absolute and served similar functions in the communities in which they performed. Recordings by "Gospel Evangelists" both before and after World War II exemplify a continuity with the past. This is amply demonstrated in **God's Mighty Hand**, an anthology of post-war recordings by proselytizers that shows characteristic links with the secular in some performances.

The term "guitar evangelist" was specially applied on record to Reverend Edward Clayborn but has long been used to identify the self-accompanied singers and "jack-leg" preachers who, lacking a church building, projected their gospel message on the sidewalks. Many were blind, like Blind Willie Davis and Blind Willie Johnson (**127**), whose songs, vocal delivery, and guitar techniques were closely related to blues singers. This affinity is evident in a number of the recordings in this CD, such as the piano accompaniment to Mary Deloatch, a singer who also recorded blues as Marylin Scott (**125**). The influence of Sister Rosetta Tharpe is marked in the playing of such singers as Lottie Bracy and Sister O.M. Terrell. Tharpe's guitar technique had been influenced by Big Bill Broonzy. She sang blues with Lucky Millinder's Orchestra and later pioneered the use of the electric guitar in gospel music, as employed in most accompaniments in this collection.

These recordings were made in locations as far apart as Miami, Charleston, Memphis, Buffalo, Chicago, Oakland, and Los Angeles, indicating the vigor and pervasiveness of black gospel music in the post-war years. In part this was due to the influence of traveling quartets and of the National Convention of Gospel Choirs organized by Thomas A. Dorsey, the former blues singer Georgia Tom (**181**, **272**). His gospel compositions, like *If I Could Only Hear My Mother Pray Again*, sung here by the Reverend A. Johnson, became part of the standard repertoire. The exchange between gospel and blues and the continuity of evolving traditions from the pre-war to post-war years is underscored by these examples, many of them having been produced by small record labels.

Pre-war recording was dominated by a few major international companies, notably Columbia, Victor (later RCA Victor) and, in the 1930s, Decca, against which smaller concerns battled and often lost, or were absorbed. Non-commercial and documentary recording was almost exclusively the outcome of fieldwork on behalf of the Archive of American Folk Song at the Library of Congress. (This is now the Archive of Folk Culture). In the 1940s many minor labels sprang up to meet local demands, some growing into a size that seriously challenged the international corporations. By the 1950s other small companies had arisen to satisfy the needs of collectors and enthusiasts. Many proprietors were motivated less by commercial interests than by the desire to document under-represented musical traditions, to record previously ignored artists, or to honour established veterans in congenial recording conditions.

A **Testament Records Sampler** is representative of such non-commercial enterprise, privately funded and founded by Pete Welding in 1963. His first issue broke new ground in documenting a songster from rural Maryland, Bill Jackson, whose *Titanic Blues* demonstrated the survival of the ballad tradition. Another previously unrecorded singer was Blind Connie Williams, who played gospel music on Philadelphia streets but also recorded blues like *One Thin Dime*. Other previously unknown singers included barrelhouse pianist Jimmy Walker and guitarist Eddie Lee "Mustright" Jones—with his family. Established blues singers were far from forgotten; among important issues were recordings of Robert Nighthawk, some with Houston Stackhouse, a rural event with Big Joe Williams, and Chicago sessions with J.B. Hutto, Johnny Shines, and Billy Boy Arnold. From Napoleon Strickland's fife and drum band to the harmonica of Dr Isaiah Ross, the recordings by this independent label, one of many, illustrate the diversity of African-American music forms which related to or were concurrent with the blues in recent years.

It is apparent that there are many facets to the blues, and to the study and appreciation of the music and its exponents. Approaches may range from the aesthetic to the analytic, the discographical to the biographical, the selective to the comparative, the musical to the social, the altruistic to the acquisitive—and many more besides.

While the ordering of the *Guide* is principally historical, it is the intention of this introductory chapter to indicate some of the related contemporary idioms and their mutual influences. Certain of these themes are expanded in the ensuing Basic Records, demonstrating that the blues did not evolve in isolation but was and remains a genre of its time, subject to the complexity of its social contexts and transcending them in a profoundly expressive vocal and instrumental music.

9 **God's Mighty Hand: Gospel Evangelists**
Various Artists
Heritage HT CD 09 (UK)
Rev. Utah Smith, *God's Mighty Hand*; Sister O.M. Terrell, *The Gambling Man*; Reverend Anderson Johnson, *Let That Liar Pass On By*; Mary Deloatch, *The Lord's Gospel Train*; Lottie Bracy, *I Had A Dream*; Henry Green, *Strange Things*; Rev. Utah Smith, *I Want Two Wings*; Reverend A. Johnson, *If I Could Only Hear My Mother Pray Again*; Willie Mae Williams, *Where The Sun Never Goes Down/Don't Want To Go There*; Evangelist Sister Winn, *Building On The Good Place/Higher & Higher*; Sister Matthews, *Stand By Me*; Rev. Charles White, *How Long*; Henry Green, *Storm Thru Mississippi*, Elder R. Wilson & Family, *This Train/Gonna Wait 'Till A Change Comes*; Elder A. Johnson, *God*

Don't Like It; Brother Willie Eason, *There'll Be No Grumblers There/I Wanna Live (So God Can Use Me)*; Joe Townsend, *If I Could Not Say A Word/Going Over The Hill*; McEnnis Jones, *Do Lord/Will The Circle Be Unbroken*

10 **Testament Records Sampler**
Various Artists
Testament TCD 4001
J.B. Hutto & The Hawks, *Pet Cream Man*; John Lee Granderson, *A Man For The Nation*; The Chicago String Band, *Railroad Blues* [Carl Martin, vocal]; Otis Spann, *Nobody Knows My Troubles*; Fred McDowell & The Hunter's Chapel Singers, *Jesus Is On The Mainline*; Eddie Taylor, *Peach Tree Blues*; Eddie Lee "Mustright" Jones, *I'm Talking About You*; Dr Isaiah Ross, *Cat Squirrel*; Robert Nighthawk, *I'm Gettin' Tired*; Jimmy Walker & Erwin Helfer, *Going Back To Texas*; Ruby McCoy, *Black Mary*; Johnny Shines, *So Cold In Vietnam*; Bill Jackson, *Titanic Blues*; Johnny Turner & Blues With A Feeling, *Don't Start Me To Talkin'*; Johnny Young, *All My Money Gone*; Blind Connie Williams, *One Thin Dime*; Fred McDowell, *Goin' Down South*; John Wrencher, *I'm Going To Detroit*; Big Joe Williams, *Annie Mae*; Napoleon Strickland Fife and Drum Band, *My Babe* [Stickland & Othar Turner, vocal], Johnny Shines, *Hoodoo Snake Doctor Blues*; Johnny Littlejohn, *Dust My Broom*; Billy Boy Arnold, *Pleading And Crying*

Basic Records

(i) Performance and Personalities

11 **Women In Blues: New York-Chicago-Memphis-Dallas, 1920–1943**
Various Artists
Fremeaux & Associés FA 018 (Fr)—*2 CD set*
DISC ONE: Mamie Smith, *Crazy Blues*; Lucille Hegamin, *Land Of Cotton Blues*; Josephine Beatty [Alberta Hunter], *Nobody Knows The Way I Feel Dis Mornin'*; Sara Martin, *Late Last Night*; Ma Rainey, *See See Rider Blues*; Bessie Smith, *Empty Bed Blues* Part 1/*Empty Bed Blues* Part 2; Clara Smith, *Shipwrecked Blues*; Martha Copeland, *Nobody Rocks Me Like My Baby Do*; Pearl Dickson, *Little Rock Blues*; Mattie Delaney, *Tallahatchie River Blues*, Lottie Beaman, *Rolling Log Blues*; Ethel Waters, *My Handy Man*; Lizzie Miles, *My Man O' War*; Ida May Mack, *Mr. Moore Blues*; Lillian Glinn, *Cravin A Man Blues*; Bertha "Chippie" Hill, *Some Cold Rainy Day*; Rosa Henderson, *Can't Be Bothered With No Sheik*; Edith Wilson, *My Handy Man Ain't Handy No More*

DISC TWO: Memphis Minnie, *Me And My Chauffeur Blues*; Lucille Bogan, *Reckless Woman*; Lil Johnson, *That Bonus Done Gone Thru*; Alice Moore, *My Man Blues*; Hattie McDaniel *I Thought I'd Do It*; Victoria Spivey, *Dirty T.B. Blues*; Mildred Bailey, *Down Hearted Blues*; Ida Cox, *Death Letter Blues*; Georgia White, *The Blues Ain't Nothin' But . . . ???*; Merline Johnson "The Yas Yas Girl", *Pallet On The Floor*; Rosetta Howard, *How Long Daddy (Will You Keep Me This Way)*; Billie Holiday, *Long Gone Blues*; Lil Green, *Why Don't You Do Right?*; Tiny Mayberry, *Mailman Blues*; Rosetta Tharpe, *Trouble*

In Mind; Wee Bea Booze, *Uncle Sam Come And Get Him*; Helen Humes, *Gonna Buy Me A Telephone*; Dinah Washington, *Salty Papa Blues*
Appropriately, Mamie Smith's *Crazy Blues* opens this collection. Her vaudeville-jazz approach, alongside Waters, Hunter, the Smiths, and Cox, is compared with the rural blues of Delaney, Dickson, Bogan, and Memphis Minnie, and the urbanity of singers of the 1930s, such as White, Howard, and Humes.

12 **Hokum Blues: Complete Recorded Works in Chronological Order (1924–1929)**
Various Artists
Document DOCD 5370 (Au)
Ukulele Bob Williams, *West Indies Blues/Go Long Mule*; The Two Of Spades, *Meddlin' With The Blues/Harmonica Blues*; Louise Ross, *No Home Blues/Can't Fool Me Blues*; Danny Small & Ukulele Mays, *Sweet Georgia Brown/Loud Speaking Papa/Sweet Man/Cecilia*; The Pebbles, *Pebble Blues/Can't Sleep Blues/Who's You Tellin'/I Mean It's Just Too Bad/Hot Pebble Blues/Deep Henderson*; Ki Ki Johnson, *Lone Grave/Look What A Hole I'm In/Lady, Your Clock Ain't Right/Wrong Woman Blues*; Feathers & Frogs, *How You Get That Way/Sweet Black Dog*; Swan & Lee, *Fishy Little Thing* (take B)/*It Sure Is Nice* (take B)
The hinterland between old-time road shows and the blues is explored. Performers include ukulele and banjo players, vocal duets and groups with repertoire ranging from the sly suggestiveness of Feathers And Frogs, or Swan And Lee, to the social implications of *West Indies Blues*.

13 **Playing With The Strings**
Lonnie Johnson [Various Artists]
JSP Records JSP CD 335 (UK)
Charlie Creath's Jazz-O-Maniacs, *Won't Don't Blues* [Johnson, vocal]; Lonnie Johnson, *Mr. Johnson's Blues/Falling Rain Blues* James "Steady Roll" Johnson, *No Good Blues/Newport Blues*; Lonnie Johnson, *Nile Of Genago/To Do This You Gotta Know How/Four Hands Are Better Than Two*; Louis Armstrong & His Hot Five, *I'm Not Rough* [Armstrong, vocal]/*Hotter Than That* [Armstrong, scat vocal]/*Savoy Blues*; Lonnie Johnson, *Playing With The Strings/Stompin 'Em Along Slow*; Duke Ellington & His Orchestra, *The Mooche* [Baby Cox, scat vocal]/*Move Over/Hot And Bothered* [Baby Cox, scat vocal]; The Chocolate Dandies, *Paducah/Star Dust*; Blind Willie Dunn's Gin Bottle Four, *Jet Black Blues* [Hoagy Carmichael, scat vocal]/*Blue Blood Blues Blues* [Hoagy Carmichael, scat vocal]; Clarence Williams' Jug Band, *Sittin' On Top Of The World/Kansas City Man Blues*; Lonnie Johnson, *I'm Nuts About That Girl/Racketeers Blues*
To Do This You Gotta Know How demonstrates Lonnie's mastery of the guitar (1926). Uniquely in this era, his record company (OKeh) chose to feature this ability with the cream of its jazz musicians. Johnson remained a commanding blues performer, however, as *Racketeers Blues* (from 1932) amply demonstrates.

14 **Great Blues Guitarists: String Dazzlers**
Various Artists
Columbia CK 47060/467894-2 (UK)
Lonnie Johnson & Eddie Lang, *Hot Fingers/A Handful Of Riffs*; Texas Alexander, *Work Ox Blues*; Sylvester Weaver, *I'm Busy And You Can't Come*

In; Georgia Bill or Blind Willie [McTell], *Georgia Rag/Warm It Up To Me*; Sylvester Weaver, *Untitled* [*Six String Banjo Piece*]; Sylvester Weaver & Walter Beasley, *Untitled* [*Me and My Tapeworm*]; Blind Willie Johnson, *When The War Was On/It's Nobody's Fault But Mine*; Big Bill Broonzy, *How You Want It Done?/Getting Older Every Day*; Casy Bill Weldon, *Guitar Swing*; Lonnie Johnson & Eddie Lang, *Bull Frog Moan*; Blind Lemon Jefferson, *Black Snake Moan*; Joshua White, *Little Brother Blues/Prodigal Son*; Tampa Red, *Denver Blues*; Lonnie Johnson, *Away Down In The Alley Blues/I Love You Mary Lou*
A collection that highlights the dexterity of well-known bluesmen for whom guitar playing is synonymous with the genre. Recorded between 1924 and 1940, several performances are instrumentals. Lonnie Johnson accompanies Alexander, while Weaver's *Six String Banjo Piece* uses an instrument associated with an earlier era.

15 **Piano Discoveries: Newly Found Title & Alternate Takes (1928–1943)**
Various Artists
Blues Documents BDCD 6045 (Au)
Ezra Howlett Shelton, *Flapper's Stomp*; Lee Green, *Five Minute Blues (15569)*; Charlie "Bozo" Nickerson, *What's The Matter Now?* Part 3/*What's The Matter Now?* Part 4; Ivy Smith & Cow Cow Davenport, *That's The Kind Of Girl I'm Looking For*; Tampa Red & Georgia Tom, *It's A Pretty Little Thing/Poor Old Bachelor Blues*; Little Brother Montgomery, *Louisiana Blues* (take B); Walter Davis, *You Don't Worry My Mind* (take 2); Leroy Carr, *Church House Blues* (take 1); Memphis Slim, *Beer Drinking Woman* (take 2); Pete Johnson & Albert Ammons, *Boogie Woogie Man* (06386-1); UNISSUED PRIVATE ACETATES: Cripple Clarence Lofton, *Deep End Boogie/I Don't Know/Fine And Mellow* [Evie Westphal, vocal]; Jimmy Yancey & Cripple Clarence Lofton, *Vocal Blues* [Lofton, vocal]/*Talking & Piano Experiment/Untitled*; Jimmy Yancey, *Boogie* No A1/*Mama And Jimmie Blues* [Mama Yancey, vocal]/*The Rocks/Untitled Blues*; Alonzo Yancey, *Unknown Rag* (at party)/*Ecstatic Rag/Everybody's Rag*
Recently recovered 78s and alternative takes by well-known singer-pianists offer opportunities for comparative listening, while home recordings eavesdrop on Cripple Clarence Lofton and the Yanceys playing in informal circumstances. Ezra Shelton's *Flapper's Stomp* is a rarity.

(ii) Parallel Traditions in Africa and the Americas

16 **Jacob Sam & Kumasi 3 [Trio] Volume 2: 1928**
Heritage HT CD 28 (UK)
Prempah Waba Part 1/*Prempah Waba* Part 2/*Akyimful Draiba Panyi/Se Minya Owu A Muwura Draiba/Kwaku Anansi* Part 1/*Kwaku Anansi* Part 2/*Nsa, Nsa, Ye, Bonun Nsa/Wie Wie Wie Mi Ye/Adjuah Yankah* Part 1/*Adjuah Yankah* Part 2/*Essie Kutah/Ababaa Wa/Wombu/Ahinkyaw/Ma Asu Awar/Se Ye Mi Ye Na W'Anye Yie A/Gyampusa Mara/Nana E GuahNi Tamar Yi A/Wie Nyanku Birebu Ya Asem A/Aven Nyi Wu*
Traveling to London from Ghana in June 1928, the Kumasi Trio cut these early examples of West African "Palm Wine" music for local consumption. Based on cosmopolitan styles by African mariners, these rhythmic and compulsive compositions were accompanied by two guitars and a drum, with vocals generally in Fanti.

17 **The West African Instrumental Quintet: 1929**
Heritage HT CD 16 (UK)
Insu Shi Wu/Ontsi Bro Fu/Bea Tsin No. 1/*Bea Tsin* No. 2/*Con Ko Bev/Ye Na Ako Fia/Kara So/Awu Raba/Som Mi Mu/On Yer Whi/Ser Akul Per/Pa Pa Bi/Tin Ka Tin Ka/Mi Wi Wi/ Ader Su* No. 1/*Ader Su* No. 2/*Alma Bou/Mia Nko/Bra Sil*
This vivacious and accomplished quintet performs in a variety of creole styles. Part of their repertoire has contemporary equivalence with pieces from the English-speaking West Indies and Europe. The exact origin of the musicians is unknown; the instruments comprise two guitars, a banjo-mandolin, ukulele or *cavaquinho*, and percussion (including tambourine).

18 **The Music of Madagascar: Classic Traditional Recordings Of The 1930s**
Various Artists
Yazoo (CD) 7003
Hiran'ny Tanoran'ny Ntao Lo, *O Lahy É [Oh! Dear Friend]*; Choeur Malgache, *Eny A Rodo Rodgrodov Ny Famindra [Echoes Of Dance Steps]*; Hiran'ny Tanoran'ny Ntao Lo, *Mam Pahory Ny Masoandro Seranin-Javona [Dark Clouds Covering The Sun Bring Sadness]*; Choeur Malgache, *Tery Mafy Loatra Ny Sain [The Mind Bound Up With Sorrow]*; Hiran'ny Tanoran'ny Ntao Lo, *Mazava Atsinana Ny Any Aminay [Clear Bright Day In My Country]*; Hiran-d Razafimahefa, *Fony Hianac Mbola Kely Sakaiza [Once When You Were A Child]*; Hiran'ny Tanoran'ny Ntao Lo, *Tanora Tsy Manaja Tena [Youths With No Self-Respect]*; Hira Malaza Taloha, *Rambalamanana* [boy's name]; Hiran'ny Tanoran'ny Ntao Lo, *O Ry Dada Sy Neny Malala Ô [Oh! Dear Father And Mother]*; Hiran-d Razafimahefa, *O Ry Fody An' Ala Ê! O! [Tribute To The Cardianl Of The Forest]*; Hiran'ny Tanoran'ny Ntao Lo, *Maraina Ny Andro [Delightful Day]*; Mpilalao Malgache, *Fikasakasana Ny eto An-Tany [Life In This World Is But Preparation]*; Hiran-d Razafimahefa, *Ry Volon-Danitra Manga [Beautiful Blue Sky]*; Hiran'ny Tanoran'ny Ntao Lo, *Raivo Ô* [girl's name]; Choeur Malgache, *Afindrafindrao* [a traditional dance]; Hiran'ny Tanoran'ny Ntao Lo, *Hadalana, Hadisoana [Folly Leads To Regrets]*; Hiran-d Razafimahefa, *O Ry T'Siriry Mandalo An' Itasy! [Bird Flying Above Lake Itaosy]*; Hira Malaza Taloha, *An'Iza-ny Basy? [Whose Gun Is This?]*; Hiran-d Razafimahefa, *Mifohaza Re Rabetorimaso [Wake Up Sleepy-head]/Indrisy Mantsy Zareo Mpilalo Tsy Manan Tiana [Pity The Musicians Who Have No Lovers])*
Stirling choral singing in harmony, with forthright lead vocalists (male or female) accompanied by fiddle, concertina, or *valia* (a unique local string instrument) mark this collection. The amalgam of different cultures contained in this island to the east of South Africa contribute to the haunting melodies and skillful interpretations.

19 **Sextetos Cubanos, Volume 1 [Sones Cubanos, 1930]**
Various Artists
Arhoolie-Folklyric CD 7003
Sexteto Munamar, *Acuérdate Bien, Chaleco [Remember Well Vest]/Vengan, Vengan [Come, Come All]/Entre Todas Las Mujeres [Amongst All Women]/Crucé Los Mares [I Crossed The Seas]/Chaquetòn [Overcoat]/Lucimí [Lucumi]/Yibiri [Yibiri]*; Sexteto Machin, *No Es Cuente, No [It's Not A Story,*

Really!]/Me Voy A Baracoa [I'm Going To Baracoa]/Reina Guajira [Guajira Queen]/El Camisón De Pepa [Pepa's Shirtdress]/Fuego En La Maya [Fire In La Maya]/Mamá Yo Quiero Un Yoyo [Mamma, I Want A Yoyo]/Avellana Y Mani [Hazelnuts And Peanuts]/A Orillas Del Ymurí [On The Banks Of The Yumuri]/El Rey Manola [King Manolo]/Sorteo De La Caridad [Lottery Drawing]/Caserita [Housewife]; Sexteto Nacional, *Suavecito [Gently]/Incitadora Región [Inciting Region]*; Sexteto Mantancero, *Son A La Mjjer Cubana [Son To A Cuban Woman]/A Una Mantancera [To A Matanzas Woman]/La Vida No Retoña [Life Cannot Be Relived]/¿De dónde Serán? (Where Are They From?)*
Call-and-response and harmonized vocals, to string accompaniment (guitar, *tres*, and bass), augmented by trumpet (or *cornetta*), claves, and bongo drums, are represented in these exceptional performances. Analogous to blues, but comprising three elements, *preludio, largo*, and *montuno*, the Cuban *son* is distilled by these artists' African-Spanish-Caribbean influences into an outstanding form of creole music.

20 **Biguine: Valse, Et Mazurka Créoles (1929–1940)**
Various Artists
Fremeaux & Associés FA 07 (Fr)—*2 CD set*
DISC ONE: L'Orchestre Antillais. Dir. M. Stellio, *Serpent Maigre*; Orchestre Creol's Band. Dir. Félix Valvert, *La Georgi-Nana/Armide*; Creol's Band Du Bal Colonial De La Rue Blomet. Dir. E. Léardée, *Pamela/Marcaïbo*; Orchestre Du Bal Antillais, Sous La Direction De M. Stellio, *A Si Paré/Soigné I Ba Moin*; Orchestre De La Boule Blanche. Dir. Charlery-Banguio, *C'Est Biguine*; Orchestre Créole Delvi, *Ba Moin En Ti Bo Doudou*; Tom Et Ses Juniors Guadeloupéens, *Robes A Queues*; Orchestre Guyanais De M. Henri Volmar, *Mouvements D'Avions*; Orchestre Créeole Delvi, *De Feu Pri En Tete Man Nordé*; Nelly Lungla Acc. De Piano Et Guitare, *Me Gadé Yo*; Duo De Guitares Par Pollo Malahel Et Benjamin Gérion, *Gros Sou*; L'Orchestre Guadeloupéen A. Kindou, *Celestin Roi Diable*; Piano Par Les Frères Martial, *Krakador Bon Ti Coin Capesterre La*; Stellio Et Son Orchestre Créole, *Èti Tintin*; Orchestre Créole Matou, *Ti Joseph A Joséphine*

DISC TWO: Rico's Creole Band, *Moin Amié Doudou Moin*; Orchestre Typique Martiniquais. Dir. Eugene Delouche, *Gepa Ka Piké*; Stellio Et Son Orchestre Créole, *Camélia /Renée*; Orchestre Del's Jazz Biguine. Dir. Eugene Delouche, *Martinique/Complainte*; Orchestre Antillais Du Bal Blomet, *Negues Bon Défençeus*; Jazz Sam Castendet, *Bossu Doudou*; Orchestre Typique Martiniquais. Dir. Eugene Delouche, *Naomi/Les Deux Jumeaux*; Orchestre Del's Jazz Biguine. Dir. Eugene Delouche, *Sous Les Tropiques*; Orchestre Antillais Du Bal Blomet, *Souvenirs De Saint-Pierre*; Roger Fanfant Et Son Orchestre Guadeloupéen, *Touloulou Mi Touloulou A Ou La/Jeanne Et Marcelle*; Marcel Yamba, Maïotte Almaby Et l'Orchestre Des Isles, *Ma Goulou Goulou*; Sosso Pé-En-Kin Et l'Orchestre Du Bal Bill Amour, *1-2-3 La Vandé*; L'Exotique Jazz, Orchestre Typique Antillais, *Sur Les Flots Aux Antilles/Pot-Pourri Biguine* African-French culture influenced music in New Orleans and the Louisiana bayous (**7**, **257**). Related developments in Trinidad (**2**), Martinique, Guadeloupe, and French Guiana feature in this superlative collection, recorded in Paris. Traditional Carnival songs (*bigunes*) are included, alongside dance pieces by creole musicians with skills equal to their counterparts in the United States.

(iii) Blues, Jazz, and Country Music—Parallel and cross-over traditions in the United States

21 **Richard M. Jones: Complete Recorded Works In Chronological Order, Volume 1, 1923–1927**
RST Records JPCD 1524-2 (Au)
Richard M. Jones, *Jazzin' Baby Blues/Twelfth Street Rag*; Richard M. Jones' Three Jazz Wizards, *New Orleans Shags/Spanish Shawl/29th And Dearborn/ Wonderful Dream*; Chicago Hottentots, *All Night Shags/Put Me In The Alley Blues*; Sara Martin acc. Richard M. Jones' Jazz Wizards, *Late Last Night/Some Sweet Day*; Bertha "Chippie" Hill acc. Richard M. Jones' Jazz Wizards, *Leavenworth Blues/Panama Limited Blues/Street Walker Blues*; Richard M. Jones' Jazz Wizards, *Kin To Kant Blues/Mushmouth Blues/Baby O' Mine*; Elzadie Robinson, *Houston Bound*; Richard M. Jones' Jazz Wizards, *Dusty Bottom Blues/Scagmore Green*; Bertha "Chippie" Hill, *Do Dirty Blues/Sport Model Mama*; Richard M. Jones' Jazz Wizards, *Hollywood Shuffle/Dark Alley*
Blues expression was assimilated by New Orleans jazz musicians such as the pianist-composer Richard M. Jones, Preston Jackson (trombone), Albert Nicholas (clarinet), and Johnny St. Cyr (banjo), who recorded blues with Jones' Jazz Wizards. So did Shirley Clay (cornet) and Artie Starks (clarinet), accompanying "Chippie" Hill on several classics of blues shouting.

22 **State Street Ramblers, Volume 2—[including] Memphis Nighthawks, Chicago Rhythm Kings—featuring Roy Palmer: Complete Recorded Works In Chronological Order (1931–1936)**
RST Records JPCD 1513-2 (Au)
State Street Ramblers, *Carless Love* (vocal)/*Kentucky Blues/I Want To Be Your Lovin' Man/South African Blues/Me And The Blues* (scat vocal)/*Sic 'Em, Tige'/ Wild Man Stomp* (scat vocal)/*Stomp Your Stuff* (scat vocal)/*Richmond Stomp* (scat vocal); Memphis Nighthawks (Alabama Rascals), *Georgia Grind* (vocal)/ *Shanghai Honeymoon* (vocal)/*Biscuit Roller* (vocal)/*Rukus Juice Shuffle/Dirty Dozens Cousins* (scat vocal)/*Nancy Jane /Jockey Stomp/Wild Man Stomp* (scat vocal)/*Come On In, Baby/Stomp That Thing* (scat vocal)/*Endurance Stomp*/[Roy Palmer and Bob Hudson] *The Trombone Slide/Sweet Feet*; Chicago Rhythm Kings, *You Battle-Head Beetle-Head* (vocal)/*It's Too Bad* (vocal)/*Shanghai Honeymoon/Little Sandwich Wagon* (vocal)
Blues flourished in small group jazz, often with a singer and rhythm section augmented by a single "front line" instrument. Roy Palmer, a trombonist from New Orleans, led most of these Chicago-based groups, with Chicagonian Darnell Howard (clarinet) and Kentucky pianist Jimmy Blythe contributing to lively performances. Big Bill Broonzy may play fiddle with the Nighthawks.

23 **Big Bill Broonzy: Complete Recorded Works In Chronological Order, Volume 3, 1934–1935**
Document DOCD 5052 (Au)
I Want To See My Baby/Serve It To Me Right/Dirty-No-Gooder/Let Her Go—She Don't Know/Hobo Blues/Prowlin' Ground Hog/C-C Rider (take A)/*C-C Rider* (take B); State Street Boys, *Mobile And Western Line* (Jazz Gillum, vocal)/*Crazy About You* (Gillum, vocal)/*Sweet To Mama* (Big Bill, vocal)/ *Rustlin' Man* (Gillum, vocal)/*She Caught The Train* (Big Bill And Jazz Gillum,

vocal)/*Midnight Special* (Gillum, vocal)/*The Dozen* (Big Bill and Jazz Gillum, vocal)/*Don't Tear My Clothes* (Big Bill, vocal); Big Bill, *The Southern Blues/ Good Jelly/C And A Blues/Somthing Good/You May Need My Help Someday/ Rising Sun Shine On*
Jazz and blues links were sustained in the 1930s by blues singer and promoter Big Bill, whose State Street Boys included the versatile Carl Martin and harmonica player Jazz Gillum (**257**). They drew on string and jug band repertoire together with blues standards. Also included are some of Broonzy's most influential songs.

24 **Clifford Hayes & The Louisville Jug Bands: Complete Recorded Works In Chronological Order, Volume 4, 1929–1931**
Various Artists
RST Records JPCD 1504-2 (Au)
Clifford Hayes' Louisville Stompers, *You're Ticklin' Me* (take 1)/*You're Ticklin' Me* (take 2)/*You're Gonna Need My Help* (Sippie Wallace, vocal); Kentucky Jazz Babies, *Old Folk's Shake/No More Blues*; Phillips' Louisville Jug Band, *Soldier Boy Blues/That's A Lovely Thing For You/Sing, You Sinners/Tiger Rag*; Kentucky Jug Band, *Walkin' Cane Stomp/Hard Hustlin' Blues*; Phillips' Louisville Jug Band, *Smackin' The Sax/That's Your Last*; Kid Coley, *Clair And Pearley Blues/Tricks Ain't Walkin' No More/Freight Train Blues*; Whistler And His Jug Band, *Foldin' Bed/Hold That Tiger*; Kid Coley, *War Dream Blues*; Jimmie Rodgers, *My Good Gal's Gone Blues* (take 2)/*My Good Gal's Gone Blues* (take 3); Ben Ferguson, *Please Don't Holler, Mama/Try And Treat Her Right*; John Harris, *Prowling Wolf Blues/Glad And Sorry Blues*
Local traditions developed in many states: Louisville, Kentucky, was the home of several jug bands—among the earliest was Whistler's raucous group. Violinist Clifford Hayes led several others; though his inclination was to jazz, he accompanied a few blues singers and the well-known white singer Jimmy Rodgers (**328**).

25 **Country: Nashville-Dallas-Hollywood, 1927–1942**
Various Artists
Fremeaux & Associés FA 015 (Fr)—*2 CD set*
DISC ONE: Sam McGee, *Railroad Blues*; G.B. Grayson, *Omie Wise*; Carolina Tar Heels, *Peg And Awl*; Buster Carter & Preston Young, *A Lazy Farmer Boy*; Buell Kazee, *The Butcher's Boy*; Kelly Harrel, *My Name Is John Jo Hannah*; Clarence Ashley, *The House Carpenter*; Williamson Brothers, *Gonna Die With My Hammer In My Hand*; Dock Boggs, *Country Blues*; Dick Justice, *Brownskin Blues*; Jimmie Tarlton, *Slow Wicked Blues*; Cliff Carlisle, *Pan American Man*; Carter Family, *John Hardy/Wildwood Flower*; Jimmie Rodgers, *Blue Yodel* No.8; Monroe Brothers, *All The Good Times Are Passed And Gone/ Sinner You Better Get Ready*; Delmore Brothers, *Brown's Ferry Blues*

DISC TWO: Jimmie Rodgers, *Jimmie's Texas Blues*; Jimmie Davis, *Rockin' Blues*; Jules Verne Allen, *The Days Of '49/The Dying Cowboy*; Tex Ritter, *Rye Whiskey*; Gene Autry, *I'll Go Ridin' Down That Old Texas Trail*; Sons Of The Pioneers, *Song Of The Bandit*; Roy Rodgers, *Cowboy Night Herd Song*; Patsy Montana, *I Want To Be A Cowboy's Sweetheart*; Bob Wills & His Texas Playboys, *What's The Matter With The Mill?/Liza, Pull Down The Shades*;

Milton Brown & His Brownies, *Hesitation Blues*; Adolf [*sic*] Hofner & His San Antonians, *Alamo Rag*; Shelly Lee Alley & His Alley Cats, *Women, Women, Women*; Jimmy Revard & His Oklahoma Playboys, *Fox And Hounds*; Roy Acuff & The Smokey Mountain Boys, *Wreck On The Highway/Fireball Mail*; Ernest Tubb & The Troubadours, *I Ain't Honky Tonkin' Anymore*
White instrumental and vocal traditions largely from the Appalachians. Seldom imitating black vocal styles, but sometimes based on the guitar patterns of Blind Lemon Jefferson and other record artists, blues were added to British ballads and the country songs and dances of "hillbilly" functions. Jimmie Rodgers even yodeled on his blues recordings.

26 **Western Swing: Texas, 1928–1944**
Various Artists
Fremeaux & Associés FA 032 (Fr)—*2 CD set*
DISC ONE: Bob Wills & His Texas Playboys, *Who Walks In When I Walk Out?*; Emmett Miller & His Georgia Crackers, *Lovesick Blues*; Milton Brown & His Musical Brownies, *Talking About You/I'll Be Glad When You're Dead, You Rascal You*; Bill Boyd & His Cowboy Ramblers, *Boyd's Blues*; The Tune Wranglers, *Red's Tight Like That/El Rancho Grande/Buster's Crawdad Song*; Jimmy Revard & His Oklahoma Playboys, *Blues In The Bottle*; Bill Boyd & His Cowboy Ramblers, *Show Me The Way To Go Home*; Cliff Bruner's Texas Wanderers, *Milk Cow Blues*; Jimmy Revard & His Oklahoma Playboys, *Ride 'Em Cowboy*; Brown's Musical Brownies, *Louise Louise Blues*; Light Crust Doughboys, *Blue Guitars*; Crystal Spring Ramblers, *Fort Worth Stomp*; W. Lee O'Daniel & His Hillbilly Boys, *Dirty Hangover Blues*; Light Crust Doughboys, *Just Once Too Often*; Modern Mountaineers, *Everybody's Truckin'*

DISC TWO: Bob Wills & His Texas Playboys, *Twin Guitar Special*; W. Lee O'Daniel & His Hillbilly Boys, *Lonesome Road Blues*; Shelly Lee Alley & His Alley Cats, *Try It Once Again*; Light Crust Doughboys, *Pussy, Pussy, Pussy*; Jimmy Revard & His Oklahoma Playboys, *Oh! Swing It*; Hank Penny & His Radio Cowboys, *Chill Tonic*; Cliff Bruner & His Boys, *Truck Driver's Blues*; Adolph [*sic*] Hofner & His Texans, *Brown Eyed Sweet*; Buddy Jones, *Settle Down Blues*; Modern Mountaineers, *Pipeliner's Blues*; Ted Daffan's Texans, *Blue Steel Blues*; Hi-Flyers, *Whatcha Gonna Do?/Juke Box Jump*; Sons Of The West, *Sally's Got A Wooden Leg*; Cliff Bruner's Texas Wandrers, *Draft Board Blues*; Bob Wills & His Texas Playboys, *Little Liza Jane*; Spade Cooley, *Shame On You*
A "Territory" (Texas-Oklahoma) combination of contemporary swing and cowboy honky-tonk music, western swing was popular in the 1930s and 1940s. Knocky Parker (pianist with Bob Wills) and the Bruner and Boyd bands featured blues and helped prepare the way for the post-war synthesis of rock 'n' roll.

(iv) Blues for Dancing—Post-war Swing, Jump, Jive, and Boogie

27 **New York City Blues: Blues Master Volume 13**
Various Artists
Rhino R2 71131
Lionel Hampton, *Hamp's Boogie Woogie*; Duke Ellington & His Famous Orchestra, *Happy Go Lucky Local* Part 1/*Happy Go Lucky Local* Part 2;

Buddy Johnson & His Orchestra, *Walk 'Em* [Johnson, vocal]; Hot Lips Page & His Orchestra, *Walkin' In A Daze* [Page, vocal]; Joe Morris & His Orchestra, *Lowe Groovin'*; Eddie Vinson & His Orchestra, *Old Maid Boogie* [Vinson, vocal]; Arnett Cobb & His Orchestra, *Smooth Sailing*; Lucky Millinder & His Orchestra, *D' Natural Blues*; Erskine Hawkins, *John Henry*; Joe Turner with Van "Piano Man" Walls & His Orchestra, *Sweet Sixteen*; Cootie Williams & His Orchestra, *'Gator Tail* Part 1/*'Gator Tail* Part 2; Johnny Hodges & His Orchestra, *Castle Rock*; Al Hibbler, *After The Lights Go Down Low*; Chuck Calhoun [Jesse Stone] & His Atlantic All Stars, *Hey Tiger* [Stone, vocal]; Big Maybelle With Orchestra Under The Direction Of Danny Mendelsohn, *I'm Getting 'Long Alright*; Sam "The Man" Taylor, *Oo-Wee*; Count Basie & His Orchestra With Joe Williams, *Every Day* Part 1/*Every Day* Part 2; Alan Freed & His Rock 'N Roll Band, *Right Now, Right Now*

By World War II big band swing and boogie woogie achieved great popularity. Centered on the headquarters of the US music business, these later examples date from 1944 (*Hamp's Boogie Woogie*) to 1956 (*Right Now, Right Now*). The last was sponsored by a pioneer rock 'n' roll disc jockey. Some traditional blues motifs remain.

28 Specialty Legends Of Jump Blues, Volume 1

Various Artists

Specialty SPCD 7058-2/Ace CDCHD 573 (UK)

Joe Liggins, *The Honeydripper*; Roy Milton, *Oh Babe!*; Joe Lutcher, *Blues For Sale*; King Perry & His Pied Pipers, *Duck's Yas Yas Yas*; Jimmy Liggins, *I Can't Stop It*; Roy Milton, *Rainy Day Confession Blues*; Nelson Alexander Trio, *Well, Well Baby*; Joe Liggins, *Rag Mop*; Buddy Banks, *Happy Home Blues*; Big Jim Wynn, *Muffle Joe Shuffle*; King Perry & His Pied Pipers, *I Ain't Got A Dime To My Name*; Jimmy Liggins, *Saturday Night Boogie Woogie Man*; Jesse Thomas, *Jack Of Diamonds*; Percy Mayfield, *I Dare You, Baby* (alternate, take 2); Herman Manzy, *I'm Your Rockin' Man*; Joe Liggins, *One Sweet Letter*; King Perry & His Pied Pipers, *Natural Born Lover*; Lester Williams, *I Can't Lose With The Stuff I Use*; Duke Henderson, *Country Girl*; Roy Milton, *The Hucklebuck*; Frank Motley & Jimmy Crawford, *Heavy Weight Baby*; Joe Lutcher, *Traffic Song*; King Perry & His Pied Pipers, *I Wonder Who's Boogin' My Woogie*; Percy Mayfield, *The Hunt Is On* (alternate, take 2); Joe Liggins, *Pink Champagne*; Jimmy Liggins, *That Song Is Gone*

Hampton, Ellington, Basie, Millinder, and their like, were superseded in ballrooms by smaller units (using amplified instruments), while jukeboxes replaced live music in dance halls and cafés. Pioneer recordings of this new "jump blues" were by West Coast companies (where the music originated), as in these selections from 1947–52.

29 House Rockin' Blues: Chess & Checker Chicago Classics

Various Artists

Ace CDCHD 610 (UK)

G.L. Crockett, *Look Out Mabel*; J.B. Lenoir, *Mama Talk To Your Daughter*; Muddy Waters, *Young Fashioned Ways*; Howlin' Wolf, *I Have A Little Girl*; Bo Diddley, *You Don't Love Me (You Don't Care)*; Morris Pejoe, *Tired Of Crying Over You*; Otis Spann, *I'm Leaving You*; John Brim, *Rattlesnake*; Willie Mabon, *Poison Ivy*; Billy Boy Arnold, *You Got To Love Me*; Little Walter,

Mellow Down Easy; Bo Diddley, *Little Girl*; Blue Smitty, *Date Bait*; John Brim, *I Would Hate To See You Go (Be Careful)*; Jimmy Rogers, *If It Ain't Me*; Howlin' Wolf, *Who Will Be Next?*; Muddy Waters, *Close To You*; Billy Boy Arnold, *Sweet On You Baby*; Sonny Boy Williamson, *The Goat*; Jimmy McCracklin, *He Knows The Rules*; Otis Rush, *I'm Satisfied*; Buddy Guy, *Let Me Love You Baby*; Elmore James, *Madison Blues*; Little Walter, *I Got To Go*; Little Luther, *The Twirl*; Robert Nighthawk, *Someday*; John Lee Hooker, *Let's Go Out Tonight*
Companies representing local music, such as Chess and Checker, made many innovations during the 1940s and 1950s. These up-tempo releases were recorded between 1952 and 1966 and epitomize Mississippi-influenced clubland blues from the "Windy City" as well as a few sides from other locations.

30 **Jiving Jamboree**
Various Artists
Ace CDCHD 561 (UK)
Louis Jordan, *Saturday Night Fish Fry*; Clarence "Frogman" Henry, *Ain't Got No Home*; Daddy Cleanhead, *Something's Going On In My Room*; Big Mama Thornton, *They Call Me Big Mama*; Joe Liggins, *The Honeydripper*; Jesse Belvin, *Love, Love Of My Life*; The Cadets, *I Want You*; The Hollywood Flames, *Buzz, Buzz, Buzz*; Chuck Higgins, *Wet Back Hop*; Wynona Carr, *Ding Dong Daddy*; Paul Gayten, *The Music Goes Round And Round*; Eugene Church, *Don't Stop Loving Me*; Jimmy Liggins, *Nite Life Boogie*; The Mills Brothers, *Opus One*; Young Jessie, *Hit, Git And Split*; Bobby Day, *Rockin' Robbin*; The Monitors, *My Baby's Rockin'*; Etta James, *That's All*; Roy Milton, *You Got Me Reelin' and Rockin'*; Camille Howard, *O Sole Mio Boogie*; The Titans, *Free And Easy*; Oscar McLollie & Jeannette Baker, *Hey Girl, Hey Boy*; Joe Houston, *Rock That Boogie*; T.V. Slim, *Flat Foot Sam*; Dolly Cooper, *My Man*
Dancers performed in a variety of musical settings. Their accompaniment ranged from big bands, to small bands, pianists, guitarists, harmonica players, solo vocalists, or vocal groups. Recorded in the decade beginning 1949, **Jiving Jamboree** is a representative sample of these different styles of black American music and emphasizes their recreational function.

31 **Boogie Woogie Riot**
Various Artists
Ace CDCHD 526 (UK)
Big Joe Duskin, *The Tribute*; Pete Johnson, *Rocket Boogie '88'* Part 2; Joe Turner with Pete Johnson, *Wine-O Baby Boogie*; Dave Alexander, *The Rattler*; Earl Hooker, *Earl's Boogie Woogie*; Robert Shaw, *The Cows*; Lightnin' Hopkins, *Lightnin's Boogie*; Piano Red, *Atlanta Bounce*; Alex Moore, *Rock And Roll Bed*; Big Joe Williams, *Throw The Boogie Woogie*; Big Joe Duskin, *Down The Road A Piece*; Robert Shaw, *Fast Santa Fe [Bear Cat]*; L.C. Williams, *Boogie All The Time*; Piano Red, *The Right String But The Wrong Yo Yo*; Pete Johnson, *Half Tight Boogie*; Lightnin' Hopkins, *Hammond Boogie [Organ Boogie]*; Mercy Dee, *Red Light*; Big Walter Horton, *Walter's Boogie*; Clifton Chenier, *Houston Boogie*; L.C. Robinson, *Pine Top's Boogie Woogie*; Katie Webster, *I Know That's Right*; Dave Alexander, *Fillmore Street Boogie*; Pete Johnson, *Skid Row Boogie*

A collection demonstrating the persistence of the boogie idiom. There are guitar interpretations (such as those by Hooker, Hopkins, and Joe Williams), an organ rendering (Hopkins), plus harmonica and accordion performances (Horton and Chenier, respectively). These stand alongside pianists associated with the style (including Duskin, Johnson, Shaw, and Webster).

(v) Blues In The Field—Non-commercial Recordings

32 **The Boogie Woogie Boys—Albert Ammons-Pete Johnson-Meade "Lux" Lewis: The Complete Library of Congress Recordings 1938; Plus Film Soundtrack 1941 in Chronological Order—*Bonus Tracks*: Alternate Takes 1936–1939**

Blues Documents BDCD 6046 (Au)

Meade "Lux" Lewis, *Honky Tonk Train* (2495 A)/*Honky Tonk Train* (2495 B)/*Honky Tonk Train* (2496 A); Albert Ammons, *Boogie Woogie* (2497 A)/*Blues* (2497 B)/*Boogie Woogie* No. 2 (2498 A); Pete Johnson, *Dying Mother Blues* [Albert Ammons, vocal] (2498 B)/*Fo' O' Clock Blues* (2499 A)/*Roll 'Em* (2499 B); Albert Ammons, *Sweet Patootie Blues* (2500 A); Pete Johnson & Albert Ammons (film soundtrack 1941), *Untitled Piano Duet*/*Boogie Woogie Dream*; BONUS TRACKS: ALTERNATE TAKES: Albert Ammons & His Rhythm Kings, *Mile-Or-Mo Bird Rag* (take B); Albert Ammons, *Shout For Joy* (take 2); Harry James And The Boogie Woogie Trio [Ammons, piano], *Woo Woo* (take 2)/[Pete Johnson, piano], *Boo Woo* (take 2)

The predominant performances are "field recordings" not intended for commercial release. Alongside piano themes by his colleagues Ammons and Johnson, Lewis describes the origin of his celebrated *Honky Tonk Train Blues*. Short motion pictures are another means of musical dissemination and their soundtracks an unusual source for recordings.

33 **I Can Eagle Rock: Jook Joint Blues From Alabama and Louisiana Library Of Congress Recordings 1940–1941**

Various Artists

Travelin' Man TM CD09 (UK)

Tom Bell, *I Can Eagle Rock, Lord I Can Ball The Jack*; Oscar Woods, *Look Here Baby, One Thing I Got To Say*; Joe Harris, *East Texas Blues*; Noah Moore, *Oil City Blues*; Kid West, *Kid West Blues*; Oscar Woods, *Sometime I Get To Thinkin'* (take 1); Tom Bell, *Cross E Shimmy Dance Tune*; Noah Moore, *Settin' Here Thinkin'*; Oscar Woods, *Don't Sell It*; Tom Bell, *New York City Blues*; Kid West, *A-Natural Blues*; Noah Moore, *Lowdown Worry Blues*; Tom Bell, *I'm Worried Now And I Won't Be Worried Long*; Oscar Woods, *Sometimes I Get To Thinkin'* (take 2); Tom Bell, *Corrina*; Noah Moore, *Jerry's Saloon Blues*; Washboard Trio [Mobile Washboard Band], *Red Cross Blues*; Tom Bell, *C-Natural Blues*; Oscar Woods, *Boll Weevil Blues*; Noah Moore, *Mr. Crump Don't Like It*; Joe Harris, *Baton Rouge Rag*; Tom Bell, *Storm In Arkansas*

Woods, Harris, and West played in restaurants and street corners in Shreveport, Louisiana; Moore was based to the north, in Oil City, while Bell resided in Livingston, Alabama. Preserved in these field recordings, their live music was soon to be replaced by the jukebox, which swept aside many opportunities for rurally based musicians.

34 **Traveling Through the Jungle: Fife and Drum Band Music From The Deep South**

Various Artists

Testament TCD 5017

J.W. Jones Fife And Drum Band, *Old Hen Cackled, Laid A Double Egg* [Ephram Carter, vocal]/*Unknown Piece/Shout, Lula With The Red Dress On* [Carter, vocal]; J.W. Jones (dancing), *Buck Dance* [with Carter, body slaps and speech]; J.W. Jones Fife And Drum Band, *I Love Jesus, Yest I Do* [Carter, vocal]; J.W. Jones (fife solo), *Wake Up, Sal, Day Done Come, Let Me Chew Your Rosin Some*; J.W. Jones Fife And Drum Band, *Old Lady Dinah Sitting By The Fire* [Carter, vocal]; Sid Hemphill Band, *Jesse James* (with vocal); Alex Askew (four-note quills, vocal effects), *Come On, Boys, Let's Go To The Ball*; Sid Hemphill Band, *The Death March* (with vocal); Sid Hemphill (ten-note quills, vocal effects), *Emmaline Take Your Time*; Sid Hemphill Band, *The Sidewalks Of New York* (with vocal); J.W. Jones (fife solo), *John Henry*; J.W. Jones Fife And Drum Band, *No Name Piece* [Carter, vocal]/*Sal, You Churn The Butter/Look Out Of The Way*; Napoleon Strickland Fife And Drum Band, *My Babe* [Strickland & Othar Turner, vocal]; Napoleon Strickland (fife), *Traveling Through The Jungle* [with Fred McDowell, waste basket]; Compton Jones (vocal, whistling, washtub), *Sitting On Top Of The World* [with Turner, vocal]; Othar Turner Fife And Drum Band, *Late At Midnight, Just A Little 'Fore Day*; Napoleon Strickland Fife And Drum Band, *Granny Will Your Dog Bite* [Turner, vocal]; Compton Jones (whistling, washtub), *Number Five*; Napoleon Strickland Fife And Drum Band, *When The Saints Go Marching In* [Strickland, vocal]; Othar Turner Fife And Drum Band, *Sitting On Top Of The World* No. 2; Unidentified Fife And Drum Band, *Fife And Drum Piece/I'm So Worried* (with vocal); Napoleon Strickland (fife solo), *Baseball Bat*; Napoleon Strickland Fife And Drum Band, *Rollin' And Tumblin'*

These field recordings appear to demonstrate African survivals in rhythm and instrumentation. J.W. Jones and his compatriots were from Georgia, but the other musicians lived in northern Mississippi. Most performances date from the 1970s. Sides by Sid Hemphill's Band and the quill solos by Hemphill and Askew were cut in 1942.

35 **Wake Up Dead Man: Black Convict Worksongs From Texas Prisons**

Various Artists

Rounder CD 2031

Benny Richardson & Group, *Jody*—cross cutting; W.D. Alexander & Group, *Julie*—logging; Joseph "Chinaman" Johnson & Group, *Long Hot Summer Days*—flatweeding; Johnny Jackson & Group, *I'm In The Bottom*—spading; Ebbie Veasley, Marshall Phillip & Theo Mitchell, *Captain Don't Feel Sorry For A Longtime Man*; Houston Page & Group, *Down The Line*—flatweeding; Willie "Cowboy" Craig & Group, *Early In The Morning*—logging; Henry Scott & Group, *Hammer Ring*—cross cutting; Joseph "Chinaman" Johnson & Group, *Fallin' Down*—cross cutting; Unidentified, *Log Loading, Talk, Yells, Chants*; Benny Richardson & Group, *Grizzly Bear*—cross cutting

Made at the conclusion of prescriptive manual labour in Texas prison farms, these *a capella* work songs were recorded as late as 1965–6. They are another example of field investigation into a form of proto-blues not originally intended for commercial release. Note the different types of work to which they are performed.

(vi) Blues: Media and Messages

36 Circle Blues Session 1946

Dan Burley, Brownie and Stick[s] McGee [McGhee], Pops Foster
Southland SCD 9
Dan Burley's Skiffle Band, *Little Cat* (test)/*Big Cat Little Cat/Shotgun House Rag/Lakefront Blues/Fishtail Blues/Three Flights Up/Hersal's Rocks/Dusty Bottom Burley/31st Street Blues/Landlady's Night*; Brownie McGhee & Sticks McGhee, *Movin' To Kansas City/Railroad Bill/Rocks In My Bed/Tennessee Shuffle/Precious Lord/If I Could Hear My Mother Pray Again*
Dan Burley (a journalist) learned to play the piano in Chicago from the legendary Hersal Thomas (**231**). Though rarely recorded, he was a strong player whose New York session with the McGhee brothers popularized the term "skiffle." The McGhees worked well together, Sticks making one of the few recordings of the ballad *Railroad Bill.*

37 18 Tracks From The Film "Chicago Blues"

Various Artists
Red Lightnin' RLCD 0080
Buddy Guy, *We're Ready—First Time I Met The Blues*; Buddy Guy & Junior Wells, *Country Girl/Hoodoo Man*; Buddy Guy, *We're Ready*—Buddy Guy & Junior Wells, *In My Younger Days*; Johnny Young, *Driving Wheel/Walking Groundhog*; Muddy Waters, *She's 19 Years Old/Hoochie Coochie Man/I Got My Mojo Working*; Mighty Joe Young, *Why You Want To Hurt Me*; Koko Taylor, *Wang Dang Doodle*; J.B. Hutto, *Speak My Mind/Come On Back Home*; Johnny Lewis, *You Gonna Miss Me/Uncle Sam/Hobo Blues*
Film-maker and blues enthusiast Harley Cokliss produced, directed, filmed, and recorded a tribute to the music of his native Chicago in February 1970, bringing the club scene to a world-wide TV audience. Waters was past his peak, but Guy, Wells, Hutto, and Joe Young were in fine form. Lewis was a guitarist from Alabama.

38 Can't Keep From Crying: Topical Blues On The Death Of President Kennedy

Various Artists
Testament TCD 5007
Big Joe Williams, *A Man Amongst Men*; James & Fannie Brewer, *I Want To Know Why*; John Lee Granderson, *A Man For The Nation*; Otis Spann, *Sad Day In Texas*; Mary Ross, *President Kennedy Gave His Life*; Bill Jackson, *The 22nd Day Of November*; James Brewer, *Why Did He Have To Go?*; Johnny Young, *I Tried Not To Cry*; Avery Brady, *Poor Kennedy*; Fannie Brewer, *When We Got The Message*; Jimmy Brown, *He Was Loved By All The People*; Johnny Young, *Tribute To J.F.K.*; Avery Brady, *Poor Kennedy* No. 2
Anthologies of blues recordings on specific themes were not uncommon on long-playing records but have been ignored on CD. An important exception is this moving collection of blues on the assassination of President Kennedy, recorded by Pete Welding. The tributes indicate the depth of blues expression that is now being overlooked.

39 **The Chicago String Band**
Carl Martin, Johnny Young, John Lee Granderson, John Wrencher
Testament TCD 5006
The Sun Is Sinking Low [Granderson, vocal]/*Trouble On Your Hands* [Martin, vocal]/*Weeping & Moaning* [Young, vocal]/*You Know I Do* [Wrencher, vocal]/ *Hoodoo Blues* [Martin, vocal]/*You Got Good Business* [Young, vocal]/*Take It Easy Baby* [Granderson, vocal]/*I Got To Find That Woman* [Granderson, vocal]/*Clean Cut Mama* [Young, vocal]/*Railroad Blues* [Martin, vocal]/*Don't Sic Your Dogs On Me* [Wrencher, vocal]/*John Henry*/*Memphis, Tenn., 1939 Blues* [Young, vocal]/*Bye Bye Pete* [Young, vocal]
An experimental re-creation of the string bands that once featured in the South and numerous cities, in which the role of harmonica and fiddle are juxtaposed. There are well-integrated performances by Young, a Mississippi mandolin player, Wrencher, a one-armed harmonica player, and guitar-violinist Carl Martin. Such reconstructions ensured that their music was not forgotten.

40 **Live! At The Long Beach and San Francisco Blues Festivals**
Clifton Chenier And The Red Hot Louisiana Band
Arhoolie CD 404
LONG BEACH BLUES FESTIVAL (1983); *Introduction & Theme* (by Band)/*I've Had My Fun (Going Down Slow)*/*Zydeco Two Step*/*Calinda*/*What'd I Say?*/*Party Down*/*I'm Coming Home*/*Pinetop's Boogie Woogie*/*They Call Me Crazy*/*Zydeco Cha Cha*/*You Gonna Miss Me*/*Caledonia*; SAN FRANCISCO BLUES FESTIVAL (1982): *New Orleans Beat*/*Clifton's Zydeco*/*Let The Good Times Roll*/*Rock Me*/ *Louisiana Two-Step*/*Cher Catin*/*I'm The Zydeco Man*
With the growth in popularity of blues in the 1960s many singers were brought to a wider audience through festivals and tours. In turn, these became a source for recordings documenting the relationship of artist to audience. Here, the "King of Zydeco" (Chenier) plays in a variety of styles to California crowds.

PAUL OLIVER

2 Songsters and Proto-Blues

Blues is a music that catches the imagination and thrills the hearts of its enthusiasts, whether they are in the United States or the United Kingdom, Toulouse or Tokyo. It seems to speak across continents and oceans and break across cultural boundaries. Why a music which is often melancholy in delivery, which is sometimes direct and sometimes obscure in its lyrics, which is limited in its structure, and which is the creation of a disadvantaged ethnic minority has this remarkable effect is beyond the scope of this book. But that it does is indisputable.

There is no simple definition of blues, for many styles of black music come within its compass, as the chapters of this book illustrate. The term "the blues" has meant a fit of depression or a state of low spirits since the 16th century, but particularly for the last hundred years or so. We do not know when it was first adopted by blacks as a description of a song type that often expressed such feelings, but the word appears in songs by black composers around 1900. Blues is a state of mind, and it is also a song or music that gives voice to that state of mind, or which releases repressed emotions. Moreover, it is a structure for doing so—most frequently as the "12-bar blues" of three lines on an *AAB* rhyme scheme. This form made improvisation of new verses and accompaniments possible during performance, though blues singers often depend on familiar lyric formulae for many of their compositions. The solo singer with his guitar or sitting at a piano may epitomize the image of the blues performer, but small groups have probably always been active, even though the blues band became more popular on record later in the history of the music. Blues is often a reflection of poor living conditions, hard times, segregation, and difficult domestic relationships, but it can also be good for dancing and entertainment; it is even humorous. It is a complex music within its stylistic constraints, and some of that variety is evident in the range of records discussed in these pages.

No one is sure precisely how, when, or even where the blues began. At one time it was customary to assume that "blues was born in slavery", but there is no conclusive evidence that it was sung or performed, at least in the forms which we now recognize until much

Sharecropper boy playing one-string Diddley Bo, Missouri, 1938 (*Russell Lee/ FSA/Library of Congress*)

later. Yet there are good grounds for believing that the blues originated in the South of the United States, and that it was a rural music before it became an urban one. Both Texas and Mississippi figured prominently in the earliest text collections that give any indication of the emergence of the music; these were compiled in the first decade of the 20th century. The earliest recollections of hearing blues, in the memories of black artists such as the composer W.C. Handy and the travelling show singer Gertrude "Ma" Rainey (**162**), also refer to this period. We may be right in assuming that the blues appeared around the end of the 19th century, and in concluding that it arose from the musical types which were prevalent among blacks at that time. This chapter is concerned with those "proto-blues" and the "songsters", among others, who played and sang them.

Essential Records

(i) Contexts and Origins

Our problem in discussing the background and origins of blues stems from the fact that there were very few people sufficiently interested in black music to note that a new form was taking shape. If there were a few examples noted down by such folklorists as E.C. Perrow, Will H. Thomas, Howard Odum, and John A. Lomax, some 20 years were to pass before commercially available recordings of any kind were made of blues. When they appeared they were issued in segregated "race record" series aimed at black purchasers. By the 1920s several kinds of blues existed side by side, but it was not until the middle of the decade that folk forms were recorded. The antecedents of blues, and the music in its formative period, have to be reconstructed from comparison between early text collections and published blues compositions, the reminiscences and playing of veteran singers, and early race and documentary records.

For examples of the kind of plantation songs sung by slaves before the Civil War we have to turn to recordings made as much as a century later. In the 1930s many were made in the field for the Archive of American Folk Song in the Music Division of the Library of Congress. John A. Lomax and his son Alan Lomax were principally involved in this work. Several invaluable documentary albums were made of this historic material, but time has not dealt kindly with these discs cut on portable equipment and they have yet to appear on CD.

Apparently the penitentiary system sustained the slave song tradition through the perpetuation of similar working conditions of forced gang labour. With the "leader-and-chorus", "chorus-and-response" form and often, antiphonal singing, this style has strong similarities with group songs from the West African savannah regions, and may well be an example of a persistent tradition in black culture with its origins in Africa.

The types of work for which gang labour was employed in the Southern penitentiaries continued until the 1960s. In 1947 Alan Lomax made a return visit to Parchman Farm, the Mississippi penitentiary where he and his father had recorded many remarkable work songs a decade earlier. Improved techniques and the opportunity to record while the men were at work produced some thrilling examples, non more so than the powerful ax-cutting version of *Rosie*, about a legendary woman whose praises are sung by a group of ten men led by "C.B.". This most popular of Mississippi work songs is also reinterpreted as a solo by a tree-felling convict (*Katy Left Memphis*) and as a double-cutting ax song by four men, led by "22" (*Early In The Morning*– a fascinating, highly syncopated and polyrhythmic *tour de force*).

All the singers are identified by nicknames or pseudonyms but "22" and his team figure prominently, especially in the hoeing songs *Prettiest Train* and *One Dollar Mamie*. Several other moving songs are included, among them *Old Alabama* by "B.B" and gang, a version of *Jumpin' Judy*, one of the most widely-dispersed of these work songs, and the sad, slow *Road Song*, redolent of oppression, from whose words the title of the CD **Murderers' Home**, is drawn.

With the cessation of slavery black Americans were enabled to cultivate their own patches and farms, and it seems likely that solo work songs, called "hollers," developed at this time. Examples of these loosely structured songs are on the same compilation such as the version by "Bama" of the ballad about the bad man hero *Stackerlee*. Many are free in form and embellished with vocal ornamentation, such as the plough-hand's holler *Whoa Back* by "C.B.". "Tangle-eye" contributes another, a contemplative lament with hummed elaborations; such free improvisations from the cotton fields are significant forerunners of the blues.

Blues may have its origins far back in African-American history, though we have no evidence to prove that this is the case. There is substantial support for the contention that proto-blues forms existed in the 19th century, to which the blues relate. Another collection, **Roots Of The Blues**, drawn from Alan Lomax's field recordings, made in the South in 1942, 1947, and 1959–60, reveals the persistence of old traditions. Over a decade after the Parchman Farm titles were made, Leroy Miller and a dozen convicts, their tools clearly audible, recorded a strong work song at Lambert, Mississippi, *Berta Berta*. There was little sign that the tradition was near an end, though changes in working patterns and conditions were to bring its demise.

A vocal technique related to lead singing in these work groups can be heard in the individual holler. Recorded in 1959, Henry Ratcliff's *Louisiana*, which is intercut with *Field Song From Senegal* (by Bakari-Badji), demonstrates this relationship and draws attention to similarities in African-American and West African styles of performance. Undoubtedly archaic in North America were the ten-note panpipes, such as those used by Sid Hemphill on *Emmaline Take Your Time*. This music is known from 19th-century reports and was rarely performed as late as 1942, when Lomax collected this example. Perhaps as old were the fife-and-drum groups of the South, one of which was led by Hemphill (**34**). In the same vein, though recorded almost 20 years later, *Jim And John* is sung and played by Lonnie and Ed Young on bass drum and cane fife respectively; the marked drum rhythms, the shrill repetitive phrases on the fife, and the chanting of the title recall recordings of African orchestras. The instrument played by Ed Young was made from stalks of sugarcane, and early reporters on black music-making commented on this practise on Louisiana plantations. On the other hand, drums were banned in much of the South through the slavery period, for fear of their potential for communicating messages that might lead to insurrection. It is easy to make assumptions as to its African nature, but fife-and-drum bands were a feature of martial music and the Young family and similar groups may relate more directly to Civil War regimental bands.

Further examples of field hollers and "moans" are to be heard on this compilation, including religious performances (see also **243** and **323/4**). *Mama Lucy* by Leroy Gary contains stanzas associated with heavy manual maintenance work on the levees, or embankments, that control the flow of the Mississippi River. The most powerful of these levee camp hollers bear comparison with Rich Amerson's *Black Woman* on **Blues Roots** (**55**). They further confirm the link between collective and solo work songs, while *Rolled And Tumbled* sung by Rose Hemphill (the daughter of Sid), accompanied by Fred McDowell on guitar, establishes the connection with instrumental blues. *Poor Boy Blues* by John Dudley, with his exemplary slide-guitar accompaniment, is another example of the continuity of old songs: a version was collected in Mississippi some 50 years earlier.

A further survivor of an old tradition was the guitar and fiddle duet. Performed by Miles and Bob Pratcher, *Buttermilk* and *I'm Gonna Live Anyhow Till I Die* are examples of raw country music, not played with particular skill, but infectious in their swing and persistent syncopated beat. *Going Down To The Races*, with Fred McDowell on slide guitar and Miles Pratcher on second guitar, was recorded in Como, Mississippi; the extraordinary sound of this dance piece is heightened by Fannie Davis' comb-and-paper complement, shifting from imitations of McDowell's voice to mimicry of his bottleneck slide whining on the strings. *Old Original Blues*, with Fred McDowell's deep-throated vocal accompanied by the riffed guitar phrases of Pratcher and Davis, hauntingly brings together some of the currents that fed the main stream of blues development.

But there were other currents, and several are represented on **Texas Worried Blues: Henry Thomas**. Thomas is probably the oldest African-American singer to be heard on record. Born of ex-slave parents in Texas in 1874, he had a repertoire which spanned the range of songs and tune types that constituted the music of the post-Reconstruction era in which he, as a young man, must have learned to perform. Black musicians were frequently employed on the plantations to play for dances at the "Big House"; their successors, the minstrels of the rural Southern communities, performed much the same role, and there is little doubt that the dance rhythms that underlie *Old Country Stomp* date back to that period. It is a reel, a country dance in which sets are called and couplets chanted. But the most notable aspect of this recording, or of another reel, *Charmin' Betsy* with its echoes of *Coming Round the Mountain*, is Thomas' breathy, syncopated playing of the reed pipes, or "quills", a form of syrinx ("panpipes") in which several reeds of graded lengths were tied together. Like the cane flutes, they seldom appeared on record.

Ballads, one of the oldest of European narrative folksong forms, were adopted by African-American musicians, though few original ballads with black heroes date from earlier than the late 19th century. One that may do is *John Henry*, which tells the story of one man's competition with a steam-driven drilling machine. The "Steel driver" fell dead in the process in Henry Thomas' version of the ballad, which is little known in Texas. Other ballads like *Bob McKinney* refer to St Louis or Arkansas. Thomas probably picked them up on his travels, for he was a hobo who "rode the blinds" on the freight trains that crossed the States, as he narrated in a remarkable monologue, *Railroadin' Some*. Thomas accompanied himself on guitar, always rhythmically arresting and often with melodic interest.

Some of Thomas' songs came straight from the minstrel show or its small-scale successor, the medicine show. Among these are *Fishing Blues*, rather bowdlerized in his version, and *Honey, Won't You Allow Me One More Chance?*, a "coon" song of 1897 written by the gifted, if perplexing black composer Irving Jones, which slipped rapidly back into the very tradition which it imitated. In Henry Thomas' rough, brusque vocal the humorous appeal of the original song was expressed as an interpersonal drama. Blues emerged when Thomas was in his late twenties and he assimilated the new song form as he did others, adapting and molding them to his performance style. It is the blues which seems to have brought out his best guitar playing, as on *Texas Easy Street*, a swinging blues with a dance lilt which had a couplet and refrain line structure: he claimed at the end of each verse "I'm goin' back to Texas, live on Easy Street." Several of his blues are in an archaic form, like *Texas Worried Blues* itself, which simply comprises three-line verses with the same words sung to each line, while *Red River Blues* has similarly basic lyrics, with the lines sung four times. Others, like *Bull Doze Blues* are irregular and half-chanted; we seem to be witnessing Henry Thomas groping for the form which was later crystallized as the familiar *AAB* structure. And there were songs which are titled as blues (which have their roots in work song) and which were known to most early singers, like *Don't Leave Me Here* (also known as *Alabama Bound*).

Henry Thomas is a perpetually fascinating hobo singer-guitarist: his capacity to synthesize new songs from the fragments garnered on his travels gives us insights into the diversity of song types at the close of the 19th century, and of the creative process among folk musicians as the blues began to take shape.

41 **Murderers' Home: An Anthology Of Negro Worksongs Compiled By Alan Lomax**
Various Artists
Sequel NEX CD 121 (UK)
Jimpson [or "Tangle-Eye"?] & Group, *Road Song [The Murderers' Home]/No More My Lawd*; Unidentified Prisoner ["Tangle-Eye"?], *Katy Left Memphis*; "B.B" & Group, *Old Alabama/Black Woman*; "Tangle-Eye", "Fuzzle Red", "Hard Hair" & Group; *Jumpin' Judy*; "C.B.", *Whoa Back*; "22" & Group, *Prettiest Train/One Dollar Mamie/It Makes A Long Time Man Feel Bad*; "C.B." & Group, *Rosie*; "Bama", *Levee Camp Holler*; [Unidentified Interviewee ("Bama"), *What Makes A Song Leader*]; "22", "Little Red", "Tangle-Eye", & "Hard Hair", *Early In The Mornin'*; [Unidentified Interviewee ("Bama"), *How I Got In The Penitentiary* (burlesque autobiography)]; "Tangle-Eye", *"Tangle-Eye" Blues*; "Bama", *Stackerlee*; Alex, *Prison Blues*; Bob & Leroy, *Sometimes I Wonder/Bye Bye Baby*

42 **Roots Of The Blues**
Various Artists
New World 80252-2
Henry Ratcliff, *Louisiana*—Bakari-Badji, *Field Song From Senegal* (intercut recordings); John Dudley, *Poor Boy Blues*; "Tangle-Eye" [or Unidentified Prisoner], *Katie Left Memphis*; Leroy Miller & Group of Prisoners, *Berta, Berta*; Fred McDowell & Miles Pratcher [& Fannie Davis], *Old Original Blues*

[*Fred McDowell Blues*]; Ed Young & Lonnie Young, *Jim And John*; Alex Askew [Sid Hemphill], *Emmaline Take Your Time*; Miles Pratcher & Bob Pratcher, *Buttermilk*; Leroy Gary, *Mama Lucy*; Miles Pratcher & Bob Pratcher, *I'm Gonna Live Anyhow Till I Die*; "Tangle-Eye" & Group of Prisoners [or Jimpson & Group]; *No More My Lord*; Rev. Crenshaw & Congregation of New Brown's Chapel, Memphis, *Lining Hymn And Prayer*; Fred McDowell, *Death Comes A-Creepin' In My Room [Soon One Mornin']*; Congregation of New Brown's Chapel, Memphis, *Church-House Moan*; Bessie Jones, *Beggin' The Blues*; Rose Hemphill [or Rosalie Hill] & Fred McDowell, *Rolled And Tumbled*; Fred McDowell, Miles Pratcher, & Fannie Davis, *Goin' Down To The Races*; Forrest City Joe, *You Gotta Cut That Out*

43 Texas Worried Blues: Henry Thomas, Complete Recorded Works 1927–1929

Yazoo (CD) 1080/1

Fishing Blues/Old Country Stomp/Charmin' Betsy/Lovin' Babe/Railroadin' Some/Don't Leave Me Here/The Little Red Caboose/Bob McKinney/Honey, Won't You Allow Me One More Chance?/Run, Mollie, Run/Shanty Blues/Woodhouse Blues/John Henry/Cottonfield Blues/Arkansas/The Fox And Hounds/Red River Blues/Jonah In The Wilderness/When The Train Comes Along/Bull Doze Blues/Don't Ease Me In/Texas Easy Street/ Texas Worried Blues

(ii) Southern Strings and Instrumentalists

In the ante-bellum South slaves who had instrumental musical abilities were in demand to play for dances up at the "Big House", and for "frolics" and dances in the more liberally run plantations. There is evidence that the gourd "banjar" was already recognized as an instrument of African origin in the 18th century. Drums were banned, as has been noted, but banjo players were joined by fiddlers, bowed instruments also having West African precedents. Similar string traditions continued well into the 20th century as black players performed for their own communities and also continued to play for white dances and functions. In spite of its late date, the recordings having been made for the Library of Congress in the 1940s, **Altamont: Black String-band Music** gives as convincing an impression of early plantation music as we are likely ever to hear.

Banjo player Nathan Frazier, and fiddler Frank Patterson were recorded in March 1942 by John Work, an African-American folklorist from Fisk University, in Nashville, Tennessee. They forced the pace on [*Old*] *Dan Tucker*, a dance tune which was already a century old. *Bile Them Cabbage Down* is probably as ancient, both themes being in the repertoire of rural string bands both black and white. The sawing fiddle against the bright, sharp banjo picking would make the dancers kick their heels, while Frazier's rough barking of the verses filled out the sound. Other tunes include *Texas Traveler* and the blues was acknowledged with one of the early standard themes, *Corinne*. The historic combination of banjo and fiddle was filled out by the guitar, when cheap instruments became available late in the 19th century. John Lusk, a fiddle player from Warren County, Tennessee, was the grandson of a slave fiddler; he led a spirited band with Murph Gribble playing banjo and Albert York on guitar.

The trio were recorded for the Library of Congress in Rocky Island, Tennessee, in 1946. "I was thunderstruck. We had never heard music like that," said Stu Jamieson who recorded the band as it pitched into *Roaring River*. We can share his amazement, listening to the virtuosity let along the sheer energy of the band as they play the old favorite of string bands, *Apple Blossom*. Their repertoire carried echoes of a darker past in *Pateroller'll Catch You*, a piece formerly known as *Run Nigger Run* which warned escaping slaves of the "patrols" that were out to catch them. Three years later Jamieson returned, to record the band again; they were in superb form on *Altamont*, from which the disc is named.

String bands were known to have been very active in Tennessee and Kentucky, but there is increasing evidence that though little recorded commercially, they were to be found throughout the South. **Texas: Black Country Dance Music** examines the tradition in Henry Thomas' home state. In Dallas, Old Man Coley's family band was a familiar sight, "serenading" in the streets or playing for dances with an instrumentation of fiddles, guitars, mandolin, and string bass. His son Coley Jones was born around 1890 and continued the family tradition with his Dallas String Band which was recorded several times by a Columbia field unit between 1927 and 1929. It was a very popular group and its appeal lay partly in the band's willingness to play a diverse range of themes. *Dallas Rag*, for instance, is a rare example of ragtime played by a string band. In its classic form ragtime was a composed music which enjoyed a vogue at the turn of the century. Although it was written mainly for piano it was influenced by black jigs and dance pieces; the Dallas recording gives us a glimpse of its antecedents.

Coley Jones leads on mandolin with great flair, taking the band through an *ABBAABCBA* sequence of successive strains. With its bright sound and faultless execution it is a masterpiece of Southern string band music. Other items are played with the same accomplishment, the lyrics on *Chasin' Rainbows* or *I Used To Call Her Baby* relating back to the "Coon song" era of the 1900s. Several tunes were drawn from black shows of the early 1920s, among them *Shine* with its jaunty introduction, or *So Tired*. A measure of mocking humor is evident in some of the vocals, as on the Clarence Williams composition

Sugar Blues. It seems that for these "serenaders" blues was another form of song rather than a means of self-expression; this is evident on *Sweet Mama Blues* and *Hokum Blues*, which opens with some minstrel-show "business."

There were other groups working in Dallas, like Frenchy's String Band, led by an excellent cornetist in the New Orleans jazz style. His identity has been much debated but he may have been Hippolyte Christian; he took the string band through two railroad blues, including *Sunshine Special*, a celebration of a famous train that served Dallas. Then there was Jake Jones and The Gold Front Boys, named after a saloon on Central Tracks, the sector of the Dallas railroad which was lined with sporting houses, saloons, and theatres. The group had an unknown personel which included a clarinetist accompanied by traditional banjo and guitar. Such string bands continued into the 1930s; the Dallas Jamboree Band appears to have been a country outfit visiting the city when it was recorded in 1935. The instrumentation was largely improvised, with Charles "Chicken" Jackson playing a domestic washboard rubbed with thimbles as a rhythm instrument; he also played the jug on *Elm Street Woman Blues*. Named after the "main stem" of the black sector of town, it featured leader Carl Davies singing a hoarse vocal and vocalizing on kazoo. *Flying Crow Blues*, with Davis playing swanee whistle, was on a popular theme about a train which ran between Port Arthur and Texakarna and beyond—a hint perhaps, of the origins of the band.

Trains figure prominently in the recordings made in the railroad nodal city of Dallas, and are imitated by harmonica player William McCoy. The harmonica was the easiest of instruments to carry—in a hip pocket or an adapted gun belt—and the relationship between the hollers of the field hands and improvisations on the "harp" is often evident. *Train Imitations And The Fox Chase* "mocked" the sounds of the locomotive and the baying of the hounds—familiar sounds in the rural South and obligatory for any harp player. *Central Tracks Blues* brilliantly evokes the sounds of the sector; McCoy squeezed out the sounds by playing in the technique known as "crossed harp" (for example, playing in the key of E on a harmonica tuned to A). He was a gifted improviser who translated the sounds that he would mimic into moving blues like *How Long Baby*.

Texas fared better than some regions in the recording of its string bands, but the commercial companies missed the celebrated Wright Brothers String Band in Texas, just as they failed to record Willie Walker's in the Carolinas, or Sid Hemphill's in Mississippi. They were more attracted to bands playing home-made and novelty instruments. These were usually string bands augmented with a domestic washboard used as a rhythm instrument by scraping forks or thimbles across its corrugations, an inverted washtub used a string bass, fiddles, and guitars made out of cigar boxes and so on. The custom arose, it seems, from the making of improvised instruments by children who wanted to form bands of their own. One such group, of white children, the Razzy Dazzy Spasm Band, was familiar in the streets of New Orleans early in the 20th century, and was even given coins by Sarah Bernhardt. But the custom goes back much longer than that: Dan Emmett's minstrels played fire-tongs and rattled the bones on-stage in the 1840s.

While the use of home-made instruments in many cases arose from genuine hardship, many bands exploited their comic appeal, reinforcing minstrel stereotypes in the process. This may account for the popularity of the jug bands. Sometimes two, or even three, jugs have been known to be played in a band, but usually there was only one. A fruity, booming sound like that of a brass bass could be obtained by blowing into the neck of a demijohn, a stovepipe or even a length of hose. **Gus Cannon**, who was born in Mississippi in 1883, led one such jug band, though his "jug" was a kerosene can with a kazoo mounted on the handle. But his real instrument was the banjo; as a child he made his first one from a bread-pan and a broom-handle. He moved to Clarksdale in the "Delta" and worked at various jobs while developing his skills as a banjo player at local dances and outdoor picnics. For many years he traveled with the medicine shows, entertainments intended to attract crowds to the vendors of patent medicines. Itinerant "doctors" gave employment on their shows to many aspiring musicians, both black and white.

Some of the medicine show songs Gus Cannon recorded were under the name of Banjo Joe. *My Money Never Runs Out* was given a sprightly treatment with clear picking; it was a comic fantasy written in 1900 by the black composer Irving Jones, who may well have been the author of the remarkable song *Can You Blame The Colored Man?*, which was a parody of the black leader Booker T. Washington and his notorious dinner with President Theodore Roosevelt at the White House in 1901. Other titles included a banjo ragtime piece, *Madison Street Rag*, an example of the kind of music which the ragtime composer adapted to piano, to which Gus gave a spoken commentary. Blues on banjo are rather rare, for the short notes do not lend themselves to vocalized treatment. But Gus Cannon played the banjo across his lap for *Poor Boy, Long Ways From Home*, stroking the strings with a slide on this, one of the earliest of blues to be noted in the field.

A couple of months later he made the first recordings of his small group, Cannon's Jug Stompers with his friend Ashley Thompson on guitar. But the outstanding musician on this and all pieces by the band was the harmonica player Noah Lewis from Henning, Tennessee (112). Strong yet sensitive, his continually inventive improvisations are heard on the band's first title, *Minglewood Blues*, and on such instrumentals as *Ripley Blues*, with the mouth-harp wailing against the paced rhythms of his companions. Classics of their kind, the recordings that followed were often lyrically interesting; *Feather Bed*, for instance, opened with a verse that referred to the years before the Civil War. Two takes of *Viola Lee Blues* exist, enabling us to study the carefully considered arrangement of the tune; the second take is a little more forceful. To a considerable extent jug bands took over the tradition of string bands, harmonica replacing fiddle as the lead instrument, and the blues bringing a new, expressive sound to their dance-based music.

44 **Altamont: Black Stringband Music from the Library of Congress**
Various Artists
Rounder CD 0238
Nathan Frazier & Frank Patterson, *[Old] Dan Tucker/Old Cow Died/Bile Them Cabbage Down/Po Black Sheep/Eighth Of January/Corinne/Texas Traveler*; Murph Gribble, John Lusk & Albert York, *Rolling River/Old Sage Friend/Apple Blossom/Pateroller'll Catch You/Across The Sea/Cincinnati/Altamont*

45 **Texas Black Country Dance Music (1927–1935): Complete Recorded Works In Chronological Order**
Various Artists
Document DOCD 5162 (Au)
Dallas String Band, *Dallas Rag/Sweet Mama Blues/So Tired/Hokum Blues/Chasin' Rainbows/I Used To Call Her Baby/Shine/Sugar Blues*; William McCoy, *Mama Blues/Train Imitations And The Fox Chase/Just It/How Long Baby/Out Of Doors Blues/Central Tracks Blues*; Will Day, *Central Avenue Blues/Sunrise Blues*; Frenchy's String Band, *Texas And Pacific Blues/Sunshine Special*; Jake Jones & The Gold Front Boys, *Monkeyin' Around/Southern Sea Blues*; Carl Davis & Dallas Jamboree Jug Band, *Elm Street Woman Blues/It May Be My Last Night/Dusting The Frets/Flying Crow Blues*

46 **Gus Cannon: Complete Recorded Works In Chronological Order, Volume 1 (1927–1928)**
Document DOCD 5032 (Au)
Banjo Joe (Gus Cannon), *Jonestown Blues/Poor Boy, Long Ways From Home/Madison Street Rag/Jazz Gypsy Blues/Can You Blame The Colored Man?/My Money Never Runs Out*; Cannon's Jug Stompers, *Minglewood Blues/Big Railroad Blues/Madison Street Rag/Springdale Blues/Ripley Blues/Pig Ankle Strut/Noah's Blues/Hollywood Rag/Heart-Breakin' Blues/Feather Bed/Cairo Rag/Bugle Call Rag/Viola Lee Blues* (take 1)/*Viola Lee Blues* (take 2)/*Riley's Wagon*

(iii) Songsters

The emphasis of traditional music-making played on the front porch or for dancing in the yard was to change under the influence of blues. Blues added new sounds to the medicine shows too, but in these and other settings, long-held traditions in black musical history continued to thrive. Black entertainers often made a distinction between the "musicianer" who played instrumental music, but did not sing, and the "songster" who accompanied his vocals on an instrument. A generation older than the majority of blues singers, the songsters were recorded in the 1920s and in some cases, much later. They were alive to songs of every description, from "sentimentals" and "heart songs" to ballads and "reels." Songsters were proud of their extensive repertoires and their skill as entertainers; few were as proud as Huddie Ledbetter.

When the Lomaxes were recording at the Louisiana state penitentiary at Angola in 1933 they encountered a "trusty" laundryman with a scar, who claimed to be the "King of the Twelve-String Guitar Players of the World". He was Huddie Ledbetter, called "Lead Belly" by his fellow convicts and now generally known as "Leadbelly." His discoverers soon found that his claim was not an idle boast; he was the most impressive single artist that they had encountered in many years of fieldwork. But Leadbelly had led a violent life and had served time for murder, attempted homicide, and assault. He recorded at Angola for a second time in 1934 (**258**). Soon after he was released, and John Lomax employed him as his driver; within six months Leadbelly was introduced to the world of folksong enthusiasts in New York.

Born in 1889 and raised on a farm near Shreveport, Louisiana, he had acquired some experience of the city having partnered Blind Lemon Jefferson in Dallas, Texas (**126**). His years in prison had exposed him to a large number of penitentiary songs, which he assimilated along with his vast store of rural dances and themes. To the eastern folklorists he was a revelation, a throwback to the presumed folk past, and many regarded him as the "last of the great blues singers." It is possible now to view Leadbelly for what he was, an exceptional songster with an unrivaled repertoire of more than 500 songs. He was from the tradition that was exemplified by Henry Thomas, who was 25 years his senior. Ledbelly's first commercial recordings did not succeed with black purchasers—they were too anachronistic—but half a century later they intimate the tremendous power of his 12-string guitar playing and the vigor of his singing which so amazed his new audience (**128**). By 1939 he was at ease in the New York environment, but still capable of drawing on his store of songs and experiences.

Leadbelly: Complete Recorded Works, Volume 4 (1944) finds him in splendid voice, and generally well recorded. The ballad *Ella Speed* is a superb example of Leadbelly at his best, with fine guitar and sparkling support on zither by Paul Mason Howard. His range was remarkable: he sang cowboy songs like *Cow Cow Yicky Yicky Yea*, and such work songs as the stirring *Take This Hammer*, the prison song *Juliana Johnson* and the unaccompanied railroad holler *Line 'Em*. The spiritual tradition which so many songsters and blues singers inherited was remembered on *The Blood Done Sign My Name* or *There's A Man Going Round Taking Names*, and which he shared with Sonny Terry and Woody Guthrie on *We Shall Be Free*. Leadbelly's remarkably varied abilities are evident throughout: the swinging country reel *Corn Bread Rough* is to his own concertina accompaniment; his barrelhouse piano playing is captured on *Eagle Rock Rag*; and there is beautiful slide (or slack string) playing on *Children's Blues*. Childhood was always in his mind and he continued to recall country dances like *Red Bird* or the excitement and disillusionment of *On A Christmas Day*.

It is not difficult to appreciate why Leadbelly made such a deep impression on the folk music specialists of New York, and why in turn, their admiration and persuasive convictions influenced him. In a period of protest song he out-composed them all with his autobiographical *Bourgeois Blues* and his equally vehement *Jim Crow Blues*, while an unknown but delighted audience joined him on the anti-war *Army Life*. Though he has often been regarded disparagingly as a "folk singer", Leadbelly was much more than this; apart from being the bearer of old African-American traditions into the mid-century he was a considerable blues singer. Some of his blues were adaptations from records he had heard in prison—from Bessie Smith's *Backwater Blues* to Leroy Carr's *In The Evenin' When The Sun Goes Down*. But others were original compositions, such as the comment on war-time California, *National Defense Blues*, or the slow drag *Easy Rider*. Leadbelly's music was memorable, and some of his songs have become undisputed classics of African-American genres—none more so than his forceful version of the work song *Rock Island Line*, with powerful vocal and thunderous guitar, or the waltz-time evergreen *Goodnight Irene*. Leadbelly was lionized in New York but he coped with the admiration of the folk audiences remarkably well, better in fact than have many blues enthusiasts who resented his popularity and overlooked his unparalleled gifts.

Leadbelly died at the age of 61. Frank Stokes was his contemporary, born in 1887 and living until 1955. Apart from a couple of years when his records were issued he remained known only to local listeners in Memphis and Mississippi. Yet he epitomized the songster in his life and his approach. Originally from a tiny rural community, he moved to Memphis when he was a boy and began playing guitar on the streets when he was 13. A strong man, he earned his living as a blacksmith, though he traveled with the medicine shows and played professionally for local events and parties. His friend Dan Sane accompanied him on two-thirds of his 40 recordings, a selection from which appear on **Frank Stokes: Creator Of The Memphis Blues**.

Medicine-show humor is evident in the self-deprecating *Chicken You Can Roost Behind the Moon*, a "coon song" of the 1900s, and in the fast, narrative *It's A Good Thing* with its sly references. *You Shall* is older, with verses that had been collected before the Civil War. Its full title was *You Shall Be Free*, which may have been too sensitive for the record company even at that late date. All these songs have a rolling quality, being played to a thumb-picked dance rhythm by Stokes and with an augmenting flat-picked (plectrum) accompaniment, executed with great skill by Dan Sane. The guitar lines of the two men integrated superbly, giving a flowing yet compelling movement to such songs as *Mr Crump Don't Like It*, a comment on the somewhat repressive regime of Mayor "Boss" Crump, and most impressively on *Beale Town Bound.* Possessing a strong, grainy voice with considerable volume, Stokes was very effective in these songs that projected to a crowd, yet he had rhythms that were ideal for dancing. He also looked to the blues, from one of the earliest collected in the field *Tain't Nobody's Business If I Do* to the established 3-line, 12-bar form of the solo *Mistreating' Blues.*

At much the same time Joshua Barnes Howell was recording in Atlanta. A songster of the same generation, he was born in 1888 in rural Georgia and farmed until he was 20. By this time he had picked up many songs and had begun to teach himself guitar. An argument with his brother-in-law led to a shooting which cost him his leg. Unable to farm any more, he moved to Alabama, where he lived by bootlegging liquor until he was sentenced to prison. On his release he played in the streets and, as "Peg Leg" Howell, became a familiar figure on Decatur Street. When Columbia began field recording he was the company's first rural singer. By the time the titles on **Peg Leg Howell & Eddie Anthony, Volume 1** (1926–1928) were made he was 40 years old and had been exposed to every kind of rural music, which he absorbed and subsequently recorded. His first title, *Coal Man Blues*, was a curious amalgam of a ballad about a coal delivery man being run over by a train (with a rhetorical question at the end of the verses), and the sales song of the coal man. *Skin Game Blues* was another ballad fragment, based on the old song in the white tradition, *The Roving Gambler.*

Howell performed in the street where he was joined by Eddie Anthony, a country fiddle player, and Henry Williams, who played second guitar. They recorded some rowdy, infectious dance pieces like *Peg Leg Stomp* or, by Anthony and Williams alone, *Geogia Crawl.* It recalled Louis Armstrong's *Georgia Grind*, while *New Jelly Roll Blues* was the same song as Jelly Roll Morton's tune, though Howell learned it from one Elijah Lawrence; it is difficult to ascertain whether they drew from common sources or whether the song had filtered back into the folk tradition. But there is no doubt that the Gang's *Hobo Blues* derived from *Cow Cow Blues* recorded by Charles "Cow Cow" Davenport. Like Leadbelly, Peg Leg Howell picked up his songs from every source, records included; several came from his experiences in prison. His voice was gruff but his guitar playing was sensitive, as on the unique *Please Ma'am*, a blues that virtually consists of one line repeated in different ways, perhaps a sole representative on record of the proto-blues type called "over-and-over." Boisterous with his Gang, his voice was lugubrious when he was alone, singing the deeply sombre *Rock and Gravel Blues*. Elemental but moving, most of his blues are on the conventional 12-bar pattern; they emphasize Peg Leg Howell's importance as one who represents the transition from songster to blues singer (**136**).

Songsters may be broadly divided between those that traveled, picking up jobs where they went, and those less extrovert artists who preferred to play for their local communities. Both are represented on the justly titled **The Greatest Songsters**. John Hurt was definitely one of the stay-at-homes. He was born in 1894 at Teoc, Mississippi, but soon moved to Avalon in Carroll County, which remained his home throughout his life. A small farmer who moved away rarely, he did have a spell working on the railroad in 1916, when he learned *Spike Driver Blues*, one of the cycle of ballads on the John Henry theme. Based on the Anglo-Scots tradition, early ballads often take a 16-bar form. Black ballads are sometimes sung as couplets with a refrain line, like *Frankie*, John Hurt's version of the Frankie and Albert story recorded by Leadbelly (**258**). His guitar accompaniment was deft and accomplished. Other ballads included *Louis Collins*, which has not been collected elsewhere, and another version of *Stack O' Lee Blues* about the Mississippi bad man, whose legendary exploits survive even today in "toasts."

As a member of his church, "Mississippi" John Hurt (the tag was a record executive's idea) knew many spirituals, and recorded a couple: *Praying On The Old Camp Ground* refers back to the camp meetings of the 19th century. He played for square dances too, often with a white fiddler, but he did not have to sing to big audiences; though husky, his voice was gentler than that of many songsters, while the subtle complexity of his three-finger picking style, with steady thumb beat, was not coarsened by the need for volume. Like other songsters, Hurt had a varied repertoire, including in *Candy Man Blues* a mildly erotic ragtime piece. He also composed his own blues and it was one of these, *Avalon Blues* that led to his rediscovery 35 years later, in 1963. With his exceptional guitar playing undiminished in quality and his voice still warm and intimate, he played briefly for folk clubs in the east before returning to his Mississippi home, where he died in 1966.

Richard "Rabbit" Brown was a notable songster who worked as a New Orleans boatman on Lake Ponchatrain. He made only a few titles but they include a singular and otherwise unrecorded black ballad, the *Mystery Of The Dunbar's Child* and the last great ballad in the genre, *Sinking Of The Titanic. Never Let The Same Bee Sting You Twice* was from the coon song era, written in 1900 and sung by Brown with a gloomy conviction which its composer Chris Smith could hardly have intended. Though Rabbit Brown had a growling voice his guitar playing was sensitive and *James Alley Blues* was a subtle composition. He too stayed in his own patch of southern Louisiana, but Hambone Willie Newbern went further afield, working for many years with the traveling medicine shows.

The catholicity of Newbern's songs is evidence of his appeal to a variety of audiences. Medicine show entertainers often worked the crowds with songs that could be locally reinterpreted—*Nobody Knows (What The Good Deacon Does)* was just such a song with its insinuating lyrics and mistrust of the cleric. *Way Down In Arkansas* is unexpected in its nostalgic sentiments, saved from sweetness by Newbern's rasping voice; it contrasted with the suggestive *She Could Toodle-Oo* on the one hand, and the original blues with its disillusioned reflection on his "dreamy-eyed woman." And in *Roll And Tumble Blues* we are witness to the beginnings of one of the classic strains in blues which was picked up many years later by a number of Chicago blues singers (**361**, **377**). In the recordings of these songsters we can see how the blues related to a variety of African-American idioms that preceded and helped to give shape to the new music.

47 Leadbelly: Complete Recorded Works 1939–1947 In Chronological Order, Volume 4, c. May to 27 October 1944
Document DOCD 5310 (Au)
In The Evening' When The Sun Goes Down/Easy Rider [See See Rider]/We Shall Be Free/Keep Your Hands Off Her/There's A Man Going Round Taking Names/Red Bird/Line 'Em/T.B. Blues/Jim Crow Blues/Bourgeois Blues/Army Life/Mr. Hitler [Hitler Song]/Juliana Johnson/Jean Harlow/Corn Bread Rough/ National Defense Blues/Children's Blues [Little Children's Blues]/The Blood

Done Sign My Name [Ain't You Glad]/Cow Cow Yicky Yicky Yea/Ella Speed/ Rock Island Line/Tell Me Baby/Take This Hammer/Irene [Goodnight Irene]/ Western Plain/On A Christmas Day/Backwater Blues/Eagle Rock Rag [Hot Piano Rag]/The Eagle Rocks

48 **Frank Stokes: Creator Of The Memphis Blues**
Yazoo (CD) 1056
Memphis Rounder's Blues; Beale Street Sheiks [Stokes & Sane], *Unnamed Blues [Jumpin' On The Hill]*; Frank Stokes, *Nehi Mamma Blues/Tain't Nobody's Business If I Do* Part 2; Beale Street Sheiks, *Mr. Crump Don't Like It*; Frank Stokes, *Mistreatin' Blues/It Won't Be Long Now*; Beale Street Sheiks, *Chicken You Can Roost Behind The Moon/You Shall/Sweet To Mama*; Frank Stokes, *Stomp That Thing*; Beale Street Sheiks, *Wasn't That Doggin' Me/Beale Town Bound/It's A Good Thing*

49 **Peg Leg Howell & Eddie Anthony: Complete Recorded Works In Chronological Order, Volume 1, 8 November 1926 to 13 August 1928**
Various Artists
Document[-Matchbox] MBCD 2004 (Au)
"Peg Leg" Howell, *Coal Man Blues/Tishamingo Blues/New Prison Blues/Fo' Day Blues*; "Peg Leg" Howell & His Gang, *New Jelly Roll Blues/Beaver Slide Rag/Papa Stobb Blues/Sadie Lee Blues/Too Tight Blues/Moanin' And Groanin' Blues/Hobo Blues/Peg Leg Stomp*; Peg Leg Howell, *Doin' Wrong/Skin Game Blues*; Henry Williams & Eddie Anthony, *Georgia Crawl/Lonesome Blues*; Peg Leg Howell, *Please Ma'am/Rock And Gravel Blues/Low-Down Rounder Blues/ Fairy Blues*; "Sloppy" Henry, *Canned Heat Blues/Say I Do It*

50 **The Greatest Songsters (1927–1929); Complete Recorded Works In Chronological Order**
Various Artists
Document DOCD 5003 (Au)
Richard "Rabbit" Brown, *James Alley Blues/Never Let The Same Bee Sting You Twice/I'm Not Jealous/Mystery Of The Dunbar's Child/Sinking Of The Titanic*; Mississippi John Hurt, *Frankie/Nobody's Dirty Business/Ain't No Tellin'/Louis Collins/Avalon Blues/Big Leg Blues/Stack O' Lee Blues/Candy Man Blues/Got The Blues Can't Be Satisfied/Blessed Be The Name/Praying On The Old Camp Ground/Blue Harvest Blues/Spike Driver Blues*; Hambone Willie Newbern, *She Could Toodle-Oo/Nobody Knows (What The Good Deacon Does)/Shelby County Workhouse Blues/Way Down In Arkansas/Hambone Willie's Dreamy-Eyed Woman's Blues/Roll And Tumble Blues*

Basic Records

(i) Contexts and Origins

51 **Elder Songsters, 1: Music From The South, Volume 6**
Various Artists
Folkways 2655—Cassette
Suddie Griffins, *I Heard The Voice Of Jesus Say/Go Preach My Gospel*;

Emmett Brand, *Most Done Traveling (Rocky Road)/Give Me That Old Time Religion/Take This Hammer/My Old Mother/Stay, John, Don't You Ride No More/The Chickens An' Crows/I'm Goin' To Cross The Rivers Of Jordan, Some Of These Days/Riding My Buggy, My Whip In My Hand/Singing On The Old Church Ground/Baby Crying'*; Wilson Boling, *I'm So Glad That I Am Free/We Have Mothers Over Yonder*; Wilson Boling, Verna Ford, *Come To Jesus*; Bessie Ford, Horace Sprott, Nellie Hastings, Annie Sprott, *O Baptise Me John In The River Of Jordan/Just Over In The Glory Land*; Jake Field, Eastman Brand, Arthur Holifield, *Father, I Stretch My Hand To Thee*; Jake Field & Group, *Down Here Lord, Waitin' On You*

These are moving and wistful field recordings, made in 1954, of elderly sharecroppers farming in the Talladega National Forest, central Alabama. Most were born in the 1870s, though Wilson Boling was born a slave. Their unaccompanied songs, including Weslyan and "Dr Watts" hymns, spirituals, field calls, and slavery songs link with the ante-bellum past.

52 **Negro Work Songs And Calls**

Various Artists

Library of Congress AFS L8—Cassette

Henry Truvillion, *Unloading Rails/Tamping Ties*; Sam Hazel, *Heaving The Lead Line*; Joe Shores, *Mississippi Sounding Call* No. 1/*Mississippi Sounding Call* No. 2; Thomas J. Marshall, *Arwhoolie (Cornfield Holler)*; Samuel Brooks, *Quittin' Time Song* No. 1/*Quittin' Time Song* No. 2; Thomas J. Marshall, *Mealtime Call*; Henry Truvillion, *Possum Was An Evil Thing/Come On, Boys, And Let's Go To Huntin'*; Moses "Clear Rock" Platt, James "Iron Head" Baker, *Old Rattler*; Baker, Platt, Will Crosby & R.D. Allen, *Go Down, Old Hannah*; Jesse Bradley & Group, *Hammer Ring*; "Lightning" & Group, *I Wonder What's The Matter*; David Pryor & Group, *Roll 'Im On Down [Bahamian Launching Song]*; Kelly Pace & Group, *The Rock Island Line*; Allen Prothero, *Track-Lining Song*

This is a selection of powerful collective work songs recorded in 1933–4, mainly at state farms and institutions in the Texas penitentiary system, and the well-known *Rock Island Line* from Cumins State Farm, Arkansas. Railroad "track-lining" calls, sounding calls on the Mississippi riverboats and "cornfield hollers" providing a cross-section of unaccompanied songs of labour.

53 **Secular Music: Negro Folk Music From Alabama, Volume 1**

Various Artists

Folkways 4417—Cassette

Joe Brown, *Mama Don't Tear My Clothes/Southern Pacific*; Rich Amerson, *Black Woman*; Red Willie Smith, *Kansas City Blues/Salty Dog*; East York Schoolchildren, *I'm Going Up North*; Lilly's Chapel Schoolchildren, *Little Sally Walker/See See Rider*; Vera Hall Ward, *Mamma's Goin' To Buy Him A Little Lap Dog*; Earthy Anne Coleman, *Soon As My Back's Turned*; Archie Lee Hill, *She Done Got Ugly*; Willie Turner, *Now Your Man Done Gone*; Annie Grace Horn Dodson *[Plantation Hollers] Field Call/Father's Field Call/Children's Call/Greeting Call*; Enoch Brown, *Complaint Call*; Rich Amerson, *Brer Rabbit And The Alligators*

This is a broad collection of secular traditions from Livingston Alabama, recorded in 1950. It includes an extended field blues and a folk tale by Rich Amerson; children's ring games, one being based on a blues; lullabies, work songs and plantation hollers; and harmonica solos and blues with guitar accompaniment.

54 **Texas Field Recordings: The Complete Recorded Works of Pete Harris, Smith Casey And Others (1934–1939)**
Document DOCD 5231 (Au)
Pete Harris, *Square Dance Calls/He Rambled/The Buffalo Skinners/Blind Lemon's Song/The Red Cross Store/ Alabama Bound/ Is You Mad At Me?/ Thirty Days In Jail/Carrie/Jack O' Diamonds* (89 B-1)/*Jack O' Diamonds* (89 B-2)/*Jack And Betsy/Standing On The Corner*; Tricky Sam, *Stavin' Chain* (210 A-1)/*Stavin' Chain* (215 A-1)/*Ella Speed*; Augustus "Track Horse" Haggerty, *I Met You Mama/I Feel That Old Black Woman Is A Jinx To Me/ Police Special/Hattie Green*; Jack Johnson, *It Was Early One Morning*; Jesse Lockett, *Worry Blues*; Smith Casey, *I Wouldn't Mind Dyin' If Dyin' Was All/When I Git Home* [duet with Roger Gill]/*Gray Horse Blues/Shorty George/West Texas Blues* [duet with Roger Gill]/*Santa Fe Blues/Hesitating Blues/Jack O' Diamonds/Mourning Blues/Two White Horses Standing In Line/East Texas Rag (Country Rag)*
Outstanding examples of the riches recorded by the Lomaxes for the Library of Congress, these items by Texas singers were mainly recorded in prison. The exception was Pete Harris, an important songster from near Houston. Smith Casey was an exceptional artist and his song *Shorty George* a memorable composition.

55 **Blues Roots: Blues Masters, Volume 10**
Various Artists
Rhino R2 71135
Jali Nyama Suso, *Kedo*; Mandingo Griots, *Tutu Jara*; Fula Flutist, *Bengsimbe*; Robert Pete Williams, *You're My All Night Steady*; Furry Lewis, *Pearlee Blues*; Ethel Perkins & Equila Hall, *My Soul Will Be Saved*; Ethel Perkins, *A Child Will Rise*; [Eddie] One String [Jones], *Rolling And Tumbling Blues*; J.D. Short, *Slidin' Delta*; Rich Amerson, *Black Woman*; Texas Prison Camp Work Gang, *Go Down Old Hannah*; Sister Dora Alexander, *Russia, Let God's Moon Alone/ Times Done Changed*; [George] Daddy Hotcakes [Montgomery], *Well, I've Been Down To Memphis*; The Mobile Strugglers, *Raise A Ruckus Tonight*; Joe Hunter, *Have You Ever Been Mistreated*; Lightnin' Hopkins, *Penitentiary Farm Blues*
African links are implied in *kore* (African lute) and flute solos by Gambian griots. Field moans, work songs, and unaccompanied anthems exemplify proto-blues, while Williams' rambling improvisation, Eddie Jones' one-string instrument and the aptly named Mobile Strugglers' *Raise A Ruckus Tonight* mark the transition to blues proper, represented by Lewis and Hopkins.

56 **"Kansas City Stomp": Jelly Roll Morton, Library of Congress Recordings, Volume 1**
Rounder CD 1091
I'm Alabama Bound No. 1/*I'm Alabama Bound* No. 2/*King Porter Stomp* No. 1/ *You Can Have It, I Don't Want It/The Miserere* ("straight" begun)/*The Miserere* ("straight" concluded)/*Sammy Davis's Style/Pretty Baby*/Tony Jackson's *Naked Dance/Honky Tonk Blues/Levee Man Blues/Aaron Harris*

Blues/Game Kid Blues (begun)/*Game Kid Blues* (concluded)/*Buddy Carter Rag/ Steal Away* and *Nearer My God To Thee/Flee As A Bird To The Mountain/Oh! Didn't He Ramble* (begun)/*Oh! Didn't He Ramble* (concluded)/*Tiger Rag: The Quadrille* (begun)/*Tiger Rag: The Quadrille* (concluded)/*Tiger Rag* (begun)/ *Tiger Rag* (concluded)/*Panama* (incomplete)/*Kansas City Stomp* (begun)/*Kansas City Stomp* (concluded)/*(Darktown) Strutters' Ball/Sweet Jazz Music/Salty Dog/Hestitating Blues/My Gal Sal/Randall's Tune/Maple Leaf Rag* "St. Louis tempo" (begun)/*Maple Leaf Rag* "St. Louis tempo" (concluded)/*Maple Leaf Rag* (Morton style)/*The Miserere* ("swung")/*Low Down Blues (New Orleans Blues)*

Recollected rags, stomps, popular songs, religious tunes, and blues, largely dating before World War I, as well as a theme from *Il Trovatore* for good measure. Morton heard legendary blues pianists in New Orleans and Memphis. With verve and sensitivity he placed their styles in the context of music of the period in these historic sessions from 1938.

57 Ain't Gonna Rain No More: An Historical Survey of Pre Blues And Blues From Piedmont, North Carolina

Various Artists

Rounder 2016—LP

John Snipes, *Snow A Little, Rain A Little*; Joe & Odell Thompson, *Old Joe Clark*; Dink Roberts, *Little Brown Jug/Roustabout*; Joe & Odell Thompson, *Rya's House*; Jamie Alston, *McKinley*; Wilbert Atwater, *Can't Get A Letter From Down The Road*; Joe & Odell Thompson, *Molly Put The Kettle On*; Jamie Alston, *Ain't Gonna Rain No More*; Dink Roberts, *Julie*; Jamie Alston, *Six White Horses*; John Snipes, *I Think I Heard The Chilly Wind Blow*; Wilbert Atwater, *Rich Girl Ride In An Automobile*; Jamie Alston, *Ain't Gonna Rain No More*; Joe & Odell Thompson, *Georgia Buck*; Dink Roberts, *Old Blue*; Wilbert Atwater, *Buffalo*; Jamie Alston, *Went Up On The Mountain*; Joe & Odell Thompson, *Going Down The Road Feeling Bad*; Guitar Slim, *Come On Down To My House*; Jamie Alston, *Goin' Away*

Veterans Snipes, Roberts, and Alston all played banjo for both black and white dances; the Thompson cousins (fiddle and banjo) often performed with whites, sharing repertoires; Atwater played guitar with banjo tuning. These 1970s recordings document Piedmont styles prevalent before the adoption of the guitar by blues singers.

(ii) Southern Strings and Instrumentalists

58 The Two Poor Boys: Joe Evans & Arthur McClain 1927–1931: Complete Recorded Works In Chronological Order

Document DOCD 5044 (Au)

Little Son Of A Gun (Look What You Done Done)/Two White Horses In A Line/John Henry Blues (take 1)/*John Henry Blues* (take 3)/*New Huntsville Jail* (take 1)/*New Huntsville Jail* (take 2)/*Take A Look At That Baby/Mill Man Blues/Oh You Son Of A Gun/Georgia Rose/Early Some Morning Blues/Cream And Sugar Blues/Old Hen Cackle/Sitting On Top Of The World/My Baby Got A Yo-Yo/So Sorry Dear/Sourwood Mountain/Down In Black Bottom* (take 1)/ *Down In Black Bottom* (take 2)/*Shook It This Morning Blues*

Reported to have come from Fairmont, Tennessee, Evans and McClain were versatile musicians who played mandolin, guitar, fiddle, and piano. Their eclectic repertoire included ballads, set dances, sentimentals, solid blues, and, in *Huntsville Jail*, parody of hillbilly singing. Alternate takes aid comparison, but expect surface noise from the rare originals.

59 Blind Roosevelt Graves: Complete Recorded Works In Chronological Order (1929–1936)

Document DOCD 5105 (Au)

Blind Roosevelt Graves & Brother, *St. Louis Ramber Blues/Guitar Boogie/ New York Blues/Bustin' The Jug/Crazy About My Baby/Staggerin' Blues/Low Down Woman/Take Your Burdens To The Lord/Take Your Burdens To The Lord* (alternate take/*Telephone To Glory/I Shall Not Be Moved/When I Lay My Burdens Down/Happy Sunshine/I'm Pressing On/Sad Dreaming Blues/Woke Up This Morning (With My Mind On Jesus)*; Mississippi Jook Band, *Hittin' The Bottle Stomp/Skippy Whippy/Dangerous Woman*; Blind Roosevelt Graves & Brother, *I'll Be Rested (When The Roll Is Called)*; Mississippi Jook Band, *Barbecue Bust*

Hailing from Hattiesburg, Mississippi, Blind Roosevelt Graves played guitar, and his brother Uaroy, tambourine. On a dozen barrelhouse titles they are accompanied by Texas pianist Will Ezell and Baby Jay on cornet (**213**). Their later, religious, titles are strongly syncopated, and their exciting Jook Band includes the legendary pianist Cooney Vaughn.

60 Mississippi String Bands & Associates: Complete Sessions 1928–1931 In Chronological Order

Various Artists

Blues Documents BDCD 6013 (Au)

Alec Johnson, *Miss Meal Cramp Blues/Sister Maud Mule/Sundown Blues/Next Week Sometime/Mysterious Coon/Toodle Doo*; Mississippi Mud Steppers, *Jackson Stomp/Farewell Waltz/Morning Glory Waltz/Alma Waltz [Ruby Waltz]*; Mississippi Blacksnakes, *Blue Sky Blues/Grind So Fine/It's All Over Now/It's So Nice And Warm*; "Sam Hill" From Louisville, *It's Gonna Stare You In The Face/Near The End*; Mississippi Blacksnakes, *Family Disturbance (Family Troubles)/Five Pound Ax Blues/Farewell Baby Blues/It Still Ain't No Good (New It Ain't No Good)/Easy Going Woman Blues*; "Sam Hill" From Louisville, *Things 'Bout Coming My Way/You Got To Keep Things Clean*; Mississippi Blacksnakes (Tennessee Shakers), *Bye Bye Baby Blues*

A varied selection of string band music as played to both black and white country audiences, not only in Mississippi but throughout the South. Alec Johnson appears to have been a minstrel show singer and his repertoire combines coon songs, novelty items, and blues, to excellent accompaniment by the McCoy Brothers. The Blacksnakes played waltzes, and, as the Mud Steppers, an outstanding *Jackson Stomp (Cow Cow Blues)*.

61 Stop And Listen

Mississippi Sheiks

Yazoo (CD) 2006

Stop And Listen Blues/Lonely One In This Town/ The World Is Going On Wrong/She Ain't No Good/Sitting On Top Of The World/Too Long/That's It/

Bootlegger's Blues/Somebody Got To Help You/Jail Bird Love Song/Shooting High Dice/Tell Me To Do Right/Sales Tax/Livin' In A Strain/Sweet Maggie/She's Crazy About Her Lovin'/Please Baby/I've Got Blood In My Eyes For You/Kind Treatment/He Calls That Religion
A dozen Chatmans played in this family string band, though only brothers Bo (Carter), Lonnie, and Sam, with their adopted brother Walter Vincson recorded (**100**, **101**, **422**). Relaxed, accomplished, and bawdily humorous, they were popular and influential. Dances and songs on fiddle and guitars are interleaved with blues in the Jackson tradition.

62 **Clifford Hayes & The Louisville Jug Bands: Complete Recorded Works In Chronological Order, Volume 2 (1926–1927)**
Various Artists
RST Records JPCD 1502-2 (Au)
Dixieland Jug Blowers, *Boodle-Am-Shake/Florida Blues/Don't Give My Lard Away/Banjoreno/Skip, Skat, Doodle-Do/Louisville Stomp/House Rent Rag/Memphis Shake/Carpet Alley-Breakdown* (take 1)/*Carpet Alley-Breakdown* (take 2)/*Hen Party Blues* (take 1)/*Hen Party Blues* (take 2); Earl McDonald's Original Louisville Jug Band, *She's In The Graveyard Now/Casey Bill/Louisville Special/Rocking Chair Blues/Mama's Little Sunny Boy/She Won't Quit But She'll Slow Down/Under The Chicken Tree/Melody March Call*; Whistler & His Jug Band, *Low Down Blues/The Vamps Of "28"/The Jug Band Special/Pig Meat Blues*
A highly entertaining selection of Kentucky "Jug bands." *Banjoreno* recalls minstrel show line-ups, while Johnny Dodds, the New Orleans clarinetist, soars above the spirited fun of *House Rent Rag*. McDonald's band played many road show songs, including Irving Jones' popular *Chicken Tree*. Don't miss Clifford Hayes' alley fiddle and Buford Threlkeld's nose-whistle!

63 **Memphis Harps & Jug Blowers (1927–1939): Complete Recorded Works In Chronological Order + 1 Alternate Take**
Various Artists
Blues Documents BDCD 6028 (Au)
Memphis Jug Band, *Memphis Jug Blues* (alternate take); Joe Williams, *I Want It Awful Bad/Mr. Devil Blues*; Jed Davenport, *How Long, How Long Blues/Cow Cow Blues*; Jed Davenport & His Beale Street Jug Band, *Beale Street Breakdown/You Ought To Move Out Of Town/The Dirty Dozen/Jug Blues/Save Me Some/Piccolo Blues*; Beale Street Rounders, *I'm Sittin' On Top Of The World/Talking 'Bout You*; Minnie Wallace & Her Night Hawks, *The Cockeyed World/Field Mouse Stomp/Let's All Do That Thing/Pick 'Em Up And Put 'Em Down*; Little Buddy Doyle, *Hard Scufflin' Blues/Grief Will Kill You/Renewed Love Blues/Bad In Mind Blues/Three-Sixty-Nine Blues/She's Got Good Dry Goods/Lost Baby Blues/Sweet Man Blues*
Jug bands in Memphis were influenced by those of Louisville but were more blues-orientated. None more so than Jed Davenport's largely anonymous group, with the leader's strongly vocalized playing on "French harp" (harmonica). The knockabout humor of Minnie Wallace's tracks with Will Shade contrast with Doyle's melancholy blues.

64 **The Tommie Bradley-James Cole Groups 1928–1932: Complete Recorded Works in Chronological Order**

Various Artists

Document DOCD 5189 (Au)

James Cole String Band, *Bill Cheatum/I Got A Gal*; Alura Mack, *Old Fashioned Blues/Seven Men Blues*; Clara Burston, *Try That Man O' Mine/Pay With Money/Can't Get Enough/Good And Hot*; Walter Cole, *Mama Keep Your Yes Ma'am Clean/Everybody Got Somebody*; Tommie Bradley, *Where You Been So Long/Adam And Eve*; James Cole's Washboard Four, *Runnin' Wild/Sweet Lizzie*; Tommie Bradley, *Pack Up Her Trunk Blues/When You're Down And Out/Please Don't Act That Way*; James Cole, *I Love My Mary*; Tommie Bradley, *Four Day Blues*; Buster Johnson, *Undertaker Blues*; James Cole, *Mistreated The Only Friend You Had*; Tommie Bradley, *Nobody's Business If I Do/Window Pane Blues*

No one is sure of the personnel of these groups or even if all items as by James Cole and Tommie Bradley are by the same two men. Believed to have come from the Ohio-Kentucky region, these obscure musicians and singers underline the repertoires, skills and pervasive influences of hillbilly and blues among the rural and urban string bands of the "border states."

65 **The Barnyard Dance**

Carl Martin, Ted Bogan, and Howard Armstrong

Rounder 2003—LP

Lady Be Good/Carl's Blues/Corinna, Corinna/Barnyard Dance/Cracklin' Hen/Sweet Georgia Brown/French Blues/Mean Mistreatin' Mama/Old Man Mose/Alice Blue Gown/Knox County Stomp

In 1930 these artists belonged to an eastern string band which played for dances, picnics, weddings, and radio. They were reunited 40 years later for this recording. Although blues singer Carl Martin (mandolin), guitarist Ted Bogan and self-educated fiddler, artist, and linguist Howard Armstrong had recorded once earlier, they are representative of the talent largely missed by recording units.

(iii) Songsters

66 **Sinners And Saints (1926–1931): Complete Recorded Works**

Various Artists

Document DOCD 5106 (Au)

T.C.I. Section Crew, *Track Linin/Section Gang Show*; Freeman Stowers, *Railroad Blues/Texas Wild Cat Chase/Medley Of Blues (All Out And Down: Old Time Blues: Hog In The Mountain)/Sunrise On The Farm*; "Beans" Hambone, El Morrow, *Beans/Tippin' Out*; "Big Boy" George Owens, *Kentucky Blues/The Coon Crap Game*; Will Bennett, *Railroad Bill/Real Estate Blues*; Lonnie Coleman, *Old Rock Island Blues/Wild About My Loving*; Nugrape Twins, *I Got Your Ice Cold Nugrape/There's A City Built Of Mansions/The Road Is Rough And Rocky/Pray Children If You Want To Go To Heaven/Nugrape—A Flavour You Can't Forget/Can't You Watch Me For One Hour*; Blind Roger Hays, *On My Way To Heaven/ I Must Be Blind, I Cannot See*; Pink Anderson & Simmie Dooley, *Every Day In The Week Blues/C.C. And O. Blues/Papa's 'Bout To Get Mad/Gonna Tip Out Tonight*

A remarkable miscellany of rural songsters, ranging from a studio recording of a work gang to Freeman Stowers' harmonica imitations, and including examples of the folksongs performed in the medicine shows by Anderson and Dooley. The Nugrape Twins harmonized while Blind Roger Hays barked his poignant religious street songs.

67 Memphis Gospel (1927–1929): The Complete Recorded Works of Rev. Sister Mary Nelson, Lonnie McIntorsh & Bessie Johnson In Chronological Order

Various Artists

Document DOCD 5072 (Au)

Rev. Sister Mary M. Nelson, *The Royal Telephone/Judgment/The Seal Of God/Isaiah-LV*; Lonnie McIntorsh, *Sleep On, Mother Sleep On/The Lion And The Tribes of Judah/Arise And Shine/How Much I Owe*; Elders McIntorsh & Edwards, *What Kind Of Man Jesus Is/Since I Laid My Burden Down/The 1927 Flood/The Latter Rain Is Fall/Take A Stand/Behold! The King Shall Reign*; Rev. Johnny Blakey, *King Of Kings/Jesus Was Here On Business/Warming By The Devil's Fire/The Devil Is Loose In This World*; Bessie Johnson, *No Room At The Hotel/Key To The Kingdom/One Day/The Whole World In His Hand*; Memphis Sanctified Singers, *The Great Reaping Day/He Got Better Things For You*

Uninhibited religious singing of the Holiness and Sanctified churches, including Sister Mary Nelson's fierce *Royal Telephone*, McIntorsh & Edwards' ring-shout *Latter Rain* and Bessie Johnson's rasping falsetto. Her powerful voice is heard on many of these tracks, some having guitar, tambourine, and hand-clapping accompaniment.

68 Guitar Evangelists (1928–1951): Complete Recorded Works In Chronological Order

Various Artists

Document DOCD 5101 (Au)

Blind Benny Paris And Wife, *I'm Gonna Live So God Can Use Me/Hide Me In The Blood Of Jesus*; Rev. I.B. Ware With Wife & Son, *I Wouldn't Mind Dying (But I Gotta Go By Myself)/You Better Quit Drinking Shine*; Blind Willie Harris, *Does Jesus Care?/Where He Leads Me I Will Follow*; Eddie Head & His Family, *Down On Me/Lord I'm The True Vine/Tryin' To Get Home/Within My Mind*; Mother McCollum, *I Want To See Him/When I Take My Vacation In Heaven/You Can't Hide/Jesus Is My Air-O-Plane/Oh Lord I'm Your Child/Glory! Glory! Hallelujah!*; Dennis Crumpton & Robert Summers, *Go I'll Send Thee/Everybody Ought To Pray Sometime*; Sister Mathews, *Stand By Me*; Rev. Charles White, *How Long*; Willie Mae Williams, *Don't Want To Go There/Where The Sun Never Goes Down*; Brother Willie Eason, *There'll Be No Grumblers There/I Want To Live (So God Can Use Me)*; Sister Elizabeth Phillips, *A Little Old-Fashioned/There's Nothing Like The Holy Spirit*

Street evangelists, some with their spouses and children, recorded in places as far apart as Philadelphia and Oakland, Atlanta, New Orleans, and Chicago. Some, like Mother McCollum, used contemporary technologies as religious metaphors. Post-war evangelists Williams, Eason, and Phillips maintained a glorious tradition.

69 **Papa Charlie Jackson: Complete Recorded Works In Chronological Order, Volume 2 (February 1926 to September 1928)**
Various Artists
Document DOCD 5088 (Au)
Papa Charlie Jackson, *Mumsy Mumsy Blues/Butter And Egg Man Blues/The Judge Cliff Davis Blues/Up The Way Bound* (take 1)/*Up The Way Bound* (take 2)/*Four Eleven Forty-Four/Your Baby Ain't Sweet Like Mine/Bad Luck Woman Blues*; Freddie Keppard's Jazz Cardinals (Papa Charlie Jackson, vocal) *Salty Dog*; Papa Charlie Jackson, *Gay Cattin'/Fat Mouth Blues/She Belongs To Me Blues/Coal Man Blues/Skoodle Um Skoo/Sheik Of Desplaines Street/Look Out Papa, Don't Tear Your Pants/Baby Don't You Be So Mean/Bright Eyes/Blue Monday Morning Blues/Long Gone Lost John/I'm Looking For A Woman Who Knows How To Treat Me Right/Ash Tray Blues/No Need Of Knockin' On The Blind/I Like To Love My Baby/Baby—Papa Needs His Lovin'/Lexington Kentucky Blues*
Charlie Jackson was the first songster/blues singer to be a popular success on record. A minstrel-show veteran from New Orleans, he usually played banjo and, infrequently, guitar. Narrative ballads, folksongs, blues songs, and a unique vocal with a New Orleans jazz band are among this varied collection.

70 **Stovepipe No. 1 & David Crockett: Complete Recorded Works In Chronological Order 1924–1930; Tub Jug Washboard Band (1928)**
Various Artists
Document DOCD 5269 (Au)
Stovepipe No. 1, *Lord, Don't You Know I Have No Friend Like You/I've Got Salvation In My Heart/Lonesome John/Cripple Creek And Sourwood Mountain/Turkey In The Straw/Fisher's Hornpipe*; Stovepipe No. 1 & David Crockett, *Court Street Blues/A Woman Gets Tired Of The Same Man All The Time/A Chicken Can Waltz The Gravy Around/Bed Slats*; King David's Jug Band, *What's That Taste Like Gravy?/Rising Sun Blues/Sweet Potato Blues/Tear It Down/I Can Deal Worry/Georgia Bo Bo*; Washboard Trio, *Washboard Rag/Lady Quit Her Husband Unexpectinly*; Tub Jug Washboard Band, *Tub-Jug Rag/San*
A "one-man-band" who played harmonica, guitar, kazoo, and stovepipe on the streets of Cincinnati, Sam Jones was the first recorded songster. His early acoustic titles included set dances and old-time tunes but guitarist Crockett extended the range. Presumably "King David", he led a raucous band with Jones playing stovepipe. The Tub Jug Washboard Band items feature home-made instruments.

71 **Jim Jackson: Complete Recorded Works In Chronological Order, Volume 1 (1927–1928)**
Document DOCD 5114 (Au)
Jim Jackson's Kansas City Blues Part 1/*Jim Jackson's Kansas City Blues* Part 2/*He's In The Jailhouse Now/Old Dog Blue* (C 1637/38)/*My Monday Blues* (C 1639)/*Mobile-Central Blues* (C 1641)/*Jim Jackson's Kansas City Blues* Part 3/*Jim Jackson's Kansas City Blues* Part 4/*My Monday Blues* (C 1647)/*I'm A Bad Bad Man/I'm Gonna Start Me A Graveyard Of My Own/My Monday Woman Blues* (take 1)/*I Heard The Voice Of A Porkchop* (take 1)/*I Heard The Voice Of A Porkchop* (take 2)/*My Monday Woman Blues* (take 3)/*My Mobile Central*

Blues (41801-4)/*Old Dog Blue* (41827)/*Bootlegging Blues*/*Policy Blues* (take 1)/*Policy Blues* (take 2)/*I'm Wild About My Lovin'*/*This Mornin' She Was Gone* (take 1)/*This Mornin' She Was Gone* (take 2)
No relation to Papa Charlie (**69**), Jim Jackson worked the medicine shows and scouted for recording talent. He made at least two versions of most of his songs, like *Old Dog Blue* on a hunting theme, and these make interesting comparison. Some of his titles, such as *I Heard The Voice Of A Pork Chop* have ironic lyrics, preparing the way for his witty blues.

72 **The Songster Tradition (1927–1935): Complete Recorded Works in Chronological Order**
Various Artists
Document DOCD 5045 (Au)
Papa Harvey Hull & Long "Cleve" Reed—The Down Home Boys, *Gang Of Brown Skin Women*/*Hey! Lawdy Mama—The France Blues*/*Two Little Tommie Blues*/*Don't You Leave Me Here*/*Mama You Don't Know How*/*Original Stack O'Lee Blues*; Big Boy Cleveland, *Quill Blues*/*Goin' To Leave You Blues*; William & Versey Smith, *I Believe I'll Go Back Home*/*When That Great Ship Went Down*/*Everybody Help The Boys Come Home*/*Sinner You'll Need King Jesus*; Luke Jordan, *Church Bells Blues* (take 1)/*Church Bells Blues* (take 2)/*Pick Poor Robin Clean* (take 1)/ *Pick Poor Robin Clean* (take 2)/*Cocaine Blues*/*Travelling Coon*/*My Gal's Done Quit Me*/*Won't You Be Kind?* Eli Framer, *Framer's Blues*/*God Didn't Make No Monkey Man*; Louie Lasky, *How You Want Your Rollin' Done*/*Teasin' Brown Blues*/*Caroline*
A beautiful collection of songster material, including the folk harmonizing of Hull and Reed, a rare example of "quill" (panpipes) playing, and the *Titanic* ballad by the Smiths. The Virginia-born songster Luke Jordan with his high, clear voice and cleanly picked guitar sings ballads and protest songs, contrasting with Lasky's rough-house blues.

73 **Kansas City Blues: The Complete Recorded Works of Lottie Beaman-Kimbrough, Winston Holmes & Charlie Turner, Sylvester Kimbrough (1924–1929)**
Document DOCD 5152 (Au)
Lottie Beaman, *Regular Man Blues*/*Honey Blues*/*Red River Blues*/*Sugar Daddy Blues*/*Low Down Painful Blues*/*Mama Can't Lose*; Lena & Sylvester Kimbrough, *City Of The Dead*/*Cabbage Head Blues*; Lottie Kimbrough & Winston Holmes, *Lost Lover Blues*/*Wayward Girl Blues*/*Rolling Log Blues*/*Goin' Away Blues*/*Blue World Blues*; Winston Holmes & Charlie Turner, *Death of Holmes' Mule* Part 1/*Death of Holmes' Mule* Part 2/*Rounders Lament*/*The Kansas City Call*/*Skinner*/*Kansas City Dog Walk*; Lottie Beaman, *Going Away Blues*/*Rollin' Log Blues*; Sylvester Kimbrough, *Garbage Can Blues*/*Bird Liver Blues*
Kansas City vocal traditions have been little documented. Lottie Kimbrough (*née* Beaman) had a strong contralto voice; her blues were accompanied by the Pruitt twins on guitar, or by the vocal effects of the entrepreneur Winston Holmes. He also performed parodies and dance pieces with the adept 12-string guitarist Charlie Turner.

74 **Gospel, Blues And Street Songs**
Reverend Gary Davis And Pink Anderson
Original Blues Classics OBCCD 524-2
Pink Anderson, *John Henry/Every Day In The Week/The Ship Titanic/Greasy Greens/Wreck Of The Old 97/I've Got Mine/He's In The Jailhouse Now*; Rev. Gary Davis, *Blow Gabriel/Twelve Gates To The City/Samson And Delilah/Oh, Lord, Search My Heart/Get Right Church/You Got To Go Down/Keep Your Lamp Trimmed And Burning/There Was A Time That I Was Blind*
Anderson, from South Carolina, performed for 30 years on one medicine show; he sang in a strong voice and played guitar with finger-picks for volume. His pieces from 1950 may be compared with earlier songster recordings. Gary Davis, from nearby, was an accomplished guitarist who turned from ragtime and blues to gospel songs after his conversion.

75 **Medicine Show Man**
Peg Leg Sam
Trix (CD) 3302
Who's That Left Here 'While Ago/Greasy Greens/Reuben/Irene, Tell Me, Who Do You Love/Skinny Woman Blues/Lost John/Ode To Bad Bill/Ain't But One Thing Give A Man The Blues/Easy Ridin' Buggy/Peg's Fox Chase/Before You Give It All Away/Fast Freight Train/Nasty Old Trail/Born In Hard Luck
Recorded as recently as 1972, while still playing harmonica with Chief Thunder cloud's Medicine Show, Peg Leg Sam (Arthur Jackson) was a veteran of carnivals, radio, and street singing. His lively, raucous singing and wailing "harp" playing includes a virtuoso version of *Fox Chase*. On some blues he is supported by guitarists Baby Tate and Rufe Johnson.

76 **Freight Train Blues And Other North Carolina Folk Songs And Tunes**
Elizabeth Cotten
Smithsonian/Folkways CD SF 40009
Wilson Rag/Freight Train/Going Down The Road Feeling Bad/I Don't Love Nobody/Ain't Got No Honey Baby Now/Graduation March/Honey Babe Your Papa Cares For You/Vastopol/Here Old Rattler Here/Sent For My Fiddle, Sent For My Bow/George Buck/Run . . . Run/Mama Your Son Done Gone/Sweet Bye And Bye/What A Friend We Have In Jesus/Oh Babe It Ain't No Lie/Spanish Flang Dang/When I Get Home
Elizabeth Cotten, from North Carolina, became famous in the 1950s through the belated popularity of her song *Freight Train*, composed when she was 12. Her impeccable dance pieces, played left-handed on banjo and mellow-toned guitar, and softly sung traditional folksongs had a universal appeal. She died age 92 in 1985.

77 **You Got To Reap What You Sow**
Mance Lipscomb, Texas Songster, Volume 2
Arhoolie CD 398
Charlie James/Come Back Baby/Spanish Flang Dang/You Got To Reap What You Sow/Cocaine Done Killed My Baby/Joe Turner Killed A Man/Bumble Bee/Boogie In "A"/Hattie Green/Silver City/The Titanic/If I Miss The Train/Lord Thomas/Tom Moore Blues/So Different Blues/Tall Angel At The Bar/Mama, Don't Dog Me/Long Way To Tipperary/Willie Poor Boy/You Rascal You/I

Looked Down The Road/And I Wondered/Sentimental Blues/Police Station Blues/Missouri Waltz
Lipscomb was a Texas sharecropper and weekend songster-guitarist. His extensive and varied repertoire is evidenced on these effortless items, recorded at a single session when he was nearly 70; more than half are issued for the first time. Standout blues are *Hattie Green* with fine guitar, *Joe Turner* with slide, and the protest blues ballad *Tom Moore*.

78 Railroad Worksong
Jesse Fuller
Lake LACD 24 (UK)
Move On Down The Line/Stealing/Ninety-Nine Years And One Dark Day/ Animal Fair/Sleeping In The Midnight Cold/Stagolee/Bill Bailey/San Francisco Bay Blues/Crazy Waltz/Railroad Worksong/Meet My Loving Mother/I Love My Baby/ Tune [Creole Love Call]/Running Wild/Stranger Blues/Hanging Around A Skin Game/The Monkey And The Engineer/Buck Dancer's Jump
Jesse Fuller called himself "The Lone Cat." A one-man-band, he played guitar, harmonica, kazoo, high-hat cymbal, and the "fotdella", a foot-operated bass of his own invention. His repertoire included comic songs, ballads, blues, and jazz themes which he performed to delighted audiences from San Francisco to London.

79 Don't Let Your Deal Go Down
John Jackson
Arhoolie CD 378
Going Down In Georgia On A Horn/Black Snake Moan/John Henry/If Hattie Wants To Lu, Let Her Lu Like A Man/Nobody's Business But Mine/John's Rag/Boats Up The River/Rattlesnakin' Daddy/Flat Foot & Buck Dance/Bear Cat Blues/Reuben/Rocks And Gravel/Going Down The Road Feelin' Bad/Police Dog Blues/Don't Let Your Deal Go Down/Muleskinner Blues/I Bring My Money/ John's Ragtime/Red River Blues/Knife Blues/Trucking Little Baby/Blind Blake's Rag/Goodbye Booze/Graveyard Blues/Early Morning Blues/You Ain't No Woman
As a songster (and gravedigger) born in Virginia in 1924, John Jackson is an anachronism and possibly the last of his tradition. He performs traditional songs that he heard in childhood and blues that he learned from disc. A skilled guitarist (*Flat Foot & Buck Dance, Blind Blake's Rag*), he also plays banjo on *If Hattie Wants To Lu*.

80 Country Negro Jam Session
Various Artists
Arhoolie CD 372
Butch Cage & Willie B. Thomas, *44 Blues*; Robert Pete Williams, *Mississippi Heavy Water Blues*; Clarence Edwards, *Smokestack Lightning*; Butch Cage & Willie B. Thomas, *Who Broke The Lock?*; Clarence Edwards, *You Don't Love Me*; Butch Cage & Willie B. Thomas, *It's The Sign Of The Judgement*; Ben Douglas, *Foxhunt*; Sally Dotson, *Your Dice Won't Pass*; Willie B. Thomas & Butch Cage, *Jelly Roll*; Rebecca Smith, *I've Got Religion*; Smoky Babe, *Going Downtown Boogie*; Clarence Edwards, *Stack O' Dollars*; Willie B. Thomas & Butch Cage, *Brown Skin Woman*; Leon Strickland, *I Won't Be Your Low-Down*

Dog No More; Butch Cage & Willie B. Thomas, *The Piano Blues*; Smoky Babe, *Cotton Field Blues*; Otis Webster, *Gettin' Late In The Evening* [mistitled *The Farm Blues*]/*The Farm Blues* No. 1 [mistitled *The Boss Man Blues*]; Butch Cage & Willie B. Thomas, *Whoa Mule!*; Otis Webster, *Boll Weevil Blues*; Clarence Edwards, *Thousand Miles From Nowhere*; Butch Cage & Willie B. Thomas, *Dead And Gone*/*Called For You Yesterday*/*Me And My Chauffeur*/*Baby Please Don't Go*

A documentary of the country music still being played in Louisiana in 1960, recorded by Dr Harry Oster and others. The exhilarating fiddle-guitar playing and rough vocals of Cage and Thomas are memorable. Webster, Williams, and Smoky Babe were survivors of an old blues tradition while Edwards was aware of current developments.

DAVID EVANS

3 Early Deep South and Mississippi River Basin Blues

The discs discussed in this chapter contain blues recorded between 1923 and 1951 by artists from the region bordering the lower Mississippi River (roughly north-eastern Louisiana, eastern Arkansas, the entire state of Mississippi, and western Tennessee) as well as musicians based in the state of Alabama and the city of St Louis, whose blues display a stylistic similarity to those of the Mississippi Valley. The early blues traditions of Louisville and Cincinnati are also included, though they are less closely connected in a stylistic sense with this region. Our view of the development of blues in the area may be somewhat skewed by the preponderance of artists from the state of Mississippi and the cities of Memphis, St Louis, Louisville, and Cincinnati; the blues of Alabama and western Tennessee are more thinly represented, while those of the sections of Arkansas and Louisiana are hardly covered. This is the fault not of our selection but of the uneven pattern of commercial recording during the period. A number of the discs listed in Chapter 2 contain proto-blues and folk-music examples that fall within the geographic, temporal, and stylistic parameters of this chapter; several discs in Chapters 5, 6, and 7 highlight down-home women blues singers, blues pianists and non-commercial artists who would also be at home in this chapter, as would the artists of the 1930s who brought a more commercial extension of Deep South blues to the northern recording studios. Chapters 10 and 11 contain discs with more recent survivals as well as commercial extensions of Deep South blues.

There is a general stylistic unity in the blues of this region. Perhaps the music's most striking characteristic is its intensity. These blues generally display powerful, steady, driving rhythms, often accelerated as a piece progresses. There is little wasted space, as performers emphasize each note through impassioned singing and wrenched timing. The voice often seems to come from the back of the singer's throat, giving it a hard, raspy quality. The lyrics also display a willingness to discuss seriously some of the blues' deepest subjects, such as death and the state of the singer's soul. Nowhere else does the genre

Ishman Bracey, Mississippi bluesman, ca 1929–30 (*coll. Blues Unlimited, courtesy Gake Dean Wardlow*)

come closer to the status of a religious experience for performers and listeners. The guitar acts as a second voice, a role often highlighted by the bending of strings and use of a slide technique. Another common stylistic feature is the percussive quality, often emphasized by striking the strings hard.

The blues of this region typically display little harmonic development. Pentatonic scales are common, and some pieces have a distinct modal character, use only two chords, or barely suggest chord changes without fully stating them. Only the essential vocal and instrumental lines are heard, and few passing notes or chords are to be found. The melodies are often close to the sounds of field hollers, and the lyrics rely heavily on a shared repertoire of traditional verse formulae. The use of short repeated ostinato phrases as well as the strongly rhythmic, percussive, and modal qualities of these blues link them closely to the tradition of African music that was brought to American by the artists' slave ancestors. Various instruments derived from the African tradition, such as the washboard, jug, and kazoo, also surface in this area's music, and lying not far in the background are other African-derived musical traditions of the banjo, fife and drum music, and home-made one-string instruments. Even at their most commercial, these blues are not far from the status of pure folk music.

Essential Records

(i) Mississippi Blues

Within the tradition of Deep South blues, there can be little doubt that the blues of Mississippi are pre-eminent; for many listeners and artists alike, they represent the epitome of the traditional blues sound. Indeed, it is quite possible that the blues originated in Mississippi, as some of the earliest notices of the music, around the beginning of the 20th century, occurred there; at any rate, they achieved an early and very intensive development in the state, which has produced an extraordinary number of outstanding blues artists. One of the chief characteristics of Mississippi blues is the extreme localism and individualism of style. Blue artists were able to synthesize stylistic elements and repertoires from an immediate environment, rich in outstanding practitioners of the folk art of blues performance. Furthermore, the music was felt within the black, largely rural, community to such a degree that highly distinctive styles were able to develop. While most of these styles conform to the general patterns of the larger region's blues traditions, the best performers are immediately recognizable one from another upon first hearing.

Nowhere did the Mississippi blues reach a greater development in the first half of the 20th century than in the state's north-west quarter, commonly known as the Delta. It was an area of incredibly rich alluvial soil, subdivided into large plantations, most of them owned by whites and worked by blacks. Much of the Delta was not opened to cultivation until the period when the folk blues tradition was beginning to take shape. Among the workers who poured into the Delta from the surrounding countryside were many musicians, each of them bringing his own regional and local folk-music traditions. The Delta plantations were close together, provided an incipient cash economy during the harvest season which was supplemented by work in the levee and lumber camps, and emphasized an intensive utilization of the environment and local resources; the social and economic conditions were much like those of an urban industrial ghetto spread out over a rural landscape. This intensity is reflected in the sound of the blues that emerged from this environment as well as in the interaction of the artists with one another. Despite their great individual stylistic distinctiveness, it is possible to trace lines of influence from Charley Patton to Willie Brown and Son House, from them to Robert Johnson and Howlin' Wolf (**363**, **410**), and from Johnson to Muddy Waters (**242**, **361**) and Elmore James (**365/6**). Another great blues artists of the present day, B.B. King (**287**, **521**), represents a further synthesis of traditional Delta and popular blues elements.

If any artist captures the essence of early Delta blues, it is Charley Patton. The 61 tracks on **Charley Patton: The Complete Recorded Works** are about two-thirds blues, the remainder being spirituals, ragtime songs, ballads, and versions of popular songs. Also included are Patton's guitar accompaniments to blues fiddler Henry (or 'Son') Sims and accompaniments to and duets with his last wife Bertha Lee. Sims and guitarist Willie Brown accompany Patton on several pieces. Patton is the first Delta artist to give us a clear and full example of the region's folk blues style. He was born in 1891 in the hill country south of the Delta. Shortly after the turn of the century his family settled on the immense Dockery's plantation between the towns of Ruleville and Cleveland. Patton lived and performed in this general vicinity until his death in 1934. The year of his birth makes him roughly of the same generation as Frank Stokes (**48**), Leadbelly (**47**, **127**, **258**), and Mississippi John Hurt (**50**, **416**). While these and most other contemporary artists sound like songsters who had incorporated blues into their repertoires, Patton appears as a thoroughgoing bluesman with some vestiges of a songster repertoire. In Patton's blues, and indeed in his spirituals, ballads, and ragtime tunes, may be found fully formed all the essential characteristics of the Deep South blues style—the gruff, impassioned voice suggesting the influence of country preaching and gospel singing style (which he displayed on his religious recordings), the percussive guitar technique, the bending of strings and use of slide style, the driving rhythms and repeated riffs, the traditional lyric formulas, and the simple harmonic structures. Patton, however, also displays one highly individual characteristic: he sings about his own experiences and events he observed—frequently ones outside the realm of the usual man-woman relationships in the blues—always shaping his lyrics from a highly personal point of view. He actually treated his own life and observations as news and helped to create his own legend (only Sleepy John Estes rivalled him in this respect). Patton was extremely popular as an artist in the Delta. His life as well as his blues inspired many other musicians, who viewed him as a "great man" and a role model.

For many listeners Patton will not be an easily acquired taste. His music is Delta blues in the raw, and the formidable surface noise on many of the original records does not help the situation. His songs lack the polish that characterizes the work of many of the Delta blues artists who came after him: they seem to be never completed, songs always still in the making. But this characteristic is part of his music's very charm. There is a sense of utter conviction in his voice and an exquisite sense of timing in his playing, his singing and his accenting of words that make his music ever fresh. And yet he is still somehow elusive, always one step ahead, ever the "Masked Marvel" (as he was billed on one of his original recordings).

Virtually all of Patton's tracks are outstanding, some particularly so. *Tom Rushen Blues, High Water Everywhere* Parts 1 and 2, *Dry Well Blues, High Sheriff Blues* and *34 Blues* contain his highly personalized views and observations on jailhouse experiences, a flood, a dry spell, and Delta plantation life. *Mississippi Boweavil Blues, Frankie And Albert* and *Elder Greene Blues* demonstrate his handling of traditional folk ballads in a style that is never far from the blues. Based on more conventional blues themes, *Down The Dirt Road Blues, Pony Blues, Banty Rooster Blues, It Won't Be Long, Going To Move To Alabama, Green River Blues, Rattlesnake Blues, Moon Going Down,* and *Bird Nest Bound* are perfect examples of what the Delta blues is all about. This collection comes with an illustrated booklet in Japanese and English by Jim O'Neal containing an essay covering Patton's life, personality, music, and influence and generally accurate lyric transcriptions to all the songs.

On **Son House And The Great Delta Blues Singers (1928–1930)** we get the evidence of Patton's influence as well as a broader view of early Deep South folk blues. Willie Brown's music provides the clearest links to Patton, for Brown was one of Pattons's earliest disciples and his sometime guitar partner over a period of about 20 years. *M & O Blues* and *Future Blues* are the only two extant songs by Brown from his session for Paramount in 1930. (He plays second guitar on four of Charley Patton's selections on the collection discussed above.) Both of Brown's songs contain melodic and instrumental ideas used by Patton and evidently learned from the older musician. Brown, unlike Patton, carefully organized these ideas and presented them as almost classic examples of basic 12-bar, three-line *AAB* blues in a Deep South style. Perhaps the difference simply reflects two opposite personalities—Brown the prepared, precise craftsman and Patton the unpredictable tinkerer exhibiting frequent strokes of brilliance. This is not to suggest that there is no sense of development in Brown's blues. In both songs there is a noticeable build-up in intensity as the pieces progress: Brown's voice becomes rougher and more strained, the tempo increases, the lyrics become more ominous, and the guitar playing becomes more percussive. In short, they appear to be a distillation of Charley Patton.

The mysterious Kid Bailey sounds very much like Willie Brown in his singing and plays identical guitar figures. This leads to speculation that Bailey was none other than Brown performing under a pseudonym. If not, he was a most faithful disciple. There is a second guitarist on his recordings, and the singing is a bit less intense than on the Brown pieces.

Son House also came under Patton's influence, but at the time of the 1930 session, when his pieces in this collection were recorded, he had known Patton for just a few weeks. House's guitar style is economical and highly percussive; no effort is wasted. He summons up all the energy and power he can muster and punches each note into the ears of the listener. The effect is heightened by his use of repeated short guitar phrases, which pull his songs out of the standard 12-bar mold, and his glistening bottleneck technique. Son House had one of the finest natural voices among early folk blues singers—strong, deep, and melismatic, with the rich inflections of a country preacher and gospel singer. He had, in fact, begun his musical career in the church and had even done some preaching, coming over to the blues only about three years before he made these recordings. This disc offers three different two-part blues masterpieces plus a newly discovered test pressing containing a second guitarist, either Patton or Brown. *Dry Spell Blues* apparently deals with the same phenomenon that Patton sang about in his *Dry Well Blues*, but while Patton weaves his own experiences of the dry spell into those of his fellow citizens of the Delta community of Lula, House takes the role of a country preacher with the Delta farmers as his congregation, ending his song with an impassioned plea to God to send down His rain. *Preachin' The Blues* uses traditional verses to poke fun at the life that House had recently abandoned, yet he sings these lyrics with such intensity that one feels the tug that the church still must have exerted upon him. (He was, in fact, known to have occasionally interrupted his blues performances by getting up on bar-room tables and preaching.) *My Black Mama* presents another sort of contrast, one between some verses that relate amusing details about the singer's "black mama" and others that tell of the death of his woman and his reaction to it. Somehow the song hangs together through the extraordinary integrity of House's performance.

Rube Lacy was another Mississippi singer and an acknowledged early influence on Son House. He grew up east of Jackson and participated in that city's blues scene in the mid-1920s, but relocated in the Delta and was based there by the time he recorded his only two issued blues in 1928. *Mississippi Jail House Groan* displays some expressive blue moaning and one-chord guitar work with a blue note built right into the tuning. Lacy's voice penetrates like a machine-gun on this piece and his equally fine *Ham Hound Crave*, where he snaps his guitar strings against the instrument's neck while poking fun at churchgoers, much in the manner of Son House on *Preachin' The Blues*. Lacy himself took the reverse path from House and became an ordained minister about ten years after he recorded these pieces. It is regrettable that he didn't leave us a larger sample of his blues repertoire before he made the change.

With the exception of Joe Calicott, who lived into the 1960s and had a brief blues revival career (**421**), the remaining artists on this disc are quite obscure figures. Blind Joe Reynolds, or Willie Reynolds as he was called on some of his recordings, was reputed to be from the Delta and did some of his recording in Memphis. Using repeated guitar figures and only rudimentary harmonic development, he sings passionately about infidelity, violence, and underworld life. His overall accusatory stance suggests that this blind singer might also have performed gospel material. *Outside Woman Blues* and *Married Man Blues* are versions of the same song, a slide guitar masterpiece that was recast in the 1960s by the British blues-rock group Cream. Garfield Akers and Joe Calicott were from the vicinity of Hernando, Mississippi, a few miles south of the city of Memphis and geographically not in the Delta but right on its edge. Jim Thompkins may have been from this area also. Akers is the most distinctive of these artists, playing a churning rhythmic guitar and singing in a rich voice reminiscent of the field holler. Calicott and Thompkins seem to display the influence of Frank Stokes (**48**) in their singing. Thompkins contributes some rough rhythmic slide guitar on his only issued recording.

On **Tommy Johnson (1928–1929)** we have an extended portrait of another of the most influential of the early Mississippi bluesmen. Every one of his six issued recordings from 1928 has been recorded more than once by other artists, who learned the songs either from Johnson's records or his live performances. In these pieces the brilliant interweaving of melodically interesting vocal and guitar lines, the memorable opening verses, and Johnson's strong, clear and sensuous voice come close to perfection. Johnson's accomplishment is even more remarkable when one considers that he was a confirmed alcoholic by the time he recorded these pieces, which he describes without apparent regret in *Canned Heat Blues, Black Mare Blues*, and *Alcohol And Jake Blues*. His prodigious drinking does seem to have affected his verbal thought processes, as some of his texts are characterized by excessive repetition and a degree of incoherence, but his complex guitar work and magnificent voice must still have been near their peak.

Johnson was an early disciple of Charley Patton and Willie Brown, the evidence of which is especially apparent in his guitar work and some of his melodic lines. Brown's influence appears to have been predominant, for Johnson's blues have the same high degree of musical organization and precision as Brown's though without Brown's building intensity. Johnson simply begins his pieces at a peak of sensitivity and feeling and maintains the same level until their conclusion. One important characteristic of his singing which is not found in the work of Patton or Brown is his ability to make effortless leaps into a falsetto register, a quality heard in *Cool Drink Of Water Blues, Big Road Blues,* and *Canned Heat Blues*. This attribute, evidently learned from other Delta bluesmen, seems to combine the influences of the field holler and the "blue yodel" of country music, two forms themselves ultimately derived from traditional African singing and German-Swiss yodelling respectively. Another fascinating aspect of Johnson's music is his ability to transpose instrumental, melodic, and lyric elements from one song to another, a characteristic possibly learned from Willie Brown. Textual and melodic phrases or variants are used in more than one song, and guitar figures and ideas are transposed to different keys or even different tunings.

While Johnson's musical ideas can stand as complete and near-perfect creations on their own, several of his recordings have additional accompaniment. The most successful are four tracks with second-guitar work by Charlie McCoy, who alternately plays mandolin-like trills, paraphrases of Johnson's guitar lines, and contrasting lines in the opposite register of Johnson's bass or treble playing. Nowhere is the folk term of "complementing" for second-guitar playing better exemplified than in these four pieces, *Cool Drink Of Water Blues, Big*

Road Blues, Bye-Bye Blues, and *Maggie Campbell Blues.* McCoy was probably taught some of his ideas by Johnson himself, who is said to have worked out second parts for many of his pieces. The accompaniment by the New Orleans Nehi Boys on *Black Mare Blues*, consisting of Charley Taylor's widely ranging piano and Kid Ernest's absurd laughing clarinet, is less effective. Other highlights of this disc are two alternate takes of *Lonesome Home Blues* and another untitled blues (none of which was ever commercially issued) and Johnson's wonderful low-register singing on *Slidin' Delta, Ridin' Horse*, and another piece with the title *Lonesome Home Blues*.

Ishman Bracey & Charley Taylor (1928–1929) contains the complete recordings of an artist who was a long-time associate of Tommy Johnson in Jackson, Mississippi. Bracey's singing style in general resembles Rube Lacy's with its moaning quality and machine-gun vibrato, while traces of Johnson's blues may be heard in some of his lyrics and perhaps in his falsetto singing in *Woman Woman Blues*. On the whole, however, Bracey is a distinctive stylist of a high order. He is a master of blue notes, which he achieves both by subtle twists of his voice and by bending the strings of his guitar. He has a punchy, minimalist approach to guitar playing, squeezing the maximum expression out of every note, and his singing has a similar quality, as he uses a rough, tense, clenched voice, particularly favouring the flattened fifth. Paul Oliver, in his notes, which offer an excellent assessment of Bracey's style and career, characterizes his music as "uncompromising"; certainly it is far removed from the usual aesthetic standards of Western music. It is not made any more accessible by the poor condition of some of the original recordings. Ishman Bracey will certainly be an acquired taste for many listeners, but his music will repay many repeated hearings for those with patience to seek out its strength and subtleties.

Perhaps Bracey's most moving pieces are the ones where he performs solo. *Woman Woman Blues* and *Suitcase Full Of Blues* are masterpieces that display the essence of Bracey's harsh vocal and guitar style. There are also two takes each of *Trouble Hearted Blues*, a moaning blues on a graveyard theme with Bracey's voice so clenched that half of the singing comes out like humming, and *The Four Day Blues*, a blues of abandonment and mistreatment. The similarity in the takes suggests that Bracey's blues were rather carefully worked out in advance. A number of them, in fact, have their own individual structures well outside the standard 12-bar blues pattern. Four other excellent selections, including two with alternate takes, have Charlie McCoy playing either second guitar or mandolin in a style similar to that which he used in accompanying Tommy Johnson. Among these is *Saturday*

Blues, the only recording of Bracey's that has been covered by other artists. Bracey's work with the New Orleans Nehi Boys is more successful than Tommy Johnson's. While these two musicians seemed to be trying to ridicule Johnson, they show respect for Bracey on four selections and let him set the pace of the songs. Of these pieces *Jake Liquor Blues* is particularly interesting, as it contains a theme similar to that of Tommy Johnson's *Canned Heat Blues* and *Alcohol and Jake Blues*; Bracey, however, warned his listeners against cheap substitutes for distilled liquor, while Johnson announced his craving for such substances in his songs. *Too Damp To Be Wet* and *Where My Shoes At?* are jiving dialogues between Bracy and Charley Taylor with a remarkable spontaneity, interspersed with bits of Taylor's fine piano work. *Mobile Stomp* and *Farish St. Rag* are piano and clarient ragtime workouts by the Nehi Boys with Kid Ernest's musicianship coming to the fore as he displays a fine slap-tongue technique. Charley Taylor plays outstanding piano in a style rather like that of Roosevelt Sykes on *Heavy Suitcase Blues* and *Louisiana Bound*, both of them solo performances.

While Tommy Johnson found solace in drink and his career went into a slow, steady decline, Ishman Bracey turned to religion and became a preacher. In the late 1960s, a few years before his death, he was as uncompromising as ever. He was still playing guitar but now in accompaniment to his spirituals. In a demonstration of his material he broke three strings from bending them so hard. He had fond memories of his blues career and was immensely proud that Louis Armstrong had recognized him from the stage at an appearance in Jackson some years previously.

The Complete Early Recordings of Skip James might serve as a good argument for the often heard, and quite untrue, statement that blues is depressing music, were it not for the uniform brilliance of the music contained therein. Although based in a local style of his native Mississippi hill country town of Bentonia, James' weird songs are shaped by the creative force of a lone and tormented genius. His sombre themes of diabolical dealings, death, abandonment, desperate poverty, drunkenness, murder, and lynching seem to express perfectly the bleakness of the Great Depression of the early 1930s in rural Mississippi. Even on a tune entitled *I'm So Glad* there is an extraordinary aura of sadness. Not even his two spirituals seem to provide any joy or uplift.

James displays a high, reedy tenor voice, sometimes employing moaning in the lower register. Most of his guitar work is in a D minor tuning and is modal in character with a tendency towards pentatonic scales, lending a particularly haunting quality to his music. Both his singing and guitar playing emphasize minor and "blue" sevenths, conferring a character of irresolution to the songs. Unlike most of his Mississippi blues contemporaries, he plays frequent guitar choruses and sometimes extends his guitar responses at the ends of vocal lines, all in an apparent attempt to display his technical mastery of the instrument. These passages, nevertheless, are always tasteful and leave the listener stunned, which was no doubt James' intention. His nimble fingers are able to execute lightning-fast runs of extraordinary delicacy and refinement in both duple and triple rhythms. His piano playing on five pieces is equally bizarre and, like his guitar work, has few parallels in recorded blues. While making a feature of darting runs and manic foot stomping, he has a tendency to play with one hand at a time or to use the left hand to punch in notes that play a melodic role. Generally he eschews the steady rhythmic role of the left hand and standard boogie-woogie and walking-bass patterns. In guitar and piano playing, singing style and mood, James sets severe stylistic limits on his music, but he is absolutely brilliant within the style he chooses.

In a disc so uniformly excellent it is difficult to pick out highlights. Nevertheless, one must point out the compelling imagery of *Devil Got My Woman, Little Cow And Calf Is Gonna Die Blues, Hard Time Killin' Floor Blues*, and *Cypress Grove Blues*, the dazzling guitar playing on *Drunken Spree, I'm So Glad,* and *Illinois Blues*, the menancing lyrics of *22–20 Blues*, the perfection of the guitar part in *Special Rider Blues*, and the wild piano of *How Long "Buck"*, which seems ready to break apart at any moment.

Robert Johnson: The Complete Recordings contains 41 tracks of 29 different blues recorded in 1936 and 1937. They represent a synthesis of everything that came before in Mississippi blues along with other elements from popular blues recordings. But while Johnson drew from the past, his greatest importance lies in that fact that his blues foretold a musical future. Unfortunately that future, which might have been launched for him personally had he appeared as scheduled at the 1938 Carnegie Hall Spirituals to Swing Concert, had to be realized by other musicians, for Johnson was dead within a few months of making his last recordings, poisoned by a jealous husband of a woman who flirted with him at a house party. Although none of his records were big commercial hits, they must have been well received by his fellow musicians, for an extraordinary number of his pieces have been covered and adapted by other artists. Johnson's general influence reaches even further and forms the core of the style of such great artists as Muddy Waters, Elmore James, Robert "Junior" Lockwood, Johnny Shines, and Eddie Taylor (Chapter 10).

Johnson absorbed influences from some of the greatest Deep South bluesmen, including Son House, Willie Brown, Skip James, and Hambone Willie Newbern. There are further echoes, though not necessarily direct borrowings, of the percussive playing of Charley Patton, the falsetto leaps of Tommy Johnson, and the clenched singing of Ishman Bracey. There is the dexterity, precision, and harmonic awareness of Lonnie Johnson. But Robert Johnson ranged even wider in creating his remarkable stylistic synthesis. In his guitar work he incorporated elements of the piano players who dominated the blues sound of the 1930s. Leroy Carr and Roosevelt Sykes in particular seem to have been influences, Carr for his lush right-hand chording and rolling rhythms and Sykes for his rumbling, churning bass patterns. There is also a new element of swing in Johnson's music. To hear this easily one may compare Johnson's *Walking Blues* with its prototype in Son House's *My Black Mama*, recorded six years earlier. Finally, there is a frantic rhythmic quality in some of Johnson's blues, which seems to foreshadow the ascendency of jive and bebop music in the late 1930s and the 1940s. One hears this especially in *32–20 Blues*, which one might compare with Skip James' piano-accompanied prototype, *22–20 Blues*, recorded five years previously (something of this same frantic quality is even evident in James' piece). By synthesizing all these diverse elements, Johnson must be credited as the man who brought Deep South folk blues out of its rural and regional isolation and into the mainstream of American music; repercussions are still being felt over 50 years after Johnson's death, and for this act he is viewed by many as the greatest blues artist of all time.

The enormous musical synthesis that Johnson achieved was held together barely long enough to be documented on recordings that could serve as a base for other, more stable, musicians to build upon. Johnsons' own personality seems to have been highly volatile and his life crossed with some sort of unexplained evil. Like many of the greatest Mississippi bluesmen, he was clearly worried about the condition of his soul, as is revealed in more than 20 percent of his songs. But while Charley Patton successfully balanced his blues career with the performance of spirituals and even preaching, while Ishman Bracey and Rube Lacy gave up the blues entirely and became preachers, while Son House vacillated over the course of a long lifetime between the Bible and the bottle, while Tommy Johnson said his "morning prayer" and spent the rest of the day in wasted inebriation, while Skip James became a bitter cynic and performed his spirituals as if they were blues, Robert Johnson seems to have fallen into a state of utter spiritual despair, a state he describes vividly in *Cross Road Blues*. In *Preaching The Blues* he equates the blues with the devil, who walks by his side in *Me And The Devil Blues*. He challenges God in *If I Had Possession Over Judgement Day.* His life seems jinxed in *Stones In My Passway*, and he is just one step ahead of his doom in *Hellhound On My Trail.* These images of despair and evil are complemented by other blues suggesting a life of compulsive wandering like some lost soul, by automobile in *Terraplane Blues*, on foot in *Walking Blues*, by train in *Rambling On My Mind*, and by riverboat in *Traveling Riverside Blues.* Other pieces, such as *Phonograph Blues, They're Red Hot, Malted Milk*, and *Drunken Hearted Man*, suggest that he plunged himself into a life of hedonism, dissipation, and self-destruction in an attempt to avoid the demons that were pursuing him.

Johnson does not have an outstanding natural singing voice and sometimes strains excessively for high notes, but he invests his performances with so much feeling and intensity that one easily overlooks his limitations. His singing is very intimate and compelling as he draws the listener into his tormented world. On the guitar he achieves with his left hand previously undreamed-of-configurations on the neck of the instrument, while his right hand displays an incredible sense of rhythmic dynamics. With only a guitar Johnson is able to suggest the sound of a full band, including piano, drums, and horns. His slide playing, which is in evidence on about one-third of his songs, has a stinging quality not heard on previous blues recordings. This package, which contains a lengthy biographical essay by Steve LaVere and complete lyric transciptions, became a huge pop music chart success more than 50 years after Johnson's death, indicating the power that his music still conveys. His recordings have influenced countless other blues, folk, and rock musicians and launched Johnson himself to a degree of fame that has made him a subject of books, films, and much speculation.

Bukka White: The Complete Sessions (1930–1940) contains four commercial recordings made in 1930, two from 1937 with an unknown second guitarist, two field recordings from 1939 made while White was an inmate in Mississippi's Parchman Penitentiary, and 12 commercial recordings made in 1940 following his release. On the latter he is backed by Washboard Sam. Born in 1909 and of the same generation as Robert Johnson, White was playing music in the delta by 1930 and was in a position to absorb and synthesize the same musical elements as did Johnson. White, however, never achieved this synthesis, and after the artistic success but commercial failure of his 1940 session he drifted off into obscurity, not recording again until his rediscovery by blues researchers in 1963.

White maintained essentially two separate musical approaches. One has its roots in his native hill country of north-east Mississippi, a region in White's youth of extreme rural isolation where the black folk-music tradition preserved many older elements. The blues of this area are characterized by a highly percussive quality and the use of repeated short instrumental phrases as a structural base; slide-guitar style is also common. These elements have their source deep in older instrumental traditions of banjo and fiddle string bands, fife and drum bands and African-derived one-string children's instruments. White uses this style in over half of these recordings, playing stunning slide guitar. It would be fair to say that he brought this archaic blues style to full perfection, perhaps matched only by Fred McDowell many years later (**409**). The style is a wonderful alternative to the often stale three-line, 12-bar blues pattern that dominated the commercial recordings of this music at the time, but White's sound was unfortunately too far outside the blues mainstream to serve as the main base for the music's future development. In fact, White compromised himself in his other approach to blues, which consisted simply of a series of borrowings from popular recording artists such as Leroy Carr (**219**) and Peetie Wheatstraw (**229**). The pieces using this approach were not particularly distinctive in their musical conception. What elevates them to a higher level is White's magnificent, rich singing voice, his powerful rhythmic drive and his sensitive lyricism, characteristics which are found in all his recordings from this period.

More than anything else, Bukka White conveys a sense of power. A baseball pitcher, boxer, merchant seaman, worker in a boiler plant, ex-convict, and hard drinker, White roars out his lyrics and batters his guitar into submission. His lyrics also display a toughness as they deal with such subjects as the death of his mother (*Strange Place Blues*), his own illness and impending death (*High Fever Blues, Fixin' To Die Blues*), mental depression (*Sleepy Man Blues*), alcoholism (*Good Gin Blues*), and his imprisonment (*When Can I Change My Clothes, Parchman Farm Blues, District Attorney Blues*). Seldom have blues on these themes been matched in the power of their imagery and delivery. Balancing these themes are two songs celebrating favorite haunts of the singer (*Pinebluff Arkansas, Aberdeen Mississippi Blues*), two dance-orientated pieces (his big hit *Shake 'Em On Down* and *Bukka's Jitterbug Swing*), and three extraordinary railroad songs from the hobo tradition in which the guitar imitates the sounds of the train. On one of the latter pieces the vocal is delivered by White's partner Napoleon Hairiston. Two spirituals from 1930 in a driving Sanctified style also have a second vocalist, a mysterious Miss Minnie. The disc contains notes by the late Simon A. Napier which give a good description of White's career and commentary on his songs.

81 **Charley Patton: The Complete Recorded Works**
P-Vine PCD 2255/6/7 (Jap)—*3 CD set/Document DOCD 5009 (Vol. 1); DOCD 5010 (Vol. 2); DOCD 5011 (Vol. 3)* (Au)—released separately
DISC ONE: *Mississippi Boweavil Blues/Screamin' And Hollerin' The Blues/Down The Dirt Road Blues/Pony Blues/Banty Rooster Blues/It Won't Be Long/Pea Vine Blues/Tom Rushen Blues/A Spoonful Blues/Shake It And Break It (But Don't Let It Fall Mama)/Prayer Of Death* Part 1/*Prayer Of Death* Part 2/*Lord I'm Discouraged/I'm Goin' Home/Going To Move To Alabama/Elder Greene Blues* (take 1)/*Elder Greene Blues* (take 2)/*Circle Round The Moon/Devil Sent The Rain Blues/Mean Black Cat Blues*

DISC TWO: *Frankie And Albert/Some These Days I'll Be Gone* (take 1)/*Some These Days I'll Be Gone* (take 2)/*Green River Blues*; Henry Sims, *Farrell Blues/Come Back Corrina*; Charley Patton, *Hammer Blues* (take 1)/*Hammer Blues* (take 2)/ *Magnolia Blues/When Your Way Gets Dark/Heart Like Railroad Steel/Some Happy Day/You're Gonna Need Somebody When You Die/Jim Lee Blues* Part 1/ *Jim Lee Blues* Part 2/*High Water Everywhere* Part 1/*High Water Everywhere* Part 2/*Jesus Is A Dying Bed-Maker/I Shall Not Be Moved/Rattlesnake Blues*

DISC THREE: *Running Wild Blues*; Henry Sims, *Tell Me Man Blues/Be True Be True Blues*; Charley Patton, *Joe Kirby/Mean Black Moan/Dry Well Blues/Some Summer Day* Part 1/*Moon Going Down/Bird Nest Bound/Jersey Bull Blues/High Sheriff Blues/Stone Pony Blues*; Bertha Lee, *Yellow Bee/Mind Reader Blues*; Charley Patton, *34 Blues/Love My Stuff/Revenue Man*; Patton & Lee, *Oh Death/Troubled 'Bout My Mother*; Charley Patton, *Poor Me/Hang It On The Wall*

82 **Son House And The Great Delta Blues Singers (1928–1930): Complete Recorded Works**
Various Artists
Document DOCD 5002 (Au)
Son House, *My Black Mama* Part 1/*My Black Mama* Part 2/*Preachin' The Blues* Part 1/*Preachin' The Blues* Part 2/*Dry Spell Blues* Part 1/*Dry Spell Blues* Part 2/*Walking Blues*; Willie Brown, *M & O Blues/Future Blues*; Kid Bailey, *Mississippi Bottom Blues/Rowdy Blues*; Garfield Akers, *Cottonfield Blues* Part 1/*Cottonfield Blues* Part 2/*Dough Roller Blues/Jumpin' And Shoutin' Blues*; Joe Calicott, *Fare Thee Well Blues/Traveling Mama Blues*; Jim Thompkins, *Bedside Blues*; Blind Joe [Willie] Reynolds, *Outside Woman Blues/Nehi Blues/Married Man Blues/Third Street Woman Blues*/Rube Lacy, *Mississippi Jail House Groan/Ham Hound Crave*

83 **Tommy Johnson (1928–1929): Complete Recorded Works In Chronological Order**
Document DOCD 5001 (Au)
Cool Drink Of Water Blues/Big Road Blues/Bye-Bye Blues/Maggie Campbell Blues/Canned Heat Blues/Lonesome Home Blues (take 1)/*Lonesome Home Blues* (take 2)/*Big Fat Mama Blues/I Wonder To Myself/Slidin' Delta/Lonesome Home Blues/Untitled Song (Morning Prayer Blues)/Untitled Song (Boogaloosa Woman)/Black Mare Blues* (take 1)/*Black Mare Blues* (take 2)/*Ridin' Horse/ Alcohol And Jake Blues*

84 Ishman Bracey & Charley Taylor: Complete Recorded Works In Chronological Order (1928–1929)
Document DOCD 5049 (Au)
Rosie Mae Moore, *Stranger Blues*; Ishman Bracey, *Saturday Blues/Left Alone Blues/Leavin' Town Blues* (take 1)/*Leavin' Town Blues* (take 2)/*Brown Mama Blues* (take 1)/*Brown Mama Blues* (take 2)/*Trouble Hearted Blues* (take 1)/ *Trouble Hearted Blues* (take 2)/*The Four Day Blues* (take 1)/*The Four Day Blues* (take 2)/*Jake Liquor Blues/Family Stirving [sic]*; New Orleans Nehi Boys, *Mobile Stomp/Farish St. Rag*; Ishman Bracey, *Woman Woman Blues/ Suitcase Full Of Blues/Bust Up Blues/Pay Me No Mind*; Charley Taylor, *Heavy Suitcase Blues/Louisiana Bound*; Charley Taylor & Ishman Bracey, *Too Damp To Be Wet/Where My Shoes At?*

85 The Complete Early Recordings of Skip James, 1930
Yazoo (CD) 2009
Devil Got My Woman/Cypress Grove Blues/Little Cow And Calf Is Gonna Die Blues/Hard Time Killin' Floor Blues/Drunken Spree/Cherry Ball Blues/Jesus Is A Mighty Good Leader/Illinois Blues/How Long "Buck"/4 O' Clock Blues/22–20 Blues/Hard Luck Child/If You Havn't Any Hay Get On Down The Road/Be Ready When He Comes/Yola My Blues Away/I'm So Glad/What Am I To Do Blues/Special Rider Blues

86 Robert Johnson: The Complete Recordings
Columbia C2K 46222/467246-2 (UK)—*2 CD set*
DISC ONE: *Kindhearted Woman Blues* (take 1)/*Kindhearted Woman Blues* (take 2)/*I Believe I'll Dust My Broom/Sweet Home Chicago/Rambling On My Mind* (take 1)/*Rambling On My Mind* (take 2)/*When You Got A Good Friend* (take 1)/*When You Got A Good Friend* (take 2)/*Come On In My Kitchen* (take 1)/ *Come On In My Kitchen* (take 2)/*Terraplane Blues/Phonograph Blues* (take 1)/ *Phonograph Blues* (take 2)/*32–20 Blues/They're Red Hot/Dead Shrimp Blues/ Cross Road Blues* (take 1)/*Cross Road Blues* (take 2)/*Walking Blues/Last Fair Deal Gone Down*

DISC TWO: *Preaching The Blues (Up Jumped The Devil)/If I Had Possession Over Judgement Day/Stones In My Passway/I'm A Steady Rollin' Man/From Four Till Late/Hellhound On My Trail/Little Queen Of Spades* (take 1)/*Little Queen Of Spades* (take 2)/*Malted Milk/Drunken Hearted Man* (take 1)/*Drunken Hearted Man* (take 2)/*Me And The Devil Blues* (take 1)/*Me And The Devil Blues* (take 2)/*Stop Breakin' Down Blues* (take 1)/*Stop Breaking Down Blues* (take 2)/*Traveling Riverside Blues/Honeymoon Blues/Love In Vain* (take 1)/*Love In Vain* (take 4)/*Milkcow's Calf Blues* (take 2)/*Milkcow's Calf Blues* (take 3)

87 Bukka White: The Complete Sessions (1930–1940)
Travelin' Man TM CD 03 (UK)
Napoleon Hairiston, *The New Frisco Train*/Bukka White, *The Panama Limited/ I Am In The Heavenly Way/Promise True And Grand/Pinebluff Arkansas/Shake 'Em On Down/Sic 'Em Dogs On/Po' Boy/Black Train/Strange Place Blues/ When Can I Change My Clothes/Sleepy Man Blues/Parchman Farm Blues/Good Gin Blues/High Fever Blues/District Attorney Blues/Fixin' To Die Blues/ Aberdeen Mississippi Blues/Bukka's Jitterbug Swing/Special Stream Line*

(ii) Memphis Blues

In the cities of the southern and border states the rural folk blues were able to reach a larger and more affluent audience, acquire a greater sophistication and become more adapted to commercial development. Some artists essentially retained the sound of rural blues that they had brought with them from the country with little or no modification. The solo blues of Memphis artists are all of this sort. Sometimes, however, these performers would meet others in the cities and form musical partnerships; it might be just a duo, or it might be a larger combination of instruments. Urban groups made up of string, wind, and sometimes percussion instruments were known variously as jug bands, bucket bands, washboard bands, skiffle bands, hokum bands, and spasm bands. Many of them were highly informal groupings, simply part of a "gang" of musicians who tended to hang out together and help one another on jobs. In Memphis and Louisville some of these jug-band groupings achieved a certain stability, no doubt caused by a sufficient demand for their services, and managed to record with some degree of frequency. Groups such as Cannon's Jug Stompers, (**46**), Jed Davenport's Beale Street Jug Band (**63**) and the Memphis Jug Band represent the peak in the development of this type of music. These were small ensembles springing wholly from the folk blues tradition and serving as prototypes for the more modern bands of today.

The Memphis Jug Band was the most prolific of all the jug bands, recording some 60 titles between 1927 and 1934. The pieces on **Memphis Jug Band** are some of its finest as well as being a good cross-section of its material and varying styles. The group was organized by guitar and harmonica player Will Shade, who was inspired by earlier recordings of jug bands from Louisville. Shade kept a jug band going in Memphis until the 1960s, but the heyday of this music was the 1920s and 1930s, when these tracks were recorded. He employed a shifting line-up of four or five musicians, sometimes with an added female vocalist (here Hattie Hart or Minnie Wallace). A number of the vocals were delivered as duets or even trios in ragged harmony. Never blessed with a great singer, the band made up for this deficiency with an unbridled collective exuberance coupled with often effective songwriting, and positively revels in its unique sound. It drew upon amateur street musicians as well as formally trained ones such as violinists Milton Robie and Charlie Pierce, who extended their musical careers by playing with jug bands after the violin had faded from more sophisticated levels of music. The jug band also served as a training ground for musicians who would have careers of their own, including guitarists Will Weldon, Vol Stevens, and Charlie Burse, and pianist Jab Jones, who usually played jug with the Memphis Jug Band. There was no standard instrumentation, but on most pieces there may be heard a rhythm guitar and three lead instruments, either the jug, kazoo, and harmonica, or two of these with a lead guitar, mandolin or violin. Altogether the Memphis Jug Band had one of the most remarkable sounds ever recorded in the blues. All the wind instruments display a raspy, buzzing sound very much within an African musical aesthetic and very far outside the Western one. The jug and kazoo, in fact, are derived from African prototypes, where they generally represent the voices of animal and ancestor spirits. Here their cultural significance appears to have been entirely reinterpreted, and they simply provide novelty entertainment and contribute to the group's hokum spirit of good times. Three different jug sounds are in evidence on this album. Jab Jones uses it at times as a melodic instrument, while Charlie Polk plays in a more conventional style imitating a plucked string bass and Ham Lewis employs an intermediate style featuring long, scooped bass notes.

The Memphis Jug Band performs good-time music, even when the song lyrics deal with serious or sad subjects. Gone are the preoccupations with sin and death of the Mississippi bluesmen. These jug-band musicians seem comfortable with the blues, able to distance themselves from its deepest emotional content and concerned mainly with producing enjoyable, entertaining music. There is considerable variety on this disc. In addition to blues on standard themes, there are older items such as *On The Road Again, Cocaine Habit Blues*, and *K.C. Moan*; dance-orientated pieces, such as *Gator Wobble, Lindberg Hop* and, *The Old Folks Started It*; blues with humorous imagery—*Oh Ambulance Man* and *What's The Matter?*; and two pieces that describe and celebrate the jug-band way of life, *Fourth Street Mess Around* and *Whitewash Station Blues*. The pieces from the 1934 session show a modernizing tendency in the incorporation of drums and scat vocal sounds of the sort popularized by Cab Calloway. Notes by Bengt Olsson, based on original research, give a good history of the group and some analysis of their material.

Memphis Blues (1928–1935) presents the entire blues output of Robert Wilkins, Tom Dickson, and Allen Shaw who are among the more enigmatic early Deep South blues artists. Robert Wilkins was born in Hernando in the Mississippi hill country in 1896 and moved to Memphis a few miles to the north about 19 years later. His 12 blues recorded between 1928 and 1930 are built mostly around repeated riffs in the manner of other hill country artists such as Fred McDowell. *Get Away Blues* is typical and uses guitar phrases similar to those of fellow Hernando artist Garfield Akers. Many of these pieces employ string bending and blue notes built into the guitar tunings. Each one is a little gem of a composition with its own distinctive melody and form and its own well-crafted theme. In fact, Wilkins' lyrics have a delicacy and strong intellectual quality that don't seem quite at home with his use of repeated rhythmic riffs and string bending. They convey a sense of repressed rage and resentment held in place by a highly creative formalism. Wilkins was preoccupied by a limited number of themes that keep recurring in these blues. Essentially they revolve around ideas of separation, departure, escape, and loss, frequently interlaced with images of death. *Rolling Stone* Parts 1 and 2, *That's No Way To Get Along, Alabama Blues, Long Train Blues, Get Away Blues, I Do Blues*, and *Falling Down Blues* all elaborate these themes. *I'll Go With Her Blues* is a graveyard piece dealing with the death of a girlfriend. Jailhouse imagery is also prominent in Wilkins' repertoire, occurring in three blues, *Jail House Blues, Nashville Stonewall Blues,* and *Police Sergeant Blues.*

After a five-year break Wilkins returned to the studio in 1935 to record five more blues. They have a generally lighter texture and sound more urban than his earlier recordings. The tracks feature Son Joe (later to be Memphis Minnie's partner and husband) on second guitar and Kid Spoons on spoons, providing an ensemble sound approaching that of the jug bands of Memphis. The lyrics include topical references and typical popular blues imagery and in general seem more self-conscious. *New Stock Yard Blues* is about the Owens Brothers' Union Stock Yard where Wilkins worked , while *Old Jim Canan's* celebrates a notorious North Memphis tavern where customers were "drinking their whisky and sniffing cocaine."

Even though Wilkins in 1935 appears to have been adapting his music successfully to modern trends, he apparently felt that he was "losin' out." Less than a year after making these recordings he abandoned the blues and joined the Church of God in Christ, eventually becoming a minister and a maker of herbal medicines. He was rediscovered in the early 1960s and induced to record an album of gospel songs with his guitar accompaniment. Several of these still showed a preoccupation with themes of traveling out in a world of sin, but now with the possibility of having God at one's side. One song, *The Prodigal Son*, substituted a biblical text for the words of *That's No Way To Get Along*, a blues Wilkins had recorded in 1929 on the theme of a prodigal son returning to his mother after being mistreated by "lowdown women." In an unlikely turn of events, the British rock group the Rolling Stones covered Wilkins' spiritual reinterpretation of the song on their big-selling *Beggars Banquet* album. This act should have boosted Wilkins' career considerably, but the result was otherwise. Wilkins became confused by the world of copyrights, licenses, and royalties and suspicious that he might not be receiving all he was due. He reacted by once again retiring from the world and into his family and church work, living in a kind of embittered obscurity for another 20 years; he died in 1987 at the age of 91.

The other two artists on this disc maintain a musical standard equal to that of Wilkins. Tom Dickson recorded in Memphis in 1928 but may have been from somewhere in the surrounding region. He displays a masterful finger-picking touch on the guitar that is thoroughly within the Deep South style. His *Happy Blues* notwithstanding, Dickson's four blues generally have sombre themes, as typified by the titles of *Death Bell Blues* and *Worry Blues*. Allen Shaw, who recorded two blues in 1934 with Willie Borum on second guitar, is more in a Memphis mold. *I Couldn't Help It* is reminiscent of some of the duets of Memphis Minnie and Kansas Joe, while *Moanin' The Blues* displays a lovely slide technique and Shaw's rich voice.

Furry Lewis (1927–1929) presents the initial recordings of an artist whose early career had much in common with that of Robert Wilkins. Lewis was born in Greenwood, Mississippi, some time between 1893 and 1900 and moved to Memphis as a teenager after he had already begun playing guitar. Like Wilkins, he performed mostly by himself, and all but three of the 25 tracks on this disc are solo pieces that betray the stylistic origins of his music. The three exceptions have an added mandolin and, like Wilkins' small ensemble pieces, have the rhythmic flavour and regularity of structure of jug-band blues.

Lewis skips around frequently from one theme to another in his lyrics, somewhat like Charley Patton but without the obvious personal element of the latter's singing. Lewis sings clearly and with great feeling and considerable poetry but without seeming to be closely involved with his songs' messages. Perhaps because he had lost a leg in a hoboing accident in his youth, he believed he had a right to sing the blues. There is an element of humor and irony in his blues, laced with a good deal of proverbial wisdom and philosophy about life. These qualities help make his blues more accessible to audiences from a social and cultural range broader than his own, even when his lyrics touch upon the deeper subjects of the blues, such as death, violence, imprisonment, and the state of the singer's soul. They also stood Lewis in good stead for the last two decades of his long life, in which he became the living embodiment of the blues tradition for thousands of young, mostly white, followers of blues and folk music (**413**).

Lewis' solo pieces provide an excellent example of how a traditional bluesman handled his lyrics and musical material in building a repertoire. He uses a limited number of melodic and guitar patterns for his basic musical structures, varying each performance with interesting little improvisations. There is even some overlap from one song to another in his lyrics, most of which are derived from formulae as part of the shared tradition of blues poetry. *Good Looking Girl Blues, Mr. Furry's Blues*, and *Rock Island Blues* all share the same musical ideas, including a guitar part in open G tuning. Similarly, *Mean Old Bedbug, Mistreatin' Mamma* and *Jelly Roll* share a guitar part based in the E position of standard tuning but with the D string tuned up to E. *Falling Down Blues* and *Judge Harsh Blues* are musically similar to one another and demonstrate lovely slide playing. The latter piece deals with a courtroom scene and contains veiled protest against a merciless legal system. Some of the songs reflect an older level of traditional material in Lewis' repertoire. *Cannon Ball Blues* and *Why Don't You Come Home Blues* are both related to the widespread *Poor Boy Long Way From Home*, one of the earliest blues to become part of the general tradition and a piece almost always performed in slide style as is the case here. *I Will Turn Your Money Green* includes a lilting melody heard widely in blues tradition and best known as a hillbilly fiddle tune, *Carroll County Blues* (**325**), named after the county where Furry Lewis was born and where he probably learned it. The two-part *Kassie Jones* is derived from a turn-of-the-century folk ballad about a Mississippi railroad wreck and is a textbook example of black handling of ballad material. The story's chronology has been completely fractured, and details of the wreck are interlaced with humorous verses and personal boasting. The emphasis is far more on Lewis' presentation of self than of the story. Musically the tune is similar to the Memphis Jug Band's *On The Road Again*. *Billy Lyons And Stack O' Lee* and the two-part *John Henry (The Steel Driving Man)* are further excellent examples of folk ballads from the same period.

88 Memphis Jug Band

Yazoo (CD) 1067

Lindberg Hop/On The Road Again/Stealin' Stealin'/Insane Crazy Blues/K.C. Moan/Cocaine Habit Blues [Hattie Hart, vocal]/*Newport News Blues* (take 1); *Whitewash Station Blues*; Minnie Wallace, *The Old Folks Started It*; Memphis Jug Band, *Everybody's Talking About Sadie Green/Memphis Jug Blues* (take 1)/ *Gator Wobble/Little Green Slippers/Taking Your Place/Sometimes I Think I Love You/Memphis Boy Blues/Aunt Caroline Dyer Blues/What's The Matter?/ Oh Ambulance Man* [Hattie Hart, vocal]/*Beale Street Mess Around/She Stays Out All Night Long/You May Leave But This Will Bring You Back/Fourth Street Mess Around*

89 Memphis Blues (1928–1935): Complete Recorded Works In Chronological Order: Robert Wilkins, Tom Dickson, Allen Shaw
Document DOCD 5014 (Au)
Robert Wilkins, *Rolling Stone* Part 1/*Rolling Stone* Part 2/*Jail House Blues/I Do Blues/That's No Way To Get Along/Alabama Blues/Long Train Blues/Falling Down Blues/Nashville Stonewall Blues/Police Sergeant Blues/Get Away Blues/I'll Go With Her Blues/Dirty Deal Blues/Black Rat Blues/New Stock Yard Blues/Old Jim Canan's/Losin' Out Blues*; Tom Dickson, *Death Bell Blues/Worry Blues/Happy Blues/Labor Blues*; Allen Shaw, *I Couldn't Help It/Moanin' The Blues*

90 Furry Lewis (1927–1929): Complete Recorded Works In Chronological Order
Document DOCD 5004 (Au)
Everybody's Blues/Mr. Furry's Blues/Sweet Papa Moan/Rock Island Blues/Jelly Roll/Billy Lyons And Stack O' Lee/Good Looking Girl Blues/Why Don't You Come Home Blues/Falling Down Blues/Big Chief Blues/Mean Old Bedbug Blues/Furry's Blues/I Will Turn Your Money Green (take 1)/*I Will Turn Your Money Green* (take 2)/*Mistreatin' Mama/Dry Land Blues/Cannon Ball Blues/Kassie Jones* Part 1/*Kassie Jones* Part 2/*Judge Harsh Blues* (take 1)/*Judge Harsh Blues* (take 2)/*John Henry (The Steel Driving Man)* Part 1/*John Henry (The Steel Driving Man)* Part 2/*Black Gypsy Blues/Creeper's Blues*

Basic Records

(i) Mississippi and Alabama Blues

91 Backwoods Blues: Complete Recorded Works (1926–1935): Bo Weavil Jackson (Sam Butler), Bobby Grant, King Solomon Hill, Lane Hardin
Document DOCD 5036 (Au)
Bo Weavil Jackson [Sam Butler], *Pistol Blues/Some Scream High Yellow/You Can't Keep No Brown/When The Saints Come Marching Home/I'm On My Way To The Kingdom Land/Why Do You Moan?/Devil And My Brown Blues/Poor Boy Blues/Jefferson County Blues/Jefferson County Blues* (alternate take)/*You Can't Keep No Brown/Christians Fight On, Your Time Ain't Long/Heaven Is My View*; Bobby Grant, *Nappy Head Blues/Lonesome Atlanta Blues*; King Solomon Hill, *Whoopee Blues* (take 1)/*Whoopee Blues* (take 2)/*Down On My Bended Knee* (take 1)/*Down On My Bended Knee* (take 2)/*The Gone Dead Train/Tell Me Baby*; Lane Hardin' *Hard Time Blues/California Desert Blues*
Jackson was a Birmingham street singer with a rough voice and often frantic guitar rhythms, sometimes played in slide style. Grant, apparently from Georgia, sings to exemplary slide guitar. Hill, allegedly from north-west Louisiana, has an individual style, with stinging slide-guitar work and high-pitched voice. Probably based in St Louis Hardin sings hauntingly to inventive guitar.

92 Jailhouse Blues
Sam Collins
Yazoo (CD) 1079
Devil In the Lion's Den/Slow Mama Slow/The Jailhouse Blues/Riverside Blues/

New Salty Dog/Yellow Dog Blues/Pork Chop Blues/Dark Cloudy Blues/Hesitation Blues/It Won't Be Long/Do That Thing/I Want To Be Like Jesus In My Heart/Loving Lady Blues/Midnight Special Blues/Lead Me All The Way/Graveyard Digger's Blues
Collins was reputedly based in south-western Mississippi with connections across the river in Louisiana. His work is somewhat eclectic and indicates a songster's approach; his best blues have a delicate slide-guitar sound that complements his high-pitched singing. Other tracks include interesting folk versions of standards.

93 **William Harris & Buddy Boy Hawkins: Complete Recorded Works in Chronological Order (1927–1929)**
Document DOCD 5035 (Au)
William Harris, *I'm Leavin' Town/Kansas City Blues/Kitchen Range Blues/Keep Your Man Out Of Birmingham/Electric Chair Blues/Bullfrog Blues/Leavin' Here Blues/Early Mornin' Blues/Hot Time Blues*; Walter "Buddy Boy" Hawkins, *Shaggy Dog Blues/Number Three Blues/Jailhouse Fire Blues/Snatch It Back Blues/Workin' On The Railroad/Yellow Woman Blues/Raggin' The Blues/Awful Fix Blues/A Rag Blues/How Come Mama Blues/Snatch It And Grab It/Voice Throwin' Blues*
Possibly from the Delta, Harris is one of the most rhythmically powerful folk blues guitarists recorded and sings with a rich voice. He mixes traditional blues and ragtime material with fine covers of recent hits. Hawkins performs a mix of blues and rags with novel themes, a distinctive guitar style, and even an example of ventriloquism.

94 **Alabama: Black Country Dance Bands: Complete Recorded Works In Chronological Order (1924–1949)**
Various Artists
Document DOCD 5166 (Au)
Daddy Stovepipe [Johnny Watson], *Sundown Blues/Stove Pipe Blues/Black Snake Blues/Tuxedo Blues*; Ben Curry ["Blind Bogus" Ben Covington], *Adam And Eve In The Garden/I Heard The Voice Of A Pork Chop/Boodle-De-Bum Blues/It's A Fight Like That/Boodle De Bum Bum/The New Dirty Dozen/Fat Mouth Blues/You Rascal You*; Mississippi Sarah & Daddy Stovepipe, *Burleskin' Blues/Greenville Strut/Read Your A.B.C.'s/Do You Love Him?/Strewin' It Out/The Spasm/35 Depression/If You Want Me, Baby*; Mobile Strugglers, *Memphis Blues/Fattenin' Frogs*
Only the Strugglers, featuring twin fiddles, live up to the description of a dance band. Stovepipe eventually became a Chicago street performer. He sang in a nasal voice and played guitar and rack harmonica. Some pieces with his wife Sarah suggest a 1920s-style vaudeville duet. Curry (possibly from Memphis) played banjo and rack harmonica, performing blues, hokum, and medicine show pieces.

95 **Jaybird Coleman & The Birmingham Jug Band: Complete Recorded Works In Chronological Order (1927–1930)**
Document DOCD 5140 (Au)
Bertha Ross, *My Jelly Blues*; Jaybird Coleman, *Mill Log Blues/Boll Weevil/Ah'm Sick And Tired Of Tellin' You (To Wiggle That Thing)/Man Trouble*

Blues/Trunk Busted—Suitcase Full Of Holes/I'm Gonna Cross The River Of Jordan—Some O' These Days/You Heard Me Whistle (Oughta Know My Blow)/No More Good Water—'Cause The Pond Is Dry/Mistreating' Mama/Save Your Money—Let These Women Go/Ain't Gonna Lay My 'Ligion Down/Troubled 'Bout My Soul/Coffee Grinder Blues/Man Trouble Blues; Birmingham Jug Band, *German Blues/Cane Brake Blues/The Wild Cat Squawl/Bill Wilson/Birmingham Blues/Gettin' Ready For Trial/Giving It Away/Kickin' Mule Blues*
Coleman was an Alabama harmonica player with superb tone and ability to achieve varied blue-note effects. Most of his blues and spirituals are solo performances. Some of these extremely rare recordings have formidable surface noise. The Birmingham Jug Band consisted of harmonica, mandolin, guitar, and jug. Their *Gettin' Ready For Trial* contains protest verses.

96 Ed Bell (Barefoot Bill/Sluefoot Joe): Complete Recorded Works In Chronological Order (1927–1930)

Document DOCD 5090 (Au)
Ed Bell, *Mamlish Blues/Hambone Blues/Mean Conductor Blues/Frisco Whistle Blues/Shouting Baby Blues/She's a Fool/Tooten' Out Blues/Grab It And Run/Leaving Train Blues/House Top Blues/Rocky Road Moan/Rosca Mama Blues/My Crime Blues/Snigglin' Blues/Big Rock Jail/From Now On*; Pillie Bolling & Barefoot Bill, *I Don't Like That/She's Got A Nice Line*; Ed Bell, *Squabblin' Blues/Barefoot Bill's Hard Luck Blues/One More Time/Bad Boy/Carry It Right Back Home/She's A Fool Gal*; Pillie Bolling, *Brown Skin Woman/Shake Me Like A Dog*
Ed Bell of Greenville, Alabama, sang in a strong voice, at times influenced by Blind Lemon Jefferson, and played guitar in an unusual arpeggiated style. St Louis guitarist-pianist Clifford Gibson accompanied on several selections. Pillie Bolling contributes two pieces in a style rather like Bell's and two duets with his compatriot.

97 Mississippi Blues: Complete Recorded Works In Chronological Order, Volume 1 (1928–1937)

Various Artists
Document DOCD 5157 (Au)
Uncle Bud Walker, *Look Here Mama Blues/Stand Up Suitcase Blues*; "Big Road" Webster Taylor, *World In A Jug/Sunny Southern Blues*; Mattie Delaney, *Down The Big Road Blues/Tallahatchie River Blues*; Louise Johnson, *All Night Long Blues/Long Ways From Home/On The Wall/By The Moon And Stars*; Mississippi [Caldwell] Bracy, *You Scolded Me And Drove Me From Your Door/Cherry Ball/Stered Gal/I'll Overcome Someday*; Geechie Wiley & Elvie Thomas, *Last Kind Words Blues/Skinny Leg Blues/Motherless Child Blues/Over To My House/Pick Poor Robin Clean/Eagles On A Half*; The Mississippi Moaner [Isaiah Nettles], *Mississippi Moan/It's Cold In China Blues*; Mose Andrews, *Ten Pound Hammer/Young Heifer Blues*
Johnson contributes exuberant singing and powerhouse piano, while Delaney performs a flood blues with excellent guitar. Of the other guitarists Wiley and Thomas sometimes perform together, singing about sex, hustling, and a wayward existence. Bracy has a lighter singing style; Taylor, Nettles and Andrews are interesting bluesmen of the second rank. Walker may be from Georgia.

98 **Mississippi Blues: Complete Recorded Works In Chronological Order, Volume 2 (1926–1935)**
Various Artists
Document DOCD 5158 (Au)
Arthur Petties, *Two Time Blues/Out On Santa Fe Blues/That Won't Do/Good Boy Blues/Quarrelin' Mama Blues/Revenue Man Blues*; Freddie Spruell, *Milk Cow Blues/Muddy Water Blues/Way Back Down Home (Milk Cow Blues)/Tom Cat Blues/Low-Down Mississippi Bottom Man/4A Highway/Don't Cry Baby/Your Good Man Is Gone/Let's Go Riding/Mr. Freddie's Kokomo Blues*; Willie "Poor Boy" Lofton, *It's Killin' Me/Poor Boy Blues/Jake Leg Blues/My Mean Baby Blues/Dirty Mistreater/Rainy Day Blues/Beer Garden Blues/Dark Road Blues*
These guitarists settled in Chicago but display downhome roots. Petties sounds like a Memphian who came into the orbit of Big Bill Broonzy. Spruell, with a crying vocal delivery and a spare guitar sound, was one of the first Delta bluesmen to record. From Jackson, Mississippi, Lofton performs in a rather frantic style based on local tradition.

99 **Charlie McCoy: Complete 1928–1932 Recordings In Chronological Order**
Blues Documents BDCD 6018 (Au)
Rosie Mae Moore, *Staggering Blues/Ha-Ha Blues/School Girl Blues*; Jackson Blue Boys, *Hidin' On Me/Sweet Alberta*; Charlie McCoy, *It Ain't No Good* Part 1/*Last Time Blues/It Ain't No Good* Part 2/*Your Valves Need Grinding/It's Hot Like That/Glad Hand Blues/Blue Heaven Blues*; Mississippi Mud Steppers, *Vicksburg Stomp/Sunset Waltz*; Charlie McCoy, *That Lonesome Train Took My Baby Away/Always In Love With You/I've Been Blue Ever Since You Went Away/You Gonna Need Me/It Is So Good* Part 1/*It Is So Good* Part 2/*The Northern Starvers Are Returning Home/Mississippi I'm Longing For You/Times Ain't What They Used To Be/Too Long*
McCoy's splendid guitar accompaniments to Moore come from the session on which he brilliantly backed Tommy Johnson (**82**) and Ishman Bracey (**84**). *Last Time* is a superb solo but most pieces find him playing mandolin with Bo Chatmon (Carter), Lonnie Chatmon, and Walter Vinson. Their repertoire included waltzes and sentimental songs for white and black audiences.

100 **Walter Vincson: Complete Recorded Works In Chronological Order (1928–1941)**
Blues Documents BDCD 6017 (Au)
Mary Butler, *Mad Dog Blues*; Walter Vincson, *Your Friends Gonna Use It Too* Part 1/*Overtime Blues/Your Friends Gonna Use It Too* Part 2/*Mississippi Yodelin' Blues/Working Man's Blues/Sheiks Special/Dear Little Girl/Mississippi Low Down/That's It*; Leroy Carter, *Can't Anybody Tell Me Blues/Black Widow Spider*; Walter Vincson, *When The Breath Bids The Body Goodbye/I Ain't Gonna Have It/Losin' Blues/The Wrong Man/How Did It Happen/Rats Been On My Cheese/Every Dog Must Have His Day/You Know What You Promised Me/Gulf Coast Bay/Rosa Lee Blues/Can't Get A Word In Edgeways/She's Leaving Me*
Vincson (or Vincent) was a member of the Mississippi Sheiks (**61**). These recordings were made mostly in the company of the same circle of musicians (**60**, **99**). He was a strong singer, good songwriter, and serviceable guitarist, backed variously by guitar, mandolin, and violin. Carter may be Vincson, who certainly accompanies, or another of the large musical Chatmon family. Butler has Charlie McCoy as guitarist.

101 Banana In Your Fruit Basket: Red Hot Blues 1931–1936
Bo Carter [Chatmon]
Yazoo (CD) 1064
Pig Meat Is What I Crave/What Kind Of Scent Is This?/Mashing That Thing/ Blue Runner Blues/Howling Tom Cat Blues/Don't Mash My Digger So Deep/Pin In Your Cushion/Ram Rod Daddy/All Around Man/Pussy Cat Blues/My Pencil Won't Write No More/Ants In My Pants/Banana In Your Fruit Basket/ Cigarette Blues
A sometime member of the Mississippi Sheiks, in a solo setting Carter shows himself as a brilliantly inventive guitarist with an advanced harmonic sense. He displays some influence from Tommy Johnson but generally has a lighter touch. Many of Carter's recordings were sold as "party records" and are heavy with *double entendre.* His lyrics make up in cleverness for what they lack in emotional depth.

102 Louisiana Blues: Sonny Boy Nelson (Eugene Powell) With Mississippi Maltida And Robert Hill (1936): Complete Recordings in Chronological Order
Wolf WSE 109 CD (Au)
Mississippi Maltilda, *A. & V. Blues/Hard Working Woman/Happy Home Blues*; Sonny Boy Nelson, *Long Tall Woman/Low Down/Lovin'Blues/Street Walkin'/If You Don't Believe I'm Leaving Baby/Pony Blues*; Robert Hill, *I Had A Gal For The Last Fifteen Years/Tell Me What's Wrong With You/You Gonna Look Like A Monkey When You Get Old/G Blues/Just Smilin'/Pal, How I Miss You Tonight/Lumber-Yard Blues/I'm Going To Write And Tell Mother/It Is So Good/Hill's Hot Sauce*
Despite the title, all the artists were from Mississippi. Nelson and Willie Harris Jr. were, in terms of technique and musical conception, spectacular. Together they accompany most of the singing. Powell's wife, Matilda, has an effective plaintive voice and contributes some strong original lyrics. Hill plays harmonica in a high-pitched squeaky style and sings a mixture of blues, hokum, country, and minstrel pieces.

103 Sonny Scott (1933)
Story of Blues CD 3525-2 (Ger)
Coal Mountain Blue/Red Rooster Blues; Water Roland & Sonny Scott, *Man, Man, Man*; Sonny Scott, *No Good Biddie/Red Cross Blues/Black Horse Blues/Firewood Man/Naked Man Blues/Highway No. 2 Blues/Try Me Man Blues/Hard Luck Man/ Early This Morning/Working Man's Moan/Rolling Water*; Walter Roland, *Frisco Blues*; Sonny Scott, *Red Cross Blues No. 2*; Walter Roland, *Overall Blues*
This collection presents Scott's complete recordings and three pieces with singing by his partner Walter Roland, who plays second guitar or piano on several selections. Scott was an accurate and very inventive Alabama guitarist as well as a sensitive singer. His blues are topical, self-conscious and typical of the 1930s.

104 Big Joe Williams: Complete Recorded Works In Chronological Order, Volume 1 (1935–1941)
Blues Documents BDCD 6003 (Au)
Little Leg Woman/Somebody's Been Borrowing That Stuff/Providence Help The

Poor People/49 Highway Blues/My Grey Pony/Stepfather Blues/Baby Please Don't Go/Stack O' Dollars/Wild Cow Blues/Worried Man Blues/I Know You Gonna Miss Me/Rootin' Ground Hog/Brother James/I Won't Be In Hard Luck No More/Crawlin' King Snake/I'm Getting Wild About Her/Peach Orchard Mama/Meet Me Around The Corner/Throw A Boogie Woogie/North Wind Blues/Please Don't Go/Highway 49/Someday Baby/Break 'Em On Down

This disc encompasses the early recordings of one of Mississippi's most distinctive and enduring blues stylists. Williams, a disciple of Charley Patton, came close to matching his mentor's power and intensity, though he lacked Patton's versatility. He performs in a rough, frantic style, and some of the songs contain unusual themes.

105 Travelin' Highway Man: Tommy McClennan, 1939–1942

Travelin' Man CD 06 (UK)

You Can Mistreat Me Here/New "Shake 'Em On Down"/Bottle It Up And Go/Whiskey Head Woman/Cotton Patch Blues/Baby, Please Don't Tell On Me/My Baby's Gone/It's Hard To Be Lonesome/Des'e My Blues/Classy Mae Blues/Travelin' Highway Man/Blues Trip Me This Morning/Roll Me, Baby/I Love My Baby/Shake It Up And Go/Blue As I Can Be/New Highway No. 51/Mr. So And So Blues/Whiskey Head Man; Robert Petway, *Boogie Woogie Woman*

McClennan had a rough, banging guitar style and a raspy, whisky-soaked voice. He performs in an almost manic style and sings from the point of view of a Mississippi sharecropper in an environment where life and love come cheap. This is blues in the raw by a Southern country boy on the loose in Chicago.

106 Mississippi Blues: Complete Recorded Works (1935–1951): Otto Virgial, Robert Petway, Robert Lockwood

Wolf WBCD 005 (Au)

Otto Virgial, *Little Girl In Rome/Bad Notion Blues/Got The Blues About Rome/Seven Year Itch*; Robert Petway, *Catfish Blues/Ride 'Em On Down/Rockin' Chair Blues/My Little Girl/Let Me Be Your Boss/Left My Baby Crying/Sleepy Woman Blues/Don't Go Down Baby/Bertha Lee Blues/Boogie Woogie Woman/Hollow Log Blues/In The Evening/My Baby Left Me/Cotton Pickin' Blues*; Robert Lockwood, *Black Spider Blues/I'm Gonna Train My Baby/Little Boy Blue/Take A Little Walk With Me/I'm Gonna Dig Myself A Hole/Dust My Broom*

Virgial displays a rich voice and a guitar style featuring repeated short phrases with some influence from Charley Patton. Petway was an associate of McClennan and his *Catfish Blues* is the earliest recording of this theme. Stepson of Robert Johnson, 'Junior' Lockwood was first to carry Johnson's stylistic synthesis to Chicago, and his first four tracks (from 1941) come close to Johnson's standard.

107 Robert Lee McCoy (Robert Nighthawk): Complete Recorded Works In Chronological Order (1937–1940)

Wolf WBCD 002 (Au)

Tough Luck/Lonesome World/G-Man/Don't Mistreat Your Woman/Prowling Night-Hawk/Sweet Pepper Mama/My Friend Has Forsaken Me/Mean Black Cat/Brickyard/Mamie Lee/Take It Easy, Baby/I Have Spent My Bonus/CNA/

Every Day And Night/Ol' Mose/You're All I've Got To Live For/She's Got What It Takes/Next-Door Neighbor/Big Apple Blues/Freight Train Blues/Good Gamblin'/Gonna Keep It For My Daddy [with Ann Sortier]; Ann Sortier, *Never Leave Me*; Robert Lee McCoy, *Mama Don't Allow Me To Stay Out All Night Long/Friar's Point Blues*

McCoy was better known for his post-war recordings as Robert Nighthawk. His early efforts display laconic singing and songwriting talents, and they foreshadow his later style from the lovely slide guitar of *Friar's Point Blues* to duo and trio performances. McCoy's girlfriend, Ann Sortier, contributes enthusiastic singing and washboard on two tracks.

(ii) Memphis Blues

108 Memphis Blues: Complete Recorded Works In Chronological Order (1927–1938)

Various Artists

Document DOCD 5159 (Au)

Ollie Rupert, *I Raised My Window And Looked At The Risin' Sun/Ain't Goin' To Be Your Low Down Dog*; Walter Rhodes, *The Crowing Rooster/Leaving Home Blues*; Pearl Dickson, *Twelve Pound Daddy/Little Rock Blues*; Madelyn James, *Stinging Snake Blues/Long Time Blues*; Charlie "Bozo" Nickerson, *What's The Matter Now?* Part 1/*What's The Matter Now?* Part 2/*Bozo's Blues* Part 1/*Bozo's Blues* Part 2; Sam Townsend, *I'm Missing That/Lily Kimball Blues*; Hattie Hart, *I'm Missing That Thing/I Let My Daddy Do That/Coldest Stuff In Town/Happy-Go-Lucky Blues*; George Torey, *Married Woman Blues/Lonesome Man Blues*; John Henry Barbee, *Six Weeks Old Blues* (take 1)/*Six Weeks Old Blues* (take 2)/*God Knows I Can't Help It/You'll Work Down To Me Someday/Against My Will*

Unusual and outstanding features include guitar duetting by the Harney brothers, behind Rhodes and Dickson, and Allen Shaw and Willie Borum, behind Hart. Judson Brown plays piano for James and Nickerson, and a jew's harp embellishes Rupert's sides. Rhodes (from Mississippi) plays accordion. It is likely the uncompromising Torey was also from Mississippi, and Townsend possibly from Georgia.

109 Memphis Jug Band: Associates & Alternate Takes (1927–1930)

Various Artists

Wolf WBCD 004 (Au)

Memphis Jug Band, *Sun Brimmer's Blues* (take 1)/*Sun Brimmer's Blues* (take 3)/*Stingy Woman Blues* (take 1)/*Newport News Blues* (take 2)/*Snitchin' Gambler Blues* (take 3)/*Lindberg Hop (Overseas Stomp)* (take 2); Will Weldon, *Turpentine Blues/Hitch Me To Your Buggy*; Vol Stevens, *Vol Stevens Blues/Baby Got The Rickets*; Will Shade, *Better Leave That Stuff Alone/She Stabbed Me With An Ice-Pick*; Minnie Wallace, *The Old Folks Started It* (take 2); Hattie Hart, *Won't You Be Kind To Me?/You Wouldn't, Would You, Papa?*; Kaiser Clifton, *Cash Money Blues/Fort Worth And Denver Blues/She'll Be Back Someday/Teach Me Right From Wrong*; Jenny Pope, *Bull Frog Blues/Tennessee Workhouse Blues/Mr. Postman Blues/Rent Man Blues*

The Jug Band tracks are all from their first few sessions. The remaining selections are by various members in a solo or duo setting or as accompanists.

Highlights include the strong vocals by the three female singers, the excellent duet work of Weldon and Stevens, and the jug and kazoo playing.

110 Jack Kelly & His South Memphis Jug Band: Complete Recorded Works In Chronological Order (1933–1939)

Blues Documents BDCD 6005 (Au)

Highway No. 61 Blues/Highway No. 61 Blues No. 2/*Red Ripe Tomatoes/Believe I'll Go Back Home*; Will Batts, *Country Woman/Cheatin' Woman*; Jack Kelly *Ko-Ko-Mo Blues/Cold Iron Bed/R.F.C. Blues/Policy Rag/President Blues*; Will Batts, *Highway No. 61 Blues/Cadillac Baby*; Jack Kelly, *Doctor Medicine/ Lightenin' Blues/Betty Sue Blues/Flower Blues/Joe Louis Special/High Behind Blues/You Done Done It/Diamond Buyer Blues/World Wandering Blues/Neck Bone Blues/Men Fooler Blues*

The 14 tracks recorded in 1933 reveal Kelly's to have been the bluesiest of the jug bands recorded in Memphis. Featured are his strong singing, songwriting, and guitar duet work with Dan Sane, and the fine fiddling of Batts. The ten tracks of 1939 lack the jug but have Kelly and Batts with an unknown second guitarist.

111 Charlie Burse-James De Berry: Complete Recorded Works in Chronological Order (1939)

Old Tramp OTCD 02 (Neth)

Charlie Burse & His Memphis Mudcats, *Beale Street Holiday/Baby, You Win/ Oil It Up And Go/What's The Matter With The Well/Good Potatoes On The Hill/Weed Smoking Mama/Dawn Of Day Blues/Goldie May/Scared To Death/ You Better Watch Out/Too Much Beef/Magic Spell Blues/It Makes No Difference Now/It's Against The Rule/Ain't Gonna Be No Doggone Afterwhile/ Memphis Highway Stomp/Brand New Day Blues*; James De Berry & His Memphis Playboys, *Touch It Up A Little/You Played A Trick On Me/Oh, Liza!/Single Man Blues/Nummy Nimmy Not/Insane Jealous Blues/Zugity Zugity Stomp/Spider Bite Blues/You Can Go*

Alongside Kelly's recordings of 1939, these are virtually the only glimpses we have of blues activity in Memphis between 1930 and 1950. Burse synthesizes jug-band influences with lowdown and hokum blues, rags, pop, and country music. De Berry suffers from occasional timing problems, while his material is more restricted to blues. Both groups are counterparts of contemporary western swing bands.

(iii) West Tennessee Blues

112 Sleepy John Estes: First Recordings, with James "Yank" Rachel, Noah Lewis

JSP Records JSP CD 601 (UK)

Sleepy John Estes, *Broken Hearted, Ragged And Dirty Too/The Girl I Love, She Got Long Curly Hair/Divin' Duck Blues*; James "Yank" Rachel *Little Sarah*; Sleepy John Estes, *Black Mattie Blues*; James "Yank" Rachel, *T-Bone Steak Blues*; Noah Lewis, *Chickasaw Special/Devil In The Woodpile*; Sleepy John Estes, *Milk Cow Blues/Street Car Blues/Expressman Blues/Watcha Doin'?/Poor John Blues/Stack O' Dollars/My Black Gal Blues/Sweet Mama*; Noah Lewis, *Like I Want To Be*; Noah Lewis's Jug Band, *Ticket Agent Blues/New Mingle-*

wood Blues/Selling The Jelly [Mrs Van Zula Carter Hunt, vocal]/*Bad Luck's My Buddy*
Estes, from Brownsville, was a limited guitarist but sang in a distinctive high-pitched crying voice. Local mandolinist Rachel joins him on these recordings of 1929–30 along with Jab Jones on piano for an unusual and highly successful combination. Lewis, a brilliant harmonica player from nearby Henning, contributes three instrumental solos and Hunt provides a raunchy vocal.

113 **James "Yank" Rachel: Complete Recorded Works 1934–1941 In Chronological Order, Volume 1 (1934–1938)**
Wolf WBCD 006 (Au)
Yank Rachel, *Blue And Worried Woman/Sugar Farm Blues/Stack O'Dollars Blues/Night Latch Blues/Squeaky Work Bench Blues/Gravel Road Woman*; Elijah Jones, *Katy Fly/Big Boat/Only Boy Child/Lonesome Man/Mean Actin' Mama/Stuff Stomp*; Yank Rachel, *J.L. Dairy Blues/Rachel Blues/Lake Michigan Blues/I'm Wild And Crazy As I Can Be/When You Feel Down And Out/Texas Tommy/It's All Over/My Mind Got Bad*
Rachel sings in a melismatic style that may be a link between Peetie Wheatstraw and Robert Johnson, particularly in the use of falsetto. On six pieces from 1934 Dan Smith provides a rough second guitar with an unusual rhythmic quality. Rachel uses mandolin on his and Elijah Jones' recordings of 1938, with John Lee "Sonny Boy" Williamson playing harmonica.

114 **"Brownsville" Son Bonds–Charlie Pickett: Complete Recorded Works In Chronological Order (1934–1941)**
Wolf WBCD 003 (Au)
Son Bonds, *All Night Long/She Walks Like My Woman/Weary Worried Blues/Back And Side Blues/I Want To Live So God Can Use Me/Ain't That News?/Give Me That Old Time Religion/In My Father's House/Trouble Trouble Blues/Tennessee Worried Blues/I'll Work Up To You Someday/Old Bachelor Blues*; The Delta Boys, *Black Gal Swing/Get Up And Go/Every Time My Heart Beats*; Son Bonds, *80 Highway Blues/A Hard Pill To Swallow/Come Back Home, Little Girl*; Charlie Pickett, *Crazy 'Bout My Black Gal/Trembling Blues/Let Me Squeeze Your Lemon/Down The Highway*
Bonds and his harmonica and jug-playing partner Hammie Nixon perform duets similar to those later recorded by Estes and Nixon (**256**). In 1938 and 1941 Estes paired with Bonds for guitar duets and hokum by The Delta Boys. Pickett, also from Brownsville, was not only a splendid singer with a rich voice but an inventive guitarist and songwriter.

(iv) St Louis Blues

115 **St. Louis Country Blues: Complete Recorded Works in Chronological Order (1929–1937): Henry Spaulding, Henry Townsend, J.D. Short**
Document DOCD 5147 (Au)
Henry Spaulding, *Cairo Blues/Biddle Street Blues*; Henry Townsend, *Henry's Worry Blues/Mistreated Blues/Long Ago Blues/Poor Man Blues/No Home Blues/Take A Chance/She's Got What I Want/My Sweet Candy/Sick With The Blues/Don't Love That Woman/She's Got A Mean Disposition/Lose Your Man/All I've Got's Gone/A Ramblin' Mind/Now I Stay Away*; Jaydee Short,

Telephone Arguin' Blues/Lonesome Swamp Rattlesnake/Snake Doctor Blues/ Barefoot Blues/Grand Daddy Blues/It's Hard Time/Back Door Blues

Raised in Cairo, Illinois, Spaulding and Townsend brought the Southern sound to St Louis. Spaulding's guitar playing features string snapping and Townsend's a duple-triple rhythmic flexibility. Four tracks have Townsend playing piano in the manner of Roosevelt Sykes. Short's Delta origins are apparent in his guitar rhythms and urgent singing; his songs also display surrealistic imagery.

116 Charley Jordan: Complete Recorded Works In Chronological Order Volume 1 (1930–1931)

Document DOCD 5097 (Au)

Charley Jordan, *Stack O'Dollars Blues/Dollar Bill Blues/Keep It Clean/Big Four Blues/Just A Spoonful/Two Street Blues/Raiding' Squad Blues/Hunkie Tunkie Blues/Running Mad Blues/Gasoline Blues*; St. Louis Bessie [Bessie Mae Smith], *Sugar Man Blues* Part 1/*Sugar Man Blues* Part 2; Charley Jordan, *Lost Ship Blues/Hungry Blues/My "Lovin' Good" Blues/Tough Times Blues/Cheating Blues/Starvation Blues/Keep It Clean* No. 2/*You Run And Tell Your Daddy/ Tight Haired Mama Blues/Days Of The Weeks Blues*

Jordan was an inventive St Louis guitarist and songwriter. He is heard as a soloist and in duos backed by pianist Peetie Wheatstraw. They also back vocalist Bessie Mae Smith on two tracks. Jordan's blues are a mixture of serious and hokum themes. Some of his guitar work shows ragtime influence.

117 Beat You Doing It

Clifford Gibson

Yazoo (CD) 1027

Bad Luck Dice/Levee Camp Moan/Hard Headed Blues/Blues Without A Dime/ Jive Me Blues/Society Blues/Ice And Snow Blues/Drayman Blues/Old Time Rider/Tired Of Being Mistreated Part 1/*Brooklyn Blues/Beat You Doing It/ Sunshine Moan/Stop Your Rambling*

Clifford Gibson was a splendid guitarist who rivaled Lonnie Johnson (also based in St Louis in the 1920s) in technical mastery of the instrument and lyrical and musical inventiveness. His rhythms are stronger than Johnson's, and he sings in a pleasing, though not very intense voice.

(v) Louisville and Cincinnati Blues

118 Sylvester Weaver: Complete Recorded Works In Chronological Order, Volume 1 (1923–1927)

Document DOCD 5112 (Au)

Sylvester Weaver, *Guitar Blues/Guitar Rag/Weaver's Blues/Smoketown Strut/ Mixing Them Up In C/I'm Busy And You Can't Come In*; Instrumental Trio [E.L. Coleman], *Steel String Blues*; Martin-Weaver-Withers, *Where Shall I Be?/ I Am Happy In Jesus*; Sara Martin, *Gonna Ramble Blues/Teasing Brown Blues*; Sylvester Weaver, *True Love Blues/Poor Boy Blues/Six-String Banjo Piece/ Damfino Stump/Guitar Rag*; Sara Martin, *Loving Is What I Crave/Useless Blues/Black Hearse Blues/Orn'ry Blues*; Sylvester Weaver, *Dad's Blues/What Makes A Man Blue*

Weaver was the first black folk blues guitarist to make commercial records. He was master of ragtime progressions as well as the slide style, and his *Guitar Rag* became a country music standard under the name of *Steel Guitar Rag*. Martin, a popular Louisville vaudeville singer, admired his talents and sounds quite comfortable accompanied by his guitar and on two strong spirituals with Withers.

119 **John Byrd & Walter Taylor (1929–1931)**
Story of Blues CD 3517-2 (Ger)
John Byrd, *The White Mule Of Sin/The Heavenly Airplane/Narrow Face Blues/Wasn't It Sad About Lemon/Insurance Man Blues/Overall Cheater Blues/Disconnected Mama/Billy Goat Blues/Old Timbrook Blues*; Walter Taylor, *Thirty-Eight And Plus/Deal Rag/Corrine Corrine/Yo-Yo Blues/Broadcasting Blues/You Rascal, You/Diamond Ring Blues/Coal Camp Blues/Do You Love Me Blues*
Byrd on guitar and Taylor on washboard formed a sort of scaled-down hokum band, whose work spanned straight blues, ragtime tunes, and hillbilly material; Byrd even contributes two comic sermons. His *Old Timbrook* is a blues version of a Kentucky racehorse ballad, while *Wasn't It Sad* is a moralistic ballad on the death of Blind Lemon Jefferson.

120 **Cincinnati Blues (1928–1936): Kid Cole, Cincinnati Jug Band, Bob Coleman, Walter Coleman**
Story of Blues CD 3519-2 (Ger)
Kid Cole, *Sixth Street Moan/Hey Hey Mama Blues/Hard Hearted Mama Blues/Niagra Fall Blues*; Cincinnati Jug Band, *Newport Blues/George St. Stomp*; Bob Coleman & Cincinnati Jug Band, *Tear It Down/Cincinnati Underworld Woman*; Bob Coleman, *Sing Song Blues*; Walter Coleman, *I'm Going To Cincinnati/Greyhound Blues/Mama Let Me Lay It On You* (take A)/*Smack That Thing/Mama Let Me Lay It On You* (take C)/*Carry Your Good Stuff Home*
The two Colemans sound alike and Cole may also be the same person. The selections from 1928–9 display string band and vaudeville influences. Some have a setting of guitar, harmonica, and jug. The latter can be heard on some Walter Coleman sides of 1936, with either two guitars or guitar and piano. This material is less emotional than blues from down-river.

BRUCE BASTIN

4 The East Coast and Texas

Blues from the south-eastern states and Texas have some similarities, not least because of their frequent use of a ragtime base and their greater clarity of diction than recorded blues from, say, the Delta country of Mississippi. The recorded evidence understandably concentrates on a few major urban centres, though most artists traveled out of state to the record companies to preserve their music. Field trips, on which the major labels such as Columbia, OKeh and Victor made periodic forays into the South to record, were limited and of lesser extent in Texas than in the East. There, Atlanta was almost exclusively the recording center outside New York, though Charlotte, North Carolina, became a valuable base also. In Texas, all recordings were made in Dallas–Fort Worth or San Antonio. A further link, which broadens our horizons extensively, was the activity of the Library of Congress, notably involving John A. Lomax, in documenting black music, as many black singers and instrumentalists recorded in state penitentiaries otherwise went undocumented (**52, 54, 258, 259**).

Texas and the south-eastern states also suffered—if that is the right word—from concentrated research into the blues of the Deep South, notably the Delta region and its environs. Near-worship by latter-day idolaters of such bluesmen as Charley Patton, Robert Johnson, Son House, and Muddy Waters, with books written and films made, transformed then into blue legends. Research into the East Coast and Texas localities was basically left to a small band of no less dedicated researchers, but neither scene ever caught the public attention.

Nonetheless, general evolutionary patterns of blues in both regions followed the now-accepted precepts of migrations; rural to urban, south to north (or west). Whereas blacks from the Deep South moved via Memphis and St Louis to Chicago and Detroit, those from the East Coast states moved via the Piedmont cities (from Atlanta, Georgia, to Richmond, Virginia) through Washington, DC, to Philadelphia, Baltimore, and ultimately the New Jersey–New York conurbation. In Texas the drift was into Houston or the Dallas–Fort Worth complex, but eventually out to California—predominantly to Los Angeles and the Oakland area of San Francisco Bay.

As always, the rural scene did not vanish as quickly as history would

Convict camp dancer, Greene County, Georgia, 1941 (*Jack Delano/FSA/ Library of Congress*)

have us believe. Rural traditions are particularly difficult to eradicate, and just because the music was no longer commercially viable did not mean that it did not exist. One mark of the persistence of researchers in these regions has been the release of recordings of older musical styles of recent vintage by bluesmen well steeped in the traditions of their regions. The blues of the 1930s was audible well into the 1970s if one knew where to search. Understandably, as a result of many influences, not least homogenization via mass audio-communications, the specific regionalisms have long since become blurred and the older music lost.

Essential Records

(i) Pre-war Blues in the South-eastern States

Blues would appear to have developed later in the south-eastern states than in the Deep South and Texas. Instances dating from the first decade of the 20th century have been noted, but interviews with surviving performers indicate the formative period in the South-east scarcely predated the first appearance of the word "blues" in print or on record. Once the northern record market began to expand in the early 1920s, companies began to look further afield for their artists, and for artists of a decidedly rural nature. The OKeh company went to Atlanta as early as 1923, but it was not until the spring of 1924 that it first recorded blues there. Other companies were slow to follow. Columbia went down in 1925, but it was November 1926 before it recorded country blues—from Peg Leg Howell. By early 1927 Victor had joined them, recording Julius Daniels in February. In the following month Columbia recorded Barbecue Bob there, following a tip from a local agent. Over the next few years Victor and Columbia shared recording honours in the city. Columbia never did venture elsewhere in the South-east, but Victor's team genuinely was mobile, recording at times from Bristol, Tennessee, to Savannah, Georgia, but usually centered on Charlotte if Atlanta was not convenient.

Only recently have we become aware of the role of agents or local A&R (Artist and Repertoire) men in determining which blues artists were recorded, especially those who performed outside the established entertainment patterns of touring show circuits. It is hardly surprising that folk musicians from the lower economic bracket did not seek out for themselves the chance to record, but a small and knowledgeable group of middlemen, invariably white, sought new material for record companies. Sometimes the performers were recorded in the locality; more often they traveled to New York or perhaps to Chicago. Once they had recorded, and if their releases sold, they might be called upon to record again. A pattern was established whereby recorded bluesmen, whose records sold predominantly in the South, in turn influenced other bluesmen from the regions. The recording industry was understandably no one's philanthropist: it was interested in making records that sold. No matter how good, if an artist didn't sell, he was passed over in preference to one who did.

Thus certain artists dominate the recorded evidence. Blind Blake, almost alone among south-eastern bluesmen, recorded prolifically in Chicago for the Paramount label for six years, releasing some 80 titles. Blind Boy Fuller, from North Carolina, had some 130 titles released, mostly for the American Record Company (ARC). From Atlanta, Barbecue Bob and Buddy Moss had more than 50 released, Blind Willie McTell almost 50, and Peg Leg Howell some 30. Inevitably, this depth of recording distorts the overall pattern. Bluesmen held in great esteem in their communities were often completely overlooked or, having recorded once, like Willie Walker or Tarter and Gay, were never recorded again.

One of the frequently overlooked aspects of blues as a music is that it was often performed in a social setting, not just for listening but for dancing. Many tunes were basically for dancing; numerous bluesmen therefore carried a high proportion of dance-type tunes in their repertoire, though this might have been distorted by their commercially recorded samples. However, among south-eastern bluesmen the proportion of recorded dance tunes remained high. On **Blind Blake: Ragtime Guitar's Foremost Fingerpicker** Blake's *Blind Arthur's Breakdown*, a ragtime dance, is a *tour de force* and *Southern Rag* and *Seaboard Stomp* are equally infectious dance numbers. In **East Coast Piedmont Style**, Blind Boy Fuller's *Rag Mama Rag* is another such tune; and his *You've Got Something There* is clearly for dancing. McTell's *Georgia Rag*, Willie Walker's stunning *South Carolina Rag* and William Moore's *Barbershop Rag* all have similar base. Many folk musicians had a phrase or tune which they made their own; no local musician would attempt Walker's *South Carolina Rag*, and the facility of his fingerwork is awesome. Several of these items are on **Ragtime Blues Guitar**.

The paradox of folk music is that on the one hand the music remains unchanged and unsullied, passed down from practitioner to follower, while on the other hand the music absorbs new trends, adapting and blending them with what is performed. Some musicians traveled extensively, thereby learning from new sources and passing on their own skills to parochial performers. Many older bluesmen themselves recalled or had heard from others that Blind Blake, a veritable enigma of a bluesman, had passed through their town. Blind

Willie McTell, whose blindness from birth seems to have enhanced his wish to travel, covered the country and was as much at home guiding a very impressionable Buddy Moss around the New York subway system as he was in directing John Lomax's car back to his hotel. McTell, many of whose best titles are on **The Definitive Blind Willie McTell**, recorded at every opportunity (as Blind Sammie, Georgia Bill, and Hot Shot Willie as well as Blind Willie), for Columbia, OKeh, Victor, and Decca, and even at the only ARC recording session on location in the South-east. Willie Walker, from South Carolina, recorded in Atlanta and was recalled traveling in Virginia.

Many musicians traveled very little outside their own limited environment. Later, some would proudly reminisce that they had journeyed all over their county, and even into neighboring counties, which actually only confirmed their parochial nature but helps to explain why their traditions persisted longer. The dividing line came, perhaps, with the degree of professionalism with which performers viewed their activity.

To think of any of these men as professionals, in the sense of performers on the shows mentioned in, say, the *Chicago Defender*, is perhaps a slight distortion, but certain of them were professionals in the sense that they made their living entirely from performance. Among these were idefatigable travelers such as Blind Blake and Blind Willie McTell or their Texas counterpart Blind Lemon Jefferson. It is no coincidence that these professionals were blind, for there would have been little else available for them as a means of livelihood; however, there were sighted professionals too. Curley Weaver, a staunch friend of McTell, with whom he shared many recording sessions (two titles from which are represented on **The Definitive Blind Willie McTell**), seems never to have had a day job. Neither did Buddy Moss, at the height of his career in the mid-1930s the most heavily recorded bluesman for ARC. Pink Anderson made his living from music (**74**), but others worked during the day and the music was secondary for them most of the time. Perhaps it came first at weekends or during the tobacco-selling season, when out-of-towners would come into Raleigh, Durham, and Winston-Salem to sell their year's crop. For a short while the population doubled or trebled, and once the crops had been sold people had money for the first time since the previous season. It was a time to relieve them of some of their spare cash, and musicians were everywhere. Sonny Terry recalled playing outside tobacco warehouses; countless amateur performers remember seeing local bluesmen, such as Gary Davis and Blind Boy Fuller, performing in public during that brief seasonal influx of money, but they also recall seeing bluesmen that they had never seen before, who had been attracted to town because of the opportunities. Sometimes they would themselves play; always they would learn.

Some musicians lived a precarious life of near-professionalism, marred either by a shortage of work or of possible restrictions of their welfare receipts. Especially vulnerable here were such blind musicians as Blind Boy Fuller and Gary Davis in Durham. Sometimes these pressures spilled over into the recording session.

Paramount's unarguable claim to be the foremost record label for country bluesmen tends to hide the fact that it was also a major recording label for black jazz bands, as well as for the classic and vaudeville female blues singers. Blind Blake appears as one of the few genuine rural bluesmen to be able to bridge the gap into a jazz format. Not only did he record *Hastings Street* with one of Paramount's leading blues pianists, Charlie Spand (**215**), but he also shared a session with one of the finest black clarinetists, Johnny Dodds. They were joined by Chicago skiffle drummer Jimmy Bertrand on *C.C. Pill Blues*. Both Dodds and Bertrand may be heard on **Ragtime Guitar's Foremost Fingerpicker**.

Blake also recorded with a number of female blues singers, and in so doing became almost the only bluesman from the South-east who could claim that distinction. Without doubt this was Paramount's policy, but Blind Lemon Jefferson was also recording for them at the time, and nowhere did he record with any—nor with a jazz group. Nonetheless, despite disparate participation with other artists on Paramount, Blake was really associated with none, being incorporated in sessions because of his skills and musical flexibility. As a performer he ran alone, and, unlike many in Atlanta, was part of no specific "set" of musicians.

While there was always some overlap between groups of musicians in various localities, certain of them would group together in personal associations in their music, hence also on record. In Atlanta, the first significant bluesman to be recorded was Peg Leg Howell. Having begun with a solo session in 1926, by the following spring he was recording with his "Gang", which generally comprised Henry Williams on guitar and Eddie Anthony on fiddle (definitely an "alley" fiddle)—(**49**, **137**). Howell's rather older style, together with the rougher sounds of his "gang" with Anthony's rural fiddle, set them apart from the slightly slicker sets of musicians who followed. Blind Willie McTell was really his own man, but he mixed with the set who grouped around Buddy Moss and Curley Weaver, and in the early 1930s they shared many sessions for ARC. With Moss and Weaver for a while was the superlative slide guitarist Fred McMullen. Because of his mid-1930s prominence one tends to move Moss to the head of this group, but he was in fact a latecomer to an established scene by the late 1920s, being but a teenager. He first appeared in the studio among the Georgia Cotton Pickers, a group that included not only Curley Weaver but also the person who headed the other mid-1920s Atlanta set, Barbecue Bob (Robert Hicks). Bob was one of Columbia's major bluesmen, and he saw to it that his brother also recorded, as Charley Lincoln.

Interestingly, very few female singers recorded with these bluesmen. Apart from such professionals on the tour circuit as the Texas performer Lillian Glinn (**167**), only Nellie Florence, who recorded with the Hicks Brothers, Blind Willie McTell's wife Kate, and Ruth Willis, who recorded with the Moss set, are known female blues singers from the South-east. Certainly we have no documentation of others, recorded or unrecorded.

Naturally Atlanta was not the only city with a strong blues scene. Doubtless most cities were able to boast some bluesmen, though we shall probably now never learn of them. Durham, North Carolina, like Atlanta, happens to be one center where considerable research has taken place, though no commercial recording sessions were ever held there. By the mid-1930s it had become a focal point for musicians; Blind Gary Davis had moved in from South Carolina and Blind Boy Fuller from elsewhere in the state. As a result of the intervention of an agent for ARC, J. B. Long, both these men came to record, and soon afterwards Long was also responsible for recording Brownie McGhee (**250**) and Sonny Terry. It was a remarkable clutch of talent. Although Gary Davis did record blues at his very first session, he converted to religion and wanted to record only religious songs. In essence this was what he purported to have done throughout his life, but in his later years he recorded many blues instrumentals, and his guitar work, let alone his declamatory vocal style, always held a blues tinge.

Without doubt, Davis was the most revered guitarist in Durham. Blind Boy Fuller, who learned a little from him (but not enough, according to Davis), was the most famous. Most of his recordings were solo efforts, but he was later teamed with a washboard player and an occasional guitarist (Floyd Council) or harmonica player (Sonny Terry) to produce a small-group dance feel. Proof of Fuller's popularity is that he recorded no title that remained unissued by the parent company.

This urban music scene was typical of smaller towns too; Greenville, South Carolina, and Spartanburg, Charlotte, and Winston-Salem were all active blues centers. Charlotte was used as a recording base by Decca and Victor in the 1930s, but by that time most sessions there were by whites or of gospel music. The city's most recorded bluesman, Julius Daniels, actually made his recordings in 1927 in Atlanta. Most bluesmen from smaller cities between Charlotte and Atlanta, including Willie Walker, Pink Anderson, and Simmie Dooley, and Lil McClintock, traveled to the latter to record. Luke Jordan even journeyed down from south Virginia. Musicians from the Virginia Eastern Seaboard, notably William Moore, were too remote to be recorded locally. Musicians from the Blue Ridge Mountains, such as Tarter and Gay, took their chance when it came and traveled to Bristol, Tennessee, to make *Brownie Blues* and *Unknown Blues*, their only recorded coupling.

Unless artists were promoted hard by their agent (such as Blind Boy Fuller) or turned up at every possible turn to promote themselves (Blind Willie McTell), they had little chance to record at all. It didn't bother them. They didn't expect to be heard far afield; many bluesmen, located at a much later date, were genuinely astonished that anyone should care. It is a truism that ephemera—and none of the bluesmen thought of their music as being anything but transitory—is of importance only to those who collect it at a later date. Nonetheless, by the 1970s some bluesmen had caught the enthusiasm of the collectors and made every effort to help document their skills and knowledge.

Few of the musicians received any recognition of their talents, apart from selling records and having some fame within their community. The vast majority went their various ways and died quietly. Brownie McGhee and Sonny Terry moved to New York and found success on Broadway and in the folk boom, becoming the nearest to household names of any bluesmen from the East Coast states. McGhee stuck firmly to his blues roots. The fame which caught him passed others by. Some, such as Buddy Moss, found that hard to live with; others simply never expected it could come their way.

All geographical regions are to some extent a convenience for those using them. Blues, with its origins still the subject of much supposition, was probably polygenetic, allowing for certain undeniable regional characteristics. Naturally, towards the edges of those regions we find a blending into other characteristics; into the Deep South of Alabama or the mountain music of Tennessee or West Virginia. Movement northwards had carried the music along the eastern seaboard states to the metropolis of New York, but it is primarily in Georgia, the Carolinas, and Virginia that we have a regional style documented in any depth.

Within this loosely defined region widely differing areas are to be found, but in general the region is one of a low-lying coastal plain with, to the west, a higher inland plain, the Piedmont, which itself gives way to the foothills of the Appalachian mountains. On this inland plain lies the string of cities from Atlanta northwards that acts as the north-south arterial routeway. These urban centers grew rapidly during the 1920s and 1930s, periods of agricultural recession, providing a strong pull-factor in population movement, rural to urban.

As was the case throughout the country, with the events of Pearl Harbor, shellac restrictions, and the recording ban of the American Federation of Musicians (AFM), blues recording virtually ceased by 1941–2. The recording of bluesmen from the South-east had ended by then, anyway. Blind Willie McTell had not taken part in a commercial session since 1936 (and the results of that had not been released), Blind Boy Fuller died in 1941, and Brownie McGhee and Sonny Terry moved further north during the early years of the war. When the recording business swung into gear once more in the mid-1940s, the music prospect had changed. The pre-war blues scene in the south-eastern states seemed to have come to an abrupt halt.

121 **Blind Blake: Ragtime Guitar's Foremost Fingerpicker**
Yazoo (CD) 1068
Diddle Wa Diddie/Come On Boys Let's Do That Messin'Around/Southern Rag/Police Dog Blues/C.C. Pill Blues/Hard Pushing Papa/Rope Stretching Blues Part 1/*Skeedle Loo Doo Blues/Chump Man Blues/Hastings St./Georgia Bound/Righteous Blues/Too Tight Blues* No. 2/*Blind Arthur's Breakdown/One Time Blues/Playing Policy Blues/You Gonna Quit Me Blues/Bad Feeling Blues/Hey Hey Daddy Blues/Black Dog Blues/Seaboard Stomp/Sweet Papa Low Down/Sweet Jivin' Mama*

122 **Ragtime Blues Guitar: Complete Recorded Works In Chronological Order (1927–1930)**
Various Artists
Document DOCD 5062 (Au)
Blind Blake, *Dry Bone Shuffle*; Willam [Bill] Moore, *One Way Gal/Ragtime Crazy/Midnight Blues/Ragtime Millionaire/Tillie Lee/Barbershop Rag/Old Country Rock/Raggin' The Blues*; Tarter & Gay, *Brownie Blues/Unknown Blues*; Chicken Wilson & Skeeter Hinton, *Myrtle Avenue Stomp/D.C. Rag/Chicken Wilson Blues/House Snake Blues/Frog Eye Stomp/Station House Rag*; Bayless Rose, *Jamestown Exhibition/Black Dog Blues/Original Blues/Frisco Blues*; Willie Walker, *Dupree Blues/South Carolina Rag* (take 1)/*South Carolina Rag* (take 2)

123 **The Definitive Blind Willie McTell**
Columbia C2K 53234/475701-2 (UK)—*2 CD set*
DISC ONE: [McTell as Blind Sammie], *Atlanta Strut/Travelin' Blues/Come On Around To My House Mama/Kind Mama/Talking To Myself/Razor Ball/Southern Can Is Mine/Broke Down Engine Blues*; [McTell as Georgia Bill], *Stomp Down Rider/Scarey Day Blues*; Mary Willis [Ruth Mary Willis], *Rough Alley Blues*; Ruth Day [Ruth Mary Willis], *Experience Blues/Painful Blues*; [McTell as Georgia Bill] *Low Rider's Blues/Georgia Rag*; Mary Willis, *Low Down Blues*; [Blind Willie & Partner—McTell & Curley Weaver], *Warm It Up*

To Me/It's Your Time To Worry/It's A Good Little Thing; Curley Weaver & Partner [Weaver & McTell], *You Was Born To Die/Dirty Mistreater*

DISC TWO: [Blind Willie & Partner], *Lord Have Mercy If You Please/Don't You See How This World Made A Change/Savannah Mama*; [McTell as Blind Willie], *Broke Down Engine/Broke Down Engine* No. 2/*My Baby's Gone/Love Makin' Mama* (take 1)/*Love Makin' Mama* (take 2)/*Death Room Blues* (take 1)/*Death Room Blues* (take 2)/*Death Cell Blues/Lord Send Me An Angel* (take 1)/*Lord Send Me An Angel* (take 2); [Blind Willie & Partner], *B & O Blues* No. 2 (take 1)/*B & O Blues* No. 2 (take 2)/*Weary Hearted Blues/Bell St. Lightnin'/Southern Can Mama/Runnin' Me Crazy/East St. Louis Blues (Fare You Well)*

124 **East Coast Piedmont Style**
Blind Boy Fuller
Columbia CK 46777/467923-2 (UK)
Rag Mama Rag/Baby You Gotta Change Your Mind/My Brownskin Sugar Plum/I'm A Rattlesnakin' Daddy/I'm Climbin' On Top Of the Hill/Baby, I Don't Have To Worry ('Cause The Stuff Is Here)/Looking For My Woman/Ain't It A Cryin Shame?/Walking My Troubles Away/Sweet Honey Hole/Somebody's Been Playing With That Thing/Log Cabin Blues/Keep Away From My Woman/Cat Man Blues/Untrue Blues/Black And Tan/Big Leg Woman Gets My Pay/You've Got Something There/I'm A Stranger Here/Evil Hearted Woman

(ii) Post-war Blues in the South-eastern States

By the time the major record companies had come to grips with the end of the AFM recording ban, they had lost control of the direction in which black music had moved. In the south-eastern states no one remained who was interested in recording the older blues styles. There was still activity in New York, and both Brownie McGhee and Sonny Terry, usually but not always teamed, recorded blues of an uncompromisingly earlier style (**36**). The pugnacious independent record company from Philadelphia, Gotham, also recorded excellent examples of the older south-eastern style of blues into the early 1950's: South Carolina-born local guitarist Doug Quattlebaum, as well as Ralph Willis and Dan Pickett, both from Alabama but bluesmen who absorbed sufficient local idiom (**140**, **429**). However, these were minor, if fascinating, aberrations to the general patterns of emerging black music. Recorded and issued as they were by such progressive independent labels as Savoy, Apollo, Gotham, Regis, 20th Century, and Red Robin, these bluesmen reflect that the music did not vanish in 1941 and that there was still a demand for it. In fact there appears to be a fair claim that on record this older style of music survived in the great metropolis longer than elsewhere in the country. **"Play My Juke Box"** is a collection of these accomplished performances, with guitarists to the fore. Some, like Boy Green, Hank Kilroy, and Guitar Shorty, were previously unrecorded. A few, such as Curley Weaver, Skoodle-Dum-Doo (Seth Richard) and Sunny (or Sonny) Jones, had made 78rpm discs before the World War II. Big Chief Ellis was a superlative pianist, originally from Alabama.

It comes as no surprise that younger, emergent forms of black music soon ousted such recordings from the catalogs. It seemed to collectors—who else was interested in this music in the 1960s?—that the older blues style was gone, so, in the true traditions of historical research, investigation began once the music was "dead." A mere handful of people began to piece together information on bluesmen who were nothing but names on record labels. The work of Sam Charters, George Mitchell, Pete Lowry, and later Kip Lornell and Glenn Hinson deserves mention here, for without their pioneering, selfless efforts our knowledge would be piecemeal at best; and we would have virtually no recent recordings of the persistence and survival of this older music.

Thus the post-1950s phase of blues investigation entered a completely different stage; that of documentation by the enthusiastic collector. This was usually carried out without any form of external support, and tiny independent labels sprang up to make the music available to a dedicated few. Eventually there was some slight institutional involvement in research, but mostly when it was too late. The one exception is the documentation of the music in the state of Virginia by the Blue Ridge Institute of Ferrum College (**144**). If only every state could have paralleled this remarkable series, then our knowledge of music in the South-east would have been as complete as one could hope for at such a late date. As it is, it remains an object lesson of what *might* have happened.

125 "Play My Juke Box": East Coast Blues 1943–1954

Various Artists

Flyright FLY CD 45 (UK)

Boy Green, *Play My Juke Box*; Curley Weaver, *Some Rainy Day*; Marylin Scott, *I Got What My Daddy Likes*; Skoodle-Dum-Doo & Sheffield, *West Kinney Street Blues*; Hank Kilroy, *Harlem Woman/Awful Shame*; Skoodle-Dum-Doo & Sheffield, *Tampa Blues*; Guitar Shorty, *I Love That Woman*; Big Chief Ellis, *Dices Dices*; Julius King, *One O'Clock Boogie*; Robert Lee Westmoreland, *Hello Central, Please Give Me 209/Good Looking Woman Blues*; Skoodle-Dum-Doo & Sheffield, *Broom Street Blues*; Jelly Belly & Guitar Slim, *Humming Blues*; Sunny Jones, *Leaving Home Blues/Don't Want Pretty Woman*; Elder R. Wilson & Family, *Better Get Ready*; Guitar Slim & Jelly Belly, *I've Been Dreaming*; Gabriel Brown, *The Jinx Is On Me*; Skoodle-Dum-Doo & Sheffield, *Gas Station Blues*; Boy Green, *A & B Blues*; Tarheel Slim, *Too Much Competition*

(iii) Pre-war Blues in Texas

Blues were documented in Texas at a very early data. "The blues come to Texas," sang Blind Lemon Jefferson on *Got The Blues*, "loping like a mule." Assuming some element of polygenesis, it is just as probable that the blue came loping *out* of Texas.

The sheer size of Texas is almost impossible to grasp. "Flying Crow leaving Port Arthur," sang Black Ivory King, of the Shreveport, Texarkana, and Kansas City-bound train (*The Flying Crow*). As the crow flies, Houston and Dallas are closer to Los Angeles than to New York. From north to south, Texas spans well over ten degrees of latitude: the British Isles from Lands End to the Orkney Islands spans only nine. Houston lies at a latitude of Tangiers. The East Coast states of Virginia, North and South Carolina, and Georgia would be lost in the area of Texas, with space for the Carolinas to fit in again—and still leave room to spare. In the south-east around Beaumont the flavour remains of the south Louisiana Cajun culture, to the north-east are the undulating pine woods, around Dallas were the fertile cotton lands, and around Houston were the rich bottom-lands with their repressive farm systems. The open, rolling plains of West Texas are awe-inspiring in their extent. Texas is a state of considerable differences—and great distances.

The vastness of the Great Plains areas and their extensions carried over into all walks of everyday life, and no less into the music. It is not romantic idea to think of these influences upon the much-traveled, itinerant bluesman such as Blind Lemon Jefferson, for most blues singers personified their music. "Good morning, Blues," sang Leadbelly on *Good Morning Blues*. "How do you do?" Something of this singular nature emerges from such songs as Blind Lemon's *Long Lonesome Blues* or Oscar Woods' *Lone Wolf Blues*. It is also reflected in the repertoire of the early songster Henry Thomas—'Ragtime Texas' (**43**).

The two greatest guitarists from that state who recorded in the 1920s helped spread the blues into every corner where blues guitar was listened to. Paradoxically, Blind Willie Johnson cut only religious music but his slide-guitar work was respected and copied everywhere in the South. **The Complete Blind Willie Johnson** contains all his sacred performances. Blind Lemon Jefferson was one of the best-known bluesmen of the 1920s, very similar in that respect to Blind Blake. Both were mainstays of the Paramount catalog whose lives grew into legends and whose passing remains—oddly—clouded in obscurity. On the one hand one might expect blues artists of their stature to have been monitored to greater effect, especially when they died, as their talents were immediately lost to the recording company. In fact, their deaths more properly epitomized their ephemeral existences. Nothing so reflects the transitory nature of their music, distorted only by the process of recording, as the fact that their going remains as much a mystery as their coming upon the scene.

Despite this lack of substance at the time such bluesmen as Blind Lemon were prominent in the record catalogs, their influence in spreading the music cannot be underestimated. Intriguingly, Blind Lemon was never recorded in his own state, and made countless journeys to Chicago as well as to Atlanta and Richmond, Indiana, to record. Like Blind Willie McTell from Georgia, he was an inveterate traveler who refused to permit his handicap to inhibit his movements. He was late for his Atlanta session because he had stopped off to "see" Shreveport, having never been there before. The sheer multiplicity of his recordings for the major blues label—almost 100 titles—attests to both his sales potential and his wide influence. Many of his best titles are on **King Of The Country Blues**. With Paramount's marketing policy of mail-order sales there can have been few nascent bluesmen outside Texas, let alone within the state, who had never heard his music. Among interviewed East Coast bluesmen active during Blind Lemon's recording career, almost all recall him as one of the first bluesmen they heard on record.

Although Paramount required its artists to travel north to record—Blind Lemon regularly commuted between Dallas and Chicago—other major labels often made field trips into the South to record new talent and to undertake repeat sessions with known artists. For some reason no trips were made into Texas before 1928, when OKeh recorded Texas Alexander in March. In October of that year both Columbia and Brunswick traveled down, committing themselves to a month-long marathon of recordings. It was probably not coincidental that these were cooler months, though Victor first came into the recording field in Texas in August 1929, when it recorded Jesse Thomas and Bessie Tucker (the company recorded Tucker the previous year in Memphis) (**164**). Victor was not to return to Dallas until February 1932, when it recorded Oscar Woods and Ramblin' Thomas. The American Record Company was late into the recording field, but made trips into Texas every year from 1934 to 1940. One of only three Decca expeditions to the South was in 1937 to Dallas, where the company recorded Black Ace and Black Ivory King as well as two of the few Texas bluesmen who recorded again after the war—pianist Alex Moore and guitarist Smokey Hogg, a most prolific recording artist. Discographical details for a number of these performers can be found in the recommendations for **Basic Records** below.

Another important regional singer, Huddie Ledbetter (Leadbelly), was incarcerated in penitentiaries in Texas and Louisiana for much of the 1920s and early 1930s (**37**, **258**). He made commercial recordings for ARC in New York in 1935 but his old-time songs were out of favor and many sides from these sessions were not issued. **King Of The 12-String Guitar** includes some of these unreleased recordings, representing strands of development in blues. His status as a songster can be gauged by this diversity. For example, in *Packin' Trunk* he plays slide guitar in the same tradition as Oscar Woods. *Honey, I'm All Out And Down* is adapted from a holler, and *Ox Drivin' Blues* is based on a work song. *Daddy I'm Coming Back To You* comes from the repertoire of Jimmie Rodgers, the famous old-time music singer (**318**). In the early years of the century Leadbelly played on the streets of Fort Worth and Dallas with Blind Lemon Jefferson and this experience is sometimes reflected in his performances. He stamped his character, however, on all his work with music that exemplifies the traditions of a region best described as greater Texas. This is true also of other significant bluesmen who played or recorded in the state but resided in neighboring communities: notably J.T. Smith and Jesse Thomas in Oklahoma and Oscar Woods in Shreveport. Smith, along with rough contemporary Little Hat Jones, remains an important figure in the evolution of Texas blues. Both men epitomize the central element of Texas blues guitar playing, the prominent use of the bass line. As with the blues of the East Coast states, there is a pronounced melody line, played cleanly with intricate finger-work. Vocals are clear, again having similarities with the East Coast style: those of both regions are markedly different from that of the intervening style from Mississippi.

Lyrically, Texas blues are highly original, given that Blind Lemon probably freely exploited floating stanzas in common usage, and many Texas artists mirror the direct repression of a harsh rural environment, more outspoken on commercial recordings than was commonplace. The penitentiary theme, which extended prominently into post-war Texas blues, is graphically covered in Texas Alexander's *Penitentiary Moan Blues* and Bessie Tucker's *Penitentiary*, hauntingly sung as "penritenshu." Personal experiences permeate these blues, and Texas Alexander's *Awful Moaning Blues* seems to say it all for many singers and musicians, but there is something numbing about Funny Papa Smith's imagery in *Hungry Wolf*: "blood in my eyes and malice [pronounced malacy] in my heart."

One divergence allowing no comparison with blues from the East Coast is a marked piano tradition, or, rather, a series of parallel traditions. Undoubtedly the vast distances necessitated movement by train, often "riding the blinds"—for it is 250 miles between the blues centers of Dallas and Houston—to enable pianists to travel the Santa Fe route and look for work. The Piney Woods of the north-east, with logging and turpentine camps, provided fixed work for pianists at the workers' bases, as did the small clubs of the growing urban centers. It is no accident that these itinerant pianists frequently made the final move to California, as migration patterns began to dictate a rural to urban, Texas to West Coast movement.

It says much of Victor that the company close to go to Dallas to re-record Bessie Tucker. It is also noticeable that the female blues singers recorded during field trips (though few were recorded more than once) came from grassroots tradition rather than the circuit stage. These women singers had powerful, untutored folk voices and their experience showed in every line. We shall never know whether they were more commonly recorded because of the whims of A & R men, as favors to various musicians, or quite simply because they were more plentiful. It cannot have been entirely by coincidence, but whatever the case may be, they were there and they recorded well.

A significant shift in recorded blues from Texas came in the 1930s. The Depression largely saw the end of the singer-guitarist as a recording artist. The demise of such labels as Columbia, OKeh and Brunswick, to say nothing of Paramount, largely terminated the field trips into the South. Texas Alexander last recorded in 1929 (apart from four sessions for ARC in 1934) and surfaced for just one obscure coupling in 1950 (**318**). Little Hat Jones last recorded in 1930 and Funny Papa Smith effectively in 1931; his 1935 solo recordings were spoiled at the time and none have been released. Blind Lemon Jefferson's last session was in 1929.

When ARC began recording after 1934 in the state, the emphasis was upon pianists. Bernice Edwards, whose previous sessions had been in 1928, recorded once in 1935 (with Funny Papa Smith, as it happens) and the new recording artists were such pianists as Black Boy Shine (whose first session also included Funny Papa Smith), Rob Copper, and Andy Boy (**153**, **231**), Joe Pullum, a vocalist, took part in four sessions from 1934 to 1936, but all had a pianist in accompaniment; only his last one featured a guitar (**254**). This session also promoted a trumpeter, marking another shift in style. By the mid- to late 1930s the pattern of small-group blues recordings had become apparent. Oscar Woods recorded solo in 1936, with a small rhythm section in 1937 and with an added trumpet in 1938 (**152**). In one sense this growth towards small combos—the Black Tams (with Texas Alexander) or the Wampus Cats (with Oscar Woods)—merely mirrored events elsewhere in the country.

126 King Of The Country Blues
Blind Lemon Jefferson
Yazoo (CD) 1069
That Crawlin' Baby Blues/Bad Luck Blues/Match Box Blues/Hot Dogs/One Dime Blues/Shuckin' Sugar/Rabbit Foot Blues/Corrina Blues/See That My Grave Is Kept Clean/Easy Rider Blues/Broke And Hungry/Black Horse Blues/Lonesome House Blues/Oil Well Blues/He Arose From The Dead/Beggin' Back/Prison Cell Blues/Rambler Blues/Gone Dead On You Blues/Wartime Blues/Booger Rooger Blues/Right Of Way Blues/Big Night Blues

127 The Complete Blind Willie Johnson
Columbia C25K 52835/472190-2 (UK)—*2 CD set*
DISC ONE: *I Know His Blood Can Make Me Whole/Jesus Make Up My Dying Bed/It's Nobody's Fault But Mine/Mother's Children Have A Hard Time/Dark Was The Night—Cold Was The Ground/If I Had My Way I'd Tear That Building Down/I'm Gonna Run To The City Of Refuge/Jesus Is Coming Soon/ Lord I Just Can't Keep From Crying* [mistitled *Lord I Can't Just Keep From Crying*]*/Keep Your Lamp Trimmed And Burning/Let Your Light Shine On Me/ God Don't Never Change/Bye And Bye I'm Goin' To See The King/Sweeter As The Years Go By*

DISC TWO: *You'll Need Somebody On Your Bond/When The War Was On/Praise God I'm Satisfied/Take Your Burden To The Lord And Leave It There/Take Your Stand/God Moves On The Water/Can't Nobody Hide From God/If It Had Not Been For Jesus/Go With Me To That Land* [mistitled *Go To Me With That Land*]*/The Rain Don't Fall On Me/Trouble Will Soon Be Over/The Soul Of Man/Everybody Ought To Treat A Stranger Right/Church I'm Fully Saved To-Day/John The Revelator/You're Gonna Need Somebody On Your Bond*

128 King Of The 12-String Guitar
Leadbelly
Columbia CK 46776/467893-2 (UK)
Packin' Trunk/Becky Deem, She Was A Gamblin' Girl/Honey, I'm All Out And Down/Four Day Worry Blues/Roberta Part 1/*Roberta* Part 2/*Death Letter Blues* Part 1/*Death Letter Blues* Part 2/*Kansas City Papa/Fort Worth And Dallas Blues/You Don't Know My Mind/Ox Drivin' Blues/Daddy I'm Coming Back To You/Shorty George/Yellow Jacket/T.B. Woman Blues/Pig Meat Papa/My Baby Quit Me.*

(iv) Post-war Blues in Texas

The essentially transitory nature of blues provided shifts in musical styles during the years documented by these CDs, the older styles vanishing rapidly with the advent of, for instance, boom-town Houston, in the days before the slump in oil prices. Lightnin' Hopkins, among the younger post-war Houston set, caught these changes of mood graphically, with a spontaneity seldom found elsewhere (**443**). As capable as anyone of feeling back to his roots—with songs such as *Grosebeck Blues* (an old Lemon Jefferson theme) and *Tim Moore's*

Farm—he nonetheless sensed the modernity about him with the likes of *Airplane Blues* and *Automobile Blues*. Made between 1947 and 1950, all these songs are represented in **The Gold Star Sessions Volume 1**, which captures the singer-guitarist in his prime.

Nonetheless, apart from ARC's annual forays into Texas to record, the last field trip made there, other than one in 1941 of limited interest, was that by Victor in 1936. The scene was changing towards one of greater homogeneity, not necessarily in style but in the approach to recording. The veritable population explosions in urban centers gave rise to the reshaping of earlier rural blues styles into a vigorous, urban phenomenon. So Oscar Woods' slide-guitar technique in small-group playing was adapted by Hop Wilson to the flat electric Hawaiian instrument (**156**). The earlier blues style of, say, Blind Lemon, melodic rather than impassioned, survived nonetheless into the 1940s in the likes of Willie Lane (**154**). In the same period, Bill Quinn recorded similar performances for his Gold Star label in Houston. Alongside Hopkins other singers appeared in his catalog, notably Lil' Son Jackson, all of whose early sides are in **Texas Blues: "The Gold Star Sessions"**. This exemplary anthology also includes representatives of the Santa Fe school of pianists—Leroy Ervin, Lee Hunter, and the impeccable Thunder Smith. Edwin "Buster" Pickens was another member of this group and accompanies the urbane Perry Cain on *All The Way From Texas*. But times, as always, were changing. The impermanence of the society mirrored in the work of these musicians brought about their own downfall. Pickens, perhaps the last of the Santa Fe pianists, was killed in 1964 in a dispute over a one-dollar kitty in a card game (as Lightnin' Hopkins casually informed me in Houston, over a quarter of a century ago, at the end of a recording session at the Gold Star Studios). The results of Hopkins' session also failed to survive and the entire episode remains only as a reminiscence pushing through from a vague memory. That this music endures on disc gives it the erroneous impression of permanence. It is really only a series of rostrum camera shots of passing change.

However, that change is never uniform and is perceived from different viewpoints by those participating in it and those coming to it as historians. After World War II the proliferation of independent record companies not only ushered in broad evidence of the ways that blues was changing, but also maintained some exposure for the earlier styles, still in demand among record buyers. Indeed, here is another parallel with the East Coast in that many examples of country blues (for want of a better term) exist from Texas during the 1940s and 1950s. The compartmentalization of the music, often valid and certainly convenient, is nevertheless arbitrary at times.

129 **The Gold Star Sessions Volume 1**
Lightnin' Hopkins
Arhoolie CD 330
Short Haired Woman/Baby Please Don't Go/Going Home Blues (Go Back And Talk To Mama)/Automobile Blues/Big Mama Jump/Loretta Blues/Seems Funny Baby/Thunder And Lightning Blues (Cooling Board Blues)/Grosebeck Blues/Tim Moor's Farm/Lighting Boogie/Traveler's Blues/Goodbye Blues/Unkind Blues/Fast Life Woman/Zolo Go [Zydeco]/You Don't Know/Treat Me Kind/Somebody's Got To Go/Death Bells/Mad With You/Airplane Blues/Racetrack Blues/Unsuccessful Blues

130 **Texas Blues: "The Gold Star Sessions"**
Various Artists
Arhoolie CD 352
Lil' Son Jackson, *Gambling Blues/Homeless Blues/Cairo Blues/Evil Blues*; Lee Hunter, *Back To Santa Fe*; L.C. Williams, *Trying, Trying/You Never Miss The Water*; Thunder Smith, *Cruel Hearted Woman/Big Stars Are Falling*; L.C. Williams, *Hole In The Wall/Boogie All The Time*; Leroy Ervin, *Rock Island Blues/Blue, Black And Evil*; Lil' Son Jackson, *Roberta Blues/Freedom Train Blues/Ground Hog Blues/Bad Whiskey, Bad Women*; Thunder Smith, *Santa Fe Blues*; L.C. Williams, *Black Woman/Strike Blues/You Can't Take It With You Baby*; Buddy Chiles, *Jet Black Woman*; Lil' Son Jackson, *No Money, No Love/ Gone With The Wind*; L.C. Williams, *I Won't Be Here Long*; Andy Thomas, *Angel Child*; Perry Cain, *All The Way From Texas*

Basic Records

(i) Pre-war Blues in the South-eastern States

131 **Nobody Knows My Name: Blues From South Carolina And Georgia**
Various Artists (anonymous)
Heritage HT 304 (UK)—*LP*
Boogie Lovin'/30 Days In Jail/Ding Dong Ring/Pick And Shovel Captain/6 Months Ain't No Sentence/Hard Times Hard Times/Trouble Ain't Nothing But A Good Man Feelin' Bad/Down In The Chain Gang/Prison Bound Blues/Georgia Chain Gang/Gonna Leave From Georgia/Black Woman/Shootin' Craps And Gamblin'/Nobody Knows My Name/Been Pickin' And Shovelin'
These are field recordings made by Lawrence Gellert in the 1920s and 1930s. Artists purposely remained anonymous and the songs have greater social comment than commercial releases. The sound quality from battered aluminum discs is poor, but the titles provide fascinating evidence for the depth and breadth of the blues tradition.

132 **Georgia Blues & Gospel (1927–1931): Complete Recorded Works In Chronological Order**
Various Artists
Document DOCD 5160 (Au)
Julius Daniels, *My Mama Was A Sailor/Ninety-Nine Year Blues* (take 1)/ *Ninety-Nine Year Blues* (take 2)/*I'm Goin' To Tell God How You Doin'/Slippin'*

And Slidin' Up The Golden Street (take 2)/*Slippin' And Slidin' Up The Golden Street* (take 3)/*Can't Put The Bridle On That Mule This Morning* (take 1)/*Can't Put The Bridle On That Mule This Morning* (take 2)/*Richmond Blues* (take 1)/ *Richmond Blues* (take 2)/*Crow Jane Blues*; George Carter, *Rising River Blues/ Hot Jelly Roll Blues/Weeping Willow Blues/Ghost Woman Blues*; Lil' McClintock, *Furniture Man* (take 1)/*Furniture Man* (take 2)/*Don't Think I'm Santa Claus/Sow Good Seeds/Mother Called Her Child To Her Dying Bed*; Lillie Mae, *Buggy Jail House Blues/Wise Like That/Mama Don't Want It/Bootie Wah Bootie*

The title is a misnomer: Daniels lived in Charlotte, North Carolina, and McClintock came from Charleston, South Carolina. Both recorded in Atlanta, Georgia, with Daniels' songs reflecting a wide repertoire. McClintock also recorded gospel and secular pieces, the latter perhaps with medicine show links. Carter and Lillie Mae might have been Georgians.

133 Carolina Blues (1937–1947): The Complete Recorded Works of Floyd Council, Eddie Kelly, Rich & Welly Trice In Chronological Order

Document DOCD 5168 (Au)

Floyd "Dipper Boy" Council, *Runaway Man Blues/I'm Grievin' And I'm Worryin'/I Don't Want No Hungry Woman/Working Man Blues/Poor And Ain't Got A Dime/Lookin' For My Baby*; Eddie Kelly Washboard Band, *Goin' Back To Alabama/Blues In The Rain/Poole Country Blues/If You Think I'm Lovin' You, You're Wrong/Corina, I'm Goin' Away/Shim Shaming/Come On Round To My House Baby* Part 1/*Come On Round To My House Baby* Part 2; Welly [Willie] Trice, *Come On In Here Mama/Let Her Go God Bless Her*; Rich [Richard] Trice, *Come On Baby/Trembling Bed Springs Blues*; Little Boy Fuller [Richard Trice], *Shake Your Stuff/Lazy Bug Blues/ Bed Spring Blues/Pack It Up And Go/Blood Red River Blues/Down-Hearted Man*

In essence this collection comprises recordings by Floyd Council and the Trice brothers, all of them close associates of Blind Boy Fuller. This is apparent in their singing and guitar playing, which sparkle with facility, and is representative of a local tradition. The inclusion of Kelly's group is incongruous.

134 The Georgia Blues 1927–1933

Various Artists

Yazoo (CD) 1012

Fred McMullen, *Wait And Listen*; Peg Leg Howell, *Rolling Mill Blues*; Blind Blake, *Police Dog Blues*; Bumble Bee Slim, *No Woman No Nickle*; Willie Baker, *Weak-Minded Blues*; Barbecue Bob, *Unnamed Blues*; Charlie Lincoln, *Doodle Hole Blues*; Sylvester Weaver, *Can't Be Trusted Blues*; Blind Blake, *That'll Never Happen No More*; George Carter, *Rising River Blues*; Gitfiddle Jim, *Rainy Night Blues*; George Carter, *Hot Jelly Roll Blues*; Willie Baker, *Crooked Woman Blues*; Gitfiddle Jim, *Paddlin' Blues*

Well-known artists feature alongside enigmatic figures such as Baker and McMullen. Kokomo Arnold (Gitfiddle Jim) and Amos Easton (Bumble Bee Slim) moved to Chicago, but McMullen, Howell, Barbecue Bob, and Lincoln exemplify different groups of musicians in Atlanta. This is an excellent guitar-orientated compilation.

135 Chocolate To The Bone
Barbecue Bob
Yazoo (CD) 2005
Motherless Chile Blues/Spider And The Fly/Yo Yo Blues/Mississippi Heavy Water Blues/California Blues; Georgia Cotton Pickers, *She's Coming Back Some Cold Rainy Day*; Barbecue Bob, *Barbecue Blues*; [Rober Hicks], *When The Saints Go Marching In*; Barbecue Bob, *Ease It To Me Blues/Poor Boy A Long Way From Home*; Georgia Cotton Pickers, *Diddle-Da-Diddle*; Barbecue Bob, *Going Up The Country/Atlanta Moan/Good Time Rounder/It's Just Too Bad/Twistin' Your Stuff* [*Twistin' That Stuff*]/*Chocolate To The Bone/Black Skunk Blues*; Nellie Florence, *Jacksonville Blues*; Barbecue Bob, *She Shook Her Gin*
A wide range of 12-string guitar accompanied material is represented, including a gospel track issued under his real name. One of the best-known of Atlanta's bluesmen, Bob is the vocalist with the Georgia Cotton Pickers. Charlie Lincoln—his brother, Charlie Hicks—probably accompanies Nellie Florence.

136 Peg Leg Howell & Eddie Anthony: Complete Recorded Works In Chronological Order, Volume 2, 13 August 1928 to 9 December 1930
Various Artists
Document[-Matchbox] MBCD 2005 (Au)
"Sloppy" Henry, *Long Tall Disconnected Mama/Royal Palm Special Blues*; Peg Leg Howell, *Banjo Blues/Turkey Buzzard Blues/Turtle Dove Blues/Walkin' Blues*; Tampa Joe & Macon Ed, *Wringing That Thing/Worrying Blues*; Peg Leg Howell, *Broke And Hungry Blues/Rolling Mill Blues*; [Peg Leg Howell & Jim Hill], *Ball And Chain Blues/Monkey Man Blues/Chittlin' Supper/Away From Home*; Macon Ed & Tampa Joe, *Everything's Coming My Way/Mean Florida Blues/Try That Thing/Tickle Britches/Tantalizing Bootblack/Warm Wipe Stomp*; Brothers Wright & Williams, *I'll Play My Harp In Beulah Land*
Several members of Howell's circle perform dances and blues, exhibiting Howell's rather archaic style, the rough fiddling of Eddie Anthony and exuberance of the pseudonymous Macon Ed and Tampa Joe. The disc is a complete contrast to the next, by Buddy Moss.

137 Buddy Moss 1930–1941
Travelin' Man TM CD05 (UK)
[Georgia Cotton Pickers], *I'm On My Way Down Home/Diddle-Da-Diddle/She Looks So Good/She's Coming Back Some Cold Rainy Day*; Buddy Moss, *Bye Bye Mama/Red River Blues* [with Ruth Willis, vocal]/*Cold Country Blues (Lousy Dime Blues)/Jealous Hearted Man*; [The Georgia Browns], *Tampa Strut/Who Stole De Lock?/Joker Man* [*Blues*]; Buddy Moss, *Dough Rolling Papa/Some Lonesome Day/Worrysome Women/Stop Hanging Around/Mistreated Boy/You Need A Woman/Joy Rag/I'm Sittin' Here Tonight/Unfinished Business*
This is a broad cross-section of Moss' work, including accompaniments from Curley Weaver, Fred McMullen, or Josh White. Brownie McGhee plays the piano on *Joy Rag*. Seven small-group titles feature Moss on harmonica, with those by the Georgia Cotton Pickers—Weaver and Barbecue Bob—some of the finest ever recorded by a blues trio.

(ii) Post-war Blues in the South-eastern States

138 **Brownie McGhee 1944–1955**

Travelin' Man TM CD04 (UK)

[Brownie McGhee & Sonny Terry], *Watch Out*; Brownie McGhee, *Dissatisfied Woman/Rum Cola Papa/Gin Headed Woman/Brownie's Guitar Boogie/Evil But Kindhearted/My Bulldog Blues/Big Legged Woman/Cheatin' And Lying/Need Someone To Love Me*; [Stick(s) McGhee & His Buddies], *Baby Baby* [*Blues*]; [Bob Harris], *Doggin' Blues*; [Big Chief (Ellis) Trio], *Big Chief's Blues*; [Brother Blues & The Backroom Boys (Jack Dupree)], *Featherweight Mama*; [Ralph Willis], *I'm Gonna Rock/Tell Me Pretty Baby*; [Champion Jack Dupree Trio], *Let's Have A Ball*; [Stick(s) McGhee & His Buddies], *Drinkin' Wine Spo-Dee-O-Dee*; [Brother Blues & The Backroom Boys (Jack Dupree)], *Day Break*; [Alonzo Scales], *My Baby Likes To Shuffle*

Alongside solo performances, one of Brownie McGhee's great skills was as an accompanying guitarist. He is featured with his brother Stick, Alabama bluesmen Ralph Willis and "Big Chief" Ellis, New Orleans pianist Jack Dupree and long-time associate Sonny Terry but the overall atmosphere is remarkably south-eastern.

139 **Whoopin' The Blues: The Capitol Recordings, 1947–1950**

Sonny Terry

Capitol 7243 8 29372 2 7/EMI CZ 546 (UK)

Telephone Blues/Custard Pie Blues/Riff And Harmonica Jump/Mad Man Blues.[Tell Me, Tell Me]/All Alone Blues/Dirty Mistreater Don't You Know/ Early Morning Blues/Whoopin' The Blues/Beer Garden Blues/Screamin' And Cryin' Blues/Crow Jane Blues/Worried Man Blues/Airplane Blues/Hot Headed Woman/Harmonica Rag/Leavin' Blues

Seminal sides by the most significant south-eastern harmonica stylist show how the pre-war blues sound transferred comfortably to post-war recordings. With Baby Dodds on drums, Stick McGhee plays guitar; otherwise his brother Brownie accompanies, with piano by "Daddy" Merritt or "Big Chief" Ellis. Sonny's remarkable harmonica and singular vocals are allowed full range.

140 **Dan Pickett & Tarheel Slim: 1949**

Flyright FLY CD 25 (UK)

Dan Pickett, *Baby How Long/You Got To Do Better/Ride To A Funeral In A V-8/Decoration Day/Drivin' That Thing/That's Grieving Me/99½ Won't Do/Baby Don't You Want To Go/Chicago Blues/Something's Gone Wrong/Early One Morning/Lemon Man/Number Writer/Drivin' That Thing* (alternate version)/*I Can Shake It*; Tarheel Slim, *Somebody Changed The Lock/You're A Little Too Slow/I Have Found No Friend/Get On The Road To Glory*

Calling himself Dan Pickett, James Founty cut these sides in Philadelphia in 1949. The vivacity of his guitar playing and singing makes him one of the most distinctive Alabama bluesmen recorded in the South-east at this time. Tarheel Slim (Alden Bunn) is represented by his first session as a blues singer.

141 **Pure Religion & Bad Company**

Reverend Gary Davis

Smithsonian/Folkways CD SF 40035

Pure Religion/Mountain Jack/Right Now/Buck Dance/Candy Man/Devil's

Dream/Moon Goes Down/Cocaine Blues/Runnin' To The Judgement/ Hesitation Blues/Bad Company/I Didn't Want To Join The Band/Evening Sun Goes Down/Seven Sisters/My Heart Is Fixed/Time Is Drawing Near/ Crucifixion
Although Davis professed to have given up playing blues, he recorded many such titles in his later years—these date from 1959. His brilliant guitar technique, without equal among East Coast musicians is everywhere evident. One can see why Carolina bluesmen viewed his guitar, which he called "Miss Gibson", with awe.

142 **The Union County Flash**
Henry Johnson
Trix (CD) 3304
Join The Army/Who's Going Home With You/Boogie Baby/Rufe's Impromptu Rag/My Mother's Grave Will Be Found/My Baby's House/Be Glad When You're Dead/Little Sally Jones/John Henry/Crow Jane/My Dog's Blues/Old Home Town/The Sign Of The Judgement
An epitome of the parochial, unknown country bluesman who never traveled more than a few miles from his Carolina home, Henry "Rufe" Johnson was nevertheless a singer and guitarist of remarkable talent. Sadly, he died before he could carry his skills to a wider audience, leaving just this one disc.

143 **Georgia Blues**
Various Artists
Rounder 2008—LP
Jessie Clarence Garmon, *Going Up The Country*; George Hollis, *You Can't Play Me Down*; Bud Grant, *Blues Around My Bed*; Willie Rockomo, *Love Her With A Feeling*; Bud White, *16 Snow White Horses*; Green Paschal, *Trouble Brought Me Down*; Cliff Scott, *Long Wavy Hair*; Bruce Upshaw, *I Wanna Love You*; Emmit Jones, *Oh Red*; Cliff Scott, *Sweet Old Tampa Blues*; Bruce Upshaw, *Rosilee*; Georgia Fife And Drum Band [J.W. Jones], *Old Hen Cackle*; J.W. Jones & James Jones, *Buck Dance*; Bud Grant, *Bud Grant's Hen Strut*; Precious Bryant, *Rock Me*; George Hollis, *Ain't Going To Germany*; Dixon Hunt, *Got On My Travelling Shoes*
This album encapsulates a rich diversity of blues talent from south-western and south-central Georgia during the 1960s. There is a wide range of musical styles from George Hollis' discordant fiddling and Cliff Scott's almost pre-blues guitar, via the only fife and drum band recorded in the South-east to the Chicago-blues-influenced playing of Bruce Upshaw.

144 **Virginia Traditions: Western Piedmont Blues**
Various Artists
Global Village (Blue Ridge Institute Series) CD 1003
Clayton Horsley, *My Little Woman*; John Tinsley, *Penitentiary Blues*; James Lowry, *Tampa Blues*; Marvin Foddrell, *Who's Been Fooling You?*; Luke Jordan, *Won't You Be Kind?*; Lewis "Rabbit" Muse, *Jailhouse Blues*; Richard Wright, *Peaksville Boogie*; Turner Foddrell, *Slow Drag*; James Lowry, *Karo Street Blues*; Luke Jordan, *My Gal's Done Quit Me*; Turner Foddrell, *Going Up The Country*; Lewis "Rabbit" Muse, *Rabbit Stomp*; Marvin Foddrell, *Looking For My Woman*; John Tinsley; *Red River Blues*; Clayton Horsley,

Don't The Moon Look Pretty; James Lowry, *Early Morning Blues*; Herbert Richardson & William Richardson, *Tell Me Baby*
A fascinating documentation of Virginia blues,* these tracks were mostly recorded in the 1970s but include Luke Jordan from 1929 and James Lowry from 1953 radio station dubs. Titles range from Foddrell's dance piece *Slow Drag* and "Rabbit" Muse's remarkable ukulele-accompanied hokum blues, to *Red River Blues*. There is delightful playing throughout.

145 **Long Steel Rail: Blues By Maryland Songster Bill Jackson**
Testament Records TCD 5014
Old Rounder Blues/Long Steel Rail/Last Go Round/Careless Love/Titanic Blues/ Freight Train Runs So Slow/Trouble In Mind/Blues In The Morning/You Ain't No Woman/Freight Train Blues/Moaning Guitar Blues/Going Back South/Blood Red River/Don't You Put Your Hands On Me/Jailhouse Blues/Key To The Highway/Master & John (story)/*Monkey, Baboon & Ape* (story)
Ballads, blues, and folk tales are all part of Jackson's repertoire. He is an excellent representative of the songster tradition, and his gentle singing and guitar playing disguise his skills as a performer. He is from one of the most underdocumented regions for black folk music in the United States.

(iii) Pre-war Blues in Texas

146 **Texas Girls (1926–1929): Complete Recorded Works In Chronological Order**
Various Artists
Document DOCD 5163 (Au)
Lillian Miller, *Kitchen Blues/Harbour Blues/You Just Can't Keep A Good Woman Down/Butcher Shop Blues/Dead Drunk Blues;* Hattie Hudson, *Doggone My Good Luck Soul/Black Hand Blues*; Gertrude Perkins, *No Easy Rider Blues/ Gold Daddy Blues*; Ida Mae Mack, *Wrong Doin' Daddy* (take 1)/*Wrong Doin' Daddy* (take 2)/*Elm Street Blues* (take 1)/*Elm Street Blues* (take 2)/*Mr. Moore Blues/When You Lose Your Daddy/Mr. Forty-Nine Blues* (take 1)/*Mr. Forty-Nine Blues* (take 2)/*Goodbye Rider* (take 1)/*Goodbye Rider* (take 2); Bobbie Cadillac, *Carbolic Acid Blues*; Bobbie Cadillac [& Coley Jones], *I Can't Stand That/He Throws That Thing/Listen Everybody/Easin' In*
A showcase for Texas pianists as well as women's blues, most of these sides were made in Dallas. Recorded in the North, however, Lillian Miller represents the Houston tradition, as do her accompanists. Generally, lyrics deal with the life of the disadvantaged. They are executed with panache by singers of accomplishment.

147 **Texan Blues (1927–1935): Complete Recorded Works In Chronological Order**
Various Artists
Document DOCD 5161 (Au)
Coley Jones, *Army Mule In No Man's Land/Traveling Man/Drunkard's Special/*

*A detailed booklet is available separately from BRI, Ferrum College, Ferrum, Virginia, 24088, USA.

The Elder's He's My Man; "Bo" Jones, *Back Door Blues/Leavenworth Prison Blues*; Little Hat Jones, *New Two Sixteen Blues/Two String Blues/Rolled From Side To Side Blues/Hurry Blues/Little Hat Blues/Corpus Blues/Kentucky Blues/ Bye Bye Baby Blues/Cross The Water Blues/Cherry Street Blues*; Oak Cliff T-Bone, *Trinity River Blues/Wichita Fall Blues*; Willie Reed, *Dreaming Blues/ Texas Blues/Leavin' Home/Goin' Back To My Baby/Some Low Down Groundhog Blues/All Worn Out And Dry Blues*

Coley Jones was a Dallas songster, as is demonstrated by his repertoire (**45**). The other guitarists on this disc are all bluesmen, some with singing styles akin to the holler, such as Bo Jones or Willie Reed. Little Hat Jones distinguishes a more sophisticated tradition, as do the earliest recordings of T-Bone Walker (Oak Cliff T-Bone).

148 Texas Alexander: Complete Recorded Works In Chronological Order, Volume 2, 16 November 1928 to 9 June 1930

Document[-Matchbox] MBCD 2002 (Au)

Penitentiary Moan Blues/Blue Devil Blues/Tell Me Woman Blues/'Frisco Train Blues/St. Louis Fair Blues/I Am Calling Blues/Double Crossing Blues/Ninety-Eight Degree Blues (take A)/*Ninety-Eight Degree Blues* (take B)/*Someday, Baby, Your Troubles Is Gonna Be Like Mine/Water Bound Blues/Awful Moaning Blues* Part 1/*Awful Moaning Blues* Part 2/*Gold Tooth Blues/Johnny Behrens Blues/Rolling Mill Blues/Broken Yo Yo/Texas Special/When You Get To Thinking/Thirty Day Blues/Peaceful Blues/Days Is Lonesome/Seen Better Days*

The sessions accompanied by south-western guitarists Little Hat Jones and Carl Davis form the core of this collection. There is also the improbable Alexander coupling with New Orleans cornetist King Oliver and sides supported by the Mississippi Sheiks. The basic elements of the field holler are seldom far from the surface.

149 Ramblin' Thomas & The Dallas Blues Singers: The Complete Recorded Works Of Ramblin' Thomas, Jess "Babyface" Thomas, Sammy Hill, Otis Harris 1928–1932

Document DOCD 5107 (Au)

Ramblin' Thomas, *So Lonesome/Hard To Rule Woman Blues/Lock And Key Blues/Sawmill Moan/No Baby Blues/Ramblin' Mind Blues/No Job Blues/Back Gnawing Blues/Jig Head Blues/Hard Dallas Blues/Ramblin' Man/Poor Boy Blues/Good Time Blues/New Way Of Living Blues/Ground Hog Blues/Shake It Gal*; Jesse "Babyface" Thomas, *Down In Texas Blues/My Heart's A Rolling Stone/Blue Goose Blues/No Good Woman Blues*; [Troy Ferguson], *Good Night*; Sammy Hill, *Cryin' For You Blues/Needin' My Woman Blues*; Otis Harris, *Walking Blues/You'll Like My Loving*

Laconic singing, original lyrics, and locally inspired guitar playing (sometimes with a slider) are the hallmark of Willard "Ramblin" Thomas. His younger brother Jesse's performances are generally more up-tempo. Both moved to Dallas from Louisiana. Sammy Hill and Otis Harris consolidate this representative sample of the greater-Texas guitar tradition.

150 Gene Campbell: Complete Recorded Works In Chronological Order (1929–1931)

Document DOCD 5151 (Au)

Mama, You Don't Mean Me No Good No How/Bended Knee Blues/Wandering Blues/Somebody's Been Playin' Papa/Wash And Iron Woman Blues/Robbin' And Stealin' Blues/I Wish I Could Die/Lazy Woman Blues/Levee Camp Man Blues/Western Plain Blues/Freight Train Yodeling Blues Part 1/*Freight Train Yodeling Blues* Part 2/*Don't Leave Me Blue Blues/Doggone Mean Blues/Married Life Blues/Fair Weather Woman Blues/Lonesome Nights Blues/Wedding Day Blues/Main Papa's Blues/Face To Face Blues/Crooked Woman Blues/Overalls Papa Blues*

These recording are all that is certain about the enigmatic Campbell, whose repertoire epitomizes Texas guitar-accompanied blues. With facile playing and pithy singing, his lyrics generally comment on unrequited love. His archetypal song about levee camp work may be autobiographical, while *Freight Train Yodeling Blues* is modeled on Jimmie Rodgers (**328**).

151 The Original Howling Wolf 1930–1931

"Funny Papa" Smith

Yazoo (CD) 1031

"Funny Papa" Smith, *Seven Sisters Blues* Part 1/*Seven Sisters Blues* Part 2/*Hungry Wolf/Corn Whiskey Blues/Hopping Toad Frog*; "Funny Papa" Smith & Magnolia Harris, *Mama's Quittin' And Leaving'* Part 1/*Mama's Quittin' And Leavin'* Part 2; "Funny Papa" Smith, *Good Coffee Blues/Honey Blues/County Jail Blues/Howling Wolf Blues* Part 1/*Howling Wolf Blues* Part 2; "Funny Papa" Smith & Dessa Foster, *Tell It To The Judge* Part 1/*Tell It To The Judge* Part 2

Coming to prominence in the early Depression years, J.T. Smith recorded surprisingly extensively, with strong confident vocals and guitar work redolent of Texas blues. All his titles were released as by "Funny Paper" Smith, the "Howling Wolf." The "Wolf" sobriquet became better known when used by a later bluesman (Chester Burnett).

152 Texas Slide Guitars

Oscar "Buddy" Woods & Black Ace: Complete Recorded Works 1930–1938 In Chronological Order

Document DOCD 5143 (Au)

[Jimmie Davis], *She's A Hum Dum Dinger (From Dingersville)*/[Shreveport Home Wreckers], *Fence Breakin' Blues/Home Wreckin' Blues*; [Jimmie Davis], *Bear Cat Mama From Horner's Corner/Saturday Night Stroll/Sewing Machine Blues/Red Nightgown Blues/Davis's Salty Dog*; Oscar Woods, *Evil Hearted Woman Blues/Lone Wolf Blues/Don't Sell It—Don't Give It Away*; [Buddy Woods], *Muscat Hill Blues/Don't Sell It (Don't Give It Away)*; [Kitty Gray & Her Wampus Cats], *Baton Rouge Rag*; [Buddy Woods], *Jam Session Blues/Low Life Blues/Token Blues/Come On Over To My House Baby*; Black Ace, *Trifling Woman/Black Ace/You Gonna Need My Help Some Day/Whiskey And Women/Christmas Time Blues/Lowing Heifer*

The disc covers commercial recordings by Oscar Woods. His slide guitar accompanies the very bluesy (and risqué) white country singer Jimmie Davis (later governor of Louisiana). There are duets with Ed Schaffer, solo performances and sides with his small combo the Wampus Cats. Black Ace learned his guitar style from Woods.

153 **Texas Santa Fe 1934–1937: The Piano Blues, Volume Eleven**
Various Artists
Magpie PY 4411 (UK)—*LP*
Son Becky, *Midnight Trouble Blues*; Black Boy Shine, *Dog House Blues*; Black Ivory King, *Working For The PWA*; Pinetop Burks, *Fannie Mae*; Alfoncy Harris, *Absent Freight Train Blues*; Pinetop Burks, *Aggravatin' Mama Blues*; Son Becky, *Sweet Woman Blues*; Bernice Edwards, Black Boy Shine & Howling Smith, *Hot Mattress Stomp*; Pinetop Burks, *Mountain Jack Blues*; Black Boy Shine, *Brown House Blues*; Bernice Edwards, *Butcher Shop Blues*; Pinetop Burks, *Jack Of All Trades Blues*; Black Ivory King, *Gingham Dress*; Son Becky, *Crying' Shame Blues*; Black Boy Shine, *Sail On Little Girl* No. 3; Pinetop Burks, *Sun Down Blues*
A cross-section of pianists is featured. Loosely termed the "Santa Fe", they followed the railroad and worked around Houston and neighboring counties. The group's rolling left-hand and ragtime-based tradition survived after the war in the music of Robert Shaw. Chapter 5 covers Shaw and others from the school (**231**, **238**).

(iv) Post-war Blues in Texas

154 **Texas Country Blues**
Various Artists
Flyright FLY CD 941 (UK)
James Tisdom, *I Feel So Good*; Andrew Thomas, *I Love My Baby*; Rattlesnake Cooper, *I Treated You Wrong*; Leroy Johnson, *No One To Love Me*; Willie Lane, *Black Cat Rag*; James Tisdom, *'51 Blues*; Monister Parker, *Black Snake Blues*; Sonny Boy Davis, *I Don't Live Here No More*; Cleo Harves, *Crazy With The Blues*; Frankie Lee Sims, *Cross Country Blues*; Sunny James, *Excuse Me Baby*; James Tisdom, *Last Affair Blues*; Rattlesnake Cooper, *Rattlesnake Blues*; Andrew Thomas, *Chicago Blues*; Mr. Honey [David Edwards], *Who May Your Regular Be*; Willie Lane, *Prowlin' Ground Hog*; Leroy Johnson, *Log House On The Hill*; James Tisdom, *Cadillac Blues*; Monister Parker, *You Gonna Need Me*; Rattlesnake Cooper, *Lost Woman*; Sunny James, *Please Mam Forgive Me*; Sonny Boy Davis, *Rhythm Blues*; James Tisdom, *Model T Boogie*
This is an anthology of rare and evocative recordings from the late 1940s to the early 1950s. They were made in Dallas-Fort Worth, Houston, South Texas, and Louisiana. Excepting Sonny Boy Davis (a pianist), all the singers are guitarists. Mr Honey is a Mississipian, accompanied by powerful Texas piano from Thunder Smith.

155 **Lucy Mae Blues**
Frankie Lee Sims
Specialty SPCD 7022-2/Ace CDCHD 423 (UK)
Lucy Mae Blues/Don't Take It Out On Me/Married Woman/Wine And Gin Bounce/Boogie 'Cross The Country/Jelly Roll Baker/I'm So Glad/Long Gone/Raggedy And Dirty/Yeah, Baby!/No Good Woman/Walking Boogie/Frankie's Blues/Cryin' Won't Help You/I Done Talked And I Done Talked/Lucy Mae

Blues Part 2/*Rhumba My Boogie*/*I'll Get Along Somehow*/*Hawk Shuffle*/*Frankie Lee's 2 O'Clock Jump*
Sims was born in New Orleans and moved to Texas when he was 12; his relatives there included Lightnin' Hopkins. His singing and guitar playing reflect Texas styles and themes, including the work-song-based *Long Gone*. These sessions date from 1953 and 1954 and epitomize tough local juke joint blues of the period.

156 **Steel Guitar Flash**
Hop Wilson & His Buddies [Various Artists]
Ace CDCHD 240
My Woman Has A Black Cat Bone (take 1)/*I Feel So Glad*/*I'm A Stranger*/*Be Careful With The Blues*/*I Ain't Got No Woman*/*My Woman Done Quite Me* [*Fenton Robinson, vocal]/*Merry Christmas Darling* (take 1)/*Dance To It*/*Rockin' In The Coconut Top* [King Ivory Lee, vocal]/*Fuss Too Much* [King Ivory Lee, vocal]/*Why Do You Twist*/*A Good Woman Is Hard To Find*/*Rockin' In The Coconut Top*/*Need Your Love To Keep Me Warm* [*Larry Davis, vocal]/*You Don't Move Me Anymore* [*Fenton Robinson, vocal]/*I Done Got Over*/*You Don't Love Me No More* [King Ivory Lee, vocal]/*Toot Toot Tootsie Goo'bye* Part 2/*Your Daddy Want's To Rock* [King Ivory Lee, vocal]/*Broke And Hungry*/*Always Be In Love With You*/*My Woman Has A Black Cat Bone* (take 2)/*I Met A Strange Woman*/*Need Your Love To Keep Me Warm* (take 2) [*Larry Davis, vocal]/*Love's Got Me All Fenced In*/*Chicken Stuff* (alternate take)/*Rockin' With Hop*/*That Wouldn't Satisfy*/*Chicken Stuff*
From the tradition of flat-picking Hawaiian-styled guitarists, Hop Wilson cut his titles in Texas and Louisiana between 1958 and 1962. Carried at times into the R&B scene by a tenor saxophone, nonetheless they have the distinct down-home feel of blues bars in Lyons Avenue or Dowling Street in Houston.

157 **I'm The Boss Card In Your Hand**
Black Ace
Arhoolie CD 374
I Am The Black Ace/*Bad Times Stomp*/*Drink On Little Girl*/*Santa Fe Blues*/*New Triflin' Woman*/*Evil Woman Blues*/*'Fore Day Creep*/*Little Augie*/*Your Legs' Too Little*/*No Good Woman*/*Santa Claus Blues*/*Golden Slipper*/*Hitch-Hiking Woman*/*Ace's Guitar Blues*/*Beer Drinking Woman*/*Ace's Guitar Breakdown*/*I've Been In Love With You Baby*/*Trifling Woman*/*Black Ace*/*You Gonna Need My Help Some Day*/*Whiskey And Women*/*Christmas Time Blues*/*Lowing Heifer*
Black Ace recorded one commercial session in 1937, included alongside titles made in 1960 when he was still close to his peak. Paralleling Oscar Woods, they are perhaps the last by an exponent of the flat-picked Hawaiian guitar-style country blues.

158 **From North Dallas To The East Side**
Whistling Alex Moore
Arhoolie CD 408
Whistling Alex Moor's Blues/*Pretty Woman With A Sack Dress On*/*Rubber*

**Idenification of vocalist by Ace Records.*

Tired Hack/You Say I Am A Bad Feller/From North Dallas To The East Side/ [New] Miss No-Good Weed/Black Eyed Peas And Hog Jowls/Boogie In The Barrel/Going Back To Froggy Bottom/July Boogie/West Texas Woman/Frisky Gal/Chock House Boogie/Miss No-Good Weed Part 1/*Alex's Boogie [Dishwasher Boogie]/You Got Me Dissatisfied [Disagreable Woman]/Alex's Rag/Alex's Blues [Slow Piano Improvisation]/Alex's Wild Blues [Fast Piano Improvisation]/Sometimes I Feel Worried/I Love You Baby/Rock And Roll Bed/ Boogiein' In Strassburg*

Recorded first in 1929, Moore was a gifted poet and blues pianist of the Dallas school (**232**). His appealing lyrical inventiveness remained when he was found in 1960, as did the vigor of his singing and playing. The disc has sides made at this rediscovery, acetates from 1947, and two titles from 1969.

159 Texas Songster

Mance Lipscomb

Arhoolie CD 306

Sugar Babe (It's All Over Now)/Going Down Slow/Freddie/Jack O' Diamonds/ Baby Please Don't Go/One Thin Dime/Shake, Shake, Mama/Ella Speed/Mama Don't Allow/Ain't It Hard/'Bout A Spoonful/Take Me Back Babe/Rag In G/Big Boss Man/You Gonna Quite Me/Blues In G/Mama Don't Dog Me/Willie Poor Boy/Tell Me Where You Stayed Last Night/Knocking Down Windows/Nobody's Fault But Mine/Motherless Children

One of the more remarkable discoveries (rather than rediscoveries) of the 1960s, Mance Lipscomb was a songster of great stature; he left a rich repository of old songs and was a magnificent guitarist. His versions of compositions such as *Sugar Babe* became part of the coffee-bar repertoire. This disc includes his first recordings.

160 The Hopkins Brothers

Lightning [Sam], Joel & John Henry

Arhoolie CD 340

Lightning, *See About My Brother John Henry*; John Henry, *Hot Blooded Woman*; Lightning & John Henry, *Black Hannah*; John Henry, *I Want To Go Fishing/Doin' Little Heiffer/Hey Baby Hey/Saddle Up My Grey Mare/Tell Me, Tell Me*; Lightning, *Little Girl/I Got A Brother In Waxahachie*; Joel, *Matchbox Blues/Home With Mama*; Lightning, *Come Down To My House*; Lightning & Joel, *Grosebeck Blues*; Lightning, speech, *The Dice Game*; Joel, *I Walked From Dallas*; Lightning & Joel, *Two Brothers Playing (Going Back To Baden Baden)*

Three generations of Texas guitar-bluesmen perform in this compelling collection, made at the instance of Chris Strachwitz. Joel (second generation) performs mainly traditional themes. Improvisations from the eldest Hopkins (John Henry) are sometimes in competition with his famous youngest brother (Lightning).

DAPHNE DUVAL HARRISON AND JOHN COWLEY

5 "Classic" Blues and Women Singers

Woman singers opened the market for blues recordings when the OKeh label issued Mamie Smith's *That Thing Called Love* and *You Can't Keep A Good Man Down* in 1920. Although these two selections were not conventional blues, their astonishing success convinced the General Phonograph Corporation, OKeh's parent company, that the black community was a potential goldmine for record sales. They followed the first recording with the now famous *Crazy Blues*, featuring a stellar group of musicians described as Mamie Smith's Jazz Hounds.

In less than two years various labels including Arto, Black Swan, Columbia, Emerson, Gennett, OKeh, and Paramount, featured black women singing the blues. Edith Wilson, Eva Taylor, Lulu Whidby, Lucille Hegamin, Lizzie Miles, and Trixie Smith were among those recorded in 1921 and 1922. The African-American community's insatiable appetite for blues inspired major labels—OKeh, Columbia, and Paramount in particular—to undertake recordings in New York and Chicago, sometimes supplemented by makeshift field studios in the South. Scouts were sent to Southern cities and towns to audition and sign on fresh talent at the well-spring of the music. The women who were destined to have the most dramatic impact on the history of American music, however, were not discovered by field audition. They were already on the show circuit, singing blues and other songs in vaudeville presentations that were popular among black people in both rural and urban areas in the South and South-west.

The blues on record were profoundly shaped by a handful of women. The best were Bessie Smith, Gertrude "Ma" Rainey, Clara Smith, and Ida Cox, but Sippie Wallace, Sara Martin, "Chippie" Hill and possibly Alberta Hunter may arguably be considered special in terms of their individual styles. All began recording careers in 1923, excepting Hunter (1921), Martin (1922), and Hill (1925). The distinctive quality of each of their voices and expressiveness in performance have stood the test of time and influenced successors in singular fashion. Their special sense of phrasing inspired instrumentalists who performed with them in recording studios and on stage. They extended the traditional 12-bar blues with antiphonal play between voice and

Lizzie Miles, New Orleans singer, 1950s (*coll. Paul Oliver*)

horn, piano or guitar. The power of the word was emphasized with vocal embellishments such as slides, moans, wails, or growls. Wit was displayed in their use of sly, risqué innuendoes, snappy admonitions, or ingratiating pleas.

Perhaps the most overlooked aspect of the early 1920s blues era was its concentration on a woman's point of view regarding the central blues themes. Although much of the music and many of the lyrics were written by men, women composed a substantial portion of the blues they performed. Some of the better-known singers produced many of the best sellers; one of Bessie Smith's hottest records, *Down Hearted Blues*, was written by Alberta Hunter. The lyrics, sometimes audacious, asserted women's attitudes towards infidelity, abandonment, mistreatment, sex, and alcohol. The subject-matter of women's blues had no limits. On the evidence of recordings, however, the language was perhaps somewhat tougher and more explicit in the blues of urban women when they discussed prostitution, violence, sex, and deviance.

(i) "Classic" and "Down-home" Singers

The repertoire of blues queens during the so-called "Classic" era (of the 1920s) is not easily categorized, owing to varied demands by black audiences. Depending on specific venues, they would sing the traditional low-down blues with a guitar or plunking piano, or a hot number backed by a swinging jazz ensemble. Some singers concentrated on heavily emotive renditions, while others focused on lighter versions of the same themes. Dance-hall blues tended to swing more to encourage terpsichorean activity at the "jazz band ball." Rowdy, ribald blues were usually reserved for the Midnight Ramble shows, rent parties, and clubs. Many examples were recorded by the end of the decade. At the same time, however, the industry began to record male singers with a decidedly rural flavor.

As has been noted, 1923 was a seminal year for the start of recording careers by major women blues singers, including the two greatest performers. Ma Rainey (sweetheart of Southern country folk) signed with Paramount—they called her "Mother of the Blues"—and Bessie Smith accepted a contract with Columbia. Usually perceived as Rainey's principal urban-based rival, Bessie became known as "The Empress."

Overshadowed but never eclipsed by these two "Classic" blues queens was Ida Cox, whose releases on Paramount preceded Rainey's by ten months. A Southerner who traveled on the TOBA (Theater Owners' Booking Agency) circuit, Cox had a defiant philosophy of life that said "don't mess with me or my man, or there will be the devil to pay." Her vaudeville performances were popular, but this acclaim increased rapidly once she was heard on record. Ida was introduced in Paramount advertisements as "the uncrowned Queen of the blues" with a picture of her bejeweled head surrounded by genuflecting subjects. **Ida Cox: Complete Recorded Works, Volume 1** covers the first seven months of her recording career—June to December 1923. These sides represent the first ten couplings she made and were issued between August 1923 and May 1924, a flow indicating something of her popularity.

Paramount's initial policy was to vary accompaniment and, excepting *Bear-Mash Blues*, this was divided exactly between sides with piano by Lovie Austin, and contributions by her Blues Serenaders (Austin, piano; Tommy Ladnier, cornet; and Jimmy O'Bryant, clarinet). Individual piano accompaniments were usually paired on release. Austin also wrote or co-wrote several of these songs with Cox. Jesse Crump, the Texas pianist whom Ida met in Indianapolis, composed *Bear-Mash* with her and plays solo piano on this track.

Ida wrote *Graveyard Dream Blues* (covered by Bessie Smith), *I Love My Man Better Than I Love Myself, Lawdy Lawdy Blues* and *Come Right In*. The latter is a precursor of *Walk Right In* by Gus Cannon's Jug Stompers (**46**), and elements from the lyrics used by these early women singers can be traced in other works recorded by "down-home" male vocalists later in the decade.

A theme of some of these recordings is travel and migration. *Bama Bound Blues* (composed by Cox and Lovie Austin) has Ida's man taking a train to Alabama and expresses her wish to follow him, but she has no "railroad fare". In the same vein, *Chicago Bound Blues* (subtitled "Famous Migration Blues") has Ida's man traveling by train to Chicago (presumably to look for work), leaving her distraught "down home" and, with her "feet" refusing "to walk", contemplating suicide. The composer credits for this track are to Cox and Williams (the latter possibly being J. Mayo "Ink" Williams, the black talent scout employed by Paramount). *I've Got The Blues For Rampart Street* has a different theme. This recalls a prime location for cabaret performances in New Orleans, where Ida wishes to go and "enjoy herself" listening to the musical attractions. The song was written by Lovie Austin, as was *Chattanooga Blues* (the subject of which is the Tennessee city where she was born). This nostalgic piece entered the repertoire of old-time music performers, with variants of the same name or *Johnson City Blues* (**321/2**).

Of the famous singers who began their recording careers in 1923, Ida was not the youngest. Born in 1896, she was two years senior to Bessie Smith, but six years younger than Ma Rainey. Bessie, who was

Rainey's junior by eight years, was a superior artist, while her singing nevertheless offers echoes of Rainey's "down-home" flavour and unadorned style. On the other hand, Rainey's recorded repertoire incorporates an urban viewpoint that denotes appeal to a widespread audience. In **Ma Rainey's Black Bottom** the listener receives a cross-section of her treatment of humorous, sexual, legendary, and traditional blues topics. Demonstrating show business acumen she adapted her vaudeville style to the recorded medium. *Oh Papa Blues* and the title song feature the honky-tonk rhythms and orchestrations of the stage band. Rainey's voice dances the Black Bottom with liberal use of drags and slides, which are interspersed with sly verbal asides. Shirley Clay's cornet provides a running commentary in the background of *Oh Papa*, while the banjo and tuba maintain oompah-pah rhythm. Rainey swings this foxtrot as if she were on the stage, giving a mock seriousness to the performance.

In contrast, *Don't Fish In My Sea* is a 12-bar blues about infidelity and "no-good trifling men." Rainey's voice, pure and unembellished, is enhanced by Jimmy Blythe's loping piano, reminiscent of Hersal Thomas. This is an urban blues, with its stride piano and *double entendre* lyrics:

> If you don't like my ocean, don't fish in my sea [*twice*]
> Stay out of my valley and let my mountain be.

Farewell Daddy Blues, with its traditional 12-bar format is an outstanding example of Rainey's raw, husky singing. The intricate guitar accompaniment by Milas Pruitt underlies the moaning vocals and emphasizes the rural quality. One of Rainey's most popular recordings, it illustrates how her emotional rendering could capture the *Angst* of a mistreated woman.

Stack O' Lee Blues is an old-time ballad, but not that usually associated with this title. Heard in many versions by different male and female singers, this is an interpretation of *Frankie And Albert* and comes close to the tent show style of the 1920s and 1930s. When she is singing *Blues Oh Blues, Screech Owl Blues*, or *Booze And Blues*, Rainey's stage persona is projected in similar manner. *Shave 'Em Dry Blues* with Pruitt, however, defies this image, with its raunchy, country approach. This is the inimitable songstress who fascinated and captivated the hearts of rugged lumber- and turpentine camp-men, and who inspired the learned musicologist John Work and the poet Sterling Brown to write so eloquently about her.

Six of the items on this disc were written or co-written by Rainey—the title song, *Blues Oh Blues, Shave 'Em Dry Blues, Screech Owl Blues, Sleep Talking Blues*, and *Don't Fish In My Sea* (the last with

Bessie Smith). They represent her interest in diverse topics and ability to perform in varied modes—saucy, boisterous, barrelhouse, and bedraggled mournful traditional blues—as well as topical themes that cut through the mire of urban living: alcohol, sexual deviance, violence, and imprisonment. The disc is representative of Rainey's art and provides a good sample of her performance style. It also demonstrates her enormous power as an artist, because her direct emotional appeal overshadows the archaic nature of some material, for example, *Georgia Cake Walk*. She strikes at the very core of attitudes to love and sex, and compels listeners to share her experiences, whether humorous, pitiful, vengeful, or reckless. Her ability is unsurpassed in this respect and remains an important force and source in blues history.

Bessie Smith's voice, interpretative ability, dramatic flair, and sense of phrasing are hallmarks of the blues women's decade. With seeming effortlessness, she sails through any song, blues or not, with a special bluesy quality, leaving a wake that swamps any singer who attempts to imitate her artistry. Some writers have stated she sings in an unembellished, direct manner unlike the sophisticated style of some of her contemporaries such as Alberta Hunter or Mamie Smith, an assessment that mistakenly underrates Bessie's ability. **Bessie Smith: The Complete Recordings, Volume 2** is effective testimony that she had a broad array of vocal devices, which she employed judiciously to maximize her musical and textual impact. The selections in this two-CD set vary in accompaniment but all feature piano (or reed organ on two tracks), and two-thirds have only one other instrument; this allows attention to be focused on her shifts in mood, tricky phrasing, and usage of guttural inflections, sliding moans, and upward and downward melisma.

In a collection that spans a period of almost two years, the first CD begins part way through a session cut on 8 April 1924 and ends with most of the sides made on 14 January 1925. All these recordings were made using the acoustic process. The second CD begins with the final two pieces from this session of January 1925 and continues with sides cut between 5 May and 18 November that year, representing the improved reproduction of electrical recordings.

From April 1924, *Moonshine Blues* is a Ma Rainey song that had been recorded by its composer at her first session for Paramount in December 1923. Bessie also cut a few similar songs written by other woman vaudeville blues singers, but none are on this disc. From September 1925, however, there is the third and final of her duets with her contemporary Clara Smith.

The decision to record Clara and Bessie together was not only good business because of their large followings, but also because it demonstrates the latter's versatility. The voices are well matched yet quite distinct in style and tonal quality. Written by Bessie, *My Man Blues* is in the form of a humorous argument between the two women over a man named "Charlie Gray". In the recording Bessie takes the first four bars of each chorus and Clara responds in the last four. Both possess strong, rich tones, but Bessie's tight control over inflection gives her voice an authority that surpasses Clara's wider range. Not quite delivering its potential (partly on account of the plodding piano), this is nevertheless a fascinating performance that confirms Bessie as the most talented blues woman in the "classic" style.

On *Work House Blues* and the next three tracks Bessie is joined on record for the first time by trombonist Charlie Green. The empathy between the two is apparent immediately, and they are augmented by Joe Smith on cornet in *Weeping Willow Blues* and *The Bye Bye Blues*. All of these feature Fletcher Henderson on piano and were made in July and August 1924. Green and pianist Fred Longshaw provide the accompaniment for *Dying Gambler's Blues* (December 1924), but some of her most musically satisfying recordings are those in which Louis Armstrong backs Bessie on cornet.

It seems Bessie viewed Armstrong as a rival soloist and there is an enhancing tension between the two in their performances that is not apparent in the cornet work of Joe Smith (her favorite accompanist on this instrument). The initial session with Louis is that which took place on 14 January 1925. Six sides were produced, the first being what has become recognized as the standard version of W.C. Handy's *St. Louis Blues*. On this and the next item, the impeccable *Reckless Blues*, Fred Longshaw plays reed organ, reverting to piano on the other four tracks.

The electrical recordings which feature Armstrong were made on 26 and 27 May, and were supported by Charlie Green on trombone and Fletcher Henderson on piano. *Nashville Women's Blues* and a version of another W.C. Handy "composition", *Careless Love*, were cut on the first day; the latter is a sublime performance. *J.C. Holmes Blues* (from 27 May) is also dramatically exciting. The song is a parody of the well-known ballad *Casey Jones* that appears in black and white tradition. Perry Bradford's *I Ain't Goin' To Play No Second Fiddle* is the final title from this foursome and sustains the high standard.

Later in the year (November) Bessie performed *Florida Bound Blues* with Clarence Williams on piano. This Williams composition was to enter the repertoire of late singers such as rural Alabama guitarist Edward Thompson, or popular Indianapolis pianist Leroy Carr (**247**). As has been mentioned, interchange, often via gramophone records, between the early woman blues singers and subsequent performers is under-appreciated. Conversely, despite the popularity of the early queens of the blues, it is also surprising how unaffected some later stylists appear to have been by these singers. One case in point is the recordings of another Bessie, whose origin was in Texas, and who cut relatively few sides at the end of the decade.

Bessie Tucker, who shared a session in Memphis, Tennessee, with fellow Texan Ida Mae Mack (**146**) in 1928, was one of the most distinctive woman blues singers from that state to be recorded in the 1920s. Unlike Lillian Glinn (**177**), with experience on the vaudeville stage, Tucker's vocal style and repertoire suggests a close relationship with less formal places of entertainment, perhaps including the dives of Dallas, the town where she recorded for a second time in 1929. All her recordings are included in Document's **Bessie Tucker**.

Her photograph, taken from a Victor catalog, gives little indication of the imposing power of her voice, or the random structure of her verses, which were closer to the holler than any other commercially recorded woman singer in the period. A clue to this, however, is provided in the three pieces she described as "moans"—*Bessie's Moan, Black Name Moan* (both from 1928), and *T.B. Moan* (1929). The subject-matter of her songs includes railroads (possibly as a result of hoboeing). A familiarity with the railroad network can also be heard in *The Dummy* (the term identifies a temporary track for logging camps and other industrial work), *Fort Worth And Denver Blues*, and *Katy Blues* (the latter from 1929). Her relationship with men is also a potent topic, with pieces such as *Fryin' Pan Skillet Blues, My Man Has Quit Me*, or *Old Black Mary*. Her most compelling sides, however, are those that deal with the levee camp, the prison camp, or similar situations. They indicate a knowledge of blatant brutality unusual in recordings from the period—except some of the songs recorded by Texas Alexander (**148**).

Penitentiary, *Got Cut All To Pieces*, *Black Name Moan*, *Key To The Bushes* and *Mean Old Master* are all exceptional in this vein. In *Penitentiary*, for example, she sings:

> Penitentiary, penitentiary gonna be my home [*twice*],
> Because my man has mistreated me, Lord, he had done me wrong;

while in *Got Cut All To Pieces*, her man takes up with another woman, after having beaten her "half dead." She swears revenge, following which "trouble" will take her away.

Key To The Bushes may be a chain gang song. The second verse runs:

> Captain, captain, what's the matter with that [*twice*],
> You have worked my partner, you have killed my pal;

and *Mean Old Master* recalls slavery or, more likely, is an account of peonage in the 1920s:

> Our boss man may come here, we' better not run [*twice*],
> Old master got a pistol, may be a great big gun.

Accompanied on all her sessions by the sensitive piano playing of K.D. Johnson (referred to as "Mr. Forty Nine" by Ida Mae Mack) there are additional instruments on her Dallas recordings. *Katy Blues* and *Better Boot That Thing* include a brass bass, and Jesse Thomas' guitar playing is featured throughout; he also sings the chorus on the latter hokum-like piece.

Although they undoubtedly shared rural origins and audiences, in contrast with Bessie Tucker's holler/work-song-like approach, the duo of Memphis Minnie and "Kansas Joe" McCoy was more sophisticated. Most of their songs are structurally thematic and have a special emphasis on adroit presentation. Hailing from the Mississippi River basin, both were skilled guitarists whose ability to entertain was enhanced by this dexterity; together with vocal styles developed for street singing and jook joint dances in the area between Memphis, Tennessee, and Jackson, Mississippi, whence they came.

All of their early sides sustain this sometimes spectacular quality, making the choice of which disc to recommend from Document's four CD chronology a difficult decision. The third volume of **Memphis Minnie & Kansas Joe 1929–1934**, however, contains varied repertoire and an association with the new decade in which it was recorded that makes it a suitable selection.

Recorded between 1931 and 1932, Minnie is the vocalist on the majority of these sides, singing two duets with Kansas Joe and contributing two scintillating instrumentals with her then husband, in which the interplay between their guitars is especially effective. These are *Pickin' The Blues* (in which one of the guitars is played bottleneck, or slide style) and *Let's Go To Town.*

Most of these songs are thematic and describe female–male relations, usually from a woman's point of view. The plight of the prostitute in Depression-riven America is the topic of *Tricks Ain't Walking No More* (1931), the only recognizable cover of a contemporary song, first recorded by Lucille Bogan in 1930 (**166**), while *Fishin' Blues* is a favorite from the repertoire of medicine shows. In the duets, Kansas Joe takes the part of the mistreated man in *Somebody's Got To Help You*, but Minnie is the offended party in *You Stole My Cake.*

Jailhouse Trouble Blues bears comparison with similar pieces in Bessie Tucker's repertoire. Unlike Tucker's work, Minnie's song is a story relating how since she left home she has experienced the jailhouse and county farm by not heeding the warnings of her mother (and in one verse her father). Interestingly Kansas Joe's *Joilet Bound* (also about crime and imprisonment) is a less thematic performance and closer to Tucker's holler-based style.

Two particular pointers to the 1930s are *Outdoor Blues* and *Socket Blues*. In the former Minnie tells how:

> One cold night I was out in the frost and snow [*twice*],
> I didn't have no penny, I couldn't find no place to go.

She sees a hoboes' fire but it is put out before she reaches it, and is rejected for having "no clothes" when seeking assistance by knocking on the door of a house. Eventually, an old lady gives her refuge at another location. This is a graphic description of an individual's hard times during the Depression.

Socket Blues (on one level a sexual metaphor) refers to the use of flat irons "down in my old home town" and the novelty of electric clothes irons in the north that require a "socket" to connect them to their source of power. Indirectly, this draws attention to life in the north and a pending migration from the south that took place during the era. Minnie herself became a Chicago-based singer in this period (**186**, **245**).

Southern imagery remained a potent element in the lyrics of blues singers throughout the 1930s and, together with strong piano accompaniment, was a feature of many of the sides cut by Lucille Bogan, an Alabama-based singer whose recording career lasted from 1923 to 1935.

In many ways, Bogan sounds distinctly rural in style. She treats her subject-matter of whiskey, abusive men, sex, and good loving with a rare individuality that makes her stand out from the vaudeville singers discussed in this section. Her lyrics, however, are thematic and akin to Memphis Minnie rather than the more archaic presentations of Bessie Tucker.

Virtually every item in **Lucille Bogan, Volume 2** was released under the pseudonym of Bessie Jackson. The first version of her Depression prostitution song *They Ain't Walking No More*, however, used her original name. She cut two other titles in 1930 that became blues standards—*Sloppy Drunk Blues* and *Black Angel Blues*, both of which were re-recorded by others during the decade and remained popular after World War II.

They Ain't Walking and *Sloppy Drunk* came from a session at which the accomplished blues pianist Charles Avery was at the keyboard. This also included *Dirty Treatin' Blues* and *Alley Boogie*. The pianist at her second session in that year is not known, but when she returned to the studios in 1933 she was partnered by the exciting Alabaman Walter Roland (**206**). Commencing with the topical *Red Cross Man* (a variant of a song known otherwise as *Red Cross Store*), this CD features his playing. He also makes vocal interjections in *Roll And Rattler* which, like several other songs, contains a reference to railroads in its title—*TN & O Blues, Forty-Two Hundred Blues* (with Roland's vocal train whistle), and *Seaboard Blues*.

In addition to her regular subject-matter, several of these songs have local topical themes. *Mean Twister* describes the devastation wrought by a tornado on the community where she lived and her desperate search for her man in the wake of the destruction. He is never found. The aforementioned *Red Cross Man* relates to relief in the Depression while *Superstitious Blues (Hooch House Blues)* has Bogan being prosecuted for violating the prohibition against the consumption of alcohol (which was rescinded in December 1933). Most interesting of this group of songs, however is *New Muscle Shoals Blues*, which begins:

> I'm going to Muscle Shoals to get my man a government job [*twice*],
> He wants to work on the lock and dam, where they don't work men so hard.
>
> They get men from the forest, and they workin' 'em on the Wilson Dam [*twice*],
> Down at Muscle Shoals, Lord, eighty miles from Birmingham.

This celebrates one aspect of President Franklin D. Roosevelt's creation of the Tennessee Valley Authority in May 1933, two months before Bogan made this recording, as part of the "New Deal" which was to benefit the lives of many black people in the aftermath of the Depression.

It is no accident that the age of the "classic" woman blues singers was the "roaring 'twenties." Their glamorous live performances in vaudeville and tent shows were part of the period's ostentation. Changes in the approach of such mainstream singers are exemplified in ASV's "Living Era" collection **Ladies Sing The Blues**. This spans the period 1923–1939 and, coincidentally, gives a glimpse of the way their performances altered in the wake of the US stock market crash of 1929.

With a few exceptions (including two sides cut by Ada Brown in St Louis in 1923), most of these titles were recorded in New York City. Brown was originally from Kansas City and her titles are accompanied by a home-town orchestra led by Bennie Moten. These pieces give a glimpse of regional vaudeville styles in the 1920s, together with Lillian Glinn's *Cravin' A Man Blues* (made with Dallas musicians in 1929) and Sippie Wallace's Chicago recording of *I'm A Mighty Tight Woman* (also from 1929). Sippie, like Lillian Glinn, was from Texas, but, as with all these singers, experience in shows had tempered local characteristics. Among this class of vocalist, such traces had virtually disappeared by the end of the 1930s.

The collection encompasses a representative sample of famous 1920s recordings including Ma Rainey's *Booze And Blues* (which influenced the repertoire of Charley Patton) (**81**), plus Bessie Smith's famous *St. Louis Blues* and celebrated two-part *Empty Bed Blues*. Adelaide Hall's well-known scat vocal on *The Blues I Love To Sing* complements a showpiece for the Duke Ellington Orchestra (1927), while Laura Smith's *Don't You Leave Me Here* (from the same year) is a variant of the familiar barrelhouse piece usually known as *Alabama Bound*. Lizzie Miles, originally from New Orleans, contributes two *double entendre* songs recorded in 1930—*Electrician Blues* and *My Man O' War*.

Victoria Spivey's *Moaning The Blues* was recorded in 1929. She was originally from Texas, and her blues career continued into the 1930s (**183**). By this time, however, most black stage and show singers who featured blues had extended their repertoire to jazz. Mildred Bailey and Billie Holiday are good examples of this type of singer. Una Mae Carlisle also took this route—interestingly *Hangover Blues* was recorded in Britain, with musicians from Barbados and Jamaica in the accompanying group.

Following the demise of their popularity in the 1920s, Ida Cox and Trixie Smith experienced a short recording revival among jazz aficionados in the late 1930s, and their tracks come from these sessions. Rosetta Howard, however, is a genuine 1930s blues woman (albeit in the wake of Billie Holiday's success) (**191**). She is accompanied by the Harlem Hamfats (**273**) on *Let Your Linen Hang Low* and *Rosetta Blues*, the former being a bawdy duet with "Kansas Joe" McCoy.

Ironically, the hundreds of women blues singers of the "classic" era were never to regain the spotlight they had captured in the 1920s. Neither would there be another period that would focus on women as solo artists, particularly as performers of the blues. The shift to swing and big bands in the 1930s left most black singers of this type without recording or stage contracts. The blues vaudevillian was replaced by ballad and jazz singers—mostly white, mostly male. Not until the emergence of a revitalized urban blues after World War II did another group of talented female singers secure the wholehearted attention of record producers and consumers. As in the past, their music was given a label to attract the market in which the recordings were distributed. This time it was called Rhythm and Blues, although the singers and listeners still considered it to be blues. These developments are considered in the next section.

Essential Records

161 **Ida Cox: Complete Recorded Works 1923–1938 In Chronological Order, Volume 1, June to December 1923**
Document DOCD 5322 (Au)
Any Woman's Blues/Bama Bound Blues/Lovin' Is The Thing I'm Wild About/ Graveyard Dream Blues (1442–1)/*Graveyard Dream Blues* (1442–2)/*Weary Way Blues/Blue Monday Blues/I Love My Man Better Than I Love Myself/Ida Cox's Lawdy Lawdy Blues* (take 3)/*Ida Cox's Lawdy Lawdy Blues* (take 4)/*Moanin' Groanin' Blues/Chattanooga Blues/Chicago Bound Blues* (take 2)/*Chicago Bound Blues* (take 3)/*Come Right In/I've Got The Blues For Rampart Street* (take 3)/ *I've Got The Blues For Rampart Street* (take 4)/*Graveyard Dream Blues* (1545–2)/*Mama Doo Shee Blues/Worried Mama Blues/So Soon This Morning Blues/ Mail Man Blues/Confidential Blues/Bear-Mash Blues*

162 **Ma Rainey's Black Bottom**
Ma Rainey
Yazoo (CD) 1071
Oh Papa Blues/Black Eye Blues (take 1)/*"Ma" Rainey's Black Bottom/Booze And Blues/Blues Oh Blues/Sleep Talking Blues* (take 1)/*Lucky Rock Blues/ Georgia Cake Walk/Don't Fish In My Sea/Stack O' Lee Blues/Shave 'Em Dry Blues/Yonder Come The Blues* (take 1)/*Screech Owl Blues/Farewell Daddy Blues*

163 **Bessie Smith: The Complete Recordings, Volume 2**
Columbia C2K 47471/468767-2 (UK)—*2 CD set*
DISC ONE: *Frankie Blues/Moonshine Blues/Louisiana Low-Down Blues/Mountain Top Blues/Work House Blues/House Rent Blues/Salt Water Blues/Rainy Weather Blues/Weeping Willow Blues/The Bye Bye Blues/Sing Sing Prison Blues/Follow The Deal On Down/Sinful Blues/Woman's Trouble Blues/Love Me Daddy Blues/Dying Gambler's Blues/The St. Louis Blues/Reckless Blues/Sobbin' Hearted Blues*

DISC TWO: *Cold In Hand Blues/You've Been A Good Ole Wagon/Cake Walkin' Babies (From Home)/The Yellow Dog Blues/Soft Pedal Blues/Dixie Flyer Blues/ Nashville Women's Blues/Careless Love Blues/J.C. Holmes Blues/I Ain't Goin' To Play No Second Fiddle/He's Gone Blues/Nobody's Blues But Mine/I Ain't Got Nobody/My Man Blues* [duet with Clara Smith]/*New Gulf Coast Blues/ Florida Bound Blues/At The Christmas Ball/I've Been Mistreated And I Don't Like It*

164 **Bessie Tucker: Complete Recorded Works In Chronological Order 1928–1929**
Document DOCD 5070 (Au)
Bessie's Moan/The Dummy/Fort Worth And Denver Blues (take 1)/*Fort Worth And Denver Blues* (take 2)/*Penitentiary* (take 1)/*Penitentiary* (take 2)/*Fryin' Pan Skillet Blues* (take 1)/*Fryin' Pan Skillet Blues* (take 2)/*My Man Has Quit Me/ Got Cut All To Pieces* (take 1)/*Got Cut All To Pieces* (take 2)/*Black Name Moan/Better Boot That Thing* (take 1)/*Better Boot That Thing* (take 2)/*Katy Blues* (take 1)/*Katy Blues* (take 2)/*Mean Old Jack Stropper Blues* (take 1)/*Mean*

Old Jack Stropper Blues (take 2)/*Old Black Mary*/*Key To The Bushes Blues*/*Bogy Man Blues*/*Mean Old Master Blues*/*Whistling Woman Blues*/*T.B. Moan*

165 **Memphis Minnie & Kansas Joe 1929–1934: Recordings In Chronological Order, Volume 3, 30 January 1931 to 4 February 1932**
Document DOCD (Au)
I Don't Want That Junk Outa You/*Crazy Cryin' Blues*/*Tricks Ain't Walking No More*/*Don't Bother It*/*Today Today Blues*/*Lay My Money Down (If You Run Around)*/*Hard Down Lie*/*Somebody's Got To Help You* [vocal duet with "Kansas Joe" McCoy]/*Pickin'*/*The Blues*/*Let's Go To Town*/*Soo Cow Soo*/*After While Blues*/*Fishin' Blues*/*Jailhouse Trouble Blues*/*Outdoor Blues*/*Where Is My Good Man*/*You Stole My Cake* [vocal duet with "Kansas Joe" McCoy]/*Kind Treatment Blues*/*You Know You Done Me Wrong* ["Kansas Joe" McCoy, vocal]/*Joilet Bound* ["Kansas Joe" McCoy, vocal]/*Stranger's Blues* ["Kansas Joe" McCoy, vocal]/*Socket Blues*

166 **Lucille Bogan (Bessie Jackson): Complete Recorded Works In Chronological Order, Volume 2, March 1930 to 20 July 1933**
Blues Documents BDCD 6037 (Au)
They Ain't Walking No More/*Dirty Treatin' Blues*/*Sloppy Drunk Blues*/*Alley Boogie*/*Crawlin' Lizard Blues*/*Struttin' My Stuff*/*Black Angel Blues*/*Tricks Ain't Walking No More*; [Bessie Jackson], *Red Cross Man*/*T & N O Blues*/*My Baby Come Back*/*Forty-Two Hundred Blues*/*Walkin' Blues*/*House Top Blues*/*Baking Powder Blues*/*Groceries On The Shelf*/*Seaboard Blues*/*Roll And Rattler*/*Superstitious Blues (Hooch House Blues)*/*Mean Twister*/*Troubled Mind*/*New Muscle Shoals Blues*

167 **Ladies Sing The Blues**
Various Artists
ASV Living Era CD AJA 5092 (UK)
Adelaide Hall, *The Blues I Love To Sing*; Mildred Bailey, *Downhearted Blues*; Una Mae Carlisle, *Hangover Blues*; Lizzie Miles, *My Man O' War*/*Electrician Blues*; Laura Smith, *Don't You Leave Me Here*; Ida Cox, *Hard Time Blues*/*Take Him Off My Mind*; Ada Brown, *Evil Mama Blues*/*Break O' Day Blues*; Trixie Smith, *Freight Train Blues*; Victoria Spivey, *Moaning The Blues*; Billie Holiday, *Billie's Blues*/*Long Gone Blues*; Rosetta Howard, *Let You Linen Hang Low*/*Rosetta Blues*; Sippie Wallace, *I'm A Mighty Tight Woman*; Mamie Smith, *Goin' Crazy With The Blues*; Lillian Glinn, *Cravin' A Man Blues*; Clara Smith, *Jelly, Jelly, Look What You Done, Done*; Ma Rainey, *Booze And Blues*/*Toad Frog Blues*; Bessie Smith, *Empty Bed Blues* Part 1/*Empty Bed Blues* Part 2/*St. Louis Blues*

(ii) From Blues (and Jazz) to Soul

The 1940s and early 1950s were fruitful years for four singers whose voices were characterized by a nasal twang, delicate vibrato, and "vulnerable-girl" quality. Helen Humes (**188/9**, **295**, **313**), Lil Green (**187**, **288**), Dinah Washington (**168**, **283**), and Ella Johnson (**289**), however, had personal styles that allowed each to make a distinct contribution to the blues idiom. From this era likewise came Esther Phillips (**199**, **305**), Big Maybelle (**169**, **290**), Ruth Brown (**192**), and Big Mama Thornton (**198**, **467**), with their dynamic voices and styling. The singing of all these women was distinguished by bold attack, sensuous vibrato, and hard driving rhythms, coupled with razor-sharp articulation. They sang in clubs and dance halls and theaters that featured live acts along with the movies.

These Rhythm and Blues vocalists inherited the legacy of Bessie Smith and Ma Rainey, which they transformed while adapting to the modern big-city lifestyles of post-war America. Rhythm and Blues was emphatically music validated by black people in cities as well as small town and rural areas. The elegant vaudeville blues queens wrapped in beaded satins and feathers were replaced by saucy, sultry sisters in bouffant hairdos and skin-tight strapless miniskirts or trousers. The music reflected these cultural and social changes.

Dinah Washington (Ruth Jones) gained her earliest singing experience in black church music—a familiar training ground for many similar performers. By the middle of World War II, however, she had switched to secular music and made her first records for Keynote in 1943 with a group led by Lionel Hampton—she was working with his band. She was then aged 19 and these recordings establish her early competence as a blues singer at the start of a dazzling career.

Washington is a special example of the process by which woman singers became Rhythm and Blues stars and branched into other musical domains with facility. **First Issue: The Dinah Washington Story** features a good mix of blues ballads and jazz recorded between 1943 and 1961. The all-star ensembles that accompany her include Hampton (who gave her the first major break), Tab Smith, Cootie Williams, Teddy Stewart, and Jimmy Cobb.

Arranged chronologically, the first disc in this two-CD compilation includes two of the Keynote tracks—*Evil Gal Blues* and *Salty Papa*—and continues with a series of selections from 1946 to 1954, with blues and standards in which the empathy between singer and accompanists is a particular feature. Whether on *Evil Gal* or *It Isn't Fair*, Washington's incredible range, sense of timing and flexible timbral variations provide tension-filled performances.

One blues of particular interest is that concerning a ban on recording by the American Federation of Musicians which took place in 1948. *Record Ban Blues* (1947) explains the expected effect on popular vocalists such as Washington in reducing the momentum of their releases. This is the only purely topical item in the collection, *T.V. Is The Thing This Year* (1953) being a *double entendre* piece. By 1954

Dinah had changed the emphasis in her recordings to mainstream popular songs, although her audience remained predominantly black. There is a stimulating extended version of Irving Berlin's *Blue Skies* from this year and the second disc begins with a moving performance of Cole Porter's *Love For Sale*. The rest of the CD contains more of this fare and only one blues—a 1957 version of Bessie Smith's *Back Water Blues*, dedicated to its composer (who wrote and recorded the song just before the Mississippi River Flood of 1927). *Crazy He Calls Me* (1954) is in the style of Billie Holiday, with small jazz band backing, but by the late 1950s many of Dinah's recordings were featuring lush string accompaniments. Her big record in this respect, which sold well to black and white purchasers, was *What A Diff'rence A Day Made*. This was cut in 1959 along with her much more satisfying duets with Brook Benton, *Baby, You've Got What It Takes* and *A Rockin' Good Way*. Friendly rivalry between the singers enhances both performances.

By the end of the 1950s the trends in black music represented in this disc had reached their zenith. Washington claimed she could sing anything and was employed to sing ballad-like songs or pieces for the rock 'n' roll audience. Blues had become a far less significant aspect of secular repertoire, which was turning to "soul" for its inspiration.

These tendencies consolidated developments that followed the decline in popularity of vaudeville women blues singers in the late 1920s. Aspirant black women vocalists of this type were just as likely to sing jazz or mainstream popular music as they were blues. Usually their credentials included church music experience and this was the case with "Big Maybelle" Smith, whose recording career began soon after that of Dinah Washington.

A major force at the peak of the R & B years in the 1950s, Big Maybelle's best recordings are included in **The Complete OKeh Sessions 1952–55**. She uses her big voice remarkably as she glides easily from deep preacher-like growls to bouncy shouts, then purrs and squeals in delight in up-beat numbers. These characteristics are evident in all the recordings in this compilation.

Her first two sessions for OKeh took place in October 1952 and comprise the first six titles on the CD. With backing by a band directed by Leroy Kirkland, and featuring the tenor saxophone of Sam "The Man" Taylor, they are of a uniformly high quality. *Gabbin' Blues* is particularly interesting in that Maybelle sings responses in slow tempo to the spoken jibes of another woman. This is an outstanding performance, as is *Rain Down Rain* with its moody lyrics and dramatic imitation of a storm by the band.

For her third OKeh session, in June 1953, Brownie McGhee took over duties on guitar (it had been played by James Cannaday on the earlier sides). This gives a mellow sound to the four performances in which *Jinny Mule* (with the band imitating the sound of the animal) and the sultry *Maybelle's Blues* are superlative. *Send For Me* is an adaptation of the familiar gospel piece *Stand By Me*

There were three sessions in 1954, the first two with Danny Mendelsohn as leader and all featuring the ringing guitar of Mickey Baker. *You'll Never Know*, Maybelle's first ballad in this series of recordings, was cut at the initial session of 1954, which also included the moody *No More Trouble Out Of Me* and *My Big Mistake*—the latter being an adaptation of Roosevelt Sykes' 1938 recording *Mistake In Life*. Two more sentimental ballads were cut at the next session, but *I'm Gettin' 'Long Alright* and the part-spoken *Hair Dressin' Women* are blues. Leroy Kirkland returned as leader for the final session of 1954 and this produced four more high-class sides, the introspective *Ain't To Be Played With* being particularly impressive, as is the raucous *One Monkey Don't Stop No Show*.

There was a change in emphasis at Big Maybelle's final OKeh session (1955). Quincy Jones was the band leader and arranger and the repertoire changed to more fashionable rhythmic music, including a version of *Whole Lot Of Shakin' Goin' On*. Maybelle's subsequent career (for other labels) continued in this manner, and included jazz interpretations.

The daughter of a famous preacher, Aretha Franklin made her first recordings as a member of her father's church around 1956. In this, like Dinah Washington and Big Maybelle, she followed the established pattern for black women singers who turned to secular music for their livelihood. Signed by Columbia in 1960, she was not yet 20 when she made the earliest of her recordings in **Aretha Franklin: Jazz To Soul**. A superior vocalist and interpreter, she demonstrates her command of voice, text, and music throughout the collection. Gospel shouts, with octave leaps and melismatic attacks, enhance and intensify hard-rocking as well as tender pensive songs.

As the title of Columbia's two-CD set implies, the label's policy in recording their young performer was to develop her potential as a singer of jazz and popular music, with only occasional glimpses of the vocal range founded in church experience. Undoubtedly, their models were singers such as Billie Holiday (*God Bless The Child*) and the later sides by Dinah Washington—several songs were recorded for a tribute LP made after Dinah's death in 1963, and are drawn from this aspect of Washington's repertoire. There were also covers of contemporary hits such as Dionne Warwick's *Walk On By* and Inez and Charlie Foxx's *Mockingbird*—all cut in 1964.

The compilation concludes in October 1965 (*Until You Were Gone*); just over a year before Aretha left Columbia for Atlantic and began a series of soul recordings that established her international reputation. In addition to the jazz and popular-orientated tracks, there are also examples of her soul singing, and the occasional blues. It is in this respect that the CDs are important, for they exemplify the way in which a key 1960s singer represents the transition from 1950s R & B to the gospel-tinged soul that has become the standard bearer for secular black music in the United States.

Links with blues are apparent in *Today I Sing The Blues*, from her first session in August 1960. They are also represented in *Muddy Water* and the emotive version of Richard M. Jones' *Trouble In Mind* (from February 1965). Aretha plays her own piano on *Maybe I'm A Fool* (1961), an attribute she shares with some of the woman blues singers of the 1920s, such as Sippie Wallace, or her niece Hociel Thomas, and fellow Texan Victoria Spivey. This gospel-flavored piece is an example of Franklin's precocious soul style, as is the earlier *Won't Be Long* (November 1960), in which the blues undergird her delivery as she caresses each note. Two sessions in 1964 also produce high-class soul. *Soulville* and *Lee Cross* were cut in February, and at the end of the year she recorded *Take It Like You Give It* (her own composition), *Can't You Just See Me* and *Bit Of Soul*. In the latter she complains "If I don't get me a hit soon, I won't be here long", but during her tenure with Columbia she never achieved the popularity that was to become the hallmark of her days with Atlantic. Blues have remained in her repertoire, but the secularization of gospel music is the core of her success, as it has been with black woman singers since the 1960s.

Essential Records

168 **First Issue: The Dinah Washington Story (the original recordings)**
Dinah Washington
Mercury 314 514841-2/514841-2 (UK)—*2 CD set*
DISC ONE: *Evil Gal Blues/Salty Papa Blues/Embraceable You/A Slick Chick (On The Mellow Side)/Postman Blues/That's Why A Woman Loves A Heel/Walkin' And Talkin'/Record Ban Blues/(What Can I Say Dear) After I Say I'm Sorry?/I'll Wait/Good Daddy Blues/I Only Know/Baby Get Lost/It Isn't Fair/I'll Never Be Free/I Wanna Be Loved/Time Out For Tears/I Won't Cry Anymore/New Blowtop Blues/Wheel Of Fortune/Trouble In Mind/I Cried For You/T.V. Is The Thing This Year/Am I Blue?/Blue Skies*

DISC TWO: *Love For Sale/I've Got You Under My Skin/I Don't Hurt Anymore/Crazy He Calls Me/Lover Come Back To Me/Teach Me Tonight/Blue Gardenia/Smoke Gets In Your Eyes/If I Had You/Sometimes I'm Happy/Keepin' Out Of*

Mischief Now/Back Water Blues/All Of Me/What A Diff'rence A Day Made/ Unforgettable/Baby, You've Got What It Takes [duet with Brook Benton]/*A Rockin' Good Way (To Mess Around And Fall In Love)* [duet with Brook Benton]/*A Bad Case Of The Blues/This Bitter Earth/September In The Rain/ Mad About The Boy*

169 **The Complete OKeh Sessions 1952–55**
Big Maybelle
Epic/OKeh/Legacy EK 53471
Just Want Your Love/So Good To My Baby/Gabbin' Blues (Don't Run My Business)/My Country Man/Rain Down Rain/Way Back Home/Please Stay Away From My Sam/Jinny Mule/Send For Me/Maybelle's Blues/I've Got A Feelin'/You'll Never Know/No More Trouble Out Of Me/My Big Mistake/Ain't No Use/I'm Gettin' 'Long Alright/You'll Be Sorry/Hair Dressin' Women/One Monkey Don't Stop No Show/Don't Leave Poor Me/Ain't To Be Played With/ New Kind Of Mambo/Ocean Of Tears/Whole Lot Of Shakin' Goin' On/The Other Night/Such A Cutie

170 **Aretha Franklin: Jazz To Soul**
Columbia C2K 48515—2 CD set
DISC ONE: *Today I Sing The Blues/(Blue) By Myself/Maybe I'm A Fool/All Night Long/Blue Holiday/Nobody Like You/Sweet Lover/Just For A Thrill/If Ever I Would Leave You/Once In A While/This Bitter Earth/God Bless The Child/ Skylark/Muddy Water/Drinking Again/What A Difference A Day Makes/Unforgettable/Love For Sale/Misty/Impossible/This Could Be The Start Of Something*

DISC TWO: *Won't Be Long/Operation Heartbreak/Soulville/Runnin' Out Of Fools/Trouble In Mind/Walk On By/Every Little Bit Hurts/Mockingbird/You'll Lose A Good Thing/Cry Like A Baby/Take It Like You Give It/Land Of Dreams/Can't You Just See Me/(No, No) I'm Losing You/Bit Of Soul/Why Was I Born?/Until You Were Gone/Lee Cross*

Basic Records

(i) "Classic" and "Down-home" Singers

171 **Classic Blues Women: Blues Masters, Volume 11**
Various Artists
Rhino R2 71134
Mamie Smith, *Crazy Blues*; Eva Taylor, *Papa De-Da-Da*; Trixie Smith, *My Man Rocks Me (With One Steady Roll)/Railroad Blues*; Ma Rainey, *Yonder Come The Blues/Countin' The Blues/Daddy Goodbye Blues*; Sippie Wallace, *Baby I Can't Use You No More*; Ida Cox, *Bone Orchard Blues*; Bessie Smith *Nobody Knows You When You're Down And Out*; Mary Johnson, *Barrel House Flat Blues*, Margaret Johnson, *When A 'Gator Holler, Folks Say It's A Sign Of Rain*; Victoria Spivey, *Any-Kind-A-Man*; Alberta Hunter, *You Can't Tell The Difference After Dark*; Edith Johnson, *Little Drops Of Water*; Billie & Dee Dee Pierce, *Married Man Blues/Careless Love*; Billie Holiday, *Stormy Blues*

From the seminal *Crazy Blues* (1920), this CD surveys a decade of popular singers. *My Man Rocks Me* (1922) epitomizes the era; other songs adapt traditional motifs, as in *Railroad Blues* (1925) and *When A Gator Holler* (1926). Wallace's side ranks with those of Cox, Rainey, and Bessie Smith. Hunter and Spivey feature recordings from the 1930s; Holiday and Billie Pierce were cut in 1954, and Edith Johnson in 1961.

172 **Young Alberta Hunter: The '20s & '30s** [also ca. 1946]
Jass J-CD-6
You Can't Tell The Difference After Dark/Second Hand Man/Send Me A Man/ Chirpin' The Blues/Down Hearted Blues (recorded 1939)/*I'll See You Go/Fine And Mellow/Yelpin' The Blues/Someday Sweetheart/The Love I Have For You/ My Castle's Rockin'/Boogie Woogie Swing/I Won't Let You Down/Take Your Big Hands Off* (recorded ca. 1946)/*He's Got A Punch Like Joe Louis* (recorded ca. 1946)/*How Long Sweet Daddy How Long/Down Hearted Blues* (recorded 1922)/*Gonna Have You Ain't Gonna Leave You Alone/You Can Have My Man If He Comes To See You Too/Bring It With You When You Come/Nobody Knows The Way I Feel Dis Mornin'/Early Every Morn/I'm Going To See My Man*
Hunter's first recording was *How Long*, here featured together with the original *Down Hearted Blues.* Backed by Louis Armstrong, *Nobody Knows* is infused with invective and moaning. Fats Waller plays organ on *I'm Going To See My Man.* The recordings of the 1930s maintain this quality, as do the sides of ca. 1946 for Juke Box.

173 **Clara Smith: Complete Recorded Works In Chronological Order, Volume 5, 1927–1929**
Document DOCD 5368 (Au)
Black Cat Moan/Strugglin' Woman's Blues/Jelly Look What You Done Done/ It's All Coming Home To You/Gin Mill Blues/Steamboat Man Blues/Sobbin' Sister Blues/Got My Mind On That Thing/Wanna Go Home/Ain't Got Nobody To Grind My Coffee/Tell Me When/Empty House Blues/Daddy Don't Put That Thing On Me Blues/It's Tight Like That/Papa I Don't Need You Now/Tired Of The Way You Do/Oh! Mr. Mitchell/Where Is My Man?/You Can't Stay Here No More/Let's Get Loose
Billed as "Queen of the Moaners", Clara was second in popularity only to Bessie. Generally to small-band backing, she sang dirges, vaudeville, and hokum pieces impressively, as in *Sobbin' Sister, It's Tight Like That, Oh! Mr. Mitchell,* and *Let's Get Loose.* Texts usually deal with human predicaments, including superstition.

174 **Bessie Smith: The Complete Recordings, Volume 4**
Columbia C2K 52838/472934-2 (UK)—*2 CD set*
DISC ONE: *Standin' In The Rain Blues/It Won't Be You/Spider Man Blues/Empty Bed Blues* Part 1/*Empty Bed Blues* Part 2/*Put It Right Here (Or Keep It Out There)/Yes Indeed He Do!/Devil's Gonna Git You/You Ought To Be Ashamed/ Washwoman's Blues/Slow And Easy Man/Poor Man's Blues/Please Help Me Get Him Out Of My Mind/Me And My Gin/I'm Wild About That Thing/You've Got To Give Me Some/Kitchen Man/I've Got What It Takes (But It Breaks My Heart To Give It Away)/Nobody Knows You When You're Down And Out/Take It Right Back ('Cause I Don't Want It Here)*

DISC TWO: *He's Got Me Goin'/It Makes My Love Come Down/Wasted Life Blues/Dirty No-Gooder's Blues/Blue Spirit Blues/Worn Out Papa Blues/You Don't Understand/Don't Cry Baby/Keep It To Yourself/New Orleans Hop Scop Blues/See If I'll Care/Baby Have Pity On Me/On Revival Day (A Rhythmic Spiritual/Moan, You Moaners/Hustlin' Dan/Black Mountain Blues/In The House Blues/Long Old Road/Blue Blues/Shipwreck Blues*
This selection ranges from 1928 to 1931 and epitomizes a vaudeville blues queen's repertoire. The Depression "anthem" *Down And Out* is a particular highlight, alongside the two-part *Empty Bed.* The Bessemer Singers join for two impressions of revival singing, and on *Keep It To Yourself* and *Hop Scop* Bessie sounds like a bright Ma Rainey.

175 Bertha "Chippie" Hill: Complete Recorded Works 1925–1929 In Chronological Order
Document DOCD 5330 (Au)
Low Land Blues/Kid Man Blues/Lonesome, All Alone And Blue/Trouble In Mind (9510)/*Georgia Man/Leavenworth Blues/Panama Limited Blues/Street Walker Blues/Pleadin' For The Blues/Pratt City Blues* (9950)/*Mess, Katie, Mess/ Lovesick Blues/Lonesome Weary Blues/Do Dirty Blues/Sport Model Mama/ Some Cold Rainy Day/Weary Money Blues/Hard Time Blues/Christmas Man Blues/Trouble In Mind* (C-2509)/*Hangman Blues*; Scrapper Blackwell & The Two Roys with "Chippie" Hill, *Non-Skid Tread*; Bertha "Chippie" Hill, *I Ain't Gonna Do It No More/Pratt City Blues* (C-3133)
The first 15 selections feature piano by Richard M. Jones. Ten are embellished by the cornet of Louis Armstrong, which enhances Chippie's resplendent diction and attack. Most later tracks feature Tampa Red (slide guitar) and Georgia Tom (piano). *Non-Skid Tread* is superior hokum and the second *Pratt City* is propelled by Bill Johnson's rhythmic bass.

176 St. Louis Girls: The Complete Recorded Works In Chronological Order of Katherine Baker, Lizzie Washington, Elizabeth Washington And The Remaining Two Titles of Johnnie Strauss 1927–1934
Document DOCD 5182 (Au)
Katherine Baker, *Chicago Fire Blues/Don't Think That You Got Your Man All By Yourself/My Man Let Me Be Blues/I Helped You, Sick Man, When You Were Sick And Down/Wild Women Blues/Daddy Sunshine Blues/Mistreated Blues/Money Women Blues*; Lizzie Washington, *Ease Away Blues/Skeleton Key Blues/East Coast Blues/My Low Down Brown/Working Man Blues/Fall Or Summer Blues/Lord Have Mercy Blues/Mexico Blues/Sport Model Mama Blues/ Brick Flat Blues/Daddy Threw Me Down Blues/Whiskey Head Blues/Every Day Blues*; Elizabeth Washington, *Riot Call Blues/You Put That Thing On Me*; Johnnie Strauss, *Hard Working Woman/St. Louis Johnnie Blues*
Baker and Washington express their vivid low-life lyrics laconically, but Washington's voice has a richer timbre. A versatile four-man group accompanies, including Lonnie Johnson (1927). *Whiskey Head* and *Every Day* feature a St Louis pianist (1929), alongside *Riot Call* and *You Put That Thing On Me* (1933, another player, and possibly singer). Strauss' deep contralto is impressive (1934).

177 **Lillian Glinn: Complete Recorded Works In Chronological Order 1927–1929**

Document DOCD 5184 (Au)

All Alone And Blue/Come Home Daddy/Doggin' Me Blues/Brown Skin Blues/The Man I Love Is Worth Talking About/Best Friend Blues/Lost Letter Blues/Packing House Blues/Shake It Down/Where Have All The Black Men Gone/I'm A Front Door Woman With A Back Door Man/Atlanta Blues/All The Week Blues/Cannon Ball Blues/Wobble It A Little Daddy/Black Man Blues/I'm Through (Shedding Tears Over You)/I Love That Thing/Don't Leave Me Daddy/Shreveport Blues/Moanin' Blues/Cravin' A Man

Born in Dallas and member of a provincial church, Glinn was sponsored by Hattie Burleson (blues singer and promoter, credited "composer" on the first four tracks). For just over two years her majestic voice and original songs were recorded regularly, in Dallas, New Orleans, or Atlanta. Small-band accompanists reflect these different locations.

178 **Ivy Smith & Cow Cow Davenport: Complete Recorded Works In Chronological Order 1927–1930**

Blues Documents BDCD 6039 (Au)

Ivy Smith, *Rising Sun Blues/Sad And Blue/My Own Man Blues/Third Alley Blues/Ninety Nine Years Blues/Cincinnati Southern Blues/Too Mean To Cry Blues/Barrel House Mojo/Shadow Blues/No Good Man Blues/Gin House Blues*; Ivy Smith & Charlie Davenport, *Mistreated Mama Blues* (vocal duet); Ivy Smith, *Doin' That Thing* (vocal trio)/*Somebody's Got To Knock A Jug* (vocal trio)/*Southern High Water Blues/Wringin' And Twistin' Papa/Got Jelly On My Mind/Gypsy Woman Blues/Milkman Blues*; Cow Cow Davenport & Iva [*sic*] Smith, *Aabammy Mistreated* (vocal duet)

Smith became a vaudeville partner of Davenport, piano blues pioneer from Alabama (**214**). Many of her mournful songs are virtually whined to somber accompaniment. Exceptions include *Barrel House Mojo* (with Davenport's proto piano-boogie motifs), showtime vocal duets and trios, and *Wringin' And Twistin' Papa.*

179 **Elzadie Robinson: Complete Recorded Works In Chronological Order 1928–1929, Volume 2; [plus] Lottie Beaman, Alternate Takes, 1924**

Document DOCD 5249 (Au)

Elzadie Robinson, *Pleading Misery Blues/Mad Blues/Wicked Daddy/It's Too Late Now/Arkansas Mill Blues/Gold Mansion Blues/Rowdy Man Blues* (take 1)/*Rowdy Man Blues* (take 2)/*Going South Blues/Need My Lovin' Need My Daddy/Unsatisfied Blues/This Is Your Last Night With Me/Cheatin' Daddy/My Pullman Porter/Driving Me South/Past And Future Blues/Ain't Got Nobody*; Lottie Beaman, *Regular Man Blues/Honey Blues/Red River Blues/Sugar Daddy Blues/Low Down Painful Blues/Mama Can't Lose*

Beaman was from Kansas City (**73**). Robinson makes reference to greater-Texas locations and is believed to be from the region. Often accompanied by pianist Will Ezell (possibly from the same area—**213**), she almost weeps as she sings. *Arkansas Mill, Rowdy Man, This Is Your Last Night With Me*, and *Past And Future Blues* are particularly effective.

180 Honey Dripper Blues
Edith Johnson
Agram Blues AB 2016 (Neth)
You Ain't Good Blues/You Know That Ain't Right; Roosevelt Sykes, *Fire Detective Blues*; Edith Johnson, *Nickles Worth Of Liver/Good Chib Blues/Can't Make Another Day/Honey Dripper Blues* (15561); Roosevelt Sykes, *Little Sow Blues/Single Tree Blues*; Edith Johnson, *Honey Dripper Blues No. 2/That's My Man/Eight Hour Woman/Nickles Worth Of Liver Blues No. 2/Honey Dripper Blues* (KC 588)/*Loving That Man Blues/Ain't No More To Be Said/Heart Aching Blues/Drive My Baby Slow/Interview*
Wife of Jesse Johnson, a St Louis talent scout, promoter and music shop owner, Edith displays knowledge of urban low life in her lyrics that belies her sonorous delivery. Accompanists include Roosevelt Sykes, Count Basie, or herself on piano, Baby James (cornet) and Ike Rodgers (trombone). The recordings from 1928–9 are supplemented by *Drive My Baby Slow* (1961) and an interview.

181 Kansas City Kitty & Georgia Tom: Complete Recorded Works In Chronological Order 1930–1934
Blues Documents BDCD 6023 (Au)
You Got That Stuff/The Doctor's Blues/Do It By Myself/Fish House Blues/Room Rent Blues/Show Me What You Got/Killing Floor Blues/How Can You Have The Blues?/Who's Been Here Since I Been Gone?/"Gym's" Too Much For Me/When Can I Get It?/That Thing's A Mess/Root Man Blues/Close Made Papa/Scronchin'/What A Fool I've Been; Kansas City Kitty, *Christmas Morning Blues/Double Trouble Blues/Leave My Man Alone/Mistreatin' Easy Rider*
Georgia Tom (Dorsey), pianist and composer, stamped his personality on Chicago blues of the 1920s. These vocal duets with "Kitty" (probably Mozelle Alderson) parallel recordings with the Famous Hokum Boys (**272**) and are risqué "good-time" pieces. In contrast, her sombre versions of *Christmas Morning* and *Double Trouble* (recorded in 1934) decry this light-voiced flippancy.

182 Lil Johnson: Complete Recorded Works In Chronological Order, Volume 1, 23 April 1929–22 April 1936
Document DOCD 5307 (Au)
Minor Blues [Mama Blues]/Never Let Your Left Hand Know What Your Right Hand Do/You'll Never Miss Your Jelly Roll Till Your Jelly Roller's Gone/House Rent Scuffle/Rock That Thing/Get 'Em From The Peanut Man (Hot Nuts) (980163-A)/*Anybody Want To Buy My Cabbage?/Shake Man Blues/Evil Man Blues/Keep On Knocking/I Lost My Baby/If You Can Dish It (I Can Take It)/I'm Bettin' On You/Press My Button (Ring My Bell)/Take It Easy Greasy/You Can't Bet On Love/That Bonus Done Got Thru* (take 1)/*That Bonus Done Got Thru* (take 2)/*Winner Joe (The Knock Out King)/Get 'Em From The Peanut Man (The New Hot Nuts)* (C-1288-1)/*Sam—The Hot Dog Man/Rag Cutter's Function/Honey You're So Good To Me*
The emphasis on sensual lyrics does not detract from Johnson's vivacious, full-voiced singing to spirited accompaniments by skilled pianists. Montana Taylor is notable on the plaintive *Minor Blues* and Charles Avery enhances *House Rent Scuffle*. Topicality is served by *That Bonus* (soldiers) and *Winner Joe* (Louis), in which Black Bob's piano is to the fore.

183 Victoria Spivey: Complete Recorded Works In Chronological Order, Volume 3, 1 October 1929 to 7 July 1936

Document DOCD 5318 (Au)

Blood Hound Blues/Dirty T.B. Blues/Moaning The Blues/Telephoning The Blues/New York Blues/Lonesome With The Blues/Showered With The Blues/Haunted By The Blues; Victoria Spivey & Harold Grey [Porter Grainger], *You've Gotta Have What It Takes* Part 1/*You've Gotta Have What It Takes* Part 2/*Baulin' Water Blues* Part 2; Magnolia Harris [probably Victoria Spivey] & Howling [J.T] Smith, *Mama's Quittin And Leaving* Part 1/*Mama's Quittin And Leavin* Part 2; Victoria Spivey, *Nebraska Blues/He Want's Too Much/Low Down Man Blues/Don't Trust Nobody Blues*; Victoria Spivey With Hunter's Serenaders, *Dreaming About My Man*; Victoria Spivey & Dot Scott's Rhythm Dukes, *Sweet Pease*; Original Victoria Spivey & Her Hallelujah Boys, *Black Snake Swing/I'll Never Fall In Love Again*; Victoria Spivey & Dot Scott's Rhythm Dukes, *TB's Got Me*

Spivey's personality, lyrics, and musical competence attracted gifted instrumentalists. The first four recordings, with Luis Russell's band, are scintillating, but duets with Grainger disconcert. If she is Harris, those with Smith (vocal/guitar) maintain the quality of those with Lonnie Johnson (**241**, **271**). *Nebraska* and *Don't Trust Nobody* are among the highlights.

184 Jailhouse Blues: Women's A Capella Songs From The Parchman Penitentiary, Library Of Congress Field Recordings, 1936 And 1939

Various Artists

Rosetta Records RR1316—LP

Mattie Mae Thomas, *Dangerous Blues*; Josephine Douglas & Group, *Noah Built The Ark*; Mattie Mae Thomas, *Workhouse Blues*; Annabell Abrahams & Group, *To Be Sho*; Beatrice Perry, *Levee Camp Blues*; Mary James, *Rabbit On A Log*; Group, *Anybody Here Want To Buy Some Cabbage*; Hattie Goff, *Railroad Man/Mr. Dooley Don't 'Rest Me*; Josephine Parker, *How'm I Doin' It/I Gotta Man In New Orleans*; Bettie Mae Bowman & Group, *Last Month Of The Year*; Eva White, *No Mo' Freedom*; Mattie Mae Thomas, *No Mo' Freedom*; Beatrice Perry, Lena Johnson, Mary Parks, *Where Have You Been John Billy*; Elinor Boyer, *Gonna Need My Help Some Day*; Edna Taylor & Group, *Susie Gal*; Group [led by Mary James], *Go 'Way Devil, Leave Me Alone*; Mary James & Group, *Make The Devil Leave Me Alone*; Elizabeth Moore, *Old Apple Tree In The Ground*; Lucille Walker, *Shake 'Em On Down*; Group, *Ricketiest Superintendent*; Mattie Mae Thomas, *Penitentiary Blues*

A total absence of hope and ever-present desolation streams from these solo and group performances, evoking the most dramatic and profound image of the dreaded Mississippi State Penitentiary. These are not simply play-party songs, hollers, and blues but the lifeline of rural women who sang them to hold on to their sanity.

185 Female Chicago Blues: Complete Recorded Works In Chronological Order, 1936–1947

Various Artists

Document DOCD 5295 (Au)

The Yas Yas Girl [Merline Johnson], *Froggy Bottom/Blues Before Daybreak/*

Two By Four Blues/Fighting Man Blues/Good Old Easy Street/How Can I Go On/Bad Whiskey Blues; Billie [Willie Mae] McKenzie, *Romeo And Juliet/That Man On The W.P.A./I'd Rather Drink Muddy Water/Get Business On Your Mind/Little Red Wagon/Oh Babe!/I'm Getting Even With You/If You Can Dish It No. 2 (I Can Take It)/Woke Up With The Rising Sun/Papa Don't Hold On Me*; Clara Morris, *Cry On Daddy/I Stagger In My Sleep/I'm Blue Daddy/Poker Playing Daddy*; Trixie Butler, *Take It Easy Greasy/You Got The Right Key/Just A Good Woman Through With The Blues*

Accompanied by Black Bob (piano), Butler sings with vaudeville ostentation (1936). McKenzie (1936–7) mixes bawdy and reflective songs to piano, and a small band (on some tracks). Her vocals are less theatrical, as are those of Morris (to piano and guitar, 1941). Johnson performs contemporary repertoire (1941, with piano and bass), plus *Bad Whiskey* (1947, with small band).

186 Memphis Minnie: Complete Recorded Works 1935–1941 In Chronological Order, Volume 5, 27 June 1940 to 12 December 1941

Blues Documents BDCD 6012 (Au)

Lonesome Shack Blues/Nothing In Rambling/Boy Friend Blues/Finger Print Blues/It's Hard To Please My Man/Ma Rainey/In My Girlish Days/Me And My Chauffeur Blues/Down By The Riverside/I Got To Make A Change Blues/Pig Meat On The Line/My Gage Is Going Up/This Is Your Last Chance/Can't Afford To Lose My Man/I'm Not A Bad Gal/You Got To Get Out Of Here/Don't Turn The Card/Looking The World Over/It Was You Baby/You Need A Friend/I Am Sailin'/Remember Me Blues; Little Son Joe [Ernest Lawlers—(Mr. Memphis Minnie)], *Black Rat Swing/Just Had To Holler*

Standing between "down-home" reflection and urbane declamation, these sessions represent another recording peak. *Nothing In Rambling* recalls past life, and *Ma Rainey* is a panegyric in which Minnie is left "to carry the good works on." This she does to effect, accompanied throughout by Little Son Joe on second guitar (including his two vocals).

187 Why Don't You Do Right? 1940–1942

Lil Green

Blues Collection 15821-2 (Fr)

Romance In The Dark/Just Rockin'/Cherry Tree Blues/What Have I Done?/Give Your Mama One Smile/My Mellow Man/Knockin' Myself Out/I Won't Sell My Love/Why Don't You Do Right/What's The Matter With Love/Love Me/ Country Boy Blues/How Can I Go On?/Hello Babe/If I Didn't Love You/ Because I Love My Daddy So/I'm Going To Start A Racket/99 Blues/Don't Know What I Will Do/You Got Me To The Place/If You Wan't To Share Your Love/If I'm A Fool/I'm Wasting My Time On You

Drawn from RCA-Bluebird recordings, these examples of Green's entreating style seem perfect in partnership with the lyrics to her *Romance In The Dark* and *Knockin' Myself Out*. *Why Don't You Do Right* is adapted from Joe McCoy's *Weed Smoker's Dream* (**273**). McCoy and Big Bill Broonzy provide other compositions and Broonzy's guitar enhances every track.

(ii) From Blues (and Jazz) to Soul

188/9 **Sammy Price And The Blues Singers**
Various Artists
Wolf WBJ CD-007 (Au)—*4 CD set*
DISC ONE: Bea Booze, *Mr. Freddie Blues/Gulf Coast Blues*; Lee Brown, *Moanin' Dove/New Little Girl, Little Girl*; Lether McGraw, *Do Your Duty/Low Down Dirty Groundhog*; Peetie Wheatstraw, *Possum Den Blues* (take A)/*A Working Man's Blues*; Harlem Stompers [Hester Lancaster, vocal], *The Monkey Swing/ My Understanding Man*; Georgia White, *Married Woman Blues/How Do You Think I Feel*; Johnnie Temple, *Good Suzie (Rusty Knees)/Stick Up Woman (Let Me Make This Trip With You)*; James Carter, *Death Letter Blues/Death Cell Blues*; Sweet Georgia Brown, *Rock Me In The Groove/These Low Down Men Blues*; Bea Booze, *If I'm A Fool/I Love To Georgia Brown So Slow*; Albina Jones, *Give It Up Daddy Blues*; Sam Price Trio, *Sammy's Boogie/ Frenchy's Blues*; Herman Ray, *Working Man (Doing The Best I Can)*

DISC TWO: NoraLee King, *Let Me Rock You Home/Why Don't You Do Right*; Yack Taylor, *My Mellow Man/Knockin' Myself Out*; Ebony Three, *Swing Low Sweet Chariot/Go Down Moses*; Ruby Smith, *Make Me Love You/Fruit Cakin' Mama*; Bea Foote, *Try And Get It/I Want A Long Time Daddy*; Pete Brown & His Band [Helen Humes, vocal], *Mound Bayou/Unlucky Woman (Unlucky Blues)*; Ruby Smith, *Black Gal/Thinking Blues*; Randy Brooks Orchestra, *After Hours*; Albina Jones, *The Rain Is Falling/Papa Tree Top Blues*; Sam Price Trio, *Eiffel Tower/Low Down Blues*; Herman Ray, *President's Blues*; Scat Man Bailey, *My Oh My/Raindrop Blues*

DISC THREE: Georgia White, *Fire In The Mountain/When The Red Sun Turns To Gray I'll Be Back*; Bea Foote, *Jive Lover*; Peetie Wheatstraw, *Possum Den Blues* (take B); Harlem Stompers [Hester Lancaster, vocal], *Jammin' In Georgia*; Gene Gilmore, *Brown Skin Woman/Charity Blues*; Peetie Wheatstraw, *Easy Way Blues*; Harlem Stompers [Hester Lancaster, vocal], *Serenade To A Jitterbug*; Sweet Georgia Brown *The Lowdown Lonely Blues/Black Cat Bone*; Yack Taylor, *You're Gonna Go Your Way And I'm Gonna Go Mine/ Don't Stop Now*; NoraLee King, *Deep Sea Diver*; Pete Brown & His Band, *Gonna Buy Me A Telephone* [Helen Humes, vocal]/*Cannonball* [NoraLee King, vocal]; Lem Johnson, *Candy Blues*; Bea Booze, *See See Rider/Let's Be Friends*; Albina Jones, *Love Is Such A Mystery*; Clyde Bernard [Bernhardt] *Pretty Mama Blues*

DISC FOUR: Bea Booze, *Uncle Sam Come And Get Him/If I Didn't Love You*; Peetie Wheatstraw, *Machine Gun Blues*; Ebony Three, *Heartbroken Blues*; Johnnie Temple, *Skin And Bone Woman*; NoraLee King, *Love Me*; Effie Scott, *Lonesome Hut Blues/Sunshine Special*; Ebony Three, *Mississippi Moan*; Bea Booze, *Catchin' As Catch Can/War Rationin' Papa*; NoraLee King, *Yump Da Da Da*; Johnnie Temple, *Fireman Blues*; Yack Taylor, *My Nightmare Jockey*; Albina Jones, *I Have A Way Of Lovin'/Song Man/Hole In The Wall*; Sam Price Trio, *Good Paree/Montparnasse*; Herman Ray, *Trouble Blues*; Monette Moore, *Another Woman's Man*; Herman Ray, *I'm A Little Piece Of Leather*; Monette Moore, *Please Mr. Blues*; Sam Price & His Rockin' Rhythm, *Ain't Nobody's Business/Back Street*

Price's role as a piano accompanist is explored, sometimes combined with small bands. Two-thirds of the recordings involve women singers, including his début, with Scott (1929). The remainder date between 1938 and 1950 when he was employed by Decca in New York. They demonstrate changes in fashion as well as unusual configurations, such as the Ebony Three (two women and a man—1938). In addition to such singers of repute as White (1939) and Humes (1942), lesser-known female vocalists also stand out: Foote (1938), McGraw (1939), Taylor (1941), and especially Booze (1942–4). Revival sides by Moore (a 1920s vaudevillian) date from 1947, but Jones (1947–9) represents post-war modernity.

190 Mutt Carey and Lee Collins [accompanists]
Hociel Thomas, Bertha "Chippie" Hill, J.H. Shayne
American Music AMCD 72
Hociel Thomas, *Gambler's Dream/Muddy Water Blues/Go Down Sunshine/ Advice Blues/Barrel House Man/Tebo's Texas Blues* (piano solo)/*Nobody Know's You When You're Down And Out*; Bertha "Chippie" Hill, *Trouble In Mind/Careless Love*; J.H. Shayne, *Mr. Freddy's Rag*; Bertha "Chippie" Hill, *Charleston Blues/How Long, How Long*; J.H. Shayne, *Chestnut Street Boogie*; Bertha "Chippie" Hill, *Steady Roll (Around The Clock)/Nobody Know's You When You're Down And Out*
Niece of Sippie Wallace, Hociel Thomas shows her ability as a singer and Texas pianist (**231**) in these stylish revival recordings (with trumpet by Carey). "Chippie" Hill's sides date from the same year (1946) and show she had lost none of her considerable vocal powers. Piano accompaniment is by Lovie Austin or Shayne; Collins is the trumpeter.

191 Rosetta Howard: Complete Recorded Works 1939–1947, In Chronological Order
RST Records JPCD-1514-2 (Au)
Come Easy Go Easy/My Blues Is Like Whiskey/The Jive Is Here/My Downfall/ Hog-Wild Blues/Plain Lennox Avenue/Men Are Like Street Cars/He's Mine All Mine/Headin' For The River/Ebony Rhapsody/I Keep On Worrying/When I Been Drinking/Help Me Baby/It's Hard To Go Thru Life Alone/Where Shall I Go/Too Many Drivers/Why Be So Blue/Sweep Your Blues Away/It Was You/You Made Me Love You/Plough Hand Blues
Rosetta's two New York sessions (1939) are similar to those with the Harlem Hamfats (1937–8). Starting with *Ebony Rhapsody*, three novel Chicago sets (1947) define war-time stylistic continuities and changes; they are accompanied by the suave Big Three Trio (**274**) or a sophisticated Big Bill Broonzy group (he composed several of her songs). Her self-possessed, mellow contralto stamps its character on each recording.

192 Miss Rhythm (Greatest Hits And More)
Ruth Brown
Atlantic 7-82061-2/Sequel RSDCD 816 (UK)
DISC ONE: *So Long/Hey Pretty Baby* [with Jimmy Brown, vocal]/*I'll Get Along Somehow* Part 1/*I'll Come Back Someday* [with the Delta Rhythm Boys, vocal]/ *Sentimental Journey* [with the Delta Rhythm Boys, vocal]/*R.B. Blues/Teardrops From My Eyes/Standing On The Corner/I'll Wait For You/I Know/Don't Cry/*

The Shrine Of St. Cecilia/It's All For You/Shine On/Be Anything/5–10–15 Hours/Have A Good Time/Daddy Daddy/Mama He Treats Your Daughter Mean/Wild Wild Young Men

DISC TWO: *Ever Since My Baby's Been Gone/Love Contest/Oh What A Dream/ Old Man River/Somebody Touched Me/Mambo Baby/I Can See Everybody's Baby/As Long As I'm Moving/It's Love Baby/I Gotta Have You* [duet with Clyde McPhatter]/*Love Has Joined Us Together* [duet with Clyde McPhatter]/*I Wanna Do More/Lucky Lips/One More Time/This Little Girl's Gone Rockin'/I Can't Hear A Word You Say/I Don't Know/Takin' Care Of Business/Don't Deceive Me*

With popular appeal that rivaled Dinah Washington's, Brown had many R & B chart successes in the 1950s. Her full-blooded vocals are heard to effect in this chronological survey of recordings for Atlantic (1949–60). Repertoire ranges from driving rhythmic numbers to contemplative ballads and blues, all performed with élan.

193 **R & B Dynamite**

Etta James

Fair/Virgin V2-86232-2/Ace CDCH 210 (UK)

W-O-M-A-N/Number One/I'm A Fool/Strange Things Happening/Hey Henry/I Hope You're Satisfied/Good Rockin' Daddy/Sunshine Of Love/That's All/How Big A Fool/Tears Of Joy/The Pick-Up/Market Place/Tough Lover/Do Something Crazy/Be My Lovey Dovey/Nobody Loves You (Like Me)/Hickory Dickory Dock/You Know What I Mean/Roll With Me Henry (or *The Wallflower*)/*Baby, Baby, Every Night/We're In Love*

James' gritty vocals blend gospel with beer-join gravel and conjure dances in smoke-filled clubs. These early West Coast tracks were made between 1954 and 1958 (with one session in New Orleans). They range from salacious (*Wallflower*) to secular copies of Sister Rosetta Tharpe (*Strange Things* and *That's All*) and confirm the explosive title of the disc.

194 **Use What You Got**

Sugar Pie De Santo

Chess CD RED 33 (UK)

[Etta James &] Sugar Pie De Santo, *In The Basement* Part 1; Sugar Pie De Santo [With Pee Wee Kingsley, vocal], *I Want to Know*; Sugar Pie De Santo, *Mama Didn't Raise No Fools/There's Gonna Be Trouble/I Don't Feel Sorry/ Maybe You'll Be There*; [Etta James &] Sugar Pie De Santo, *Do I Make Myself Clear*; Sugar Pie De Santo, *Slip-In Mules/Ask Me/Use What You Got/Can't Let You Go/Soulful Dress/I Don't Wanna Fuss/Going Back To Where I Belong/It Won't Be Long/She's Got Everything/Wish You Were Mine/It's Done And Forgotten/Tell Me What's The Matter/I Still Care/Slip-In Mules* (alternate take)

De Santo's powerful vocals are used to effect in these Checker recordings, which were made on the West Coast or in Chicago between 1959 and 1965. Expressive, self-confident imagery enhances each performance—especially *Soulful Dress, Use What You Got*, and *Slip In Mules* (a hit)—and she equals Etta James' grit in the barnstorming duets.

195 Songs We Taught Your Mother

Alberta Hunter, Lucille Hegammin, and Victoria Spivey

Original Blues Classics OBCCD 520-2

Alberta Hunter, *I Got Myself A Workin' Man*; Lucille Hegammin, *St. Louis Blues*; Victoria Spivey, *Black Snake Blues*; Alberta Hunter, *I Got A Mind To Ramble*; Lucille Hegamin, *You'll Want My Love*; Victoria Spivey, *Going Blues*; Alberta Hunter, *You Gotta Reap What You Sow*; Lucille Hegamin, *Arkansas Blues*; Victoria Spivey, *Got The Blues So Bad*; Alberta Hunter, *Chirpin' The Blues*; Lucille Hegamin, *Has Anybody Seen My Corine*; Victoria Spivey, *Let Him Beat Me*

Hunter's strong, electrifying voice has an intense vibrato, and her recorded output is of astoundingly consistent quality. She is joined in this revival session (1961) by two other pioneers, Hegamin (who had lost some of her sparkle) and Spivey (always a special performer). Old-time songs are handled effectively, to the accompaniment of an all-star band.

196 Women Be Wise

Sippie Wallace

Alligator ALCD 4817/Storyville STCD 8024 (Dan)

Women Be Wise/Trouble Everywhere I Roam/Lonesome Hours Blues/Special Delivery Blues/Murder Gonna Be My Crime/Gambler's Dream/Caldonia Blues/ You Got To Know How/Shorty George Blues/Bedroom Blues/I'm A Mighty Tight Woman*/Up The Country Blues/Suitcase Blues/You Don't Know My Mind*

Recorded in Europe in 1966, this delectable collection represents a renaissance of Sippie's heyday of the 1920s. With sensitive piano accompaniment from Roosevelt Sykes, Little Brother Montgomery, or herself (on *Up The Country*), the skill of the Texas-born blues queen is readily apparent throughout.

197 Wang Dang Doodle

Koko Taylor

Roots RTS 33030 (Belg)

I Got What It Takes/What Kind Of Man Is This/Don't Mess With The Messer/ Whatever I Am, You Made Me/I'm A Little Mixed Up/Wang Dang Doodle/Blue Heaven/I Got All You Need/Tell Me The Truth/Good Advice/Egg On The Hen/ Just Love Me/Fire/Insane Asylum/Separate Or Integrate/I Don't Care Who Knows/Love You Like A Woman/Yes, It's Good For You/Twenty Nine Ways/ Nitty Gritty/I Love A Lover Like You

This is a significant sampling from Taylor's Checker recordings, made between 1964 and 1969. She is backed by some of Chicago's best contemporary bluesmen, including Buddy Guy, Shakey Horton, Sunnyland Slim, Robert Nighthawk, Willie Dixon, and Lafayette Leake. Her aggressive shouting eradicates all stereotypes of the timid, helpless female.

198 Ball N' Chain

Big Mama Thornton

Arhoolie CD 305

Sweet Little Angle/Unlucky Girl/Swing It On Home/Little Red Rooster/Hound

*Transposed in CD tracklisting.

Dog/Your Love Is Where It Ought To Be/School Boy/My Heavy Load/I'm Feeling Alright/Sometimes I Have A Heartache/Black Rat/Life Goes On/Bumble Bee/Gimmie A Penny/Wade In The Water/Ball N' Chain
Deep-seated emotion and tremendous power are cornerstones of Thornton's highly charged performances. Fine Chicago musicians accompany most of these recordings from the 1960s, plus her own harmonica and drums on *Your Love*. Fred McDowell plays slide guitar on the superlative *School Boy* and *My Heavy Load*, while the final two titles feature a West Coast band.

199 Confessin' The Blues
Esther Phillips
Atlantic 7-90670-2/Sequel RSACD 807 (UK)
I'm Gettin' 'Long Alright/I Wonder/Confessin' The Blues/Romance In The Dark/ C.C. Rider/Cherry Red/In The Evenin'/I Love Paris/It Could Happen To You/ Bye Bye Blackbird/Blow Top Blues/Jelly Jelly Blues/Long John Blues
With a voice and style similar to Dinah Washington's, Phillips began her career aged 13 (**305**). These compelling and mature versions of blues standards date from 1966 and 1970. They highlight her unique tremolo, vulnerable yet powerful, and in non-blues demonstrate her ability to overcome mediocre material in husky, stylish renditions.

200 First Ladies Of R & B
Various Artists
Charly CDRB 9 (UK)
Barbara George, *I Know*; Inez Foxx, *Mockingbird*; Jan Bradley, *Mama Didn't Lie*; Sugar Pie De Santo, *Slip-In Mules*; Gladys Knight & The Pips, *Letter Full Of Tears*; Betty Lavette, *He Made A Woman Out Of Me*; Betty Everett, *You're No Good*; Koko Taylor, *Wang Dang Doodle*; Ella Washington, *He Called Me Baby*; The Shirelles, *Mama Said*; Laura Lee, *Dirty Man*; Bessie Banks, *Go Now*; The Jellybeans, *I Want To Love Him So Bad*; Fontella Bass, *Rescue Me*; Mitty Collier, *I Had To Take A Walk With My Man*; The Dixie Cups, *Iko Iko*; Little Esther Phillips, *Release Me*; Betty Harris, *Cry To Me*; Etta James, *Next Door To The Blues*; Irma Thomas, *Wish Someone Would Care*
Excepting Thomas (1976), this is a cross-section of recordings from the 1960s that show how womens' blues became subsumed by soul music and other influences. *Mockingbird* is based on a children's game song and *Iko Iko* a New Orleans Mardi Gras chant, but most of these strongly sung performances are far from traditional secular styles.

REGENT

MIKE ROWE

6 Piano Blues and Boogie Woogie

In the way that blues guitar probably developed from the string bands of the 1880s and 1890s, it seems that blues piano emerged as a crude offshoot of ragtime during the same years. And, like the guitarists, the pianists fashioned a diversity of styles, creating a music that could be at once simple and complex, exciting and breathtakingly beautiful. That the first piano blues recordings date from the early 1920s leaves us in some difficulty in tracing its development, but there is evidence it originated in the South and especially in the lumber, levee, and railroad camps of Texas and Louisiana. While Eubie Blake remembered its most distinctive form, boogie woogie, played by William Turk in Baltimore in 1896, Leadbelly heard it in the barrelhouses of Fannin Street, Shreveport, around 1905, Roy Carew recalled its beginnings in New Orleans about 1904 and Richard M. Jones heard it played in the railroad camps at Donaldsonville, Louisiana, in 1906. But for the way that the early piano blues sounded we must rely on the prodigious memories of Jelly Roll Morton (**56**, **212**), born in 1885, and Little Brother Montgomery, born in 1906, for a few re-creations and glimpses of a vast, unknown army of pianists—men such as Game Kid, Brocky Johnny, Skinny Head Pete, and Papa Lord God, whose soubriquets were as colorful as their music.

By the turn of the century the piano blues were on the move—spreading northwards to the cities as part of the black migration, but helped along by the peculiar mobility of the pianists who, unlike the guitarists, always had to seek out their instrument to play. That pianos were found in the barrelhouses, where chock-beer and moonshine whiskey was dispensed from a rack of barrels, and in the whorehouses meant the pianist's life was a dangerous one, with the threat of casual violence ever present. Traveling offered little respite from danger, with the pianists hoboing on freight trains from job to job, risking life and limb and at the mercy of the elements. Small wonder then, that the railroad was the greatest single influence on blues piano, as the players imitated the train rhythms in their basses and trebles. Probably each urban center of the South developed its own regional style of blues piano, a local sound dictated by the leading pianists and local preference, and these were carried northwards. On admittedly scant recorded

"Big Maceo" Major Merriweather, ca 1940 (*coll. Blues Unlimited*)

evidence (Hersal Thomas from Houston, whose *Fives*—**211**—was recorded only as a piano roll in 1924, and Will Ezell from Shreveport—**213**), the newly arrived pianists in the early 1920s were still playing in their particular Southern tradition, and the emergence of a northern (say, Chicago) style was a slowly maturing process. This happened in 1929 with the release of Clarence "Pine Top" Smith's massively engaging *Pine Top's Boogie Woogie*, which fused the elements of the walking bass (used on earlier recordings, Cow Cow Davenport's *Cow Cow Blues*, for example), treble breaks of great suspense and right-hand variations into a dynamic and uniquely exciting whole. Smith's recording ushered in a Golden Age of blues piano, which lasted until the depths of the Depression.

Essential Records

(i) The Golden Age

There is a limpid grace to *Pine Top's Boogie Woogie* notwithstanding the powerful undercurrent of rolling bass figures, its most striking feature. The record launched "boogie woogie" as a term of the English language as well as a discrete musical style and there has been almost as much contoversy about one as the other. From Pine Top's calls followed by the suspense of the breaks and eventual release by the boogie bass it seems that his boogie woogie was a dance step which gains some credence from his introduction of this lesser-known B take on **Vocalion, 1928–1930** as, "This is Pine Top's Trouble" (which was actually the title in the files for his first, unissued version a few weeks earlier). If he is actually saying "strut" and not "trouble," as is very possible, then it is even more significant, of course. The fact that he didn't seem to distinguish musically between blues and boogie woogie—his blues sides, especially *Pine Top Blues*, are performed with similar bass figures—lends further support that, to Pine Top, boogie woogie was a dance. He was just playing the blues.

The term as applied to a form of blues piano playing is claimed to have been originated by Cow Cow Davenport who, discovering Smith in a joint in Sachem Alley, Pittsburgh, told him, ". . . you sure have got a mean boogie woogie" and, according to Davenport, "That's where the name boogie woogie derived from." Unfortunately Cow Cow didn't offer any explanation of the term, and Pine Top didn't live long enough to confirm its provenance. What is certain is its perfect onomatopoeia—the insistent and repetitious bass patterns seem completely described by "boogie woogie."

Whatever else may be his due credit, Davenport, who was already a veteran of the recording studios by 1928, recommended Smith to his recording company Vocalion and its manager Mayo Williams. When we read of Davenport's assertion that Pine Top "didn't know what he way playing," it is implied that boogie woogie was already a style that was known, if not well known by that name. Some of the characteristic basses had appeared on record before, the earliest in 1923 in *The Rocks*, a piano solo by Clay Custer (who may or may not have been George W. Thomas of Houston; if they were not the same man they were closely connected, and Thomas, anyway, picked up the bass as his trademark)—(**231**). Clarence Williams, a music publishing associate of George Thomas in New Orleans around 1917, published the latter's *New Orleans Hop Scop Blues*, which was the first published piece to incorporate the bass fragments. Thomas often used the same bass in his own performances, according to his younger sister Sippie Wallace. Moreover, George taught his younger brother Hersal, who, as something of a child prodigy, was to display a precocious talent; his recording of *Suitcase Blues* in 1925 also hinted at the mature style to come. By then George, Hersal, and Sippie were living in Chicago and Hersal was playing with, and greatly impressing, Albert Ammons. Davenport himself had contributed in 1925 what was to become almost an anthem of boogie woogie in *Cow Cow Blues* (**214**). This was a vocal version, which he recorded again in 1927 (also as a piano roll—**211**) and then, in a definitive version, as a pure piano solo for Vocalion in July 1928. The previous year *Jockey Blues*, by the obscure Sammy Brown, which employed some of the *Cow Cow Blues* motifs, was another precursor; the much more famous *Honky Tonk Train Blues* by Meade "Lux" Lewis dates from the same year. But nobody was calling the style boogie woogie, although the term was in use as in Chicago jazz pianist Jimmy Blythe's *Boogie Woogie Blues* of 1927 (**211**), which only hints at the style. Ironically it is Blythe's *Chicago Stomp* from 1924 (and a piano roll cut in 1927—**211**) which could probably be considered the first actual boogie woogie on record.

One idea that suggests itself amidst all the conjecture is the possible vaudeville origins of the style. Many of our prime suspects here (except Blythe) had a vaudeville background, especially multi-instrumentalist George Thomas. Davenport spent some years on the TOBA circuit, as did Pine Top Smith. It makes sense that the distinctive boogie woogie bass originated as an amusing novelty effect among vaudeville pianists—perhaps to imitate thunder or horse trotting, or a train, of course. They might have tossed in a few bars in the middle of some popular or ragtime melody; but what Pine Top succeeded in doing was to create a whole number out of it, and a big success. Unfortunately, on the eve of his follow-up recording session he was accidentally shot by a stray bullet during a dance-hall brawl. Vocalion and its sister label Brunswick needed a replacement and looked for a successor among such new talent as Montana Taylor, Romeo Nelson, and Speckled Red. Neither were the lessons of *Pine Top's Boogie Woogie* lost on the other companies catering to a black market, and Paramount especially recorded boogies by Will Ezell and introduced Charles Avery, Charlie Spand, and Little Brother Montgomery the same year, followed by Wesley Wallace, Jabo Williams, and Louise Johnson in the early 1930s. That there are two discs of Paramount material, one of Vocalion and another composed largely of Vocalion/ Brunswick and Paramount recordings among this group of five CDs reflects the huge contribution of these labels to what is, after all, a tiny legacy of the great blues piano performances. (OKeh had earlier recorded Hersal Thomas, who also died tragically young, and in 1929, that watershed year again, recorded Roosevelt Sykes. But Columbia showed little interest, as did Victor until the worst of the Depression years were over and the company started its cheap Bluebird label.)

Most of the piano players were obscure, even by blues standards, and our knowledge of all but the most popular is scant indeed. Thus, of the 35 pianists represented in this section about 20 are complete biographical blanks; our knowledge is confined to those who enjoyed a professional career of some longevity, such as Little Brother Montgomery and Roosevelt Sykes, or the few who were rediscovered. About the others we can only make educated guesses from their style or perhaps from their titles or clues hidden in their songs. So the ragtime beat and title of Blind Leroy Garnett's *Louisiana Glide* (on **Paramount, Volume 1, 1928–1932**) suggest an older, probably first generation, pianist from Texas or Louisiana. *Chain 'Em Down*, with its ragtime feel and varying basses, is a looser and beguiling admixture of ragtime and blues, while *Forty-Four Blues*, where he accompanies the deep-voiced James Wiggins, is an intriguing and fairly straight version of the classic and very difficult theme originated by Little Brother Montgomery, another Louisiana pianist. From Shreveport (or possibly Texas), but sharing a similar sawmill background with Little Brother, Will Ezell shows a huge ragtime influence in his playing of *Heifer Dust*, but *Playing The Dozen* (on **Paramount, Volume 2, 1927–1932**) is an up-tempo boogie with a light swinging touch. From September 1929, with the Graves brothers on guitar and tambourine, and a cornetist, Baby James, came a more recognizable *Pitchin' Boogie*, which is particularly interesting: along with a session-mate under Roosevelt Graves' name, it is the first example of a small group playing the style and, incidentally, is only the second recording with "boogie" in the title. Cow Cow Davenport was from Anniston, Alabama; his great technical ability and flair for invention encompasses the pure ragtime and stride piano of *Texas Shout* and the prototypical boogie woogie of *Cow Cow Blues*. His trademark of the walking octave bass is evident, too, in *Slum Gullion Stomp* and *Back In The Alley*, which also contains quotes from *Cow Cow Blues*.

Wherever he came from, by 1929 Charlie Spand was living in Detroit's Black Bottom, perhaps on Brady Street—which is actually the subject of *Hastings St.*, Spand's celebrated duet with the ragtime guitarist Blind Blake (on **Paramount, Volume 1**). Spand plays a storming up-tempo boogie while Blake matches him on guitar. Blake is also present on *Moanin' The Blues*, a heavy eight-to-the-bar boogie with splendid right-hand embellishments, on which he shadows the piano bass with guitar figures of his own. Spand seems to be playing the new music of the house-rent parties of Detroit or Chicago rather than that of the barrelhouses of Texas or Louisiana. A regular boogie bass has replaced the stride or ragtime elements to a large degree. The music is more *bluesy*.

Coming just a few months after Pine Top's recording, Spand's mature boogie blues suggests that the music was already developed in the northern cities, probably via the institution known as the house rent party, where a piano player would be hired, admission charged, and food and beer sold to raise the rent. Romeo Nelson has recalled the parties and the early mornings when "you could get away with anything—just hit the keyboards with your elbows and fists, it didn't make no difference to them, they were so drunk by then." Charles Avery's only solo, *Dearborn Street Breakdown*, a driving up-tempo boogie, was set firmly in the Chicago mold, as was Raymond Barrow's *Walking Blues*, that pianist's only known title. He may well have been the "Raymond" whose mother, Rose, ran a rent party at 45th and State streets and with a leap of the imagination, even at "four-five-oh-six" to where Rudy Foster invites his listeners in *Corn Trimmer Blues*. Not that this necessarily refers to Chicago, but if one accepts that the unknown Foster plays his own piano accompaniment then there seems a strong northern connection—a heavy, rhythmically coherent boogie—although to tie him in with Romeo Nelson's father in-law, a Mr Foster, is perhaps just too fanciful! Bob Call raises questions, but not of locale. His one solo, *31 Blues* strongly suggests he had listened to Cow Cow Davenport but seems at odds with the later accompaniments to Chicago artists and a post-war jump blues session. But this is explained by Call, probably alone among his contemporaries, going to music school to study. One could not imagine this of Piano Kid Edwards, a rough and eclectic barrelhouse pianist who must have sounded old-fashioned even by 1930. With two of his four tracks devoted to gambling it seems likely that the Piano Kid had another profession even more risky than piano playing. Although not a pianist, James Wiggins is interesting for his material: his three issued sessions with accompaniments from Call, Garnett, and an unknown pianist result in interpretations of four popular blues standards and a cover of Memphis Minnie and Kansas Joe's *Frisco Town*.

More is known about two of the finest blues pianists that Vocalion recorded in 1929. Iromeio "Romeo" Nelson was born in Springfield, Tennessee, in 1902 and learned piano in East St Louis from a river-front musician named "Window" around 1915. By 1919 he was in Chicago playing at the parties (he claimed to be influenced by Pine Top Smith and, inexplicably, by Clarence Williams) and gambling for a living. A friendship with Tampa Red resulted in an audition for Mayo Williams, and Nelson's classic rent-party piece, *Head Rag Hop*, was recorded. Pine Top's influence is apparent as Romeo similarly exhorts an imaginary dancer in a virtuoso performance of matchless treble runs against a rolling eight-to-the-bar boogie. His inimitably performed *Gettin' Dirty Just Shakin' That Thing*, with its sly verses, seems to be a first cousin to *The Dirty Dozen*. The month after Pine Top's death Vocalion found another worthy successor in Montana Taylor. Arthur Taylor was born in 1903 in the unlikely city of Butte, Montana, where his father ran the Silver City Club. Later the family moved to Chicago, and then to Indianapolis where, around 1919, Taylor learned to play by associating with local pianists Tom and Phil Harding, Funky Five, and Slick and Jimmy Collins. Four years later Montana earned his first money playing at the Hole in the Wall, at Goosie Lee's Rock House and at rent parties. From the 1929 Vocalion session came four issued sides—four of the finest boogie-woogie solos ever made. *Detroit Rocks* is a composition of quiet majesty played with immense feeling and taste—not the most common quality found among boogie-woogie pianists. Nor is it a quality shared by the Jazoo Boys, an unsuitable duo who detract from the piano on *Whoop And Holler Stomp*. *Indiana Avenue Stomp*, with Taylor solo again, is another peerless performance. Montana Taylor's recordings further reveal the truth of the coded fragments pieced together in the haphazard history of piano blues recordings; that boogie woogie was already a fully developed style by the time Pine Top perhaps unwittingly put a name to it. Pine Top made only four blues recordings, and *Jump Steady Blues* was unusual in exploring as delicately and gracefully as ever further possibilities of the walking octave bass.

Meade "Lux" Lewis's was a curious case. In 1927 he recorded

Honky Tonk Train Blues, a seminal boogie-woogie performance, but Paramount didn't release it until 1929 and never recorded another solo by Lewis, though they used him as accompanist on some drab sides by George Hannah and Bob Robinson. By then Mayo Williams had left the company, eventually to join Vocalion, and Paramount relied on such talent scouts as Harry Charles in Birmingham and H. C. Speir in Mississippi, who supplied the company with some of the finest country blues artists. In 1930 Louise Johnson, from Robinsonville, Mississippi, traveled to the studios in Grafton, Wisconsin, with Son House and Charley Patton; this resulted in four outstanding sides under her name which have been a source of great controversy ever since. It was thought that the pianist was Cripple Clarence Lofton because of the similarity of style and theme, and his usage, later, of snatches of the same lyrics. *On The Wall* (on **Paramount, Volume 2**) used the *Cow Cow Blues* tune just as Lofton was to use it for his *Streamline Train*, while the lyrics of this truly barrelhouse song used the folk fragments of "you can hang it on the wall, throw it out the window see if you can catch it 'fore it falls," which he was to use five years later. But careful comparison with Lofton's work suggests that Son House's testimony is correct and that Louise Johnson, in her teens, was the pianist and a remarkably aggressive one too. But hers is unlike any other Mississippi piano blues style on record. The same could be said about Charley Taylor from Sumner, Mississippi, whose two intense blues solos have hammered treble cascades over an irregular bass reminiscent of the Texas pianists. Representative of Louisiana would be the gifted Little Brother Montgomery from Kentwood, a sawmill town where his father owned a honky tonk and Little Brother learned from the itinerant pianists. *No Special Rider* (on **Paramount, Volume 1**) is an insistent and intricate boogie, while *Vicksburg Blues* is the great piano set-piece, the "Forty-Fours," which he learned in his teens and taught to Lee Green. Green in turn taught it to Roosevelt Sykes, and both of them beat Little Brother to the recording studios with their versions. *Memphis Fives* was Lee Green's most attractive number—a string of mildly insulting and obscure verses sung over a jaunty, varied bass to a distinctive melody.

Green was a big influence on Roosevelt Sykes, from Elmar, Arkansas (born in 1906), who was brought up in Helena and St Louis. From his first session in 1929, when he cut his version of *44 Blues* and a slick cover of *Boogie Woogie*, Sykes was hardly out of the studios, and, assisted by a variety of pseudonyms, he continued to record throughout the Depression. As he was the accompanist to more than 30 singers, one gets some idea of his popularity. After his discovery by Jesse Johnson, who supplied most of the St Louis talent, Sykes became almost a talent scout himself. Genial, professional and above all reliable, he was always the first choice of the record companies for soloist or accompanist. There were several characteristics of a Roosevelt Sykes performance—an unsyncopated single-note bass and a treble of great rhythmic complexity, or sometimes a chorded bass, which gave the "hollow" sound that typifies so many St Louis piano blues. There was a sophistication, too, about his playing (he said that until Lee Green taught him the blues he used to be "on the jazz side"), which is controlled in his best numbers but clearly evident on *Nasty But It's Clean* and a fast solo such as *Kelly's Special* (for Victor he was Willie Kelly). *You So Dumb*, another up-tempo talking blues, has the single-note bass with a fugitive resemblance to the mysterious Wesley Wallace. It is a fact that Sykes' considerable technical abilities can often blind one to his blues feeling but this blues feeling may be seen in *I Love You More And More, Drinkin' Woman Blues*, or *Cotton Seed Blues* and with guitarist Henry Townsend, *Hard Luck Man Blues* and *As True As I've Been To You*, all of which are fine blues. Sykes was probably the most important blues pianist of the 1930s—and certainly the most visible.

Joe Dean's *So Glad I'm Twenty-One Years Old Today* (on **Vocalion, 1928–1930**) has a little of Sykes' pyrotechnics, with its single-note bass and breakneck speed; it was Sykes who encouraged him to record. Henry Brown, who recorded with trombonist Ike Rodgers and tough-voiced Mary Johnson for Brunswick and Paramount, was not as accomplished as Sykes or Joe Dean, but his easy-paced solos and accompaniments were just as satisfying. Brown is the most representative pianist of the important St Louis school. The chorded bass of *Eastern Chimes Blues* gives a hollow sound to the appealing melody, while the single-note bass variations of *Deep Morgan Blues* afford a contrast to the treble clusters in a performance of some power. On *Henry Brown Blues*, with its more striding than walking bass, he shows similarities in style to Sykes, but *Blind Boy Blues*, with Ike Rodgers, has Brown in familiar territory—a rock-steady accompaniment and the distinctively hollow treble. Brown, like most of the archetypal St Louis blues artists, had moved to the city from the South (Troy, Tennessee, in his case).

The most exciting and fascinating of the St Louis pianists was Wesley Wallace, thought to be from Alton, Illinois. He recorded a couple of lackluster accompaniments to other singers and two solos of immense quality that stamp him as one of the greatest blues pianists of all time. *Fanny Lee Blues* (on **Paramount, Volume 1**), taken at medium tempo, is powerful and inventive, with treble after treble embellishment over a thundering boogie bass; but *No. 29*, a talking blues describing hoboing on a train from Cairo to East St Louis, is an amazing experience as Wallace imitates the sound of the train's whistle, its speed and his painful descent to the ground, all the time carrying on a ferocious bass and treble independently of each other. This virtuoso performance is justly the most famous of all train blues. Paramount had another piano genius with St Louis connections in "Jabo" Williams, who was originally from Birmingham, Alabama. There is a pronounced ragtime flavor to Williams' music, as in *Pratt City Blues*, which celebrates this suburb of Birmingham in a joyously forthright manner; *Jab Blues* is a similarly exciting performance, with "bugle call" breaks and flying treble patterns. Jabo Williams and Paramount disappeared after this session of 1932, and an ill-deserved obscurity beckoned nearly all the pianists who had contributed so colourfully to the great piano blues explosion of 1929. Most were unknown even when they were recording; nothing is known about Bert Mays, Dan Stewart, or Jim Clarke. Barrel House Welch would be better remembered for a rare accompaniment by Louis Armstrong than for his other sides, and Freddie Brown and Lonnie Clark were just names on a record label. Bill O'Bryant wasn't even that—his was a name in the Vocalion files as piano player on Tampa Red's *Black Hearted Blues*, his only excursion on record. He was just one more of the excellent boogie pianists to disappear into the depths of Depression America. Mississippi country blues guitarist Skip James fared better than most through his rediscovery in the 1960s (**402**), but had his only recorded legacy been his highly idiosyncratic piano-accompanied titles, he would no doubt have shared the same fate.

201 Paramount, Volume 1, 1928–1932: The Piano Blues
Various Artists
Magpie PYCD 01 (UK)
Charlie Spand, *Moanin' The Blues*; Blind Leroy Garnett, *Chain 'Em Down*; Little Brother Montgomery; *No Special Rider*; Wesley Wallace, *Fanny Lee Blues*; Louise Johnson, *By The Moon And Stars*; Will Ezell, *Pitchin' Boogie* Blind Leroy Garnett, *Louisiana Glide*; Blind Blake [with Charlie Spand] *Hastings St.*; Skip James, *If You Haven't Any Hay*; Jabo Williams, *Fat Mama Blues*; James "Boodle It" Wiggins, *Evil Woman Blues*; Lonnie Clark, *Down In Tennessee*; Charles Avery, *Dearborn Street Breakdown*; Charlie Spand, *Mississippi Blues*; Will Ezell, *Heifer Dust*; Little Brother Montgomery, *Vicksburg Blues*; Wesley Wallace, *No. 29*; James Wiggins, *Forty-Four Blues*; Henry Brown, *Henry Brown Blues*; Louise Johnson, *All Night Long Blues*

202 Paramount, Volume 2, 1927–1932: The Piano Blues
Various Artists
Magpie PY CD 05 (UK)
"Jabo" Williams, *Pratt City Blues*; Henry Brown, *Eastern Chimes Blues*;

Freddie Brown, *Raised In The Alley Blues*, Skip James, *22–20 Blues* Raymond Barrow, *Walking Blues*; Charley Taylor, *Heavy Suitcase Blues*; Barrel House Welch, *Dying Pickpocket Blues*; Louise Johnson, *Long Ways From Home*; "Jabo" Williams, *Polock Blues*; James Wiggins, *Weary Heart Blues*; Will Ezell, *Old Mill Blues*; Henry Brown & Ike Rodgers, *Blind Boy Blues*; Louise Johnson, *On The Wall*; Charley Taylor, *Louisiana Bound*; Barrel House Welch, *Larceny Woman Blues*; Meade Lux Lewis, *Honky Tonk Train Blues*; Will Ezell, *Playing The Dozen*; Freddie Brown, *Whip It To A Jelly*; Henry Brown, *Deep Morgan Blues*; "Jabo" Williams, *Jab Blues*

203 **Vocalion 1928–1930: The Piano Blues**
Various Artists
Magpie PYCD 03 (UK)
Cow Cow Davenport, *Back In The Alley*; Bert M. Mays, *Michigan River Blues*; Joe Dean (From Bowling Green), *I'm So Glad I'm Twenty-One Years Old Today*; Lee Green, *Memphis Fives*; Jim Clarke, *Fat Fanny Stomp*; Cow Cow Davenport, *Cow Cow Blues*; Romeo Nelson, *Gettin' Dirty Just Shakin' That Thing*; Dan Stewart, *New Orleans Blues*; Pine Top Smith, *Pine Top's Boogie Woogie* (take B); Bert M. Mays, *You Can't Come In*; Montana Taylor, *Indiana Avenue Stomp*; Cow Cow Davenport, *Slum Gullion Stomp*; Pine Top Smith, *Pine Top Blues*; Montana Taylor, *Detroit Rocks*; Tampa Red, *Black Hearted Blues*; Pine Top Smith, *Jump Steady Blues*; Joe Dean (From Bowling Green), *Mexico Bound Blues*; Romeo Nelson, *Head Rag Hop*; Cow Cow Davenport, *Texas Shout*; Montana Taylor, *Whoop And Holler Stomp*

204 **Boogie Woogie & Barrelhouse Piano, Volume 2, 1928–1930**
Various Artists
Document DOCD 5103 (Au)
"Boodle-It" Wiggins, *Keep A-Knockin' An You Can't Get In/Evil Woman Blues*; Bob Call, *31 Blues*; Raymond Barrow, *Walking Blues*; "Boodle-It" Wiggins, *My Loving' Blues/Weary Heart Blues*; Blind Leroy Garnett, *Chain 'Em Down/ Louisiana Glide*; "Boodle-It" Wiggins, *Forty Four Blues/Frisco Bound*; Marie Griffin, *What Do You Think This Is?/Blue And Disgusted*; James "Boodle-It" Wiggins, *Corrinne Corrina Blues/Gotta Shave 'Em Dry*; Romeo Nelson, *Head Rag Hop/Gettin' Dirty Just Shakin' That Thing/Dyin' Rider Blues/1129 Blues (The Midnight Special)*; Rudy Foster, *Black Gal Makes Thunder/Corn Trimmer Blues*; Piano Kid Edwards, *Gamlin' Man's Prayer Blues/Hard Luck Gamblin' Man/Piano Kid Special/Give Us Another Jug*

205 **Roosevelt Sykes: Complete Recorded Works In Chronological Order, Volume 2, 12 June 1930 to 10 June 1931**
Document DOCD 5117 (Au)
Willie Kelly [Sykes], *32–20 Blues/Give Me Your Change/I Love You More And More/Kelly's 44 Blues*; Dobby Bragg [Sykes], *3–6 And 9/We Can Sell That Thing/Conjur Man Blues*; Easy Papa Johnson [Sykes], *Cotton Seed Blues/No Good Woman Blues/Drinkin' Woman Blues/Papa Sweetback Blues*; St Louis Bessie, *He Treats Me Like A Dog/Meat Cutter Blues*; Willie Kelly [Sykes], *Side Door Blues/Big Time Woman/Thanksgivin' Blues/Kelly's Special/Don't Put The Lights Out/No Settled Mind Blues/As True As I've Been To You/Hard Luck Man Blues/Don't Squeeze Me Too Tight/You So Dumb/Nasty But It's Clean*

(ii) Urban Blues

When the Depression-hit Race record companies regrouped to battle for a market shrunk to a tenth of its former size, they cut back their catalogs accordingly, relying on a handful of their most popular artists, and reduced the price of their records. Vocalion/Brunswick, under new ownership, continued to record Leroy Carr (**247**), and Gennett's cheap label Champion, though barely active, did record Turner Parrish and Frank James. Paramount shut its doors in 1932, Columbia/OKeh was in trouble and only Victor continued under the same ownership. Victor recorded Roosevelt Sykes persistently (**253**), and introduced Walter Davis in 1930 and the Sparks Brothers in 1932 (**224**). Then in 1933 the company started a new cheap label, Bluebird, following the lead of the American Record Company (ARC was launched in 1930 and quickly merged with Vocalion/Brunswick), whose "dime-store" labels sold for only 25 cents. As the economic climate brightened, another competitor, the English Decca company, entered the field in 1934 with its 35-cent label and an aggressive marketing policy, with Mayo Williams in charge.

However, there had been a subtle change in the market for piano blues. Those pianists such as Leroy Carr (**219**), Walter Davis (**221**), and even Roosevelt Sykes (**226**) who had lasted out the Depression were popular for their songs and singing; that they played piano was incidental. While the sawmill pianists played for dancers and had to survive on pianistic prowess, the blues pianist of the urban 1930s had to achieve success as a singer or songwriter. Piano blues had been taken out of the lumber camps and whorehouses and into the homes of an increasingly sophisticated urban audience. This accent on the content of the song meant that pianists had little encouragement to stretch themselves, and Davis or Peetie Wheatstraw, for example, could make recording after recording using the same introduction and tempo, which tended to mask their abilities as pianists. Boogie woogie had become integrated into blues accompaniments, and ragtime was all but eliminated. There was a smoother, more regular sound to the 1930s piano blues, and although a few field trips by Bluebird, Decca, and ARC preserved some regional styles, and the iconoclastic Texas piano in particular, it was the cities such as Chicago and St Louis that provided the bulk of the artists.

With Brunswick/Vocalion and ARC in the same ownership from December 1931 Birmingham singer Lucille Bogan's last Brunswick sides were reissued on ARC's cheap labels, and in 1933 the company recorded her, as Bessie Jackson, with guitarist Sonny Scott and pianist-guitarist Walter Roland, both from Birmingham (**166**). Roland's first recording, *Red Cross Blues* (as Alabama Sam), must have impressed ARC, as between them they cut four different versions in as many days.

An unusually constructed blues, which played on the black audience's suspicion of the Red Cross Flood Relief station's role as unofficial army recruitment centers, it was an immediate success. Roland went on to make about 40 sides under his own name and more than 50 accompaniments, of some variety considering there were only three trips to the New York studios. His music ranged from the ragtime flavor of *Piano Stomp*, the hokum of *Hungry Man's Scuffle* and *Whatcha Gonna Do?* to the strong boogie of *Jookit Jookit*, his version of Pine Top's classic with its driving bass and Roland's characteristic right-hand flourishes. Some of fellow Birmingham pianist Jabo Williams' influence is heard in the leisurely rolling basses and triplets as well as in songs such as *House Lady Blues*. But Roland always brought a lot of his own ideas to someone else's numbers; this is also evident on *Early This Morning ('Bout The Break Of Day)*, which is based on Charlie Spand's *Soon This Morning*. His blues are sung in a soft, melancholy voice, not unlike Leroy Carr's, with great warmth and feeling. The slow *Black Door Blues* is another example, beautifully sung and played, with the mellowest of walking basses.

Before she teamed with Walter Roland, Lucille Bogan had a ten-year career and a variety of piano accompanists, including Will Ezell and Charles Avery. In Roland, however, she found the perfect foil (**227**). Whether it was her usual themes of mistreatment, prostitution, lesbianism, and low life in general, or of loving tenderness (*Changed Ways Blues*, for example), Roland's playing fitted all moods—with sometimes a quietly understated backing or, at others, a rolling and emphatic support. *B.D. Woman's Blues*, Bogan's song about lesbianism, has one of his finest accompaniments to one of her typically robust vocals, and *Stew Meat Blues* (the kind of culinary metaphor she so enjoyed) is another perfect marriage of voice and instrument. Theirs was one of the great blues partnerships on record. It ended abruptly in 1935 when after two years of solid recording activity they disappeared from the scene, never to be heard of again. The market may have declined for Roland's wistful, reflective blues, but ARC was still recording similar material down South to compete with the brasher offerings from the Chicago studios. ARC's left hand, Vocalion, had Memphis Minnie, Big Bill Broonzy and Bumble Bee Slim in Chicago, who were making a noisier blues sound, often using small groups with trumpets or clarinets (**244**, **245**, **263**).

The same year that ARC dropped Bogan and Roland, it recorded two Chicago pianists of particular interest. One, Cripple Clarence Lofton, became more famous in collectors' circles in the 1940s, while the other, George Noble (**217**), had a recording career of just over a month, ending on the same day as Walter Roland's.

Cripple Clarence Lofton was one of the most creative of boogie-woogie pianists, his powerful and precise boogie bass was matched by a hugely percussive treble to create moody, introspective blues or rollicking up-tempo boogies of great color and imagination. Lofton's is the music of Chicago and of the rent parties, in that he is a pianist and not a singer. He was also a supremely tasteful accompanist, and the tight, controlled boogie backing to Red Nelson's *Crying Mother Blues* is one of the best examples. That he could supply such a sympathetic backing to other artists is surprising in view of his egotism and the descriptions of his uninhibited live performances, when he would leap up from the piano, run around the back, snap his fingers, whistle and dance. Some of this rowdy good humor trickles through his songs—the four vocals with Broonzy are all sung in a coarse voice with humorous undertones. *Strut That Thing* is a *tour de force* evoking his eccentric live performances. The romping *Brown Skin Girls* has lyrics from Hull's and Reed's *Gang Of Brown Skin Women* (recorded in 1927—**72**) and a syncopated walking bass, while the two blues have great, stomping boogie passages between the mocking verses. The accompaniments to Red Nelson, for Decca, came the next year; among them was *Streamline Train*, his individual adaptation of *Cow Cow Blues* and the source of the Louise Johnson controversy. He made another four versions of the song and each time played it slightly differently. Like most pianists, Lofton had a limited number of themes, and the tune he used for *When The Soldiers Get Their Bonus* cropped up in his later solo recordings, but with subtle variations. He was born in Kingsport, Tennessee, in 1887 and had been in Chicago since about 1920. Washing cars by day and seeking out a piano to play at night, he cut a lonely and eccentric figure even among his peer group of rent-party pianists. Eye-witness accounts date from 1939, when he was a frequent visitor to Jimmy Yancey's house and played at a saloon called the Big Apple on South State Street, where his second, short, recording career began.

By the late 1930s the dominant sound of the blues was that of the Chicago singers and their small groups, most of whom recorded for Bluebird. Piano was an important ingredient of the "Bluebird Beat," as it was neatly dubbed by Sam Charters, but it was usually provided by the house pianists, few of whom could fulfill a solo role. Notable exceptions, though, were Broonzy's accompanist, Memphis Slim, and Tampa Red's pianist, Big Maceo Merriweather. Maceo was born in 1905 in Newnan, Georgia, and learned his piano playing in Atlanta around 1920. After moving to Detroit in 1924 he kept up his playing at house parties while working by day at a succession of laboring jobs and, during the Depression, for the Works Progress Administration (WPA).

In 1941 he went to Chicago to try and get a recording contract, and Big Bill and Tampa Red introduced him to Lester Melrose. In a matter of days Maceo recorded his classic *Worried Life Blues*, a clever variant of Sleepy John Estes' *Someday Baby*. He had inherited his singing talent from a family of gifted singers, and his smoky brown voice and songs steeped in a quiet fatalism were an affecting combination. The songs were all important, but Maceo was also a fine pianist with an unusually powerful style. He was left-handed, and his heavy bass was a trademark, along with the drive and energy of his playing. While he too drew upon earlier piano styles, he used them as a framework to create new compositions, such as *Ramblin' Mind Blues*, which is reminiscent of Sykes' *Highway 61 Blues*. Maceo's performances are always so distinctive that it is almost with surprise that one detects any outside influences, such as Leroy Carr's *How Long* in *Tuff Luck Blues* and the weird *Dirty Dozen* introduction to *I Got The Blues*. There are other songs that show a debt to *Someday Baby*, the theme reappearing in *Some Sweet Day* and, from 1945, *I'm So Worried* and *Things Have Changed*; the influence of Maceo's best seller was never very far away. The rowdiest and most traditional theme is a toast from the well of black folklore, *The Monkey And The Baboon*, which turns up as *Can't You Read*. A number popular from the house parties, it was always known as *'Filte Fish*, a reminder of the original Jewish settlement area that was Hastings Street until the 1920s. It is significant that this obvious novelty is the only up-tempo number from his three pre-war sessions on this disc. There are no piano solos and it is titles such as *Bye Bye Baby*, *Anytime For You* and *So Long Baby* that speak of a deeply traditional singer and composer, however innovative a pianist he was. Big Maceo had a big influence on the post-war Chicago blues, with his music carried on by his pupils Little Johnny Jones, Henry Gray, and Otis Spann, the new generation of Chicago blues band pianists. But Maceo himself did not profit from it: a stroke effectively ended his playing career and he died in 1953.

206 Walter Roland: Complete Recorded Works In Chronological Order, Volume 1 (1933)

Document DOCD 5144 (Au)

Alabama Sam [Roland], *Red Cross Blues*; Walter Roland [originally attributed to Sonny Scott], *Red Cross Blues* No. 2; Walter Roland, *T Model Blues*; Walter Roland & Sonny Scott, *Man, Man, Man*; Sonny Scott, *No Good Biddie*; Alabama Sam [Roland], *You Gonna Need Me*; Walter Roland, *Slavin' Blues/Last Years Blues*; Sonny Scott, *Early This Morning/Working Man's Moan/Rolling Water*; Jolly Jivers [Roland], *Jookit Jookit/Piano Stomp*; Walter Roland, *Back Door Blues*; Jolly Two, *Guitar Stomp/Railroad Stomp*; Walter Roland, *Frisco Blues/House Lady Blues*; Jolly Jivers [Roland], *Whatcha Gonna*

Do?; Walter Roland, *Early This Morning ('Bout Break Of Day)*; Jolly Jivers [Roland], *Hungry Man's Scuffle*; Jolly Two, *Come On Down*; Walter Roland, *Overall Blues*

207 **Cripple Clarence Lofton: Complete Recorded Works In Chronological Order, Volume 1 (1935–1939)**
Blues Documents BDCD 6006 (Au)
Strut That Thing/Monkey Man Blues; Albert Clemens [Lofton]; *Policy Blues (You Can't 3–6–9 Me)*; Cripple Clarence Lofton, *Brown Skin Girls/You Done Tore Your Playhouse Down*; Red Nelson, *Crying Mother Blues/Streamline Train*; Al Miller & His Swing Stompers, *Its Got To Be Done/Juicy Mouth Shorty*; Red Nelson, *Sweetest Thing Born/When The Soldiers Get Their Bonus (Even If It Don't Last Long)*; Cripple Clarence Lofton, *Traveling Blues/Streamline Train/I Don't Know/Mistaken Blues/Pitchin' Boogie/Mercy Blues/Had A Dream/Streamline Train* (R 2772)/*I Don't Know* (R 3361)

208 **Big Maceo: The King Of Chicago Blues Piano**
Arhoolie Folklyric CD 7009
Worried Life Blues/Ramblin' Mind Blues/County Jail Blues/Can't You Read/So Long Baby/Texas Blues/Tuff Luck Blues/I Got The Blues/Bye Bye Baby/Poor Kelly Blues/Some Sweet Day/Anytime For You/My Last Go Round/Since You Been Gone/Kidman Blues/I'm So Worried/Things Have Changed/My Own Troubles/Maceo's 32–20/Texas Stomp/Winter Time Blues/Detroit Jump/Won't Be A Fool No More/Big Road Blues/Chicago Breakdown

(iii) Boogie Woogie

Outside the mainstream development of black blues piano there was an important revival of boogie woogie in the late 1930s, which took the genre out of the rent parties and bars and established it as a separate style of jazz, as opposed to blues, piano. Collector-inspired, it resulted from John Hammond getting together Albert Ammons, Meade Lux Lewis, Pete Johnson, and vocalist Joe Turner for the historic Carnegie Hall "From Spirituals to Swing" concert in December 1938. It was so successful that another was held the following December (**8**). Ammons, a native Chicagoan, had learned piano from Pine Top Smith and Hersal Thomas, and both he and Lewis had been influenced by Jimmy Yancey. In the 1920s Lewis, also born in Chicago but raised in Louisville, Kentucky, was living with Smith and Ammons on Chicago's Prairie Avenue. Pete Johnson, from Kansas City, learned piano from his uncle after working first as a drummer. He met Joe Turner in the clubs and they eventually teamed up together in the 1930s. In 1935 Lewis had been actively sought out by Hammond to re-record his famous *Honky Tonk Train Blues*, which was followed by sessions for Decca and Victor. Ammons, who was leading a band, had recorded with his Rhythm Kings in 1936. It was the Carnegie Hall dates that brought all three to the notice of a white public and tumultuous acclaim. The interest sparked off a stream of recording activity, with opportunities for the big three and immediate orchestration of the style by the white swing bands. In the end the relentless commercialization, as the popular music industry joined in, diluted and destroyed a highly idiosyncratic and attractive little tributary of jazz piano.

There was a legitimate folk interest in the performers as well, and the day after the first concert Alan Lomax recorded Ammons, Lewis, and Johnson for the Library of Congress (**32**). The next week they recorded for Vocalion as a trio and Ammons and Lewis made some solos. Days later both Ammons and Lewis recorded for the newly formed Blue Note record company. Previously unknown recordings have also surfaced and with the rare Carnegie Hall titles are of great historic and musical interest. From the concert, Lewis' *Honky Tonk Train Blues* was his fifth recording of the title, and he had also previously recorded *Yancey Special*, a tribute to Jimmy Yancey. Ammons' *Boogie-Woogie Stomp* was his explosive version of *Pine Top's Boogie Woogie*, to which title he reverted for the 1938 concert and repeated the next year as *Boogie-Woogie Stomp*. It remains a testimony to his prodigious technique. His playing was characterized by the clarity and precision with which he hit the notes, apparently the result of teaching himself by copying the sound of piano rolls. The duets and trios were an outcrop of the boogie craze; there had been such duos before—Blythe & Clark, Blythe & Burton, and Smith & Irvine for example—but significantly they involved jazz pianists or, at the very least, not strictly blues artists. Of course boogie woogie was an ideal vehicle, given the distinctive functions of left and right hands, for this kind of exploitative novelty. Enjoyable though the Ammons & Johnson duets are, they merely emphasize that in their own ways the "Big Three" were jazz pianists. Johnson would continue to play in and lead small groups while Lewis (who may have been setting down some kind of marker when he chose *Solitude* and *Melancholy* for his first Blue Note recordings) would incorporate stride elements and explore a solo career of increasing sophistication.

Ammons' slow blues sometimes showed a harmonic diversion in common with Lewis and Johnson which engage the attention of the jazz lover more than the blues enthusiast. This is not surprising, as Ammons had been playing in bands from the 1930s and even took lessons in order to do so. He took part in one more solo session in 1944 but after that all his recordings were made with small groups, including guitar, bass, and drums, and occasionally trumpet and tenor saxophone (often played by his son Gene); even so, the other musicians never intrude too much. From 1945 until his untimely death in 1949 he recorded for Mercury and these commercial recordings of Ammons as piano-playing band leader may show where his heart really lay (**235**).

However, there were other specialists in Chicago who were untouched by the boogie craze—except to share in some recording opportunities—whose music was contained in the small bars of the South Side or at private parties, out of the glare of the commercial spotlight (**15**). Cripple Clarence Lofton recorded again, for Solo Art and then for Phil Featheringill's Session label, as did Jimmy Yancey. But Yancey had some intervening exposure on major labels too, for Victor/Bluebird and Vocalion, for which he laid down the definitive statement of his few themes with an eloquent and moving dignity. The most striking feature of Yancey's music was the "Spanish tinge"—a bass figure, rhythmically rather like the habanera, that he habitually used. The only other blues examples of this figure on record are by the obscure Little David Alexander from Chicago and Doug Suggs from St Louis, a close friend and workmate of Yancey's. But Estelle "Mama" Yancey, Jimmy's wife, was adamant that Jimmy never learned anything from Suggs. A possibility is that he picked it up as a child when he was a dancer in vaudeville and the habanera was sweeping the country. Having retired from the stage in his teens, he learned piano from the pianists at the house parties; it is fascinating to imagine what the piano blues sounded like in Chicago around 1916. Although he influenced very few, he was a popular and well-respected pianist (Papa Yancey to colleagues just a few years younger) who made a good living on the rent-party circuit. He never sought a professional career, preferring to play for friends or at home, where he and Estelle held open house for piano players.

Yancey may have had only a dozen or so themes, which cropped up again and again under different titles on his recordings, but they were all unmistakably his own, and the gentle and haunting melodies he put together seemed an extension of his personality. However, he could also play a heavy boogie woogie, as hinted at by the medium-tempo *Yancey Stomp*, also known as *The Fives*, and *Midnight Stomp*. But Yancey's artistry is most obvious on a number such as *State Street Special*, a slow and masterly exercise in suspense, finally resolved when he breaks into a regular eight-to-the-bar boogie for the last choruses, or on *Five O'Clock Blues*, which after the introduction settles down into Yancey's version of *How Long Blues*, the sparsest and most affecting of all his blues. This Victor session was followed by one the next year which Lester Melrose placed with Vocalion and consisted of two Yancey solos and two exquisite accompaniments to the adenoidal Faber Smith, once thought to be Yancey himself. But Smith was actually an alto saxophonist in his brother Lloyd Smith's band and a near neighbor of Yancey's. Another session for Victor later that year was the last time a major company dallied with Yancey—he was not going to be part of the boogie craze. He was, though, to be part of the great piano blues tradition, and to be respected as a man who loved and understood the blues—a man who; as Mama Yancey told me, would "play anytime—if he got up early enough in the morning and felt like it, take him a drink, sit down and play him a piece before he went to work."

209 Boogie Woogie Boys 1938–1944
Various Artists
Magpie PYCD 21 (UK)
Meade Lux Lewis, *Honky Tonk Train Blues*; Albert Ammons, *Pine Top's Boogie Woogie*; Meade Lux Lewis, *Yancey Special*; Pete Johnson, *Low-Down Dog* [Joe Turner, vocal]; Albert Ammons, *Boogie-Woogie Stomp*; Albert Ammons, Pete Johnson & Meade Lux Lewis, *Jumpin' Blues*; Meade Lux Lewis, *Honky Tonk Train Blues*; Albert Ammons & Meade Lux Lewis, *Double-Up Blues*; Albert Ammons & Pete Johnson, *Boogie-Woogie Man* (take 1)/ *Boogie-Woogie Man* (take 2)/*Barrel House Boogie/Cuttin' The Boogie/Foot Pedal Boogie/Walkin' The Boogie/Sixth Avenue Express/Pine Creek/Movin' The Boogie/Boogie Woogie Prayer/Foot Pedal Boogie/Jumpin' The Boogie/Cutting' The Boogie/St Louis Blues/Lady Be Good/The Sheik Of Araby/Pistol Packin' Mama/Rumboogie/Boogie Woogie Man*

210 Jimmy Yancey: Complete Recorded Works 1939–1950 In Chronological Order, Vol. 1 May 1939 to February 1940
Document DOCD 5041 (Au)
Jimmy's Stuff [Jimmy's Stuff No. *2]/The Fives/La Salle Street Breakdown/Two O'Clock Blues/Janie's Joys/Lean Bacon/Big Bear Train/Lucille's Lament/Beezum Blues/Yancey Limited/Rolling The Stone/Steady Rock Blues/P.L.K. Special/ South Side Stuff/Yancey's Getaway/How Long Blues/How Long Blues* No. *2/ Yancey Stomp/State Street Special/Tell 'Em About Me/Five O'Clock Blues/Slow And Easy Blues/The Mellow Blues*; Faber Smith, *I Received A Letter/East St. Louis Blues*

Basic Records

(i) Pre-war

211 Boogie Woogie Blues: Piano Roll Solos
Various Artists
Biograph BCD 115
Cow Cow Davenport, *Cow Cow Blues/5th Street Blues/Hurry And Bring It Home Blues*; James P. Johnson, *Harlem Choc'late Babies On Parade/ Birmingham Blues*; Clarence Williams, *Sugar Blues/Papa De Da Da*; Clarence Johnson, *Gulf Coast Blues/You're Always Messin' Round With My Man/Low*

Down Papa; Jimmy Blythe, *Chicago Stomp/Society Blues/Boogie Woogie Blues*; Everett Robbins, *Hard Luck Blues*; Hersal Thomas, *The Fives*; Lemuel Flowler, *Down And Out Blues*
Vitally important both historically and musically: two Davenport numbers never committed to wax; Blythe's *Chicago Stomp*, his later piano-roll version of the earliest recognizable boogie-woogie solo; and Hersal Thomas' only rendering of *The Fives*, a tune that only Lofton recalled.

212 **Winin' Boy Blues: The Library Of Congress Recordings, Volume 4**
Jelly Roll Morton
Rounder CD 1094
Freakish/Pep/Card Dealer's Song/New Orleans Blues/Creepy Feeling (begun)/*Creepy Feeling* (concluded)/*The Crave/Mamanita/Can-Can/If You Don't Shake/Spanish Swat/Ain't Misbehavin'/I Hate A Man Like You/Michigan Water Blues/Winin' Boy Blues* No. 2 (begun)/*Winin' Boy Blues* No. 3 (concluded)/*Buddy Bertrand's Blues* No. 1—*Mamie's Blues* (combined)/*Boogie Woogie Blues/Albert Carroll's Tune/Buddy Bertrand's Blues* No. 2/*L'il Liza Jane/Tricks Ain't Walkin' No More*
This extraordinary document of jazz history throws an interesting sidelight on the early unknowns of blues piano. *Winin' Boy* with its unexpurgated whore-house lyrics and *Mamie's Blues* are outstanding, as are the jazz solos with an exquisite Spanish tinge, while the only known "original" version of *Tricks Ain't Walkin'* is a curiosity.

213 **Will Ezell: Complete Recorded Works In Chronological Order, 1927–1931**
Blues Documents BDCD 6033 (Au)
Marie Bradley, *Stormy Hailing Blues*; Ora Brown, *Jailhouse Moan/Restless Blues*; Bertha Henderson, *Black Bordered Letter/Six Thirty Blues*; Will Ezell, *Barrel House Man/West Coast Rag/Old Mill Blues* (take 1)/*Old Mill Blues* (take 2)/*Mixed Up Rag/Ezell's Precious Five/Crawlin' Spider Blues/Barrel House Woman* (take 1)/*Barrel House Woman* (take 2)/*Bucket Of Blood/Heifer Dust/Playing The Dozen/Just Can't Stay Here/Pitchin' Boogie/Freakish Mistreater Blues/Hot Spot Stuff*; Slim Tarpley, *Try Some Of That/Alabama Hustler*
Listening to Ezell is like eavesdropping at the birth of piano blues. Outside the authority of his ragtime playing, he haltingly samples different basses and trebles to fascinating (if untidy) effect and works up to the finished product—the enthusiastic *Pitchin' Boogie*. His walking bass on *Barrel House Man* is again before Pinetop Smith.

214 **Cow Cow Davenport: Complete Recorded Works In Chronological Order, Volume 1, 1 October 1925 to 1 May 1929**
Document DOCD 5141 (Au)
Dora Carr, *Cow Cow Blues*; Davenport & Carr; *Alabama Mis-Treater*; Cow Cow Davenport, *Jim Crow Blues/Goin' Home Blues/New Cow Cow Blues/Stealin' Blues/Cow Cow Blues* (take A)/*Cow Cow Blues* (take B); Cow Cow Davenport & Ivy Smith, *State Street Jive* (take A); Cow Cow Davenport, *State Street Jive* (take B)/*Chimin' The Blues*; Cow Cow Davenport & Ivy Smith, *Alabama Strut*; Cow Cow Davenport, *Alabama Mistreater/Dirty Ground Hog Blues*; Charlie Davenport [Cow Cow Davenport], *Chimes Blues/Struttin'*

The Blues/Givin' It Away/Slow Drag/Atlanta Rag; Cow Cow Davenport & Sam Theard, *That'll Get It/I'm Gonna Tell You In Front So You Won't Feel Hurt Behind*; Sam Theard [Lovin' Sam From Down In 'Bam], *State Street Blues*; Cow Cow Davenport, *Back In The Alley/Mootch Piddle*
This disc illustrates Cow Cow's pioneering blues style in all its variety—as accompanist, as vaudeville performer with fellow conspirator Sam Theard and as solo ragtime and blues pianist. The 1928 Vocalion solos of *Cow Cow Blues* and *State Street Jive* reveal the full maturity of his blues and boogie piano.

215 Charlie Spand: The Complete Paramounts In Chronological Order, 1929–1931
Document DOCD 5108 (Au)
Soon This Morning Blues/Fetch Your Water/Good Gal/Ain't Gonna Stand For That/Moanin' The Blues/Back To The Woods Blues; Blind Blake [with Charlie Spand], *Hastings St.*; Charlie Spand, *In The Barrel Blues/Levee Camp Man/Breakdown/Mississippi Blues/45th St. Blues/Got To Have My Sweetbread* (take 3)/*Got To Have My Sweetbread* (take 4)/*Room Rent Blues/Mistreatment Blues/Soon This Morning* No. 2/*She's Got Good Stuff/Thirsty Woman Blues/Dreamin' The Blues/Big Fat Mama Blues/Hard Time Blues/Georgia Mule Blues/Tired Woman Blues/Evil Woman Spell*
Charlie Spand, immediately successful with his excellent boogie *Soon This Morning*, went on to record regularly until the Depression. *Levee Camp Man*, perhaps a clue to his background, sounds archaic, and the ragtime influence is strong, but the heavy boogies, with *Hard Time Blues* outstanding, show a music in transition.

216 Piano Blues: Complete Recorded Works In Chronological Order, Volume 1, 1927–1936 (+ Bonus Tracks 1955)
Various Artists
Document DOCD 5192 (Au)
Bert Mays, *Midnight Rambler's Blues/Oh-Oh Blues/Troublesome Mind Blues/Mama's Man Blues*; Bert M. Mays, *Michigan River Blues/You Can't Come In*; Blind Clyde Church, *Number Nine Blues/Pneumatic Blues*; Dan Stewart, *New Orleans Blues*; Jim Clarke, *Fat Fanny Stomp*; Judson Brown, *You Don't Know My Mind Blues*; Joe Dean (From Bowling Green), *Mexico Bound Blues/I'm So Glad I'm Twenty-One Years Old Today*; James "Bat" Robinson, *You Left Me Alone/Bat's Own Blues/Humming Blues*; Pigmeat Terry, *Moaning The Blues/Black Sheep Blues*; Jesse James, *Sweet Patuni/Southern Casey Jones/Lonesome Day Blues/Highway 61*; Bat "The Hummingbird" Robinson, *Bat's Blues/Four O'Clock*
Only Joe Dean and "Bat" Robinson of St Louis are known. Bert Mays was probably from Texas; Stewart and Clark (discoveries of Richard M. Jones), and Jesse James probably from Cincinnati, but by the 1930s regional influences have disappeared. Outstanding are the dazzling Joe Dean, the moving Jesse James, and the quirky Jim Clarke.

217 Chicago Piano: The Complete Recorded Works of Eddie Miller, John Oscar, George Noble (1929–1936)
Document DOCD 5191 (Au)
John Oscar, *In The Gutter/Mama Don't Allow No Easy Riders Here*; Eddie Miller, *Good Jelly Blues/Freight Train Blues/School Day Blues*; John Oscar,

Dyin' Mother Blues/Whoopee Mama Blues; Big Oscar [John Oscar], *Mistreatment Blues/Other Man Blues*; Eddie Morgan, *My Gal Blues/Rock House Blues*; Eddie Miller, *I'd Rather Drink Muddy Water* (take 1)/*I'd Rather Drink Muddy Water* (take 2)/*Whoopie*; Willie Mae McKenzie, *I'd Rather Drink Muddy Water/Get Business On Your Mind*; George Noble, *New Milk Cow Blues/On My Death Bed/The Seminole Blues/Sissy Man Blues/Bed Springs Blues/If You Lose Your Good Gal, Don't Mess With Mine/T.B. Blues*
These pianists show the range of the developed Chicago piano sound of the 1930s from the accomplished Miller's lighter St Louis touch to the mysterious John Oscar, Eddie Morgan's boogies and the dour if eclectic George Noble's thunderous basses. Probably from Cincinnati, Morgan was certainly not Eddie Miller.

218 St. Louis Barrelhouse Piano: The Complete Recordings of Wesley Wallace, Henry Brown & Associates 1929–1934
Document DOCD 5104 (Au)
Bessie Mae Smith, *St. Louis Daddy/Farewell Baby Blues*; Robert Peeples, *Wicked Devil's Blues/Fat Greasy Baby*; Wesley Wallace, *No. 29/Fanny Lee Blues*; Robert Peeples, *Dying Baby Blues/Mama's Boy*; Sylvester Palmer, *Do It Sloppy/Broke Man Blues/Mean Blues/Lonesome Man Blues*; Henry Brown, *Stomp 'Em Down To The Bricks*; Ike Rodgers & His Biddle Street Boys, *Malt Can Blues*; Henry Brown, *Twenty First Street Stomp/It Hurts So Good/Henry Brown Blues/Screening The Blues*; Henry Brown & Ike Rodgers, *Blues Stomp/Blind Boy Blues*; Henry Brown, *Eastern Chimes Blues/Deep Morgan Blues*; Dolly Martin, *All Men Blues*; Tee McDonald, *Beef Man Blues*; Peetie Wheatstraw & His Blue Blowers, *Throw Me In The Alley Blues*
Wesley Wallace's accompaniments suffer in comparison with his virtuoso solos. He has been linked with Sylvester Palmer but Palmer, fine though he is, lacks Wallace's brilliance. Henry Brown, a dependable accompanist and solid soloist is more the mainstream St Louis blues pianist; he also forged a unique partnership with trombonist Ike Rodgers.

219 Leroy Carr 1930–1935: The Piano Blues
Magpie PYCD 07 (UK)
Barrel House Woman No. 2/*Good Woman Blues/Ain't It A Shame/George Street Blues/Just A Rag/Alabama Woman Blues/I Believe I'll Make A Change/Don't Start No Stuff/You Left Me Crying/Suicide Blues/How Long Has That Evening Train Been Gone/Eleven Twenty-Nine Blues/Take A Walk Around The Corner/New How Long How Long Blues* Part 2/*Four Day Rider/Rocks In My Bed/Sloppy Drunk Blues/Going Back Home/Big Four Blues/It's Too Short*
The hugely popular and influential Indianapolis pianist Leroy Carr was the prime shaper of the urban blues. He was a deceptively fine pianist of great variation, and his music here ranges from the beautiful slow blues of *Ain't It A Shame* to the powerful boogie of *Barrel House Woman*, and a little hokum too.

220 Barrelhouse Women, 1925–1933. The Piano Blues, Volume Nineteen
Various Artists
Magpie PY 4419 (UK)—*LP*
Cow Cow Davenport & Ivy Smith, *State Street Jive*; Dorotha Trowbridge,

Slavin' Mama Blues; Margaret Thornton, *Texas Bound*; Elzadie Robinson, *St Louis Cyclone Blues*; Mary Johnson, *Mean Black Man Blues*; Lucille Bogan, *Coffee Grindin' Blues*; Margaret Whitmire, *That Thing's Done Been Put On Me*; Ida Mae Mack, *Goodbye Rider*; Lillian Miller, *Kitchen Blues*; Elzadie Robinson, *The Santa Claus Crave*; Mozelle Alderson & Blind James Beck, *State Street Special*; Evelyn Brickey, *Down In The Valley*; Mary Johnson, *Black Man Blues*; Elizabeth Washington, *Riot Call Blues*; Mary Johnson, *Morning Sun Blues*; Lil Johnson, *You'll Never Miss Your Jelly Till Your Jelly Roller's Gone*
As notable for its vocal variety as for its piano accompanists, this album includes styles ranging from the professional to the decidedly amateur, but with no slackening of interest or enjoyment. Sweet-voiced Margaret Thornton and pianist Blind James Beck, Lucille Bogan, and Mary Johnson are a few among many highlights.

221 Walter Davis: Complete Recorded Works 1933–1952 In Chronological Order, Volume 1, 2 August 1933 to 28 July 1935
Document DOCD 5281 (Au)
Red Cross Blues/L & N Blues/Moonlight Blues/Life Boat Blues/Night Creepin'/Evil Woman/You Don't Smell Right/All Worn Out/Oil Field Blues/What's The Use Of Worrying/Stormy Weather Blues Part 1/*Stormy Weather Blues* Part 2/*What You Got On Your Mind/Poor Grinder Blues/Red Cross Blues* Part 2/*Sloppy Drunk Again/Travelin' This Lonesome Road/Sad And Lonesome Blues/Minute Man Blues* Part 1/*Minute Man Blues* Part 2/*Sweet Sixteen/Wonder Where My Baby's Gone/Lay Around On Your D.B.A./Dentist Blues/Root Man Blues*
The under rated Walter Davis was enormously popular in the 1930s for songs and performances steeped in the deepest melancholy. Even his pornographic blues were bluer than most. Sykes accompanied his first recordings, but once Davis played his own piano he revealed a distinct style and talent to move his listeners.

222 Barrelhouse Piano Blues And Stomps: The Complete Recorded Works Of Herve Duerson, Turner Parrish, Kingfish Bill Tomlin 1929–1933
Document DOCD 5193 (Au)
Alura Mack, *I'm Busy You Can't Come In*; Herve Duerson, *Avenue Strut/Naptown Special/Easy Drag/Evening Chimes Waltz*; Teddy Moss, *Texas Dream Blues (Dreamin' Of Texas)/Ocean Wave Blues/Dyin' In The Electric Chair/You Broke My Heart Baby/Heart-Breaker Blues/Back-Biter Blues*; Dudley Brown [Turner Parrish], *Wake Up In The Morning Blues/Western Traveller Blues*; Teddy Moss, *Sympathizin' Blues (Sorry Blues)/Easy Papa*; Harry Campbell, *You'll Be Sorry One Day*; Turner Parrish, *Graveyard Blues/Ain't Gonna Be Your Dog No More/Trenches/Fives*; Kingfish Bill Tomlin, *Dupree Blues/Army Blues/Hot Box/Mean And Unkind Blues*
Duerson's mixture of ragtime, jazz, and light blues contrasts strongly with Turner Parrish's solid blues and boogies, the breakneck *Trenches*, and the more leisurely *Fives*, which is like no other. Tomlin is mostly notable for *Hot Box* and *Mean And Unkind*, with the enticing suggestion of Louise Johnson as pianist.

223 **Little Brother Montgomery: Complete Recorded Works 1930–1936 In Chronological Order**

Document DOCD 5109 (Au)

No Special Rider Blues/Vicksburg Blues; "E" Montgomery, *Louisiana Blues/Frisco Hi-Ball Blues*; Little Brother Montgomery, *The Woman I Love Blues/Pleading Blues/Vicksburg Blues* No. 2/*Mama You Don't Mean Me No Good*; Little Brother, *Misled Blues/The First Time I Met You/A. & V. Railroad Blues/Tantalizing Blues/Vicksburg Blues* Part 3/*Louisiana Blues* Part 2/*Santa Fe Blues/West Texas Blues/Never Go Wrong Blues/Sorrowful Blues/Mistreatin' Woman Blues/Chinese Man Blues/Farish Street Jive/Crescent City Blues/Shreveport Farewell*

Little Brother's wanderings led to his playing in barrelhouse, jazz, and swing bands, followed by a Chicago career of jazz, blues, R & B, and popular music; finally, he became legendary on the rediscovery circuit. He was the originator of *Vicksburg Blues* (or the *44's*) and these early sides show most facets of an extraordinary talent.

224 **The Sparks Brothers: Complete Recorded Works In Chronological Order 1932–1935**

Document DOCD 5315 (Au)

Pinetop & Lindberg, *Louisiana Bound/I Believe I'll Make A Change/4–11–44/East Chicago Blues*; Elizabeth Washington, *Riot Call Blues/Whiskey Blues/Mistreated Blues*; Tecumseh McDowell, *My Man Blues/So Called Friend Blues*; Dorotha Trowbridge, *Bad Luck Blues/Slavin' Mama Blues*; Sparks Brothers, *61 Highway/Down On The Levee/Chicago's Too Much For Me*; Flyin' Lindburg [Milton Sparks], *I.C. Train Blues/No Good Woman Blues*; Pinetop [Aaron Sparks], *Tell Her About Me/Every Day I Have The Blues/Got The Blues About My Baby/Workhouse Blues*; Milton Sparks, *Erie Train Blues/Ina Blues/Grinder Blues/I Wake Up In The Morning*

St Louis blues from pianist Pinetop (Aaron) and his twin brother, vocalist Lindberg (Milton) Sparks. Restrained accompaniments and easy-paced boogies like *4–11–44, East Chicago*, or *Tell Her About Me* abound. *Believe I'll Make A Change* and two seminal performances of *Every Day I Have The Blues* (one version as *Whiskey Blues*) give much food for thought.

225 **Deep South Blues Piano 1935–1937: Complete Recorded Works In Chronological Order**

Various Artists

Document DOCD 5233 (Au)

Harry Chatmon, *Please Don't Do It No More/Letter From Texas/Hoo Doo Blues/Smoke-Stack Blues/Deep Blue Ocean Blues/These Jackson Women Will Not Treat You Right/Black Ants Blues/Quarrelin' Mama Blues*; Blind Mack, *Rootin' Ground-Hog Blues/Keep Your Good Woman Home*; Kid Stormy Weather, *Short Hair Blues/Bread And Water Blues*; Mack Rhinehart & Brownie Stubblefield, *If I Leave Here Running/Dirty No Gooder/Clay County Blues/Lonesome House Blues/Lost Woman Blues/You Don't Know My Mind/Broke And Hungry/T.P.N. Moaner/I Can't Take It Anymore/Uptown Blues/Blues After Sundown/Open Back Door Blues*

Regional characteristics are thin on the ground here. Kid Stormy Weather's is a rare example of 1930s New Orleans blues piano; Harry, one of the lesser-known Chatmon brothers, may be representative of the under-recorded Mississippi piano blues but Mack Rhinehart, from Tennessee perhaps, shows more the influence of his contemporaries.

226 Roosevelt Sykes: Complete Recorded Works In Chronological Order, Volume 4, 18 August 1934 to 22 May 1936
Various Artists
Document DOCD 5119 (Au)
Roosevelt Sykes, *D.B.A. Blues/Ethel Mae Blues*; Johnnie Strauss, *Radio Broadcasting Blues/Old Market Street Blues*; Arthur McKay, *Central Limited Blues/ Heavy Stuff Blues*; Dorothy Baker, *Steady Grinding Blues*; Roosevelt Sykes, *D.B.A. Blues* No. 2/*Dirty Mother For You* (60503-A)/*Dirty Mother For You* (60503-D)/*The Cannon Ball/Jet Black Snake/She Left Me Cold In Hand/Driving Wheel Blues/Barrel House Man/Second Floor Blues/Sister Kelly Blues/Soft And Mellow/Sugar Hill Blues/Take Off Box/The Honeydripper/Dirty Mother For You* (90738)
During the mid-1930s Sykes settled down into a rocking blues style, lyrically as inventive as ever. Along with his mastery of the "blue blues" are other intriguing songs—*Sugar Hill*, the curiously downbeat *Barrel House Man, The Cannon Ball* (a vocal and piano *tour de force* of *Cow Cow Blues*) and his classic *Driving Wheel Blues*.

227 Lucille Bogan (Bessie Jackson): Complete Recorded Works In Chronological Order, Volume 3, 30 July 1934 to 8 March 1935
Blues Documents BDCD 6038 (Au)
Bessie Jackson, *You Got To Die Someday/Lonesome Midnight Blues/Boogan Ways Blues/My Man Is Boogan Me/Pig Iron Sally/I Hate That Train Called The M. And O./Drinking Blues/Tired As I Can Be/Sweet Man, Sweet Man/ Down In Boogie Alley/Changed Ways Blues/Bo-Easy Blues/That's What My Baby Likes/Shave 'Em Dry* (take 1)/*Shave 'Em Dry* (alternate take 1)/*Shave 'Em Dry* (alternate take 2)/*Barbecue Bess/B.D. Woman's Blues/Jump Steady Daddy/Man Stealer Blues/Stew Meat Blues/Skin Game Blues*
Perfect piano accompaniments by Walter Roland to the tough-voiced Lucille Bogan (Bessie Jackson) in all moods. Whether understating or rolling out an emphatic boogie, Roland was the perfect foil. Even to her more robust songs he brings an inner mournfulness much like Walter Davis.

228 Speckled Red: Complete Recorded Works 1929–1938
Document DOCD 5205 (Au)
House Dance Blues/The Dirty Dozen/Wilkins Street Stomp/The Dirty Dozen No. 2/*We Got To Get That Fixed/Speckled Red's Blues/The Right String But The Wrong Yo Yo/Lonesome Mind Blues/Welfare Blues/Down On The Levee/Do The Georgia/Early In The Morning/Take It Easy/Try Me One More Time/Louise Baltimore Blues/What Makes You Treat Me Mean?/St. Louis Stomp/You Got To Fix It*; Willie Hatcher, *They're Mean To Me/So Unkind*; Speckled Red, *Dad's Piece/Oh Red!/Early In The Morning*
These complete pre-war recordings show Speckled Red's boisterous talent and sense of good-timing. Like all barrelhouse players, he was strident voiced; his

main trademark was an unusually melodic boogie bass into which he would break at the least provocation. Bonus tracks from 1956 show no lessening of his exuberance.

229 Peetie Wheatstraw, The Devil's Son-In-Law: Complete Recorded Works In Chronological Order, Volume 1, 13 September 1930 to 17 March 1932

Document DOCD 5241 (Au)

Tennessee Peaches Blues/Four O'Clock In The Morning/Don't Feel Welcome Blues/Strange Man Blues/School Days/So Soon/So Long Blues/Mama's Advice/ Ain't It A Pity And A Shame?/Don't Hang My Clothes On No Barb Wire Line/ C And A Blues/Six Weeks Old Blues/Devil's Son-In-Law/Pete Wheatstraw/ Creeping Blues/Ice And Snow Blues; Pretty Boy Walker, *The Breaks I'm Gettin'/Hog-Love Blues*; Peetie Wheatstraw, *Police Station Blues/All Alone Blues/Can't See Blues/Sleepless Nights Blues*

St Louis bluesman Peetie Wheatstraw favored a quiet accompaniment to his songs, with a characteristic piano introduction and similar, unvarying tempos. He was a competent and distinctive pianist, and, in line with other 1930s blues artists, his singing and lyrics, rather than his piano playing, accounted for his popularity.

230 Peter Chatman As Memphis Slim: The Complete Recordings 1940–1941

Blues Collection 158032 (Fr)

Peter Chatman & His Washboard Band, *Diggin' My Potatoes* No. 2/*The Jive Blues/Last Pair Of Shoes Blues/Miss Ora Lee Blues/Blue Evening Blues/Blues At Midnight*; Memphis Slim, *Beer Drinking Woman/You Didn't Mean Me No Good/Grinder Man Blues/Empty Room Blues/Shelby County Blues/I See My Great Mistake/Old Taylor/I Believe I'll Settle Down/Jasper's Gal/You Got To Help Me Some/Two Of A Kind/Whiskey Store Blues/Maybe I'll Loan You A Dime/Me, Myself And I/Whiskey And Gin Blues/You Gonna Worry Too/This Life I'm Living/Caught The Old Coon At Last/Don't Think That You're Smart/ Lend Me Your Love*

Massive over-exposure on record has tended to diminish Memphis Slim's reputation, but this excellent collection of his first recordings from the 1940s would restore it. Solid, swinging piano showing a debt to Sykes, and fine, often slyly humorous lyrics make this CD one of the best examples of the Bluebird blues.

(ii) Texas

231 Texas Piano, Volume 1: The Complete Recorded Works Of George And Hersal Thomas, Moanin' Bernice Edwards (1923–1935)

Document DOCD 5224 (Au)

Clay Custer, *The Rocks*; George Thomas, *Fast Stuff Blues/Don't Kill Him In Here*; Hersal Thomas, *Suitcase Blues*; Hociel Thomas, *I Can't Feel Frisky Without My Liquor/Worried Down With The Blues* (12188)/*I Must Have It*; Hersal Thomas, *Hersal Blues*; Hociel Thomas, *Worried Down With The Blues* (9167)/*Fish Tail Dance*; Moanin' Bernice Edwards, *Sunshine Blues/Lonesome Longing Blues/Mean Man Blues/Long Tall Mama/Moaning Blues/Southbound*

Blues/Hard Hustling Blues/High Powered Mama Blues/Low Down Dirty Shame Blues/Born To Die Blues/Two-Way Mind Blues/Jack Of All Trades; Bernice Edwards, *Bantam Rooster Blues*; Bernice Edwards, Black Boy Shine & Howling Smith, *Ninth Street Stomp/Hot Mattress Stomp*; Bernice Edwards, *Butcher Shop Blues*

Historically important reissue of the influential Thomas family of Houston (excluding only Sippie (Wallace) Thomas). Elder brother George Thomas was perhaps the first to use elements of boogie woogie; younger brother Hersal was a big influence on the Chicago piano players and Albert Ammons in particular; George's daughter Hociel sang and later played piano on her rediscovery recordings (**190**). Bernice Edwards, a family friend, was a fine-voiced but limited pianist of the Santa Fe school.

232 Dallas 1927–1929: The Piano Blues

Various Artists

Magpie PYCD 15 (UK)

Texas Bill Day & Billiken Johnson, *Elm Street Blues*; Whistlin' Alex Moore, *Heart Wrecked Blues*; Billiken Johnson & Neal Roberts, *Frisco Blues*; Texas Bill Day, *Goin' Back To My Baby*; Hattie Hudson, *Doggone My Good Luck Soul*; Billiken Johnson & Fred Adams, *Sun Beam Blues*; Whistlin' Alex Moore, *Blue Bloomer Blues*; Bessie Tucker, *Penitentiary/The Dummy*; Texas Bill Day, *Good Morning Blues*; Whistlin' Alex Moore, *They May Not Be My Toes*; Ida Mae Mack, *When You Lose Your Daddy/Elm Street Blues*; Texas Bill Day & Billiken Johnson, *Billiken's Weary Blues*; Billiken Johnson & Neal Roberts, *Wild Jack Blues*; Whistlin' Alex Moore, *West Texas Woman*; Bobbie Cadillac, *Carbolic Acid Blues*; Texas Bill Day, *Burn The Trestle Down*; Billiken Johnson & Fred Adams, *Interurban Blues*; Whistlin' Alex Moore, *Ice Pick Blues*

This Dallas collection from 1927–9 shows how obstinately individual the Texas piano blues were: quiet, reflective accompaniments in that idiosyncratic jazz-blues style often at odds with the exceptional colour of the lyrics. Billiken Johnson's vocal effects are an oddity; more representative are Moore, Hudson, and Cadillac.

(iii) Boogie Woogie

233 Cripple Clarence Lofton: Complete Recorded Works In Chronological Order, Volume 2, 1939–1943

Blues Documents BDCD 6007 (Au)

Pine Top's Boogie Woogie/More Motion/Sweet Tooth/Sixes And Sevens/Clarence's Blues/Lofty Blues/House Rent Struggle/Juice Joint/Salty Woman Blues/Blue Boogie/Streamline Train (125)/*I Don't Know* (126)/*Policy Blues/I Don't Know/The Fives/Deep End Boogie (South End Boogie)/In De Mornin'/Early Blues/I Don't Know* (No. 2) (142)/*Streamline Train* (143)

Lofton's Solo Art and Session recordings were mainly a return to his great original themes—the staggering *Pine Top's Boogie Woogie* always an exception—but he did re-create Hersal Thomas' *Fives* (reflected here in three versions: *Sixes And Sevens, Clarence's Blues,* and *The Fives*). Totally new for Session were two more masterpieces, *Deep End Boogie* and the delightful and magical *In De Mornin'*.

234 **Montana Taylor With Chippie Hill And Almond Leonard**
Southland SCD 30
Bertha "Chippie" Hill, *Worried Jailhouse Blues/Black Market Blues*; Montana Taylor, *Low Down Bugle* (take 11B)/*Low Down Bugle* (take 11C); Bertha "Chippie" Hill, *Mistreatin' Mr Dupree*; Montana Taylor, *Sweet Sue/In The Bottom/Rotten Break Blues/I Can't Sleep/'Fo Day Blues/Detroit Rocks/Indiana Avenue Stomp/Montana's Blues/Five O'Clocks* (broadcast)/*I Can't Sleep* (broadcast)
The Circle rediscovery recordings from 1946 include as a wonderful bonus clean copies of the two air-shots, *I Can't Sleep* and the arm-busting *Five O'Clocks*, and, never before issued, an alternate take of *Low Down Bugle* and a jaunty *Detroit Rocks*.

235 **Albert Ammons, The King of Boogie Woogie (1939–1949)**
Blues Classics BC 27—LP
Monday Struggle/Boogie Woogie/Boogie Woogie Blues/Boogie Woogie Stomp/Chicago In Mind/Bass Goin' Crazy/Boogie Woogie At The Civic Opera/I Don't Want To See You [Jack Cooley, vocal]/*Swanee River Boogie/The Clipper/Ammons Stomp/Why I'm Leaving You* [Jack Cooley, vocal]/*Tuxedo Boogie/Baltimore Breakdown*
Ammons is on display here as both superb solo boogie pianist and superb band boogie pianist. The beautiful solos *Monday Struggle, Boogie Woogie Blues*, and *Chicago In Mind* contrast with the small group jazz of the disarming *Swanee River Boogie*, the near R & B of drummer Jack Cooley's two vocals and the dangerous riffs of *Ammons Stomp* and *Baltimore Breakdown*. The wheel had turned full circle from 1936.

(iv) Post-war and the Revival

236 **Champion Jack Dupree 1945–1953**
Krazy Kat KK CD 08 (UK)
Stumbling Block Blues/Number Nine Blues; Champion Jack Dupree With Big Chief Ellis & His Blues Stars, *Deacon's Party/I'm Gonna Find You Someday*; Bob Harris, *Up And Down The Hill*; Jack Dupree Trio, *I Think You Need A Shot*; Champion Jack Dupree, *Drunk Again*; Duke Bayou & His Mystic Six [Dupree], *Rub A Little Boogie*; Lightning Junior & The Empires [Dupree], *Ragged And Hungry*; Meat Head Johnson & His Blues Hounds [Dupree], *Barrel House Mama/Goin' Back To Louisiana/Old, Old Woman/Mean Black Snake*; Bob Harris, *Baby You Say You Love Me*; Lightning Junior & The Empires [Dupree], *Somebody Changed The Lock*; Jack Dupree & His Quartet, *Fifth Avenue Woman/Highway 31*; Champion Jack Dupree, *Shake Baby Shake/Highway Blues*' Bob Harris, *Drinkin' Little Woman*; Jack Dupree & His Band, *Mean Mistreatin Mama*; Champion Jack Dupree, *Shim Sham Shimmy*
Jack Dupree's engaging personality played some part in a career spanning almost 50 years, but he was also able to adapt his limited, but always attractive, driving piano to the demands of the small-group R&B of the 1940s and 1950s, as on these excellent New York sides.

237 Unfinished Boogie: Western Blues Piano, 1946–1952
Various Artists
Muskadine 104—LP
Thunder Smith, *Thunder's Unfinished Boogie/New Worried Life Blues*; Jimmy McCracklin, *Highway 101/Street Loafin' Woman*; Thunder Smith, *Little Mama Boogie*; Mercy Dee, *Straight And Narrow*; Little Son Willis, *Howling Woman/ Roll Me Over Slow*; Little Willie Littlefield, *Little Willie's Boogie*; Thunder Smith, *West Coast Blues/Low Down Dirty Ways*; Luther "Rocky Mountain" Stoneham, *Mable Blues*; Mercy Dee, *The Pay Off/Baba-Du-Lay Fever (G.I. Fever)*; Little Son Willis, *Skin And Bones*; Jimmy McCracklin, *Baby Don't You Want To Go*
Texas, always independent, could still produce notable post-war pianists, as here, with only McCracklin from outside the state. But now the influences on Santa Fe pianist Thunder Smith and Willie Littlefield are the urban 1930s and Pete Johnson respectively; only Willis and Mercy Dee remain true to the rich tradition of Texas.

238 The Ma Grinder: Texas Barrelhouse Piano
Robert Shaw
Arhoolie CD 377
The Ma Grinder/Hattie Green/The Fives/Black Gal/Put Me In The Alley/ Groceries On My Shelf (Piggly Wiggly)/The Clinton/People, People/The Cows/ Whores Is Funky/Here I Come With My Dirty, Dirty Duckings On/Saturday Night Special/Jim Nappy/Fast Santa Fe (Bear Cat)/Mobile & K.C. Line/Going Down To The Gulf/She Used To Be My Baby (Ma Grinder No. 2*)*
With Buster Pickens, Robert Shaw was the last of the pianists who followed the Santa Fe railroad. Retired, Shaw played for his own pleasure and in 1963 recorded the well-known and lesser-known anthems of the Santa Fe, *The Cows*, *The Ma Grinder*, and *The Clinton*, with all the verve of a lifetime of music-making.

239 Atlanta Bounce
Piano Red
Arhoolie CD 379
Atlanta Bounce/Ten Cent Shot/Pushing That Thing/Red's How Long Blues/ Corrine, Corrina/You Ain't Got A Chance/My Baby Left Me/Let's Get It On/ Got You On My Mind/Boogie Time/Blues, Blues, Blues/Please, Baby, Come On Home/Telephone Blues/Do She Love Me/Right String But The Wrong Yo-Yo (recorded 1972)/*Right String But The Wrong Yo-Yo* (recorded 1956)/*Don't Get Around Much Anymore/Umph-Umph-Umph/Got You On My Mind/Rockin With Red/Red's Boogie*
Both "Piano Red" (Willie Perryman) and his elder brother "Speckled Red" (Rufus Perryman) had engaging boogie piano styles. Piano Red's career in R & B bands, however, means that his material was much more commercial and often less interesting. As well as the more commercial offerings, solo recordings from 1972 show the man hidden behind the "Dr Feelgood" soubriquet.

240 Otis Spann Is The Blues
Otis Spann & Robert Lockwood Jr
Candid CCD 79001
Otis Spann, *The Hard Way*; Robert Lockwood Jr, *Take A Little Walk With*

Me; Otis Spann, *Otis In The Dark*; Robert Lockwood Jr, *Little Boy Blue*; Otis Spann, *Country Boy/Beat-Up Team*; Robert Lockwood Jr, *My Daily Wish*; Otis Spann, *Great Northern Stomp*; Robert Lockwood Jr, *I Got Rambling On My Mind* No. 2; Otis Spann, *Worried Life Blues*

With Robert Lockwood Jr on guitar, Otis Spann, the natural inheritor of Big Maceo's piano stool, had the chance in 1960 to make the definitive post-war piano solo album for a small jazz label. The result is modern Chicago blues piano playing and singing of the highest order.

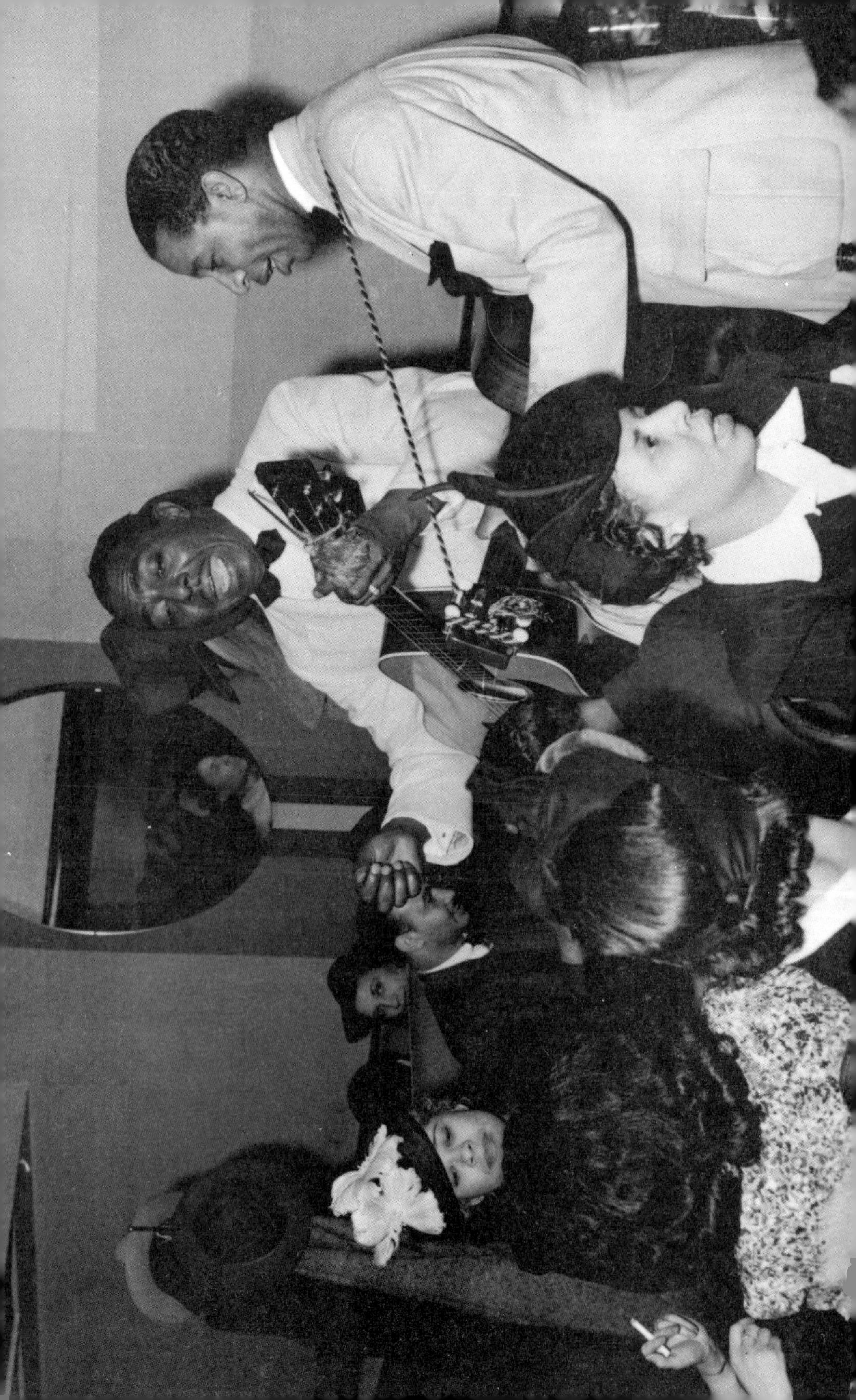

JOHN COWLEY

7 The 1930s and Library of Congress

The decade of the 1930s is often considered a time during which blues became ossified by commercial pressures. As with most generalizations, this contains a grain of truth. A much more complex picture emerges, however, if one adopts an open mind to the era's recordings and scrutinizes the historical material. It must also be remembered that the music usually reflects only one segment of the black community—the artisan and less-skilled employee.

Beginning in the depths of economic depression, this decade is the most rewarding and best-documented encapsulation of black music in North America. Commercial recordings provide a great deal of evidence for the dynamics of musical continuity and change. The "race record" market was dominated by RCA Victor (the Bluebird label), Columbia (a variety of marques), and Decca (which started trading in 1934). From 1933, Roosevelt's New Deal encouraged popular recognition for the most disadvantaged and this allowed a corresponding series of field recordings to be sponsored by the Library of Congress. The results constitute an unparalleled archive of rural black folk music and allow comparison between commercial and non-commercial approaches to recording in the same period.

Both methods of securing performances confirm regional styles. A tendency towards uniformity in commercial recordings was tempered by migration of rural tradition bearers (and their patrons) to urban centers, or segregated people from one urban center to another. There is variety in repertoire and the use of musical instruments to accommodate disparate audiences. Library of Congress recordings, with an emphasis on older folk styles, provide further evidence along these lines. They also demonstrate how traditions were sustained in tandem with newer styles, readily available from record shops.

Essential Records

(i) "News & The Blues" and the Library of Congress

From slavery, topicality has been a particular feature of African-American song, referred to by many observers of differing musical

Lonnie Johnson (right) plays in Tavern, Chicago South Side, 1941 (*Russell Lee/FSA/Library of Congress*)

styles across the continents, North and South. This is true for both sacred and secular traditions and, as the CD title **News & The Blues** implies, includes many blues recordings.

The songs in this collection range from sides made in the 1920s to the 1950s, with three religious items that stand alongside the secular topics. Of these, Blind Willie Johnson's *God Moves On The Water* is a religious ballad about the sinking of the SS *Titanic* in 1912, while the title of Sister Terrell's *The Gambling Man* is self-explanatory.

Many of the topics covered revolve around the hard times occasioned by the economic depression of the 1930s—*W.P.A. Blues, Unemployment Stomp, '29 Blues, Three Ball Blues*. Others are panegyrics for particular personalities; famous blues singers like Leroy Carr and Ma Rainey, or black heroes such as the boxer Joe Louis. Mississippi John Hurt's *Frankie* is a version of the black murder ballad *Frankie And Albert*, while Victoria Spivey's *Dope Head Blues* deals with drug addiction. Bessie Smith's famous *Black Water Blues* records the consequences of Mississippi River flooding and Charlie Patton's *34 Blues* looks with pessimism at the year it was recorded (and in which he died). This self-reflection is also evident in Bukka White's *Parchman Farm Blues* (commenting on the prison farm where he served time). A melancholy attitude is also expressed in Homer Harris' *Atomic Bomb Blues* (1946), based on the terrifying events that accelerated the end of World War II. Poverty and lack of permanent accommodation remained among the black community even after the war-time economic recovery. Willie "Long Time" Smith's 1947 recording *Homeless Blues*, while reporting this desperation, expresses the hope that "the time going to be better."

This hope had been sustained by the New Deal, following Roosevelt's election as President of the United States in 1933. From this time a changed attitude towards public spending boosted the collection of folk music by the Library of Congress. Its Archive of Folk Song (now Archive of Folk Culture) had been in existence singe 1928. The thrust of the New Deal, combined with the push of John A. Lomax and his son Alan Lomax, however, allowed it to become a major repository of recorded American folk music. This heyday lasted from 1933 (when the Lomaxes started their expeditions) to 1942, when World War II brought regular field recording assignments to a halt.

Most field trips took in several states, but in 1941–2 there was a special survey of black music in Coahoma County, Mississippi. Alan Lomax's celebrated recordings in 1941 of McKinley Morganfield—later to become well known as the Chicago bluesman Muddy Waters—were one result. **The Complete Plantation Recordings** contains all the known sides supervised by Lomax at this historic occasion in

August 1941, and at a session cut in July the year following. Recorded in 1941, *I Be's Troubled* was Waters' personal holler, set to slide-guitar accompaniment and based on a church song. He was to record it in Chicago as *I Can't Be Satisfied* (**361**). His style of guitar playing was patterned on Son House, one of the most popular north-Mississippi blues musicians of the 1930s, whose influence can also be heard in the lyrics to Muddy's *Country Blues*. Muddy also sang *Burr Clover Farm Blues*, duetting on guitar with Son Sims (formerly Charlie Patton's fiddle player). This commemorates the development of "burr clover" on the Stoval plantation where Waters worked.

In 1942 there was a concerted effort to record something of the repertoire of the string band with which Muddy played (the Son Simms Four). With Sims on fiddle throughout, Waters took the vocal on *Ramblin' Kid Blues* and *Roaslie*. Louis Ford, an old-time musician who played mandolin, sang a very early blues *Joe Turner* (about a prison turnkey) and Percy Thomas (a guitarist) was the singer on *Pearlie Mae Blues*. The latter was closer to the more modern repertoire featured in Muddy's individual recordings, which included his version of *Take A Walk With Me*, popularized by Robert Lockwood in 1941 (**106**). On some sides Muddy was accompanied on second guitar by either Son Sims or Charley Berry. The latter was also a slide-guitar player and, in accompaniment to Waters' moaned vocals, the echo of their slide-guitar duets on the two versions of *I Be Bound To Write To You* create a particularly haunting sound. The lyrics to Muddy's second *Country Blues* show considerable difference when compared with his recording of 1941.

On advice from Muddy Waters, Son House was found by Lomax in 1941. Son also recorded on both of the Coahoma County expeditions. **The Complete Library Of Congress Sessions 1941–1942** contains all of these sides. He had made significant commercial recordings in 1930, which represent a record company's view of his music at that time (**82**). His sessions of 1941–2, however, explore his repertoire in the context of early influences and employment of different musical styles.

House had one of the most distinctive singing voices in blues and was an emotive slide-guitar player. In 1941 he recorded three pieces with a small band, comprising Willie Brown on second guitar, Fiddlin' Joe Martin on mandolin, and Leroy Williams on harmonica. Brown had been an associate of Charlie Patton, and a key member of the school of blues that developed in Drew, Mississippi (**81**, **82**, **83**). Two of the three songs were versions of the same theme—*Levee Camp Blues* and *Government Fleet Blues*—and reflect on the lives of workers who maintained Mississippi River embankments, or levees. The third piece was a rendering of *Walking Blues*, one of the most influential songs in

Son's repertoire. This was a remake of one of his unissued recordings from 1930, but had been learned in person from House by both Robert Johnson (**86**) and Muddy Waters. In addition Son performed *Shetland Pony Blues* (displaying guitar-picking skills), the traditional *Delta Blues* to his own guitar and Williams' harmonica and, with Martin and Brown, an unaccompanied *Camp Hollers* (relating to levee construction). Son's recordings in 1942 include: *Special Rider Blues*, the earliest song he learned (from Willie Williams of Mattson, Mississippi); and *Depot Blues* (also picked up from Williams, of Greenwood [*sic*], Mississippi). There was a demonstration of one of his guitar tunings, *They Key Of Minor*, and another version of *The Pony Blues*, which he told Lomax he had been taught by Willie Brown. Likewise, the two affecting recordings of *The Jinx Blues* reflect the influence of Brown (and the Drew school). The piece Son called *Walking Blues* in 1942 is more akin to *My Black Mama*, from his session of 1930 (**82**). He also performed contemporary songs.

The recordings by House and Waters are a watershed for blues in the 1930s and the social changes signaled by World War II. House, the old-time Mississippi performer, whose repertoire was captured so fortuitously, was soon to move to Rochester, New York, where he eventually settled and retired from music. Muddy Waters, his young disciple, was also to migrate, but to Chicago, where he became a leading pioneer in the rejuvenation of commercially recorded blues in the late 1940s (**361**).

241 **News & The Blues: Telling It Like It Is**
Various Artists
Columbia CK 46217/467249-2 (UK)
Bessie Smith, *Black Water Blues*; Victoria Spivey, *Dope Head Blues*; Blind Willie Johnson, *If I Had My Way I'd Tear The Building Down*; Mississippi John Hurt, *Frankie*; Blind Willie Johnson, *God Moves On The Water*; Lucille Bogan, *Groceries On The Shelf*; Charlie Patton, *'34 Blues*; Casey Bill Weldon, *W.P.A. Blues*; Big Bill Broonzy, *Unemployment Stomp*; Alfred Fields, *'29 Blues*; Jack Kelly, *Joe Louis Special*; Blind Boy Fuller, *Three Ball Blues*; Bukka White, *Parchman Farm Blues*; Bill Gaither, *Life Of Leroy Carr*; Memphis Minnie, *Ma Rainey*; Peter Cleighton, *Moonshine Man Blues*; Big Bill Broonzy, *In The Army Now*; Sister O.M. Terrell, *The Gambling Man*; Homer Harris, *Atomic Bomb Blues*; Willie "Long Time" Smith, *Homeless Blues*

242 **The Complete Plantation Recordings—The Historic 1941–42 Library of Congress Field Recordings**
Muddy Waters
MCA Chess CHD 9344
Country Blues No. 1/*Interview* No. 1/*I Be's Troubled*/*Interview* No. 2/*Burr Clover Farm Blues*/*Interview* No. 3; Son Simms Four [Waters, vocal], *Ramblin'*

Kid Blues (partial)/*Ramblin' Kid Blues*/*Roaslie*/*Joe Turner* [Louis Ford, vocal]/ *Pearlie Mae Blues* [Percy Thomas, vocal]; Muddy Waters, *Take A Walk With Me*/*Burr Clover Blues*/*Interview* No. 4/*I Be Bound To Write To You* No. 1/*I Be Bound To Write To You* No. 2/*You're Gonna Miss Me When I'm Gone* No. 1/ *You Got To Take Sick And Die Some Of These Days*/*Why Don't You Live So God Can Use You*/*Country Blues* No. 2/*You're Gonna Miss Me When I'm Gone* No. 2/*32–20 Blues*

243 **The Complete Library Of Congress Sessions 1941–1942**
Son House
Travelin' Man TM CD 02 (UK)
Levee Camp Blues/*Government Fleet Blues*/*Walking Blues*/*Shetland Pony Blues*; [Fiddlin' Joe Martin], *Fo' Clock Blues*; Son House [with Martin & Willie Brown], *Camp Hollers*; Son House [& Leroy Williams], *Delta Blues*; Son House, *Special Rider Blues* (test)/*Special Rider Blues*/*Low Down Dirty Dog Blues*/*Depot Blues*/*The Key Of Minor* (interview)/*American Defense*/*Am I Right Or Wrong*/*Walking Blues*/*County Farm Blues*/*The Pony Blues*/*The Jinx Blues* Part 1 [No. 1]/*The Jinx Blues* Part 2 [No. 2]

(ii) Chicago and Indianapolis

Migration of black people from Southern states to Chicago, and other urban centers in the north, has been a continuing process for 150 years or more. This has been not simply from a rural to an urban environment, but from urban center to urban center. The treck northwards was in search of better employment prospects, and included musicians.

An established place for staging entertainments of all types, from the 1920s, the "Windy City" (as Chicago is known) gained a status as a permanent recording location for blues singers. The development of the genre in the city, therefore, is documented on record much more extensively than in most other locations.

Many performers gained their reputations in Chicago clubs and recording studios, including Big Bill Broonzy. Originally from Mississippi, the singer-guitarist was a well-established Chicago resident by the early 1930s and was known as an accompanist as well as a solo artist. On *I Can't Be Satisfied* in the collection **Good Time Tonight**, Broonzy is joined on second guitar by Frank Brasswell. This ragtime-like piece dates from 1930 and adjoins similar guitar-orientated sides from 1932—*Long Tall Mama, Worrying You Off My Mind* Part 1, and *Too Too Train Blues.* They serve as a useful starting-point in a selection of his repertoire devoted otherwise to the period 1937–1940, when he was at the height of his popularity. At this time Broonzy was playing with small bands that usually comprised piano, bass, and drums, but were sometimes augmented with a trumpet, saxophone, or clarinet. He was a prolific composer of his own songs, which were usually of a formal thematic nature rather than employing the traditional stanza-orientated lyrics of less city-wise performers. The majority of Bill's lyrics deal with male–female relationships, more often than not from the point of view either of a boastful male or a rejected male lover. Many of his songs became standards; an example in this collection is *Too Many Drivers*, which the New Orleans bluesman Smiley Lewis recorded for Imperial in 1950 (**482**). *Woodie Woodie* is based on the boogie-woogie motifs that had become highly fashionable by 1939 (the year of its recording).

With his longstanding popularity, it is probably significant that Broonzy is one of the few bluesmen to have written his own biography–*Big Bill Blues* (1955). It places his life and activities in relation to his contemporaries, one of whom was Memphis Minnie.

Minnie had begun her recording career in 1929, making a string of scintillating sides with her then husband "Kansas Joe" (McCoy). Both were fine singers and these early sessions are justly prized (**165**). By 1935 Minnie and Joe had dissolved their partnership. She had begun recording on her own two years earlier and **Hoodoo Lady**, Columbia's collection of her 1930s sides, includes *My Butcher Man* and *Ain't No Use Tryin' To Tell On Me* from this occasion in 1933. In this respect the CD parallels its companion Big Bill compilation. A sample of solo-guitar-orientated recordings feature alongside later pieces in small-band setting. Of the latter, some of the most distinctive are five titles from a 1938 session that included Charlie McCoy, the brother of her erstwhile partner, on mandolin, together with Minnie's own guitar, a pianist and a string bass player—*I Hate To See The Sun Go Down, Has Anyone Seen My Man?, Good Biscuits, I've Been Treated Wrong*, and *Keep On Eatin'*.

Like most of the songs in this collection (the others were recorded in 1936 and 1937), they deal with male–female relations. *Hoodoo Lady* mixes this with superstition, as do *I'm A Bad Luck Woman* and *Black Cat Blues* (which also contains sexual metaphor).

Minnie's popularity continued into the early 1940s (**186**), by which time she had teamed with another male guitarist–Ernest Lawlars (Little Son Joe). Along with Big Bill, she maintained her recording career into the 1950s (**368**), though Broonzy broadened his audience by playing in Europe in this period.

Another contemporary who moved to Chicago during the 1930s was singer and harmonica player John Lee Williamson. Better known as Sonny Boy Williamson, he came originally from Jackson, Tennessee, and began his recording career in 1937. This was cruelly cut short by his murder in 1948, by which time he had become the most recorded blues harmonica player, with an extensive catalog to his credit.

Williamson was an inventive performer, with a very distinctive style. A slight stammer could be heard in his singing and added engagingly to the attraction of his vocals. *Sugar Mama Blues*, from his first session, was one of his most popular songs. This is contained in **Sonny Boy Williamson: Complete Recorded Works In Chronological Order, Volume 1 (5 May 1937 to 17 June 1938)**, which concentrates on the earliest phase of his career. Other important sides from this session are *Good Morning, School Girl, Blue Bird Blues*, and *Got The Bottle Up And Gone*. They comprise a superb set of recordings, accompanied by the twin guitars of Mississippians Big Joe Williams and Robert Lee McCoy.

At his second session for Bluebird in 1937, Williamson was joined by Walter Davis on piano for *Up The Country Blues* and for the 1930s topical standard *Collector Man Blues*. Additional accompaniment was provided throughout the session by two guitarists, probably Robert Lee McCoy and Henry Townsend. *Early In The Morning* is another piece that became well known; there are also several songs about male–female relations, including the topically titled *Project Highway*.

At his next recording session, which took place in March 1938, there was another group of backing musicians, which included Yank Rachel on mandolin and Elijah Jones on guitar. On the CD, this commences with *My Little Cornelius*. Many of Williamson's pieces at this time are taken at a slow or medium temp, but *You Can Lead Me* and *I'm Tired Trucking My Blues Away* break with this pattern and are performed in a fast dance rhythm. Two of the most familiar sides from this occasion are *Decoration Blues* and *Beauty Parlour* (better known as *Miss Sadie Mae*), which became blues standards. *Honey Bee Blues* (another standard), dates from June 1938.

Williamson proved adept at changing and developing his style and his post-1942 sides are represented in Chapter 10, devoted to Chicago and the North (**373**).

That the migration of black musicians has been a complicated pattern is demonstrated by the careers of two blues pianists who based themselves in Indianapolis, Indiana. The first is Leroy Carr, one of the most popular urban singers of the late 1920s and early 1930s. Although he was born in Tennessee, his singing and playing epitomized sophistication, an urbanity consolidated on record by scintillating guitar accompaniment from Francis "Scrapper" Blackwell (originally from North Carolina).

Beginning with the highly successful *How Long–How Long Blues*, made in June 1928, Carr cut a stream of successful recordings in a career that lasted until his death in April 1935. For virtually the whole of this period he combined with Blackwell to create one of the most distinctive sounds in blues. His generally mournful and wistful vocals, to mellow piano accompaniment, were juxtaposed with the ringing sound of Blackwell's expertly played steel-bodied guitar.

Magpie's **Leroy Carr Vol. 2 1929–1935** draws together recordings from most of this productive period, and contains several songs that became blues standards—*Blues Before Sunrise, Mean Mistreater Mama*, and *When The Sun Goes Down.* The two-part *Straight Alki Blues* (which may be autobiographical–Carr died of alcoholism and nephritis) was also adopted by other performers. Examples include John Lee Williamson's *Shannon Street Blues* (recorded in 1938), or Big Mama Thornton's *Unlucky Girl* from 1965 (**198**).

By no means all of Leroy's pieces were dirges. *Gettin' All Wet* (on which Blackwell shares vocals in the chorus), *Papas's On The House Top, Barrel House Woman* and *Bread Baker* do not fit this pattern. *Carried Water For The Elephant* is a humorous account of gaining free access to a circus and hints at a performance for the vaudeville stage. Carr's high reputation, however, was based on his ability to summarize the melancholy in succinct, well-crafted subjective songs, and *Midnight Hour Blues, Florida Bound Blues* (written by Clarence Williams), and the prophetic *Six Cold Feet In The Ground* (recorded two months before his death) are prime examples of this skill.

Champion Jack Dupree moved from New Orleans, Louisiana, to Indianapolis in the 1930s. A former boxer, he learned piano technique in the dives of New Orleans, but polished his style in "Naptown." Here he came under the influence of Carr, and Dupree's early recorded performances reflect absorption of the traditions of both cities. By 1940 his singing and piano-playing ability had attracted the attention of the Chicago talent scout Lester Melrose, who organized the sessions issued in **New Orleans Barrelhouse Boogie**.

New Orleans blues pianists were not well represented in gramophone record catalogs before World War II. Jack Dupree's early performances, therefore, are especially important. Several of the songs mention the city, and others have musical themes that can be readily identified with post-war styles recorded there–*Heavy Heart Blues*, or *Junker Blues* (Chapter 13). Southern topics include the stomping [*Good Old*] *Cabbage Greens* (a sexual metaphor based on an earlier minstrel-like piece) and the descriptive *Chaing Gang Blues* (about conditions in a Georgia chain gang). In *Black Woman Swing*, the singer is returning from poverty and the hostile climate of the North to his "good for the soul" and "black as coal" woman in the South; and the subject of the somber *Angola Blues* is the well-known Louisiana State Penitentiary.

Many of Dupree's lyrics are organized around traditional stanzas and imagery. Some, however, are topical, such as *Warehouse Man*

Blues (from 1940), in which he complains of the withdrawal of Works Progress Administration relief in New Orleans, and also mentions the bonus owing to veteran soldiers. There were a number of similar topical blues and old-time music songs by white performers in this era, reflecting the view of the underprivileged towards the Depression and the New Deal. Some are printed in Alan Lomax's *Hard Hitting Songs For Hard-Hit People*, which documents the music of the period.

In addition to powerful and percussive piano playing, sometimes augmented by superb string bass from Wilson Swain or Ransom Knowling, Jack Dupree adopted the understated singing style favored by Leroy Carr. The popular ballad-like *All Alone Blues* (1941) is the best example, pinpointing the underlying richness of Dupree's voice that adds a cutting edge to the understatement. In this recording, *Jackie P. Blues* (about the generosity of a friend), and several other tracks, he is accompanied on guitar by Jesse Ellery, in the ringing Indianapolis-style pioneered by Scrapper Blackwell. Two previously unissued sides from the session provide useful pointers to the influence of earlier recordings on repertoire and the distribution of traditional themes. With minor lyrical variations, *Shady Lane* is the same song recorded as *Shady Lane Blues* by Leroy Carr in 1934. *Hurry Down Sunshine* (another Carr title from the same year), however, has just the line "Hurry down sunshine, see what tomorrow brings" in common with this piece. The latter, in which the line ends rather than opens the performance, is sung to the "44s" a traditional piano blues accompaniment represented on record by Little Brother Montgomery (*Vicksburg Blues*, **201**, **223**) and Roosevelt Sykes (**205**) among others.

While Indianapolis was his residence, Chicago was the place where Champion Jack Dupree was recorded, and this was usually the case for the few Indianapolis blues musicians who made records in the 1930s. New York City, however, was sometimes favored for sessions by the principal recording companies. Street singers, based on the Eastern Seaboard, or performers touring with established bands of musicians were joined occasionally by those who usually recorded in Chicago. Conversely, Eastern Seaboard artists sometimes traveled to the 'Windy City' to make their recordings.

244 Good Time Tonight

Big Bill Broonzy
Columbia CK 46219/467247-2 (UK)
Sammy Sampson [Big Bill], *I Can't Be Satisfied*; Big Bill, *Long Tall Mama/ Worrying You Off My Mind* Part 1/*Too Too Train Blues/Come Home Early/ Hattie Blues/I Want My Hands On It/Make A Date With An Angel (Got No Walking Shoes)/Horny Frog/I Believe I'll Go Back Home/Good Time Tonight/ Flat Foot Susie With Her Flat Yes Yes*; Big Bill & The Memphis Five, *W.P.A.*

Rag/Going Back To Arkansas; Big Bill, *It's A Low Down Dirty Shame/Too Many Drivers/Woodie Woodie/Whiskey And Good Time Blues/Merry Go Round Blues/You've Got To Hit The Right Lick*

245 **Hoodoo Lady (1933–1937) [1938]**
Memphis Minnie
Columbia CK 46775/467888-2 (UK)
Down In The Alley/Has Anyone Seen My Man?/I Hate To See The Sun Go Down/Ice Man (Come On Up)/Hoodoo Lady/I'm A Bad Luck Woman/Caught Me Wrong Again/Black Cat Blues/Good Morning/Man, You Won't Give Me No Money/Keep On Eatin'/I've Been Treated Wrong/Good Biscuits/Ain't No Use Tryin' To Tell On Me (I Know Something On You)/My Butcher Man/My Strange Man/If You See My Rooster (Please Run Him Home)/My Baby Don't Want Me No More/Please Don't Stop Him/I'm Going Don't You Know

246 **Sonny Boy Williamson: Complete Recorded Works In Chronological Order, Volume 1 (5 May 1937 to 17 June 1938)**
Document DOCD 5055 (Au)
Good Morning, School Girl/Blue Bird Blues/Jackson Blues/Got The Bottle Up and Gone/Sugar Mama Blues/Skinny Woman/Up The Country Blues/Worried Me Blues/Black Gal Blues/Collector Man Blues/Frigidaire Blues/Suzanna Blues/Early In The Morning/Project Highway/My Little Cornelius/Decoration Blues/You Can Lead Me/Moonshine/Miss Louisa Blues/Sunny Land/I'm Tired Trucking My Blues Away/Down South/Beauty Parlour/Until My Love Come Down/Honey Bee Blues

247 **Leroy Carr Vol. 2 1929–1935: The Piano Blues**
Magpie PYCD 17 (UK)
Straight Alki Blues Part 1/*Straight Alki Blues* Part 2/*Gettin' All Wet/Papa's On The House Top/Carried Water For The Elephant/Low Down Dog Blues/Papa's Got Your Water On/Gone Mother Blues/Midnight Hour Blues/Blues Before Sunrise/Court Room Blues/Mean Mistreater Mama/Blue Night Blues/Barrel House Woman/Florida Bound Blues/Tight Time Blues/Bread Baker/When The Sun Goes Down/Bad Luck All The Time/Six Cold Feet In The Ground*

248 **New Orleans Barrelhouse Boogie**
Champion Jack Dupree
Columbia CK 52834/472192-2 (UK)
Gamblin' Man Blues/Warehouse Man Blues/Chain Gang Blues/New Low Down Dog/Black Woman Swing/Cabbage Greens No. 1/*Cabbage Greens* No. 2/*Angola Blues/My Cabin Inn/Bad Health Blues/That's All Right/Gibing Blues/Dupree Shake Dance/My Baby's Gone/Weed Head Woman/Junker Blues/Oh, Red/All Alone Blues/Big Time Mama/Shady Lane/Hurry Down Sunshine/Jackie P. Blues/Heavy Heart Blues/Morning Tea/Black Cow Blues*

(iii) The Eastern Seaboard

One Eastern Seaboard musician who made his first recordings in Chicago was the Tennessee-born singer-guitarist Walter "Brownie"

McGhee. He had been engaged in August 1940 by J.B. Long, the manager of Blind Boy Fuller, in Durham, North Carolina, as a substitute for this popular East Coast singer (**124**, **279**), whose terminal illness meant he was no longer able to perform. A proportion of Brownie's first records, therefore, were released under the soubriquet "Blind Boy Fuller No. 2." In order to maintain Fuller's ethos, George Washington (Bull City Red), one of Blind Boy's circle, was added as a washboard player. Together with McGhee's regular harmonica player, Jordan Webb, they cut two sessions at this time, creating an effective imitation of the infirm singer's earlier recordings.

Columbia's double CD **The Complete Brownie McGhee** contains all the sides made by Brownie following the arrangement with J.B. Long, and spans the period 1940–41.

At the 1940 sessions, there was a proportion of popular pieces already in the recorded repertoire, such as *Picking My Tomatoes* (adapted from a 1939 Chicago recording by Washboard Sam–*Diggin' My Potatoes*), or *Black Door Stranger* (also recorded by Sam as *Back Door*, in 1937). Like most blues in this period, the subject of Brownie's songs was male–female relations, though *Born For Bad Luck* also has a superstitious theme and *Not Guilty Blues* pleads against legal discrimination. McGhee's adaptation of Fuller's *Step It Up And Go* was not issued until this collection, nor was the topical *Coal Miner Blues*.

There was more of the same at the next three sessions, cut in May 1941. Fuller had died (in February) and Brownie composed a commemorative *Death Of Blind Boy Fuller*. There were also religious pieces using a common Fuller/Bull City Red pseudonym, Brother George. The washboard on these sessions, however, was Brownie's regular accompanist Robert Young (known as Washboard Slim) and, with Jordan Webb on harmonica, the threesome again re-create something of the atmosphere of Fuller's recordings. McGhee's guitar-picking style, however, was less fluid and his diction had a hard edge not noticeable in Blind Boy's vocals. Webb sings on *What Will I Do (Without The Lord?)*. *Key To The Highway 70* (previously unissued) is another variant of a tune earlier recorded by Chicago-based musicians. By far the most interesting topical performance is *Million Lonesome Women*, which revolves around US male mobilization, in the light of the war then waging in Europe, and the consequent availability of "unattached" females.

Before the United States became involved directly in the war (December), Brownie cut two more sessions (October), but this time in New York. Many of these sides are issued here for the first time. *Workingman's Blues* was released, however, and this was the first 78rpm record on which McGhee was joined by Fuller's former harmonica player Sonny Terry, a partnership consolidated from that time (**138, 139**). Jordan Webb also played on certain sides, as did washboard players Washington and Young. A second guitarist was also present, Buddy Moss (**137**), and he accompanies Brownie on *Swing, Soldier, Swing*. The song returns to the theme of women available because of the military mobilization, and the "studio chatter" contributes to our understanding of the process by which such lyrics were composed.

New York, of course, was the headquarters of the US music business and for black performers the key city in which to create a favorable impression. Out-of-town blues singers like Fuller or McGhee were peripheral to this activity. They just traveled to the metropolis to make records and return home—J.B. Long scheduled trips for holidays from his regular work. Sophisticated singers and jazz bands, with which they might sing, cut a much higher profile with impresarios and big-city audiences.

Before the 1930s, many of these units started as "territory bands" that played for audiences in states such as Oklahoma, Missouri, or Kansas. Some traveled as far as California. These areas were also traversed by migrant singers, ranging from lone bluesmen to those who sang with bands.

One singer who fits this pattern is Jimmy Rushing, who was born in Oklahoma City (in 1903) and had a circle of acquaintances that came to include many "territory" musicians. One of these was Walter Page, with whose band he cut his first record *Blue Devil Blues* in Kansas City in 1929. This and four other early sides, recorded with Benny Moten's Kansas City Orchestra, open **Mr. Five By Five**, the Topaz Blues collection of his pre-war sides. Moten's orchestra was taken over by band leader/pianist William "Count" Basie, with whom Rushing was associated for much of his career.

With clear diction, impeccable timing, and a feeling for blues shouting that mirrored his knowledge of the work of the best women stylists (such as Ida Cox or "Chippie" Hill), Jimmy was a singer of class. In this he fitted his role perfectly with Basie's band of superlative musicians.

Count Basie's orchestra cut a series of innovative and sparkling sides following their contract with Decca in 1937, most of them in New York and a few in Chicago. Despite some omission, this CD represents Rushing's best blues with Basie's band. *Good Morning Blues* (1937) was a favorite (*That Too, Doo Blues*, from 1930, is another version), and he always acknowledge his liking for the work of Leroy Carr (*How Long Blues* is from 1939).

Another song, *I'm Gonna Move To The Outskirts Of Town*, serves to indicate post-war developments in recorded blues during this period. The piece had first been recorded by Chicago singer and steel-guitar player Casey Bill (Weldon) in 1936. The lyrics revolve around male suspicion of female infidelity and Weldon is credited as composer on all subsequent versions. Rushing's *I'm Gonna Move* was an attempt to cash in on the commercial success of recent popular recordings. Louis Jordan had cut the side for Decca in Chicago in 1942. It was followed in March by a version by Big Bill Broonzy for Columbia's Vocalion marque, with small-group support. The Count Basie rendering for Columbia (with Rushing's vocal) was made in April and Jordan responded with *I'm Gonna Leave You On The Outskirts Of Town* on 21 July. Within nine days Decca's other rival, Bluebird (Victor), had organized a cover recording by the popular Chicago blues harmonica player and vocalist Jazz Gillum.

Such close-knit commercial rivalry did not last. It was broken by World War II shellac rationing, which limited manufacture, and a ban on recording by the American Federation of Musicians—a dispute over revenues. Although all these performers continued their careers after the hiatus, the changed circumstances were to force a dilution of the three-company monopoly and, therefore, revised attitudes to marketing. These trends are explored in subsequent chapters.

249 The Complete Brownie McGhee
Brownie McGhee
Columbia C2K 52933/475700-2 (UK)—*2 CD set*
DISC ONE: *Picking My Tomatoes/Me And My Dog Blues/Born For Bad Luck/I'm Callin' Daisy/Step It Up And Go/My Barkin' Bulldog Blues/Let Me Tell You 'Bout My Baby/Prison [Poison] Woman Blues/Back Door Stranger/Be Good To Me/Not Guilty Blues/Coal Miner Blues*; [McGhee as Blind Boy Fuller No. 2], *Step It Up And Go* No. 2/*Money Spending Woman*; Brownie McGhee, *Death Of Blind Boy Fuller* (take NG-1)/*Death Of Blind Boy Fuller* (take 2); [McGhee as Blind Boy Fuller No. 2], *Got To Find My Little Woman/I'm A Black Woman's Man* (take NG-1)/*I'm A Black Woman's Man* (take 2)/*Dealing With The Devil/Double Trouble* (take NG-1)/*Double Trouble* (take 2) [as Brownie McGhee]/*Woman I'm Done*

DISC TWO: [McGhee as Blind Boy Fuller No. 2], *Key To My Door/Million Lonesome Woman/Ain't No Tellin'/Try Me One More Time*; Brother George & His Sanctified Singers [McGhee, vocal], *I Want To See Jesus/Done What My Lord Said/I Want King Jesus*; [Jordan Webb, vocal], *What Will I Do (Without The Lord?)*; [McGhee as Blind Boy Fuller No. 2], *Key To The Highway 70* (take NG-1)/*Key To The Highway 70* (take 2)/*I Don't Believe In Love/So Much Trouble/Goodbye Now/Jealous Of My Woman/Unfair Blues/Barbecue Any Old Time/Workingman's Blues/Sinful Disposition Woman/Back Home Blues/Deep Sea Diver/It Must Be Love/"Studio Chatter"* [preceding–]/*Swing, Soldier, Swing* (take NG-1)/*Swing Soldier Swing* (take 1)

250 **Mr. Five By Five**
Jimmy Rushing
Topaz Blues TPZ 1019 (UK)
Walter Page's Blue Devils, *Blue Devil Blues*; Benny Moten's Kansas City Orchestra, *That Too, Doo Blues/Liza Lee/Now That I Need You/New Orleans*; Count Basie & His Orchestra, *Exactly Like You/Boogie Woogie (I May Be Wrong)/Listen My Children (And You Shall Hear)/Good Morning Blues/Don't You Miss Your Baby?/Blues In The Dark/Sent For You Yesterday (And Here You Come Today)/The Blues I Like To Hear/Do You Wanna Jump Children?/ You Can Depend On Me/Nobody Know/How Long Blues/I Left My Baby/Blues (I Still Think Of Her)/Take Me Back Baby Blues/Harvard Blues/I'm Gonna Move To The Outskirts Of Town*

Basic Records

(i) "News & The Blues" and the Library of Congress

251 **Legends Of The Blues: Volume 2**
Various Artists
Columbia CK 47467/468770-2 (UK)
Roosevelt Sykes, *Henry Ford Blues*; Texas Alexander, *Ninety-Eight Degree Blues*; Oak Cliff T-Bone [Aaron T-Bone Walker], *Trinity River Blues*; Barbecue Bob [Robert Hicks], *She Shook Her Gin*; Tampa Red "The Guitar Wizard", *Turpentine Blues*; Curley Weaver, *No No Blues*; Bessie Jackson [Lucille Bogan], *Bo-Easy Blues*; Walter Roland, *School Boy Blues*; Bumble Bee Slim [Amos Easton], *Cold Blooded Murder* No. 2; Buddy Moss, *My Baby Won't Pay Me No Mind*; Robert Wilkins, *Old Jim Canan's*; Lil Johnson, *Take It Easy Greasy*; Casey Bill Weldon, *Two-Timin' Woman*; Victoria Spivey, *Down Hill Pull*; Curtis Jones, *Down In The Slums*; The Yas Yas Girl [Merline Johnson] With The Louisiana Kid, *Separation Blues*; Charlie Spand, *Soon This Morning* No. 2; Bill McKinley [Bill "Jazz" Gillium], *Is That A Monkey You Got*; Champion Jack Dupree, *Hurry Down Sunshine*; Brownie McGhee, *Goodbye Now*
An exemplary collection of recordings from the 1930s demonstrating regional styles and repertoire and giving weight to piano blues, alongside those of the guitarist. The first three tracks were recorded in 1929. Chicago sessions predominate, but variety is maintained by the mix of male and female vocalists, as well as differing accompaniments.

252 **The Slide Guitar: Bottles Knives & Steel Volume 2**
Various Artists
Columbia CK 52725/47191-2 (UK)
Allen Shaw, *Moanin' The Blues*; Sam Collins, *Slow Mama Slow*; The Georgia Browns, *Decatur Street 81*; Sam Montgomery, *Where The Sweet Oranges Grow/Low In Mind Blues*; Nellie Florence, *Midnight Weeping Blues*; Tampa Red & Georgia Tom, *Dead Cats On The Line*; Tampa Red, *Things 'Bout Coming My Way*; The Hokum Boys, *Caught Us Doing It*; Helen Humes, *Cross-Eyed Blues/Alligator Blues*; Buddy Moss, *Jealous Hearted Man/Hard Times Blues*; Tampa Red & Georgia Tom, *Things 'Bout Coming My Way* No. 2/*No Matter How She Done It*; Walter Beasley, *Toad Frog Blues*; Buddy Moss,

Hard Road Blues; Papa Too Sweet, *Big Fat Mama*; Tampa Red (The Guitar Wizard), *Western Bound Blues/Sugar Mama Blues* No. 1
Humes and Beasley represent Kentucky traditions (1927), while Florence, Moss, and the Georgia Browns were from Atlanta (1928 and 1933 respectively). Montgomery was also from the East Coast, but Collins was from Mississippi and Shaw resided in Tennessee. The others were from Chicago. A predominantly 1930s collection exemplifying regional playing styles.

253 Roosevelt Sykes: Complete Recorded Works In Chronological Order, Volume 3, 19 September 1931 to 11 December 1933
[Various Artists]
Document DOCD 5118 (Au)
Emerson Houston, *Hard Luck Blues/Strange Man Blues*; James "Stump" Johnson, *Sail On Black Sue/Barrel Of Whiskey Blues*; Matthew McClure [Southern Blues Singer], *Prisoner's Blues*; Mosby & Sykes, *Mosby Stomp*; Roosevelt Sykes, *Mr. Sykes Blues/Highway 61 Blues*; Ethel Smith, *Jelly Roll Mill*; Isabel Sykes, *In Here With Your Heavy Stuff/Don't Rush Yourself*; Willie Kelly [Roosevelt Sykes], *I Done You Wrong/Sad And Lonely Day*; Clarence Harris, *Try My Whiskey Blues/Lonesome Clock Blues*; Frank Pluitt, *Found A Note On My Door*; Roosevelt Sykes, *New 44 Blues/Working Dollar Blues/Big Legs Ida Blues/Devil's Island Gin Blues*; Carl Rafferty, *Dresser With The Drawers/Mr. Carl's Blues*; Napoleon Fletcher, *She Showed It All*
A singer-pianist, Sykes recorded prolifically from 1929 as an accomplished solo artist (**250**, **226**) and as accompanist. A well-traveled record-company talent spotter, with family links in Helena, Arkansas, he was based in St Louis, Missouri. Many of his vocalists came from that city and this is reflected in their repertoire.

254 Joe Pullum: Complete Recorded Works 1934–1935, In Chronological Order, Volume 1
Document DOCD 5393 (Au)
Black Gal What Makes Your Head So Hard/CWA Blues/Woman Oh Woman/Cows, See That Train Comin'/McKinney Street Stomp; Rob Cooper, *West Dallas Drag*; Joe Pullum, *Black Gal What Makes Your Head So Hard* No. 2/*Black Gal* No. 3/*Black Gal* No. 4/*Married Woman Blues/Rack It Back And Tell It Right/Careful Drivin' Mama/Mississippi Flood Blues*; Rob Cooper, *West Dallas Drag* No. 2; Joe Pullum, *Blues With Class/Hard-Working Man Blues/Traveling Blues/Bad Break Blues/Hustler's Blues/I Believe You/Telephone Blues/I Can't Control Myself/Some Day/Dixie My Home*
A Texas vocalist, Pullum was complemented by gifted pianists of the Santa Fe school (**153**). *Black Gal* was his most famous song, but he recorded topical themes and the *Cows* (a local traditional melody). Cooper's superlative technique is evident in *West Dallas Drag*. Andy Boy accompanies *Hard-Working Man Blues* and subsequent sides.

255 Lonnie Johnson: Complete Recorded Works 1937—June 1947, In Chronological Order, Volume 1, 8 November 1937 to 22 May 1940
Blues Documents BDCD 6024 (Au)
Man Killing Broad/Hard Times Ain't Gone No Where/Food Water Blues/It Ain't What You Usta Be/Swing Out Rhythm/Got The Blues For The West End/

Something Fishy (Don't Lie To Me)/I'm Nuts Over You (But You Just A Teaser/Friendless And Blue/Devil's Got The Blues/I Ain't Gonna Be Your Fool/ Mr. Johnson Swing/New Falling Rain Blues/Laplegged Drunk Again/Blue Ghost Blues/South Bound Backwater/Why Women Go Wrong/She's Only A Woman/ She's My Mary/Nothing But A Rat/Trust Your Husband/Jersey Belle Blues/The Loveless Love/Four-O-Three Blues/Be Careful/I'm Just Dumb/Don't Be No Fool
A consummate guitarist, Johnson resided for a time in St Louis. Often touring with jazz bands and vaudeville shows he had a long recording career, beginning in 1925 (**13**). This varied selection presents stylish performances, featuring his singing, guitar instrumentals, and a model session with Roosevelt Sykes on piano.

256 Sleepy John Estes: Complete Recorded Works In Chronological Order, Volume 2, 2 August 1937 to 24 September 1941
Document DOCD 5061 (Au)
Floating Bridge/Need More Blues/Jack And Jill Blues/Poor Man's Friend (T Model)/Hobo Jungle Blues/Airplane Blues/Everybody Ought To Make A Change/Liquor Store Blues/Easin' Back To Tennessee/Fire Department Blues (Matha Hardin)/Clean Up At Home/New Someday Baby/Brownsville Blues/ Special Agent (Railroad Police Blues)/Mailman Blues/Time Is Drawing Near/ Mary Come On Home/Jailhouse Blues/Tell Me How About It (Mr. Tom's Blues)/Drop Down (I Don't Feel Welcome Here); [The Delta Boys], *Don't You Want To Know/You Shouldn't Do That/When The Saints Go Marching In*; Sleepy John Estes, *Lawyer Clark Blues/Little Laura Blues/Working Man Blues*
Estes was one of the foremost rurally based singer-guitarists of the 1930s to perform topical blues. His recording career began in 1929 (**112**). The songs deal with home-town events in Brownsville, Tennessee, railroad company special agents (when hoboing to a recording session), and more general human relations.

257 Louisiana Cajun And Creole Music, 1934: The Lomax Recordings
Various Artists
Swallow LP 8003-2—2 LP Set
[RECORD ONE] SIDE ONE–THE HOFFPAUIR FAMILY: Elita, Mary, & Ella, *Six Ans Sur Mer [Six Years At Sea]*; Elita, *Les Clefs De La Prison [The Prison Keys]*; Elita, Mary, & Ella, *J' Ai Vu Lucille [I Saw Lucille]*; Julian, *La Belle Et Le Capitaine [The Fair Maiden And The Captain]/Une Fille De Quatorze Ans [A Young Girl Of Fourteen]/Mademoiselle Emélie [Miss Emélie]*; Elita, *Tout Un Beau Soir En Me Promenant [One Fine Evening While Out Walking]*

SIDE TWO–FIDDLES AND ACCORDIONS: Unknown, *Cajun Waltz*; Wayne Perry, *Creole Blues/Cajun Waltz* No. 1/*Cajun Waltz* No. 2/*Cajun Two-Step*; Segura Brothers, *Viens Donc t' Assir Sur La Coix De Ma Tombe [Come And Sit On Top Of My Tomb]*; Edier Segura, *Joe Féraille [Little Joe Féraille]/Un Té Pas Gain De L' Air [One Didn't Have Any Air]*; Oakdale Carrière, *Catin, Prie Donc Pour Ton Nègre [Honey, Please Pray For Your Man]*; Paul Junius Malveaux & Ernest Lafitte, *Bye-Bye, Bonsoir, Mes Parents [Goodbye, Goodnight, My Family]/Tout Les Samedis [Every Saturday]*

[RECORD TWO] SIDE THREE–BALLADS, LAMENTS, AND DRINKING SONGS: Mr. Bornu, *Belle [Sweetheart]*; Jesse Stafford, *Je M' Endors [I'm Sleepy]*; Fenelon

Brasseaux, *Je Me Suis Marié [I Married]*; Fenelus & Cleveland Sonnier, *Trinquons [Let's Toast]*; Fenelon Brasseuaux, Isaac Sonnier, & Cleveland Sonnier, *La Chanson Des Savoy [Savoy's Song]*; Fenelus Sonnier, *La Chanson De Théogène Dubois [Théogène Dubois' Song]*; Lanese Vincint & Sidney Richard, *J' Ai Marié Un Ouvrier [I Married A Carpenter]/Madame Gallien/Je M' Ai Fait Un Maîtresse [I Had A Mistress]*; Davous Bérard, *Les Amours [Et Les Beaux Jours] Sont Courts [Love And Good Days]/Mes Amis, Je Suis Gris [My Friend, I'm Drunk]*; Edier Segura, *Le Pays Des étrangers [The Land Of Strangers]*

SIDE FOUR–ZARICO, JURE, AND THE BLUES: Wilfred Charles, *Dégo*; Jimmy Peters & Ring Dance Singers, *J' Ai Fait Tout Le Tour Du Pays [I Went All Around The Land]/S'En Aller Chez Moreau [Going To Moreau's]/Je Veux Me Marier [I Want To Marry]*; Joseph Jones, *Blues De La Prison [Prison Blues]*; Cleveland Benoit & Darby Hicks, *Là-Bas Chez Moreua [Over At Moreau's]*; Austin Coleman, Washington, & Sampson Brown, *Feel Like Dying In His Army*; Jimmy Peters & Ring Dance Singers, *Rockaway*
Excepting Amédé Ardoin (**516**), few black French musicians were recorded commercially during the 1930s. Selections in this important collection, therefore, are especially significant. In addition to dance pieces accompanied by accordion and harmonica (**SIDE TWO**: Carrière, Malveaux & Lafitte), they include voice-only secular and religious ring shouts (*juré*) not otherwise documented (**SIDE FOUR**). The remaining performers are white.

258 Midnight Special–The Library Of Congress Recording, Volume One
Leadbelly
Rounder CD 1044
Irene Part 1/*Irene* Part 2/*Matchbox Blues/Midnight Special/Governor O.K. Allen/Frankie & Albert/Ella Speed/[Which Way Do The] Red River [Run]/Get [Got] Up In The Mornin' [So Doggone Soon]/You Don't Know My Mind/I'm Sorry Mama/Take A Whiff On Me/De Kalb Blues/Roberta/Careless Love*
Collected by the Lomaxes, this is an exemplary anthology of Texas–Louisiana ballads, blues, and barrelhouse songs recorded by the famous songster in 1934 and 1935. *Governor O.K. Allen* (a pardon song) was once said to have influenced Leadbelly's release from the Louisiana State Penitentiary, where it was recorded.

259 Red River Blues 1934–1943
Various Artists
Travelin' Man TM CD 08 (UK)
Blind Joe, *When I Lie Down [Last Night]/In Trouble*; Reese Crenshaw, *Trouble*; Robert Davis, *Poor Joe Breakdown*; Jimmie Owens, *Not Satisfied*; Willie Williams, *Red River Blues*; J. Wilson, *Barrel House Blues*; Allison Mathis, *Mama You Goin' To Quit Me*; Jimmie Strothers, *Goin' To Richmond*; Smith Band, *Fort Valley Blues*; Buster Brown, *War Song*; Gus Gibson, *Milk Cow Blues*; Sonny Chestain, *Po' Boy Long Way From Home*; Buster Brown, *I'm Gonna Make You Happy*; Gus Gibson, *Railroad Song*; James Sneed's Washboard Band, *Southern Rag*; Allison Mathis & Jesse Stroller, *John Henry*; Gabriel Brown, *Talking In Sebastopol*; Booker T. Sapps, *Alabama Blues* Part 1/ *The Weeping Worry Blues*; Willy Flowers, *Levee Camp Holler*; Brooker T. Sapps, *Boot That Thing*

These exciting guitar and jook-band Library of Congress field recordings, from Florida, Georgia, North Carolina, and Virginia, help greatly in documenting Eastern Seaboard music (Chapter 4). Some sides were made by prison inmates.

260 The Devil Is Busy: Library Of Congress Field Recordings
Sampson Pittman
Laurie Records LCD 7002
I['ve] Been Down In The Circle Before/Interview No. 1/*Levee Camp Story/ Highway 61 Blues/Brother Low Down And Sister Do-Dad* Parts 1, 2, [and 3 *sic*]/ *Brother Low Down And Sister Do-Dad* (version 2)/*Cotton Farmer Blues/ Interview* No. 2/*Welfare Blues/Interview* No. 3/*Joe Louis/Interview* No. 4/*John Henry*
Sampson Pittman was a migrant from Arkansas to Detroit, Michigan, and his performances are special, his repertoire outstanding. Field recordings were not often made in urban centers. Some songs represent unusual topics, such as *Down In The Circle* (about Mississippi River levee contractors), or his *Welfare Blues* (critical of welfare in Detroit).

261 Mississippi Blues: Library of Congress Recordings 1940–1942
Various Artists
Travelin' Man TM CD 07 (UK)
Leroy Williams, *Uncle Sam Done Called*; [David] Honeyboy Edwards, *Water Coast Blues/Army Blues*; Fiddlin' Joe Martin, *Going To Fishing*; [David] Honeyboy Edwards, *Spread My Raincoat Down/Wind Howlin' Blues*; Willie Brown, *Make Me A Pallet On The Floor*; [David] Honeyboy Edwards, *Roamin' & Ramblin' Blues*; Lucious Curtis, *High Lonesome Hill*; Willie Ford, *Pay Day*; Lucious Curtis, *Train Blues/Lonesome Highway Blues/Mississippi River Blues/ Stagolee/Farmin' Man Blues*; Willie Ford, *Santa Field Blues [sic]/Sto' Gallery Blues*; Lucious Curtis, *Rubber Ball Blues*; Willie ["61"] Blackwell, *Junio's A Jap Girl's Christmas For His Santa Claus [sic]*.
Williams, Edwards, Martin, Brown, and Blackwell were recorded by Alan Lomax during the Coahoma County study (1941–2). John A. Lomax located Curtis and Ford further south, in Natchez, in 1940. There is a mixture of blues, ballads, and barrelhouse songs, and contemporary reflections on the build-up to World War II. A guitar-orientated collection.

262 Blues In The Mississippi Night
Various Artists
Rykodisc RCD 90155
[Memphis Slim], *Life Is Like That*; [Unidentified Group], *Long Meter Hym [And Pitied Every Groan]*; [Sonny Boy Williamson & Memphis Slim], *I Could Hear My Name Ringing [My Black Name]*; [Memphis Slim], *Ratty [Ratty] Section*; [Memphis Slim & Big Bill Broonzy], *I'm Going To Memphis [Work Songs]*; [Memphis Slim & Sonny Boy Williamson], *[Bama's* (*sic*)*] Stacker Lee*; [Unidentified Convict Group(s)], *[Oh] 'Berta/Murderers' Home [I Ain't Got Long]/Don't You Hear Your [Poor] Mother Calling*; [Memphis Slim], *Slow Lonesome Blues [Piano Blues]*; [Unidentified female Vocalist], *Another Man Done Gone*; [Memphis Slim], *Fast Boogie [Piano Blues* No. 2*]*
Recorded in 1947, this documentary features recollections of life in the South during the 1930s. Three famous Chicago-based bluesmen of the period explain

segregation through stories and associated songs. Group work songs and sacred performances are added where appropriate. This classic exposition was made by Alan Lomax.

(ii) Chicago and Indianapolis

263 **Bumble Bee Slim (Amos Easton): Complete Recorded Works In Chronological Order, Volume 5, 18 July 1935 to 6 February 1936**
Document DOCD 5265 (Au)
[Slim as Shelly Armstrong], *How Long How Long Blues/You Don't Mean Me No Good/New B & O Blues/Prison Bound Blues*; Bumble Bee Slim, *My Old Pal Blues (Dedicated To The Memory Of Leroy Carr)/Last Respects (Dedicated To The Memory Of Leroy Carr)*; [as Shelly Armstrong], *Sloppy Drunk Blues/ D.B.A. Blues*; Bumble Bee Slim & His Rhythm Riffers, *I'll Take You Back/Sick And Tired Of Singing The Blues*; Bumble Bee Slim, *New When The Sun Goes Down/ Happy Life Blues/When Somebody Loses (Then Somebody Wins)/ Ramblin' With That Woman/This Old Life I'm Living/Dumb Tricks Blues* (take 1)/*Dumb Tricks Blues* (take 2)/*New Orleans Stop Time* [with interjections by Memphis Minnie]/*You Got To Live And Let Live/Hard Rocks In My Bed/ Who's Been Here Today/I Done Caught My Death Of Cold/No More Biscuit Rolling Here* (take 1)/*No More Biscuit Rolling Here* (take 2)
Based in Chicago for most of the 1930s, Slim performed in a style influenced by Leroy Carr. The appeal of his songs lies in the varied experience of black city life. His finest piano accompanist was Myrtle Jenkins, on several tracks here. Others feature the steel-guitar playing of Casy Bill Weldon.

264 **Kokomo Arnold: Complete Recorded Works In Chronological Order, Volume 3 (22 May 1936 to 12 March 1937)**
[Various Artists]
Document DOCD 5039 (Au)
[Alice Moore], *Grass Cutter Blues/Telephone Blues/Dark Angel/Money Tree Man*; [Signifying Mary Johnson], *Delmar Avenue*; [Alice Moore], *I'm Going Fishing Too/Three Men*; Kokomo Arnold, *Shake That Thing*; [Oscar's Chicago Swingers], *Try Some Of That/My Gal's Been Foolin' Me*; Kokomo Arnold, *Running Drunk Again/Coffin Blues/Lonesome Road Blues/Mister Charlie/Black-fence Picket Blues/Fool Man Blues/Long And Tall/Salty Dog/Cold Winter Blues/Sister Jane 'Cross The Hall/Wild Water Blues/Laugh And Grin Blues*
An incisive singer and master slide-guitar player, Arnold stamps his character on every recording. The St Louis vocalists Moore and Johnson are respectively accompanied on piano by Peetie Wheatstraw and Roosevelt Sykes; and Oscar's Chicago Swingers may include piano from Albert Ammons. *Mister Charlie* refers to the white bossman.

265 **Georgia White: Complete Recorded Works In Chronological Order, Volume 3 (5 October 1937 to 18 May 1939)**
Document DOCD 5303 (Au)
Georgia Man/All Night Blues/Away All The Time/The Stuff Is Here/Strewin' Your Mess/Fare Thee Honey Fare Thee Well/Careless Love/Rock Me Daddy/ Red Cap Porter/Alley Boogie/I'm Blue And Lonesome/Almost Afraid To Love/

Too Much Trouble/Crazy Blues/'Tain't Nobody's Business If I Do/Holding My Own/The Blues Ain't Nothin' But . . .??/Dead Man Blues/Love Sick Blues/My Worried Mind Blues/The Way I'm Feelin'/Married Woman Blues
One of the most popular women singers in Chicago during the 1930s, White was an evocative vocalist and competent pianist. Her solo career spanned the years 1935–41. She performed past and contemporary songs, accompanied by small groups and string or jazz bands.

266 Washboard Sam: Complete Recorded Works In Chronological Order, Volume 3, 14 March to 16 December 1938
Document DOCD 5173 (Au)
It's Too Late Now/Barbecue/Down At The Old Village Store/The Gal I Love/Bucket's Got A Hole In It/Save It For Me/Serve It Right/Cruel Treatment/Jumpin' Rooster/I'm Gonna Keep My Hair Parted/Sophisticated Mama/Policy Writer's Blues/I'm Gonna Pay/When My Love Change/You Waited Too Long/Gonna Kill My Baby/Suspicious Blues/Walkin' In My Sleep/Washboard Swing/Hand Reader Blues/Rack 'Em Back/I'll Be Up Some Day/Warehouse Blues/CCC Blues
Sam was one of the few washboard players to record as a lead vocalist, displaying a rich baritone timbre. He was also a prolific writer of topical and other songs. As on this disc, he was usually accompanied by Big Bill Broonzy and other Chicago instrumentalists.

267 Jazz Gillum: Complete Recorded Works In Chronological Order, Volume 2, 16 December 1938 to 4 July 1941
Document DOCD 5198 (Au)
Let Her Go/Get Away Old Woman/Stavin' Chain/She Won't Treat Me Kind/I'll Get Along Somehow/Got To Reap What You Sow/Big Katy Adams/Against My Will/Keyhole Blues/Talking To Myself/Hard Drivin' Woman/Somebody's Been Talking To You/One Time Blues/It Sure Had A Kick/She Belongs To Me/Longest Train Blues/Key To The Highway/I'm Still Walking The Hi-Way/Get Your Business Straight/Muddy Pond Blues/Little Woman; [Bill McKinley (Jazz Gillum)], *Poor Boy Blues/Is That A Monkey You Got?*; Jazz Gillum, *Riley Springs Blues/That's What Worries Me*
With a singing voice that matched the buzzy intonation of his harmonica playing, Gillum did not achieve the renown of John Lee Williamson. His innovative approach, however, usually with the support of Big Bill and other Chicago-based musicians, stands out alongside his contemporaries. This disc encompasses traditional and popular themes.

268 Tampa Red: Complete Recorded Works In Chronological Order, Volume 12, 24 June 1941 to 5 July 1945
Document DOCD 5212 (Au)
Georgia Georgia Blues/I Got A Right To Be Blue/Don't Deal With The Devil/She's Love Crazy/It's A Low Down Dirty Shame/You Better Be Ready To Go/No Baby No/So Far So Good/My First Love Blues/Gin Head Woman/Don't Jive It Mama/Gypsy Lady Blues/Mean And Evil Woman/Let Me Play With Your Poodle/She Want To Sell My Monkey/You Gonna Miss Me When I'm Gone/I Ain't Fur It/The Woman I Love/Detroit Blues/Sure Enough I Do/Lula Mae/Mercy Mama/I Can't Get Along With You

From the start of his career in 1928, Tampa Red was one of the most versatile and recorded of bluesmen. Primarily a singer-guitarist and composer, he also played piano and kazoo. Several facets of his ability are represented in these influential sides, accompanied by the peerless piano of Big Maceo (**208**).

269 Bill Gaither (Leroy's Buddy): Complete Recorded Works In Chronological Order, Volume 4, 13 September to 22 October 1939
Document DOCD 5254 (Au)
Army Bound Blues/Sing Sing Blues/Kentland Blues/Lazy Woman Blues/See Me Grieve Blues/Wintertime Blues/Another Big Leg Woman/Greyhound Blues/Changing Blues/Jungle Man Blues/Hard Way To Go/New So Much Trouble/Mean Devil Blues/Stony Lonesome Graveyard/Cheatin' Blues/Bloody Eyed Woman/Bachelor Man Blues/Evil Yalla Woman/It's Too Late Now/Sweet Woman Blues/Triflin' Woman Blues/Rainy Morning/Fairy Tale Blues
A Kentucky singer-guitarist based in Indianapolis, Gaither was a successor on record to Leroy Carr. The only performer from that city to have been recorded regularly from 1935, he was usually accompanied on piano by Honey Hill. Varied repertoire and relaxed vocals are well documented in this collection.

(iii) Good-time Blues and Hokum

270 Good Time Blues: Harmonicas, Kazoos, Washboards & Cow Bells
Various Artists
Columbia CK 46780/467891-2 (UK)
Mississippi Jook Band, *Hittin' The Bottle Stomp/Skippy Whippy*; Memphis Jug Band, *Mary Anna Cut Off/Gator Wobble*; Son Becky, *Mistreated Washboard Blues*; Charlie Burse & His Memphis Mudcats, *Baby You Win/Oil It Up And Go*; The Georgia Browns, *Tampa Strut*; Georgia Cotton Pickers, *Diddle-Da-Diddle/She's Coming Back Some Cold Rainy Day*; Big Joe [McCoy] & His Washboard Band, *If You Take Me Back/I'm Through With You/When You Said Goodbye/I Love You Baby*; Buddy Moss, *Struggle Buggie/I'm Sittin' Here Tonight*; Mississippi Jook Band, *Dangerous Woman/Barbecue Bust*; Peter Chatman [Memphis Slim], *Diggin' My Potatoes* No. 2/Sonny Terry & Jordan Webb, *Touch It Up And Go*; Bernice Edwards, *Ninth Street Stomp*
The unusual instruments are associated with all facets of good-time music. They accompany vocalists from several regions, performing individually, or with string and other groups. The Jook Band features Coony Vaughn (a legendary Mississippi pianist), with Becky and Edwards representing Texas piano stylists, and Chatman those from Tennessee. Recordings range from 1930 to 1941.

271 Raunchy Business: Hot Nuts & Lollypops
Various Artists
Columbia CK 46783/467889-2 (UK)
Lil Johnson, *Sam–The Hot Dog Man/My Stove's In Good Condition*; Lonnie Johnson, *Wipe It Off/The Best Jockey In Town*; Lucille Bogan, *Shave 'Em Dry* [No. 1]/*Shave 'Em Dry* [No. 2]; Lillie Mae Kirkman, *He's Just My Size*; Barrel House Annie, *If It Don't Fit (Don't Force It)*; Lonnie Johnson & Victoria Spivey, *Furniture Man Blues* Part 1/*Furniture Man Blues* Part 2; Bo Carter, *My Pencil Won't Write No More/Banana In Your Fruit Basket*; Lil Johnson, *Get*

'Em From The Peanut Man (Hot Nuts)/Get 'Em From the Peanut Man (The New Hot Nuts); Mississippi Sheiks, *Driving That Thing/Bed Spring Poker*; Hunter & Jenkins ["Coots" Grants & "Socks" Wilson], *Lollypop/Meat Cuttin' Blues*; Buddy Moss, *You Got To Give Me Some Of It*; Bernice Edwards, *Butcher Shop Blues*

Excepting Spivey and Johnson (1928) these are recordings from the 1930s. Titillation is common in hokum, but some sides are more openly suggestive. There is variety from string bands (the Sheiks), to vaudeville (Hunter and Jenkins). Barrelhouse themes include *Shave 'Em Dry* (by Jackson) and *Butcher Shop Blues* (by Edwards). Others are more urbane.

272 Famous Hokum Boys: Complete Recorded Works In Chronological Order, Volume 2 (16 September 1930 to January 1931)

Wolf WBCD 012 (Au)

[Bill Williams], *Mr. Conductor Man*; [Bill Williams & Sammy Sampson (Big Bill)], *No Good Buddy*; [Georgia Tom & Hannah May], *What's That I Smell/It's Been So Long/Terrible Operation Blues/Rent Man Blues*; Famous Hokum Boys, *Pie-Eating Strut/It's All Used Up*; [Georgia Tom & Jane Lucas], *What's That I Smell/Terrible Operation Blues/Where Did You Stay Last Night?/Fix It/Ain't Goin' There No More* No. 2/*That's The Way She Likes It/Double Trouble Blues/Leave My Man Alone* (take A)/*Leave My Man Alone* (take B); [Hokum Boys & Jane Lucas], *Hip Shakin' Strut/Hokum Stomp*; [Harum Scarums], *Come On In (Ain't Nobody Here But Me)/Where Did You Stay Last Night?/Alabama Scratch* Part 2/*Alabama Scratch* Part 1/*Sittin' On Top Of The World*

In 1930 Big Bill Broonzy, Georgia Tom (Dorsey), and others formed this group to perform fast raggy pieces and risqué songs. They backed Hannah May (pun intended) in ribald duets with Dorsey. She sometimes used the names Jane Lucas or Kansas City Kitty (**181**). These are accomplished and entertaining recordings.

273 Harlem Hamfats: Complete Recorded Works In Chronological Order, Volume 1, 18 April to 13 November 1936

Document DOCD 5271 (Au)

Oh! Red/Lake Providence Blues/Live And Die For You/New Oh! Red/What You Gonna Do?/She's Gone Again/Let's Get Drunk And Truck/Move Your Hand/Sales Tax On It (But It's The Same Thing)/You Done Tore Your Playhouse Down/Little Girl/Southern Blues/My Garbage Man/Weed Smoker's Dream (Why Don't You Do Now?)/If You Want To Live/I Feel Like A Millionaire/Bad Luck Man/My Daddy Was A Lovin' Man/She's Trickin' Me/We Gonna Pitch A Boogie Woogie (take A)/*We Gonna Pitch A Boogie Woogie* (take C)/*Hamfat Swing/Who Done It?/Growling Dog*

True to hokum spirit, these skilful Southern instrumentalists dubbed themselves the Harlem Hamfats ("hamfat" meaning an indifferent musician). Spirited New Orleans jazz is combined with Mississippi string-band styles—by Joe McCoy (vocal, guitar) and his brother Charlie (mandolin). The songs are a mixture of jazz, blues, and hokum.

274 Willie Dixon: The Big Three Trio

Columbia CK 46216/467248-2 (UK)

Big 3 Boogie/If The Sea Was Whiskey/I Ain't Gonna Be Your Monkey Man

[No More]/88 Boogie/Money Tree Blues/Big 3 Stomp/Since My Baby [Been] Gone/Hard Notch Boogie Beat/No One To Love Me/Don't Let The Music Die/ It's All Over Now/Tell That Woman/Got You On My Mind/Etiquette/You Don't Love Me No More/Come Here Baby/O.C. Bounce/Cool Kind Woman/Juice-Head Bartender/What Am I To Do/Signifying Monkey
Harmony singing, mixed with hokum, jive, boogie, and sentimentality, links these sides with pre-war recordings by the Hamfats and others. The trio comprised Leonard Caston Sr (vocal, piano), Ollie Crawford (vocal, guitar), and Willie Dixon (vocal, string bass). Slick performance disguises some traditional themes. Dixon later produced particular songs with 1950s Chicago bluesmen.

(iv) The Eastern Seaboard

275 **Butterbeans & Susie**
JSP Records JSP CD 329 (UK)
You're A No 'Count Triflin' Man/Mama's Gonna Shorten Your Days/Gonna Make You Sorry (For Everything You Do)/I Ain't Scared Of You/Fast Fadin' Papa/Been Some Changes Made (Since You Been Gone)/Watch Your Step/ Gonna Start Lookin' For A Man To Treat Me Right/Put Your Mind Right On It/Get Away From My Window (Stay Away From My Door)/I Want A Good Man And I Want Him Bad/That's More Than I Can Stand/Get Yourself A Monkey Man (And Make Him Strut His Stuff)/Radio Papa (Broadcastin' Mama)/Broke Down Mama/You Dirty Mistreater/What It Takes To Bring You Back (Mama Keeps It All The Time)/Better Stop Knockin' Me Around/Ain't Gonna Do That No More/Times Is Hard (So I'm Savin' For A Rainy Day)/ Elevator Papa, Switchboard Mama/Deal Yourself Another Hand/Papa Ain't No Santa Claus (Mama Ain't No Christmas Tree)
Jodie Edwards and his wife Susie were a famous vaudeville duo whose effortless performances belied their professionalism in maintaining dialogs interspersed with vocals, to instrumental accompaniment. Their lyrics use vernacular motifs and are often insinuating but never vulgar. Mainly recorded in the 1920s, they continued to perform into the next decade.

276 **The Henry Allen Collection, Volume 1**
Various Artists
Collectors Classics COCD 1 (Dan)
Billy Banks & His Orchestra, *Bugle Call Rag* (take 1)/*Oh! Peter (You're So Nice)* (take 1) [vocal, Henry Allen]/*Margie* [vocal, Billy Banks]/*Oh! Peter (You're So Nice)* (take 3) [vocal, Billy Banks]/*Spider Crawl* [vocal, Billy Banks]/*Who's Sorry Now* [vocal, Billy Banks]/*Take It Slow And Easy* [vocal, Billy Banks]/*Bald-Headed Mama* [vocal, Billy Banks]; The Rhythm Makers, *I Would Do Anything For You* (take 1) [vocal, Billy Banks]/*Mean Old Bed Bug Blues* (take 1) [vocal, Billy Banks, Fats Waller]/*Yellow Dog Blues* (take 3) [vocal, Billy Banks]/*Yes Suh!* (take 2) [vocal, Billy Banks]; Jack Bland & His Rhythm Makers, *Who Stole The Lock (On The Hen House Door)* [vocal, Henry Allen]/*A Shine On Your Shoes* [vocal, Chick Bullock]/*Someone Stole Gabriel's Horn* [vocal, Henry Allen]; Billy Banks & His Orchestra, *Bugle Call Rag* (alternate take)/*Oh! Peter (You're So Nice)* (take 2) [vocal, Henry Allen]/ *Oh! Peter (You're So Nice)* (take 4) [vocal, Billy Banks]; The Rhythm Makers,

I Would Do Anything For You (take 2) [vocal, Billy Banks]/*Mean Old Bed Bug Blues* (take 2) [vocal, Billy Banks, Fats Waller]/*Yellow Dog Blues* (take 2) [vocal, Billy Banks]/*Yes Suh!* (take 1) [vocal, Billy Banks]
This is exciting hokum-inspired blues and jazz from high-class New York-based musicians. Henry "Red" Allen adds a virtuoso New Orleans flavor with inspired trumpet playing and vocals, alongside the voluble Banks, or more urbane Bullock (on one session). *Who Stole The Lock?* occurs in both black and white repertoire.

277 **At The Swing Cat's Ball—The Early Years 1937–1939**
Louis Jordan
JSP Records JSP CD 330 (UK)
Chick Webb & His Orchestra [Louis Jordan, vocal], *Gee But It's Swell/Rusty Hinge/It's Swell Of You*; Louis Jordan's Elk's Rendevous Band [Rodney Sturgis, vocal], *Toodle-oo On Down/So Good/Away From You*; [Louis Jordan, vocal], *Honey In The Bee Ball/Barnicle Bill The Sailor*; Louis Jordan & His Tympany Five, *Flat Face/Keep-A-Knockin'/Sam Jones Done Snagged His Britches/Swingin' In The Cocoanut Trees/Doug The Jitterbug/At The Swing Cats' Ball/Jake What A Snake/Honeysuckle Rose/'Fore Day Blues/But I'll Be Back/You Ain't Nowhere/You're My Meat*
Jordan's earliest sides, as a feature musician with other orchestras and leading his own groups, demonstrate instrumental ability as well as skills as a dead-pan vocalist. The songs range from hokum and novelty numbers to straightforward blues. These styles were to sustain his reputation into the 1950s (**281**).

278 **The Chronological Blue Lu Barker 1938–1939**
Classics 704 (Fr)
Blue Lu Barker With Danny Barker's Fly Cats, *You're Going To Leave The Old Home Jim/New Orleans Blues/He Caught That B & O/Don't You Make Me High/I Got Ways Like The Devil/That Made Him Mad/Scat Skunk/Nix On Those Lush Heads/Georgia Grind/You Ain't Had No Blues/Marked Woman*; Blue Lu Barker, *Midnight Blues/Down In The Dumps/Blue Deep Sea Blues/Never Brag About Your Man/He's So Good/I Don't Dig You Jack/Handy Andy/Jitterbug Blues/You Been Holding Out Too Long/Lu's Blues*
Louisa and her husband Danny were from New Orleans. Working in New York, Danny assembled groups of top-flight Southern musicians for the six sessions represented on this disc. Lu's suave vocals are tinged with an aggressive edge. There are blues standards and original songs, performed with panache.

279 **Blind Boy Fuller 1935–1940**
Travelin' Man TM CD 01 (UK)
Baby You Gotta Change Your Mind/Baby, I Don't Have To Worry [(Cause' The Stuff Is Here)]/Looking For My Woman/Somebody's Been Playing With That Thing/Mama Let Me Lay It On You/Boots And Shoes/Truckin' My Blues Away No. 2/*My Best Gal Gonna Leave Me/Too Many Women Blues/Oozin' You Off My Mind/Shake That Shimmy/Heart Ease Blues/Georgia Ham Mama/Jivin' Woman Blues/You Got To Have Your Dollar/Bye Bye Baby*; [Brother George & His Sanctified Singers], *No Stranger Now/Must Have Been My Jesus/Jesus Is A Holy Man/Precious Lord* [Bull City Red, vocal]

These titles range from Blind Boy Fuller's first session (with Gary Davis on guitar) to his last. Including Sonny Terry on harmonica and Bull City Red on washboard, they cover Fuller's performance spectrum, from dance tunes to blues, as well as his final gospel recordings.

280 Mean Old Blues 1943–1949
Gabriel Brown
Flyright FLY CD 59 (UK)
I Get Evil When My Love Comes Down/You Ain't No Good/Black Jack Blues/Going My Way/Down In The Bottom/Bad Love/I Got To Stop Drinkin'/Cold Love/Not Now, I'll Tell You When/I'm Gonna Take It Easy/I've Done Stopped Gamblin'/It's Getting Soft/Don't Worry About It/Hold That Train/Boogie Woogie Guitar/That't Alright/Stick With Me/Doing My Best/Good-Time Papa/Baby, Boy, Baby/Mean Old Blues/You Have To Be Different/The Jinx Is On Me/It's Time To Move/Hold Me Baby/Nobody Loves Like My Little Girl
Migrating to New York from Florida (**259**), Brown's career epitomizes the pattern for many Eastern Seaboard blues musicians. This collection of his commercial recordings demonstrates sensitive singing and guitar picking as well as his ability as a slide guitarist, the accompaniment to his angry *I'm Gonna Take It Easy* being particularly effective.

DAVE PENNY

8 Rhythm and Blues

How can one define "Rhythm & Blues" or "R & B"? Like the racially insulting "sepia" or "race music" used before World War II, it seems that the generic label "Rhythm & Blues" has been popularly applied to all post-war black musics from the powerhouse swing bands of the 1940s to present-day soul and rap. Indeed, at the time of writing, the US music paper *Billboard* still lists its black music chart under the title "R&B". This blanket term, therefore would include the majority of the artists discussed in this book from this chapter onwards (excluding Chapter 9). Among those cognizant with the music, however, it is evident that "Rhythm & Blues" was a style that developed alongside, rather than out of, its contemporary the blues.

Having its roots in the novelty jazz and vaudeville blues of such pre-war catalysts as Cab Calloway, Fats Waller, Slim Gaillard, and Lucky Millinder, R&B was born kicking and screaming into a musical world in turmoil: the big swing-jazz bands were in creative and economic decline and had already begun to splinter into small groups of bebop and jump units. The latter retained the elements of the big bands that had started to become popular with the masses—the histrionic tenor saxophonist, the strong-voiced blues shouter, the blues-based jump, boogie and shuffle rhythms, and that upstart the electric guitar—and rearranged them for the use of a smaller unit usually consisting of a trumpet and/or trombone, two or three saxes, piano, guitar, bass, and drums.

Throughout the 1940s R&B retained strong links with both jazz and blues, mainly due to the fact that its main purveyors were the talented musicians who had served their apprenticeships in the big jazz orchestras, but by the early 1950s, the new generation of record buyers wanted their own younger heroes, and as these had not had the musical training of their older predecessors, the style of R&B they produced was on the whole a wild, chaotic and, some might say, amateurish mutation that only vaguely resembled the original: certainly the form of R&B that immediately predated the emergence of rock 'n' roll in the mid-1950s seemed to be a music created for the young by the young and, like most rebellious offspring, caring little for its earlier roots and influences, turned its back on the blues and jazz elements of its upbringing.

Wynonie Harris, 'Hot Lips' Page, Joe Knight, and Marion Abernathy (*coll. Blues Unlimited*)

As this volume is concerned first and foremost with the recorded history of the blues and the history of R&B is much too diverse to cover in 40 CDs, this chapter will concentrate on the prime years when the music was popularly tagged "jump blues" and was compounded from the twin elements of jazz and blues. Of later recordings, only those by important performers who retained a strong blues styling could be included. In addition to considering mainly the shouters, singers, guitarists, and pianists of the 1940s and 1950s, it would be negligent not to include a small representation of the honkers and squealers of the R&B saxophone style; although not always very bluesy, their music is synonymous with the genre.

Essential Records

(i) Forget Your Troubles and Jump Your Blues Away

The early blues shouters and jump blues combos, as previously mentioned were revitalized from the fractured parts of the large black swing orchestras that had developed in the 1930s. Such 16- or 18-man leviathans had become turgid by the end of the decade and increasingly inflexible to innovative musical ideas, so small units of kindred spirits began breaking away to create the sort of improvisational music they were now denied. Some of these tentative experiments resulted in bebop and cerebral modern jazz which did not achieve widespread popularity immediately, but many musicians persevered with the dance music of the day—a form of rough-house small band swing that metamorphosed through Harlem jump into jump blues. These musicians included popular small-band leaders like Hot Lips Page, Pete Brown, Buddy Tate, Illinois Jacquet, and others, and the role model for all who developed in his wake, Louis Jordan. Jordan had learned his trade as a reedman with, among others, the orchestras of Louis Armstrong, Clarence Williams, and Chick Webb (**277**), before forming his own small group and signing a long-term recording contract with the far-sighted Decca recording company, which lasted from the end of 1938 to the beginning of 1954.

The Best Of Louis Jordan is a collection of 20 of the biggest hits from the Decca years, from *Knock Me A Kiss* (1941) to *Nobody Knows You When You're Down and Out* (1954). Exactly half of Jordan's 18 number one R&B chart hits are included together with a further 11 popular songs from his repertoire, many of which are suffused with his wicked, although admittedly diluted, ethnic humor. The earliest tracks cast Jordan's combo, the Tympany Five, in the role of the small Harlem swing band, though the earthy humor of jump blues is already in evidence on such a title as *What's The Use Of Gettin' Sober*, Jordan's greatest successes at this time were the swinging, good-time ditties like *Five Guys Named Moe*.

In 1945 Jordan decided to inject some new blood into the Tympany Five. The result was a louder, brasher style—still with an impeccable jazz pedigree—as can be heard from the very first post-war Decca session which produced *Somebody Done Changed The Lock On My Door, Buzz Me*, and *Caldonia*; the last two of these showcase a rejuvenated Jordan with a strident vocal style and a buzz-toned sax. *Somebody Done Changed The Lock On My Door* was written by Arkansas bluesman Casey Bill Weldon, while the theme of *Caldonia*, if not the title, had been used in earlier recordings by Hot Lips Page and the Spirits Of Rhythm, but Jordan had the gift of taking other's songs and making them his own.

During the rest of his career Jordan would occasionally return to the odd ballad like *Don't Let The Sun Catch You Cryin'* or try his hand at a new trend such as the calypso sound of *Run Joe*, but his forte was the jazzy jump 'n' jive novelty which he took to the top of the R&B charts again and again: *Choo Choo Ch'Boogie, Ain't Nobody Here But Us Chickens* (both 1946), *Run Joe* (1947), *Beans And Corn Bread, Saturday Night Fish Fry* (both 1949), and *Blue Light Boogie* (1950) followed *What's The Use Of Gettin' Sober, Caldonia*, and *Buzz Me* to the number one slot. Not quite as commercially successful but just as innovative was the mock gospel-preaching of *Beware!*, the hillbilly/R&B mix of *Barnyard Boogie*, the latin blues of *Early In The Mornin'* and the syncopated rapping of *I Want You To Be My Baby*. Other lesser hits, such as *Let The Good Times Roll* and *School Days*, were simply powerfully influential milestones that affected the musical formation of later heroes like B.B. King, Ray Charles, Chuck Berry, and James Brown.

Louis Jordan was born in Brinkley, Arkansas, on July 8, 1908, and his experience virtually spanned the entire spectrum of 20th-century black popular music. He was basically a big-band swinger at heart, and even though he formed one of the first small jump combos, he invariably utilized a two- or three-man front line to produce an effect emulating the big bands. In 1951, at the tail-end of the swiftly closing big-band era, Jordan made a vain attempt to revitalize the style by forming a 16-piece orchestra and left Decca three years later to pursue his recording career on Aladdin and, less satisfyingly, with RCA's "X" subsidiary. The material Jordan recorded for Mercury in the late 1950s (**Mercury R&B (1946–62)**) under Quincy Jones' direction, was better, but for Jordan the old spark was gone. Records were now selling to a more juvenile market that demanded backbeats and inane rock 'n' roll lyrics; the sublime subtlety of a *Somebody Done Changed The Lock On My Door* or a *Buzz Me* was lost on the newer, younger audience, and Jordan, who died in 1974, spent the last 14 years of his life recording for a handful of tiny US labels or making the occasional European tour. He has posthumously led the R&B reissue onslaught to such an extent that there is very little of his recorded work left unreissued. So readers who find the recordings on this CD to be to their taste need not go hungry for more.

Jay "Hootie" McShann was only six months younger than Jordan, and developed along similar lines, but whereas Jordan was one of the first to embrace the small-combo format, McShann was one of the last band leaders in Kansas City to suffer the economic problems of trying to maintain a large territory orchestra. His band will always be best known as the incubator of a true jazz genius, Charlie Parker, but the inclusion here of **Blues From Kansas City** is solely on account of the presence of McShann's true blues genius: Walter Brown. Jay McShann's Orchestra recorded fewer than two dozen sides for Decca between April 1941 and December 1943, and 12 of those numbers bore the legend "vocal chorus by Walter Brown". Aside from using an alternate take of *New Confessin' The Blues* in place of the issued take, **Blues from Kansas City** delivers the complete Decca recordings of the McShann band, which includes fine boogie instrumentals by the rhythm section, like *Vine Street Boogie, Hold 'Em Hootie*, and *So You Won't Jump*, and powerful big-band blues instrumentals such as *Swingmatism, Dexter Blues*, and *Sepian Bounce* featuring exciting solos from the likes of Parker and John Jackson, as well as the dozen perfectly formed Walter Brown blues which were to have a profound influence on the likes of Jimmy Witherspoon (**291**, **303**, **480**), Wynonie Harris (**285**, **302**, **312**), and the younger shouters.

Born around 1917 in Dallas, Texas, Brown began singing in the Dallas and Kansas City areas where he no doubt came across band blues singer Jimmy Rushing (**250**). Jay McShann was in Dallas in April 1941 to record his band's début session for Decca, and ten days before, according to legend, he heard Brown singing *Roll 'Em Pete!* at a barbecue stand—McShann, who had previously led an all-instrumental band, immediately engaged the blues shouter to sing with the band at the recording session. Walter sang two blues at the début, both written by the singer with McShann. *Hootie Blues* features the full band and is remembered as much for Parker's spine-tingling alto sax solo as Walter's innovative blues vocal, but it was the second song, *Confessin' The Blues*, recorded simply with piano, bass, and drums, that became the hit, selling over half a million copies and in the process becoming an anthem of R&B that would be covered by artists as diverse as Wynonie Harris, Little Walter, Chuck Berry, B.B. King, and Esther Phillips.

Subsequently, Decca lost all interest in McShann's redoubtable young musicians unless they were being used to back another blues sung by Walter Brown; the second Decca session, in Chicago in November 1941, resulted in eight masters consisting of just one instrumental and seven more Walter Brown blues. Highlights included the erotic *'Fore Day Rider*, the jumping *Hootie's Ignorant Oil*, the swinging *Baby Heart Blues*, and the classic *Red River Blues*.

McShann finished off his Decca contract with two sessions in as many years, and was rewarded with a minor hit in *The Jumpin' Blues* in which Brown advises:

> If you're feelin' lonely and nothing seems o.k. [*twice*]
> Don't drink no whiskey, just jump your blues away!
>
> You can't drown your troubles, boys, that's all a lie [*twice*]
> But I'll be jumpin' the blues until the day I die!

Sadly, it seems that Brown did not practice what he preached, and his heavy drinking and drug habit started to take its toll on McShann and his musicians. The leader began experimenting with new vocalists, like the urbane Al Hibbler, who performs the ballad *Get Me On Your Mind*, and trumpeter Bob Merrill, who describes his *Wrong Neighborhood*. He eventually disbanded in the mid-1940s, at which time Walter Brown began touring as a solo performer and resumed his recording career on Queen and Signature. He later ironed out his differences with McShann and the pianist backed his recalcitrant vocalist on sides recorded for Mercury, Capitol, and Peacock, but surprisingly, despite the honor being bestowed on other, lesser talents, Brown (who is reported to have died from drug-related complications in Lawton, Oklahoma, in June 1956) has not had much of his own work reissued.

Another vocalist who spent her formative years performing with a first-rate black orchestra was Dinah Washington. In direct contrast to Walter Brown, however, Washington was seldom given the chance to record with Lionel Hampton's band during her full two-year tenure. Due to the wide popularity of Hampton's blasting big-band instrumentals, Decca was happy to record as few vocals as possible, and although the release of concert and radio broadcasts of the time have since shown that Washington was very much in evidence "live," only one studio track was made during the Hampton years, except for the four illicit sides made for Eric Bernay's Keynote label in 1943.

Dinah Washington was born Ruth Lee Jones in Tuscaloosa, Alabama, on August 29, 1924; when she was a small child her family moved north to Chicago. At a very early age she was taught to sing and play piano with the various gospel choirs and quartets that visited her local Baptist church on Chicago's South Side. For a while she toured the country giving recitals, and then joined the female gospel group led by the famous Sallie Martin. In 1941 she returned to Chicago and began singing blues ballads and jazz in the style of Billie Holiday, and was in fact standing in for the ailing Lady Day at the Garrick Bar when she caught the attention of band leader Lionel Hampton, who promptly employed Ruth Jones and gave her the name of Dinah Washington. Although Hampton was obviously enamored of his new singer's gospel-inflected vocal style, his Decca bosses were happy enough with the hugely popular big-band boogies and so Washington was shelved as a recording star. It was British-born music critic and jazz aficionado Leonard Feather who instigated her recording début, and it was his songs that became her earliest successes.

The four illicit masters, recorded in December 1943 with a sextet from the Hampton band, were *Salty Papa Blues*, *Homeward Bound*, the saucy *I Know How To Do It*, and her first hit, *Evil Gal Blues*, which Feather had originally written as *Evil Man Blues* for the Hot Lips Page Trio in 1940. This superb jazz-blues session was packed with quality solos by the likes of Milt Buckner on piano, Rudy Rutherford on clarinet and Texas tenorman Arnett Cobb, who, like Washington, was making his long-overdue recording début. Decca relented 15 months later, and Washington cut her only studio track with the full Hampton band when Leonard Feather persuaded the label to let her record his *Blow-Top Blues*, the wickedly amusing saga of a nervous breakdown. Sadly, Decca kept this master in the can until 1947 when Dinah started to appear in the charts with her early Mercury records.

Having been deprived of adequate exposure on record with Hamp's band, Washington was easily persuaded to leave in December 1945 when Apollo Records offered her a short-term recording contract; the 12 sides recorded in Hollywood with an all-star group led by tenorman Lucky Thompson are arguably her finest blues recordings, and Arnold Shaw wrote of them in his book *Honkers and Shouters*: "The sensuous ballad style that influenced virtually every black female vocalist came later, but even in these blues, her voice had a velvet sheen, and, in its bluer moments, it tore like silk, not satin." Washington's unique vocal style does not deserve all the credit for making her Apollo recordings so special, however; a nod of appreciation is due to the steel filigree of 21-year-old Lucky Thompson's tenor sax and the flawless support of his band: Karl George (trumpet), Jewel Grant (alto sax), Gene Porter (baritone sax and clarinet), Wilbert Baranco (piano), Charlie Mingus (double bass), Lee Young (drums), and Milt Jackson (vibraphone).

Undoubtedly the jewel in the Apollo crown is Baranco and Mingus' composition *Pacific Coast Blues*, with its excellent arrangement, vibe/piano and piano/tenor sax obbligatos, baritone sax solo and stunningly evocative lyrics:

> Well the morning sun is rising and I'm sitting on your back door step,
> I'm just a fugitive from slumber—can't count one hour that I've slept,
> I'm just as blue as the Pacific and I know my eyes are just as wet.

Dinah Washington's Keynote, Decca, and Apollo recordings have been reissued on several compilations over the years, but this is the first time we have had the benefit of them all on one release, and **The Complete Dinah Washington—Volume 1** is unreservedly recommended as the place to start before exploring her hit period with Mercury Records (**168**, **289**). She died in 1963 from an accidental overdose of diet pills.

281 The Best Of Louis Jordan
Louis Jordan & His Tympany Five
MCA MCAD-4079
Choo Choo Ch'Boogie/Let The Good Times Roll/Ain't Nobody Here But Us Chickens/Saturday Night Fish Fry Part 1/*Saturday Night Fish Fry* Part 2/*Beware!/Caldonia/Knock Me a Kiss/Run Joe/School Days (When We Were Kids)/Blue Light Boogie* Part 1/*Blue Light Boogie* Part 2/*Five Guys Named Moe/What's The Use Of Gettin' Sober (When You Gonna Get Drunk Again)/Buzz Me/Beans And Corn Bread/Don't Let The Sun Catch You Cryin'/Somebody Done Changed The Lock On My Door/Barnyard Boogie/Early In The Mornin'/I Want You To Be My Baby/Nobody Knows You When You're Down And Out*

282 Blues From Kansas City
Jay McShann Orchestra
MCA GRP16142
Swingmatism/Hootie Blues [Walter Brown, vocal]/*Dexter Blues/Vine Street Boogie/Confessin' The Blues* [Walter Brown, vocal]/*Hold 'Em Hootie/One Woman's Man* [Walter Brown, vocal]/*'Fore Day Rider* [Walter Brown, vocal]/*So You Won't Jump/New Confessin' The Blues* [Walter Brown, vocal] (alternate take)/*Red River Blues* [Walter Brown, vocal]/*Baby Heart Blues* [Walter Brown, vocal]/*Cryin' Won't Make Me Stay* [Walter Brown, vocal]/*Hootie's Ignorant Oil* [Walter Brown, vocal]/*Lonely Boy Blues* [Walter Brown, vocal]/*Get Me On Your Mind* [Al Hibbler, vocal]/*The Jumpin' Blues* [Walter Brown, vocal]/*Sepian Bounce/Say Forward, I'll March/Wrong Neighborhood* [Bob Merrill, vocal]/*Hometown Blues* [Walter Brown, vocal]

283 The Complete Dinah Washington—Volume 1 1943–1945
Official 83004 (Dan)
Dinah Washington With The Keynotes, *Evil Gal Blues/I Know How To Do It/Salty Papa Blues/Homeward Bound*; Lionel Hampton & His Septet, *Blow-Top Blues* [Dinah Washington, vocal]; Dinah Washington With Lucky Thompson's All Stars, *Wise Woman Blues/Walking Blues/No Voot No Boot/Chewing Mama*

Blues/My Lovin' Papa/Rich Man's Blues/All Or Nothing/Begging Mama Blues/ Mellow Mama Blues/My Voot Is Really Vout/Blues For A Day/Pacific Coast Blues

(ii) I Woke Up Hollerin' and Screamin'

During the early 1940s, along with the rise of the powerhouse black big-bands, a new, arrogant style of blues vocalist emerged. Taking their stylistic blueprint from early protagonists like Jimmy Rushing and Walter Brown, this new generation of band blues singers decided that they would not quietly accept their grievances with the society in which they lived, nor even deliver a poignant song to exorcise them like the old country bluesmen. Instead they decided they should shout, holler, scream, yell—and having to sing in front of a 12- or 16-piece band they would need to do it loudly.

Big Joe Turner was an early example of a blues shouter, preferring the power of his voice over the pitch of, say Jimmy Rushing, and preceded both Dinah Washington and Walter Brown in making records; indeed the Louis Jordan band beat him to it by only a matter of ten days. But from the outset it was Big Joe who was the star of the show—the record labels usually bore his name, not "the so-and-so orchestra" in big letters with "vocal refrain by Joe Turner" hidden somewhere else in smaller typeface. He was most certainly a band blues singer, but for many of his earliest releases he was coupled with a lone pianist—invariably Pete Johnson—or a small rhythm trio, settings which starkly revealed the potency of his voice.

Born Joseph Vernon Turner in Kansas City, Missouri, on May 18, 1911, he left school following the death of his father to find bar work in the city's myriad nightclubs and speakeasies where he was eventually employed as a performer. Occasionally touring with the local territory bands led by Bennie Moten, George E. Lee, Andy Kirk, and Count Basie, Turner was more comfortable in a small group setting, or accompanied just by the piano of his friend Pete Johnson. In 1938, having failed there two years earlier, Turner and Johnson returned to New York City where they were booked for John Hammond's "From Spirituals To Swing" concert (**8**, **209**) and for Benny Goodman's "Camel Caravan" radio show. This time they became the talk of the town and ignited the boogie-woogie fever that subsequently swept the nation.

Often in the company of the era's most talented jazzmen, Turner recorded extensively from 1938 to 1944 for major companies like Vocalion, Varsity, OKeh, and Decca; when he won *Esquire* magazine's silver award kiss-of-death for "best male vocalist," however, he was paradoxically dropped by the majors and started label-hopping through the independent record companies, including National, Aladdin, RPM, Freedom (**304**, **318**) and Imperial.

Tell Me Pretty Baby collates 24 tracks from the period 1947–9 when Big Joe was recording on the West Coast for Jack Lauderdale's Down Beat label and Dootsie Williams' Coast Records; the latter's unissued masters were sold to, and released on, new major-league player M-G-M Records. On all these sides Big Joe is reunited with his friend Pete Johnson on piano and accompanied by little big-bands including trumpets and saxes, with arrangements by Maxwell Davis, the doyen of West Coast R&B. In addition to the complete Joe Turner Down Beat and M-G-M recordings there are four band boogie instrumentals led by Pete Johnson from the same sessions and a salaciously retrospective slice of the old pre-war Turner & Johnson duo with *Around The Clock Blues* from 1947 and San Francisco's Stag Records.

As fine as these recordings are, one-off record deals are not good career moves for any recording artist of stature and by the turn of the decade Turner's career was at its lowest ebb. When approached by Ahmet Ertegun of the relatively new independent label, Atlantic, in the spring of 1951, he was no doubt resigned to more rehashes of his old hits *Roll 'Em Pete, Low Down Dog* or *Cherry Red.* Fortunately, Ertegun had greater ideas, and the incongruous second career of Joe Turner as a 40-odd-year-old rock 'n' roll singer was started. Superb musicians, excellent arrangements, witty songs, and, above all (figuratively and literally), Big Joe's magnificent voice made huge hits out of *Chains Of Love, Sweet Sixteen, Honey Hush, Shake, Rattle & Roll*, etc (**315**, **316**). Far from being a one-off deal, Big Joe stayed with Atlantic from 1951 to 1961, revitalizing his career with a momentum that would carry him for the rest of his life and make him a favorite with blues, jazz, R&B, and rock 'n' roll fans. He died on November 24, 1985 after shouting those blues for more than 50 years.

Almost as influential as Big Joe, certainly to the younger generation of blues shouters in the mid-1940s, was the charismatic Wynonie "Mr Blues" Harris, a hard-drinking, hard-living, boastful braggart who made some of the most indispensable records in this (or any other) style of music. Born on August 24, 1913 in Omaha, Nebraska, Harris found employment locally as a comedian and dancer in the mid-1930s. Teaching himself to play drums, he formed his own combo, but switched to singing the blues in the late 1930s after hearing Big Joe Turner in Kansas City, and subsequently moved to Los Angeles to pursue his career as a vocalist. Harris diversified in California, and was MC at Central Avenue's famous Club Alabam, producing stage shows and revues at the Lincoln Theatre, even appearing as a dancer in the film *Hit Parade of 1943*. By that time he was making his name as a talented blues shouter and by 1944 his reputation had spread enough to result in residencies in Chicago and Kansas City as well as Los Angeles. Word of his prowess eventually brought him to the attention of band leader Lucky Millinder, who needed a replacement for his popular singer Trevor Bacon; this, and more was found in Mr Blues.

Like Walter Brown with Jay McShann, within days of Harris having joined the Millinder Orchestra, he was cutting his two début sides for Decca Records, making the cover versions of Benny Carter/Savannah Churchill's *Hurry, Hurry*! and the Sunset Orchestra's *Who Threw The Whiskey In The Well?* his own. Nevertheless within a few months he was back in Los Angeles; perhaps, like his idol Big Joe, the strictures of big-band life disagreed with him, but it was highly likely that the arrogant Mr Blues and his ego made life on the road unbearable for the other musicians.

Apart from a solitary air-shot recorded as a guest with the Lionel Hampton Orchestra in 1948, Harris recorded continuously and prolifically in his own name from 1945 to 1964 for Philo/Aladdin, Apollo (**302**), Hamp-Tone, Bullett, Aladdin again, Atlantic, Roulette, and Chess respectively, usually in the company of impeccable jazz musicians. His most abundant and successful period was slotted between his second stint with Aladdin and Roulette when he spent a decade recording for Syd Nathan's King label from 1947 to 1957 after being recommended by another great blues shouter, Gatemouth Moore. **Good Rocking Tonight** features 20 of his greatest commercial and artistic successes cut between 1947 and 1953 for King Records.

The well-known title song was actually offered to Harris as a gift by its writer, a then unknown, as yet unrecorded local blues shouter while he was touring New Orleans, but Harris in his arrogance dismissed the song and its writer. Within a few months, the composer, Roy Brown, had recorded the song for Deluxe with great success and Harris was forced by King to eat humble pie and cover it together with the record's erotic B-side, *Lollipop Mama*. Nevertheless, with the valuable accompaniment of the Hot Lips Page band, Wynonie overtook Roy Brown's massive sales to surface as the definitive version, itself going on to influence a certain young Memphis truck driver who would record the song with some success in the mid-1950s (**330**).

Usually billed as his "All Stars," Harris' musicians on the King sessions were just that; superb veterans culled from the Lips Page, Todd Rhodes, Lucky Millinder, Joe Morris, or Sonny Thompson bands, providing a flawless backdrop to deliciously obscene, barely *double-entendre* classics such as *Sittin' On It All The Time, I Like My Baby's Pudding, I Want My Fanny Brown,* and *Keep On Churnin' ('Til The Butter Comes),* as well as the odd ballad like *Luscious Woman* or jazzy tenor sax showcase like *Blow Your Brains Out*, in which Harris' improvisational skills are outstanding.

His last known professional appearance was at the famous Apollo Theater in 1967 where he stunned the audience with his power-packed performance. On June 14, 1969 the hard-living and hard-drinking finally took their toll and Wynonie Harris died largely forgotten by all but his closest friends and fans.

Walter Brown, Big Joe Turner and even Wynonie Harris were products of the late 1930s, learning their craft from a mixture of territory band jazz vocalists and classic blues singers, but during the late 1940s another strain of blues shouter emerged, who relied less on the power and timbre of the voice and more on the soulful melisma practiced by the gospel singers of sacred music. This melismatic way of singing the blues—by bending, stretching, and worrying key words and phrases of the song—burgeoned in the Southern cities, particularly in Atlanta, Memphis, and New Orleans, and one of its first masters, perhaps the originator of soul music, was Roy Brown—the master of both the heart-rending, crying blues and the joyous, soulful jump blues. Born on September 10, 1925 in New Orleans, Brown formed his own gospel quartet, the Rookie Four, in the late 1930s and moved to Los Angeles in 1942. By 1945 he was singing professionally in the Shreveport area and later around Galveston, where he unknowingly made his recording début for Goldstar Records when the small Texas label made clandestine recordings during a club performance. Brown returned to New Orleans in 1947, where he was introduced to Jules Braun of Deluxe Records by Cecil Gant (**297**) and he took part in his first bona fide recording session the very next day; the first song recorded was Brown's original *Good Rocking Tonight*, backed with *Lolly Pop Mama*.

Blues Deluxe consists of 24 consecutive masters recorded over six sessions between April 1950 and September 1951, so it fails to deliver earlier successes like *Good Rocking Tonight, Lolly Pop Mama, Fanny Brown* or *Boogie At Midnight*. It does, however, include even bigger hits such as *Love Don't Love Nobody, Long About Sundown, Cadillac Baby, Big Town,* and *Bar Room Blues*, which spent 18 weeks on the *Billboard* R&B chart and reached the number one position. The genius behind these successes was arranger and producer Henry Glover, who would often augment or even replace some of Roy Brown's working band with other available musicians to produce a different effect; therefore the *Hard Luck Blues* session features elements from the bands of Tiny Bradshaw (**299**) and the Griffin Brothers, and this explosive mixture climaxes in a barely controlled *New Rebecca* with an urgent solo from Roy's regular tenor player, Johnny Fontenette, and a blistering trombone solo from the assisting Jimmy Griffin:

> When it comes to making love it's a natural fact,
> Rebecca satisfies or gives your money back!

Many of Brown's jump tunes were salacious, but so were some of his straight blues. *Too Much Lovin' Ain't No Good* sounds like another of his "crying" blues, until you listen closely to the lyrics about his girlfriend who has a job "working like a carpentry man." Backed by the effectively plangent guitar chords of Edgar Blanchard, Roy wails:

> Now she takes her screwdriver when there's special work to do,
> And the whole day long she don't do a doggone thing but screw.

At the time of the sides here, Brown's contract and all of his Deluxe masters had been purchased by King Records, although they continued to release singles on Deluxe until 1952, when Brown was switched to the King label proper. In 1956 Brown went to Imperial Records where he had his last hit with a cover of Buddy Knox's rock 'n' roll hit *Party Doll*, and returned to King for a couple of sessions in 1959, but his recordings on these and later labels lacked the spark of the classic Deluxe sides.

In the late 1970s, Brown made something of a comeback and toured Europe, where his fans discovered that his voice was virtually undiminished by the intervening years. Sadly this Indian summer was short-lived: he died on May 25, 1981.

B.B. King is the odd man out here, being the only living legend among those discussed so far. His style, an explosive fusion of Roy Brown's soulful vocal technique and a similarly melismatic adaption of T-Bone Walker's single-string electric guitar playing, has influenced all subsequent so-called soul bluesmen from Freddy King (**311**) to Robert Cray (**448**).

Just six days younger than Roy Brown, born on a Mississippi plantation between Itta Bena and Indianola, Riley B. King began singing in local churches at the age of four and later joined his school's spiritual quartet. Around the age of 15, while working as a farmhand, King taught himself guitar and formed the Elkhorn Singers Quartet. After briefly serving with the US Army in 1943 he joined the St John Gospel Singers, who performed on radio shows broadcast from Greenwood. In 1946 King moved to Memphis, where he began playing the blues on street corners and soon graduated to become a member of the mythical Beale Streeters—a group of Memphis bluesmen said to include Bobby Bland, Johnny Ace, Rosco Gordon (**320**), and Earl Forest.

In 1949 King became a celebrated personality in the Memphis area, both as a performer and as a disc jockey on radio station WDIA. The result of this fame was that he began recording, initially for Nashville's Bullet Records under the name B.B. King (the initials are those of his

WDIA radio persona, "Blues Boy" King) and, from 1950, for the Bihari brothers' RPM label, based in California. He recorded most of his early sides at Sam Phillips' famous Sun studios, later traveling to Houston to record, and eventually to the West Coast. Remaining with the Biharis for 12 years, King left in 1962 to record for ABC Paramount (**521**), although he had moonlighted to record for Peacock in Houston in 1953 and Chess in Chicago in 1958, and had even inaugurated his own record label, Blues Boy Kingdom, in the mid-1950s.

Singin' The Blues/The Blues is a value-for-money package in which B.B.'s first two LPs have been combined on one CD; it features his finest RPM tracks, spanning the Memphis recordings of 1951 to his Los Angeles masters of 1954–8, taking in the Houston recordings of 1952–3 on the way. As well as being his finest cuts, many are also his greatest hits: *Three O'Clock Blues* (coupled with *That Ain't The Way To Do It*) and *You Know I Love You* both reached the number one position on *Billboard's* R&B chart, while *Boogie Woogie Woman, Woke Up This Morning (My Baby's Gone), Please Love Me, You Upset Me Baby, Everyday (I Have the Blues), What Can I Do? (Just Sing The Blues), Crying Won't Help You, Sweet Little Angel,* and *I Want To Get Married* all earned high R&B chart placings, as did their reverse sides.

While the earliest sides are interesting, it is the later recordings made in Houston and, particularly, Los Angeles that bear the mark of polished professionalism. In Houston, B.B. was teamed with the local band led by Bill Harvey as both a touring and a studio unit, and this becomes obvious on the effortlessness of tracks like *Please Love Me,* the latin-flavored *Woke Up This Morning,* and the intense *Blind Love.* King's musical maturity was completed when his recording company eventually brought him to Los Angeles in 1954, where he was set to work with the redoubtable Maxwell Davis, a musician, band leader, arranger and A&R (Artist and Repertoire) man of unmatchable talent, whose skills were pursued by all of the West Coast labels. His faultless arrangements for King of Memphis Slim's *Nobody Loves Me* via Lowell Fulson's retitling to *Everyday I Have The Blues,* Roy Hawkins' *Why Do Everything Happen To Me?,* Gatemouth Moore's *Did You Ever Love A Woman?,* and Tampa Red's *Sweet Little Angel* and *Crying Won't Help You,* are perfect examples of Davis' art of taking older blues styles and marrying them to contemporary, soulful horn charts, producing a sound that was fresh and new—and successful. The legacy of such recordings, coupled with King's grueling touring schedule over the last 40 years have earned him the love and respect of the music business and the title "Ambassador of the Blues."

284 **Tell Me Pretty Baby**
Big Joe Turner
Arhoolie CD 333
Joe Turner With Pete Johnson & His Orchestra, *Wine-O Baby Boogie/B & O Blues*; Pete Johnson Sextet, *Rocket Boogie "88"* Part 1; Joe Turner With Pete Johnson & His Orchestra, *Old Piney Brown's Gone/Baby Won't You Marry Me*; Pete Johnson Sextet, *Skid Row Boogie*; Joe Turner With Pete Johnson & His Orchestra, *Christmas Date Boogie/Radar Blues/Tell Me Pretty Baby;* Pete Johnson Sextet, *Rocket Boogie "88"* Part 2; Joe Turner With Pete Johnson & His Orchestra, *Trouble Blues*; Pete Johnson Sextet, *Half Tight Boogie*; Joe Turner, *Mardi Gras Boogie/My Heart Belongs To You/So Many Women Blues/ Messin' Around/I Don't Dig It/Rainy Weather Blues/Boogie Woogie Baby/ Married Woman Blues/Feelin' So Sad/Moody Baby*; [as Big Vernon], *Around The Clock Blues* Part 1/*Around The Clock Blues* Part 2

285 **Good Rocking Tonight**
Wynonie Harris
Charly CD Charly 244 (UK)
Wynonie Harris, *Good Rocking Tonight*; Wynonie Harris & His All Stars, *She Just Won't Sell No More*; Wynonie Harris, *Blow Your Brains Out*; Wynonie Harris & His All Stars, *I Want My Fanny Brown/All She Wants To Do Is Rock*; Wynonie Harris, *Lollipop Mama*; Wynonie Harris & His All Stars, *Baby, Shame On You/I Like My Baby's Pudding*; Wynonie Harris, *Wynonie's Boogie*; Wynonie Harris & His All Stars, *Sittin' On It All The Time/Good Morning Judge/I Feel That Old Age Coming On*; Wynonie Harris With Todd Rhodes Orchestra, *Lovin' Machine*; Wynonie Harris & His All Stars, *Mr Blues Is Coming To Town*; Wynonie Harris, *Quiet Whiskey*; Wynonie Harris & His All Stars *Rock Mr Blues/Bloodshot Eyes*; Wynonie Harris With Todd Rhodes Orchestra, *Luscious Woman*; Wynonie Harris, *Down Boy Down*; Wynonie Harris With Todd Rhodes Orchestra, *Keep On Churnin' ('Til The Butter Comes)*

286 **Blues Deluxe**
Roy Brown
Charly CD Charly 289 (UK)
Roy Brown & His Mighty-Mighty Men, *Cadillac Baby/Hard Luck Blues/New Rebecca/Sweet Peach/Love Don't Love Nobody/Dreaming Blues/Good Man Blues/Too Much Lovin' Ain't No Good/Teenage Jamboree/Train Time Blues/Bar Room Blues/Long About Sundown/Beautician Blues/Drum Boogie/Double Crossin' Woman/Swingin' With Johnny/Wrong Woman Blues/Good Rockin' Man/I've Got The Last Laugh Now/Big Town/Brown Angel/Rock-A-Bye Baby/ Lonesome Lover/Answer To Big Town*

287 **Singin' The Blues/The Blues**
B.B. King
Virgin/Flair V2-86296 (US)/*Ace CDCHD 320* (UK)
B.B. King & His Orchestra, *Please Love Me*; B.B. "Blues Boy" King & His Orchestra, *You Upset Me Baby/Everyday (I Have The Blues)/Bad Luck*; B.B. King & His Orchestra, *Three O'Clock Blues/Blind Love (Who Can Your Good Man Be?)/Woke Up This Morning (My Baby Was Gone)/You Know I Love*

You; B.B. "Blues Boy" King & His Orchestra, *Sweet Little Angel/Ten Long Years (I Had a Woman)/Did You Ever Love A Woman?/Crying Won't Help You* B.B. King, *Why Do Everything Happen To Me?*; B.B. "Blues Boy" King & His Orchestra, *Ruby Lee/When My Heart Beats Like A Hammer*; B.B. King & His Orchestra, *Past Day (Don't Have To Cry)/Boogie Woogie Woman/Early Every Morning*; B.B. King, *I Want To Get Married*; B.B. King & His Orchestra; *That Ain't The Way To Do It*; B.B. King, *Troubles, Troubles, Troubles*; B.B. "Blues Boy" King & His Orchestra, *Don't You Want A Man Like Me?*; B.B. King, *You Know I Go For You*; B.B. "Blues Boy" King & His Orchestra, *What Can I Do? (Just Sing The Blues)*

(iii) A Blues & Rhythm Melting-Pot

As the six-decade history of R&B is so diverse, it is sensible for novices to begin their collections with the more varied "various artists" compilations in order to discover whether they prefer the 1940s sound to that of the 1950s or 1960s; whether the jazzier end of the spectrum is found to be more stimulating than black proto-rock 'n' roll or whether their taste is for vocal groups rather than solo blues shouters. The recent surge of interest in blues and R&B, coupled with a pleasing catholicism of taste, has resulted in a number of excellent boxed sets containing two, three, or even more CDs which will provide endless listening pleasure for newcomer and expert alike.

The RCA Victor Blues & Rhythm Revue is a surprisingly welcome release, for, although there have periodically been reissues of the fine jazz and blues recordings from the vaults of RCA Victor and its subsidiaries, the company has seldom seen fit to dip into its equally fine R&B catalogue. These 28 tracks make a thoughtful, interesting, but most importantly, immensely enjoyable set spanning the years 1940–59, beginning with two titles from the urbane Lil Green, supported by Big Bill Broonzy, on her hit *Romance In The Dark* and the irresistible *Why Don't You Do Right?* The latter became a hit for Peggy Lee, and deserves special mention due to its importance at the very roots of R&B music, because it was composed by "Kansas Joe" McCoy, who recorded it as *Weed Smoker's Dream* in 1936 with the Harlem Hamfats (**273**).

Avery Parrish's piano feature *After Hours* was such an artistic success and so ground-breaking stylistically that it was necessary for all serious musicians to learn it note-for-note, no matter what instrument they played, and it has been echoed many times throughout R&B's long history. Likewise, Billy Eckstine's blues recorded while he was vocalist with Earl Hines' Orchestra, *Stormy Monday* and *Jelly, Jelly*, were very influential in their day, with his rich bass-baritone setting the standard for all subsequent big-band blues singers. Among women singers Billie Holiday was no less influential, as is evident in the work of Etta Jones. The doyen of jump blues tenor saxophone, Illinois Jacquet, blows an ultrafast bop blues, *Hot Rod*, based on his pioneering 1942 solo on Lionel Hampton's *Flying Home*, while the Delta Rhythm Boys proffer two performances in differing stylings: *Dry Bones*, the ancient traditional song, takes us back to the roots of the vocal group style and to groups such as the Mills Brothers; and Duke Ellington's signature tune, *Take The "A" Train*, brings us bang up to date with a modern vocalised arrangement of the instrumental.

When the popular Charles Brown quit Johnny Moore's Three Blazers (**441**), his replacement, Billy Valentine, was compared unfavorably with his predecessor. *Rock With It* proves how unfair this was: Valentine turns in a marvelous vocal and piano solo, while Johnny's brother Oscar adds a fine guitar break. Despite boasting the same instrumentation, *Two Guitar Boogie* from Rene Hall's trio four years later is not quite in the same league, being a rocking guitar-led instrumental with an over-forceful backbeat.

The big bands of Cab Calloway, Lucky Millinder, Count Basie, and Buddy Johnson were all catalytic in the evolution of R&B, their bands incubating the future heroes of the music. Calloway sings Jessie Mae Robinson's amusing *Rooming House Boogie*, recorded by Amos Milburn just a few weeks previously (**442**); Calloway's version benefits from a tenor sax solo by one of those embryonic R&B heroes—Sam "The Man" Taylor. Having employed some of early R&B's finest vocalists, Lucky Millinder rarely sang on his recordings of the 1940s and 1950s. Annisteen Allen's powerful voice was a match for any male blues shouter and effortlessly cuts through Lucky's 20-piece orchestra on *Moanin' The Blues*, whereas the instrumental *D'Natural Blues* (on which *The Hucklebuck*, a best seller of 1949, was based) spotlights a fine tenor sax solo by Slim Henderson. One of the Basie band's greatest gifts to the development of R&B was Jimmy Rushing—the original blues shouter. *Hey Pretty Baby* (1947) is suffused with Rushing's characteristic melancholic tone, which, although not strictly a shout, influenced all who came after him. Two years later Basie covered Buddy Johnson's rip-roaring *Did You See Jackie Robinson Hit That Ball?*, proving that jump blues was not just about sex and alcohol.

Cole Slaw introduces us to Jesse Stone (RCA Victor's answer to Louis Jordan), who was a talented singer, songwriter, pianist, band leader, arranger, and talent scout. Before joining the staff at Atlantic Records, he recorded witty jump tunes such as this one, which has a fine tenor sax solo by Eddie "Lockjaw" Davis. It was swiftly covered by both Jordan and Frank "Floorshow" Culley (**315**). Similarly, William "Mr Sad Head" Thurman was RCA's clone of the popular

Wynonie "Mr Blues" Harris, but, despite the support of Billy Ford's band with young Wayne Bennett on guitar, his song is a little too close to Harris' *Good Morning Judge* (**285**) for comfort.

RCA's flirtation with Atlanta R&B was much better, as Clyde "Blow-Top" Lynn's *Reliefin' Blues* and Little Richard's two contributions testify. The first is sung by the wickedly underrated Melvin Smith, who wails in a soulful, typically Atlantan style. *Get Rich Quick* was Little Richard's recording début in 1951; written by Leonard Feather, it is an optimistic jump blues, very much in the Roy Brown style. Although Richard's own song, *Thinkin' 'Bout My Mother*, is doom-laden and full of self-pity and remorse, it gives the singer a chance to show off his superb melisma (learned from local hero Billy Wright) and also allows guitarist Wesley Jackson the opportunity to shine.

During the 1940s and 1950s another interesting facet of R&B was the rise of the vocal group. Such 1940s units as the Delta Rhythm Boys were the inspiration for the next generation, for example the West Coast's The Robins (whose career began with Johnny Otis's band) and the East Coast's Du Droppers, which evolved, like many of the early groups, from a gospel quartet. The more obscure Heartbreakers were associated with Frank Motley, a band leader from Washington DC, although *Rockin' Daddy-O* is accompanied by a combo led by the important R&B arranger and pianist Howard Biggs. The Treniers were another of the older-style vocal acts who toughened up their approach with the advent of "hard" R&B, resulting in the most popular rock 'n' roll cabaret act of the 1950s. Milt Trenier had the strongest voice of all the brothers, and proves it on the powerful *Squeeze Me*, backed by an all-star band of West Coast Cool Jazz musicians under the critic-dodging pseudonym of Boots Brown & His Blockbusters.

Recorded in 1956, *Open Up* is from the tail-end of the so-called golden years of R&B, but this *tour de force* by King Curtis is ironically a throwback to the seminal days of jump blues saxophone and Illinois Jacquet's histrionic displays at "Jazz at the Philharmonic". Last on this disc, *Shout* points to the future of R&B, and is therefore a little out of place here with its schizophrenic mixture of R&B, rock 'n' roll and early soul. Nevertheless, the Isley Brothers indicate the way to the next great era of black music and the Motown explosion of which they were a part.

Not as venerable as RCA, Mercury records was founded by Louis Jordan's agent Berle Adams in 1945 but soon muscled its way into the premier league of major record companies with its strong roster of blues, jazz, and R&B stars such as Dinah Washington, Eddie "Mr

Cleanhead" Vinson, Jay McShann, and Walter Brown. Like RCA Victor, Mercury is long overdue for an extensive reissue program, but in the meantime has produced a rhythm and blues collection entitled **Mercury R&B (1946–62)**. Starting with the company's biggest star, Dinah Washington, the first CD offers three of Leonard Feather's songs from her illicit session for Keynote Records in 1943 and then launches into Mercury product proper. *New Blow-Top Blues* is a smart revision of her solitary disc with Lionel Hampton's Orchestra; *Trouble In Mind* is a nice remake of the classic blues song penned by Richard M. Jones; and *Fat Daddy*, aptly, is a bouncy little R&B song dominated by Jackie Davis' organ and Paul Quinichette's tenor sax. The other songs depict Dinah's departure from the R&B market to the more lucrative popular charts; nevertheless the consummate *I Don't Hurt Anymore* reached number 3 on *Billboard's* R&B chart.

Eddie "Mr Cleanhead" Vinson has been undeservedly neglected as far as CD reissues are concerned. A small, dapper, bald-headed man, he was an exciting and innovative alto saxophonist in R&B, while shouting the blues with a unique Texas squeak. Born in Houston, Texas, on December 19, 1917, Vinson learned his craft in the territory bands of Chester Boone and Milt Larkin, alongside the likes of Arnett Cobb, T-Bone Walker and Illinois Jacquet. Leaving for the big time and Chicago, in 1942 Vinson joined the Cootie Williams Orchestra and spent three years recording for OKeh, Hit, and Majestic, laying down some of the first bona fide recordings in the blues shout idiom. He formed his own band in late 1945 and began a four-year association with Mercury, re-recording some of the hits he had with the Williams Orchestra. Examples include his version of Big Joe's *Cherry Red Blues*, and favorite songs like Big Bill Broonzy's *Just A Dream*, which Big Bill had taught to Eddie when they were both accompanying singer Lil Green on tour in 1941. Most of Mr Cleanhead's songs were earthy, bawdy, and downright funny—original pieces about drunken or promiscuous women and his own lack of money or hair. His showstopper, *Cleanhead Blues*, is a perfect example:

> If it wasn't for you women, I'd have my curly locks today [*twice*]
> But I've been hugged, kissed and petted, 'til all my hair's been rubbed away!

Vinson's biggest hit came with the double-header *Kidney Stew Blues/Old Maid Boogie* in 1947, but the American Federation of Musicians' strike of 1948 interrupted the flow and he left Mercury in 1949 to record successfully for King Records. From the 1960s onwards, Vinson's potent cocktail of Texas blues hollering and Charlie Parker-like alto sax made him a headliner at most of the US and European jazz and blues festivals, and right up until his death from cancer on July 2, 1988, Mr Cleanhead was touring and performing in a style largely unchanged from that of his heyday.

Roy Byrd is covered more extensively in Chapter 13 under his more colorful soubriquet Professor Longhair. His Mercury recordings came in 1949, between his recording début on Talent records and his more famous Atlantic sessions, accompanied by his Blues Jumpers consisting of Robert Parker on sax, Walter "Papoose" Nelson on guitar, and drummer Al Miller. The four sides here are neatly split between the mid-tempo blues of *Her Mind Is Gone* and *Byrd's Blues*, with Byrd's idiosyncratic boogies displayed on *Oh Well* and *Baldhead* (the latter had been recorded earlier as *She Ain't Got No Hair*).

The enigmatic Eagles were a vocal group whose only claim to fame was that they recorded the original version of *Tryin' To Get To You*, which was latter cut for Sun Records by Elvis Presley (**330**) It is interesting to note that, on this evidence, Presley's "unique" vocal style was apparently taken directly from the lead singer of the Eagles.

The orchestra led by Buddy Johnson was immensely important in the history of early R&B. Paradoxically, to date there has been no CD reissue of the essential prime recordings cut for Decca Records, but virtually everything else recorded by the band is available digitally. Johnson was born in Darlington, South Carolina, on January 10, 1915. In 1938, as a professionally trained pianist and arranger, he moved to New York City, where he formed a jazz group and began recording for Decca in 1939. He was joined the following year by his younger sister Ella, a peerless singer of blues and blues ballads, and the hits started flowing: *Please Mr Johnson, Since I Fell For You, I Still Love You* and *That's The Stuff You Gotta Watch* are just a handful of the standards Buddy and Ella Johnson gave to blues and R&B.

In 1953, Decca let the Johnson band go to Mercury, and here they continued their chart run by re-recording some of their biggest Decca successes as well as original, more contemporary, R&B hits like *Hittin' On Me, I Don't Want Nobody (To Have My Love But You)* and *(Gotta Go) Upside Your Head.* In addition to Ella, Buddy usually carried a male singer in the Billy Eckstine mold and a hard blues shouter, like Ricky Harper, who delivers *Shut Your Big Mouth* and *A Pretty Girl (A Cadillac And Some Money).*

Buddy Johnson continued successfully with his big R&B band longer than most, but he eventually retired in the mid-1960s and died in New York City on February 9, 1977.

Like Buddy Johnson, Louis Jordan joined Mercury after spending the 1940s and early 1950s with Decca (**281**), also recording a mixture of old successes and more modern R&B originals. *Caldonia, Let The*

Good Times Roll, and *Salt Pork, West Virginia* were all re-recordings of Decca hits with smart new arrangements by Quincy Jones and a band that included New York City's R&B session whizz-kids Sam "The Man" Taylor and Mickey Baker. Despite this seemingly faultless formula, Jordan's Mercury sales were very disappointing.

Clyde McPhatter went to Mercury Records in June 1960 after a successful career as lead singer in some of the best R&B vocal groups of the 1950s. Born in Durham, North Carolina, on November 15, 1932, he joined the Mount Lebanon Gospel Singers shortly after arriving with his family in New York City in 1947. Having made successful appearances at the Apollo Theater's infamous Amateur Nights, he was approached by arranger Billy Ward to sing lead with his new vocal group, The Dominoes, who recorded successfully for King's Federal subsidiary with songs like *Have Mercy Baby* and the passionate *Do Something For Me.* In early 1953 McPhatter left The Dominoes to lead his own group, The Drifters, on Atlantic Records (**316**), recording R&B classics like *Money Honey, White Christmas,* and *Such A Night*, and from 1955 recorded solo.

McPhatter's solo efforts never quite had the impact of his electrifying lead vocals with the vocal groups and in spite of hits like *A Lover's Question, Ta Ta, I Never Knew, Lover Please,* and a cover of Thurston Harris' *Little Bitty Pretty One,* they remained an uncomfortable blend of pop R&B and early soul. His success declined in the 1960s and he died on June 12, 1972.

Even older than RCA Victor, which was incorporated in 1901, was the pioneering Columbia Records, which was founded around 1865, began recording jazz in 1917 and blues in 1921. They took over OKeh records in 1926. Although viewed as a "popular music" label, Columbia created a spectacular catalog of black music from very early on, and increasingly from the mid-1940s recorded some of the best early Chicago blues and up-town R&B. **The OKeh Rhythm & Blues Story 1949–1957** picks up the tale with a revitalized OKeh label and the signing of jazzy jump groups like Philadelphia's Chris Powell & The Five Blue Flames and jive groups like Kansas City's The Five Scamps, who would provide cover versions of popular R&B hits such as Jimmy Preston's *Rock The Joint*, Amos Milburn's *Chicken Shack Boogie* and *Red Hot*, which is a thinly disguised rewrite of Red Callender/Roy Milton's *Red Light*, as well as their own material.

Having recorded such popular blues artists as Big Bill, Memphis Minnie, Buster Bennett, and Willie Dixon's Big Three Trio (**274**) in the mid- to late 1940s, Columbia constantly had an eye on the Chicago scene and came up trumps again in 1950 with Red Saunders' Orchestra featuring young Joe Williams. Joe would later find fame as Jimmy

Rushing's replacement in the Count Basie band of 1954, but as a raw young shouter he comes across powerfully on these his first recordings, particularly on the song in tribute to his adopted hometown, *CHI.* OKeh had discovered its biggest star, crooner Johnnie Ray, in Detroit's Flame Show Bar, and returned to sign Show Bar R&B band Maurice King & His Wolverines and its featured vocalists Ruby Jackson and Dolores "Bea" Baker. Nothing more is known of Jackson, but "Bea" became LaVerne Baker, finding success on Atlantic in the mid-1950s (**316**) and Maurice King became an arranger and "artists development" coach with Motown Records.

Joe "Mr Google Eyes" August was a young blues shouter from New Orleans whose contract was acquired by OKeh from Coleman Records and his two best Coleman masters were re-recorded by OKeh. Subsequently OKeh trawled the Crescent City for R&B talent and signed Earl Williams, later buying a package of important New Orleans artists from the financially insecure Regal Records that included Paul Gayten, Annie Laurie, Larry Darnell, and Sammy Cotton who made some of their best records for the Columbia subsidiary.

OKeh targeted the artists of Atlanta, Georgia, in the early 1950s, acquiring minor signings like The Royals but striking gold with major blues stylists; these included singer/songwriters Titus Turner and the tragic Chuck Willis. He had five top ten R&B hits during his OKeh tenure; he left in 1955 for similar success with Atlantic Records but died in 1958.

The tightly knit West Coast scene was scrutinized but the combination of a thriving independent record business and the ideal climate made OKeh a bad move for Californian musicians. Nevertheless, OKeh hired the occasional Los Angeles studio to record pianist/vocalist Hadda Brooks, the bands of saxophonists Little Brother Brown and Chuck Thomas and their vocalists Irlton French and Pearl Traylor to tap into the classic West Coast jump sound. And vocal groups were not neglected, from the precursors of the doo-wop sound, The Ravens, through the jive style of The Shufflers, the parody of Big John and The Buzzards, to the fully fledged rock 'n' roll style of Little Joe and The Thrillers and The Marquees featuring Marvin Gaye.

As R&B became more generic, with local trends melding to form a single style, OKeh continued to rediscover stars like Big Maybelle, a big-voiced shouter who recorded powerful blues, such as her *Gabbin' Blues*, along with proto-rock 'n' roll like *One Monkey Don't Stop No Show* and *Whole Lotta Shakin' Goin' On* (also **169**). Other artists included the aforementioned Treniers, whose OKeh recordings of *The Moondog* and *Poontang* predated and influenced the first rock 'n' roll showbands led by Bill Haley and Freddie Bell, and the bizarre, but highly original Screamin' Jay Hawkins, who gave the eldritch *I Put A Spell On You* to the world of popular music and spawned a batch of disciples including Lloyd Fatman (Smith). **The OKeh Rhythm and Blues Story** offers an unparalleled insight into the broad spectrum of 1950s R&B. There are the jump bands of Chris Powell and Billy Ford, the jive rhythm of Bill Davis Trio, the city blues of guitarist Leroy Johnson, and the soulful voice of Billy Stewart. Alongside these is the blues shouting of Pinnochio James and Jumpin' Joe Williams, jazzy stylings from Clifford "King" Solomon and Red Rodney, and novelty rock 'n' roll by Andre Williams and Hurricane Harry. This is a solid springboard from which to test the deep waters of a varied music.

288 The RCA Victor Blues & Rhythm Revue
Various Artists
RCA 8423-2
Lil Green, *Romance In The Dark/Why Don't You Do Right?*; Erskine Hawkins & His Orchestra, *After Hours*; Earl Hines & His Orchestra, *Stormy Monday Blues* [Billy Eckstine, vocal]/*Jelly, Jelly* [Billy Eckstine, vocal]; Etta Jones With J.C. Heard & His Band, *I Sold My Heart To The Junkman*; Illinois Jacquet & His Orchestra, *Hot Rod*; Delta Rhythm Boys, *Dry Bones/Take The "A" Train*; Johnny Moore's Three Blazers, *Rock With It* [Billy Valentine, vocal]; Rene Hall Orchestra, *Two Guitar Boogie*; Cab Calloway & His Cab Jivers, *Rooming House Boogie*; Lucky Millinder & His Orchestra, *Moanin' The Blues* [Annisteen Allen, vocal]/*D'Natural Blues*; Count Basie & His Orchestra, *Hey, Pretty Baby* [Jimmy Rushing, vocal]/*Did You See Jackie Robinson Hit That Ball?* [Taps Miller, vocal]; Jesse Stone & His Orchestra, *Cole Slaw*; Mr Sad Head, *Butcher Boy*; Blow-Top Lynn & His House Rockers, *Reliefin' Blues* [Melvin Smith, vocal]; Little Richard, *Get Rich Quick/Thinkin' 'Bout My Mother*; Milt Trenier & His Solid Six [Boots Brown & His Blockbusters], *Squeeze Me*; The Heartbreakers, *Rockin' Daddy-O*; The Robins, *All Night Baby*; Du Droppers, *Bam Balam/Boot 'Em Up*; King Curtis, *Open Up*; The Isley Brothers, *Shout* Part 1/*Shout* Part 2

289 Mercury R&B (1946–62)
Various Artists
Polygram/Mercury 838 243-2—2 CD set
DISC ONE: Dinah Washington With The Keynotes, *Evil Gal Blues/I Know How To Do It/Salty Papa Blues*; Dinah Washington With Nook Shrier's Orchestra, *New Blow-Top Blues*; Dinah Washington With Jimmy Cobb's Orchestra, *Trouble In Mind/Fat Daddy*; Dinah Washington With Hal Mooney's Orchestra, *I Don't Hurt Anymore;* Dinah Washington, *I Just Couldn't Stand It No More*; Eddie "Mr. Cleanhead" Vinson & His Orchestra, *Cherry Red Blues/Just A Dream*; Eddie Vinson & His Orchestra, *Cleanhead Blues/When A Woman Loves Her Juice/Kidney Stew Blues/Old Maid Boogie/Some Women Do/You Can't Have My Love No More*; Roy Byrd & His Blues Jumpers [Professor Longhair],

Her Mind Is Gone/Baldhead/Oh Well/Byrd's Blues; The Eagles, *Tryin' To Get To You*

DISC TWO: Buddy Johnson & His Orchestra, *That's How I Feel About You* [Ella Johnson, vocal]/*Hittin' On Me* [Ella Johnson, vocal]/*Shut Your Big Mouth Girl* [Ricky Harper, vocal]/A Pretty Girl (A Cadillac And Some Money) [Ricky Harper, vocal]/*(Gotta Go) Upside Your Head* [Ella Johnson, vocal]/*I Don't Want Nobody (To Have My Love But You)* [Ella Johnson, vocal]/*That's What You Gotta Do* [Ella Johnson, vocal]/*I Still Love You* [Ella Johnson, vocal]; Louis Jordan & His Tympany Five, *Caldonia/Let The Good Times Roll/Big Bess/Cat Scratchin'/Salt Pork, W. Va [West Virginia]/Fire/Ella Mae/Sweet Hunk Of Junk*; Clyde McPhatter, *Ta Ta/I Never Knew/Lover Please/Little Bitty Pretty One*

290 The OKeh Rhythm & Blues Story 1949–1957
Various Artists
Sony/Epic E3K 48912—3 CD set
DISC ONE: Chris Powell & The Five Blue Flames, *Rock The Joint/That's Right!*; The Five Scamps, *Chicken Shack Boogie*; Mr Google Eyes With Billy Ford & His Musical V-8's, *No Wine, No Women*; The Five Scamps, *Red Hot*; Mr Google Eyes With Billy Ford & His Musical V-8's, *Rough and Rocky Road*; Chris Powell & The Five Blue Flames, *Hot Dog*; The Five Scamps, *Fine Like Wine*; Jumpin' Joe Williams With Red Saunders & His Orchestra, *CHI (Chicago)/Lyin' Girl Blues*; The Ravens, *Gotta Find My Baby*; Chuck Willis, *Let's Jump Tonight*; Maurice King & His Wolverines, *I Want A Lavender Cadillac* [Bea Baker, vocal]; Earl Williams, *If You Ever Had The Blues*; The Bill Davis Trio, *Catch 'Em Young, Treat 'Em Rough, Tell 'Em Nothin'*; Jumpin' Joe Williams With Red Saunders & His Orchestra, *Weekday Blues*; Irlton French With Chuck Thomas & His All Stars, *My Run Around Baby*; The Five Scamps, *Stuttering Blues*; Leory Johnson, *She Did Me Wrong*; The Ravens, *Honey, I Don't Want You*; Larry Darnell, *Work Baby Work*; Pinnochio James, *Camp Meeting*; Pearl Traylor With Chuck Thomas & His All Stars, *Come On Daddy (Let's Go Play Tonight)*; Maurice King & His Wolverines, *I Feel So Good (I Must Be Dead)* [Ruby Jackson, vocal]; Pearl Traylor With Chuck Thomas & His All Stars, *Three Ball Sam (The Pawn Shop Man)*; Little Brother Brown, *Brother's Blues*

DISC TWO: Jumpin' Joe Williams With Red Saunders & His Orchestra, *Hey Bartender Give That Man A Drink*; Little Brother Brown, *Goof Boogie*; Chuck Willis, *I Rule My House*; Pinnochio James, *Pinnochio's Blues*; Larry Darnell With Leroy Kirkland's Orchestra, *I'll Be Sittin', I'll Be Rockin'*; Annie Laurie, *It's Been A Long Time*; Hadda Brooks, *Jump Back Honey*; Titus Turner, *Got So Much Trouble*; The Royals, *Gas Happy Mama*; Chuck Willis With The Royals, *My Story*; Big Maybelle With Leroy Kirkland's Orchestra, *Gabbin' Blues*; The Treniers, *The Moondog*; Annie Laurie, *Stop Talkin' And Start Walkin'*; Red Rodney Sextet, *Dig This Menu Please!* [Morty Perry, vocal]; Paul Gayten Orchestra, *It Ain't Nothing Happening*; Chuck Willis, *You Broke My Heart*; The Treniers, *Poontang*; Hadda Brooks, *Brooks' Boogie*; Big Maybelle With Leroy Kirkland's Orchestra, *Jinny Mule*; Titus Turner, *Livin' In Misery*; Jumpin' Joe Williams With Red Saunders & His Orchestra, *Voodoo Blues*; The Bill Davis Trio, *Bring The Money In*; Sammy Cotton With

Leroy Kirkland's Orchestra, *You The Kind Of Women*; Annie Laurie, *I'm In The Mood For You*; Chuck Willis, *Make Up Your Mind*; Paul Gayten Orchestra, *Cow Cow Blues*

DISC THREE: Cliff "King" Solomon, *But Officer!*; Sammy Cotton With Leroy Kirkland's Orchestra, *Give Me One More Drink*; Annie Laurie, *Leave It To Me*; Cliff "King" Solomon, *Square Dance Boogie* [Ernestine Anderson, vocal]; Big John & The Buzzards, *Your Cash Ain't Nothin' But Trash*; Big Maybelle With Leroy Kirkland's Orchestra, *One Monkey Don't Stop No Show*; Titus Turner, *My Lonely Room*; The Treniers, *Uh Oh (Get Out Of The Car)*; Paul Gayten Orchestra *Creole Alley* [Lee Allen, saxophone]; Larry Darnell, *Give Me Your Love*; The Shufflers, *Bad, Bad Women*; Big Maybelle, *I'm Gettin' 'Long All Right*; Big John & The Buzzards, *Oop Shoop*; The Shufflers, *Jump Ted!*; Big Maybelle, *Ocean Of Tears*; Chuck Willis, *Ring Ding Doo*; Screamin' Jay Hawkins With Leroy Kirkland's Orchestra, *Little Demon/I Put A Spell On You*; Andre Williams [Mr Rhythm], *Bacon Fat*; Hurricane Harry, *The Last Meal*; Little Joe & The Thrillers, *Let's Do The Slop*; Lloyd Fatman, *Where You Been?/Miss Mushmouth*; The Marquees, *Wyatt Earp* [Marvin Gaye with Bo Diddley, guitar]; Billy Stewart *Billy's Heartache* [Bo Diddley, guitar]; Screamin' Jay Hawkins With Leroy Kirkland's Orchestra, *Yellow Coat*

Basic Records

(i) Forget Your Troubles and Jump Your Blues Away

291 **Jumping On The West Coast**
Buddy Tate & Friends
Black Lion BLCD 760175 (UK)
Buddy Tate Orchestra, *Tate's A Jumpin'* (take A4)/*Blue and Sentimental*/*Vine Street Breakdown* (take A4)/*Ballin' From Day To Day* [C.Q. Price, vocal]/*Six Foot Two Blues* [Jimmy Witherspoon, vocal]/*Kansas City Local* (take A3)/ *Kansas City Local* (take A5)/*The Things You Done For Me Baby* [C.Q. Price, vocal]/*Vine Street Breakdown* (take A1)/*Early Morning Blues* [Jimmy Witherspoon, vocal]/*Good Morning Judge* [C.Q. Price, vocal]/*Tate's A Jumpin'* (take A2); Earl Jackson's Band, *Kansas City Jump* (take 2); Pete Peterson Band, *Rock Bottom*/*Long Gravy*; Jay McShann Quartet, *McShann Stomp*; Jimmy Witherspoon, *Wanderin' Gal Blues*; Earl Jackson Orchestra, *Kansas City Jump* (take 1)
Among the most fertile seedbeds for early R&B and jump blues musicians were the territory bands of the South-western and Mid-western states. Few were recorded until the mid-1940s when many diminished units received this chance. An exciting Count Basie combo led by Tate features the blues shouting of Price and Witherspoon.

292 **Be Bop Baby Blues**
Johnny Otis Band
Night Train International NTI CD 7003
Johnny Otis, His Drums & His Orchestra, *Alligator Meat* [Joe Swift, vocal]/ *Crazy 'Bout Your Cooking* [Joe Swift, vocal]/*That's Your Last Boogie* [Joe Swift, vocal]/*Be Bop Baby Blues* [Joe Swift, vocal]; Earl Jackson Orchestra,

Kansas City Jumps/Talking To Myself [Walter Roberts, vocal]/*A Woman Don't Want A Good Man No More* [Walter Roberts, vocal]/*Take Out The Squeal* [Luther Luper, vocal]; Clifford Blivens, *Fat Man Blues/Crying Blues*; Johnny Crawford Orchestra, *Texas Woman* [Larry Costello, vocal]; Johnny Otis, His Drums & His Orchestra, *Train Blues* [Joe Swift, vocal]/*Lovin' Baby Blues* [Joe Swift, vocal]/*Alligator Meat*
Johnny Otis's greatest R&B-era triumphs were to come with his Savoy contract, but these sides are taken from his first recordings on the West Coast while leading one of the last of the big territory bands. The compilation includes tracks by other Californian band leaders spotlighting their powerful blues shouters.

293 Two Timin' Baby
Jack McVea & His Door Openers
Jukebox Lil RBD 612 (Swe)
Scrub, Sweep and Mop [Cappie Oliver, vocal]/*New Worried Life Blues* [Rabon Tarrant, vocal]/*House Party Boogie/Listen Baby Blues* [Rabon Tarrant, vocal]/ *Silver Symphony/Frantic Boogie/Lonesome Blues* [Rabon Tarrant, vocal]/ *Richard Gets Hitched* [Rabon Tarrant, Jack McVea & Tommy Kahn, vocals]/ *Two Timin' Baby* [Rabon Tarrant, vocal]/*Bulgin' Eyes/Jam Boogie/Slowly Goin' Crazy Blues* [Rabon Tarrant, vocal]/*Groove Juice (I Need It Bad)* [Band, vocal]/*Blues With A Feeling* [Rabon Tarrant, vocal]/*Swing Man* [Sammy Yates, vocal]/*Fightin' Mama Blues* [Rabon Tarrant, vocal]
Already a veteran of the California jazz scene and a Lionel Hampton alumnus, saxophonist Jack McVea formed his own jump band in 1944 and had an international hit three years later with *Open The Door, Richard.* The follow-up *Richard Gets Hitched* and some wonderful blues by the band's drummer Rabon Tarrant are featured.

294 Bad Man Jackson, That's Me
Bullmoose Jackson
Charly CD Charly 274 (UK)
Big Ten Inch Record (take 7)/*Bad Man Jackson, That's Me/Jammin' And Jumpin'/We Ain't Got Nothin' (But The Blues)/Bullmoose Jackson Blues/The Honeydripper/Hold Him Joe/I Want A Bowlegged Woman/Oh John/Fare Thee Well, Deacon Jones, Fare Thee Well/Nosey Joe/Bearcat Blues/Why Don't You Haul Off And Love Me/Cherokee Boogie/Meet Me With Your Black Dress On/ Hodge Podge/Big Fat Mamas Are Back In Style Again/(Let Me Love You) All Night Long/Bootsie/If You Ain't Lovin' (You Ain't Livin')/I Wanna Hug Ya, Kiss Ya, Squeeze Ya/Big Ten Inch Record* (take 9)
Benjamin Jackson was a saxophonist in the Lucky Millinder Orchestra until he stood in for Wynonie Harris, and his rise in popularity as a singer was meteoric. His success was due mainly to his bass-baritone crooning, but he also cut some of the most salacious songs in the history of R&B.

295 Be-Baba-Leba
Helen Humes
"Whiskey, Women, and . . ." Record Company RBD 701 (Swe)
Be-Baba-Leba/Fortune Tellin' Man/Every Now And Then/Central Avenue Boogie/He Don't Love Me Anymore/Voo-It/Pleasing Man Blues/It's Better To

Give Than To Receive/They Raided The Joint/Airplane Blues/I Hear A Rhapsody/Loud Talkin' Woman/You Played On My Piano/Helen's Advice/All Night Long/If I Could Be With You One Hour Tonight
Humes made her recording début aged 14 in 1927 (**252**) and later replaced Billie Holiday in Count Basie's Orchestra; she then went solo and revitalized her career with *Be-Baba-Leba* in 1945. Her music is traced from 1944 to 1952 and includes some of the best West Coast R&B by one of the finest female singers.

296 Ugly Papa
Julia Lee & Her Boyfriends
Jukebox Lil RBD 603 (Swe)
Do You Want It?/Dream Lucky Blues/Lotus Blossom/Ugly Papa/Julia's Blues/If You Hadn't Gone Away (I Wouldn't Be Where I Am)/Bleeding Hearted Blues/Oh Chuck It (In A Bucket)/It Won't Be Long/Decent Woman Blues/Scream In The Night/I Know It's Wrong (The Diet Song)/Bop And Rock Lullaby/Goin' To Chicago/King Size Papa/Scat You Cats
Pianist and vocalist Julia Lee was another veteran whose career began in the 1920s; she was most famous in the mid- to late 1940s when she recorded for Capitol. She excelled in "blue" songs, and this compilation, while including a quota of ribaldry, presents her in her capacity as a blues and R&B singer.

297 Cecil Gant
Krazy Kat KK CD 03 (UK)
Cecil Boogie/Hit That Jive Jack/Hogan's Alley/I Gotta Gal/Boogie Blues/Little Baby You're Running Wild/Long Distance/Am I To Blame?/Rock The Boogie/Blues In L.A./Cecil Boogie No. 2/*What's On Your Worried Mind/Stuff You Gotta Watch/Syncopated Boogie/Time Will Tell/Cecil's Mop Mop/Train Time Blues/Ninth Street Jive/Playing Myself The Blues/Sloppy Joe's*
Gant is best known for his seminal hit *I Wonder* (1944) and other melancholic ballads. This CD selects the best of his slow West Coast blues, a few jive novelties, and his idiosyncratic piano boogie instrumentals which show why he was such an influential figure among his peers.

298 Road House Boogie
Big Jay McNeely
Saxophonograph RBD 505 (Swe)
Blow Big Jay/Road House Boogie [Ted Shirley, vocal]/*Willie The Cool Cat/Midnight Dreams* [Clifford Blivens, vocal]/*Hoppin' With Hunter/K & H Boogie/Gingercake/Boogie In Front/Junie Flip* [Clifford Blivens, vocal]/*Jaysfrantic/Real Crazy Cool/Tondalayo/Deac's Blowout/Let's Split/Just Crazy/Penthouse Serenade*
A controversial R&B saxophonist, McNeely proved early that he was a consummate musician who could play his tenor sax literally standing on his head, as well as numerous other acrobatics while honking and squawking. The bluesier side of the showman is presented along with accompaniments to some obscure West Coast shouters.

299 Breaking Up The House
Tiny Bradshaw
Charly CD Charly 43 (UK)
Breaking Up The House/Walk That Mess/Train Kept A-Rollin'/T99/Bradshaw

Boogie/Walkin' The Chalk Line/Mailman's Sack/Snaggle Tooth Ruth/Rippin' And Running' [Tiny Kennedy, vocal]/*The Blues Came Pouring Down/Two Dry Bones On The Pantry Shelf/Brad's Blues/Boodie Green/Well Oh Well/Newspaper Boy Blues* [Tiny Kennedy, vocal]/*One, Two, Three, Kick Blues* [duet with Dorena Dean]

An orchestra leader of the Cab Calloway school for 15 years, Bradshaw started a second career as a blues shouter on King Records in 1949. This disc includes powerful jump tunes as well as several fine blues performances, spotlighting exceptional musicians like guitarist Willie Gaddy.

300 Tiny Grimes And His Rocking Highlanders

Krazy Kat KK CD 01 (UK)

Call Of The Wild (take 1)/*Call Of The Wild* (take 2)/*St Louis Blues* (take 1)/*St Louis Blues* (take 2)/*Tiny's Jump/Howlin' Blues/Marie/1626 Boogie/Rockin' & Sockin'/Frankie And Johnny Boogie* (take 1)/*Frankie And Johnnie Boogie* (take 2)/*Am I Blue?/Hawaiian Boogie/Pert Skirt/Ho Ho Ho* [Band, vocal]/*Drinking Beer* [J.B. Summers, vocal]/*Hey Mr J.B.* [J.B. Summers, vocal]/*Battle Of The Mass/I'm In Love With You Baby* [George Grant as Haji Baba, vocal]/*My Baby's Cool* [Claudine Clark, vocal]

An adept guitarist in the Charlie Christian style, Grimes became a popular R&B band leader in the late 1940s; his tartan-clad Rocking Highlanders included young Red Prysock and Benny Golson on tenors. This CD shows off the band's ingrained jazz musicianship mixed with the vigor and urgency of R&B.

301 Jumpin' The Blues

Various Artists

Ace CDCHD 941 (UK)

Stomp Gordon, *Damp Rag*; Margie Day With Paul Williams Band, *Take Out Your False Teeth Daddy*; Willie Brown, *Cadillac Boogie*; Harold Burrage With Horace Henderson Band, *Hi-Yo Silver*; Cecil Payne, *Block Buster Boogie*; Stomp Gordon, *Fat Mama Blues*; Doles Dickens Quintet, *We're Gonna Rock This Morning* [Joe Gregory, vocal]; Tiny Davis & Her Orchestra, *How About That Jive?*; James Von Streeter & His Wig Poppers, *Chit'lins*; Zilla Mays & The Blues Caravan, *Nightshift Blues*; Big Bob Dougherty & His Orchestra, *Big Bob's Boogie*; Tiny Davis & Her Orchestra, *Race Horse*; Waymon Brown, *The Six Hundred Block*; Joey Thomas, *Hobo Boogie*; Cecil Gant, *Rock Little Baby*; Johnnie Brown, *I'm Gonna Stop (Foolin' Around)*; Goree Carter, *I'm Your Boogie Man/I've Got News For You*; Willie Brown, *Easter Bunny Boogie*; John Godfrey Trio, *Yes Ya Do*; Connie Jordan, *I'm Gonna Rock (Till My Rocker Breaks Down)*; Eunice Davis, *Work Daddy Work*

American Decca with the help of contracted bands like those of Count Basie, Louis Jordan, Hot Lips Page, Jay McShann, Lucky Millinder, Lionel Hampton, and Buddy Johnson, ushered in the R&B era. These lesser-known artists recorded for Decca and its subsidiaries Coral and Brunswick during 1949–54.

(ii) I Woke Up Hollerin' and Screamin'

302 **West Coast Jive**
Various Artists
Delmark DD 657
Cee Pee Johnson & His Band, *The "G" Man Got The "T" Man*; Duke Henderson With Lucky Thompson's All Stars, *H.D. Blues*; Al "Stomp" Russell Trio, *Let's Go Down The Road*; Wynonie "Mr Blues" Harris With Jack McVea & His All Stars, *Somebody Done Changed The Lock On My Door*; Cee Pee Johnson & His Band, *Without You*; Frank Haywood With Monroe Tucker & His All Stars, *You Gotta Give It Up*; Wynonie "Mr Blues" Harris With Johnnie Alston & His All Stars, *Playful Baby*; Cee Pee Johnson & His Band, *When You're Alone*; Duke Henderson With Shifty Henry's All Stars, *Get Your Kicks*; Al "Stomp" Russell Trio, *Let's Get Together*; Wynonie "Mr Blues" Harris With Illinois Jacquet & His All Stars, *Wynonie's Blues*; Cee Pee Johnson & His Band, *I'm So Lonesome*; Al "Stomp" Russell Trio, *Give Me My Money Back*; Duke Henderson With Lucky Thompson's All Stars, *Not Worth A Dime*; Cee Pee Johnson & His Band, *Hour After Hour*; Frank Haywood With Monroe Tucker & His All Stars, *Now Or Never*; Duke Henderson With Shifty Henry's All Stars, *Don't Slam The Door*; Cee Pee Johnson & His Band, *Miss Jiveola Brown*
Los Angeles in the mid-1940s was a hot and hip place where many forms of proto-R&B competed for popularity: the novelty jazz and jump of Cee Pee Johnson, the cool rhythm trio style of Stomp Russell and Frank Haywood, and the horny jump-blues of Duke Henderson and the awesome Wynonie Harris.

303 **Blowin' In From Kansas City**
Jimmy Witherspoon
Flair/Virgin V2-86299-2/Ace CDCHD 279 (UK)
Jimmy Witherspoon, *Love My Baby/There Ain't Nothing Better* [duet with "His Girl Friday" (Mickey Champion)]/*Love and Friendship*; Jimmy Witherspoon With Al Wichard's Sextette, *T.B. Blues*; Jimmy Witherspoon, *Goin' Around In Circles* (alternate take); Jimmy Witherspoon With Hootie McShann's Sextette, *Geneva Blues [Evil Woman]* (alternate take); Jimmy Witherspoon, *I'm Just A Country Boy*; Jimmy Witherspoon With Buddy Floyd's Orchestra, *Good Jumping [Jump Children]* (alternate take); Jimmy Witherspoon, *Slow Your Speed/Blowing The Blues/It's Raining Outside/I'm Just A Lady's Man/I'm Just Wandering* Part 1/*I'm Just Wandering* Part 2/*Who's Been Jivin' You* (alternate take); Jimmy Witherspoon With Hootie McShann's Sextette, *Sweet Lovin' Baby/Thelma Lee Blues*; Jimmy Witherspoon, *The Doctor Knows His Business [Doctor Blues]* (alternate take)/*Rain, Rain, Rain* (alternate take)/*Baby, Baby*
Like Walter Brown, whom he replaced, Witherspoon came to fame with Jay McShann's exciting territory orchestra in the mid-1940s. The earliest of these tracks feature Witherspoon accompanied by McShann and various all-star units. They are taken from the singer's prime years with Modern records in the late 1940s and early 1950s.

304 **Shouting The Blues**
Various Artists
Specialty SPCD 7028-2/Ace CDCHD 439 (UK)
Joe Turner, *Adam Bit The Apple/Still In The Dark/Feelin' Happy/Midnight Is*

Here Again [Dawn Is Breakin' Through]/I Want My Baby [When The Rooster Crows]/Life Is A Card Game/After A While You'll Be Sorry/Just A Travelin' Man; Big Maceo, *Big City Blues/Do You Remember/Just Tell Me Baby/One Sunday Morning*; Don Johnson Orchestra, *State Street Boogie* [Smilin' Smokey Lynn, vocal]/*Jackson's Blues* [Smilin' Smokey Lynn, vocal]/*Chesterfield Baby* [Smilin' Smokey Lynn, vocal]; Smilin' Smokey Lynn, *Lonesome Lover Blues*; Johnny Crawford & His Orchestra, *Run, Mister Rabbit, Run* [Larry Costello, vocal]; Smilin' Smokey Lynn, *Feel Like Ballin' Tonight/Rock-A-Bye Baby/ Hometown Baby (Hip Cat)*; H-Bomb Ferguson, *She's Been Gone/You Made Me Baby*

West Coast independent Specialty is best known for the wild rock 'n' roll of Little Richard, Larry Williams, and Lloyd Price, although it started recording a full ten years before their era. This CD recalls the day of the blues shouter, including Big Joe Turner's Houston sides from 1949–50.

305 Better Beware

Little Esther

Charly CD Charly 248 (UK)

Little Esther With Earl Warren & His Orchestra, *Looking For A Man*; Little Esther With The Dominoes, *Other Lips, Other Arms/The Deacon Moves In*; Little Esther With Earl Warren & His Orchestra, *I'm A Bad, Bad Girl* [duet with Mel Walker]/*Crying And Singing The Blues/Ring-A-Ding Doo* [duet with Mel Walker]; Little Esther, *Hold Me/Better Beware/Aged And Mellow Blues/ Ramblin' Blues/The Storm/Hollerin' And Screamin'*; Little Esther With The Robins, *Saturday Night Daddy* [duet with Bobby Nunn]/*Mainliner/You Took My Love Too Fast* [duet with Bobby Nunn]; Little Esther With Little Willie Littlefield & His Orchestra, *Last Laugh Blues* [duet with Little Willie Littlefield]/*Flesh, Blood And Bones/Turn The Lamps Down Low* [duet with Little Willie Littlefield]; Little Esther, *Cherry Wine/Hound Dog*

Esther was star vocalist with the Johnny Otis Orchestra, featured here under a pseudonym for contractual purposes. These Federal recordings from 1951–3 are as good as her contemporary sides with Otis for Savoy and feature musicians of the caliber of Ben Webster and Pete Guitar Lewis (**460**).

306 Early R&B Volume One—Chicago Jump Bands

Various Artists

RST Records RST 91577-2 (Au)

Charles Gray & His Rhumboogie Five, *I'm A Bum Again/Crazy Woman Blues*; Robert Caffery, *Ida Bee* [Little Bluitt, vocal]/*Blodie's Blues* [Little Bluitt, vocal]; Memphis Seven, *Farmer's Daughter Blues* [Cozy Eggleston, vocal]/*Grunt Meat Blues* [Cozy Eggleston, vocal]; Chicago Allstars, *No No Baby* [Eddie "Sugarman" Penigar, vocal]/*I Love You Mama* [Eddie "Sugarman" Penigar, vocal]/*Hey Hey Big Mama* [Johnny Morton, vocal]/*Green Light* [Johnny Morton, vocal]/*Strange Strange Lover* [Clarence "Pro" McClam, vocal]/*Are You Getting Married, Brother?* [Cozy Eggleston, vocal]; Bill Crosby & His Band, *That's My Gal/Come For A Ride/Those Dog-Gone Blues* [Eddie "Sugarman" Penigar, vocal]/*Eat, Drink And Be Merry/Hip Chick Blues/Sneaking Woman Blues*; Big Bertha Henderson With Al Smith's Band, *Rock, Bertha, Rock/Tears In My Eyes*; Mitzi Mars With Sax Mallard's Orchestra, *I'm Glad/Roll 'Em*

Before Muddy Waters led the Chess brothers to experiment with heavily amplified down-home blues, conceiving what is now called Chicago Blues, the city was a hive of fine jump blues. This is reflected in the recordings of artists such as Roosevelt Sykes, Sonny Thompson, and the performers on this important CD.

307 **The Seventh Son**
Willie Mabon
Charly 44, CD BM 44 (UK)
I Don't Know/I'm Mad/Got To Have It/Beggar Or Bandit/You're A Fool/Monday Woman/I'm Tired/Lonely Blues/Willie's Blues/Poison Ivy/He Lied/Someday You Gotta Pay/The Seventh Son/Knock On Wood/Why Did It Happen To Me/I'm Mad At You
A fine, witty songwriter as well as a talented singer-pianist, Mabon hit big in 1952 with his first Chess single, a version of Cripple Clarance Lofton's *I Don't Know*. His lyrics often display knowledge of urban violence that belies the sophisticated image of early publicity photos, and his music is similarly urbane.

308 **Trailblazer**
Ike Turner's Kings Of Rhythm
Charly CD Charly 263 (UK)
Ike Turner's Kings Of Rhythm, *The Big Question* [Clayton Love, vocal]; Billy Gayles With Ike Turner's Kings Of Rhythm, *Just One More Time*; Jackie Brenston With Ike Turner's Kings Of Rhythm, *The Mistreater*; Billy Gayles With Ike Turner's Kings Of Rhythm, *No Coming Back*; The Gardenias With Ike Turner's Kings Of Rhythm, *You Found The Time*; Ike Turner's Kings Of Rhythm, *She Made My Blood Run Cold* [Clayton Love, vocal]; Billy Gayles With Ike Turner's Kings Of Rhythm, *I'm Tore Up*; Ike Turner's Kings Of Rhythm, *Trail Blazer/You've Changed My Love* (take 5) [Clayton Love, vocal]; Billy Gayles With Ike Turner's Kings Of Rhythm, *Let's Call It A Day*; Jackie Brenston With Ike Turner's Kings Of Rhythm, *Much Later*; The Gardenias With Ike Turner's Kings Of Rhythm, *Miserable*; Ike Turner's Kings Of Rhythm, *Do You Mean It?* [Clayton Love, vocal]; Jackie Brenston With Ike Turner's Kings Of Rhythm, *Gonna Wait For My Chance*; Billy Gayles With Ike Turner's Kings Of Rhythm, *If I Never Had Known You*; Ike Turner's Kings Of Rhythm, *Rock-A-Bucket*; Billy Gayles With Ike Turner's Kings Of Rhythm, *Sad As A Man Can Be*; Jackie Brenston With Ike Turner's Kings Of Rhythm, *What Can It Be?*; Billy Gayles With Ike Turner's Kings Of Rhythm, *Do Right Baby*; Ike Turner's Kings Of Rhythm, *You've Changed My Love* (take 1) [Clayton Love, vocal]; The Gardenias With Ike Turner's Kings Of Rhythm, *My Baby's Tops*; Billy Gayles With Ike Turner's Kings Of Rhythm, *Take Your Fine Frame Home*
Long before Tina Turner brought him fame and fortune, Ike was a successful musician, talent scout, and band leader. His Federal recordings from 1956–7, overlaid with Ike's wild guitar, focuses on the band's fine singers: the prodigal Jackie Brenston, the soulful Clayton Love, and the charismatic Billy Gayles

309 **The Formative Years 1951–1953**
Little Richard
Bear Family BCD 15448 AH (Ger)
Little Richard, *Get Rich Quick* (take 1)/*Get Rich Quick* (take 2)/*Why Did You Leave Me?/Taxi Blues/Every Hour/I Brought It All On Myself* (take 1)/*I Brought It All On Myself* (take 2)/*Ain't Nothing Happenin'/Thinkin' About My Mother*

(take 1)/*Thinkin' About My Mother* (take 2)/*Please Have Mercy On Me* (take 1)/*Please Have Mercy On Me* (take 2); Little Richard With The Johnny Otis Orchestra, *Little Richard Boogie*/*Directly From My Heart* (take 1)/*Directly From My Heart* (take 2)/*I Love My Baby* (take 1)/*I Love My Baby* (take 2)/*Maybe I'm Right*; Tempo Toppers With The Deuces Of Rhythm, *Ain't That Good News* [Little Richard, vocal]/*Fool At The Wheel* [Little Richard, vocal] Tempo Toppers With Little Richard, *Rice, Red Beans And Turnip Greens*/*Always*
Before recording rock 'n' roll classics on Specialty in the mid-1950s, the androgynous Little Richard Penniman had closely studied Atlanta blues shouter Billy Wright and practiced his early R&B style on the mighty RCA Victor and, aptly, the independent Texas company Peacock Records

310 **Roots Of A Revolution**
James Brown
Polydor 817 304-2 (UK)
James Brown & The Famous Flames, *I Feel That Old Feeling Coming On*/*No, No, No*/*Hold My Baby's Hand*/*Chonnie-On-Chon*/*Just Won't Do Right*/*Let's Make It*/*Fine Old Foxy Self*/*Why Does Everything Happen To Me? [Strange Things Happen]*/*Begging, Begging*/*That Dood It*/*There Must Be A Reason*/*I Want You So Bad*/*Don't Let It Happen To Me*/*Bewildered*; James Davis, *Doodle Bug*; James Brown, *This Old Heart*/*I'll Never, Never Let You Go*/*You've Got The Power* [duet with Bea Ford]/*Baby, You're Right*/*I Don't Mind*/*Come Over Here*/*And I Do Just What I Want*/*Just You And Me, Darling*/*So Long*/*Tell Me What You're Gonna Do*; James Brown Presents His Band, *Hold It*; James Brown, *Dancin' Little Thing*/*You Don't Have To Go*/*Lost Someone*/*Shout And Shimmy*; Yvonne Fair & James Brown Band, *I Found You*; James Brown, *I Don't Care*/*I've Got Money*/*Mashed Potatoes U.S.A.*/*Signed, Sealed And Delivered*/*Prisoner Of Love*; Tammy Montgomery & James Brown Band, *I Cried*; James Brown & The Famous Flames, *Oh Baby Don't You Weep* Part 1/*Oh Baby Don't You Weep* Part 2/*(Do The) Mashed Potatoes*/*Maybe The Last Time*
"Soul Brother Number One," Brown stood in awe of Louis Jordan, Ray Charles, and Billy Wright and adopted elements of their styles. Between 1956 and 1964 he took the R&B of his predecessors and slowly molded it into the new form called soul music.

311 **Blues Guitar Hero—The Influential Early Sessions**
Freddy King
Ace CDCHD 454 (UK)
Hideaway/*Lonesome Whistle Blues*/*San-Ho-Zay*/*I'm Tore Down*/*See See Baby*/*Christmas Tears*/*You've Got To Love Her With A Feeling*/*Have You Ever Loved A Woman*/*You Know That You Love Me (But You Never Tell Me So)*/*I Love The Woman*/*It's Too Bad (Things Are Going So Tough)*/*Sen-Sa-Shun*/*If You Believe (In What You Do)*/*Takin' Care Of Business*/*The Stumble*/*Sittin' On The Boat Dock*/*Side Tracked*/*What About Love*/*Come On*/*Just Pickin'*/*I'm On My Way To Atlanta*/*In The Open*/*The Welfare (Turns Its Back On You)*/*She Put The Whammy On Me*
Borrowing stylistically from his namesake B.B. King, Texan guitarist and vocalist Freddy King enjoyed huge success on Federal. This selection draws on his best and most influential sides from these early sessions of 1960–62. They were produced and arranged by pianist Sonny Thompson, whose band accompanies.

(iii) A Blues & Rhythm Melting-Pot

312 **Ride, Daddy Ride! And Other Songs Of Love**

Various Artists

Charly CD Charly 272 (UK)

Fats Noel, *Ride, Daddy, Ride*; The Four Jacks, *Sure Cure For The Blues*; Bullmoose Jackson With Tiny Bradshaw's Orchestra, *Big Ten Inch Record*; The Drivers, *Smooth, Slow And Easy*; Dorothy Ellis, *Drill, Daddy, Drill*; The Swallows, *Roll, Roll, Pretty Baby*; Fluffy Hunter, With Jesse Powell's Orchestra, *The Walkin' Blues (Walk Right In, Walk Right Out)*; Todd Rhodes & His Orchestra, *Rocket 69* [Connie Allen, vocal]; The Sharps & Flats, *I Knew He Would*; Lil Greenwood & The Four Jacks, *Granpa Can Boogie Too*; Bullmoose Jackson & His Buffalo Bearcats, *I Want A Bowlegged Woman*; Wynonie Harris & His All Stars, *I Want My Fanny Brown*; Fluffy Hunter With Jesse Powell's Orchestra, *My Natch'l Man*; Pete Guitar Lewis, *Chocolate Pork Chop Man*; The Swallows, *It Ain't The Meat*; The Lamplighters, *Ride, Jockey, Ride*; Eddie Davis & His Band, *Mountain Oysters*; Wynonie Harris & His All Stars, *Triflin' Woman*; Dave Bartholomew & His Orchestra, *My Ding-A-Ling*; The Four Jacks, *The Last Of The Good Rocking Men*; Todd Rhodes & His Orchestra, *Your Daddy's Doggin' Around* [Connie Allen, vocal]

If nothing else, R&B should be remembered for being one of the last popular "adult" musics of the 20th century, dealing amusingly with sex, violence, and alcohol. The disc features songs of a decidedly *single entendre*, that entertain to the accompaniment of orgasmic saxes, rampant guitars, and climactic rhythms.

313 **Blues Jubilee**

Various Artists

Vogue 600171 (Fr)

Dinah Washington, *Cool Kind Papa/It Isn't Fair/Baby, Get Lost/I Wanna Be Loved/Fast Movin' Mama*; Jimmy Witherspoon, *Ain't Nobody's Business/No Rollin' Blues/Big Fine Girl/Falling [sic—Failing] By Degrees/New Orleans Woman/I Gotta Gal [Roll 'Em, Pete]*; Helen Humes With Roy Milton's Band, *Million Dollar Secret/E Baba Le Ba/I'm Gonna Let Him Ride [He May Be Your Man]/If I Could Be With You*; Big Joe Turner, *Flip, Flop And Fly/3 O'Clock In The Morning [Chains Of Love]/Up, Up And Away [The Chicken And The Hawk]/Blues [Honey Hush]*

During the late 1940s and early 1950s, Californian DJs Frank Bull and Gene Norman produced popular "Just Jazz" and "Blues Jubilee" concerts. This collection has highlights from some of R&B's biggest stars recorded at these dates, a rare opportunity for fans of R&B—and blues in general—to hear vintage concert and live radio broadcast material.

314 **Let's Have A Ball Tonight—The Pioneers Of Rhythm And Blues**

Various Artists

Natasha NI-4025

AMERICAN FORCES RADIO BROADCASTS: Louis Jordan & His Tympany Five, *Five Guys Named Moe/I'm Gonna Move To The Outskirts Of Town/Infantry Blues/Knock Me A Kiss*; The Duke Of Iron, *Marry A Woman Uglier Than*

You; Meade Lux Lewis, *Honky Tonk Train Blues*; Ernie Morris, *In The Mood*; Sister Rosetta Tharpe, *This Train*; APOLLO THEATRE RADIO BROADCASTS: Joe Liggins & His Honeydrippers, *Pink Champagne*; Johnny Otis & His Orchestra, *Harlem Nocturne*; Amos Milburn, *I'm Just A Fool In Love*; Eddie "Cleanhead" Vinson, *Charmaine*; Sister Rosetta Tharpe, *Didn't It Rain, Children*; Bullmoose Jackson, *Time Alone Will Tell*; Ensemble, *Let's Ball Tonight*; BIRDLAND RADIO BROADCASTS: Big Jay McNeely, *The Goof/Serenade In Blue/Deacon's Parade/ Boogie In The Front/Body And Soul/Deacon's Hop*
This disc provides probably the only example we are likely to get of a full broadcast of a concert from the prime years of R&B. Most of the tracks are preceded by a radio announcement and some humorous jive talking between the MC and the artists. If only they had been filmed . . .

315 **Atlantic Rhythm And Blues, Volume 1 (1947–1952)**
Various Artists
Atlantic 781 293-2
Joe Morris Orchestra, *Lowe Groovin'*; Tiny Grimes Quintet, *That Old Black Magic/Annie Laurie/Midnight Special*; Joe Morris Orchestra, *The Applejack*; Frank Floorshow Culley, *Cole Slaw*; Stick McGhee & His Buddies, *Drinkin' Wine Spo-Dee-O-Dee*; Ruth Brown With Eddie Condon's TV Orchestra, *So Long*; Ruth Brown With Budd Johnson's Orchestra, *I'll Get Along Somehow*; Roland Byrd [Professor Longhair], *Hey Little Girl*; Professor Longhair & His New Orleans Boys, *Mardi Gras In New Orleans*; Harry Van Walls With The After Hours Session Boys, *Tee Nah Nah* [Brownie McGhee as Spider Sam, vocal]; Al Hibbler With Billy Kyle's Orchestra, *Danny Boy*; Joe Morris Orchestra, *Anytime, Anyplace, Anywhere [Laurie Tate, vocal]; Ruth Brown, Teardrops From My Eyes*; Stick McGhee, *One Monkey Don't Stop No Show*; The Clovers, *Don't You Know I Love You*; The Cardinals With Jesse Stone's Orchestra, *Shouldn't I Know*; Big Joe Turner, *The Chill Is On/Chains Of Love*; The Clovers, *Fool, Fool, Fool/One Mint Julep*; The Cardinals, *Wheel Of Fortune*; Big Joe Turner, *Sweet Sixteen*; Ruth Brown, *5-10-15 Hours*; Willis Gatortail Jackson, *Gator's Groove*
This disc shows the earliest successes of the fledgling label: Morris, Grimes, and Culley were local band leaders with recording careers but it was the acquisition of the huge hit *Drinkin' Wine Spo-Dee-O-Dee* that enabled major signings like Brown, Turner, and Hibbler, as well as vocal groups such as The Clovers and The Cardinanls.

316 **Atlantic Rhythm And Blues, Volume 2 (1952–1954)**
Various Artists
Atlantic 781 294-2
The Clovers, *Ting-A-Ling*; Ruth Brown & The James Quintet, *Daddy Daddy*; Ray Charles; *The Midnight Hour*; The Diamonds, *A Beggar For Your Kisses*; Ruth Brown, *Mama, He Treats Your Daughter Mean*; The Clovers, *Good Lovin'*; Ruth Brown, *Wild Wild Young Men*; Ray Charles, *Mess Around*; Big Joe Turner With Pluma Davis' Orchestra, *Honey Hush*; LaVern Baker, *Soul On Fire*; Clyde McPhatter & The Drifters, *Money Honey*; The Clovers, *Lovey Dovey*; Clyde McPhatter & The Drifters, *Such A Night*; Professor Longhair & His Blues Scholars, *Tipitina*; Clyde McPhatter & The Drifters, *White Christmas/Honey Love/Whatcha Gonna Do?*; Big Joe Turner, *Shake Rattle & Roll*; The Chords, *Sh-Boom*; Ruth Brown & Her Rhythm Makers, *Oh What a*

Dream; Tommy Ridgley & His Band, *Jam Up*; Al Hibbler, *After The Lights Go Down Low*; LaVern Baker & The Gliders, *Tomorrow Night/Tweedlee Dee*; Ray Charles & His Orchestra, *I Got A Woman/Greenbacks*
This volume delivers the classic recordings of 1950s New York City R&B: Big Joe Turner, Ray Charles, Ruth Brown, and LaVern Baker shouting the blues with the best of Atlantic's vocal groups contributing doo-wop hot and cool. Professor Longhair and Tommy Ridgely's recordings are the worthy results of the label's continuing forays into New Orleans R&B.

317 **Best Of Gotham R&B**
Various Artists
Krazy Kat KK CD 04 (UK)
Ernie Fields Orchestra, *Butch's Blues*; Roy Milton's Solid Senders, *Milton's Boogie*; The Jones Boys, *I Ain't Mad At You*; Jesse Price & His Jump Jivers, *Creepin' And Peepin' [Tippin' In]*; Jimmy Rushing, *Fool's Blues*; Lil Armstrong & Her Chicago Boys, *Rock It*; Johnny Sparrow & His Bows & Arrows, *Sparrow In The Barrel*; The Cats & The Fiddle, *Movin' Out Today*; Tiny Grimes & His Rocking Highlanders, *Why Did You Waste My Time?* [Screamin' Jay Hawkins as Jalacy Hawkins, vocal]; J.B. Summers With Tiny Grimes & His Rocking Highlanders, *Hey Now*; Bill Jennings, *Alexandria, Va*; Harry Crafton With Doc Bagby's Orchestra, *It's Been A Long Time*; Jimmy Preston & His Prestonians, *Rock The Joint*; Leo Parker & His Mad Lads, *Woody*; The Three Peppers, *Three Little Words*; Frank Motley & His Orchestra, *Bow Wow Wow* [T.N.T. Tribble, vocal]; Panama Francis All Stars, *Jitterbug Jump*; T.N.T. Tribble & His Band, *She Walk Right In* [Whiskey Sheffield, vocal]; The Rhythm Rockers, *Love Muscle Boogie*; Mike Pedicin Quartet, *Disc Jockey's Boogie*
Whereas Southern independent labels largely nurtured local talent, the more affluent Northern ones experimented with purchased masters and their output was often more varied. Gotham mixed big bands, jive vocal groups, and blues shouters with saxophonists, guitarists, drummers, and pianists from Oklahoma, California, Washington DC, and New York City as well as its Philadelphia locale.

318 **Come On Let's Boogie—Freedom Records: Texas Blues Anthology**
Various Artists
P-Vine PCD 2482/3 (Jap)—*2 CD set*
DISC ONE: Goree Carter, *Sweet Old Woman's Blues*; Goree Carter & His Hepcats, *Back Home Blues/Rock Awhile/I'll Send You/How Can You Love Me?/My Love Is Coming Down/Hoy Hoy/I Just Thought Of You*; Goree Carter, His Guitar & Rocking Rhythm Orchestra, *She's Just Old Fashioned/Working With My Baby/Is It True?/What A Friend Will Do/She's My Best Bet*; Goree Carter, *Serenade/Come On Let's Boogie/Lonely World*; Texas Alexander With Benton's Busy Bees, *Crossroads/Bottom's Blues*; Carl Campbell & Orchestra, *Gettin' High/Between Midnight And Dawn*

DISC TWO: Little Willie Littlefield, *Littlefield Boogie*; Jesse Thomas, *Let's Have Some Fun/Guess I'll Have To Walk Alone*; Joe Turner & His Orchestra, *Adam Bit The Apple/Life Is Like A Card Game*; L.C. Williams Orchestra, *I Don't Want Your Baby*; L.C. Williams With J.C. Conney's Combo, *Ethel Mae*; Lonnie Lyons' Combo, *Flychick Bounce/Faraway Blues*; Sammye Harris' Band,

Fatso [Leon Whitehead, vocal]; Connie McBooker, *Loretta*; Clarence Samuels & Orchestra, *She Walk, She Walk* Part 1/*She Walk, She Walk* Part 2; Leroy "Country" Johnson, *No One To Love Me/Log House On The Hill*; Joe Turner & His Orchestra, *Still in The Dark*; Joe Turner Combo, *Jumpin' At The Jubilee*; Clarence Samuels & Orchestra, *Low Top Inn/Lost My Head*; L.C. Williams Orchestra, *Won't You Please Come Back*; L.C. Williams With J.C. Conney's Combo, *Jelly Roll*

While any mention of Texas usually brings to mind downhome bluesmen such as "Country" Johnson, the state also has a long tradition of sophisticated jazz blues and R&B. A 2-CD set from the vaults of an independent Houston label bears witness to the quality of jump blues and R&B produced by such small concerns.

319 Regal Records In New Orleans

Various Artists

Specialty SPCD 2169-2/Ace CDCHD 362 (UK)

Paul Gayten Orchestra, *I'll Never Be Free* [duet with Annie Laurie]/*Yeah! Yeah! Yeah!/You Ought To Know/You Shouldn't/Confused/Bear Hug/Oooh La La/My Last Good-Bye/I Ain't Gonna Let You In* [duet with Annie Laurie]/*Kickapoo Juice/Each Time/Fishtails/Suzette/Happy Birthday To You/For You My Love/Back Trackin' [Dr. Daddy-o]/Gold Ain't Everything*; Annie Laurie With Paul Gayten's Band, *Baby, What's New/My Rough And Ready Man/I Ain't Gonna Let You In* [alternate take]; Annie Laurie With Dave Bartholomew's Orchestra, *Low Down Feeling/3 × 7 = 21/Don't Marry Too Soon*; Dave Bartholowmew & His Orchestra, *Messy Bessy/Nickel Wine*; Roy Brown With Paul Gayten's Band, *Riding High/Brand New Baby*

Before Fats Domino (**483/4**) and the "Gumbo" sound of classic New Orleans R&B, the Cresent City was dominated by Gayten, Brown, and Bartholomew (**481**) who played in the more familiar jump style. Had it not been for Northern labels like Regal, much of this earlier music would have gone unrecorded, including the very underrated Annie Laurie.

320 The Sun Blues Archives Volume Two: Bootin' Boogie

Various Artists

Charly/Sun CD Sun 30 (UK)

Rosco Gordon, *I Don't Like It/Don't Take It Out On Me/If You Want Your Woman/You Been Cheatin' On Me/Hey Hey Girl/Mean Woman/Real Pretty Mama/Shoobie Oobie* (alternate take)/*Sally Joe* (alternate take); Vincent "Guitar Red" Duling, *Go Ahead On* (alternate take)/*Baby Please Don't Go* (alternate take); Little Junior Parker & His Blue Flames, *Love My Baby* (alternate take)/*Sittin' At The Window/Feelin' Bad/Sittin' At The Bar/Love My Baby* (alternate take); Eddie Snow With Elven Parr's In The Groove Boys, *Don't Dog Me Around/Mean Mean Woman/Skin and Bone* (take -1)/*Skin And Bone* (take -2); Billy "The Kid" Emerson, *No Teasing Around* (alternate take)/*When My Baby Quit Me/I'm Not Going Home* (alternate take)/*Hey Little Girl*

Probably the most famous independent label in the history of US popular music, Sun Records of Memphis, Tennessee, is renowned for many of rock 'n' roll's original heroes. This disc introduces the raw and wild Southern jump music of the early 1950s which influenced Presley, Perkins, Lewis, and other rockabillies (**330**, **354**, **355**).

NORM COHEN

9 Southern Crossovers

The New World musical interchange between immigrants of African and European heritage began with the importation of the first slaves from Africa in the early 17th century. What we know, musically speaking, of the next two centuries is sketchy at best, documented by only a handful of written references and fleshed out by unabashed conjecture, often by writers with weighty political or social axes to grind. Much can be inferred if one accepts the assumption that African-American and Anglo-American music before interchange began can be approximated by the better-documented African and British music of the late 19th century.

Interchange during the 17th century took place in every respect, from cultural to recreational to procreational, notwithstanding the enormous social gulf that separated the African-Americans from their white owners and masters. Such assimilations as language and basic musical conventions will be largely taken for granted in this essay; the aim is rather to explore the musical interaction between the African-American and Anglo-American traditions after the Civil War.

Naturally, the emphasis will be on blues as the aspect of African-American music of particular relevance—in which case the direction of borrowing will almost always be from African- to Anglo-American. One then thinks of "white blues" as the pallid reflection of the black blues tradition. Nevertheless, it makes sense to consider the wider matrix in which blues is enmeshed, and comment on influences not directly subsumed under this rubric, in all its variations. Many of the selected recordings, therefore, will not fall into the category of blues (or white blues) per se; all, however, have bearing on that broader subject of cross-cultural musical borrowings.

The attention paid to country music recordings dating before 1942 (often referred to as "old-time" or "hillbilly") has consistently lagged behind that given to blues—both in depth of scholarship and quantity of reissues. This is true also for CD reissue programs, so that at the time of writing there is an extreme dearth of older material available on CD. In fact, one would be hard-pressed to find 40 "essential" CDs applicable to the topic at hand, though it is very likely that this situation will change.

Country string band, Maggie Valley, North Carolina, Teddy Sutton, banjo, 1972 (*Paul Oliver*)

The material in this review is divided into four disparate categories: (i) Roots of the Black—White Interchange; (ii) The Southern Mountains: Old Timey and Bluegrass; (iii) The South-West: Western Swing and Country & Western; and (iv) Post-war: Rockabilly and Modern Country. They are disparate in the sense that the first is thematic, the next two are geographical, and the last is chronological. The fourth category may require clarification: with few exceptions, "post-war" is construed to mean the 1940s and 1950s. After that era, the notion of regionality becomes eroded, as Southerners of both African- and Anglo-American heritage migrated into Northern urban centers and facilitated a nation-wide diffusion of what were once strictly Southern traditions.

Commentators on American popular music have observed that since the Civil War its history can be seen as a progression of African-American infusions into the Anglo-American-controlled music industry: minstrel, ragtime, jazz, blues, gospel, swing, R&B soul. More broadly, variegated American musical styles blossom and flourish when cross-pollinated by different vernacular musical idioms—not only African-American, but also Cajun and Creole in Louisiana; French-American in Missouri; German-American and Czech-American in the Midwest; Mexican-American in Texas and the South-west; Jewish-American in the urban North; Irish-American around Boston; Puerto Rican in New York; and French Canadian in the North-east. Not all ethnic centers are as geographically compact as this statement suggests, nor are they all confined to the South, but it is fair to characterize the Southern regions as the most fertile seedbed for new musical ideas.

Essential Records

(i) Roots of the Black-White Interchange

The lamentable institutions of slavery and segregation, most visible but never confined to the South, contributed to the persistence of a strong African-American culture. It was in the South, therefore, that Anglo-Americans were most widely exposed to African-American music and gradually incorporated elements of it into their own. Broadly speaking, rhythm was only very primitively developed in Anglo-American music and, when one finds any Anglo-American musical tradition with other than metronomically regular 4/4 or 3/4 beats, one can probably find other borrowings from African-Americans. This can be heard when comparing the rigidly tight fiddle styles of the North-east and Midwest with the fluid, bluesy bowing of certain Southern regions. Comparison might also be made with antebellum hymns and spirituals, and revivalist spirituals and gospel music; fife and drum marching music of the North-east with marching brass bands of New Orleans; or the play party song games of Appalachia with the ring dances and shouts of Mississippi.

Some of these comparisons and contrasts are evident in two admirable collections, each set comprising four CDs. The most ambitious project of its kind to date, **Roots n' Blues: The Retrospective (1925–1950)** , samples a mix of some of the best commercial "hillbilly" (Anglo-American) and "race" (African-American) recordings. Most are from the three exciting decades following the recognition by commercial phonograph companies of potential profits in recording local artists and marketing the material regionally, in the communities whence they came. The white artists all represent a wide range of Southern traditions and, as such, most show some evidence of African-American contacts. **Sounds Of The South** makes available on CD the seven-album set of LPs issued in November 1960, after an extensive field trip during summer 1959, through the South by Alan Lomax (and a follow-on visit the next year to Virginia and the Georgia Sea Islands). The revised format maintains aspects of the original albums but contrasts related black and white musical traditions in particular discs. Paired with **Roots n' Blues,** it provides a glimpse of Southern rural music a generation after the preceding compilation, though focusing more intensively on a smaller number of performers, many of whom did not make a living from playing music professionally.

Older traditional fiddle music of England and New England provides a benchmark against which Southern fiddling can be measured for evidence of African-American influences. On **Roots n' Blues** the styles range from the square rhythms of Ernest Stoneman's band on *Untitled [Fly Around My Pretty Little Miss]* or Freeny's Barn Dance Band *(Don't You Remember The Time),* to the more fluid fiddling of Posey Rorer in *Whitehouse Blues* (Charlie Poole's North Carolina Ramblers) and *Darn Good Girl* (with Buster Carter and Preston Young). *Sweet Milk And Peaches* by the Mississippi duo Narmour and Smith is very heavily accented, as is the bluesy *D Blues* by the Blue Ridge Ramblers. Narmour and Smith were obviously in contact with African-American musicians in their native Carroll County; in fact, they recommended the black songster Mississippi John Hurt to their A&R (Artist and Repertoire) man as a strong prospective recording artist.

The few black fiddlers who were recorded in the 1920s are at the far end of the continuum. Late 18th- and 19th-century sources suggest that black slaves frequently took up the white man's fiddle, learned his dance tunes and entertained him at local dances. By the early 1920s, however, black fiddlers were becoming scarce. The Mississippi Sheiks are among the few well-documented examples of a black string band. They played with equal ease for black and white audiences and had a repertoire that fitted each requirement, such as *The Jazz Fiddler*.

The range of approaches to rhythm is, if anything, dramatically more evident when Anglo-American and African-American singing styles are compared. As with fiddle music, artists closest to the Anglo ideal sing with metronomic regularity; two stellar examples are Almeda Riddle and Mrs Texas Gladden, both heard in a selection of children's songs on **Sounds Of The South.** Contrast their approach to that of Vera Hall or Bessie Jones on the same set. Riddle and Gladden are not dull, uninspired singers, but renowned in their idiom; their range of vocal ornamentation can be great, but they certainly cannot be said to "swing". Hall and Jones do just that (compare the latter's *Sometimes*).

Rivaling these borrowings in importance was the banjo, an instrument adapted from Africa in the New World and readily taken up by white people. After the Civil War it became one of the mainstays of traditional music in the South-east. One of the earliest references to a string band was in Nicholas Cresswell's *Journal* (1774), in which he records: "A great number of young people met together [in Virginia] with a Fiddle and Banjo played by two Negroes, with plenty of Toddy." Hillbilly string band music of the first decades of the 20th century and its successor, bluegrass music, are almost unthinkable without the banjo. At its most sophisticated, the instrument's role was on a par with that of the fiddle (listen to Charlie Poole's banjo on *Whitehouse Blues*), though it was common for it to take the duties of rhythm back-up (for example, *Washington County Fox Chase* or *Soldier's Joy*). By the late 1930s, the banjo had begun to disappear from country music, except in the hands of comic performers. This trend was reversed dramatically in the 1940s and afterward by bluegrass music (Bill Monroe's *Goodbye Old Pal* is a particular example). In African-American music the banjo had begun its disappearing act much earlier. With the important exception of the New Orleans jazz scene, by the heyday of "race" recordings in the 1920s there were hardly any banjo players in the catalogs. In both cases, the trend was influenced by social factors: in the late 19th century, to many black people the banjo represented music played by subservient "Uncle Tom" for bossman "Mister Charley"; to white country artists in the 1930s seeking social status, the instrument conjured up the image of the backwoods rube. To all, the imagery of blackface minstrelsy (whites imitating blacks imitating whites) provided another negative cultural association. As the banjo receded into the hills (the possibility must be acknowledged of a more vigorous "underground" tradition than the recorded documentation suggests), white country music turned to jazz and swing for inspiration. Most of the more successful aggregations of the 1930s and 1940s were heavily jazz-influenced in their instrumentation and styles—The Prairie Ramblers, Light Crust Doughboys, and Brown County Revellers are good examples.

Since World War II the guitar has been identified as the pre-eminent folk musician's instrument, both in Anglo-American and African-American traditions. The evidence of commercial recordings in the 1920s, however, suggests that the guitar was just becoming familiar among Anglo-American folk musicians, and was more frequently used for rhythmic back-up than as a lead instrument. This was not true among African-Americans, and one can only conclude that African-American folk artists took up the guitar first, probably at the end of the 19th century; they had developed the instrument's potential long before there were any virtuoso guitarists among rural Anglo-Americans. Of course, only slightly earlier, the guitar had become an Anglo-American parlor instrument of the upper classes-one that well-bred young ladies learned to play, much as they did the piano in different generations.

By the late 1920s there was a handful of skilled Anglo-American guitarists who recorded solos; among the best guitar instrumentals were the several duets by Roy Harvey and Leonard Copeland (whose *Back To The Blue Ridge* was never issued on 78). Almost all Anglo-Americans who played in slide-guitar style in the 1920s acknowledged that they learned from African-American musicians, who may have originated the technique or adapted it from touring Hawaiian musicians. Sherman Tedder (whose *untitled* instrumental was also never issued on 78) was clearly an adept slide guitarist. Better known in this style is Frank Hutchison, who was heavily influenced in his youth by African-American labourer musicians. His *Last Scene Of The Titanic* is an unusual *cante fable* (a partly sung story), narrating an accident that left a deep mark on folk and popular music in the 1910s and 1920s among both Anglo- and African-Americans. By the 1930s the once-common line-up of fiddle, banjo, and guitar was becoming less common among professionally orientated Anglo-American string band musicians. The banjo was set aside, to be replaced by steel guitar or mandolin; string bass and other back-up instruments also became more common. More drastically, the string band, which primarily represented a dance music ensemble, found itself being replaced by other combinations—in particular two or more guitars (exemplified by the Callahan Brothers' *Brown's Ferry Blues*), one of which might be played slide style. Tom Darby and Jimmy Tarlton pioneered this combination in the 1920s; the latter was an outstanding steel guitarist, as is evident on *Lonesome Frisco Line* (previously unissued). As hillbilly music evolved into the Nashville-dominated country music of post-war years, the role of the guitar was often reduced to that of a backing instrument. This was not true among those folk musicians who remained closer to earlier traditions; in fact, the incorporation of a variety of flat-picking and finger-picking styles, learned from jazz and blues guitarists, respectively, fortified the importance of the guitar. Estil C. Ball had been recorded by Alan Lomax in the 1930s for the Library of Congress; in 1959 Lomax revisited him with newer equipment and recorded a much broader range of material. Ball's bouncy finger-picking (as on *When I Get Home*) and rich, rhythmic back-up attest to African-American influences but well integrated into an Anglo-American matrix.

In religious, as in secular traditions, musical exchange across the ethno-social barrier flowed sturdily, though in many cases the direction of borrowing was not so obvious (at least in the 19th century). In fact, the question of who borrowed from whom burdened early 20th-century scholars of folksong, among whom were partisans who could not accept that African-Americans might create anything worthwhile artistically; they simply must have borrowed it from their social and artistic white superiors. Today this notion of black creativity no longer falls on credulous ears. While white America's earliest religious musical expressions, psalms and hymns, were of European origin, by the 19th century they had become mixed inextricably with African-American elements—first spirituals (whose origins were once the subject of bitter contention), then gospel music.

The first commercial documentation of Southern musical culture (in the 1920s) came at a time when hymns had become rare and psalms were nearly extinct. The major folk religious musical expression of the region and period remained the fa-so-la idiom, sometimes called "Sacred Harp" music after one of the most popular and long-lived set of songbooks to be published. A number of such groups were recorded commercially in the 1920s. Though they must have represented an "old-fashioned" survival to corporate executives, there were still numerous practitioners to be found (whether they bought records is another question). The Daniels-Deason Sacred Harp Singers (*Hallelujah*) and the OKeh Atlanta Sacred Harp Singers (*Ortonville*) provide two examples of this archaic idiom, though the former group is much too stilted and awkward to be taken as the best of Sacred Harp music (the original 78rpm recording was never issued). A better example is afforded by the 1959 recordings on **Sounds Of The South.** Alan Lomax made these at the three-day Sacred Harp Convention in Ffyfe, Alabama, where he heard the Alabama Sacred Harp Singers sing *Windham, Antioch,* and *Calvary.*

Gospel music emerged in the 1870s, associated with the revival movement of Moody and Sankey, who created a new religious style by borrowing heavily from then-contemporary secular idioms. Though strongly reviled by many contemporary critics, the music served its purpose of strengthening religious attendance by making it more accessible to church worshipers. The first phase of borrowing turned to the Anglo-American popular music of the last decades of the 19th century. By the early 20th century, however, gospel music had become more dependent on jazz and other African-American forms, and was associated primarily with African-American fundamentalist church groups; during the next few decades it was characterized by the dynamism of a music still evolving stylistically. There was a distinct white gospel style by the 1930s, but its musical debt to African-American music remained audible (particularly in Pentecostal churches), and the two church movements continued to share numerous texts and tunes. Estil and Orna Ball and friends provide two representative examples of white gospel quartet style with *The Cabin On The Hill* and *Lonesome Valley* (though both pieces have many spiritual characteristics), while the Mountain Ramblers provide bluegrass gospel at its best in *Baptizing Down By The Creek* and *The Old Country Church*, all reissued on **Sounds Of The South.** From the preceding decade is Molly O'Day's *Heaven's Radio*, typical of gospel texts of the 1920s and 1930s that co-opt new technological imagery in the service of the Lord.

Rhythm was not the only African-American gift to the lighter-skinned neighbors; an entirely different approach to narrative was born and nourished in black oral literature—one that bore the same relationship to the strict chronological story that polyrhythms and swing did to four-square metrical regularity. The Anglo-American ballad evolved out of the matrix of medieval western European narratives such as the epic, the lay, and the romance. By the 17th century several cultures had an established story song that we now call "ballad." Unlike the earlier forms, the ballad tended to focus on a single incident, retell the story dramatically with strong emphasis on action, and little editorializing or moralizing. It was cast in two- or four-line stanzas set to a simple, recurring melody. This pattern has survived in America from the days of the first settlers to the present, though it has also spawned variant styles. Estil Ball's rendition of *The Farmer's Curst Wife* shows the New World transformation of a British ballad, once laden with supernatural elements. Hobart Smith's *Poor Ellen Smith*, Bob Carpenter's *Kenny Wagner*, and Neil Morris' and Charley Everidge's *Jesse James* exemplify ballads that treat actual events in the United States. Considerably removed stylistically from the oldest British ballads, they represent a later style (typically 18th and

19th century) that lacks many of the striking poetic devices of the earlier phase (incremental repetition, extensive dialog, elaborate structural patterns), and tends toward a more sentimentalized narrative. The most divergent narrative to emerge sheds both the strict chronological mold and the coolly objective viewpoint. These are replaced with a song that stresses attitudes and feelings over actions, commenting on an incident presumably already well known and not needing detailed retelling. How this form originated is still unclear, but the fact that it shares some traits with the blues is very suggestive of African-American influence if not origin. This looser, more disjointed, more subjective way of telling a story is now called the "blues ballad." Its relationship with African-American musical traditions is further supported by the fact that blues ballads are most likely to be sung by African-American musicians.

One of the best examples of a blues ballad, certainly the one most widely known in both Anglo-American and African-American traditions, is *John Henry*, which the Mountain Ramblers offer in bluegrass style on **Sounds Of The South**. Charlie Poole and the North Carolina Ramblers' rendition of *Whitehouse Blues*, dealing with the assassination of President McKinley at the Pan American Exposition in Buffalo, New York, in 1901, is another example, generally found only in white tradition. The great African-American singer, Vera Hall, offers a *Boll Weevil Holler* that shows the blues ballad with its narrative element practically stripped bare; it is the other end of the continuum that starts with *The Farmer's Curst Wife*.

The final factor to keep in mind in assessing cross-cultural borrowings is the number of texts—whether secular or religious—that occur in both traditions. **Sounds Of The South** contains a handful of examples: *All Night Long, Death Have Mercy, Go Tell Aunt Nancy, Frog Went A-Courtin', Boll Weevil Holler,* and *On That Rock* all have close relatives on the other side; and Wade Ward's banjo rendition of *Chilly Winds* is basically the same tune as the *Going Down The Road Feeling Bad/Lonesome Road Blues*.

For didactic purposes, I have stressed particular elements of these two outstanding boxed sets; I would do my readers a disservice if I did not assure them that both contain many more remarkable selections than have been mentioned. Columbia (and its successor, American Record Corporation) was such an important entity in the 1920s and 1930s that a selection such as **Roots n' Blues**, taken entirely from its catalog, can indeed be described as presenting some of the best hillbilly and race recordings of the period. Alan Lomax had a knack for finding and recording some of the best folk musicians alive. **Sounds Of The South** offers some of the greatest performers to be found in the 1950s:

African-American (Vera Hall, Fred McDowell, Bessie Jones); and Anglo-American (Almeda Riddle, Texas Gladden, Hobart Smith, Wade Ward). Add to the music itself the handsome, and lavishly illustrated booklets that accompany each, and one has two excellent packages that could, if nothing else were available, provide a foundation for understanding African-American and Anglo-American music of the last seven decades and for recognizing their great mutual indebtedness.

321/2 **Roots n' Blues: The Retrospective (1925–1950)**
Various Artists
Columbia C4K 47911/471832-2 (UK)—*4 CD set*
DISC ONE: Charlie Poole With The North Carolina Ramblers, *Whitehouse Blues*; Aiken County String Band, *High Sheriff*; Frank Hutchison, *The Last Scene Of The Titanic*; Hersal Thomas, *Suitcase Blues*; Rev. J.M. Gates, *Death's Black Train Is Coming*; Dora Carr, *Cow-Cow Blues*; Vance's Tennessee Breakdowners, *Washington County Fox Chase*; Fiddlin' John Carson, *I'm Going To Take The Train To Charlotte*; Ernest V. Stoneman's Trio, *Untitled [Fly Around My Pretty Little Miss]*; Whistler & His Jug Band, *Low Down Blues*; Washington Phillips, *Paul & Silas In Jail*; Barbecue Bob, *Blind Pig Blues*; Austin & Lee Allen, *Chattanooga Blues*; Sherman Tedder, *Untitled*; Dallas String Band With Coley Jones, *Hokum Blues*; Gladys Bentley, *Worried Blues*; Elizabeth Johnson, *Empty Bed Blues* Part 1/*Empty Bed Blues* Part 2; South Georgia Highballers, *Blue Grass Twist*; Charlie Bowman & His Brothers, *Moonshiner And His Money*; Clarence Green, *Johnson City Blues*; Reverend Johnny Blakey, Assisted By The Sanctified Singers, *Warming By The Devil's Fire*; Papa Too Sweet & Harry Jones, *(Honey) It's Tight Like That*; Mississippi John Hurt, *Big Leg Blues*; Daniels-Deason Sacred Harp Singers, *Hallelujah*

DISC TWO: Herschel Brown & His Happy Five, *Liberty*; Mamie Smith, *My Sportin' Man*; Blues Birdhead, *Mean Low Blues*; Pink Anderson & Simmie Dooley, *C. C. & O. Blues*; The OKeh Atlanta Sacred Harp Singers, *Ortonville*; Slim Doucet, *Dear Black Eyes [Chere Yeux Noirs]*; Roosevelt Sykes, *Roosevelt Blues*; Hokum Boys, *Gin Mill Blues*; Joe Falcon, Accompanied By Clemo & Ophy Breaux, *Osson*; W. T. Narmour & S. W. Smith, *Sweet Milk And Peaches* [Breakdown]; Gid Tanner & The Skillet Lickers, With Riley Puckett & Clayton McMichen, *Soldier's Joy*; Whistlin' Alex Moore, *They May Not Be My Toes*; Mississippi Sheiks, *The Jazz Fiddler*; Lonnie Johnson, *I Have To Do My Time*; Tom Darby & Jimmie Tarlton, *Lonesome Frisco Line*; Roy Harvey & Leonard Copeland, *Back To The Blue Ridge*; Buster Carter & Preston Young, *Darn Good Girl*; Bo Carter, *West Jackson Blues*; Lonnie Johnson & Clara Smith [As Violet Green], *You Had Too Much*; Silver Leaf Quartet, *Oh! Glory Glory*; Freeny's Barn Dance Band, *Don't You Remember The Time*; Pelican Wildcats, *Walkin' Georgia Rose*; Peetie Wheatstraw [The Devil's Son-in-Law], *Police Station Blues*; Tindley Quaker City Gospel Singers, *Hallelujah Side*; Will Batts, *Highway No. 61 Blues*

DISC THREE: W. Lee O'Daniel & His Light Crust Doughboys, *Doughboys Theme Song* No. 1; W. Lee O'Daniel & His Hillbilly Boys, *Ida (Sweet As Apple Cider)*; W. Lee O'Daniel & His Light Crust Doughboys, *Doughboys Theme Song* No. 2; Blind Willie [McTell] & Partner, *Bell Street Lightnin'*; Charlie Patton, *Jersey*

Bull Blues; Walter Roland, *Every Morning Blues*; Blue Ridge Ramblers, *D Blues*; Breaux Freres, *La Valse Des Yeux Blue [Blue Eyes Waltz]*; Lucille Bogan [as Bessie Jackson], *Skin Game Blues*; Leroy Carr With Scrapper Blackwell, *Good Woman Blues*; Josh White [as Pinewood Tom], *Sissy Man*; Rhythm Wreckers, *Blue Yodel No. 2 (My Lovin' Gal Lucille)*; Anglin Twins [Jack & Jim], *Just Inside The Pearly Gates*; Bumble Bee Slim [Amos Easton], *Hard Rocks In My Bed*; The Two Charlies, *Tired Feelin' Blues*; Eldon Baker & His Brown County Revelers, *One Eyed Sam*; A'nt Idy Harper & The Coon Creek Girls, *Poor Naomi Wise*; [Kid] Prince Moore, *South Bound Blues*; Big Bill Broonzy, *C & A Blues*; George Curry, *My Last Five Dollars*; The Nite Owls, *Memphis Blues*; The Alley Boys Of Abbeville, *Pourquoi Tu M'Aime Pas*; Rev. Benny Campbell [Meetin' House In Dixie], *Have Mercy On Me*; Albert Ammons, *Shout For Joy*; Jack Kelly, *Flower Blues*; Cliff Carlisle [as Bob Clifford], *Onion Eating Mama*; Callahan Brothers, *Brown's Ferry Blues*; Little Buddy Doyle, *Slick Capers Blues*; Bill "Jazz" Gillum [as Bill McKinley], *Poor Boy Blues*

DISC FOUR: Frank Edwards, *We Got To Get Together*; Sweet Violet Boys, *You Got To See Mama Ev'ry Night (Or You Can't See Mama At All)*; The Humbard Family, *I'll Fly Away*; Tony Hollins, *Cross Cut Saw Blues*; Peter Cleighton, *Black Snake Blues*; Black Cats & The Kitten, *Step It Up And Go*; Bob & Randall Atcher, *Papa's Going Crazy, Mama's Going Mad*; Adolf Hofner & His San Antonians, *Cotton-Eyed Joe*; Poor Boy Burke, *Old Vets Blues*; Little Son Joe, *Black Rat Swing*; Big Maceo Merriweather, *Macy Special*; Light Crust Doughboys, With J. B. Brinkley, *It's Funny What Love Will Make You Do*; Hank Penny & His Radio Cowboys, *Army Blues*; James [Beale Street] Clark, *Who But You*; Homer Harris, *Tomorrow May Be Too Late*; Muddy Waters [as McKinley Morganfield], *Burying Ground Blues*; Bill Monroe & His Blue Grass Boys, *Goodbye Old Pal*; Gene Autry, *Dixie Cannonball*; Bill Landford & The Landfordaires, *Run On For A Long Time*; Joe Williams, *Baby, Please Don't Go*; Sister Myrtle Fields, Accompanied By Austin McCoy Trio, *I'm Toiling*; Willie [Boodle It] Right, *Two By Four Blues*; Bailes Brothers, *You Can't Go Halfway (And Get In);* Molly O'Day & The Cumberland Mountain Folks, *Heaven's Radio*; Rosetta Howard, *Plow Hand Blues*; Memphis Seven, *Grunt Meat Blues*; Deep South Boys, *Until I Found The Lord*; Brother Porter & Brother Cook, *I Know My Jesus Won't Deny Me*

323/4 Sounds Of The South: A Musical Journey From The Georgia Sea Islands To The Mississippi Delta

Various Artists

Atlantic 7 82496-2—4 CD set

DISC ONE—SOUNDS OF THE SOUTH/BLUE RIDGE MOUNTAIN MUSIC: Neil Morris & Charley Everidge, *The Banks Of The Arkansas/Wave The Ocean*; Lonnie Young, Ed Young, & Lonnie Young, Jr., *Hen Duck*; Estil C. Ball, *The Farmer's Curst Wife*; Vera Hall, *Boll Weevil Holler*; Mountain Ramblers, *Jesse James*; Neil Morris, *Jesse James*; Bob Carpenter, *Kenny Wagner*; Vera Hall, *Trouble So Hard*; Rev. W. A. Donaldson, *Baptizing Scene*; Viola James & Congregation, *Is There Anybody Here That Love My Jesus*; Alabama Sacred Harp Singers, *Windham*; [Mississippi] Fred McDowell, *Keep Your Lamps Trimmed And Burning*; Sid Hemphill & Lucius Smith, *Come On Boys Let's Go To The Ball*; John Davis & Group, *Join The Band*; Ed Lewis, *Lucky Holler*; Ed Lewis & Group, *I Be So Glad When The Sun Goes Down*; Mountain Ramblers,

Cotton Eyed Joe [Cullen Gaylen, vocal]/*Big Tilda*; Estil C. Ball & Orna Ball, *Jennie Jenkins*; Mountain Ramblers, *John Henry* [Cullen Gaylen, vocal]/ *Rosewood Casket* [Eldridge Montgomery, vocal]/*Silly Bill*/*Big Ball In Boston* [Thurman Pugh, vocal]; Wade Ward, *Chilly Winds*; Mountain Ramblers, *The Old Hickory Cane* [Thurman Pugh, vocal]; Hobart Smith, *John Brown*/*Poor Ellen Smith*; Mountain Ramblers, *Shady Grove* [Thurman Pugh, vocal]

DISC TWO—ROOTS OF THE BLUES/THE BLUES ROLL ON: Lonnie Young, Ed Young, & Lonnie Young, Jr., *Jim and John*; Vera Hall, *Wild Ox Moan*; [Mississippi] Fred McDowell, *Been Drinkin' Water Out of A Hollow Log*; Miles Pratcher & Bob Pratcher, *All Night Long*; [Mississippi] Fred McDowell, Miles Pratcher, & Fannie Davis, *Shake 'Em On Down*; Forrest City Joe, *Levee Camp Reminiscence*; Lonnie Young, Ed Young, & Lonnie Young, Jr., *Chevrolet*; Johnny Lee Moore, *Levee Camp Holler*; Johnny Lee Moore & 12 Mississippi Penitentiary Convicts, *Eighteen Hammers*; Forrest City Joe, Sonny Boy Rogers, & Thomas Morgan, *Drink On Little Girl*; [Mississippi] Fred McDowell, *Drop Down Mama*; Boy Blue, Willie Jones, & Joe Lee, *Boogie Children*; Forrest City Joe, Sonny Boy Rogers, & Thomas Morgan, *She Lived Her Life Too Fast*; Lonnie Young, Ed Young, & Lonnie Young, Jr., *Sittin' On Top Of The World*; John Dudley, *Cool Water Blues*; Forrest City Joe, Sonny Boy Rogers, & Thomas Morgan, *She Don't Love Me That Way*/*Stop Breaking Down*; Boy Blue, Willie Jones, & Joe Lee, *Joe Lee's Rock*; Rosalie Hill, *Bullyin' Well*; [Mississippi] Fred McDowell, *When You Get Home, Write Me A Few Little Lines*; Forrest City Joe, *Red Cross Store*; Forrest City Joe, Sonny Boy Rogers, & Thomas Morgan, *Forrest City Jump*

DISC THREE—NEGRO CHURCH MUSIC/WHITE SPIRITUALS: Vera Hall, *Death, Have Mercy*; James Shorty & [Mississippi] Fred McDowell, *I Want Jesus To Walk With Me*; Mrs. Mary Lee & Congregation, *Jesus Is Real to Me*; Rev. R. C. Crenshaw & Congregation, *I Love The Lord*; Rev. G. I. Townsel, *Sermon Fragment*; Rev. R. C. Crenshaw & Congregation, *I'm Goin' Home On The Mornin' Train*; Madam Mattie Wigley & Congregation, *Power*; Viola James, Lonnie Young, & Ed Young, *On That Rock*; James Shorty, Viola James, & Congregation, *Jesus On The Main Line*; Henry Morrison & St. Simon's Island Singers, *I'm Gonna Sail Like A Ship On The Ocean*; John Davis, Bessie Jones, & St. Simon's Island Singers, *Blow Gabriel*; Bernice McClellan & Congregation, *What Do You Think About Jesus (He's All Right)*; Estil C. Ball, Lacey Richardson, & Blair Reedy, *Tribulations*; Estil C. Ball & Blair Reedy, *When I Get Home*; Estil C. Ball, *Poor Wayfaring Stranger*; Mountain Ramblers, *Baptizing Down By The Creek*; Rev. I. D. Back & Congregation, *Sermon And Lining Hymn*; Alabama Sacred Harp Singers, *Antioch*/*Calvary*; Estil Ball & Lacey Richardson, *Please Let Me Stay A Little Longer*; Estil C. Ball, *Father, Jesus Loves You*; Estil C. Ball, Lacey Richardson, Blair Reedy, & Orna Ball, *Lonesome Valley*; Estil C. Ball, *Father Adieu*; Mountain Ramblers *Old Country Church*; [Thurman Pugh, vocal], Estil C. Ball, Lacey Richardson, Blair Reedy, & Orna Ball, *The Cabin On The Hill*

DISC FOUR—AMERICAN FOLK SONGS FOR CHILDREN: Mainer Band, *Johnson's Old Gray Mule*; Almeda Riddle, *My Little Rooster*; Mainer Band, *Whoa Mule*; Almeda Riddle, *Frog Went A-Courtin'*; Mainer Band, *Glenn's Chimes*; Almeda Riddle, *Chick-a-le-lee-lo*; Mountain Ramblers, *Old Joe Clark*; Almeda Riddle, *Go Tell Aunt Nancy*; Mainer Band, *Train 111*; Bessie Jones & Group, *Johnny*

Cuckoo; Almeda Riddle, *Mama Buy Me A Chiney Doll*; Hobart Smith, *Soldier, Soldier*; Jesse Pratcher, Mattie Gardner, & Mary Gardner, *Mary Mack*; Bessie Jones & Group, *Hambone*; Hobart Smith, *Banging Breakdown*; Jesse Pratcher, Mattie Gardner, & Mary Gardner, *Green Sally, Up*; Bessie Jones & Group, *Sometimes*; Hobart Smith, *The Arkansas Traveler*; Estil C. Ball & Orna Ball, *Paper Of Pins*; Mrs. Texas Gladden, *The Little Dappled Cow*; Bessie Jones & Group, *Go To Sleep Little Baby*;* SOUNDS OF THE SOUTH: Wade Ward, Charley Higgins, & Charley Poe, *Paddy On The Turnpike*; BLUE RIDGE MOUNTAIN MUSIC: Spence Moore & Roy Birns, *Jimmy Sutton*; Mountain Ramblers, *Liza Jane*; ROOTS OF THE BLUES: Lonnie Young, Ed Young, & Lonnie Young, Jr., *Oree*; Forrest City Joe, *Train Time*; [Mississippi] Fred McDowell, *Freight Train Blues*; NEGRO CHURCH MUSIC: James Shorty, Viola James, & Congregation, *This Little Light Of Mine*; Felix Dukes & [Mississippi] Fred McDowell, *Motherless Children*; WHITE SPIRITUALS Neil Morris, *Little Moses*

(ii) The Southern Mountains: Old Timey and Bluegrass

The most visible influence of African-American music on hillbilly musicians in the 1920s and 1930s was in the genre called "white blues." These were songs in three-line stanzas (generally *AAB*, rhymed) with 12 bars to the line; usually one or two singers were accompanied by guitar (though occasionally something more elaborate). The themes were rarely narrative, but lyrical, dealing with anything from love, to work, the economy, or relations with one's in-laws. By virtue of geographical proximity, many Anglo-American musicians had ample opportunity to learn from rural bluesmen. The recurrence of elements that must have been taken from the very popular blues recording artists such as Blind Lemon Jefferson, however, strongly suggests that they learned as much from phonograph records as from direct contact. This would also account for the almost exclusive reliance on the classic 12-bar *AAB* blues stanza—an idealized form characteristic of classic city blues but only approximated by rural bluesmen.

White Country Blues (1926–1938): A Lighter Shade Of Blue is an admirable collection of recordings from Columbia's vaults that amply demonstrates some of the best recordings of the genre. Though many of the artists appear also on **Roots n' Blues**, there is only one duplicated title. While there are numerous examples included in the 12-bar blues format, some of the selections are bluesy in spirit only. Among the most striking of the classic blues renditions are Clarence Green's *Johnson City Blues* and Larry Hensley's *Matchbox Blues*. Remarkably, Neither Green nor Hensley recorded any other guitar solos. Green was an outstanding fiddler from North Carolina who made numerous

*The disc continues with items issued on the original long playing records under the generic headings expressed in small capitals.

string band recordings; Hensley was the back-up guitarist for Walker's Corbin Ramblers, from Kentucky. Hensley may have learned his piece from Blind Lemon Jefferson's recordings (**126**), but his text is considerably different, and he has smoothed out Lemon's metrical irregularities. The source of Green's *Johnson City* is Ida Cox's *Chattanooga Blues* (**161**). It is cut from the same cloth as *Deep Elem Blues*, and was closely copied by the Allen Brothers in their version of *Chattanooga* (on **Roots n' Blues**). A good hot country version of *Deep Elem Blues* is provided by the Prairie Ramblers. West Virginian steel guitarist Frank Hutchison was primarily known as a blues guitarist and all four of his selections on this set are very close to African-American tradition. Riley Puckett was the decade's pre-eminent back-up guitarist, mostly with Gid Tanner's Skillet Lickers, but (on the basis of aural evidence) he also accompanied at least one African-American singer (Virginia Childs). He made a pair of guitar solos of which *Darkey's Wail*, an instrumental steel-guitar version of *John Henry*, is the more successful—learned, he says in his spoken introduction, from "an old southern darkey . . . comin' down Decatur Street [Atlanta]."

Tom Darby and Jimmie Tarlton were a remarkable pair on disc, but bitter rivals and deeply suspicious of one another (Tarlton made up a tune for one of his oldest ballads so that Darby would not learn the "real tune" from his recording). They blend well together (Darby on straight guitar/vocal, Tarlton on slide guitar/vocal)-except for Jimmie's occasional tendency to try to drown out Darby by outsinging or outplaying him. Many years later, Tarlton would deny in interviews any African-American influences whatever, though his music incontrovertibly suggests otherwise. Their *Frankie Dean* is a folk version of one of the most widely known blues ballads of the early decades of the century, *Frankie And Johnny* (or *Frankie And Albert*). Charlie Poole's *Leaving Home* is derived from the popular version of the same ballad; his *If The River Was Whiskey* and *Ramblin' Blues* are respectively W. C. Handy's *Hesitating Blues* and *Beale Street Blues*, two of the earliest blues songs published in sheet music form (1915 and 1916 respectively). The blues rubric must have been very popular commercially, because many songs were titled "blues" although they were not. Cast in standard *ABC* quatrain format, but with the ever-popular yodelling refrain, good examples are Cliff Carlisle's novelty songs *Chicken Roost Blues* (to the tune of *Polly Wolly Doodle All Day*) and *Tom Cat Blues*, together with Cox and Hobbs' *Oozlin' Daddy Blues* (Bob Wills' rewrite of the Delmore Brothers' *Brown's Ferry Blues*, another version of which is on **Roots n' Blues**). Laughing and crying records were quite popular during the 1910s and 1920s—they must have made good party records—and the Allen Brothers' *Drunk And*

Nutty Blues is essentially in this form. In fact, earlier Columbia executives thought their *Laughing And Crying Blues/Chattanooga Blues* sounded so bluesy they were issued in the 14000—D race records series, rather than the 15000—D hillbilly series. The Allens were hardly flattered, and brought a lawsuit against Columbia. Their *Chattanooga Mama* is another variant of *Chattanooga Blues*. Mention should also be made of the *double entendre* blues, which were a major African-American sub-genre, but much less frequent in white blues. In the latter idiom, they tended too much toward formulaic and cliche-ridden verses to compete poetically with their black counterparts. Cliff Carlisle's *Ash Can Blues* (issued under the pseudonym of Bob Clifford) is a fair example. The other major musical style in the "white blues" genre is the "blue yodel," popularized (if not invented) by Jimmie Rodgers, though probably named by the talent scout Ralph Peer. It consists of an *AAB* blues stanza with a yodeling refrain. Examples on this set are W. Lee O'Daniel's band's *Dirty Hangover Blues* (a version of *Blue Yodel* No. 10), and Ramblin' Red Lowery's *Memphis Yodel No. 1*. The "blue yodel" was so popular that the Mississippi Sheiks even titled one of their pieces *Yodeling Fiddling Blues* (**331**).

"Bluegrass music" means many things to different people. It was the creation of Bill Monroe and his Blue Grass Boys, who began developing the form in 1939. Most critics regard classic bluegrass to be the style that Monroe's band recorded in 1946–8: a hard-driving, fast-paced music (for listening, not dancing) with tense-voiced, high-pitched vocals. The characteristic instrumentation was fiddle, mandolin, and banjo alternating on lead, with rhythm back-up by guitar and upright bass. Unlike earlier hillbilly music, the instruments rotated leads, following the pattern established by New Orleans jazz bands. The first fiddler in Monroe's band was Chubby Wise, whose fluid, bluesy bowing established a model for bluegrass fiddle that persists to this day. At the time, the pre-eminent banjo player in the band was Earl Scruggs, who built on earlier three-finger picking styles to develop patterns that enabled very fast melodic runs much more intricate than previously thought possible. Monroe has always been ready to acknowledge the influence of African-American music on his style—in particular, one Arnold Shultz, a local fiddler/guitarist who also taught the musicians from whom fellow Kentuckian Merle Travis learned. Within a decade, a handful of bands through the South-east were playing the music professionally, on the radio and in live concerts. While the new bands wrote many of their own songs, a strong tendency remained to play older, traditional material with which the musicians, all Southerners, had grown up. This was given fresh impetus a decade later when bluegrass bands began playing to

Northern college audiences, where the urban folksong revival was raising interest in traditional mountain music.

Recorded and edited by Mike Seeger, mostly in New York, Boston and the Baltimore-Washington area, **Mountain Music Bluegrass Style** presents bluegrass music as it was being played in the late 1950s by bands other than the handful who were commercially prominent at the time. The emphasis is on the older facet of the musicians' repertoires. Earl Taylor's band has been a mainstay in Washington-Baltimore for decades; their hard-driving playing and Taylor's intense singing style offer an exciting introduction to the music for novices. Their *White-house Blues* recasts the Charlie Poole blues ballad about the McKinley assassination in the up-tempo bluegrass style. Virtuoso instrumentalist Smiley Hobbs' repertoire includes *Nine Pound Hammer*, a lyric on the John Henry story familiar in both Anglo-American and African-American traditions. *All The Good Times Have Passed And Gone*, by Earl Taylor, and *Drifting Too Far From The Shore*, by Bob Baker's band, offer bluegrass gospel at its best. Bluegrass has matured and diversified greatly since these recordings were made; also a great deal has been written about the music from a sophisticated, analytic point of view. None of this should detract from the significance of Seeger's efforts to define and explain a new musical phenomenon: the music was (and still sounds) first rate.

When Ralph Rinzler and Gene Earle first encountered Arthel "Doc" Watson in the course of locating old-time banjo player and singer Clarence Ashley, he was recommended to them as a musician of prodigious talents. At the time, however he was playing electric guitar in a rockabilly band in order to supplement his farm income and was not particularly receptive to performing the kind of music they were seeking. Through Rinzler's urging he returned to his older musical roots and created a new (and commercially far more successful) career for himself. Though Doc Watson is a competent banjo and harmonica player, it is as a guitarist that he has few (if any) peers—whether finger-picking, flat-picking, or playing back-up. It was probably his dazzling ability to transpose fiddle tunes to flat-picked guitar that really launched him into stardom. In the decades since his discovery, Watson's repertoire has broadened from the older, traditional material he knew as a child and the hillbilly and blues music he learned from 78rpm records in the 1930s and later; he now includes folk, country, blues, bluegrass, and other styles with which he came into contact during his travels as a professional musician. All of the nearly three dozen albums that Watson has recorded include at least one bluesy number, and he never fails to play some blues in his concerts.

Pickin' The Blues is a frank testimonial to Watson's appreciation for

African-American music; his notes tell us where he obtained each song and what they mean to him. *Mississippi Heavy Water Blues* he learned from a 78 by Barbecue Bob (**135**), and *I'm A Stranger Here* from Brownie McGhee and Sonny Terry. These are the only selections on the CD obtained directly from African-American musicians, though Watson listened to, and learned from, recordings by Skip James, Mississippi John Hurt, and Cannon's Jug Stompers. Several other selections are in the white blues category: *Jailhouse Blues*, taken from the Delmore Brothers, *Freight Train Blues* from Roy Acuff's band, *Carroll County Blues* from Narmour and Smith (**325**), and *Honey Babe Blues* from Clarence Ashley—all excellent sources for anyone. Doc shares equal title billing with his son Merle, whom he taught and worked into his act as soon as Merle (named after guitarist Merle Travis) was old enough. Over the years, Merle's proficiency on guitar continued to grow, and his tragic death in a tractor accident on their farm was a great musical as well as personal loss to Watson. Since Doc Watson rose to national prominence in the folk festival circuit in the 1960s, many other flat-picking guitarists have learned from him and/or carried the style into other directions. While there are faster pickers, there are none who can match Watson's impeccable taste and ingratiating warmth.

325 White Country Blues (1926–1938): A Lighter Shade Of Blue
Various Artists
Columbia C2K 47466/472886-2 (UK)—*2 CD set*
DISC ONE: Frank Hutchison, *K. C. Blues/Cannonball Blues*; Charlie Poole With The North Carolina Ramblers, *Leaving Home/If The River Was Whiskey*; Cauley Family, *Duplin County Blues*; Tom Darby & Jimmie Tarlton, *Sweet Sarah Blues/Frankie Dean*; Riley Puckett, *Darkey's Wail*; Clarence Green, *Johnson City Blues*; Carolina Buddies, *Mistreated Blues*; Tom Ashley, *Haunted Road Blues*; Roy Acuff & His Crazy Tennesseans, *Steel Guitar Blues*; Carlisle & Ball, *Guitar Blues/I Want A Good Woman*; Cliff Carlisle, *Ash Can Blues*; Val & Pete, *Yodel Blues* Parts 1 and 2; Mr. & Mrs. Chris Bouchillon, *Adam And Eve* Part 2; W. T. Narmour & S. W. Smith, *Carroll County Blues*; Charlie Poole With The North Carolina Ramblers, *Ramblin' Blues*; Frank Hutchison, *Worried Blues/Train That Carried The Girl From Town*; Roy Harvey & Leonard Copeland, *Lonesome Weary Blues*; W. Lee O'Daniel & His Hillbilly Boys, *Bear Cat Mama.*

DISC TWO: Blue Ridge Ramblers, *Jug Rag*; Prairie Ramblers, *Deep Elem Blues*; Clayton McMichen, *Prohibition Blues*; Larry Hensley, *Matchbox Blues*; Callahan Brothers, *Somebody's Been Using That Thing*; Homer Callahan, *Rattlesnake Daddy/My Good Gal Has Thrown Me Down*; W. Lee O'Daniel & His Hillbilly Boys, *Dirty Handover Blues/Tuck Away My Lonesome Blues*; Asa Martin & His Kentucky Hillbillies, *Lonesome, Broke And Weary*; Cliff Carlisle, *Chicken Roost Blues/Tom Cat Blues*; Bill Cox & Cliff Hobbs, *Oozlin' Daddy Blues/Kansas City Blues*; Ramblin' Red Lowery, *Ramblin' Red's Memphis Yodel* No. 1; Anglin Brothers, *Southern Whoopie Song*; Allen Brothers, *Drunk*

And Nutty Blues/Chattanooga Mama; Smiling Bill Carlisle, *String Bean Mama/ Copper Head Mama*; Bill Cox, *Long Chain Charlie Blues/ Georgia Brown Blues*; Al Dexter, *New Jelly Roll Blues*; Rhythm Wreckers, *Never No Mo' Blues*

326 **Mountain Music Bluegrass Style**
Various Artists
Smithsonian/Folkways CD SF 40038
Tex Logan, *Katy Hill*; Don Stover, Bea Lilly, & Chubby Anthony, *Katy Cline*; Earl Taylor & The Stoney Mountain Boys, *Short Life Of Trouble*; Bob Baker & The Pike County Boys, *Philadelphia Lawyer/Little Willie*; Smiley Hobbs, *Leather Britches*; Tex Logan, *Natchez Under The Hill*; Mike Seeger, Eric Weissberg, & Bob Yellin, *Old Joe Clark*; Don Stover, Bea Lilly, & Chubby Anthony, *There Ain't Nobody Gonna Miss Me When I'm Gone*; Earl Taylor & The Stoney Mountain Boys, *Whitehouse Blues/They're At Rest Together/Foggy Mountain Top*; Smiley Hobbs, *Nine Pound Hammer*; Don Stover & Chubby Anthony, *Cricket On The Hearth*; Anthony Seeger & Yellin, *New River Train*; Earl Taylor & The Stoney Mountain Boys, *Fox Chase*; Bob Baker & The Pike County Boys, *Feast Here Tonight/Snow Dove/Drifting Too Far From The Shore*; Jerry Stuart, Smiley Hobbs, Pete Kuykendall, & Tom Gray, *Rockey Run*; Don Stover, Bea Lilly, & Chubby Anthony, *Bile 'Em Cabbage Down*; Earl Taylor & The Stoney Mountain Boys, *All The Good Times Have Past And Gone/Sally Ann*

327 **Pickin' The Blues**
Doc and Merle Watson
Flying Fish FF 70352
Mississippi Heavy Water Blues/Sittin' Here Pickin' The Blues/ Stormy Weather/ Windy And Warm/St. Louis Blues/Jailhouse Blues/Freight Train Blues/Hobo Bill's Last Ride/Carroll County Blues/Blue Ridge Mountain Blues/I'm A Stranger Here/Honey Babe Blues

(iii) The South-west: Western Swing and Country-Western

Jimmie Rodgers has rightly been called the "father of Country Music." He certainly marked the transition from the regional rural string band music of the early 1920s to the smoother, professional, almost nationalized music that steadily evolved into today's familiar Nashville-dominated product. Born in Mississippi in 1897, Jimmie spent his early years working on the M & O Railroad, where numerous contacts with African-American laborers and musicians afforded ample opportunity to acquire a comfortable familiarity with their music. In 1924 tuberculosis forced him to give up that strenuous life, and he turned to music for a livelihood that was very slow in coming. His fame skyrocketed a year after his first recordings in 1927, and he had a brilliant career until his death in 1933. Rodgers was largely responsible for many changes in country music, most important of which in the context of this discussion was his popularization of white blues, in particular his own innovation, the "blue yodel." Two blue yodels—*California Blues*

[*Blue Yodel* No. 4] and *Anniversary Blue Yodel* [No. 7]—are included in **Train Whistle Blues**, a set stressing the railroad-related aspect of his repertoire. Rodgers' long association with Mississippi African-Americans is evident in many of his lyrics, not just the blue yodels. Essentially in blues format are *Let Me Be Your Side Track, Brakeman's Blues, Train Whistle Blues*, and *Memphis Yodel.* Despite their titles, *Travellin' Blues* and *Jimmie's Mean Mamma Blues* are not in the accepted pattern. Also not a blues is one of Rodgers' most influential and best-selling recordings *Waiting For A Train*, a turn-of-the-century hoboing song that was circulating in many versions in the 1920s, but became practically frozen into Rodgers' rendition after he recorded it. A good later example is *Helping Hand* by Fats Domino (**483/4**).

Most of his blues share phrases or verses with African-American equivalents. For example, *Train Whistle Blues* has one couplet in common with *Freight Train Blues* by Clara Smith and that recorded by Trixie Smith (**167**), and another with Maggie Jones' *Box Car Blues. Brakeman's Blues* uses phrases that also appear in Charlie Patton's *Hammer Blues* (**81**), Bo Chatman's *Shake 'Em On Down*, and Ma Rainey's *Southern Blues.* I am not asserting that he learned from these particular recordings (a few, in fact, post-dated his records), but rather that Rodgers felt free to draw upon the collective body of imagery and versification that constituted the African-American blues tradition. However, the borrowing was far from one-way; stanzas from his songs turn up in many blues recordings, and Dave Evans has interviewed a number of Mississippi bluesman who either knew Rodgers or listened to his records. Skip James, for example, sang *Waiting For A Train.* The same is doubtless true in other locales. Needless to say, Rodgers' influence among country musicians has been strong ever since his death: discs cited in this chapter by Bob Wills, Merle Haggard, Doc Watson, and Bill Monroe all include items from the Rodgers catalog.

Rodgers' other musical contributions are secondary in terms of Southern crossovers, but were revolutionary in terms of the history of country music. They include his emphasis on new material, rather than older standards; his use of studio musicians, including Hawaiian-style and jazz artists (Louis Armstrong, Boyd Senter, Mickey Bloom, and possibly Earl Hines); his stress on the vocals as primary and the instruments as secondary; and overall his stylistic eclecticism that brought country music into much closer proximity with more popular styles of the day. In his music, South-eastern and South-western styles entered into a partnership of equals that has remained intact at the core of country music. (In the 1940s, region-specific trade terms such as "hillbilly," "old-time," and "cowboy" were replaced with the more generic—and less offensive—term, "country-western"—now "country.")

In the late 1920s American vernacular music embraced a host of styles. Jazz itself, originally an African-American creation in the deep South, had proliferated numerous offshoots, engulfed the earlier ragtime idiom, and struggled with a color barrier that was enforced much more stringently in public venues than among musicians behind closed doors. A particularly identifiable jazz style was beginning to emerge that become almost the musical icon of the Depression years: big band swing. Rural South-eastern string bands were still a thriving if localized tradition, and Jimmie Rodgers and a host of his imitators were bringing urban and rural styles together in a new successful hybrid. In the Southwest, traditional cowboy musicians rubbed shoulders with German and Bohemian brass bands, *latino mariachi* and *conjunto* bands, and Louisiana Cajun and Creole musicians. Texas and Oklahoma vernacular musicians absorbed elements of all of these styles and created a new amalgam, first to be recorded in the early 1930s. It is now generally dubbed "western swing," though that appellation was first applied in Los Angeles to Spade Cooley's musical aggregation in the 1940s. In the 1930s the music was variously called "hot dance music," "Okie jazz," "western," "hot western," or "hot string band." **Okeh Western Swing** provides a good survey of the music during its halcyon years of 1935 to 1950, with emphasis on the 1930s. Of particular interest are the two opening tracks featuring earlier ensembles that illustrate the musical ties between western swing and its antecedents. Al Bernard was one of the last generation of minstrel musicians, turning to vaudeville and later formats in the 1920s. His rendition of the W. C. Handy favorite *Hesitation Blues* presages the treatment given the same piece by western ensembles in the next few years. More important in the history of country and western music was Southern-born Emmett Miller, whose long years in blackface and minstrel shows are evident in his *Lovesick Blues*, the source of Hank Williams' million-selling hit two decades later. When the CD picks up western swing itself, with the next selection by Roy Newman from 1935, the principal difference is in the emphasis on strings—though by no means to the exclusion of woodwinds or horns. To the inexperienced listener one of the most striking aspects of this style must be the almost uniformly high level of musicianship. True, most of the musicians were self-taught, but many were formally schooled, even classically trained; and clearly, many of the bands were keen students of contemporary blues and jazz records. This level of musical sophistication and discipline was a necessary concomitant of the large bands that Bob Wills, Spade Cooley, Tex Williams, and other fronted—sometimes exceeding a dozen instruments. One of western swing's more erudite practitioners was John "Knocky" Parker, who later earned his PhD in music and has taught at university level; his solos on the Light Crust Doughboys' *Knocky, Knocky* owe much to jazz and boogie piano. Adolf Hofner's previously unissued *Gulf Coast Special* and Spade Cooley's *Three-Way Boogie* similarly skate back and forth between jazz/boogie and western swing with impunity.

Bob Wills himself is justly remembered as the "king of western swing," and he dominates this CD with seven of the 28 selections. Four titles are pop or jazz standards; on the others, he takes composer's credits but, as mentioned, *Oozlin' Daddy Blues* is a scarcely disguised variant of *Brown's Ferry Blues*. Texas-born Wills learned to fiddle from his father, a champion old-time fiddler, but as his band grew in size he buttressed himself with one or two other fiddle players. It could easily take three fiddles not to be drowned out by the sprawling Wills aggregations that sported horns, reeds, drums, piano, and plectrum banjo. It is often suggested that the ponderous size of western swing bands was necessitated by the noisy, rowdy honky-tonks and bars where the musicians tried to make themselves heard. More of Wills' music can be heard on **348**.

Western swing bands, unlike their South-eastern counterparts, rarely included religious music in their repertoire, but the Sons of the Pioneers' *One More River To Cross* is a satisfactory example. The Swift Jewel Cowboys' rendition of Bob Miller's *When I Put On My Long White Robe* verges on parody at one point, almost lapsing into *Turkey In The Straw*.

328 Train Whistle Blues
Jimmie Rodgers
ASV Living Era CD AJA 5042 (UK)
Jimmie's Mean Mamma Blues/The Southern Cannonball/Jimmie The Kid/Travellin' Blues/The Mystery of No. 5/Memphis Yodel/Blue Yodel No. 4/*Hobo Bill's Last Ride/Waiting For A Train/Ben Dewberry's Final Run/My Rough And Rowdy Ways/Blue Yodel* No. 7/*Brakeman's Blues (Yodeling The Blues Away)/Let Me Be Your Side Track/Hobo's Meditation/Train Whistle Blues*

329 OKeh Western Swing
Various Artists
CBS Special Products A 37324
Al Bernard, Accomp. By Goofus Five, *Hesitation Blues*; Emmett Miller & His Georgia Crackers, *Lovesick Blues*; Roy Newman & His Boys, *Sadie Green*; Blue Ridge Playboys, *Give Me My Money*; Range Riders, *Range Riders' Stomp*; W. Lee O'Daniel & His Hillbilly Boys, *There'll Be Some Changes Made*; Crystal Springs Ramblers, *Fort Worth Stomp*; Bob Wills & His Texas Playboys, *Get With It/Who Walks In When I Walk Out/Too Busy/Playboy Stomp/Oozlin' Daddy Blues/Pray For The Lights To Go Out/The Girl I Left Behind Me*; Saddle Tramps, *Hot As I Am*; Sons Of The Pioneers, *One More River To Cross*; Light Crust Doughboys, *Knocky, Knocky*; Hi Neighbor Boys, *Zeke Terney's Stomp*; Hank Penny & His Radio Cowboys, *Chill Tonic*; Swift Jewel Cowboys, *When I Put On My Long White Robe*; Sweet Violet Boys, *I*

Love My Fruit; Ocie Stockard & His Wanderers, *Bass Man Jive*; Hi-Flyers, *Reno Street Blues*; Sons Of The West, *Panhandle Shuffle*; Adolf Hofner & His Orchestra, *Gulf Coast Special*; Slim Harbert & His Boys, *Brown Bottle Blues*; Spade Cooley & His Orchestra, *Three-Way Boogie*; Leon McAuliffe & His Western Swing Band, *Take It Away, Leon*

(iv) Post-war: Rockabilly and Modern Country

"If I could find a white man who had the Negro sound and the Negro feel, I could make a billion dollars." That was Sam Phillips talking—at least, he has been quoted as saying it so often, it must be so. Elvis revolutionized popular music around the world, beginning with his seminal recordings for Phillips' Sun label in 1954–5. This handful of discs has been reissued and repackaged so many times, and pop music has changed so much since the 1950s, that it may be difficult for anyone to recapture the sense of excitement and power that Elvis' hits exuded when they first tumbled out of a tiny one-man recording operation in Memphis, Tennessee. **The Sun Sessions CD** is a particularly valuable package, not only because all the original Sun releases are included but because of Peter Guralnick's notes, which clarify the process by which Presley, Moore, and Black perspired their way to reify the vision that haunted Phillips. The several unissued and alternate takes vividly illustrate the group's gropings toward success. The brochure provides probable sources for all of Elvis' selections, which were split between: blues and R&B (Arthur Gunter's *Baby, Let's Play House*, Wynonie Harris' *Good Rockin' Tonight*, Arthur Crudup's *That's All Right,* Lonnie Johnson's *Tomorrow Night*); country (Bill Monroe's *Blue Moon Of Kentucky*, the Shelton Brothers' *Just Because*); and pop artists. (His *Milkcow Blues Boogie* could have come from Kokomo Arnold's original or one of several covers, including—but not very probably—Bob Wills' *Brain Cloudy Blues*: the latter can be heard on **348**.) Phillips' role is all the more transparent when one realizes that the songs that Presley was prepared to audition were all slow ballads; it took 12 months of false starts and fresh encouragements to tease out of him the style with which he eventually became identified.

Without detracting from Elvis' astonishing success, it must be acknowledged that Phillips' dream of African-American music in Anglo colors was not totally unprecedented: this entire chapter is testimony to the contrary. More specifically, after World War II many country artists turned to blues, R&B, Boogie, and jazz for fresh inspiration. The Delmore Brothers were among the most successful in completely refurbishing their older pure (i.e. Anglo-American) hillbilly sound with echo and electrical amplification that were "trademarks" of Syd Nathan's King studios in Cincinnati a decade before Presley first walked into Phillips' office. In addition, too many other artists were achieving successes in 1954–5 to assert that without Elvis rock 'n' roll would never have happened.

Nevertheless, while crossing the artistic color line was often ventured, any such social navigations were still taboo, leading to the incongruities and contortions that could only bewilder the politically naive. Merle Haggard turned out some excellent country blues songs, but when he wrote and sang about integration in his song *Irma Jackson*, he met with stiff reproach. African-American harmonica player De Ford Bailey was treated like a mascot on the Grand Ole Opry for decades, but other black people were not allowed in the auditorium. Chuck Berry's first view of the Opry was off-stage in the wings because he could not join the audience. Painfully slow but inexorable political change since the mid-1950s has eased social tensions, but country music still remains predominantly the domain of white artists, notwithstanding the much more openly acknowledged debt to African-American music. Charley Pride is still the only major black country music performer, and his music is virtually free of traces of the blues. Conversely, the number of Anglo-American artists performing blues and R&B is quite large—though in many cases one can question their artistic success.

330 **The Sun Sessions CD**
Elvis Presley, Scotty Moore, Bill Black
RCA 6414-2-R
[MASTER TAKES]: *That's All Right/Blue Moon Of Kentucky/Good Rockin' Tonight/I Don't Care If The Sun Don't Shine/Milkcow Blues Boogie/You're A Heartbreaker/Baby, Let's Play House/I'm Left, You're Right, She's Gone/ Mystery Train/I Forgot To Remember To Forget/I Love You Because/Blue Moon/Tomorrow Night/I'll Never Let You Go (Little Darlin')/Just Because/ Trying To Get To You;* [OUT-TAKES]: *Harbor Lights/I Love You Because* (take 2) / *That's All Right/Blue Moon Of Kentucky/I Don't Care If The Sun Don't Shine/I'm Left, You're Right, She's Gone* (take 9) / *I'll Never Let You Go (Little Darlin')/When It Rains It Really Pours;* [ALTERNATE TAKES]: *I Love You Because* (take 3)/*I Love You Because* (take 5) / *I'm Left, You're Right, She's Gone (My Baby's gone)* (take 7)/*I'm Left, You're Right, She's Gone (My Baby's Gone)* (take 12)

Basic Records

(i) Roots of the Black-White Interchange

331 **Blacks, Whites, and Blues**
Various Artists
CBS 52796 (UK)—*LP*
Dallas String Band, *Dallas Rag*; Charlie Poole With The North Carolina Ramblers, *Coon from Tennessee*; Lil McClintock, *Don't Think I'm Santa Claus*;

Frank Hutchison, *K. C. Blues*; Macon Ed & Tampa Joe, *Tickle Britches*; Austin & Lee Allen, *Chettanooga Blues*; Mississippi Sheiks, *Yodeling Fiddling Blues*; "Ramblin' Red" Lowery, *Ramblin' Red's Memphis Yodel* No. 1; Tom Darby & Jimmie Tarlton, *Sweet Sarah Blues*; Too Tight Henry, *Charleston Contest* Part 2; Cliff Carlisle, *Ash Can Blues*; Georgia Browns [Buddy Moss, Fred McMullen, & Curly Weaver], *Decatur Street 81*; Prairie Ramblers, *Jud Rag*; Hokum Boys, *Caught Us Doing It*; Bob Wills & His Texas Playboys, *Brain Cloudy Blues*; Earl Hooker, *Walking The Floor Over You/Steel Guitar Rag*
Tony Russell edited this LP companion to his book of the same title, one of the best surveys available of the topic. Divided between African-American and Anglo-American performers, it concludes with Earl Hooker's renditions of two country standards, one from Ernest Tubb, the other from Bob Wills. The Sheiks' piece owes a considerable debt to Jimmie Rodgers.

332 **The Gospel Tradition: Roots And Branches, Volume 1**
Various Artists
Columbia CK 47333
Keaton Sextette, *Jubilee*; Price Family Sacred Singers, *Ship Of Glory*; Brantly & Williams With Their Versatile Four, *When God Made Me He Didn't Make A Monkey Man*; Brothers Wright & Williams, *I'll Play My Harp In Beulah Land*; Sister Clara Hudman, *Now Is The Needy Time*; Bessie Smith, *Moan, You Moaners*; Blind Willie Johnson, *Church, I'm Fully Saved Today*; Washington Phillips, *What Are They Doing In Heaven Today?*; Wilmoth Houdini, *Happy Land Of Canaan*; Carter Family, *On The Rock Where Moses Stood*; Bob Wills, *No Disappointment In Heaven*; Mitchell's Christian Singers, *Them Bones*; Sons Of The Pioneers, *One More River*; The Blue Chips, *Crying Holy Unto The Lord*; Humbard Family, *What A Wonderful Feeling*; Josh White, *Trouble*; Wright Brothers, *Gospel Train*; The Charioteers, *All God's Chillun Got Shoes*; Sister Myrtle Fields, *Jesus At The Well*; The Landfordaires, *Trouble Of This World*; Jackson Gospel Singers, *Count Your Blessings*; Sister O. M. Terrell, *God's Little Birds*; Chuck Wagon Gang, *I'm Headed For The Promised Land*; Leonard De Paur Infantry Chorus, *In That Great Gettin' Up Mornin'*
A good cross-section of three decades of Anglo- and African-American gospel styles, including some artists not usually associated with sacred music—the calypsonian Houdini, Bessie Smith (the song sounds almost like a parody), the Sons Of The Pioneers and Bob Wills. Some recordings are not easy to identify as black or white.

333 **Primitive Baptist Hymns Of The Blue Ridge**
Various Anglo-American and African-American Baptist Churches of Virginia
University of North Carolina Press (ISBN 0-8078-4083-1)—LP
Hylton Thessalonia Primitive Baptist Church,* Patrick County, *Dunlap* ("Dark was the night and cold the ground"); Danville Primitive Baptist Church, *Dunlap* ("My God the spring of all my joys"); Union Primitive Baptist Church, Floyd County, *Devotion* ("Poor and afflicted, Lord are thine"); Shady Grove Primitive Baptist Church,* Floyd County, *Devotion* ("Twas on that dark, that

*These congregations are African-American.

doleful night"); Elder Bennie & Edrie Clifton, *Pilgrim* ("On Jordan's stormy banks I stand"); Ephesus Primitive Baptist Church,* Henry County, *Jesus Is A Rock*; Old Republican Primitive Baptist Church, Franklin County, *Pisgah* ("I'm not ashamed to own my Lord"); Tatum Macedonia Primitive Baptist Church,* Patrick County, *Pisgah* ("Amazing grace! how sweet the sound"); Old Republican Primitive Baptist Church, Franklin County, *Wayfaring Stranger* ("Come thou long-expected Jesus"); Hylton Thessalonia Primitive Baptist Church,* Patrick County, *I Heard The Voice Of Jesus Say* ("I heard the voice of Jesus say"); Carolina Springs Primitive Baptist Church,* Franklin County, *Condescension* ("Firmly I stand on Zion's hill"); Ephesus Primitive Baptist Church,* Henry County, *Long Sought Home*
Tune titles are followed by the first line of text, a common identifier. Brett Sutton collected these hymns in African-American and Anglo-American churches of Virginia in 1976. Three paired renditions from the two different traditions illustrate similarities and differences.

334 Step By Step: Lesley Riddle Meets The Carter Family: Blues, Country And Sacred Songs
Lesley Riddle
Rounder CD 0299
Little School Girl/Frisco Blues/Broke And Weary Blues/Hilltop Blues/Motherless Children/Titanic/I'm Out On The Ocean A-Sailing/I'm Working On A Building/I Know What It Means To Be Lonesome/Red River Blues/One Kind Favor/If You See My Savior/The Cannon Ball/Step By Step
Riddle (1905–80) accompanied A.P. Carter of the celebrated Carter family on numerous song-collecting trips about 1927–32. African-American, he taught the Carters many songs and guitar techniques, providing one of the most direct examples of black influence among early hillbilly musicians. These recordings were made by Mike Seeger in 1965–78.

335 String Bands 1926–1929: Complete Recorded Works In Chronological Order
Various Artists
Document DOCD 5167 (Au)
Kansas City Blues Strummers, *Broken Bed Blues/String Band Blues*; Old Pal Smoke Shop Four, *Surprised Blues/Black Cat Blues*; Taylor's Kentucky Boys, *Gray Eagle/Forked Deer/Soldier Joy/Maxwell Girl*; Booker Orchestra, *Camp Nelson Blues*; Georgia Yellowhammers [with A & J. Baxter], *G. Rag*; A & J Baxter *Bamalong Blues /K. C. Railroad Blues/The Moore Girl/Georgia Stomp/ Forty Drops/It Tickles Me/Dance The Georgia Poss*; Hayes & Prater, *Somethin' Doin'/Easy Winner/Nothin' Doin'/Prater Blues*; Alabama Shieks, *Travellin' Railroad Man Blues/Sittin' On Top Of The World/New Talkin' 'Bout You/Lawdy Lawdy Blues*
Alongside several interesting examples of African-American string bands

*These congregations are African-American.

(featuring banjos, fiddles, or mandolins), two otherwise white bands have black fiddlers: Taylor's Kentucky Boys with Jim Booker and the Georgia Yellowhammers with Andrew Baxter.

336 **Harp Blowers: Complete Recorded Works In Chronological Order (1925–1936)**
Various Artists
Document DOCD 5164 (Au)
John Henry Howard, *Black Snake/Do Lord Do Remember Me/I've Started For The Kingdom/Gonna Keep My Skillet Good And Greasy*; De Ford Bailey, *Pan-American Blues/Dixie Flyer Blues/Up Country Blues/Evening Prayer Blues/Muscle Shoals Blues/Old Hen Cackle/Alcoholic Blues/Fox Chase/John Henry/Ice Water Blues/Davidson County Blues*; D. H. "Bert" Bilbro, *C. & N. W. Blues/Mohana Blues/Yes, Indeed I Do/We're Gonna Have A Good Time Tonight/Chester Blues*; George Clarke, *Prisoner Blues/Court-House Blues/More Blues (Harmonica Blues)*
Blues harpists have often been able to conceal their racial identity; Howard and Bilbro are probably white, but there is some question. Bailey, the diminutive (in physical stature only) African-American who was a fixture on Grand Ole Opry for many years, was more the beneficiary of Southern paternalism than of early integrationism.

337 **Minstrels and Tunesmiths: The Commercial Roots of Early Country Music**
Various Artists
JEMF LP-109—LP
Don Richardson, *Mississippi Sawyer*; Dan Quinn, *Drill Ye Tarriers, Drill*; Len Spencer & Charles D'Almaine, *Arkansas Traveler*; Uncle Josh, *Ticklish Reuben*; Bentley Ball, *The Dying Cowboy*; Billy Golden & James Marlowe, *Listen To The Mockingbird/She's A Dandy*; Harry McClaskey, *When You And I Were Young, Maggie*; Tuskegee Institute Singers, *I Want To Be Ready*; George P. Watson, *Sleep, Baby, Sleep*; Arthur Collins, *Minstrel*; Harry C. Browne & Peerless Quartette, *Hear Dem Bells*; Kitty Cheatham & Vess L. Ossman, *Scandalize My Name/Satidy Night/Georgia Buck*; Fred Van Eps, *Turkey In The Straw Medley*; May Irwin, *The Bully*; Carroll C. Clark & Vess L. Ossman, *De Little Old Log Cabin In De Lane*; Billy Golden & Joe Heins, *Good And Bad*; Wendell Hall, *It Ain't Gonna Rain No Mo'*
Early students of hillbilly music stressed its traditional Anglo-American folk roots. This LP explores another major source—commercial popular music of 1840–1920.* All selections are "pop" recordings of songs, tunes, and humorous sketches (1902–23) taken into the hillbilly repertoire. One side stresses Anglo-American influences, the other African-American (though the performers are almost all Anglo-American).

*The sequencing on the jacket is incorrect, with one omission and one selection from side A moved to side B.

(ii) The Southern Mountains: Old Timey and Bluegrass

338 **Ragged But Right: Great Country String Bands Of The 1930's**
Various Artists
RCA 8416-2-R
Riley Puckett & Ted Hawkins, *Ragged But Right*; Gid Tanner & His Skillet Lickers, *Ida Red/Soldier's Joy/On Tanner's Farm*; Ted Hawkins & Riley Puckett, *Hawkins' Rag/Tokio Rag*; Prairie Ramblers, *Go Easy Blues/Blue River/ Kentucky Blues/Shady Grove My Darling/Tex's Dance*; Patsy Montana, *Montana Plains*; J. E. Mainer's Mountaineers, *Maple On The Hill/Seven And A Half/Johnson's Old Grey Mule*; Wade Mainer & Zeke Morris, *Short Life And It's Trouble*; Wade Mainer, Zeke Morris, & Steve Ledford, *Riding On That Train 45*; Wade Mainer & Sons Of The Mountaineers, *Mitchell Blues*
Some of the most disparate and commercially successful aggregations are highlighted. The Skillet Lickers exemplify the wild approach of North Georgia, while the Mainers represent North Carolina, where generally a smoother style prevailed, with banjos being plucked rather than frailed. The Prairie Ramblers feature a jazzy technique akin to western swing.

339 **Are You From Dixie?: Great Country Brother Teams Of The 1930's**
Various Artists
RCA 8417-2-R
Allen Brothers, *Jake Walk Blues/Roll Down The Line/A New Salty Dog*; Lone Star Cowboys, *Deep Elm Blues/Crawded Song/Just Because*; Delmore Brothers, *I've Got The Big River Blues/Blow Yo' Whistle, Freight Train/Nashville Blues*; Dixon Brothers, *Weave Room Blues/Intoxicated Rat/Down With The Old Canoe*; Monroe Brothers, *Nine Pound Hammer Is Too Heavy/Roll In My Sweet Baby's Arms/Have A Feast Here Tonight*; Blue Sky Boys, *I'm Just Here To Get My Baby Out Of Jail/Katie Dear/Are You From Dixie?*
A companion to the preceding CD, this features six of the best duets of brothers—a very popular combination during the 1930s. Each but one sported different instruments: Allens, guitar and banjo; Attleseys (Lone Star Cowboys), mandolin and jug or ukulele; Delmores, guitar and tenor guitar; Dixons, guitar and steel guitar; Monroes and Bolicks (Blue Sky Boys), mandolin and guitar.

340 **Something Got A Hold Of Me: A Treasury Of Sacred Music**
Various Artists
RCA 2100-2-R
Carter Family, *I'm Working On A Building/Something Got A Hold Of Me*; Monroe Brothers, *On That Old Gospel Ship/What Would You Give In Exchange*; Bill Monroe & His Blue Grass Boys, *Cryin' Holy Unto My Lord*; Blue Sky Boys, *Only One Step More/Where The Soul Of Man Never Dies*; Bill Carlisle, *The Heavenly Train*; Grady & Hazel Cole, *Tramp On The Street*; Dixon Brothers, *I Didn't Hear Nobody Pray*; Blind Alfred Reed, *Always Lift Him Up And Never Knock Him Down/There'll Be No Distinction There*; Wade Mainer & The Sons Of The Mountaineers, *Mansions In The Sky/Farther Along*; J. E. Mainer's Mountaineers, *Just Over In the Glory Land*; Uncle Dave Macon, *Just One Way To The Pearly Gates*
These recordings include some of the most popular 1930s hillbilly artists released by RCA's budget Bluebird label. *Tramp On The Street* is an

outstanding example of country music social theology that has become a standard. *There'll Be No Distinction There* promises social equality in the hereafter for those less fortunate in the present.

341 **Mountain Blues**
Various Artists
County 511—LP
Sam McGee, *Railroad Blues*; Lowe Stokes & His North Georgians, *Left All Alone Again Blues*; Jimmie Tarlton, *Careless Love*; Leake County Revelers, *Leake County Blues*; Carolina Tar Heels, *Farm Girl Blues*; Dock Boggs, *Down South Blues*; Frank Hutchison, *Cannon Ball Blues*; W. T. Narmour & S. W. Smith, *Carroll County Blues*; Dick Justice, *Brown Skin Blues*; R. D. Burnett & Leonard Rutherford, *Curley Headed Woman*; Doc Roberts, *Cumberland Blues*; Clarence Green, *Johnson City Blues*
Blues influences are sampled in string-band and guitar adaptations in the hillbilly tradition. The North Georgians, Leake County Revelers, Burnett and Rutherford, and Doc Roberts trio are fiddle-led units, while the Tar Heels is a banjo and harmonica band. The blues elements is subdued, though without African-American borrowings each piece would be quite different.

342 **Mister Charlie's Blues (1926–1938)**
Various Artists
Yazoo L-1024—LP
Wesley Long, *They Are Wild Over Me*; Herschel Brown, *Spanish Rag*; Dick Justice, *Black Dog Blues*; Sam McGee, *Buck Dancer's Choice*; Buster & Jack, *Cross Tie Blues*; Larry Hensley, *Match Box Blues*; South Georgia Highballers, *Blue Grass Twist*; Allen Brothers, *Maybe Next Week Sometime*; Roy Harvey & Leonard Copeland, *Just Pickin'*; Dick Justice, *Cocaine*; Sam McGee, *Franklin Blues*; Buster & Jack, *Pouring Down Blues*; Anglin Brothers, *Southern Whoopee Song*; South Georgia Highballers, *Bibb County Grind*
This album presents some of the most heavily African-American-influenced (and musically exciting) of the hillbilly white blues artists of their day. In consequence, it may offer the most listenable introduction to the genre for pure blues aficionados. The liner notes discuss musical characteristics in terms of African-American and Anglo-American idioms.

343 **Old-Time Songs Recorded From 1925 to 1930**
Charlie Poole and the North Carolina Ramblers
County CO-CD-3501
White House Blues/Sweet Sunny South/Shootin' Creek/He Rambled/The Letter That Never Came/Mountain Reel/You Ain't Talkin' To Me/Sweet Sixteen/Leaving Home/Took My Gal A'Walkin'/Monkey On a String/Ramblin' Blues/Flying Clouds/Falling By The Wayside/Don't Let Your Deal Go Down/Take A Drink On me
This CD is a sampler of one of the most popular string bands of the 1920s, whose uncluttered banjo/fiddle/guitar/vocals provided inspiration for city revival groups decades after they disbanded. *White House Blues* and *Don't Let Your Deal Go Down* were two of their most requested numbers, the latter surely African-American-inspired.

344 **Dock Boggs' Original Records**
Dock Boggs
Folkways [RBF] 654—Cassette
Country Blues/Danville Girl/Down South Blues/False Hearted Lover's Blues/ Hard Luck Blues/Lost Love Blues/New Prisoner's Song/Old Rub Alcohol Blues/ Pretty Polly/Sammie, Where Have you Been So Long?/Sugar Baby/Will Sweethearts Know Each Other There
"Dock" Boggs (1897–1971) created an unforgettably intense combination of vocal and banjo. Though he first learned to frail, he developed a picking style in his youth derived from a black banjoist who him impressed deeply. All twelve of his recordings from 1927–9 are reissued in this collection.

345 **The Train That Carried My Girl From Town**
Frank Hutchison
Rounder 1007—LP
All Night Long/C. And O. Execursion Train/Chevrolet Six/Coney Isle/Hell Bound Train/Hutchison's Rag/Johnny And Jane Part 1/*Johnny And Jane* Part 2/ *K. C. Blues/Last Scene Of The Titanic/Miner's Blues/Old Rachel/Railroad Bill/ Train That Carried The [Sic] Girl From Town/Wild Hogs In The Red Brush/ Worried Blues*
Many of these selections from 1927–9 evoke black tradition: *Railroad Bill* and the less familiar blues ballads *Old Rachel* and *Johnny And Jane*; the blues-structured *Miner's* and *Worried Blues;* and the celebrated *Train That Carried My Girl From Town.* Hutchison (1897–1945) was heavily influenced by a black guitarist in his youth, both in style and repertoire.

346 **Mule Skinner Blues**
Bill Monroe And His Blue Grass Boys
RCA 2494-2-R
Mule Skinner Blues/No Letter In the Mail/Cryin' Holy Unto The Lord/Six White Horses/I Wonder If You Feel The Way I Do/Katy Hill/Tennessee Blues/ Shake My Mother's Hand For Me/Were You There?/Blue Yodel No. 7/*The Coupon Song/Orange Blossom Special/Honky Tonk Swing/In the Pines/Back Up And Push*
This includes all of Monroe's first "bluegrass" recordings of 1940–41—among which were two Jimmie Rodgers songs and several common in African-American tradition (if not originating there). Four songs are religious, and bluegrass still retains a high proportion of sacred material.

347 **Mountain Songs And Instrumentals**
Arthur Smith, Sam and Kirk McGee
Folkways 2379—Cassette
Bile 'Em Cabbage Down/Buck Dancer's Choice/Coming From The Ball/Cumberland Gap/Dusty Miller/Green Valley Waltz/Guitar Waltz/Hell Among The Yearlings/Hollow Poplar/House Of David Blues/Jim Sapp Rag/Kilby Jail/ Knoxville Blues/Needlecase/Polly Ann/Railroad Blues/Rock House Joe/Roll On Buddy/Sally Long/Sixteen On Sunday/Snowdrop/Whoop 'Em Up Cindy
Sam was one of the first hillbilly guitar pickers (as distinguished from accompanists), and very influential following his initial recordings in 1926. Mike Seeger made these sides in 1957. In their sixties, the McGees were still brilliant

instrumentalists. Generally overshadowed by Sam in the 1930s, Kirk reveals himself as a virtuoso of comparable skill on banjo.

(iii) The South-west: Western Swing And Western Country

348 The Bob Wills Anthology
Sony Music WK 75055
Osage Stomp/Spanish Two Step/Maiden's Prayer/Mexicali Rose/Old Fashioned Love/Sittin' On Top Of The World/Steel Guitar Rag/Blue Yodel No. 1/*Silver Bell/That's What I Like 'Bout The South/I'll See You In My Dreams/The Waltz You Saved For Me/Corrine Corrina/Time Changes Everything/Big Beaver/Honey What You Gonna Do?/I Found A Dream/Take Me Back To Tulsa/New San Antonio Rose/I Knew The Moment I Lost You/Twin Guitar Special/Mississippi Delta Blues/Roly Poly/Brain Cloudy Blues*
Wills did not originate the style, nor was he the first exponent, but he is justifiably dubbed "the King of Western Swing", and recorded extensively for three decades. *Steel Guitar Rag* was taken from bluesman Sylvester Weaver (**118**), *Sittin' On Top Of The World* from the Mississippi Sheiks (**61**); and *Brain Cloudy Blues* from Kokomo Arnold (**264**).

349 Under The Double Eagle: Great Western Swing Bands Of The '30s
Milton Brown and his Musical Brownies; Bill Boyd and his Cowboy Ramblers
RCA 2101-2-R
Milton Brown, *Brownie's Stomp/Do the Hula Lou/Joe Turner Blues/Garbage Man Blues/Where You Been So Long, Corrine/Talking About You/Just Sitting On Top Of The World/Get Along Cindy/Loveless Love;* Bill Boyd, *I'm Gonna Hop Off The Train/Ridin' Old Paint And Leadin' Old Ball/Train Song/Under The Double Eagle/Evil In You Children/When The Sun Goes Down Again/The Sweetest Girl/I Can't Tame Wild Women/Get Aboard That Southbound Train*
These recordings of 1934–5 present two of the most popular Texas swing bands of the 1930s. Brown's group was particularly noted for listening to all the new jazz and blues records as they came out (*Corrine* was probably learned from a Cab Calloway record) and working the material into their repertoire.

350 Texas Stomp: Hot 'n' Bluesy, 1934– 1940
Hugh and Karl Farr
Country Routes RFD CD 11 (UK)
Blues In E/Main Street/Buglers Blues/Bluebird Rhythm/Fire Alarm Blues/Milenberg Joys/Cajun Stomp/St. Louis Blues/Kilocycle Stomp/Outlaw Rag/Riddle Rhythm/'Deed I Do/Lazy River/Now Or Never/Swingin' The Bow/Cricket Hop/Dance Of The Dogies/Cactus Swing/Heart To Heart/I Said Goodbye/Comin' Thru The Rye/Memories In Blue/Dark Eyes/Texas Stomp/Farr Away Stomp/The Knock Me Over, Easy Mama, Don't Take All My Spending Money, I'll Buy That New Car For You Blues
The Farr Brothers were regulars in the Sons Of The Pioneers, providing skilled guitar and fiddle back-up. Here they shine in their characteristic instrumental virtuosity that easily evokes thoughts of Django Reinhardt and Stephane Grappelly or of Eddie Lang and Joe Venuti—and compares favourably.

351 **Rockin' Blues**
Jimmie Davis
Bear Family BFX 15125 (Ger)—*LP*
There's Evil In Ye Children, Gather 'Round/Red Nightgown Blues/Davis' Salty Dog/Saturday Night Stroll/Sewing Machine Blues/Easy Rider Blues/1982 Blues/High Behind Blues/Rockin' Blues/Home Town Blues/Tom Cat And Pussy Blues/Organ Grinder Blues/Penitentiary Blues/She Left A'Runnin' Like A Sewing Machine/Lonely Hobo/Arabella Blues
The former governor of Louisiana enjoyed writing and recording blues, many of them risqué. Abandoning the style when he turned to politics, he circumvented charges of hobnobbing with blacks yet his music demonstrates this influence. On several tracks he is joined by African-American blues guitarists Ed Schaffer and Oscar Woods (**152**) and jazz guitarist Eddie "Snoozer" Quinn.

(iv) Post-war: Rockabilly and Modern Country

352 **Delmore Brothers**
Ace CDCH 455 (UK)
Blues Stay Away From Me/Freight Train Boogie/Trouble Ain't Nothin' But The Blues/Boogie Woogie Baby/Rounder's Blues/Mobile Boogie/Used Car Blues/Pan American Boogie/Field Hand Man/Brown's Ferry Blues/Peach Tree Street Boogie/Blues You Never Lose/Steamboat Bill Boogie/Muddy Water/Sand Mountain Blues/Hillbilly Boogie/You Can't Do Wrong And Get By/Kentucky Mountain/Weary Day/Take It To The Captain
The Delmores, star musicians of the 1930s (see also **332**), adapted as well as anyone to the R&B-influenced stylistic changes of the post-war decade. Electrified instruments, heavy echo, and rolling bluesy tempos fitted in well with the rockabilly craze.

353 **Folksongs Of The Hills (Back Home/Songs Of The Coalmines)**
Merle Travis
Bear Family BCD 15636 AH (Ger)
Nine Pound Hammer/That's All/John Bolin/Muskrat/Dark As A Dungeon/John Henry/Sixteen Tons/Possum Up A 'Simmon Tree/I Am A Pilgrim/Over By Number Nine/Barbara Allen/Lost John/Black Gold/The Harlan County Boys/Pay Day Comes Too Slow/The Browder Explosion/Bloody Brethitt County/Here's To The Operator, Boys/The Miner's Wife/The Courtship Of Second Cousin Claude/Miner's Strawberries/Paw Walked Behind Us With A Carbide Lamp/Preacher Lane/Dear Old Halifax
This reissues two significant LPs of the 1940s. Travis listened to, and learned from, many blues artists and recordings. His African-American borrowings are more successful when less overt, as on *John Henry, I Am A Pilgrim, Nine Pound Hammer,* or *Lost John,* than subsequent attempts copied from recordings at the end of his career.

354 **18 Original Sun Greatest Hits**
Jerry Lee Lewis
Rhino R2 70255
Whole Lotta Shakin' Goin' On/Great Balls Of Fire/Breathless/High School

Confidential/What'd I Say/Drinkin' Wine Spo-dee-o-dee/Matchbox/Jambalaya/When The Saints Go Marchin' In/Lewis Boogie/It'll Be Me/All Night Long/Big Blon' Baby/Crazy Arms/Ubangi Stomp/Big Legged Woman/Put Me Down/Wild One

John Ruskin's comment about Beethoven ("sounds like the upsetting of bags of nails, with here and there an also dropped hammer") is better applied to Lewis. Supercharged keyboard antics and vocal gymnastics make him a high point of rockabilly, qualified only by lack of stylistic breadth. Sacred and secular are shamelessly indistinguishable in when *The Saints Go Marchin' In.*

355 **Memphis Rocks: Rockabilly In Memphis, 1954–1968**

Various Artists

Smithsonian Press RD 051

Ray Harris, *Come On Little Mama*; Warren Smith, *Rock 'n' Roll Ruby*; Billy Lee Riley & The Little Green Men, *Red Hot*; Sonny Burgess, *Red Headed Woman*; Charlie Feathers, *Stutterin' Cindy*; Carl Mann, *Mona Lisa*; Malcolm Yelvington, *Rockin' With My Baby*; Carl McVoy, *You Are My Sunshine*; Ray Smith, *Why Why Why?*; Carl Perkins, *Boppin' The Blues/Matchbox*; Charlie Feathers, *Peepin' Eyes*; Johnny Cash & The Tennessee Two, *Get Rhythm/I Walk The Line*; Jerry Lee Lewis & His Pumping Piano, *High School Confidential/Whole Lotta Shakin' Goin' On*; Roy Orbison & The Teen Kings, *Ooby Dooby*; Warren Smith, *Ubangi Stomp*

These recordings provide a good sampling of Sam Phillips' Memphis studio, the birthplace of the rockabilly sound. Cash, Lewis, Perkins, and Orbison are probably the best-remembered artists from this period, though Cash's later career meandered far from these beginnings. Perkins' *Matchbox* provides the bridge between Blind Lemon's original and the Beatles' later re-creation.

356 **Get Hot Or Go Home: Vintage RCA Rockabilly, '56–'59**

Various Artists

Country Music Foundation CMF-014-D

Joe Clay, *Duck Tail/Sixteen Chicks/Doggone It/Goodbye Good-bye/Slipping Out And Sneaking In/Get On The Right Track/You Look That Good To Me/Cracker Jack/Did You Mean Jelly Bean (What You Said Cabbage Head)*; Ric Cartey, *Ooh-Eee/Heart Throb/I Wantcha To Know/Let Me Tell You About Love/Born To Love One Woman/Mellow Down Easy/My Babe*; Homer & Jethro, *Two Tone Shoes*; Pee Wee King, *Catty Town*; David Houston, *Sugar Sweet*; Tommy Blake & The Rhythm Rebels, *Honky Tonk Mind (Woman I Need)/All Night Long*; Martha Carson, *Now Stop*; Janis Martin, *Love Me To Pieces/Two Long Years/All Right Baby*; Dave Rich, *Chicken House*; The Sprouts, *Teen Billy Baby*; Milton Allen, *Don't Bug Me Baby*; Morgan Twins, *Let's Get Goin'*; Jimmy Dell, *Rainbow Doll*; Gordon Terry, *It Ain't Right*; Roy Orbison, *Almost Eighteen*; Hoyt Johnson, *Little Boy Blue*

Despite doubts, RCA Victor purchased the Elvis masters from Sam Phillips at A&R man Steve Sholes' urging, and the cash register proved him right. Promotion of RCA's other rockabilly artists was tentative, however, and many will not be remembered. Houston and King are better known for their recordings of straight country music and Carson for her gospel singing.

357 **Berry Pickin' In The Country**
Jim and Jesse [McReynolds] and the Virginia Boys
Epic LN 24176—LP
Memphis/Johnny B. Goode/Sweet Little Sixteen/Roll Over Beethoven/Reelin' And Rockin'/Maybellene/Bye Bye Johnny/Too Much Monkey Business/Back In The USA/Brown Eyed Handsome Man
This remarkable album of Chuck Berry songs in bluegrass style was cut in 1965, at the conclusion of Berry's most successful decade (**393**). The notion of a top bluegrass band recording covers of a major R&B artist was revolutionary at a time when different musical genres were more carefully separated from one another.

358 **Cajun Music And Zydeco**
Various Artists
Rounder CD 11572
Dennis McGee, *Rosa, Tomorrow Is Not Sunday*; Alphonse "Bois-Sec" Ardoin & Canray Fontenot, *Hack A 'Tit Moreau*; Aldus Roger, *KLFY Waltz*; Clifton Chenier, *Zydeco Sont Pas Salé*; Felix Richard, *La Valse du Grand Chemin*; Boozoo Chavis, *Paper In My Shoe*; Zachary Richard, *Madeleine*; John Delafose & The Eunice Playboys, *La Misère M'a Fait Brailler*; Savoy-Doucet Cajun Band, *Marie*; Preston Frank, *Why Do You Want To Make Me Cry?*; Dewey Balfa, *Quand J'Etais Pauvre*; Zydeco Force, *Zydeco Extravaganza Theme*; Beausoleil, *Peirrot Grouillette et Mamselle Josette*; Buckwheat Zydeco, *Zydeco Boogaloo*; Bruce Daigrepont, *Disco et Fais Do-Do*; Nathan & The Zydeco Cha Chas, *Slow Horses And Fast Women*; Steve Riley & The Mamou Playboys, *Mardi Gras Jig/Scott Playboys Special*
Few non-English vernacular traditions have had an impact on mainstream country and R&B, but the Franco-American music of Louisiana, both Cajun (white) and Zydeco/Creole (black), is a vigorous exception. Companion to a book by Barry Jean Ancelet and Philip Gould, the CD is a good introduction to these genres and their influences on each other.

359 **Best Of Country Blues**
Merle Haggard
Curb CD D2-77368
Workin' Man Blues/Blues Stay Away From Me/Moanin' The Blues/Blues For Dixie/Mississippi Delta Blues/White Man Singin' The Blues/Cotton Patch Blues/T. B. Blues/Gamblin' Polka Dot Blues/Brain Cloudy Blues
Overall, Haggard successfully captures a variety of bluesy moods. *Mississippi Delta* is a Dixieland rendition of the Jimmie Rodgers favorite; *Gamblin' Polka Dot Blues* is from the same source. *White Man Singin' The Blues* made a warm interracial statement at a time when it was not so popular in country music.

360 **Rhythm Country And Blues**
Various Artists
MCA MCAD-10965
Vince Gill & Gladys Knight, *Ain't Nothing Like The Real Thing*; Al Green & Lyle Lovett, *Funny How Time Slips Away*; Aaron Neville & Trisha Yearwood, *I Fall To Pieces*; Little Richard & Tanya Tucker, *Somethin' Else*; Patti Labelle & Travis Tritt, *When Something Is Wrong With My Baby*; Sam Moore &

Conway Twitty, *Rainy Night In Georgia*; Clint Black & Pointer Sisters, *Chain Of Fools*; Natalie Cole & Reba McEntire, *Since I Fell For You*; Chet Atkins & Allen Toussaint, *Southern Nights*; Staple Singers & Marty Stuart, *The Weight*; George Jones & B. B. King, *Patches*

This fitting conclusion to a survey of Southern crossovers is based on a television special, which paired top country and R&B artists in duets that challenged their ability to bring two idioms into euphonious concert. Its success is testament to the continuing influence of R&B singing styles on today's country singers.

PAUL GARON

10 Post-War Chicago and the North

The new Chicago sound of Muddy Waters, Howlin' Wolf, and Elmore James was brash, piercing, and most of all, electric. Not only did amplification enable the singers to be heard at noisy clubs and house parties, but the technology itself was compelling in its modernity. For many singers, the adoption of the new and the modern signaled a rebellion against earlier blues traditions and forms, and against the way of life from which those traditions sprung. This notion of rebellion is evident in Louis Myers' remembrance that the new amplified sound he and Little Walter took on the road vanquished 10- and 12-piece bands that never had a chance against their power. They were not the only band to engage in the demolishing of bigger bands, for Jimmy Rogers and Muddy Waters did it, too.

As much as the new blues reflected the "sounds of the city" and the rhythms of the industrial work site, so did they reflect and exemplify the angry urgency of the times. This was the era of the Brown desegregation decision (1954); the reminiscences of blues artists like Hound Dog Taylor, J.B. Lenoir, Bobo Jenkins, and many others underscore how keenly they were interested in these struggles. Many songs also reflected the economic uncertainties of the time: J.B. Lenoir's bitter *Eisenhower Blues* (1954) is an excellent example, as is the earlier *Stockyard Blues* by Floyd Jones (1947). But tough times are not date-stamped in the blues.

The first incarnation of the "Chicago blues" was an earlier sound produced by artists under the control of powerful A&R man Lester Melrose in the late 1930s and 1940s. Sonny Boy Williamson, Big Joe Williams, Dr Clayton, and many others who met for rehearsals at Tampa Red's house created an urban, swinging, combo sound with bass, drum, piano, and occasional horn backing. While their tendency to record together resulted in a routine face, their swinging, danceable rhythms were exceedingly popular with the growing urbanized audience that purchased blues records.

By the late 1940s, however, such Melrose artists as Big Bill Broonzy often found themselves being replaced by R&B or jump bands at the clubs where they had appeared, while smaller clubs were hiring new and younger blues artists, such as Jimmy Rogers or Snooky Pryor,

Maxwell Street Jimmy plays on Maxwell Street, Chicago (*Mike Rowe/Blues Unlimited*)

whose pay demands were low. Thus, Bluebird and Columbia were terminating their blues artists' contracts at precisely the time that the new independent companies Chess and J.O.B. were signing up Muddy Waters and Eddie Boyd in Chicago, and Staff recorded Baby Boy Warren in Detroit.

Many of the new singers came due North to Chicago from the Mississippi Delta region, and these roots are clearly manifest in the Chicago sound. The number of Chicago blues standards derived from the country blues of Delta heroes like Charley Patton or Robert Johnson alone is suggestive: *Sweet Home Chicago, Rollin' and Tumblin',* and *Smokestack Lightnin'* only scratch the surface. But perhaps the strongest and most pervasive sign of Delta infiltration was the influence of Muddy Waters.

Essential Records

(i) Chessmen

Muddy Waters had listened to Son House and the recordings of Robert Johnson and he learned his lessons well. In 1944, shortly after arriving in Chicago, he began to play electric slide guitar, adding a bubbling, piercing element to an already razor-sharp style; he also absorbed a few modern, non-slide techniques from Blue Smitty. Sunnyland Slim arranged for Muddy to record for the Chess brothers' Aristocrat label, but this foray brought little success.

In early 1948, however, Muddy was called back into the studio, and this time he fell back on his slide-guitar style and his old Library of Congress pieces (**242**). Leonard Chess didn't know what to make of *I Can't Be Satisfied,* but within half a day, the first pressing sold out. Thousands of record buyers would pay to hear Muddy's imposition of an urban tone on essentially rural material, played in a down-home style. The Chicago blues stars of an earlier generation, unlike Muddy, had urbanized their style, their material, and their tone. But it was Muddy's unconventional combination of the lure of the city with the spirit of the Delta that was to make him one of the most influential blues artists ever.

Muddy Waters: The Chess Box, a three-CD set complete with elegant booklet, provides excellent documentation of the evolution of Waters' style, from the 1950 *Rollin' Stone,* a version of *Catfish Blues* that finds Muddy accompanied only by his guitar and Big Crawford's bass, to his first national hit, *Louisiana Blues* and beyond. *Louisiana Blues,* which climbed the *Billboard* R&B charts in early 1951, was a steamy voodoo number calling on down-home forces to come to Chicago for a new kind of ritual; and it was one of Muddy's first records to feature Little Walter. Henceforth the harp, and especially Little Walter's harp, would be a major component of Muddy's sound. It was already a major component of Chicago blues.

She Moves Me is a low-key tune that gave Walter time for a little exploration over Muddy's slide. In *Still A Fool* (1951) Walter switched to guitar, playing in a style that bubbles with distortion as it attempts to evoke the industrial grit tracked into the clubs where Muddy and Walter performed. It was another *Catfish* relative, with repeated trailing phrases; and its famed ending, a *tour de force* with Muddy shouting, "She's all right, she's all right", from one end of the stage to the other, had to be seen to be believed.

Hoochie Coochie [I'm Your Hoochie Coochie Man] was one of Muddy's biggest hits ever, selling 4,000 copies in its first week and immediately entering the charts nation-wide. It has a powerful stop-time beat carried by the whole band, with Walter's harp honking in the low registers on the chorus. Written by Willie Dixon, *Hoochie Coochie* was one of Muddy's most forceful and commanding numbers.

Rock Me is a brilliant integration of Otis Spann's lilting piano accents with a solid, insistent rhythm supplied by Jimmy Rogers on second guitar, a bass, and Francis Clay on drums. Muddy's guitar is secondary to James Cotton's harp on this number, but comparing it with the tenor sax and the Pat Hare lead on the up-tempo *Good News* (cut only six months later) gives a clear picture of the breadth of Waters' repertoire. One of his best-known works, *Got My Mojo Working,* shares a rhythmic similarity with *Rock Me,* and it became a best seller, especially after it was introduced to white audiences at the Newport Folk Festival in 1960. Two years later Muddy made his second tour in the UK and his fame began to spread.

Waters never forgot his roots, and this set contains a number of exciting tributes to singers of earlier decades: Leroy Carr's *Blues Before Sunrise,* Big Bill's *Southbound Train,* and Memphis Minnie's and Kansas Joe's *What's The Matter With The Mill?* all appear here in compelling versions, the last mentioned as *Can't Get No Grindin'. Elevate Me Mama* (alternate take) makes eager use of Spann's piano, Cotton's harp, and Luther Tucker's guitar, and as such is representative of Muddy's sound of the early to mid-1960s. Emblematic of the end of the period surveyed by this sumptious set is *Bird Nest On The Ground,* a modern piece recorded in 1967 with two guitars, piano, and organ that nonetheless reaches all the way back to Charley Patton and 1930 for its source (**81**). But that was Muddy!

More diversity was added to Chicago blues when Little Walter began recording under his own name for Chess in 1952. John Lee "Sonny

Boy" Williamson may have established the harmonica's strategic importance, but Little Walter extended its dominance until the playing of the harp became synonymous with the sound of the Chicago blues. He saw the harp as a capable but crude horn substitute, giving it a quality of earthiness and grit. It was characteristic of the great blues artists that they would excite the contradictions that seemed to constrain them, and Walter's expansive harp style, when combined with the Aces' backing, produced a sound both sophisticated and raw.

Walter left the South in 1947 and was drawn to Chicago's Maxwell Street area, playing with Johnny Young, Othum Brown, and others. He had carefully absorbed the music of both Rice Miller and John Lee Williamson, having heard the former in the South and the latter on record. But he had also listened carefully to Louis Jordan's jump band, especially Jordan's alto solos. For Walter, hearing something once was usually enough; he'd be playing it in a few minutes and saying he wrote it in a few more. Like Muddy Waters, his effect on the Chicago blues was beyond measure.

Muddy had recorded his band's on-stage theme song at a session in 1952, and while they were on the road, it was released under Walter's name as *Juke*. It was a light but lively tune that well displayed Walter's agility. He was relying less on the chordal style of Sonny Boy Williamson and the influence of horn conceptions was evident. It was this tune that catapulted Walter into the limelight. He was so excited to hear it that he abandoned the band on the road and hurried back to Chicago to start his own band. He joined with the Aces while that group's harp player, Junior Wells, took Walter's place with Muddy.

The Essential Little Walter is as good as its title, and we see in this two-CD set the full range of Walter's talent. *Mean Old World,* like many songs on this collection, was a nation-wide hit. His voice was limited in range and was neither subtle nor supple, yet was nonetheless successful for its expressiveness in tone. On this simple blues Walter's harp and Louis Myers' guitar perform simultaneous treble fill-ins. On other tunes like *Sad Hours,* Louis would carry part of the melody, sometimes in front, sometimes behind, always seeming to mesh perfectly with the harmonies. Walter was able to wring many distinctive sounds from his instrument, suggesting a lunch whistle, a train stopping, or traveling at great speed.

Off The Wall is a jump tune in which the harp alternates soft and loud passages, and often comes close to defying the separation between raucous and strident. *Tell Me Baby* is another up-tempo tune, and this vivacity gave Walter his greatest hit ever, *My Babe*. Willie Dixon had written a simple number inspired by the gospel standard *This Train,* and he'd brought home another winner. It has a spirited boogie bass over which Walter could stretch out without ever abandoning the implicit langor of his vocal.

Blues With A Feeling is one of Walter's best performances. His harp seems to summon new elements to the blues; the song has a shouted climax and an unusually expressive ending, albeit aggressively spat out. In *Last Night,* on the other hand, he retains the slow and melancholy mood of the song even while his harp attains a certain ferocity. Nonetheless, the rhythmic lightness of the piece was a dimension that the blues of Muddy Waters and Howlin' Wolf would never have.

While Walter's later repertoire lacked the intensity of some of his earlier pieces, he did not lose his touch. Indeed, his *Key To The Highway,* sensitively supported by Spann, Luther Tucker, and Muddy, and *Worried Life [Blues]* were both traditional pieces that Walter helped recover from history.

The presence of Walter and Muddy Waters alone would be enough to give Chess Records control of the Chicago blues scene, but in the early 1950s they added another star to their roster, Howlin' Wolf.

Howlin' Wolf was born in 1910 and grew up in the Delta region where the legendary Charley Patton played a crucial role in his musical development. He traveled with Robert Johnson and with Rice Miller from whom he learned harp. He moved to Memphis in 1948 where he organized a crackling electric band featuring Willie Johnson on guitar and "Destruction" on piano (**410**). The band's sound was more modern than Muddy's, but Wolf's own singing and harp work were more primitive. In 1952 he moved to Chicago, where he was already well known, and the rough sound and ragged edges of his band began to disappear. Despite this new location however, his market was concentrated more in the South than either Little Walter's or Muddy's.

Howlin' Wolf: The Chess Box, a three-CD set with a handsome booklet, documents his recording career from his first session in 1951, *Moanin' At Midnight* and *How Many More Years,* to the 1973 recording of *Moving*. Wolf's genius and talent are apparent even on his first recording date. Cut in Memphis (as all his songs were for the next two or three years), his early pieces demonstrate an important element in the formation of his sound. Unlike Muddy Waters, whose Delta slide style continued to develop in Chicago after his move there in 1947, Wolf allowed his music to mature in Memphis for a number of years before moving north. Thus of the four most dynamic instigators of the new electric sound, Muddy and Walter forged their new styles *in* Chicago, Elmore James in the area of Jackson, Mississippi, and Wolf in Memphis, Tennessee. This demography accounts for many of the differences in their styles.

The songs that Wolf recorded in Memphis for Sam Phillips of Sun Records is one part of a Memphis tale, but Phillips' role in leasing recordings of Southern artists to companies like Chess is an important episode in the history of the post-war era.

From the first eerie howl to the perfectly timed entrance of the distortion-bent guitar, the band playing with a fierce insistence that almost overwhelms the listener, *Moanin' At Midnight* is the perfect introduction to the Howlin' Wolf phenomenon. In contrast with this intensity, *How Many More Years* starts with a soothing Ike Turner piano introduction, but we soon hear Wolf's vibrato echoing from deep within, finally issuing forth as a vicious nasal twang. *All Night Boogie* has Wolf's harp gasping and panting.

No Place to Go (1954) was Wolf's first hit. It is as dark and brooding as his next hit that year, *Evil,* in which he alternates throaty verses and nasal choruses to achieve a chilling effect and Otis Spann adds a considered piano solo. *Forty-Four,* recorded in 1954, is the famous virtuoso piano piece, and Wolf's version is perhaps the most sinister on record. The song appears in only a few post-war Chicago repertoires, and here it is used mainly as a vehicle for Hubert Sumlin, an accomplished guitarist who had joined Wolf earlier that year. Sumlin's unusual highlighting became more and more conspicuous as his career with Wolf lengthened, perhaps peaking with the shared-solo masterpieces with Buddy Guy like *Killing Floor* (1964) and *I Walked From Dallas.*

I Asked for Water (She Gave Me Gasoline) is Wolf's rendering of Tommy Johnson's *Cool Drink Of Water Blues* (**83**). Johnson was an archetypal developer of the falsetto break and he was a powerful influence on Wolf, who, however, had little room and no mercy for the fragility of Johnson's guitar and voice. *Smokestack Lightnin'* (1956) is another Delta classic and one of Wolf's best-known pieces. It was inspired by Charley Patton's *Moon Going Down* (**81**), but it becomes an intensely personal statement for Wolf. Indeed, Wolf was always the pyrotechnician, and with his nerve, his guts, and his music, he was one of the few Chicago stalwarts to challenge Muddy Waters' crown.

Rice Miller, the second Sonny Boy Williamson, was another Chess notable. He spent much of his time in the South, playing with Robert Johnson, Robert Nighthawk, Elmore James (**406**), and many others. The role he played in blues radio, as well as in introducing the amplified harp to the post-war blues scene, was a pioneering one, notwithstanding Little Walter's claim to this distinction. Rice began recording for Chess's Checker label in Chicago after moving to Milwaukee in 1955. By the late 1950s, he was playing in Detroit, but he grew discouraged with that city's blues scene when harps seemed to be going out of fashion. With his services less in demand, he returned to the South where he could easily raise money playing on the corner.

It has been said that Rice did not have the technical virtuosity of Little Walter, but the two-CD set **The Essential Sonny Boy Williamson** reveals that this was not necessarily so. Certainly what Little Walter achieved with energetic adroitness, Sonny Boy sought with more subtlety and a genius of his own, although he did not seem to have Walter's reach or breadth. His tone harkened back to Memphis and Noah Lewis instead of forward to the harsh new inflections of industrial modernism. Big Walter (Shakey) Horton, another Memphis harpist, also demonstrated a bit of this seasoned and mellow tone.

Rice's interesting repertoire saw him through the lean years and he continued to record for Chess until shortly before his death in 1965. His Chess career began in the mid-1950s, just as rock 'n' roll was beginning to cast a cold shadow over the careers of other Chicago blues veterans. But in these years, Rice was hitting his stride. *Don't Start Me ToTalkin'* dates from his first Checker session in 1955. In his lyrical, quivering voice, he seems to demand that the listener discover the nature of "signifying" in the very depths of his song. This same notion is faintly echoed in *All My Love In Vain*, where Rice complains, "You whip her when she need it and the judge won't let you explain". For most of his sessions, Sonny Boy would be accompanied by the Chicago "standard" band: piano, two guitars, bass, drum, and, of course, a harp.

Keep It To Yourself relies on a medium tempo characteristic of many of his pieces, but here Rice takes an almost Walter-like solo, keeping extra busy and hitting more single notes than usual. In *The Key (To Your Door)*, Miller's long-time friend and lead guitarist Robert Jr Lockwood supplies an uncommon chorded rhythm over which Sonny Boy imposes some light, simple harp thrusts, but he does stretch out in a solo where he is really able to test the reeds. The tune's eccentric rhythm predominates, however, and the song remains infused with an oddly mysterious feel. Rice's lyrics are more intricate and gratifying than those of many of his colleagues, and in *Fattening Frogs For Snakes* he cleverly builds a folk expression into a fully developed song. In *Ninety Nine*, the air of intrigue that Rice so often brings to his pieces is dominant.

I Don't Know is a modest and palatable number in spite of the absence of a piano that prevailed for a few sessions in 1956–7. In *Cross My Heart*, especially, Lockwood's comfort and experience in playing with Sonny Boy is palpable, as he picks mellow chords over

Otis Spann's rapid treble explorations, all just slightly below the surface of Rice's vocal. *Your Funeral And My Trial* displays his tight combo sound at its best, this time with Lafayette Leake's inventive piano background, both lilting and frolicsome, over an up-beat tempo engineered by Lockwood and the full rhythm section. Leake was a regular on the Rice Miller sessions and many later pieces like *Down Child* are enlivened by his presence. There is a comic aspect that pervades many of Rice's songs, and we may enrich our appreciation of his music if we are consistently alive to this possibility. Thanks to the presence of *Little Village,* we are not likely to forget it.

361 **Muddy Waters : The Chess Box**
MCA Chess CHD3 80002—3 CD set
DISC ONE: *Gypsy Woman/Good Looking Woman/Mean Disposition/I Can't Be Satisfied/I Feel Like Going Home/Train Fare Home Blues/Mean Red Spider/ Streamline Woman/Little Geneva/Rollin' And Tumblin'* Part 1/*Rollin' Stone/ Walkin' Blues/Louisiana Blues/Evans Shuffle/Long Distance Call/Honey Bee/She Moves Me/Still A Fool/Stuff You Gotta Watch/Standing Around Crying/Flood/ Baby Please Don't Go/Blow Wind Blow/Hoochie Coochie/[I'm your Hoochie Coochie Man]*

DISC TWO: *I Just Want To Make Love To You/I'm Ready/Smokestack Lightnin'/ Young Fashioned Ways/Mannish Boy/Trouble No More/Forty Days And Forty Nights/Just To Be With You/Don't Go No Further/Diamonds At Your Feet/I Love The Life I Live, I Live The Life I Love/Rock Me/Look What You Done/ Got My Mojo Working/Good News/Evil/She's Nineteen Years Old/Close To You/Walkin' Thru The Park/Blues Before Sunrise/Lonesome Road Blues/Take The Bitter With The Sweet* (alternate take)/*She's Into Something/Southbound Train/Double Trouble*

DISC THREE: *I Feel So Good/ You Shook Me/You Need Love/Twenty Four Hours/Elevate Me Mama* (alternate take)/*So Glad I'm Living/My Love Strikes Like Lightning/You Don't Have To Go* (alternate take)/*Things That I Used To Do/My Home Is In The Delta/Good Morning Little School Girl/The Same Thing/You Can't Lose What You Never Had/Short Dress Woman/Making Friends/Black Night/Bird Nest On The Ground/Country Boy/Sugar Sweet* (alternate take)/*All Aboard* (alternate take)/ *Going Down Slow/Who's Gonna Be Your Sweet Man When I'm Gone/Can't Get No Grindin'*

362 **The Essential Little Walter**
MCA Chess CHD2 9342—2 CD set
DISC ONE: *Juke/I Can't Hold Out Much Longer/Boogie/Blue Midnight* (alternate take)/*Mean Old World/Sad Hours/Don't Need No Horse/Tell Me Mama/Off The Wall/Quarter To Twelve/Blues With A Feeling/Too Late/Fast Boogie/Lights Out/Fast Large One/You're So Fine/Oh Baby/I Got To Find My Baby/Last Night* (first version)/ *You Better Watch Yourself/Mellow Down Easy/My Babe/ Roller Coaster/Little Girl*

DISC TWO: *I Hate To See You Go/Boom, Boom Out Goes The Light/It Ain't Right/It's Too Late Brother/Just A Feeling/Ah'w Baby/I've Had My Fun* (alternate take)/*Confessin' The Blues/Key To The Highway/Walkin' On/You Gonna Be Sorry (Someday Baby)* (alternate take)/*Crazy Mixed Up World/ Worried Life [Blues]/Everything's Gonna Be Alright/Back Track/Blue And Lonesome/I Don't Play/As Long As I Have You/ Just Your Fool/Up The Line/ Southern Feeling/Dead Presidents*

363 **Howlin' Wolf: The Chess Box**
MCA Chess CHD3 9332—3 CD set
DISC ONE: *Moanin' At Midnight/How Many More Years/Howlin' Wolf Boogie/ The Wolf Is At Your Door/Mr. Highway Man/Howlin' Wolf Talks* No. 1/ *Bluebird/Saddle My Pony/(Well) That's All Right/My Last Affair/Just My Kind/Work For Your Money/Mama Died And Left Me/All Night Boogie [All Night Long]/Streamline Woman/Crazy About You Baby/You Gonna Wreck My Life [No Place To Go]* (alternate take)/*Neighbors/Howlin' Wolf Talks* No. 2 / *I'm The Wolf/Rockin' Daddy/Baby How Long/Evil/I'll Be Around /Forty-Four/ Who Will Be Next/Don't Mess With My Baby*

DISC TWO: *Smokestack Lightnin'/You Can't Be Beat/Howlin' Wolf Talks* No. 3/*I Asked For Water/The Natchez Burnin'/Who's Been Talking/Tell Me/Sittin' On Top Of The World/I Didn't Know/Moaning For My Baby/Change My Way/I Better Go Now/Howlin' For My Darling/I've Been Abused/Mr. Airplane Man* (alternate take)/*Wang Dang Doodle/Back Door Man/Howlin' Wolf Talks* No. 4/ *Spoonful/Down In The Bottom/ Shake For Me/The Red Rooster/You'll Be Mine/ Just Like I Treat You/I Ain't Superstitious/Goin' Down Slow/Tail Dragger*

DISC THREE: *Hidden Charms/Three Hundred Pounds Of Joy/Built For Comfort/ Love Me Darlin'/Killing Floor/My Country Sugar Mama/Louise/I Walked From Dallas/Tell Me What I've Done/Don't Laugh At Me/Ooh Baby (Hold Me)/New Crawlin' King Snake/My Mind Is Ramblin'/Commit A Crime/Dust My Broom/ I'm The Wolf* (acoustic)/*Ain't Goin' Down That Dirt Road/Mary Sue/Hard Luck/The Red Rooster* (later version)/*Moving*

364 **The Essential Sonny Boy Williamson**
MCA Chess CHD2 9343—2 CD set
DISC ONE: *Good Evening Everybody/Don't Start Me To Talkin'/All My Love In Vain/You Killing Me/Let Me Explain/Your Imagination/Don't Lose Your Eye/ Keep It To Yourself/The Key (To Your Door)/Have You Ever Been In Love/ Fattening Frogs For Snakes/I Don't Know/Like Wolf/Cross My Heart/Ninety Nine/Born Blind/Little Village/Unseen Eye/Your Funeral And My Trial/Keep Your Hands Out Of My Pocket/Unseeing Eye/Let Your Conscience Be Your Guide/The Goat*

DISC TWO: *Cool Disposition/Santa Claus/Checkin' Up On My Baby/Temperature 110/Lonesome Cabin/Somebody Help Me/Down Child/Trust My Baby/Too Close Together/Too Young To Die/She's My Baby/Stop Right Now/Too Old To Think/ One Way Out/Nine Below Zero/Help Me/Bye Bye Bird/Bring It On Home/ Decoration Day/Trying To Get Back On My Feet/Close To Me/I Can't Be Alone*

(ii) A Wide Range of Feeling

One of the most important post-war stylists, Elmore James was associated with Rice Miller and Robert Johnson, and his experiences with them in the 1930s and 1940s in the Delta were formative and critical. It was, of course, from Robert Johnson that he learned the guitar riff for his famous versions of *Dust My Broom*, his first record (1952) and his first hit (**406**), but it was Kokomo Arnold who first sang "I believe I'll dust my broom", in *Sagefield Woman Blues*, cut in 1934, several years before Johnson recorded.

James represents an important synthesis of the Delta traditions and the modern electric sound. That James brought his heady mixture to a boil while still in the South is worth re-emphasizing: in the mid- to late 1940s Elmore was leading an electrified, six-piece blues band while Muddy was yet to make his first commercial record. As one authority noted, Muddy updated the blues for his early audience, but Elmore modernized them for all time. James sang and played with a remarkable emotional intensity, and his bands had amazing drive.

Like most of his cohorts, Elmore broadcast on Southern radio, but he preferred juke joints and club appearances to broadcasting, and he was so hesitant to sign a recording contract that he had to be tricked into making his first record for Trumpet, a small company in Jackson, Mississippi. For many years he lived and worked in the South, also returning there while based in Chicago.

Arthur "Big Boy" Crudup was responsible for putting Bobby Robinson of Fire Records in touch with Elmore, and it was with Fire that some of his most exciting recordings were made. All of these are collected on **King Of The Slide Guitar,** a four-disc set from Charly. Included are Elmore's recordings for Chief as well as his Checker/ Chess material; the Chess session of April 1960 may be Elmore at his best, thanks not only to the excellent arrangements but to the presence of J.T. Brown on sax, Elmore's cousin Homesick James on second guitar, and Johnny Jones on piano.

The Sun Is Shining, while less well known than *The Sky Is Crying*, features the same personnel. Elmore here uses his voice as a separate instrument, drawing words out into extra syllabic moans, as he does in *I Can't Hold Out* (originally released by Chess coupled with *The Sun Is Shining*), an up-tempo number also featuring segments of the *Dust My Broom* riff. J.T. Brown's backgrounding makes Elmore's version of T-Bone Walker's *Stormy Monday Blues* unusually appealing, but it is on *Madison Blues*, an infectious dance number, that Brown really shines: his two solos are alluring and lovely in tone, and in the second he has a compelling exchange with the guitars.

The Twelve Year Old Boy, *Coming Home*, *Knocking At Your Door*, *Elmore's Contribution To Jazz*, *Held My Baby Last Night*, and *Dust My Broom* were also recorded in Chicago; the last two of these, also featuring J.T. Brown on tenor, Johnny Jones on piano, and Homesick James on bass or second guitar, are especially well articulated. *The Twelve Year Old Boy* (a later version appears here, too) is a humorous tale of being cuckolded by a twelve-year-old, while *Coming Home* features a very brash *Dust My Broom* riff, achieved by Elmore and two other guitars playing simultaneously through the same amplifier. *Held My Baby Last Night* (1959) has a lovely J.T. Brown background over which James alternates husky imperatives with understatement—for Elmore, an unusual figure.

Dust My Broom (track 18 on the first disc) is a far fuller and richer rendition than his earlier hit, thanks in large part to the horn section, but Elmore's vocal is commanding and authoritative. The song also reappears as *My Baby's Gone*, and *I Believe My Time Ain't Long* (the original version, from Elmore's first session in 1951).

The New York sessions that combined sophisticated jazz accompaniments with James' roughly hewn and dramatic delivery have done much to codify how modern the down-home blues can be. *Elmore's Contribution To Jazz* is a frantic instrumental cha-cha-cha. Johnny Jones seems to pound the keyboard to pieces, while Elmore's guitar sounds equally maniacal. *Done Somebody Wrong* is one of Elmore's masterpieces, a powerful stop-time tune with slashing vocal and pile-driving guitar. James' ability to communicate such intense emotion with his abrasive groans and cries is one of his hallmarks. *Fine Little Mama* is a rocking presentation of the *Dust My Broom* melody, with more power if a bit less subtlety; Elmore's vocal is fiercer, while the tune is fast and infectious.

The *Dust My Broom* riff is (again) superimposed over the lush, heavy horn rhythms of *Early One Morning*, but listen closely: the rhythmic saxes are playing the melody of another Fire hit, Buster Brown's *Fannie Mae*. *Look On Yonder Wall*, recorded in New Orleans, has an earthy and down-home feel largely attributable to Sammy Myers' harp; combined with the icy insinuations of James' vocal, however, this version of "Big Boy" Crudup's song is among Elmore's best achievements.

For his first session for Fire in 1961, Elmore recorded the blues standard *Stranger Blues* in an unusual rhythm and a remarkable performance of *Anna Lee*, derived in part from Robert Nighthawk but with greater vocal intensity. Further, the unusual horn and reed work by Danny Moore and two unidentified musicians make this an incomparable performance, even if judged by its last verse alone.

This session can also teach us something about Southern sources.

While many listeners believe that slide techniques originated in Mississippi, it is often forgotten that Tampa Red, of Florida, was one of the foremost innovators and the main source of inspiration for the slide guitar of Robert Nighthawk. In the session under discussion we not only hear examples of Tampa Red's bottleneck style, but one of his and Georgia Tom's songs as well, *Stranger Blues* (in this instance without slide guitar).

James' mastery is amply demonstrated in *My Bleeding Heart*, a slow blues with complex, improvisatory trumpet and sax filling in between the lines—but from a great distance, while James pleads a case of intense melancholy. The interplay between voice and guitar as a means of articulating pain is almost uncanny, and one could be forgiven for claiming that the blues exist so that songs like this one may be played and heard.

Elmore had always suffered from ill-health. When he left the Navy in 1945, he knew he had a heart problem, and this condition, together with a natural shyness or cautiousness, kept him returning to the South. He played for years in the area around Canton, Mississippi, before ever going to Chicago and New York to record, but inevitably he returned to the Canton area and old friends like Sonny Boy Williamson (Rice Miller). In May 1963, Elmore James had his third heart attack, and he died at Homesick James' house on Wieland Avenue on Chicago's near north side.

Jimmy Reed also came from Mississippi and, like many of the above musicians, made his way North in the early 1940s. He played in the clubs with his childhood friend Eddie Taylor, as well as Floyd Jones, Snooky Pryor, and John and Grace Brim, all of whom would help to found the Chicago blues in just a few years. The simplicity of Reed's style, which owed a large measure of its success to Eddie Taylor, belied the fact that it was not widely imitated, although a few singers have had varied success emulating him. Otis "Big Smokey" Smothers, Frank Frost, and Louisiana Red, all played more or less like Reed; but the inability of most performers to capture his distinctive qualities should not obscure the fact that in more subtle ways, he was one of the most influential blues singers of all time.

Reed was also the most commercially successful blues singer, and easily the most popular of the Delta bluesmen, appealing to large masses of white record buyers at a time when Howlin' Wolf or Muddy Waters appealed to only a few, and B.B. King to only a few more. Reed had 11 records in the *Billboard* Hot 100 pop charts between 1956 and 1961, less than Chuck Berry but more than Bo Diddley; and 14 Reed hits made the R&B chart. Most of these are collected on **"Speak The Lyrics To Me, Mama Reed"**

Reed's sustained and sweet harp tones glided smoothly over the softly muffled bass, and his occasional treble forays on guitar did nothing to dispel the aura of supreme comfort. Reinforcing this langorous atmosphere was Reed's lazy and slurred vocal style, which paradoxically engendered a feverish energy in his dancing listeners.

Reed and Taylor played for years in the Chicago taverns as well as in Gary clubs like the Pulaski Bar. When Chess rejected their first recording attempts in 1953, they went over to Vee Jay. Reed's first discs were unsuccessful, but his third record, *You Don't Have To Go*, was a hit. Coarser and more industrial than his later hits would be, it reflected his years of playing in rough joints and bars. Mary Lee ("Mama") Reed wrote many of Jimmy's songs, softly whispered the lyrics to him (hence the title of this CD), and could occasionally be heard on his records. Sometimes they were able to write a song, work it up in the studio, and record it on the spot, and *You Don't Have To Go* was one of these. The guitar introduction even hints at things to come from Bo Diddley and Billy Boy Arnold.

In *You Got Me Dizzy*, Reed still sported the rough voice and sound that was popular in the clubs, but by 1957 he was recording more songs like *Honest I Do*, a supple and mellow tune whose lushness was broken only by an occasional, carefully timed cymbal crash from Earl Phillips. Reed was developing a more polished and accessible sound, as is evident on *Baby What You Want Me To Do*, recorded in 1959, a huge crossover hit that paved the way for future successes like *Big Boss Man*. The special popularity of the former is probably derived from the fact that by this time Vee Jay was using three guitars and a bass on his records; it was the first Reed song to catch the imagination of a wider range of listeners, specifically young whites, and this new coterie would account for a larger and larger proportion of Reed's success in the future. Songs like *Hush Hush*, *Found Love* and *Big Boss Man* all featured three guitars and sold well in the white market. The latter tune was co-written by Chess producer Willie Dixon, who makes a rare Vee Jay appearance as bassist on *Big Boss Man*, giving the song a special bounce. Like John Lee Hooker, Reed was an original, and he has had no true successors.

The next two selections, **Blues Is Killing Me** and **The Cobra Records Story,** exemplify the various styles of the post-war Chicago sound, with Floyd Jones and Baby Face Leroy Foster representing the more industrial and gritty small combos that recorded for J.O.B., while Otis Rush, Magic Sam, and Buddy Guy represent the polished stylists that recorded for the West Side labels like Cobra and Artistic.

It is no accident that Sunnyland Slim covers the full spectrum of these styles. It was Sunnyland who arranged for Muddy to accompany him on his Aristocrat sessions. Muddy also played with Slim in his early Chicago days, as did Jimmy Rogers, Walter, and others. Indeed, Sunnyland probably played with every Chicago blues musician at one time or another. As he was house pianist for J.O.B., he can be heard here accompanying Baby Face Leroy and Floyd Jones.

Baby Face was a popular performer who, in his early days, regularly performed with Muddy, Walter, and Jimmy Rogers (he died young on account of chronic drinking problems). Songs like *Pet Rabbit* and *Louella* have achieved cult status among post-war blues fans, both for their heavily amplified guitar sound and the Sonny Boy Williamson-influenced vocals with their drawn-out inflections.

Floyd Jones' *Dark Road* shows the influence of Tommy Johnson but has a darker mood that is characteristic of all his records. He was ultimately one of the most significant post-war songwriters and performers, and images of the road—*Dark Road, On The Road Again*—and tough times accurately reflect the nature of his life and work.

Floyd also heard Charley Patton, as well as the diverse artists on the records his family purchased from the drug store, but his mother's musical talent was his greatest inspiration. He began performing at the height of the Depression, and always had to supplement the income from his musical career with other jobs, ranging from the Civilian Conservation Corps to the stockyards for Swift. He characterizes his own early style as "fast" or "jumping", as on *Skinny Mama*, but the predominant mood of his 78rpm releases is somber, brooding and slow as can be heard on the murderous *I Lost A Good Woman*.

Floyd played on Maxwell Street, near home, but he also worked the Madison Street clubs, sometimes with the crew in Moody Jones' band or with Sunnyland Slim or Little Walter. Eventually, Floyd teamed with Snooky and Moody while Muddy teamed with Jimmy Rogers and Little Walter. Some may argue over whether Muddy or Floyd "originated" the Chicago blues; it is more likely that they simultaneously developed their own separate strands of the post-war sound.

Memphis Minnie's career spanned a quarter of a century, beginning with virtuoso acoustic guitar duets at the advent of the Depression (**165**) and ending with her session for J.O.B. in 1953. In that session she was assisted by Little Brother Montgomery on piano, turning in an especially evocative performance of *World Of Trouble* and a humorous version of the old Memphis Jug Band favorite, *Fishing In the Dark* (here reworked into *Kissing In The Dark*). These sides marked the successful end of one of the most remarkable blues careers on record. Her husband, Little Son Joe, accompanies her on these sides and sings lead on two others, also present here.

Little Hudson (Hudson Showers) gave one of his most interesting performances on *Things Going So Tough With Me*, sung to the *44 Blues* melody. Based on Big Maceo's *Tuff Luck Blues* (**208**), the lyrics were used eight years later (without the *44 Blues* motif) in Freddy King's *It's Too Bad* (*Things Are Going So Tough*) (**311**). Despite his distinct vocal nuances and the piano work of Lazy Bill Lucas (rather than Sunnyland Slim). Little Hudson's pieces seem to wear the J.O.B. brand. In fact, J.O.B. itself has come to typify a certain aspect of the post-war, Northern sound: rougher edged than Muddy (either in his early solo days or with his modern combo) such artists as Floyd Jones and Baby Face were always available to show what Chicago blues sounded like beforehand.

Otis Rush is a stylistic innovator whose influence is widespread, and his Cobra recordings, collected on **The Cobra Records Story,** are often stunning. Born in Mississippi in 1934, Rush went to Chicago in 1949 and quickly began playing in clubs. Hearing T-Bone Walker and B.B. King, Rush was impressed by the distance between their styles and that of Muddy Waters and his colleagues, and he began to tailor his own style to the cleaner sound evident on this two-CD set. Thus, the "West Side sound" went beyond the Chicago blues to draw its chief inspiration from other urban performers. Further, the "heavy chords" and other distinguishing traits of this style were derived from artists like Rush adapting the role of the guitar in larger bands to small bands of their own and also reconceiving horn parts for guitar.

Rush's first record, *I Can't Quit You Baby*, was a *Billboard* "R&B Best Buy" and it reached number nine on the national R&B charts. His second release, *My Love Will Never Die*, emphasized trembling, extended cries of anguish interspersed with haunting falsetto breaks, and its minor key setting became a Rush trademark, as did the refinement of his guitar technique. *Checking On My Baby* is one of the highspots of Otis' early work, his eerie falsetto weaving in and out of a melancholy half-shouted moan and the sax honking in derision at the song's unfortunate protagonist. Rush's virtuoso phrasing has few rivals. His vocal on *Double Trouble* is stark and textured, polished yet still gritty. *All Your Love* shows Otis in top form: halfway through, he abandons the Latin beat for a medium tempo, straight blues bridge, and this releases a great deal of energy. *My Baby Is A Good 'Un* is a high-spirited rocker with a forceful stop-time rhythm. Otis' two guitar choruses underline his status as a modern master.

Buddy Guy had played professionally in Louisiana before leaving for Chicago. He learned from phonograph records and, especially, from Guitar Slim whose stage act had been influential in getting him to perform standing up instead of sitting down (**497**). In Chicago he was hired by Rufus Foreman to play in his band at the Big Squeeze on the

West Side. Meeting Otis Rush and Magic Sam at the Blue Flame was critical, however, and it was Sam who took him to Eli Toscano at Cobra. One of Guy's first tunes, *You Sure Can't Do*, owed much to Guitar Slim, and *This Is The End* owed much to B.B. King, but these two sides are nonetheless among the most powerful blues of the decade. Wherever his indebtedness lay, it was clear that Guy also brought much originality.

Like Guy, Magic Sam had a magnetic personality and an infectious warmth, as can be heard on *Easy Baby*. In many ways his performances seem derived from Rush's, but during the 1960s he began to define his own territory. Comparing his releases on **The Cobra Records Story** and those on **West Side Guitar** (384) with his later work shows the breadth he established.

The Cobra Records Story is by no means a simple showcase for Rush Guy, and Sam, however. Syl Johnson's powerfully articulated guitar phrasing combined with Shakey Jake's hoarsely shouted vocals make *Call Me If You Need Me* of more than passing interest, and the presence of Little Willie Foster is an added bonus. Alas, Foster's passionate cries and emotive harp were little recorded. The six Ike Turner cuts feature moving vocals by the sophisticated Jackie Brenston and the more colorful Tommy Hodge, thus stretching the connection between Chicago blues and the world of rhythm and blues, while demonstrating the breadth of Cobra's recording ambitions.

365/6 **King Of The Slide Guitar**

Elmore James

Charly CD RED Box 4 (UK)—*4 CD set*

DISC ONE: *I Believe My Time Ain't Long [Dust My Broom]/Country Boogie/I See My Baby/She Just Won't Do Right/My Best Friend/Whose Muddy Shoes/The Twelve Year Old Boy/Coming Home /It Hurts Me Too/Knocking At Your Door/Elmore's Contribution To Jazz/Cry For Me Baby/Take Me Where You Go/ Bobby's Rock/ The Sky Is Crying/ Baby Please Set A Date/Held My Baby Last Night/ Dust My Broom*

DISC TWO: *The Sun Is Shining/I Can't Hold Out/Stormy Monday Blues/Madison Blues/The Sun Is Shining* (alternate take)/ *Strange Angels/Rollin' And Tumblin'/Done Somebody Wrong/Something Inside Me/I'm Worried/Fine Little Mama/I Need You/She Done Moved/I Can't Stop Loving You/Early One Morning/Stranger Blues*

DISC THREE: *Stranger Blues* (alternate take)/*Anna Lee/Standing At The Crossroads/My Bleeding Heart/My Kind Of Woman/Got To Move/So Unkind/Person To Person/One Way Out/Go Back Home Again/Look On Yonder Wall/Shake Your Money Maker* (take 1—false start)/*Shake Your Money Maker* (take 2)/*Mean Mistreatin' Mama* (take 1)/*Mean Mistreatin' Mama* (take 2)/*Sunnyland Train/You Know You're Wrong/ Mean Mistreatin' Mama* (take 3)/*You Know*

You Done Me Wrong/My Baby's Gone/Find My Kind Of Woman/Look On Yonder Wall/Find My Kinda Woman

DISC FOUR: *It Hurts Me Too/Dust My Broom/Pickin' The Blues/Everyday (I Have The Blues)/I've Got A Right To Love My Baby/The Twelve Year Old Boy/She's Got To Go/I Gotta Go Now/Talk To Me Baby/Make My Dreams Come True/Hand In Hand* (take 1)/*Hand In Hand* (take 3)/*Conversation (Back In Mississippi)/Hand In Hand* (take 4)/*I Can't Stop Loving My Baby/Up Jumped Elmore/I Believe*

367 **"Speak The Lyrics To Me, Mama Reed"**
Jimmy Reed
Vee Jay NVD2-705
High and Lonesome/ You Don't Have To Go/Shoot My Baby/You Upset My Mind/Ain't That Lovin' You Baby/Can't Stand To See You Go/You Got Me Dizzy/Honey, Where You Going/Little Rain/The Sun Is Shining/Honest I Do/ My Bitter Seed/I'm Gonna Get My Baby/Going To New York/I Told You Baby/ Take Out Some Insurance/Baby What You Want Me To Do/Hush Hush/Found Love/Big Boss Man/Close Together/Bright Lights, Big City/Oh John/Shame, Shame, Shame/I'm The Man Down There

368 **Blues Is Killin' Me**
Various Artists
Paula PCD-19/Flyright FLY CD 28 (UK)
[Baby Face (Leroy Foster) & Sunnyland Trio], *Pet Rabbit/Louella/Late Hours At Midnight/Blues Is Killin' Me*; Floyd Jones [& His Trio], *Dark Road/I Lost A Good Woman/Skinny Mama/Rising Wind/On The Road Again;* [Little Hudson's (Hudson Showers) Red Devil Trio], *Where Have You Been So Long; Rough Treatment/I'm Looking For A Woman/Things Going So Tough With Me/Don't Hang Around;* Memphis Minnie [& Her Combo], *Kissing In The Dark/World Of Trouble/In Love Again/What A Night;* Little Son Joe [Ernest Lawlars], *Ethel Bea/A Little Too Late*

369 **The Cobra Records Story**
Various Artists
Capricorn 9 42012-2—2 CD set
DISC ONE: Otis Rush, *I Can't Quit You Baby* (alternate take 1A); [Louie Meyers & The Aces] Louis Myers, *Just Wailin'*; Otis Rush, *I Can't Quit You Baby* (alternate take B)/*Sit Down Baby* (alternate take)/ *I Can't Quit You Baby;* The Clouds, *Rock and Roll Boogie* (alternate take); Shakey Horton [Walter Horton], *Need My Baby/Have A Good Time*; Otis Rush & His Band, *My Love Will Never Die* (alternate take)/*Violent Love*; Sunnyland Slim, *Highway 61/It's You Baby*; Otis Rush, *Groaning The Blues/If You Were Mine*; Little Willie Foster, *Crying The Blues/Little Girl*; Harold Burrage, *I Don't Care Who Knows* (alternate take); Magic Sam, *All Your Love/Love Me With A Feeling*; Otis Rush, *Love That Woman/Jump Sister Bessie*; Harold Burrage, *Satisfied* (alternate take); Betty Everett, *My Love* (alternate take); Duke Jenkins & His Orchestra, *Shake It* (alternate take); Magic Sam, *Look Whatcha Done/Everything Gonna Be Alright*; Sunnyland Slim & Walter "Shakey" Horton |?|, *Eli Toscano Blues*

DISC TWO: Otis Rush & Willie Dixon Band, *Three Times A Fool/She's A Good 'Un*; Betty Everett, *I Ain't Gonna Cry* (alternate take); Magic Sam, *All Night Long*; Harold Burrage With Willie Dixon Band, *I Cry For You* (alternate take); Magic Sam, *All My Whole Life*; Otis Rush, *It Takes Times/ Checking On My Baby*; Charles Clark [& Willie Dixon Band], *Row Your Boat*; Buddy Guy & His Band, *Sit And Cry (The Blues)/Try To Quit You Baby*; Magic Sam, *Easy Baby* (alternate take)/ *21 Days In Jail* (alternate take); Shakey Jake & Willie Dixon Band, *Call Me If You Need Me/Roll Your Moneymaker*; Otis Rush & His Band, *Double Trouble/Keep On Loving Me Baby*; Buddy Guy & His Band, *This Is The End/You Sure Can't Do*; Otis Rush & His Band, *All Your Love (I Miss Loving)/My Baby Is A Good 'Un;* Ike Turner's Kings Of Rhythm, *Matchbox* [Tommy Hodge, vocal]/*You've Got To Lose* [Jackie Brenston, vocal]/ *Box Top* [Ike Turner & Carlson Oliver, vocal]/*You Keep On Worrying Me* [Jackie Brenston, vocal]/ *(I Know) You Don't Love Me* [Tommy Hodge, vocal]/ *Down And Out* [Tommy Hodge, vocal]

(iii) Detroit Blues

John Lee Hooker was born on a farm near Clarksdale, Mississippi, in 1917. He learned his unique guitar playing from his stepfather, Will Moore, an associate of the legendary Delta bluesman Charley Patton. Hooker listened to many blues stars on the phonograph, as is obvious from his repertoire, but he particularly stressed the influence of Blind Lemon Jefferson, Tony Hollins, and Tommy McClennan on his own style. Hooker's songs are eminently original works, even when they are reworkings of classics. One of McClennan's songs, *Bottle It Up And Go* (**105**), is at the root of *Momma Poppa Boogie*, although (as with all of his pieces) the finished product is far removed from the sound of the original. The unstructured, half-spoken, half-sung, *cante fable* delivery of *Momma Poppa Boogie* is rarely heard in the work of other recording artists.

Hooker left home early and stopped in Memphis for a few years, playing house parties for a few drinks while he was still too young to play clubs. During these years, he worked at regular day jobs, devoting only the evenings and weekends to his music. When he arrived in Detroit in 1943, he easily found employment. He continued to work in the auto plants until 1948, when Elmer Barber heard him play at a house party. Barber took him to Bernie Besman who quickly signed him and arranged for a release on the Bihari brothers' Modern label. With his first record, *Boogie Chillen*, Hooker topped the charts (an alternate take, *Henry's Swing Club*, appears on **Graveyard Blues**). He went on the road with Besman while his releases continued to score national success. It was Besman's idea to use plywood on the floor under Hooker's foot, heard to good advantage in *Hastings Street Boogie*, an alternate take which highlights the same infectious beat as the original.

It was also Besman who had him recording for numerous labels under many pseudonyms, from Texas Slim to Delta John to Birmingham Sam. When Hooker went to Vee Jay in 1955, he began to develop a more modern sound which took a few years to jell, but which paid off in 1961 with the crossover hit *Boom Boom.* Only a year or two before this success, he had already stepped back across the line to record a few LPs of "authentic folk blues", and this would be a line that he would traverse many times during his still-continuing career.

Hooker's style is sufficiently personal to invite no comparisons, although his voice is recognizably Delta-bred, with its dark, brooding intensity. *Burnin' Hell* is a fast shuffle with powerful harp backing by Eddie Burns. The piece draws on Son House for some of its lyrics, while Hooker's guitar has an abrasive demonic quality. But it is in *Graveyard Blues* that he goes beyond the typical blues of his day. In this extended moan, with repeated and half-whispered droning lines, Hooker's ardent cries seem closer to the field holler. This ability to evoke trance-like states and arouse in his listeners the darkest forebodings of the future makes him one of the few adepts of the Delta blues. Hooker's style was atavistic by any standard, but while his Delta cohorts were exercising their new electric combos, he was still performing his darkly fierce solos like *Alberta*, accompanied only by his guitar.

The unrelenting and familiar rhythm of *Huckle Up Baby*, recorded in 1950, is only one sign of the nature of Hooker's influence on rock 'n' roll. He is often called the "King of the Boogie," and if he is entitled to this accolade, it is because of the depth of his influence in the white music world as well as the black. Artists from Eddie Kirkland to the rock group Canned Heat have absorbed something from him, although no one has ever claimed to match his playing of the blues.

370 **Graveyard Blues**
John Lee Hooker
Specialty SPCD 7018-2/Ace CDCHD 421 (UK)
War Is Over (Goodbye California)/Henry's Swing Club/Alberta/Hastings Street Boogie/Build Myself A Cave/Momma Poppa Boogie/Graveyard Blues/Burnin' Hell/Sailing Blues/Black Cat Blues/Miss Sadie Mae/Canal Street Blues/Huckle Up Baby/Goin' Down Highway 51/Sail On, Little Girl, Sail On/Alberta Part 2/My Baby's Got Something/Boogie Chillen No. *2/21 Boogie/Rollin' Blues*

Basic Records

(i) The Melrose Years

371 **That's All Right Mama**
Arthur "Big Boy" Crudup
Bluebird RCA Heritage 61043-2
If I Get Lucky/Gonna Follow My Baby/Mean Old 'Frisco Blues/Cool Disposi-

tion/Rock Me Mama/Keep Your Arms Around Me/That's Your Red Wagon/She's Gone/So Glad You're Mine/Chicago Blues/Crudup's After Hours/That's All Right/Shout, Sister, Shout/She Ain't Nothing But Trouble/My Baby Left Me/Too Much Competition/Second Man Blues/I'm Gonna Dig Myself A Hole/Mr. So And So/My Wife And Woman/I Love You/She's Got No Hair

"Big Boy" Crudup's guitar style bridged the gap between country and city, and his songwriting talent produced *Mean Old 'Frisco Blues* and countless other classics; but he is still best known as Elvis Presley's source for *My Baby Left Me*, and for providing a foundation for rock 'n' roll (**330**).

372 Doctor (Peter) Clayton: Complete Pre-War Recordings In Chronological Order (1935–1942)

Document DOCD 5179 (Au)

Peter's Blues/Yo Yo Jive/Roaming Gambler/Slick Man Blues/False Love Blues/Something Going On Wrong/Black Snake Blues/'41 Blues/Moonshine Man Blues/Back Door Man Blues/Jitterbug Swing/Love Is Gone/Confessin' The Blues/Streamline Love/Doctor Clayton Blues/Watch Out Mama/Cheating And Lying Blues/Gotta Find My Baby/Honey Stealin' Blues/My Own Blues/On The Killing Floor/Moonshine Woman Blues/Pearl Harbor Blues/Ain't No Business We Can Do

This disc shows how Clayton's vocal style tightened while his imagination broadened increasingly in his compositions. Clayton was an important influence on B.B. King. *'41 Blues, Moonshine Woman Blues* (recorded by B.B. as *The Woman I Love*), and *Pearl Harbor Blues* are all noteworthy.

373 Sonny Boy Williamson: Complete Recorded Works In Chronological Order, Volume 5 (1945–1947)

Document DOCD 5059 (Au)

Early In The Morning/The Big Boat/Stop Breaking Down/You're An Old Lady/Sonny Boy's Cold Chills/Mean Old Highway/Hoodoo Hoodoo/Shake The Boogie/Mellow Chick Swing/Polly Put Your Kettle On/Lacey Belle/Apple Tree Swing/Wonderful Time/Sugar Gal/Willow Tree Gal/Alcohol Blues/Little Girl/Blues About My Baby/No Friend Blues/I Love You For Myself/Bring Another Half A Pint/Southern Dream/Rub A Dub/Better Cut That Out

Many of Sonny Boy's songs are regularly performed by others, notably *Stop Breaking Down* and *Alcohol Blues*, and this (besides the omnipresent harp in Chicago blues) is a measure of his powerful influence. His later pieces like *Wonderful Time* suggest the power of his inspiration on *Little* Walter.

374 Big Joe Williams: Complete Recorded Works in Chronological Order Volume 2 (1945–1949)

Blues Documents BDCD 6004 (Au)

Drop Down Blues/Somebody's Been Worryin'/Wanita/Vitamin A/His Spirit Lives On/Baby Please Don't Go/Stack of Dollars/Mellow Apples/Wild Cow Moan/P Vine Blues/Bad And Weakhearted Blues/King Biscuit Stomp/I'm A Highway Man/Banta Rooster Blues/Mean Step Father Blues/House Lady Blues/Don't You Leave Me Here/Jivin' Woman/She's A Married Woman; Chasey Collins, With Big Joe Williams, *Walking Blues/Atlanta Town*

This disc is more down-home in flavor than the preceding. The sensitive interaction between Big Joe and Sonny Boy Williamson captures the essence of the rural tendency of the Melrose sound. This trend, when combined with electrification, however, contributed vital ingredients to the nascent Chicago blues.

(ii) Small Labels: The Industrial Sound

375 **Johnny Shines And Robert Lockwood**
Paula PCD 14/Flyright FLY CD 10 (UK)
Johnny Shines, *Ramblin'/Fishtail/Cool Driver/Ain't Doin' No Good/Evening Sun/No Name Blues/Brutal Hearted Woman/Gonna Call The Angel/Gonna Call The Angel* (alternate take)/*Evening Shuffle*; Robert Lockwood, *Dust My Broom/Pearly B/Aw Aw Baby/Sweet Woman From Maine*; [Alfred Wallace], *You've Got To Stop This Mess/Glad I Don't Worry No More* [Wallace, vocal]; [Sunnyland Slim & His Trio], *Down Home Child* [Slim, vocal]/*Sunny Land Special*; [Sunnyland Trio], *Leaving Your Town* [Slim, vocal]; Robert Lockwood, *Dust My Broom* (alternate take)
Tradition-based Johnny Shines and progressive Robert Lockwood have both redefined the limits of Robert Johnson's legacy. From the jazz-influenced modernism of Lockwood's *Pearly B* to Shines' ringing eloquence on *No Name Blues*, it is clear that both men saw Johnson's style as mileposts on the road, meant only for passing.

376 **Snooky Pryor**
Snooky Pryor, Floyd Jones, and Moody Jones
Paula PCD 11/Flyright FLY CD 20 (UK)
Floyd Jones [With Snooky & Moody], *Keep What You Got/Stockyard Blues*; [Snooky & Moody] Snooky Pryor, *Boogie/Telephone Blues*; [Man Young] Johnny Young, *Let Me Ride Your Mule/My Baby Walked Out On Me;* Snooky Pryor, *Fine Boogie/I'm Getting Tired*; Moody Jones, *Rough Treatment/Why Should I Worry*; Snooky Pryor, *Going Back On The Road/Real Fine Boogie/Hold Me In Your Arms*; Moody Jones, *Rough Treatment* (alternate take); Snooky Pryor, *Harp Instrumental/Stop The Train Conductor/Walking Boogie/My Head Is Turning Grey/Uncle Sam Don't Take My Man/Boogie Twist*
Pryor was an amplified harp innovator, and Moody Jones an exceptional guitarist. The work of Snooky, Moody, and Floyd Jones did as much to bring about the birth of the Chicago blues as the Chess records by Muddy, Walter, and Wolf. *Real Fine Boogie* and *Boogie Twist* may convince you, too.

377 **The Blues World Of Little Walter**
Various Artists
Delmark DD 648
[Little Walter Trio], *I Just Keep Loving Her/Muskadine Blues;* [Baby Face Leroy Trio], *Rollin' And Tumblin'* Part 1/*Rollin' And Tumblin* Part 2/*Boll Weevil*; [Little Walter Trio], *Bad Acting Woman*; [Baby Face Leroy Trio], *Red Headed Woman*; [Little Walter Trio], *Moonshine Blues*; J.B. Lenoir, *I Wanna Play A Little While/Louise*; [J.B. Lenore & His Combo], *People Are Meddlin' In Our Affairs*; Sunnyland Slim, *I Done You Wrong/Low Down Sunnyland Train*
No cross-section of the Chicago blues is complete without the eight legendary sides cut at the Parkway session in 1950. With vocals by Baby Face Leroy (*Rollin' And Tumblin'* and *Boll Weevil*) and Little Walter (*I Just Keep Loving Her*), these pieces are virtually maps of the evolving genre.

378 **Hand Me Down Blues, Chicago Style**
Various Artists
Relic 7015
Henry Gray, *Watch Yourself/That Ain't Right/Goodbye Baby/You Messed Up*; Dusty Brown, *He Don't Love You/Yes She's Gone/Hurry Home/Rusty Dusty*; Albert King, *Hand Me Down Blues/Little Boy Blues*; John Brim [& His Stompers], *Gary Stomp*; Sunnyland Slim, *Going Back To Memphis/Devil Is A Busy Man*; Snooky Pryor, *Crosstown Blues/I Want You For Myself*; Little Willie Foster, *Four Day Jump*
The expressive Henry Gray is the star of any disc on which he appears, and these four piano sides from a "lost" session are no exception. Combined with John Brim's fierce *Gary Stomp*, four tracks by Dusty Brown, and diverse appearances by Snooky Pryor, this collection is a Chicago harp fan's delight.

379 **Memphis Slim At The Gate Of Horn**
VeeJay NVB2-800
The Comeback/Steppin' Out/Blue And Lonesome/Mother Earth/Slim's Blues/Gotta Find My Baby/Messin' Around/Wish Me Well/My Gal Keeps Me Crying/Lend Me Your Love/Sassy Mae/Rockin' The Blues
Some of the smoothest and the most compelling post-war blues are on this CD, drawn from a Chicago studio session of 1959. There are three saxes, Slim's piano and characteristic vocals, all highlighted by guitar master Matt Murphy. *Sassy Mae* is their version of *Dust My Broom*. Try this if you need converting.

380 **Third Degree**
Eddie Boyd
Charly CD BM 42 (UK)
Picture In The Frame/I Got The Blues/Got Lonesome Here/Blues For My Baby/Cool Kind Treatment/24 Hours/Hard Time Getting Started/Best I Could/The Tickler (alternate take) */Third Degree/Rattin' And Runnin' Around/Just A Fool/Hush Baby Don't You Cry/Nothing But The Blues/I Got The Blues/Driftin'/Got Me Seein' Double/I'm A Prisoner/Treat Her Right/Come On Home*
With one foot in the Melrose camp and the other pressing the pedals at Chess, Boyd is always impressive in his breadth and polished style. His lyrics are often thoughtful, as in the hits *24 Hours* and *Third Degree*, and he embodies an important facet of Chicago blues.

381 **Junior Wells 1957–1963**
Paula PCD 03/Flyright FLY CD 03 (UK)
Come On In This House/Little By Little/ So Tired/She's A Sweet One/It Hurts Me Too/Universal Rock/Messin' With The Kid/Prison Bars All Around Me/You Couldn't Care/I Could Cry/You Sure Look Good To Me/When The Cat's Gone The Mice Play/Two-Headed Woman/Cha Cha Cha In Blues/Lovey Dovey Lovey One/I'm A Stranger/The Things I'd Do For You/I Need Me A Car/I'll Get You Too/One Day (Every Goodbye Ain't Gone)/Calling All Blues/Love Me/Galloping Horses A Lazy Mule
All of Wells' Chief/Profile output is gathered here, reflecting the sophistication he had achieved since his earliest recordings with the States label. *It Hurts Me Too* and the influential *Messin' With The Kid* are especially powerful, and Earl Hooker's presence on numbers like *So Tired* adds an enviable elegance.

382 **Chicago Piano 1951–1958**
Various Artists
Paula PCD 15/Flyright FLY CD 31 (UK)
Sunnyland Slim, *Highway 61* (alternate take)/*It's You Baby*; [John Brim Trio], *Over Night* [Sunnyland Slim, vocal]; Sunnyland Slim [& His Playboys], *That Woman/'Fore Day Bounce*; Floyd Jones, *Big World*; [Sunnyland (Slim) Trio], *Mary Lee*; Eddie Boyd, *Five Long Years/Hard Headed Woman/It's Miserable To Be Alone*; Charles Clark [& Willie Dixon Band], *Row Your Boat* (alternate take); Memphis Slim, *I Wonder What's The Matter/I Can't Live Without You/ Best Gal I Ever Had/So Tired*; Shakey Horton [Walter Horton], *Need My Baby* (alternate take); Little Brother Montgomery, *Keep Drinkin'/Boogie*; Moody Jones, *Please Somebody*; J.T. Brown, *Short Dresses*
With Eddie Boyd's pre-eminently influential *Five Long Years* establishing the mood, this selection of Chicago piano blues exemplifies an aspect of the Chicago sound that is often overlooked. Billy Howell's tasteful trumpet on Floyd Jones' *Big World* accentuates this point, as do Little Brother's two piano trio cuts.

383 **Chicago Blues Harmonicas**
Various Artists
Paula PCD 07/Flyright FLY CD 11 (UK)
Baby Face Leroy [& His Trio], *My Head Can't Rest No More/Take A Little Walk With Me;* Snooky Pryor, *Boogy Fool/Raisin' Sand/Cryin' Shame/Eighty Nine Ten;* John Lee Henley, *Rythm [sic] Rockin' Boogie/Knockin' On Lula Mae's Door;* Little Willie Foster, *Crying The Blues/Little Girl;* [Louie Meyers (Louis Myers) & The Aces] *Bluesy;* Arbee Stidham, *When I Find My Baby;* [Louie Meyers (Louis Myers) & The Aces] *Just Whaling;* Sonny Boy Williamson, *Steady Rollin' Man/Take Your Hand Out Of My Pocket;* Charles Clark [& Willie Dixon Band], *Row Your Boat;* Shakey Horton [Walter Horton], *Need My Baby/Have A Good Time;* Sunnyland Slim, *Highway 61*
While Little Willie Foster's *Crying The Blues* is one of the most powerful post-war performances ever recorded, this selection of Chicago classics is remarkable not only for its consistency but for its diversity as well. John Lee Henley, Louis Myers, and Arbee Stidham are all an important part of the Chicago picture.

(iii) West Side Polish and South Side Soul

384 **West Side Guitar: Magic Sam, 1957–1966**
Paula PCD 02/Flyright FLY CD 02 (UK)
Everything Gonna Be Alright/Look Whatcha Done/All My Whole Life/Love Me With A Feeling/All Your Love/Call Me If You Need Me/Roll Your Money Maker/Easy Baby/Magic Rocker/Love Me This Way/21 Days in Jail/All Night Long/Out of Bad Luck/Every Night About This Time/Blue Light Boogie/You Don't Have To Work/My Charlie/My Love Is Your Love/She Belongs To Me/ Respect Me Baby/A Hard Road
One of the most popular blues artists in Chicago, Sam died at 32, having made relatively few records. But many of these, like the minor-key *All Your Love,* the rocking *Every Night About This Time,* or the well-known *All Night Long* became standards in many Chicago repertoires.

385 **Bad Boy**
Eddie Taylor
Charly CD BM 35 (UK)
Bad Boy/E.T. Blues/Ride 'Em On Down/Big Town Playboy/You'll Always Have A Home/Don't Knock At My Door/I'm Gonna Love You/Lookin' For Trouble/ Find My Baby/Stroll Out West/I'm Sitting Here/Do You Want Me To Cry/ Train Fare/Leave This Neighborhood/Somethin' For Nothin'
Taylor's considerable skills as a bluesman are often overshadowed by his role as second guitarist for Jimmy Reed, but his hard-driving versions of *Big Town Playboy,* the gambling blues *Ride 'Em On Down,* and *Leave This Neighborhood,* reveal him to be an artist of remarkable talent.

386 **The Way I Feel**
Various Artists
Flyright FLY CD 43 (UK)
Homesick James, *Crossroads;* Jesse Fortune, *Heavy Heart Beat;* Detroit Junior, *Call My Job;* J.B. Lenoir & His African Hunch Rhythm, *I Feel So Good;* Jesse Fortune, *Good Things;* Homesick James, *My Baby's Sweet;* Andrew Brown, *You Better Stop* Harold Burrage [With Willie Dixon Band], *I Cry For You;* Willie Mabon, *Somebody Got To Pay;* Jesse Fortune, *Too Many Cooks;* T.V. Slim [Oscar Wills], *You Can't Love Me;* Detroit Junior, *The Way I Feel;* Willie Mabon, *Some More;* Koko Taylor, *Honky Tonk;* Willie Mabon, *New Orleans Blues;* Big Moose [John Mayon Walker], *Rambling Woman;* Fenton Robinson, *Say You're Leavin';* Lillian Offitt, *Oh Mama;* Mighty Joe Young, *Hard Times;* Willie Mabon, *Something For Nothing/Some Time I Wonder*
An excellent sampler of the modernization of the 1950s Chicago blues sound. From the rich slide on Homesick James' *Crossroads* and the humor of Detroit Junior's *Call My Job* to Buddy Guy's dextrous accompaniment to Jesse Fortune, these sides (originally recorded for the USA label) point to where the blues was going in the early 1960s.

387 **I Wish You Would**
Billy Boy Arnold
Charly CD BM 34 (UK)
Sweet On You Baby/You Got To Love Me/I Wish You Would/I Was Fooled/ Don't Stay Out All Night/I Ain't Got You/Here's My Picture/You've Got Me Wrong/My Heart Is Crying/Kissing At Midnight/Prisoner's Plea/No, No, No, No, No/Everyday, Every Night/Rockinitis
Billy Boy's first record for Vee Jay, *I Wish You Would,* was an instant success. He had idolized John Lee Williamson, but he also learned from Little Walter and Junior Wells. Arnold had earlier teamed with Bo Diddley, and his hit had the Latin beat that created influential ripples throughout the blues community.

(iv) Chess

388 **The Complete Chess Studio Recordings**
Buddy Guy
MCA Chess CHD2 9337—2 CD set
DISC ONE: *First Time I Met The Blues/Slop Around/I Got My Eyes On You/ Broken Hearted Blues/Let Me Love You Baby/I Got A Strange Feeling/Gully*

Hully/Ten Years Ago/Watch Yourself/Stone Crazy/Skippin'/I Found A True Love/Hard But It's Fair/Baby (Baby, Baby, Baby)/When My Left Eye Jumps/ That's It/The Treasure Untold/American Bandstand [American Bandstand Thing]/No Lie/$100 Bill/My Love Is Real/Buddy's Boogie

DISC TWO: *Worried Mind [Stick Around]/Untitled Instrumental/Moanin'/I Dig Your Wig/My Time After A while/Night Flight/Crazy Love (Crazy Music)/Every Girl I See/The Many Ways/Leave My Girl Alone/Got To Use Your Head/Keep It To Myself [Keep It To Yourself]/My Mother/She Suits Me To A Tee/Mother-In-Law Blues/Buddy's Groove/Going To School/I Cry And Sing The Blues/Goin' Home/I Suffer With The Blues/Lip Lap Louie/My Time After Awhile* (alternate take)/*Too Many Ways* (alternate take)/*Keep It To Myself* (alternate take)/ *I Didn't Know My Mother* (alternate take of *She Suits Me To A Tee)*
Buddy Guy's Chess output virtually represents a sub-genre of Chicago blues. Fans can also hear how Jarrett Gibson's and Bob Neely's horns contributed to the Chess sound so strongly associated with Guy's slashing guitar.

389 **Hard Working Man**
Jimmy Rogers
Charly CD BM 3 (UK)
I Used To Have A Woman/Hard Working Man/My Little Machine/Give Love Another Chance/What's The Matter/Blues Leave Me Alone/Sloppy Drunk/If It Ain't Me/One Kiss/I Can't Believe/What Have I Done/Trace Of You/Don't Turn Me Down/Don't You Know My Baby
Rogers' ability as a singer and guitarist was an important element in the 1950s sound. Walter Horton's freewheeling harmonics support on the tightly knit *If It Ain't Me* and the classic version of Lucille Bogan's *Sloppy Drunk* are obvious highspots, but even the pop "standards" played a significant role in modern Chicago repertoires.

390 **Natural Man**
J.B. Lenoir
MCA Chess CHD 9323
Natural Man/Don't Dog Your Woman/Let Me Die With The One I Love/Carrie Lee/Mama, What About Your Daughter/If I Give My Love To You/Five Years/ Don't Touch My Head/I've Been Down So Long/What Have I Done/Eisenhower Blues/Korea Blues/Everybody Wants To Know/I'm In Korea
Lenoir had a unique sound, and this selection is a gem, ranging in style from the topical *Eisenhower Blues* to the saxophone collage of *If I Give My Love To You.* The sophisticated integration of styles that often took place in the Chicago bands is discernible in *Don't Dog Your Woman*, which has a soft horn background.

391 **Drop Down Mama**
Various Artists
MCA Chess CHD 93002
Johnny Shines, *So Glad I Found You;* Robert Nighthawk, *Sweet Black Angel/ Anna Lee;* Big Boy Spires, *One Of These Days;* Honey Boy Edwards, *Drop Down Mama;* Floyd Jones, *Playhouse;* Big Boy Spires, *Murmur Low;* Floyd Jones, *You Can't Live Long;* Johnny Shines, *Joliet Blues;* Robert Nighthawk,

Jackson Town Gal/Return Mail Blues; Blue Smitty, *Crying/Sad Story;* Floyd Jones, *Dark Road*

From Robert Nighthawk's Tampa Red-inspired slide on *Anna Lee* to Big Boy Spires' reworking of Tommy Johnson's *Big Fat Mama Blues* in *Murmur Low,* this is a collection to treasure. Two sides by the obscure Blue Smitty and two previously unreleased tracks by Johnny Shines add to the pleasure. Top-notch Chicago guitars.

392 **Bo's Blues**

Bo Diddley

Ace CDCH 396 (UK)

Down Home Special/You Don't Love Me (You Don't Care)/Blues, Blues/500% More Man/Live My Life/She's Fine, She's Mine/Heart-O-Matic Love/Bring It To Jerome/Pretty Thing/You Can't Judge A Book By The Cover/The Clock Strikes Twelve/Cops And Robbers/Run Diddley Daddy/Before You Accuse Me/ Diddy Wah Diddy/Bo's Blues/Little Girl/I'm A Man/I'm Bad/Who Do You Love/I'm Looking For A Woman/Two Flies

This and the next CD demonstrate clearly why blues is called the foundation of rock 'n' roll. *Before You Accuse Me* and *Blues, Blues* are explicitly blues, yet they both have the resonance of rock 'n' roll that made Bo Diddley popular with buyers of "Top 40" records.

393 **On The Blues Side**

Chuck Berry

Ace CDCH 397 (UK)

Confessin' The Blues/Run Around/Worried Life Blues/The Things That I Used To Do/Blues For Hawaiians/Wee Wee Hours/I Still Got The Blues/Down The Road Apiece/No Money Down/Stop And Listen/Blue On Blue/Sweet Sixteen/I Got To Find My Baby/I Just Want To Make Love To You/Merry Christmas Baby/Deep Feeling/Wee Hour Blues/Don't You Lie To Me/Ain't That Just Like A Woman/Driftin' Blues/Blue Feeling

Berry wields Dr Clayton's (and B.B. King's) *I Got To Find My Baby* with an expertise that matches the ease he brings to Charles Brown's *Driftin' Blues,* demonstrating that he was not only a vital transitional figure, but a master of whatever suited his fancy. His sonorous use of the *Dust My Broom* riff in *Run Around* is instantly captivating.

(v) Pastmasters . . . Live!

The following CDs were originally recorded as LPs (not singles).

394 **Hawk Squat**

J.B. Hutto and his Hawks

Delmark DD 617

Speak My Mind/If You Change Your Mind/Too Much Pride/What Can You Get Outside That You Can't Get At Home/The Same Mistake Twice/20% Alcohol/ Hip-Shakin'/The Feeling Is Gone/Notoriety Woman/Too Late/Send Her Home To Me/Hawk Squat

The substitution of a tenor saxaphone for a harmonica gives this set a contemporary feel, but all of J.B.'s usual intensity and flare still come to the fore. The best full CD of his later work.

395 **Beware of the Dog**
Hound Dog Taylor
Alligator ALCD 4707
Give Me Back My Wig/The Sun Is Shining/Kitchen Sink Boogie/Dust My Broom/Comin' Around The Mountain/Let's Get Funky/Rock Me/It's Allright/ Freddie's Blues
No one but Hound Dog combined a slashing slide guitar with an almost hypnotic "boogie" sensibility, and this compilation covers the range of everything in between. Elmore's forceful and brooding *The Sun Is Shining* and the jumping *Kitchen Sink Boogie* embody the house-rocking music for which Hound Dog was famous.

396 **The Earthshaker**
Koko Taylor
Alligator ALCD 4711
Let The Good Times Roll/Spoonful/Walking The Back Streets/Cut You Loose/ Hey, Bartender/I'm A Woman/You Can Have My Husband/Please Don't Dog Me/Wang Dang Doodle
Taylor directly descends from Howlin' Wolf and Muddy Waters, as *Spoonful* and *Wang Dang Doodle* make clear, and as she herself insists. If you don't know why Taylor consistently wins "Female Vocalist" awards, this CD will tell you.... You'll even wonder why the band doesn't garner its own share of trophies.

397 **Johnny Littlejohn Chicago Blues Stars**
Arhoolie CD 1043
What In The World You Goin' To Do/Treat Me Wrong/Catfish Blues/Kiddeo/ Slidin' Home/Dream/Reelin' and Rockin'/Been Around The World/How Much More Long/Shake Your Money Maker/I'm Tired/Nowhere To Lay My Head
Littlejohn's gripping slide style, midway between Robert Nighthawk and Elmore James, is given deserved exposure here, and songs like *Dream* reveal him to have been a bluesman of rare talent. *Been Around The World* highlights the cleanly articulated phrasing of his non-slide playing, and, with *Kiddeo,* demonstrates the breadth of his achievement.

398 **Chicago/The Blues/Today**
Various Artists
*Vanguard VMD 79216 (Vol. 1); VMD 79217 (Vol. 2); VMD 79218 (Vol. 3)— 3 CD set**
VOLUME ONE: Junior Wells, *A Tribute To Sonny Boy Williamson/It Hurts Me Too/Messin' With The Kid/Vietcong Blues/All Night Long;* J.B. Hutto, *Going Ahead/Please Help/Too Much Alcohol/Married Woman Blues/That's The Truth;* Otis Spann, *Marie/Burning Fire/S.P. Blues/Sometimes I Wonder/Spann's Stomp*

*each CD also available separately.

VOLUME TWO: James Cotton, *Cotton Crop Blues/The Blues Keep Falling/Love Me Or Leave Me/Rocket 88/West Helena Blues;* Otis Rush, *Everything's Going To Turn Out Alright/It's A Mean Old World/I Can't Quit You Baby/Rock/It's My Own Fault;* Homesick James, *Dust My Broom/Somebody Been Talkin'/Set A Date/So Mean To Me*

VOLUME THREE: Johnny Young, *One More Time/Kid Man Blues/My Black Mare/ Stealin' Back/I Got Mine In Time/Tighten Up On It;* Johnny Shines, *Dynaflow Blues/Black Spider Blues/Layin' Down My Shoes And Clothes/If I Get Lucky;* Big Walter Horton With Memphis Charlie, *Rockin' My Boogie;* Johnny Shines, *Mr. Boweevil/Hey Hey*
J.B. Hutto's spare, tight and hard-punched *That's The Truth* demonstrates a high level of performance skill, as does Otis Rush's rendition of *It's My Own Fault,* highlighted by the elegant support of Robert "Sax" Crowder. Johnny Shines' fierce, declamatory *Dynaflow Blues* may be his best performance ever.

(vi) Detroit

399 John Lee Hooker And Eddie Burns, 1950–1952
Flyright FLY CD 23 (UK)
John Lee Hooker, *House Rent Boogie/Wandering Blues;* Eddie Burns, *Making A Fool Out Of Me;* John Lee Hooker, *Questionnaire Blues/Real Gone Gal;* Eddie Burns, *Squeeze Me Baby;* John Lee Hooker, *Feed Her All Night;* Eddie Burns, *Gangster Blues/Where Did You Stay Last Night;* John Lee Hooker, *My Daddy Was A Jockey/Little Boy Blue/How Long Must I Be Your Slave;* Eddie Burns, *Grieving Blues;* John Lee Hooker, *Ground Hog/Mean Old Train/Catfish;* Baby Boy Warren, *My Special Friend Blues/Nervy Woman Blues*
Eddie Burns' vocals, backed with his harp and John Lee Hooker's guitar, make compelling listening, as *Squeeze Me Baby* attests, and Hooker's own cuts are among his best performances. Baby Boy Warren was one of the most important Detroit performers, and his two rare cuts are an added treat.

400 Detroit Blues: The Early 1950s
Various Artists
Blues Classics BC 12—LP
Baby Boy Warren, *Sanafee/Baby Boy Blues/Mattie Mae/Chicken;* Dr. Ross, *Thirty-Two Twenty;* Bobo Jenkins, *10 Below Zero/Baby Don't You Want To Go;* Eddie Kirkland, *No Shoes;* Detroit Count, *Hastings Street Opera* Parts 1 and 2; L.C. Green, *Remember Way Back;* Big Maceo, *Big City Blues;* John Lee Hooker, *House Rent Boogie;* One String Sam, *I Need $100;* Brother Will Hairston, *Alabama Bus*
No CD yet adequately portrays the breadth of Detroit Blues. On this vinyl release, Baby Boy Warren's *Sanafee* and *Mattie Mae* are lyrically and musically alluring; Bobo Jenkins' *10 Below Zero* is the definitive version, and his *Baby Don't You Want To Go* is on a par with any version of *Sweet Home Chicago.*

BOB GROOM

11 Down-Home Post-War Blues

During the immediate post-war years the focus of blues recording, long concentrated on Chicago, shifted to the West Coast. Chicago did not begin to regain much of its pre-eminence until the early 1950s, when heavily electrified blues bands produced the powerful sound that restored Mississippi—based blues to the R&B charts. In the meantime, the "country," "rural", or "down-home" blues (i.e. solo or small group performances by artists using older blues styles, often with acoustic, rather than electrified instrumental accompaniments) was rarely recorded by the major companies, or even the leading independents, though once in a while a company such as Atlantic would pay tribute to its roots by recording an obscure country bluesman such as Lawyer Houston. It was largely left to a proliferation of small independent record labels across the South to record the down-home blues that continued to be performed in every state from Texas across to Florida. Such sessions were speculative and often resulted in little return for the (often short-lived) recording company and even less for the artist, but there was always the outside chance of a big hit if the record caught on, repeating the success of Elmore James with *Dust My Broom* or Lightnin' Hopkins serenading his *Short Haired Woman*.

Far from down-home blues withering away with the success of the big-city sound, it seemed as if there was a continuing social need for the local bluesman, even if it often meant recasting the popular Chicago or West Coast hits in down-home guise. The advent of rock 'n' roll in the mid-1950s drove this music still further underground, even affecting the sales of such big names as Muddy Waters and B.B. King. However, a blues revival blossomed in Europe in the early 1960s and then spread back across the Atlantic, and in order to satisfy this rapidly growing interest many blues artists were sought out for recording and concert appearances. Soon young white researchers were tracing legendary figures from the pre-war era and encouraging their return to regular performing. Organized programs of field research located major talents who had never been recorded before, and studies were made of particular blues traditions.

The records selected for this chapter are in various down-home blues styles and their recording dates span the five decades since the end of

Roosevelt Sykes, Smithsonian Festival of American Folklife, Montreal, Canada, 1972 (*Paul Oliver*)

World War II. About half were recorded in professional studios, the remainder "in the field," taped in the home of the artist or in some makeshift local studio. Several of the studio-recorded sets comprise anthologies or compilations of solo artists' recordings for commercial companies. Some of these center on Memphis, Tennessee, and the Mississippi Delta area and come from the late 1940s and the 1950s when such music continued to flourish, having a limited but enthusiastic black audience.

Although almost all the artists selected for the list of Essential Records, as well as many in the Basic list, came from this region, it should be stressed that a significant number of outstanding blues performers were to be found in other parts of the South. As musicians from Mississippi, Tennessee and Arkansas tended to head north to Chicago, so some from Texas went west to California while others from the Atlantic seaboard states recorded in New York. Although the East Coast states, Louisiana, and Texas receive separate coverage in the *Guide*, representative albums by several important artists from these areas, as well as four significant anthologies, are included in this chapter.

Many of the down-home artists to be found on the anthologies are little known and did not record extensively, but their musical worth should not be equated with their relative lack of success. Limitations of space preclude detailed discussion of their recordings but their contribution to the story of the blues should not be underestimated. In the final analysis the continuance of the blues tradition has relied as much on the "minor" as the "major" artists.

Essential Records

(i) The Living Legends

Billed as the "Living Legends" on a record featuring concert recordings by all three, Son House, Skip James, and Bukka White were all rediscovered after decades in obscurity. Even at the remove of a quarter of a century, the rediscovery of Eddie James (Son) House stands as one of the most significant events of the blues revival. At the time it seemed amazing that a revered bluesman, then known only from the reissue of two obscure but magnificent 78rpm recordings from 1930 and half an album of Library of Congress recordings, had emerged from the mists of time. House was located after a long search, not in his natal state of Mississippi but a thousand miles north-east, way up in Rochester, New York, on Lake Ontario, where he had moved in 1943. It took some time for him to regain profiency on the guitar and to recall his old songs, but within a few months he was making concert appearances and impressing audiences with the total commitment he made to his music.

A coup on the part of his manager, Dick Waterman, was to secure a recording session for a major company, Columbia, thus testifying to the recognition House had received as one of the greatest blues singers of all time. (Most of the other rediscoveries recorded for small, specialist concerns.) At the time Columbia's producer for blues, folk, and jazz recordings was John Hammond, internationally famous for having launched Bob Dylan's recording career. It was Hammond who had arranged Bessie Smith's final recording session and the "From Spirituals to Swing" concerts of 1938–9 (**32**); he had also overseen Robert Johnson's reissue album in 1961, among many other projects.

Columbia ensured excellent sound quality and good distribution. The question was—could House produce the kind of performance required when, in April 1965, he entered a recording studio for the first time since his very first session 35 years earlier? (His Library of Congress recordings had been made in the field: **243**.) The Columbia recordings were an unqualified success and the resultant album enshrined a number of memorable performances. Mustering much of his old power, the toll of the years thrust aside, House sang and played as if his very life depended upon it. Much credit for the session was due to Al Wilson, who a few years later achieved fame as the lead vocalist on two big hits by electric blues group Canned Heat. Apart from encouragement in the studio, Wilson sensitively supported House on several performances, playing harmonica on two versions of Son's magnificent *Levee Camp Moan*, and second guitar on the rolling train blues *Empire State Express* and the traditional *Yonder Comes My Mother*.

The original LP issue of nine selections (all on DISC ONE) was rather pretentiously titled **Father Of Folk Blues**; the present CD version (which includes all the remaining recordings on DISC TWO) is also misleadingly titled, **Father Of The Delta Blues**. Son House was certainly a Master of the Delta Blues but his music had antecedents. Born in the vicinity of Clarksdale, Mississippi, in (probably) March 1902, House spent much of his childhood with his mother in Louisiana and was a grown man when he returned to the Delta and became interested in the blues performed by local musicians—James McCoy, Willie Wilson, Rube Lacy. He soon became a more than proficient slide guitarist and after meeting Willie Brown and Charlie Patton (who arranged House's Paramount recording session in 1930) extended his repertoire (**81, 82**).

Son's father (Eddie James House Sr), a Delta plantation worker, played in a brass band; he was a part-time preacher but also, at times, a heavy drinker. In the latter respects the son followed the father. Son House's intensely religious upbringing influenced him throughout his life but, unlike many blues singers, he showed no fear of mixing the sacred and the secular in composing his classic *Preachin' Blues*. The recordings of 1965 are by no means replicas of the two-part classic of 1930 as Son includes several different verses and develops the song more coherently.

Perhaps the most affecting of all Son's recordings for Columbia was his *Death Letter*. In Chapter 7 the development of this theme from 1930 to 1942 is mentioned. Here, 23 years on, is its final flowering, the grim lyrics honed down to a cutting edge: "I got a letter this morning, how do you reckon it read?" This version has an urgency somehow lacking in the Library of Congress recording (*Walking Blues*), which was in more reflective mood. *Pearline* is a country dance tune with fragmentary lyrics, related performances include Mississippi John Hurt's *Pera Lee*. Elijah Brown's *Pearline*, and *Pearlee Blues* by Furry Lewis. Only one take was made of this and the doleful *Louise McGhee*, a tribute to a former girlfriend. Also captured in one take were *Empire State Express*, a song inspired by a dozen or so years spent, working for the New York Central Railroad, and a beautiful performance of *Sundown* in which Son recounts how when he is troubled he takes a seat at the edge of town to watch the evening sun go down.

After his rediscovery House made a practise of including some monologs and *a capella* vocals in his concert performances, perhaps to ease the tension and allow him to recover from the emotional involvement of his guitar-accompanied blues. Possibly the best of his little homilies was *Grinnin' In Your Face*. with its simple message that "a true friend is hard to find." *John The Revelator* is an unaccompanied spiritual that harks back to his youth.

The seven songs not included on the vinyl issue are all of interest. Two are sensitive renditions of old spirituals. *A Down The Staff* is a guitar workout. The tribute to *President Kennedy* uses the melody of Son's *American Defence* (1942); *Pony Blues* derives from a Charlie Patton recording, as does *Shake It And Break It*, Son recorded a related performance for the Library of Congress as *Am I Right Or Wrong*.

Less than ten years after his rediscovery, Son House retired from recording and performing. Later he and his wife moved from Rochester to Detroit, where Son died in November 1988, at the advanced age of 86. Most of his rediscovery recordings are worth hearing but those he made for Columbia are unsurpassed in their passion and musical quality, evoking the very essence of Mississippi Delta blues and timeless in their ability to move the listener.

Nehemiah (Skip) James was born on the Woodbine plantation near Bentonia, a small town in Yazoo County, Mississippi, in June 1902. He showed an early interest in music and his mother fostered this by sending him for piano lessons at the Yazoo City High School. He learned songs such as the *Devil Blues* from older black musicians, notably Henry Stuckey, and adapted them to his own style. *Devil Got My Woman* earned him a long session for the by then ailing Paramount company in 1931 (**85**). It was to be 33 years before he recorded again. In June 1964 he was located in the Tunica County Hospital; a move to Washington, DC brought an improvement in his condition. Still sick, he appeared at the Newport Festival the following month and captured the audience with his strange and moving music. Several recording sessions were not wholly satisfactory but those for Vanguard produced two albums that did full justice to his music, the first being **Skip James/Today.**

Not immediately accessible like some blues, James' music repays careful listening, with its intricate, almost ornate guitar lines and his falsetto floating above the accompaniment, sounding almost ethereal in contrast with the deep-voiced singers from the Mississippi Delta region. Its seeming fragility is deceptive, however, for although better educated than most country blues singers and with a positive penchant for using such archaisms as "thee" and "damsel", James still came up in a hard school, as the bitterness of *Hard Time Killin[g]Floor Blues* attests. Skip James first recorded at the height of the Depression, when there were "hard times here, hard times everywhere I go"; his musical career never really materialized, his original recordings hardly sold and, like Son House's, are now extremely rare collectors' items. His disillusionment over this kept him from trying to record again and, by the time white audiences began to become interested in his music 35 years later, it was already too late to bring him much material reward. However, James was a proud, almost unbending character and always fervently (and justifiably) believed that he had the qualities of genius.

Crow Jane was the very first song James learned, back before World War I, and variants were recorded by other bluesmen such as Big Bill Broonzy (1957) and Carl Martin (1935). He relishes the lyrics, which remind the "high-falutin'" of their mortality. James' own mortality had been brought home to him in hospital, and his *Washington D.C. Hospital [Center] Blues* both describes his experiences there and pays tribute to those who saved his life. *Special Rider Blues* is a theme of particular beauty, both lyrically and instrumentally, inspired by a Little Brother Montgomery piano piece. Since the surviving 78 of this song from 1931 used for reissue is badly worn, it is fortunate that we have this crystal-clear recreation on disc. *Drunken Spree*, a sprightly piece learned from Rich Griffith, an early Bentonia musician, gives a delightful change of mood. Other recorded versions include *Late Last Night* by Sara Martin (1926). *Cherry Ball* [*Cherryball*] was originally a spontaneous improvisation in the Paramount studio: "I love my little Cherry Ball, better than I do myself." *How Long*, freely adapted from the Leroy Carr standard, and *All Night Long* both feature James' idiosyncratic uptempo piano playing; the latter was recorded in 1931 as *If You Haven't Any Hay, Get On Down The Road.* In complete contrast, the beautiful but somber *Cypress Grove* has an eerie-sounding guitar accompaniment which chillingly underscores the lyrics (James normally used the unusual open D minor tuning, which he called "cross-note tuning"). *Look Down The Road* combines traditional elements, but in true Skip James fashion it comes out as a cohesive whole, sounding like no other recording; the light but insistent guitar riff adds great appeal.

My Gal derives from a 1934 blues hit by Texas bluesman Joe Pullum, *Black Gal What Makes Your Head So Hard (***254***)*, but, characteristically, James' version is no copy and the song suits his voice perfectly. *I'm So Glad*, a comparatively light-weight but enjoyable romp which showed off his lightning guitar speed when first recorded in 1931, brought James his only big royalty payments, the song having been recorded by the pop-blues group Cream, featuring Eric Clapton. It is ironic that perhaps his most inconsequential piece should be the one to be heard all round the world, but Skip James' life was full of contradictions and frustrations. He died in October 1969 in Philadelphia, his concert career having largely petered out.

Booker T. Washington White (later dubbed Bukka by his second recording company) first recorded for Victor in 1930, producing the greatly esteemed train blues *The Panama Limited.* He had a hit in 1937 with *Shake 'Em On Down*, eventually followed up with two sessions of sustained brilliance in 1940 (**87**). But White was a victim of changing tastes, and these Chicago recordings were his last for a black audience. From the early 1940s he was resident in Memphis, doing day jobs and occasionally playing for dances. He was still there in the summer of 1963 when two researchers came knocking on his door. Unknown to White there had already been much interest in the reissue of his old recordings, particularly when a version of his *Fixin' To Die Blues* had been recorded by Bob Dylan and included on Dylan's first album, issued in March 1962. Three Bukka White LPs were recorded before the end of 1963.

White went back on the road and made many successful concert appearances, presenting the ultimate in barrelhouse blues, sensitive, yet full of power. At his very best, as he certainly was when John Fahey and Ed Denson recorded Bukka soon after locating him, he could almost recapture the quality of his celebrated OKeh session (1940), which produced such classics as *Aberdeen, Mississippi Blues*, a tribute to the nearest big town to the place of his birth (Houston, in November 1906). His voice had coarsened somewhat with the years and his slide-guitar playing had lost a little of its old subtlety, but with his National steel guitar in his hands and in the right environment he was still one of the most powerful and impressive down-home blues singers, outclassing most others in the field.

Apart from re-creating some of his old recordings, including *Parchman Form Blues* (actually *When Can I Change My Clothes?*), *Poor Boy Long Ways From Home* (previously recorded for the Library of Congress), and the spiritual *I Am In The Heavenly Way* (originally a 1930 duet with "Miss Minnie"), White also recorded some new material for the session. *Baby Please Don't Go* is a particularly powerful version of a song normally associated with Big Joe Williams but which has traditional roots. *New Orleans Streamline* and *The Atlanta Special* are improvised songs loosely based on earlier train blues (*Special Streamline* and *The Panama Limited*), in which fantasy and past experience are inextricably woven together. *Drunk Man Blues* offers a rare opportunity to hear Bukka accompanying himself on piano. His tongue-in-cheek *Army Blues* has the same idea as Brownie McGhee's blues of World War II *Million Lonesome Women*, requesting Uncle Sam to "leave me alone, I got to watch these pretty women while the other men is gone" (**249**).

Remembrance of Charlie Patton is of particular interest. Bukka talks reverentially about the great Mississippi blues singer who, he claimed, gave him his first taste of whiskey and became his musical hero, although such was White's compositional ability that he never felt the need to record any of the great man's songs.

Bukka died in 1977, mourned by the whole Memphis blues community and admirers all over the world. Lest it be thought that his vibrant music was that of a bygone era and had little relevance when he performed in the 1960s and 1970s, one should pause to think that one of the most important post-war blues singers, B.B. King, acknowledged a musical debt to his cousin, none other than Booker T. Washington White.

401 Father Of The Delta Blues: The Complete 1965 Sessions
Son House
Columbia C2K 48867/471662-2 (UK)—*2 CD set*
DISC ONE: *Death Letter/Pearline/Louise McGhee/John The Revelator/Empire State Express/Preachin' Blues/Grinnin' In Your Face/Sundown/Levee Camp Moan*

DISC TWO: *Death Letter* (alternate take)/*Levee Camp Moan* (alternate take)/ *Grinnin' In Your Face* (alternate take)/*John The Revelator* (alternate face)/ *Preachin' Blues* (alternate take)/*President Kennedy*/*A Down The Staff*/*Motherless Children*/*Yonder Comes My Mother*/*Shake It And Break It*/*Pony Blues*/ *Downhearted Blues*

402 **Skip James/Today**
Skip James
Vanguard VM CD 7310 (US)/*VMD 79219* (UK)
Hard Time Killin[g]/Floor Blues/Crow Jane/Washington D.C. Hospital [Center] Blues/Special Rider Blues/Drunken Spree/Cherry Ball [Cherryball]/How Long/ All Night Long/Cypress Grove/Look Down The Road/My Gal/I'm So Glad

403 **Mississippi Blues: Legacy of the Blues Vol. 1**
Bukka White
Takoma CDP 72701/Sonet SNTCD 609 (UK)
Aberdeen, Mississippi Blues/Baby Please Don't Go/New Orleans Streamline/ Parchman Farm Blues/Poor Boy Long Ways From Home/Remembrance of Charlie Patton/Shake 'Em On Down/I Am In The Heavenly Way/The Atlanta Special/Drunk Man Blues/Army Blues

(ii) Mr DownChild

Big Joe Williams was the ultimate itinerant blues singer; although he died in the next county (Noxubee) to the one in which he was born (Oktibbeha, a Cherokee Indian name; Williams like a surprisingly large number of other blues singers, had Indian blood) in October 1903, he had traveled many thousands of miles in between. He was on the road early, driven from home by the "mean stepfather" he sings about so vehemently on his first Arhoolie album. He criss-crossed the United States many times over the next 50 years, singing and playing his guitar wherever he could. In the 1960s and 1970s his horizons broadened and he toured Europe and Japan. Admittedly his last few years were spent in his home town of Crawford, Lowndes County, Mississippi, living in a trailer home, his legs troubling him greatly, but even then he still loved to travel. A month or so before he died, in December 1983, he was playing in Memphis.

In 1935 he recorded for Bluebird as Poor Joe Williams and had a hit with *Baby Please Don't Go* (**104**). He continued to record for the company until 1945, having another hit in 1941 with *Crawlin' King Snake*. In 1947 he took part in a couple of sessions for Columbia with Sonny Boy Williamson (**374**). Staying power was the hallmark of Williams' recording career. When the big companies began to lose interest in recording blues, he moved to the new independent companies. In 1957 he made contact in St Louis with Bob Koester, who recorded him extensively for Delmark over a number of years.

A session for Arhoolie held at Los Gatos, California, in October 1960 found Williams in exceptional form. He had just had a most unpleasant brush with the law and his performances were imbued with great emotion and urgency, lifting them to the level of greatness. *Greystone Blues* actually explores his recent, painful experiences; as he sings with vehemence, "no one would go Big Joe's bail", resulting in his being transferred from the Oakland city jail to the altogether more unpleasant correctional facilities in Pleasanton.

Williams worked regularly with John Lee (Sonny Boy) Williamson in Chicago and recorded with him several times before Williamson was brutally murdered in 1948. As a tribute to his old partner he revived a number that Williamson had recorded successfully in 1941 and again in 1947, *Sloppy Drunk Blue* (**373**). Williams' incredible bass-string slapping on this and the traditional *Forty Four Blues* is as powerful as a string bass and develops tremendous momentum. Although he used a conventional six-string guitar on his first recordings, by the 1940s he was using a unique, home-made, nine-string guitar, with the first, second, and fourth strings doubled.

Brother James is a faster version of a grim number about a car wreck in Mississippi, that he had first recorded in 1937. *Shake Your Boogie* is an uninhibited version of another Sonny Boy Williamson number, while *She Left Me A Mule To Ride* reworks a piece that Williams recorded several times in the 1950s, again derived from a popular recording by Williamson. *Vitamin A Blues* revives one of his recordings of 1945, but with frank references to Mary (then his common-law wife) and his recent experience, "I been in trouble, I don't know what's been going on", "she may be in love with some other man, because she don't never have no pep for me", turning it into another emotional performance. *So Glad* is a most moving evocation of home-coming, prefaced by the remark that it was his "dear old mother's favorite song, before she died." *Yo Yo Blues*, when issued on LP, was subtitled *(A) Levee Camp Moan*, and is entirely different to the song of the same title recorded by Barbecue Bob and other Georgia bluesmen. *President Roosevelt* is a superb variant of Williams' 1945 recording *His Spirit Lives On* for the small Chicago label, one of a number of tributes to Franklin D. Roosevelt, savior of the nation through the Depression and World War II. Only three years later Joe composed a moving tribute to President Kennedy (**38**). Mary Williams spiritedly performed the old gospel number *I Want My Crown*, with Joe supporting on guitar.

Nine years after his first session for Arhoolie, Big Joe again recorded for Chris Strachwitz. *Thinking Of What They Did To Me* referred to Joe's earlier troubles but the emotional mood was naturally less intense on this session. Nonetheless, performances like *Killing Floor Blues* and *Take Me Out Of The Bottom* are delivered with considerable power and conviction. Over a recording career lasting nearly half a century, Joe Williams seldom gave less than his best.

Sleepy John Estes must be counted as one of the major blues songwriters—his *Someday Baby* (usually titled *Worried Life Blues*) has been recorded by artists as diverse as Big Maceo, Ray Charles, and Chuck Berry—as well as a moving vocalist, employing a style that Big Bill Broonzy graphically described as "crying the blues." Born out in the country near Ripley, Tennessee, in January 1904, John Adam Estes was virtually the same age as Big Joe Williams (it has been suggested that both were about four years older than their official birth years suggest; but we shall never know for certain). It was Williams who was responsible for Estes' return to recording. Blues researchers had assumed that Estes was dead, but Williams knew that he was still living in Brownsville, Tennessee, and told fellow bluesman Memphis Slim; the latter relayed the information to David Blumenthal, who was making a documentary film *Citizen South—Citizen North* and who visited Estes. Later Blumenthal mentioned his find to Bob Koester of Delmark Records, who lost no time in bringing him to Chicago for an exploratory recording session early in 1962. On the strength of this he was signed up for the label.

Estes' rediscovery sent shock waves through the blues world, some diehard collectors even refusing to believe that he could still be alive. (At this time his unissued sessions for Ora Nelle, Sun, and Bea & Baby were unknown to blues collectors.) His first LP, aptly titled **The Legend Of Sleepy John Estes** (and retained for this CD), confounded the sceptics, demonstrating that he was still in full possession of his musical powers, and initiating a series of albums that presents one of the most fully rounded aural portraits of any major down-home blues artist.

The very first track, a post-war composition, takes the listener straight into the harsh environment of the poor Southern black; even then Estes tinges the bleakness with humor:

> Oh them rats is mean in my kitchen, I have ordered me a mountain cat [*twice*]
> The way they 'stroyin' my groceries, I declare you know it's tight like that.

There is no doubt that Estes was in penury when Delmark rescued him from obscurity, and that the modest income he received from recordings and concert appearances over the next 15 years never really lifted him out of the poverty-stricken circumstances he had endured for much of his life.

The rapport with harmonica player Hammie Nixon, who had accompanied Estes on many of his classic recordings for Champion and Decca in 1935 and 1937 (**256**), contributes greatly to the success of eight of the 12 recordings. A dozen years younger than Estes, Nixon "came up" under the influence of the older man, "seconding" him at medicine shows and in juke joints in the South and later venturing up to Chicago with him, where Mayo Williams secured them a recording contract. The four songs without Nixon have a sparer sound. *Milk Cow Blues* in its original version (**112**) inspired the Kokomo Arnold hit of 1934, which in turn was recorded by Elvis Presley for Sun in 1954 (**330**). On the grim *Death Valley Blues*, first recorded by Big Boy Crudup in 1941, and a new version of *Down South Blues*, in which he expresses his intention to go south to escape the rigors of winter, a bass player supports. Knocky Parker's piano further strengthens the sound on the up-tempo stomp *Stop That Thing* and the cynical *Who's Been Telling You, Buddy Brown*. In another classic, *Married Woman Blues*, Estes advises against taking up with a married woman as she will "take all your money" and then leave. *You Got To Go* and *I'd Been Well Warned* are two affecting post-war compositions. The first concerns the draft, while the second movingly tells how Estes lost his eyesight completely in 1950, having been blind in one eye since childhood. He had then left Memphis and returned to Brownsville, married, and raised a family. He was still living in Brownsville in the environment in which he felt most comfortable when he died suddenly in June 1977.

Rice Miller, better known as the second Sonny Boy Williamson, was one of the blues' most enigmatic and mysterious figures. For ten years he was a successful recording artist for Chess in Chicago (**364**), and he developed a considerable following when he appeared in concert in Europe in 1963–4. Impressive as a harmonica wizard, he was a hawk-like figure, hovering at the microphone and swooping into a demonstration of astonishing virtuosity on the instrument. He even recorded with prominent rock and blues groups of the day, such as the Yardbirds. By 1965, having returned to his home in Helena, Arkansas, he was dead. His gravestone in Turwiler, Mississippi, states that he was born in 1908, his passport said 1909, but he was certainly older than this and was born in Glendora, Mississippi, probably about 1901. His real name was thought to be Alex (or Aleck) Miller, but he was also known as Willie Miller or Williams(on). In the final analysis, all that really matters is that he was an outstanding blues artist.

Long before his belated success Miller had tramped the Mississippi Delta and surrounding areas, playing in the dangerous world of juke joints, levee camps, and Saturday night dances for decades, learning his craft and just scuffling to stay alive. In 1938 his first real break came when he started broadcasting over KFFA radio in Helena. It was to be another dozen years, however, before he made his first recordings for the Trumpet label in Jackson, Mississippi.

Then aged about 50, with a lifetime in the blues behind him, Miller produced a consistently excellent series of recordings, the first 16 of which are included on the Arhoolie CD. Its title, **King Biscuit Time**, comes from the KFFA show that he played on for many years and *V-8 Ford, Stormy Monday, Right Now*, and *Come Go With Me* were actually recorded during a broadcast in 1965. (Elmore James sometimes appeared on KFFA and Miller played harmonica on Elmore's first recording, *Dust My Broom.*) Alongside him in the band was guitarist Joe Willie Wilkins, whose playing was an important factor in the success, musically and commercially, not only of Miller's but also of many other recording for Trumpet. Wilkins did not play on Miller's first recording, *Eyesight To The Blind*, with its startling imagery, and instead the piano is well featured; coupled with the up-tempo *Crazy About You Baby*, it sold well. Trumpet soon had another session set up, with Miller complaining to his woman in *Stop Crying* that "all you throwing away is mine", but on the other hand encouraging her in *Do It If You Wanna*, which is primarily an instrumental showcase. Rapid tempos were a feature of this session and Miller can often be heard finger-clicking and shouting encouragement to the band. On *Cool, Cool Blues* guitar and harmonica interweave while Miller sings of leaving a hopeless situation and finding some new place to go. *Come On Back Home* and *I Cross My Heart* are fast blues, the latter coupled with the best song from the session, *West Memphis Blues*. This recounts how the house Miller had bought there three years earlier had burned down.

Sonny Boy's Christmas Blues, from the next session, is outstanding; Miller is on top form as he recounts that he tried to "fetch" religion but the devil would not let him pray, so he had to stay drunk all Christmas Day, his woman having left him alone. *Pontiac Blues* was inspired by a car owned by Mr and Mrs McMurry, the proprietors of Trumpet Records, which he liked and was sometimes allowed to drive. (Miller was usually on foot as he tended to spend his money on alcohol). In lively vein he sings about cruising down Highway 49.

The third and final session included the unusual feature of Cliff Givens on vocal bass. He is most effective on the atmospheric *Mighty Long Time*, jelling with the simple guitar figure while Miller moodily sings the superb lyrics describing how his woman had been away so long that the carpet had faded on the floor. The stabbing harmonica phrases echo the mood of desolation. The use of echo presages Sun's use of this effect on its hits a few years later. The record was a hit, not the least because it was coupled with *Nine Below Zero*, which matches it lyrically, with Miller declaring that his woman had been so heartless as to put him out for another man while the temperature was below freezing. *She Brought Life Back To The Dead* employs even more bizarre imagery than his first recording, while *Too Close Together* and *Stop Now Baby* are fast, jive blues *Mr. Downchild*, reputedly a Robert Johnson piece, suits Miller's style admirably, and perhaps sums up much of his life before his last few years of recognition as a fine singer and one of the greatest blues harmonica players of all time.

404 **Shake Your Boogie**
Big Joe Williams
Arhoolie CD 315
Sloppy Drunk Blues/Yo Yo Blues [A Levee Camp Moan]/President Roosevelt/Forty-Four Blues/Greystone Blues/I Want My Crown [Mary Williams, vocal]/*Mean Stepfather/Brother James/Shake Your Boogie/Vitamin A Blues/She Left Me A Mule To Ride/So Glad/Louisiana Bound/Killing Floor Blues/Throw The Boogie Woogie/Dirt Road Blues/Montreal Blues/Take Me Out Of The Bottom/Thinking Of What They Did To Me/The Death Of Dr. Martin Luther King/Army Man In Vietnam/Creole Queen/Remember Way Back/King Jesus*

405 **The Legend of Sleepy John Estes**
Sleepy John Estes
Delmark DD 603
Rats In My Kitchen/Someday Baby/Stop That Thing/Diving Duck Blues/Death Valley Blues/Married Woman Blues/Down South Blues/Who's Been Telling You, Buddy Brown/Drop Down Mama/You Got To Go/Milk Cow Blues/I'd Been Well Warned

406 **King Biscuit Time**
"Sonny Boy Williamson" [Rice Miller]
Arhoolie CD 310
Do It If You Wanna/Cool, Cool Blues/Come On Back Home/Stop Crying/Eyesight To The Blind/West Memphis Blues/I Cross My Heart/Crazy About You Baby/Nine Below Zero/Mighty Long Time/She Brought Life Back To The Dead/Stop Now Baby/Mr. Downchild/Sonny Boy's Christmas Blues/Pontiac Blues/Too Close Together/[Radio program (KFFA)]: *V-8 Ford/Stormy Monday/Right Now/Come Go With Me;* Elmore James, *Dust My Broom*

(iii) Time Has Made a Change

John Lee Hooker has cast a long shadow over the blues world for the past 50 years. His first hit, *Boogie Children*, is reputed to have sold a million copies and was certainly hugely successful. Hooker never looked back, recording for a bewildering number of labels, often under pseudonyms such as Texas Slim or Birmingham Sam, (**370**, **399**). He continued to have hits, though none was as big as his first. In the mid-

1950s he signed with Vee Jay Records and produced both new material and smoother but almost equally effective versions of his earlier recordings, with band accompaniment.

During the 1960s, Hooker was lifted to pop star status with the new white audience for blues, and he recorded with rock stars and electric blues groups such as Canned Heat. In June 1964 he actually penetrated the UK Top 30 with *Dimples*, later repeating this success with *Boom Boom*. In the disco era of the 1970s he issued his *Endless Boogie*, and the blues quality became somewhat diluted. Hooker remains a major figure, however, and can still sing the blues like few others. In the summer of 1988 he returned to England after a long absence and played to packed houses, his status undiminished. The following year *The Healer* album was released and was awarded a platinum disc. John Lee Hooker became a superstar, with his albums in every record store.

Hooker was 31 years old when in November 1948 he made his first recording in Detroit, Michigan, his base through the 1950s. His musical roots were back in Mississippi Delta country—he was born in Clarksdale, its principle town, in August 1917—and in Memphis, where he worked on Beale Street before moving north. He learned guitar from his stepfather and was probably influenced to some extent by such artists as Tony Hollins and Big Joe Williams, but everything to be heard on these early recordings is pure Hooker. He sounds little like anyone else, even on a well-known number such as Sonny Boy Williamson's *Decoration Day Blues*. What he was playing during the period covered by the reissue CD **No Friend Around**, the first two years of his recording career, was pure down-home blues, but his heavily amplified guitar and boogie patterns somehow made it sound of the city, and it appealed to black record buyers in the North as well as in the South. Although recorded in relatively primitive conditions, such as the back room of a record shop, and with inevitable surface noise, Hooker may still be heard clearly throughout.

The opening and closing tracks are largely instrumental: *Stomp Boogie* emphasizes his foot-stomping, which is as much as integral part of the performance as his dynamic guitar playing; the anarchic *Do The Boogie* features a pianist and has shouted dance instructions. *Black Man Blues* is Hooker at his best, an intense performance by a man alone with his guitar, expressing his troubles in song to dispel his violent mood. *Helpless Blues* conveys his powerlessness to stop his woman leaving. Listening to *Goin' Mad Blues* is an amazing experience: Hooker's guitar becomes overwhelming as he becomes more and more intense, sounding like a man on the edge of disintegration. *Morning Blues* is another song of despair, Hooker literally moaning the blues. *Roll 'n' Roll* derives from the traditional *Roll And Tumble Blues*, but as expected it bears little relationship to any other recorded version. The title track, *No Friend Around*, is a theme to which Hooker often returned on later recordings, "T. B.'s killing me." This is the definitive expression of it.

Low Down Midnight Boogie and *House Rent Boogie* are pure enjoyment, as Hooker presents a humorous side to his music: he didn't have the rent and out the door he went. *Wandering Blues* reworks Charles Brown's big hit *Drifting Blues*, personalizing the lyrics. *Landing Blues* describes his experience down at the landing looking for his woman to come off the "Big Boat." *My Baby's Got Somethin'* is up-tempo, with Hooker throwing in some wordless "doodle-oos" while his guitar acts as a second voice.

Born in Frayser, Tennessee, in the same month (April) and year (1915) as Muddy Waters, Johnny Shines also made his first commercial recordings for Columbia in 1946. Neither artist had the results of their session issued, but Muddy Waters soon went on to success with Chess, whereas Shines made a few magnificent but poor-selling recordings in Chicago between 1950 and 1953 (**375**) and then faded from the scene, visiting the clubs only to photograph other blues artists. Preoccupied with the need to keep body and soul together, he reverted to day work and for ten years virtually gave up music. He was persuaded to start recording again in 1965 and quickly made a name for himself, both as a solo performer and in a band context (often with long-time associate Walter "Shakey" Horton) (**398**). He has many splendid LPs to his credit (not all of which have been reissued on CD), but it is those that reflect his Memphis and Mississippi Delta roots that seem the most impressive. In his youth he was inspired by Howlin' Wolf and traveled with both Robert Johnson (**86**) and Rice Miller.

In 1968 Shines recorded for the UK Blue Horizon label in Chicago. Horton (harmonica) and Clifton James (drums) are present on several tracks, including *Baby Don't You Think I Know* —a high energy adaptation of *Baby Don't You Want To Go (Sweet Home Chicago)*— and *Pipeline Blues* (imaginatively developed from Robert Johnson's *I'm A Steady Rollin' Man*), which also features pianist Otis Spann. However, **Last Night's Dream** (reissued as a CD under the Sire marque) is not really a band album. Willie Dixon's bass is an unobtrusive pulse on *Solid Gold, I Had A Good Home*, and the title track, on all of which Johnny plays stunning slide guitar. These sublime performances are essentially solo Delta blues, with strong echoes of Son House and Robert Johnson. Quite different are *From Dark 'Till Dawn* ("no one will steal my woman, it'll be too dangerous to try"), *I Will Be Kind To You* with its insistent rhythms and almost Faustian message ("give me your soul, I'll give you silver and gold") and the lyrically adventurous *Mean Fisherman*, a most unusual piece with its philosophical tone, loose structure, and sensitive use of falsetto singing. Shines is in magnificent voice throughout the session, sometimes squalling like the *Black Panther* he sings about in his revival of an old Sonny Boy Williamson blues or in contrast sombre and restrained as in *I Don't Know*, with its overtones of Johnson's *Ramblin' On My Mind*. Johnny continued to record and play concerts through the 1970s, making several tours overseas, but his considerable reputation as a performer was rarely matched with press recognition and commensurate financial reward (his unpublished autobiography was ironically titled *Success Is My Downfall*). A stroke interrupted his career around 1980 and although he continued to perform, his guitar playing was severely affected. In later years Johnny escaped from the urban pressures of Chicago and made his home in Tuscaloose, Alabama, where he died in April 1992.

Only a few of the many blues performers recorded on field trips in the South during the past three decades achieved much more than passing interest when their recordings were first made available. Attention has always focused more strongly on the "name" artists who had recorded previously, whether only a couple of 78s or successfully over a long period. An outstanding exception to this general rule is "Mississippi" Fred McDowell, who was born just over the state line in Rossville, Tennessee, in about 1904. He spent his formative years in that state, but had been long resident in Como, Mississippi, when he was discovered by the noted folklorist Alan Lomax who, assisted by Shirley Collins, spent two months in the summer of 1959 making recordings right across the South. This major field trip produced over 20 albums of material, issued in separate series by Atlantic (**313/14**), Prestige and, subsequently, New World Records (**42**). Much worthwhile music was included, but it was the recordings made of McDowell that seized the attention of the expanding white blues audience. So impressed was Chris Strachwitz of Arhoolie Records that, when the opportunity came, he visited Fred in Como (which lies east of the Delta proper, in Panola County) and recorded what can only be described as one of the most impressive début albums of all time.

You Gotta Move incorporates this album. When first issued the CD was entitled "Mississippi Delta Blues" but in fact McDowell was an exponent of what might be termed a "North Mississippi" blues style. Similar sounding artists include R. L. Burnside, Rosa Lee Hill, and old-timer Eli Green, from whom McDowell learned several pieces, among them *Write Me A Few Lines*. (Green also recorded with McDowell, his guitar playing sounding not dissimilar to that of Son House.) Apart from his warm and modest personality (not qualities displayed by all blues singers), McDowell's great attributes were his truly brilliant slide-guitar playing (he usually used a metal slide, with his guitar in an open tuning), his unerring sense of rhythm and timing, and his strong, expressive voice. His material was a potent mixture of original songs, reworkings, and traditional material, but everything came out sounding like Fred McDowell.

The disc commences with one of his strongest numbers, previously recorded for Lomax: "When you get home, baby, write me a few of your lines, that'll be consolation to my worried mind." The pace never slackens as guitar answers voice in call-and-response pattern. Johnny Temple's very popular 1936 recording *Louise Louise Blues* established the song as a blues "standard" and McDowell recorded several versions of it; none better than this, the first. *I Heard Somebody Call* includes traditional verses such as the intriguing one beginning "I got a girl in Cuby, I got three in Spain." The road that gives its name to *61 Highway*, the "longest road I know", runs from Memphis through the Delta country and has been the subject of several blues *Mama Don't Allow [Me]* is taken very fast, and McDowell's control over his bottle-neck-guitar playing at this speed is breathtaking; his version is quite different in concept to that by Sleepy John Estes (as *Drop Down Mana*: **405**). *Kokomo Blues* had been widely recorded in a number of different guises; one variant by Robert Johnson produced the post-war standard *Sweet Home Chicago* also reflected in Johnny Shines' version, mentioned above.

Fred's Worried Life Blues was his own reworking of the Sleepy John Estes composition so widely recorded by blues singers of several generations. *You Gonna Be Sorry, My Trouble Blues*, and *That's Alright* are slow and brooding. *Shake 'Em On Down* is perhaps the highlight of the whole CD, the power and urgency of McDowell's slide-guitar playing being particularly exhilarating. The song is the classic Bukka White composition (**87**, **403**), but is treated very differently to the original. *Black Minnie* is a song well known in Mississippi and Tennessee; Tommy McClennan recorded it in 1940 but Sleepy John Estes called it *Black Mattie Blues* when he made it in 1929 (**112**).

The final six tracks (originally included on Fred's second Arhoolie LP) were recorded a couple of years later and include two Eli Green vocals (*Brooks Run Into The Ocean* and *Bull Dog Blues*) with the almost eerie sound of two slide guitars accompanying. *You Gotta Move* was arguably Fred's strongest recording of a gospel piece; it was later "adopted" by the Rolling Stones. McDowell often recorded spirituals with his wife Annie Mae, and she took the vocal on *When I Lay My Burden Down*. Fred laid his burden down in July 1972, when he died in a Memphis hospital.

Chester Arthur Burnett was born in West Point, Mississippi, not many miles away from Bukka White's birthplace, Houston, in June 1910 (making him a year older than Robert Johnson). Unlike White, however, he did not become a recording artist until well after the end of World War II. His youth was spent working as a plantation hand in the Delta but, like White, he developed an enthusiasm for the blues of Charlie Patton and his disciples. He began to sing and play guitar around 1928 and later learned blues harmonica from his brother-in-law, Rice Miller (the second Sonny Boy Williamson), acquiring several nicknames along the way, including one reflecting an aspect of his massive 6' 3", 20-stone frame, "Big Foot". However, "Howlin' Wolf" was the one that stuck.

Music was only a sideline for Wolf through the 1930s as he farmed with his father, Dock Burnett, and after army service he went back on the farm. In 1948 he moved to West Memphis, Arkansas, and around that time his father died. Wolf became heavily involved in the local music scene and for the first time formed a band—The House Rockers—to play the clubs there and across the Mississippi River in Memphis, Tennessee. Several artists who later became big names in their own right played with him, including harmonica players Junior Parker and James Cotton and guitarist Matt Murphy, but the band's line-up eventually stabilized with Wolf playing harmonica and sometimes second guitar, Willie Johnson (or sometimes Pat Hare) playing lead guitar, pianist "'Struction", and drummer Willie Steele. A regular half-hour program on radio station KWEM, West Memphis, was the springboard to success for Wolf. Musician and entrepreneur Ike Turner introduced him to Sam Phillips, who had set up his Memphis Recording Service in 1950 to record local black artists performing both sacred and secular music.

There is a popular misconception, often repeated in print, that Howlin' Wolf recorded for Sun Records. In fact, although during 1951 Sam Phillips supervised a number of recording sessions by Howlin' Wolf in what was to become the Sun studio, he didn't yet have his own record label and was leasing material to various independent companies. By the time the Sun label was launched in March 1952, Wolf was signed to an exclusive contract with Chess Records and the following year he moved to Chicago, remaining with Chess for the rest of his life (**363**). Despite Supervising Wolf's sessions only at the beginning of his recording career, Sam Phillips was tremendously impressed by him as a singer and performer, many years later rating him the most exciting he ever recorded, white or black.

Confusion surrounds Howlin' Wolf's earliest recordings. The first, early in 1951, may have been two audition acetates of a Wolf song (he wrote much of his own material in those days) known as *Riding In The Moonlight* or *Baby Ride With Me*, both included in the CD **Howling Wolf Rides Again**. Phillips sent them to Modern Records of Los Angeles, who expressed interest, but in the meantime he sold recordings made in May 1951 of *Moanin' At Midnight* and *How Many More Years* to Chess, who issued them in August and were rewarded with fast sales (**363**). The Bihari brothers, who owned Modern/RPM, were furious about this and terminated their arrangement with Phillips. In September they signed Wolf to a recording contract and immediately contacted talent scout Ike Turner to set up a session for him in West Memphis.

Wolf recut the exhilarating *Riding In The Moonlight* with Turner on piano and Willie Johnson sharpening up the rather restrained guitar accompaniment he used on the earlier acetates. RPM lost no time in issuing this tremendous version (included on the CD but not with the echo added to the vocal chorus as on the original 78 and its vinyl reissue) coupled with a remake of *Moanin' At Midnight* to "cover" the Chess issue. From around the same time comes *Keep What You Got*, possibly inspired by a similar recording under the same title made by Floyd Jones with Snooky and Moody in 1947. Taken very fast, it seems to explode with power as the guitarist takes a shattering solo after Wolf's ferocious harp choruses. Surprisingly, neither this nor the recut of the somber *How Many More Years (Dog Me Around)* were issued until included on a Crown LP in 1961.

At the beginning of October, Wolf was again recorded for RPM, this time at the black YMCA building in Memphis with Joe Bihari supervising, as before, and Ike Turner on piano. In the mistitled *House Rockin' Boogie* (the real one was issued by Chess as *Howlin' Wolf Boogie!*) Wolf gives a namecheck to the members of his band ("play that guitar Willie Johnson, till it smokes") and extolls the virtues of the state of California ("a swell place"). *Crying At Daybreak* was the first recorded version of a song better known as *Smokestack Lightning*, the 1956 recording of which had success in the R&B charts and even brushed the bottom rungs of the UK Top 40 in June 1964. The version of 1951 is different to (but almost the equal of) the Chess masterpiece, Wolf's falsetto whoops echoing Jimmie Rodgers and Tommy Johnson. Coupled with the faster *Passing By Blues* it was quickly issued as a follow-up to the first RPM disc. *My Baby Stole Off* (a poorish dub) and *I Want Your Picture* comprised Wolf's third and last RPM record.

In November and December both companies' versions of *Moanin' At Midnight* appeared on the R&B charts and their dispute came to a head. In February 1952 Modern/RPM recorded Howlin' Wolf again but no titles were issued as that month the disagreement was resolved with Wolf becoming exclusively a Chess artist. A couple later surfaced on the Crown LP, one version of *Chocolate Drop* (as *Brownskin Woman*) and the exciting *Worried About My Baby*, reputedly a song that St Louis Jimmy had given to Wolf, which is taken at a torrid pace with sizzling guitar by Willie Johnson and the big man in tremendous voice. *Driving This Highway* is a lyrically distinct variant of a song recorded for Chess as *Cadillac Daddy* but issued as *Mr. Highway Man, The Sun Is Rising*, a pure delta blues, first appeared on a Kent LP in 1969, as did *My Friends*, in which Wolf displays the paranoid side of his personality, fearing that they are "stealing my clothes", and the self-descriptive *I'm The Wolf* ("that comes out of the woods").

The music created by Howlin' Wolf and his band at this time was certainly full of raw power but in no sense can it be described as "crude" or "primitive." Combining elements of traditional Mississippi blues with rocking R&B rhythms and featuring superb instrumental work (solid drumming, Wolf's propulsive harp playing and Willie Johnson's almost jazzy guitar playing) and the magic of Howlin' Wolf's vocals, these timeless recordings sound fresh and ear-catching in an era when spontaneity has largely been sacrificed in the relentless pursuit of technical perfection.

407 No Friend Around
John Lee Hooker
Red Lightnin' RLCD 0093 (UK)
Stomp Boogie/Black Man Blues/Helpless Blues/Goin' Mad Blues/Morning Blues/Roll 'N' Roll/No Friend Around/Low Down Midnight Boogie/House Rent Boogie/Wandering Blues/Landing Blues/My Baby's Got Somethin'/Decoration Day Blues/Do The Boogie

408 Last Night's Dream
Johnny Shines
Sire 45285-2
Solid Gold/From Dark Till Dawn/I Will Be Kind To You/Last Night's Dream/Baby Don't You Think I Know/Pipeline Blues/I Don't Know/Black Panther/I Had A Good Home/Mean Fisherman

409 You Gotta Move [formerly Mississippi Delta Blues]
Fred McDowell
Arhoolie CD 304
Write Me A Few Lines/Louise/I Heard Somebody Call/61 Highway/Mama Don't Allow [Me]/Kokomo Blues/Fred's Worried Life Blues/You Gonna Be Sorry/Shake 'Em On Down/My Trouble Blues/Black Minnie/That's Alright/When I Lay My Burden Down [Annie Mae McDowell, vocal]/*Ain't Gonna Be Bad No Mo'/Do My Baby Ever Think Of Me*; Eli Green, *Brooks Run Into The Ocean/Bull Dog Blues*; Fred McDowell, *Frisco Line/You Gotta Move*

410 **Howling Wolf Rides Again**
Howling Wolf
Ace CHCHD 333
House Rockin' Boogie/Crying At Daybreak/Keep What You Got/Dog Me Around/Moaning At Midnight/Riding In The Moonlight/Chocolate Drop/My Baby Stole Off/I Want Your Picture/Passing By Blues/Worried About My Baby/ Chocolate Drop (alternate version)/*Driving This Highway/The Sun Is Rising/ Riding In The Moonlight [Baby Ride With Me/*(audition version A)*] My Friends/I'm The Wolf/Riding In The Moonlight [Baby Ride With Me]* (audition version B)

Basic Records

(i) Memphis and the Delta

411 **Memphis Blues Piano Today**
Mose Vinson and Booker T. Laury
Wolf CD 120.928 (Au)
Booker T. Laury, *Next Time You See Me/Big Legged Woman/Blues With A Feeling/Booker T's Memphis Blues/Night Time Is The Right Time/Sweet Root Man/You Can Go Your Way/Booker's Boogie*; Mose Vinson, *Blues Jump The Rabbit/Tell Me Like It Is/Boogie Woogie Blues/Good Morning Memphis/44 Blues/4'O Clock Blues/You're Not Too Old/Lost My Mule Blues*
Vinson, born in 1917, has survived from the shadowy band of juke-joint and dance-hall pianists to record old-time blues and boogies. Also recorded in 1990, Laury works through an excellent program of blues and barrelhouse numbers, including *Big Legged Woman*, which he performed in the film *Great Balls of Fire*.

412 **Boogie Disease**
Dr. Ross
Arhoolie CD 371
Boogie Disease (take 5)/*Going To The River/Good Thing Blues/Turkey Leg Woman/Country Clown/My BeBop Gal/Memphis Boogie (Juke Box Boogie,* take 1)/*Shake' Em On Down/Down South Blues/Shake A My Hand/Little Soldier Boy/Mississippi Blues (Cat Squirrel)/Going Back Down South/Dr. Ross (Chicago)/Breakdown* (take 2)/*Taylor Mae/Texas Hop/Chicago Breakdown* (take 3)/*Juke Box Boogie* (take 2)/*Feel So Sad/Polly Put Your Kettle On/Industrial Avenue Boogie/Downtown Boogie*
After moving to Detroit, Dr Ross achieved a measure of fame as a one-man band. These first recordings, most previously unissued, were made by Sam Phillips in Memphis between 1951 and 1954. On some he is accompanied only by his own guitar and harmonica, on others by a small band; they are uniformly excellent.

413 **Furry Lewis**
Folkways 3823—Cassette
Longing Blues/John Henry/I Will Turn Your Money Green/Early Recording Career/Pearlee Blues/Judge Boushay Blues/I'm Going To Brownsville/The Medicine Shows/Casey Jones/East St Louis Blues

Furry Lewis is another pre-war recording artist (**90**) who had sunk into obscurity when he was located and recorded in Memphis in 1959. He reminisces about his recording career and medicine-show days and performs several of his best pieces with bottleneck-guitar accompaniment. He continued to record through the 1960s and 1970s.

414 **The Be-Bop Boy**
Joe Hill Louis, with Walter Horton and Mose Vinson
Bear Family BCD 15524 AH (Ger)
Joe Hill Louis, *She Treats Me Mean And Evil/Dorothy Mae/Sweetest Gal In Town/Keep Your Arms Around Me/Got A New Woman/I'm A Poor Boy*; Walter Horton, *In The Mood* (instrumental)/*West Winds Are Blowing/Little Walter's Boogie* (take 1)/*We All Got To Go* (*Sometime*); Joe Hill Louis, *We All Gotta Go Sometime* (take 3); Walter Horton, *Little Walter's Boogie* (take 2); Joe Hill Louis, *Tigerman* (demo); Mose Vinson, *44 Blues*; Joe Hill Louis, *My Love Has Gone*; Mose Vinson, *Mistreatin' Boogie/My Love Has Gone/Worry You Off My Mind/Reap What You Sow*; Walter Horton, *Walter's Instrumental*; Joe Hill Louis, *Hydramatic Woman/Tigerman/Keep Your Arms Around Me* (alternate take)/*She Comes To See Me Sometime/We All Gotta Go Sometime* (take 2)/ *Shine Boy*
Louis shares this CD with harmonica ace "Shaky" Horton pianist Mose Vinson. Joe was an exceptionally gifted bluesman, singing and playing guitar and harmonica, sometimes operating as a one-man-band. He died in 1957, missing the blues revival of the 1960s which would have showcased his talents.

415 **The Ultimate Memphis Blues Collection**
Various Artists
Memphis 07 (Neth)—*2 CD set*
DISC ONE: Joe Hill Louis, *Boogie In The Park*; Lost John Hunter & The Blind Bats, *Cool Down Mama*; Sleepy John Estes, *Runnin' Around*; Hotshot Love, *Hormonica Jam*; Mose Vinson, *Mistreatin' Boogie*; Sleepy John Estes, *Registration Day Blues*; Howlin' Wolf, *Highway Man*; Charlie Booker, *Walked All Night*; Joe Hill Louis, *We All Gotta Go Sometime*; Pinetop Perkins, *Pinetop's Boogie Woogie*; Howlin' Wolf, *My Troubles And Me*; Houston Stokes, *You'll Be Sorry*; Jimmy De Berry, *Take A Little Chance*; Memphis Ma Rainey, *Baby No. 10*; Sammy Lewis & Willie Johnson Combo, *I Feel So Worried*; Walter Horton, *Easy*; Howlin' Wolf, *Everybody's In The Mood*; Joe Hill Louis, *Hydramatic Woman*; Johnny O'Neal, *Ugly Woman*; Sammy Lewis & Willie Johnson Combo, *So Long Baby, Good Bye*; Jimmy DeBerry, *Before Long*; Tot Randolph, *Blues Train*; Willie Nix, *Prison Bound Blues*; Doctor Ross, *Boogie Disease*; Johnny O'Neal, *Dead Letter Blues*; Houston Boines, *Carry My Business On*; Walter Horton, *Walter's Instrumental*; Howlin' Wolf, *Come Back Home*

DISC TWO: Houston Stokes, *Baby Gone And Left Me*; Jackie Brenston, *Rocket 88*; Junior Parker, *Feelin' Good*; Willie Nix, *Baker Shop Boogie*; Little Milton, *Beggin' For My Baby*; Billy "The Kid" Emerson, *Shim Sham Shimmy*; Rufus Thomas, *Save That Money*; Pat Hare, *Bonus Pay*; Jackie Brenston, *My Real Gone Rocket*; Roscoe Gordon, *I Found A New Love*; Eddie Snow, *Bring Your Love Back Home*; Junior Parker, *Love My Baby*; Doctor Ross, *Juke Box Boogie*; Billy "The Kid" Emerson, *When It Rains It Really Pours*; James

Cotton, *My Baby*; Roscoe Gordon, *Cheese And Crackers*; Little Milton, *Lookin' For My Baby*; Rufus Thomas, *Tiger Man*; Junior Parker, *Mystery Train* ; James Cotton, *Cotton Crop Blues*; Eddie Snow, *Ain't That Right*; Billy "The Kid" Emerson, *Red Hot*; Rufus Thomas, *Bear Cat*; Little Milton, *If You Love Me*; Pat Hare, *I'm Gonna Murder My Baby*; Billy "The Kid" Emerson, *Move Baby Move*; Willie Nix, *Midnight Showers Of Rain*; Roscoe Gordon, *I'm Gonna Shake It*
Illustrating the depth and breadth of recordings made by Sam Phillips between 1950 and 1956, this compilation ranges from out-and-out country blues—Estes, De Berry—to Brenston's irresistible R&B smash *Rocket 88*, and Gordon's novelty *Cheese And Crackers*. There are acknowledged and lesser-known down-home classics. *Mystery Train* and *When It Rains It Pours* were later recorded by Elvis Presley (**330**).

416 **Avalon Blues**
Mississippi John Hurt
Flyright FLY CD 06 (UK)
Avalon Blues/Richlands Women Blues/Frankie And Albert/Louis Collins/Stackolee/Coffee Blues/Slidin' Delta/Corrine Corrina/Nobody'd Dirty Business/Monday/Morning Blues/Hey Baby Right Away/Spanish Flangdang/Pay Day/Talking Casey Jones/Let The Mermaids Flirt With Me/Got The Blues That Can't Be Satisfied/Stocktime/Candy Man/Pera-Lee/Trouble I've Had It All My Days
Still resident in Avalon, Mississippi, 35 years after his first recordings (**50**) songster John Hurt was located by researchers early in 1963. In July he was extensively recorded for the Library of Congress. These selections are from those sessions and feature many of the strongest pieces in the repertoire.

417 **Roots Of Rhythm And Blues: A Tribute To The Robert Johnson Era**
Various Artists
Columbia CK 49584/472264–2 (UK)
Johnny "Ned" Shines & Ensemble, *Sweet Home Chicago*; Lonnie Pitchford, *Come On In My Kitchen*; Moving Star Hall Singers, *You've Got To Move*; Henry Townsend, *All My Money's Gone*; Robert Junior Lockwood, *How Long, How Long Blues*; David Honeyboy Edwards, *That's Alright*; Jessie Mae Hemphill, *Train, Train*; Elder Roma Wilson, *This Train*; Phil Wiggins, *Silver Comet Train*; Railroad Maintenance Crew, *Captain Can't Read*; Johnny "Ned" Shines, *Satisfied/Watermelons*; David Savage, *I'm Going Home*; John Cephas & Phil Wiggins, *The Brownsville Blues*; Johnny "Ned" Shines & Ensemble, *Loved And Lost*; Lonnie Pitchford, *Walking Blues*; Johnny "Ned" Shines, *Tell Me Daddy, How You Want Your Rolling Done*; David Savage, *Bertha*; Moving Star Hall Singers, *If You Miss Me*; Johnny "Ned" Shines & Ensemble, *The Moon Is Rising*; Robert Junior Lockwood, *Kind Hearted Woman*; Toshi Reagon, *I Hate To See The Sun Go Down*; Lonnie Pitchford, *Terraplane Blues*; Johnny "Ned" Shines & Ensemble, *Milkcow Blues/Fat Mama*
Selected from a program at the Smithsonian Folklife Festival in July 1991, this CD includes gospel music, worksongs, and a variety of down-home blues as a backcloth to Johnson's recordings. Interpretations are performed by close associates Shines and Lockwood and the much younger Lonnie Pitchford. The musical quality is very high and the idea most laudable.

418 **Delta Blues 1951**
Various Artists
Alligator ALCD 2702
Big Joe Williams, *Delta Blues/Mama Don't Allow Me/She Left Me A Mule/Bad Heart Blues/Juanita/Friends And Pals/Over Hauling Blues/Whistling Blues*; Luther Huff, *1951 Blues/Dirty Disposition/Bull Dog Blues/Rosalee*; Willie Love, *Everybody's Fishing/My Own Boogie/74 Blues/Shady Lane Blues/21 Minutes To Nine/Vanity Dresser Boogie*
Big Joe is in commanding form, updating his sound with heavy amplification. The Huff brothers sound more "central Mississippi" than Delta. Vocalist/pianist Love is accompanied by such guitar luminaries as Elmore James, Joe Willie Wilkins and Little Milton. All were recorded in the space of a year for Trumpet in Jackson, Mississippi.

419 **Mississippi Delta Blues: Blow My Blues Away, Volume 1**
Various Artists
Arhoolie CD 401
Napoleon Strickland & The Como Drum Band/*Oh Baby/Como Breakdown*; Johnny Woods & Fred McDowell, *Three O'Clock In The Morning/My Jack Don't Need No Water (Long Haired Doney)*; Teddy Williams, *Catfish Blues/Down Home Blues*; Do-Boy Diamond, *Long Haired Doney (My Jack Don't Need No Water)/Hard Time Blues/The Shaggy Hound/Going Away Blues*; Walter Miller, *Stuttgart, Arkansas/Vicksburg Blues*; Robert Diggs, *Mississippi Goin' To Be My Home/Dangerous Slim/Drink, Drink, Drink*; Rosa Lee Hill, *Pork And Beans*; Dewey Corley, *Fishing In The Dark/Tri-State Bus*; Tom Turner, *Gonna Bring Her Right Back Home*; Peck Curtis & The Blues Rhythm Boys, *The Death Of Sonny Boy Williamson*; Robert Nighthawk & The Blues Rhythm Boys, *Nighthawk Boogie* (instrumental) /*You Call Yourself A Cadillac* [Carey Mason, vocal]/*Blues Before Midnight* (instrumental)
George Mitchell's Mississippi field trips in 1967 and 1968 produced a wealth of down-home blues recordings, mostly by artists who had never been recorded, illustrating the continuing strength of the music. The Como Drum Band represents a previously little known local fife-and-drum band tradition (**35**).

420 **Mississippi Delta Blues: Blow My Blues Away, Volume 2**
Various Artists
Arhoolie CD 402
Joe Callicott, *Lonesome Katy Blues/Come Home To Me Baby/Fare You Well Baby Blues/Country Blues/Laughing To Keep From Crying/Love Me Baby Blues (France Chance)/I Rolled And I Tumbled/Old Bo Weevil/Up Town Blues/Traveling Mama Blues/Fare Thee Well Blues*; R.L. Burnside, *Poor Black Mattie/Long Haired Doney/Going Down South/Skinny Woman/I's Be Troubled/Catfish Blues/See My Jumper Hangin' Out On The Line/I Rolled And I Tumbled/Walking Blues/Nightmare Blues*; Houston Stackhouse & The Blues Rhythm Boys, *Cool Water Blues/Big Road Blues/Right Around The Corner* [Peck Curtis, vocal]/*Canned Heat*
Mitchell discovered Burnside in Coldwater, to the east of the Delta. He was an exponent of the popular local percussive style and these are perhaps his best recordings. Callicott was found a few miles north, in Nesbit. He made one 78

in 1930 (included, arguably inappropriately) and his delicate, early style is well sampled. Stackhouse was a Tommy Johnson disciple (**83**).

421 **All Night Long**
Junior Kimbrough & The Soul Blues Boys
Fat Possum FP 1002/Demon FIEND CD 742 (UK)
Work Me Baby/Do The Romp/Stay All Night/Meet Me In The City/You Better Run/Done Got Old/All Night Long/I Feel Alright/Nobody But You/Slow Lightnin'
Proving downhome blues is alive and well in Marshall County, Mississippi, this CD (recorded in 1993) presents the authentic juke-joint sound of singer-guitarist Kimbrough, supported by drums and bass. Constructed from old and new song elements, his powerfully hypnotic pieces are rooted in the highly rhythmic, percussive blues tradition peculiar to the area east of the Delta.

(ii) Behind The Sun: Central/South Mississippi and Louisiana

422 **The Mississippi Sheik**
Sam Chatmon
Blue Goose 2006—LP
Go Back Old Devil/B & Blues/Love Come Falling Down/Make Me A Pallet On The Floor/Vacation Blues/Last Chance Shaking In The Bed With Me/Blues In E/Stretching Them Things/Brownskin Women Blues/Fool About My Loving/Turnip Greens/Cold Blooded Murder Blues/Sam's Rag/Cross Cut Saw Blues/Kansas City Blues
Chatmon was a blues singer-cum-songster who for many years was in the shadow of his more famous brother, Bo Carter (**101**). He came into his own in the 1970s when, with his varied repertoire and compelling vocal and guitar style, he was comprehensively recorded. This particular album provides a satisfying selection of his best work.

423 **Cat Iron Sings Blues And Hymns**
Folkways 2389—Cassette
Poor Boy A Long, Long Way From Home/Don't Your House Look Lonesome/Tell Me, You Didn't Mean Me No Good/Jimmy Bell/I'm Goin' To Walk Your Log/Got A Girl In Ferriday, One In Greenwood Town/Well, I'm In Your Hand/When I Lay My Burden Down/Old Time Religion/Fix Me Right/O, The Blood Done Signed My Name/When The Saints Go Marching Home
This cassette preserves the only recordings of an old-time performer of blues and country gospel material, made by Frederic Ramsey Jr in Natchez, Mississippi. Playing his guitar flat with a small medicine bottle in open D tuning, Cat Iron attacks his songs with fierce vocal power.

424 **Catfish Blues: Mississippi Blues From Jackson & Crystal Springs 1951–1967**
Various Artists
Blue Moon CDBM 090 (UK)
Bobo Thomas & Sonny Boy Williamson, *Catfish Blues*; Tommy Lee Thompson, *Highway 80 Blues/Packin' Up Blues*; Little Milton Anderson & Eddie White, *Little Milton's Boogie/Mistreated Baby Blues*; Little Milton's Juke Band, *Blow It Down/Jackson Juke*; Mager Johnson, *Travelling Blues*; Houston Stackhouse &

Carey "Ditty" Mason, *Mercy Blues* [Mason, vocal]/*Few Clothes*/[Mason, vocal]/*Boogie*/*I Hate To Hear My Good Gal Call My Name* [Mason, vocal]/*Big Road Blues* [Stackhouse, vocal]/*Talkin' 'Bout You* [Stackhouse, vocal]/*That's Alright* [Stackhouse, vocal]/*Pony Blues* [Stackhouse, vocal]/*Kind Hearted Woman* [Stackhouse, vocal]

The first seven recordings were made in Jackson, Mississippi, in the early 1950s. The remainder were recorded by researcher David Evans in Crystal Springs, Mississippi, in 1967. Of particular interest is the fine performance by Tommy Johnson's younger brother, Mager.

425 **Louisiana Country Blues**

Smoky Babe; Herman E. Johnson

Arhoolie CD 440

Smoky Babe, /*I'm Broke And I'm Hungry*/*Too Many Women*/*Two Wings* [duet with William Dotson]/*Mississippi River*/*My Baby She Told Me*/*Rabbit Blues* [duet with Sally Dotson]/*Black Ghost* [duet with Sally Dotson]/*Ain't Got No Rabbit Dog*/*Bad Whiskey*/*Black Gal*/*My Baby Put Me Down*/*Going Back Home*/*Regular Blues*; Herman E. Johnson, *I Just Keeps On Wanting You*/*You Don't Know My Mind*/*Motherless Children*/*Depression Blues*/*She's A-Looking For Me*/*She Had Been Drinking*/*I'm Growing Older*/*Po' Boy*/*Leavin' Blues*/*Piano Blues*/*Where The Mansion's Prepared For Me*

Born in Mississippi, but resident in Louisiana when recorded in 1960–1, Smoky Babe maintains a high level of vocal and instrumental performance. His slide-guitar playing on *Bad Whiskey* is especially fine. Another Louisiana-based bluesman, Herman E. Johnson, also played slide guitar and composed distinctive blues about his life as well as more traditional material.

426 **Free Again**

Robert Pete Williams

Original Blues Classics OBCCD 553

Free Again/*Almost Dead Blues*/*Rolling Stone*/*Two Wings*/*A Thousand Miles From Nowhere*/*Thumbing A Ride*/*I've Grown So Ugly*/*Death Blues*/*Hobo Worried Blues*/*Hay Cutting Song*

Discovered by Dr Harry Oster, at the Angola penitentiary in Louisiana in 1958, Williams proved to be a truly great blues singer with a unique guitar style and the ability to compose moving blues about his life. These vital recordings were made when he was on parole, working long hours on a farm.

(iii) Blues Coast To Coast

427 **The Fifties: Juke Joint Blues**

Various Artists

Flair/*Virgin V2-86304*/*Ace CDCH 216* (UK)

B.B. King, *Three O'clock Blues*; Elmore James, *Long Tall Woman*; Boyd Gilmore, *Ramblin On My Mind*; Baby Face Turner, *Gonna Let You Go*; Bobby Bland & Junior Parker, *Love My Baby*; Howling Wolf, *Ridin' In The Moonlight*; Dudlow & Peck Curtis, *44 Blues*; Sunny Blair, *Step Back Babby*; James Reed, *This Is The End*; Lightnin' Hopkins, *Jake Head Boogie*; Little George Smith, *Down In New Orleans [Hey Mr Porter]*; Dixie Blues Boys, *Monte Carlo*; Floyd Dixon, *Doin' The Town*; Rosco Gordon, *Just In From*

Texas; Jimmy Nelson, *Big Mouth*; Mercy Dee, *Have You Ever*; Walter Robertson, *Sputterin' Blues*; Johnny Fuller, *Prowling Blues*; Kid Tanner, *Going To New Orleans*; Joe Hill Louis, *Good Morning Little Angel*; Jimmy McCracklin, *The Panic's On*; Walter Horton, *What's The Matter With You*
A rewarding cross-section from the South or West Coast. It ranges from the raw country blues of Gilmore, Turner, Dudlow & Curtis, and Blair (recorded in Arkansas and Mississippi) to sophisticated, but still very down-home, sounds of Dixon, Mercy Dee, Fuller, and McCracklin. Big names like King, James, and Hopkins also contribute outstanding performances.

428 **Rural Blues: Complete Recorded Works In Chronological Order, Volume 1 (1934–1949)**
Various Artists
Document DOCD 5223 (Au)
"Little Brother," *Up And Down Building K.C. Line*; Willie Lane, *Prowlin' Ground Hog/Too Many Women Blues/Howling Wolf Blues/Black Cat Rag/Black Cat Rag* (alternate take); Black Diamond, *T.P. Railer/Lonesome Blues*; Goldrush, *All My Money Is Gone*; Monroe "Moe" Jackson, *Move It On Over/ Go 'Way From My Door*; Johnny Beck, *Locked In Jail Blues/You've Gotta Lay down Mama*; John Lee, *Baby Blues/Baby Please Don't Go/Down At The Depot/ Alabama Boogie/Blinds Blues*; Julius King, *Mississippi Boogie/One O'Clock Boogie/If You See My Lover/I Want A Slice Of Your Pudding*; D.A. Hunt, *Lonesome Old Jail/Greyhound Blues*; One String Sam, *My Baby Ooo/I Need A Hundred Dollars*
A broad-based selection made for small labels in the 1940s and 1950s, excepting the first title, a Library of Congress recording from 1934. "Moe" Jackson is a pseudonym for a white western swing performer. The tracks by One String Sam are unusual in having been recorded as a "commercial" 78 featuring a one-string instrument.

429 **Drove From Home Blues**
Various Artists
Flyright FLY CD 48 (UK)
Wright Holmes, *Good Road Blues/Alley Special*; Sonny Boy Johnson, *Quinsella*; Wright Holmes, *Drove From Home Blues*; David Pete McKinley, *Ardelle*; Stick Horse Hammond, *Little Girl/Truck 'Em On Down*; [Detroit Slim] Sonny Boy Johnson *[sic], Netta Mae/She's Alright With Me/I Done Got Tired*; David Pete McKinley, *Shreveport Blues*; Ralph Willis, *So Many Days/ That Gal's No Good*; Doug Quattlebaum, *Don't Be Funny Baby*; Ralph Willis, *Goin' to Chattanooga/New Goin' Down Slow*; Sonny Terry, *News For You Baby/No Love Blues*; Ralph Willis, *Steel Mill Blues/I Will Never Love Again*; Sonny Terry, *Lonesome Room/Baby Let's Have Some Fun*; Muddy Waters [as James Carter], *Mean Red Spider*
Of the guitar players, Quattlebaum migrated from South Carolina to Philadelphia and Mississippi-born Waters achieved success in Chicago. Holmes was a Texan and Hammond and McKinley from Louisiana. Willis (an Alabaman) cut sides in New York, alongside Georgia-born harmonica wizard Terry. Johnson, from the West Coast, had John Lee Williamson as his harmonica model but three attributions are to a Detroit performer.

430 **Bluesville Volume 1: Folk Blues**
Various Artists
Ace CDCH 247 (UK)
Furry Lewis, *Judge Boushay Blues*; Memphis Willie B, *Country Girl Blues*; K.C. Douglas, *Big Road Blues*; Big Joe Williams, *Levee Camp Blues*; Robert Curtis Smith, *Catfish*; Memphis Willie B, *Highway 61*; Furry Lewis, *Shake 'Em On Down*; Sidney Maiden, *San Quentin Blues*; Wade Walton, *Big Fat Mama*; Pete Franklin, *Grievin' Me*; Sidney Maiden, *Hand-Me-Down Baby*; Blind Willie McTell, *The Dyin' Crapshooter's Blues* (with spoken introduction); Blind Snooks Eaglin, *Alberta*; Lonnie Johnson, *Fine Booze And Heavy Dues*; Scrapper Blackwell, *Blues Before Sunrise*; Doug Quattlebaum, *You Is One Black Rat*; Blind Snooks Eaglin, *Brown Skinned Woman*; Reverend Gary Davis, *You Got To Move*; Baby Tate, *See What You Done Done*; Scrapper Blackwell, *Goin' Where The Monon Crosses The Yellow Dog*; Brownie McGhee & Sonny Terry, *Pawn Shop*
A sampler from some of the best down-home blues albums issued on Prestige's Bluesville labels in the 1960s. Some of the artists are well known, others relatively obscure; all performances are excellent.

431 **The Lowdown Backporch Blues**
Louisiana Red
Sequel NEX CD 213 (UK)
Ride On Red, Ride On (alternate take A)/*I Wonder Who* (alternate take 3)/ *Red's Dream/Working Man's Blues/I'm Louisiana Red/Sweet Alesse/Keep Your Hands Off My Woman/I'm A Roaming Stranger/Ride On Red, Ride On/I Wonder Who/The Seventh Son/Sad News/Two Fifty Three/Don't Cry/Sugar Hips/I'm Too Poor To Die/Don't Cry* (with harmonica overdub)/*Ride On Red, Ride On* (alternate take B)
Red was born in Vicksburg, Mississippi, raised in Louisiana, and later resident in Pittsburgh, Pennsylvania. He made a few disparate recordings in the 1950s (influenced by both John Lee Hooker and Muddy Waters) and recorded his first LP in 1962, an album containing a dozen original and ear-catching songs. This CD includes all those items and some supplementary titles.

432 **Down At The Depot**
John Lee
Rounder 2010—LP
Down At The Depot/Mama's Dead/You Know You Didn't Want Me/Nobody's Business What I Do/Lonesome Blues/Take Me Back, Baby, Try Me One More Time/Blind Blues/Northbound Blues/She Put Her Hand Where My Money Was/ Dago Hill/Somebody's Been Fooling You/Mule Blues
Alabama has been neglected as regards field research, but John Lee's music indicates a rich vein of blues in that state. *Blind Blues*, with slide guitar, re-creates his outstanding recording of 1951. All the guitar-accompanied performances are excellent; those with piano are slightly less successful.

433 **Last Session**
Blind Willie McTell
Original Blues Classics OBCCD 517–2
Baby, It Must Be Love/The Dyin' Crapshooter's Blues/Don't Forget It/Kill It

Kid/That Will Never Happen No More/Goodbye Blues/Salty Dog/Early Life/ Beedle Um Bum/A Married Man's A Fool/A To Z Blues/Wabash Cannonball/ Pal Of Mine/Kill It Kid/Broke Down Engine Blues**
Arguably the greatest of the Georgia bluesmen, McTell made his last recordings for the owner of an Atlanta record shop in 1956. Still in good voice and accompanying himself of 12-string guitar, he worked through a program of pre-war blues, bawdy numbers, and popular songs.

434 **Done Some Travelin'**
Frank Edwards
Trix (CD) 3303
Throw Your Time Away/Good Morning, Little School Girl/Goin' Back And Get Her/She is Mine/Mean Old Frisco/Key To The Highway/I Know He Shed The Blood/When The Saints Go Marching In/Chicken Raid/Mini Dress Wearer/ Alcatraz Blues/Love My Baby/Put Your Arms Around me
Frank Edwards was born in Georgia and raised in Florida. He recorded in 1941 and 1949, singing and playing guitar and harmonica together in a distinctive style. This was still evident in 1972, when he performed this well-chosen program of original songs and standards, including two spirituals, on one of which he plays slide.

435 **Blind James Campbell And His Nashville Street Band**
James Campbell's Friendly Five
Arhoolie CD 438
Have I Stayed Away Too Long?/I'm Crazy About You Baby/Buffalo Gal/Will The Circle Be Unbroken/The Moon May Rise In Blood/John Henry/Baby Please Don't Go/Jimmy's Blues/Monkey Man Blues/This Little Light Of Mine/Detroit Blues/Beauford's Breakdown/Gambling Man/Sittin' Here Drinking/Jam Piece (George's Boogie)/I Never Had Nothing/Do You Remember (theme song)/*My Gal Got Evil/Beauford's Boogie Woogie/When The Saints Go Marching In/I Am So Blue When It Rains/Pick And Shovel Blues/Detroit Jump*
Recorded in Nashville, Tennessee, in 1962–3, Campbell's was a true street band, a rarity at that date. Instrumentation included guitar, fiddle, banjo, trumpet, and tuba, with Campbell singing. Repertoire comprises blues, dance tunes, ballads, gospel pieces, and popular songs. The performances range from rough and raucous to sensitive and affecting.

436 **Carolina Blues Jam**
Big Boy Henry
Erwin Music EM9301
The New "Mr. President"/Corrine/John Henry/My Baby Won't Let Me In/ Airport Blues/Lookin' For My Woman/Holland Boogie/My Little Dog/Goodbye Little Girl/Talkin' With Mr. Henry/Rockin' Little Woman/Just Like My Child (She Looked Me Dead In The Eye)/Big Boy's Jump/Do Lord
A North Carolina artist, first recorded in 1947, Henry began performing regularly at concerts in the 1980s. His strong singing recalls the vintage era of Piedmont blues. Although influenced by such musicians as Fuller and McGhee,

*1949 recordings leased from Atlantic Records.

(**124, 249**) he is very much his own man. Instrumental support includes Gary Erwin on piano and British guitarist Dave Peabody.

437 **Carolina Slim: Complete Recorded Works In Chronological Order (1950–1952)**

Blues Documents BDCD 6043 (Au)

Mama's Boogie/Come Back Baby/Black Chariot Blues/Pleading Blues/Jivin' Woman/I'll Get By Somehow/Blues Knocking At My Door/Worry You Off My Mind/Blues Go Away From Me/Shake Boogie/Worrying Blues/Slo-Freight Blues/ Rag Mama/Sugaree/Carolina Boogie/Since I Seen Your Smiling Face/Your Picture Done Faded/Ain't It Sad/One More Time/Mother Dear Mother/Side Walk Boogie/I'll Never Walk In Your Door/Black Cat Trail/Georgia Woman/ Money Blues/Wine Head Baby/(Pour Me) One More Drink

Ed Harris, recorded as Carolina Slim in 1950. These (and some later) titles were influenced by Texas bluesman Lightnin' Hopkins. In 1951–2, using pseudonyms, he recorded guitar-accompanied blues and boogies in the tradition of his home area, some reminiscent of Blind Boy Fuller. He was no mere copyist, and his music stands up to repeated listening.

438 **Lightnin' Hopkins**

Smithsonian Folkways CD SF 40019

Penitentiary Blues/Bad Luck And Trouble/Come Go Home With Me/Trouble Stay 'Way From My Door/See That My Grave Is Kept Clean/Goin' Back To Florida/Reminiscences Of Blind Lemon/Fan It/Tell Me, Baby/She's Mine

The most heavily recorded post-war Texas singer-guitarist Hopkins recorded prolifically between 1946 and 1953 (**129, 438**). He was in a commercial trough when Sam Charters made these recordings in January 1959, including brooding performances like *Penitentiary Blues*, and lighter pieces like *Fan It*. The original album relaunched his career.

439 **River Blues**

Lowell Fulson

Arhoolie C 2003—Cassette

Western Union Blues/Lazy Woman Blues/River Blues Part 1/*River Blues* Part 2/*I Walked All Night/Midnight And Day/Three O'Clock Blues/The Blues Is Killing Me/Did You Ever Feel Lucky?/I'm Wild About You/Blues With A Feeling/Why Can't You Cry For Me/There Is A Time For Everything/Lowell Jumps One*

A Texas style singer/guitarist based in California, Fulson often performed in a West Coast setting, with band accompaniment (**447, 469**). Many of these recordings from 1948, however, had only his brother Martin (second guitar) in support and these are very much in the down-home blues idiom. *River Blues* is a variant of the traditional Texas *Penitentiary Blues.*

440 **Mercy's Toubles/Troublesome Mind**

Mercy Dee [Walton]

Arhoolie CD 369

Have You Ever Been Out In The Country/Five Card Hand/After The Fight/ Lady Luck/Betty Jean/One Room Country Shack/Mercy's Troubles/Sugar

Daddy/Red Light/Walked Down So Many Turnrows/Call The Asylum/Mercy's Shuffle/Troublesome Mind/Shady Lane/Eighth Wonder Of The World/I Been A Fool

This gifted song composer, vocalist, and pianist moved from Texas to the West Coast, and had a national R&B hit with *One Room Country Shack* (**453**). After a series of recordings on several labels, he was extensively recorded by Arhoolie's Chris Strachwitz, often in the company of Mississippi guitarist K.C. Douglas, Sidney Maiden (harmonica), and drummer Otis Cherry.

DICK SHURMAN

12 Post-War Texas and the West Coast

Vast in terms of both musical breadth and geographical area, the post-war blues of Texas and the West Coast are inexorably linked. The Black population of California in the mid-to-late 1940s consisted principally of emigrants from the South-west, initially attracted by the war-time defense industry boom; many of them enjoyed the music they brought from back home.

It was an exciting time as entrepreneurial independent labels emerged from war-time recording restrictions to capitalize on changing tastes. Commercially, there were only a few major successes in Texas, such as Don Robey's Houston recording and management empire Duke/ Peacock Records and Buffalo Booking. Most of the vital enterprises were in California, especially Los Angeles, where companies like Aladdin, the Bihari brothers' Crown-RPM-Modern-Kent complex, Black & White, Exclusive, Imperial, Specialty, Supreme, Swing Time, and others set the pace on the charts.

The tastes of the migrants ranged from crude country guitar blues and cool piano-led small combos to big band swing and jump. Aladdin searched for a new Leadbelly in 1946 and found Houston artists Lightnin' Hopkins and Amos Milburn; both achieved quick success. In Los Angeles pioneering hits such as *I Wonder* by pianist Cecil Gant (**297**) and *Drifting Blues* by Johnny Moore's Three Blazers (featuring Charles Brown) revealed stylistic and business opportunities virtually neglected by major recording companies. During the late 1940s emerging labels in Texas, Los Angeles, and the San Francisco Bay Area recorded scattered down-home blues, with Hopkins as the role model. T-Bone Walker and a host of followers such as Gatemouth Brown and Pee Wee Crayton did much to define modern electric guitar blues in a band setting. Lowell Fulson straddled both camps and set a lofty standard as a singer (**439**). Stripped-down big bands led by the likes of Roy Milton, Johnny Otis (**292**), or master Los Angeles arranger and tenor saxophonist Maxwell Davis founded what came to be known as rhythm and blues. Davis became the most ubiquitous force associated with top West Coast R&B recordings. Vocalists such

Pee Wee Crayton (*Sugar Ray, coll. Blues Unlimited*)

as Jimmy Witherspoon (**303**), Percy Mayfield, and Big Joe Turner (**284**) set the pace, while Dinah Washington (**168, 283**) proved a model for Little Esther Phillips (**199, 305**) and many others. Johnny Otis helped develop Esther and the adolescent dynamo Etta James (**193**). Pianists by the score, including Ray Charles, emulated Brown and Milburn, using motifs derived either from the jumping R&B bands or the hugely popular Nat "King" Cole Trio. In the Bay Area, less celebrated artists such as Johnny Fuller, Jimmy Wilson, and Jimmy McCracklin achieved initial, if often fleeting, success. In the mid-1950s another boom was spearheaded by the increasingly polished gospel blues stylings of B.B. King (**284**) and Bobby Bland, which served as the precedent for many recordings over the next two decades. But the musical tidal wave of rock 'n' roll washed away much of this impetus and many careers.

The interest of white collectors during the 1960s resulted in many rediscoveries, new specialist labels, and revived careers; this trend continued even while Chicago blues were in greater vogue in the psychedelic ballrooms. By the 1980s, with a resurgence of interest in R&B, Texas-styled guitarists, like Albert Collins, and their lineage, such as Robert Cray, were at the commercial forefront of the music.

Representation of vintage post-war Texas and West Coast blues on CD is improving, but some of the most historic and enjoyable vinyl has been neglected. Recent reissues of small-label Texas R&B are wildly variable in quality of compilation and documentation. Most of the important vaults have been plumbed to some extent. Leading candidates for improvement, however, are second-echelon R&B figures and the down-home Bay Area productions of Bob Geddins. While many who defined the genre 40 years ago are gone, eminent performers like Bland, Fulson, Gatemouth Brown, and Charles Brown remain active and excellent. The Austin scene based around Antone's night club and record label has received acclaim as a melting-pot for older and younger musicians from Chicago and Texas, blurring regional distinctions further, but epitomizing a healthy rejuvenation and continuity. California in September is virtually one long blues festival. The ongoing popularity of Texas and West Coast blues and its derivatives indicates a durable and dynamic form that continues to speak powerfully across the generations.

This assessment concentrates on artists who did their parts in establishing and popularizing the regions' modern styles of blues guitar, piano, vocals, and arrangements, with emphasis on bands and amplification. Pertinent gems can also be found in other chapters, especially 4, 8, and 13.

Essential Records

(i) Pioneers: Rhythm And Blues Piano And Blues Ballads

As a youth in Texas, Charles Brown became immersed in learning to play the piano. One of the most influential Texas–California blues figures, he trained as a chemist in college and eventually moved to Los Angeles. After winning a talent contest playing a classical piece, he was recorded by Philo Records in 1945. Singing and playing as a member of Johnny Moore's Three Blazers, with accompaniment by Moore (guitar), Eddie Williams (bass), and the addition of Johnny Otis (drums), he came up with a spare, wistful composition from his youth, *Driftin' Blues*. The subdued, brooding vocal became the prototype for a generation of "cocktail blues" vocalists, also under the influence of the King Cole Trio and Leroy Carr. Brown's fluent piano playing and Moore's exquisitely melodic, glissando-laden guitar work defined a scaled-down form of up-town blues which proved to have astonishing appeal. The ambience is decidedly sentimental, understated and "after-hours", with the inference of an ache rather than a sharp stab of pain; even up-tempo pieces convey an underlying suggestion of pervasive melancholy.

Brown was also a frequent and accomplished balladeer. This component of R&B was prevalent among the smoother pianists such as himself and Ivory Joe Hunter, but extended to the basic repertoires of guitarists, including T-Bone Walker, Pee Wee Crayton, Lowell Fulson, and Gatemouth Brown.

The popular Three Blazers turned out 78s for several labels—usually silky blues or ballads interspersed with occasional jump vocals or instrumentals—and spawned imitators with regularity. Sometimes they were augmented by the likes of Moore's regularly poll-winning guitarist brother Oscar, or by Maxwell Davis playing an unusually subdued tenor saxophone. Aladdin, which acquired Philo, continued to have hits with Brown even after he and the Three Blazers parted company somewhat acrimoniously in 1948. Songs such as *Black Night* (1950), *Trouble Blues, Fool's Paradise,* and even *Merry Christmas, Baby* are still components of any basic blues repertoire and have inspired an array of singers and instrumentalists.

While Mosaic has gathered all the 1945–56 Philo-Aladdin sides into a five-CD box, the Collectables CD **Driftin' Blues, The Best Of Charles Brown** is a succinct survey of highlights. The previously mentioned moody masterpieces are complemented by the still morose but comparatively energetic *Please Don't Drive Me Away,* and insinuating blues like *My Baby's Gone* and the early Lieber-Stoller composition

Hard Times. Advanced devices such as the use of double time during the last verse of *Driftin' Blues,* the breaks in *Please Don't Drive Me Away,* and the departures from the standard *AAB* blues verse structure in *Black Night* reveal the "cool" sophistication. While a pop orientation is evident on a number of tracks, his classic performances are essential for understanding later modern blues developments. Brown has made a number of laudable albums over the years, is still playing robustly and his voice is remarkably intact.

Amos Milburn was an associate and contemporary of Charles Brown; the two even recorded and lived together at various times. Milburn could convey the toned-down wistfulness that made Brown a blues immortal, but his enduring persona is that of a hard-driving extrovert—pounding out boogie woogie and exhorting audiences to celebration and intoxication over a riffing band led by blasting tenor saxophone. He made his recording début in 1946, when he was taken from Houston by his manager Lola Anne Cullum to shop for a deal in Los Angeles and was signed by Aladdin. Some of Milburn's earlier efforts relied only on rhythm accompaniment (most were based either on eight-to-the-bar boogie woogie or forceful rhythmic triplets) but it was Maxwell Davis' arrangement of *Chicken Shack Boogie* that made his name. Don Wilkerson was Milburn's tenor saxophonist from about 1948 to 1952; he later became a mainstay in Ray Charles' group, contributing some of the most famous solos in R&B. Milburn's vibrato-laden, declamatory vocals were also well suited to songs concerning drinking, and he had hits with *Bad, Bad Whiskey, One Scotch, One Bourbon, One Beer* and *Vicious, Vicious Vodka*. Ballads like *Bewildered* sold well. His years for Aladdin culminated in the mid-1950s with a searing remake of *Chicken Shack Boogie* featuring the New Orleans tenor saxophonist Lee Allen. Although the track became a standard and was incipient rock 'n' roll, Milburn did not weather the trend. His later association with King Records led to little that was memorable. He cut one of the first Motown albums, but it soon sank into obscurity. A stroke complicated his impoverished last years and his final album for Johnny Otis is more pathetic than affirmative.

The Best Of Amos Milburn: Down The Road Apiece is a generally solid 1946–57 cross-section from Aladdin, though the second *Chicken Shack Boogie* is omitted. It conveys the crackling, relentless boogie-woogie energy that made such memorable and exciting celebrations of the roadhouse spirit as *Down The Road Apiece, Roomin' House Boogie, Sax Shack Boogie, Roll, Mr. Jelly* and *House Party (Tonight)*. There is also a useful share of the best known drinking songs and calls to good times. These include *Real Pretty Mama Blues, Let's Have A Party,* and *Hold Me Baby* (separate fragments of which were transformed on wax by B.B. King and Little Walter). Milburn's slow blues chops are present on *It Took A Long Time* (suggesting his considerable influence on Fats Domino), but Amos Milburn collections are not oriented toward quiet reflection. As this CD demonstrates, he could rattle the walls with rhythm backing, or match the power of a jump band with ease. In this respect his imitators included Domino, Floyd Dixon, Little Willie Littlefield, and Jimmy McCracklin. From there it was a short step to Little Richard or Jerry Lee Lewis, who reinforced the energy of these enduring R&B celebrations and converted it into primal rock 'n' roll. (All 145 Aladdin tracks have been released in a 7-CD Mosaic box set.)

441 **Driftin' Blues, The Best Of Charles Brown**
Charles Brown
Collectables COL 5631
Driftin' Blues/Homesick Blues/Get Yourself Another Fool/In The Evening When The Sun Goes Down/A Long Time/It's Nothing/Trouble Blues/My Baby's Gone/Black Night/I'll Always Be In Love With You/Seven Long Days/Hard Times/Evening Shadows/I Lost Everything/Lonesome Feeling/Cryin' Mercy/I've Been Savin' My Love For You/Fool's Paradise/Please Don't Drive Me Away/Merry Christmas, Baby

442 **The Best Of Amos Milburn: Down The Road Apiece**
Amos Milburn
EMI 7243 8 27229-2/EMI CZ 526 (UK)
Down The Road Apiece/Hold Me Baby/Chicken Shack Boogie/It Took A Long Time/Empty Arms Blues/Bewildered/In The Middle Of The Night/Roomin' House Boogie/Walking Blues/Real Pretty Mama Blues/Sax Shack Boogie/Let's Rock A While/Bad, Bad Whiskey/Tears, Tears, Tears (Tears In My Eyes)/Thinking And Drinking/Put Something In My Hand (I Know You Love Me, Baby)/Roll, Mr. Jelly/Let Me Go Home, Whiskey/One Scotch, One Bourbon, One Beer/Let's Have A Party/Good, Good Whiskey/Milk And Water/Vicious, Vicious Vodka/I Done Done It (Don't Do It)/House Party (Tonight)/Soft Pillow

(ii) Texas Troubadour

Sam "Lightnin" Hopkins (1912–82) was the archetypal troubadour—a distillation of the Texas blues tradition and the spiritual and cultural progeny of the African griot who, like all great folk artists, transcends regionalism. Indeed, he and his peer John Lee Hooker are linked as masters of the spontaneous: iconoclasts who break many conventional rules of performance and composition but ironically became models for widespread inspiration and derivation.

The young Hopkins was profoundly influenced by his encounter with Blind Lemon Jefferson, the prototype Texas blues guitarist **(126)**

Further elements of his craft were acquired from another renowned vocalist, and elder cousin, Alger (Texas) Alexander (**148**). (Albert Collins was a younger cousin.) Hopkins, however, was largely self-taught, and preferred live performances to recording. Rather than viewing them as fixed, he tailored his blues to a specific setting or current event. He was a consummate master of "air music," pulling his material from the forces in the wind at any given moment. As Pete Welding, the compiler and annotator of **The Complete Aladdin Recordings,** put it: "Before long, Lightnin' Hopkins was Houston's best-known and most popular blues artist, the King of Dowling Street, shaman, poet, jester, maker of songs and chronicler of life and times of Houston's black community."

With the pianist Wilson Smith (quickly dubbed "Thunder" by Aladdin Records), the two went to Los Angeles in 1946, at the instance of the Houston talent scout Lola Anne Cullum. (They were accompanied by Amos Milburn, making his second recording trip.) *Katie May,* from the first session in Lightnin's long career, was an instant hit. It is a deliberate yet majestic blues, typical of Hopkins, and has the lyric poet's common touch, also showing him to be an eloquent (if limited) guitarist; his vocals are worldly and unpretentious. The duo's second Los Angeles session (1947) generated the equally famous *Short Haired Woman,* in a similar vein. Lightnin's subsequent Aladdin recordings were solos, made in Houston, producing masterpieces like the much-covered *Shotgun.* Hopkins soon shifted from Aladdin to a dazzling succession of labels (for example **129**) and remained among the blues pantheon as the self-described "Po' Lightnin'" until his death. He occasionally used an amplified band, but the Aladdin sides remain a definitive catalogue of his assets and standard for his greatness.

443 The Complete Aladdin Recordings

Lightnin' Hopkins

EMI CDP 7 96843-2—2 CD set

DISC ONE: *Katie May/Feel So Bad/Blues (That Mean Old Twister)/I Can't Stay Here In Your Town;* Thunder Smith, *Can't Do Like You Used To/West Coast Blues;* Lightnin' Hopkins, *Short Haired Woman;* Thunder Smith, *L.A. Blues/Big Mama Jump (Little Mama Blues);* Lightnin' Hopkins, *Down Baby/Let Me Play With Your Poodle/Fast Mail Rambler/Thinkin' And Worryin'/Can't Get That Woman Off My Mind/Woman Woman (Change Your Way)/Picture On The Wall/You're Not Goin' To Worry My Life Anymore/You're Gonna Miss Me/Sugar On My Mind/Nightmare Blues/Someday Baby/Come Back Baby*

DISC TWO: *Lightnin's Boogie/Baby You're Not Going To Make A Fool Out Of Me/Daddy Will Be Home One Day/Moon Rise Blues/Howling Wolf/Morning Blues/Have To Let You Go/Mama's Baby Child/Mistreated Blues/My*

California/Honey Babe/So Long/See See Rider/Unpredictable Woman/I Just Don't Care/Drinkin' Woman/Abilene/Shotgun/Rollin' And Rollin'/Tell It Like It Is/Miss Loretta

(iii) Foundations of Electric Blues Guitar

As much as anyone, Aaron "T-Bone" Walker (1910–75) carved out the essence of modern electric-guitar blues. Predecessors such as Lonnie Johnson (**255**) and Blind Lemon Jefferson foreshadowed the kind of vocal-guitar relationship perfected by Walker. It is T-Bone's jazzy, percussive fills, chording, bent strings, and dynamics, however, that have anchored the vocabulary of most band-orientated blues guitarists since World War II. His highly syncopated use of hammered-on notes has been adapted throughout blues and jazz as a rhythmic device; the arpeggiated augmented chord made famous in *Call It Stormy Monday* suggests a whole style to blues veterans. Walker also popularized the Texas guitar shuffle, an apparently eternal forum for flashiness, imagination, and rhythmic accessibility, without which it is virtually impossible to imagine the musical conceptions of Gatemouth Brown, Albert Collins, Guitar Slim (Eddie Jones) (**497**), and countless heroes of the electric era. (Louis Jordan also did much to popularize the shuffle in the blues world: **281**.)

Walker led Blind Lemon Jefferson around the streets of Dallas when he was a youth and made his recording début in 1929 (**147**). In the late 1930s he became one of the first to amplify his guitar, moved to Los Angeles and worked for a while as a sideman and featured performer with the Les Hite Orchestra. Although he performed guitar solos on some recordings with Hite, in *T-Bone Blues,* which became his vocal speciality, he abandoned the instrument and was accompanied by Hawaiian guitar in the vein of Floyd Smith's popular *Floyd's Guitar Blues.* This and his output from the ensuing 14 years (including approximately two dozen alternate takes) is gathered into the historic **Complete Recordings Of T-Bone Walker 1940–1954.** A session for Capitol in 1942, which yielded *I Got A Break Baby* and *Mean Old World,* was the first to highlight the key elements of Walker's approach. After the war-time recording ban he cut a handful of highly influential sides in Chicago, with orchestral backing, which consolidated his revolutionary impact on blues guitar. These included *You Don't Love Me Blues, T-Bone Boogie,* and *I'm Still In Love With You.* For the remainder of the decade he recorded in Los Angeles for a number of labels; Capitol eventually acquired all the masters. The spare accompaniment of the initial Capitol sides is countered by the jumping trumpet, tenor saxophone, and piano on the other recordings.

Call It Stormy Monday from 1947 remains the quintessential modern slow blues; Walker's solo typically relies on teasing the beat as well as on the release of the created tension. *Bobby Sox Blues* is another wonderfully dynamic slow blues. *T-Bone Shuffle* became an anthem as well as a musical prototype. The remaining tracks from this period are fairly well divided between the jump exemplified by *Hypin' Woman Blues* and *You're My Best Poker Hand,* and slow blues such as *Born To Be No Good* and *West Side Baby*. The quality of these recordings cast a shadow over succeeding generations of blues players. As B.B. King put it: "That was the best sound I ever heard."

Walker continued his illustrious career with Imperial Records. These sessions reflect the gradual transition from a swing band to R&B orchestration. He remained at his inventive, torrid best with landmarks like *Strollin' With Bone, You Don't Love Me, You Don't Understand, Welcome Blues, Tell Me What's The Reason, Cold, Cold Feeling,* and *Love Is A Gamble*. The six-CD set is available from Mosaic via mail order only, but EMI have released separate sets of Walker's Capitol and Imperial recordings.

Although T-Bone's health was beginning to slow him down in the mid-1950s, his later recordings for Atlantic are also worthwhile. He remained prolific and was a popular attraction in Europe right up to his death. Much of his later work has merit. It is no slight, however, to say that it joins almost all modern guitar blues recordings in being on a lower plane than the pioneering sides issued by Mosaic, which remain a bulwark of contemporary blues.

Clarence "Gatemouth" Brown, born in 1924, was one of the first of Walker's disciples to achieve prominence. While he never matched T-Bone's national appeal, the two were dominant figures in post-war Texas. Brown took Walker's showmanship even further, and added a fierce aggressiveness. His extremely idiosyncratic guitar style involves the use of a capo and an unorthodox, percussive plucking approach with his right hand. One key point of departure from his mentor is the pursuit of diversity. In addition to big-band jazz and jump blues, Brown added numerous strains of Cajun and country music to his musical brew, and complemented his flashiness and fluidity on guitar with a command of violin and harmonica. A persistent thread of whimsy runs through his music, chiefly amusing gimmicks or sudden quotations from *White Christmas* or *Pop Goes The Weasel,* as his mind wages an apparent battle between agility and concentration. Today he is billed as the "High Priest of Texas Swing" and vehemently resists any attempts at categorization. He proved long ago that he is more than just a great bluesman, but it was in this capacity that he captured the spotlight.

In the late 1940s Brown was being managed by Don Robey. Frustrated by Aladdin's lack of support for Brown's recording début (with backing by Maxwell Davis' combo, of course), Robey started Peacock (named after a Houston nightclub he operated) and began recording Brown himself. The arrangement lasted through the 1950s and generated dozens of memorable exercises in extroverted innovation. **Original Peacock Recordings** on Rounder is the best starting-point on CD. Although Gate's later work was more varied, this disc shows his prowess and includes harbingers on a solid blues foundation. Some have called *Okie Dokie Stomp* from 1954 the perfect shuffle, and if imitation is a barometer, it does not fall far short. *Midnight Hour* did not become such a staple, but is another shuffling *tour de force,* this time with a vocal. One of two previously unissued cuts from a session in 1956, *That's Your Daddy Yaddy Yo* begins with an explosive guitar introduction. *Ain't That Dandy* is another shuffle instrumental with excellent orchestration, which remains in Brown's working repertoire, often as a set opener. *Sad Hour, Dirty Work At The Crossroads* (with Jimmy McCracklin on piano), and the previously unissued *Good Looking Woman* are typical of his slow guitar blues. *Gate's Salty Blues* explains much about where his disciple Albert Collins acquired his sound, and is also the first recorded example of Brown's harmonica playing. The atmospheric *Just Before Dawn* is his first fiddle excursion. While Brown's stage presence can only be subliminally felt in these recordings, it is easy to understand why guitar players are drawn to him. This has kept many of his licks and tricks in the contemporary blues lexicon, and sustained the legend of his Peacock years and bandstand performances. Brown would be the last to consider these Peacock gems representative of his current music, but they remain a hallmark for the emergent Texas shuffle blues. After a recording lull in the 1960s, punctuated by scattered 45s and a period leading the house band for *The Beat* (a syndicated TV show with Nashville disc jockey Hoss Allen), a European tour in 1971 opened the door to revitalized international acclaim and a prolific studio career.

Whereas Brown's breadth incorporated many non-blues forms into his music, Lowell Fulson's recording portfolio is remarkable for the masterful variety he brought to the blues. Born in Oklahoma in 1921 and from an African-American-Amerindian heritage, he worked as a youth in country string bands and as an accompanist to Texas Alexander. While overseas on military duty during World War II, he developed a liking for jazz and bigger bands. He then settled in the East Bay Area in California, singing blues and gospel. Local impresario Bob Geddins discovered him, and a stream of recordings ensued. While many placed Fulson with small combos, some of the most striking were country duets with his guitarist brother Martin; these included *3 O'Clock In The Morning* (**439**), which B.B. King adapted for his first hit (**287**). Fulson then turned to Los Angeles as his recording base, and an alliance with pianist-arranger Lloyd Glenn provided him with an especially sympathetic foil; he also developed a less nasal vocal style. Post-war staples such as *Every Day I Have The Blues, Blue Shadows, Sinner's Prayer* and *Guitar Shuffle* resulted, and Fulson's band nurtured future stars such as Ray Charles and tenor saxophonist Stanley Turrentine. A fixture on jukeboxes with his compelling mixture of primitive and sophisticated, Fulson was the embodiment of a hard-edged modern bluesman who could evoke good times downtown or scuffling across the tracks with equal authority.

He began an affiliation with Chess/Checker in 1954, which reflected less breadth than his previous recordings, but refined and focused most of his major strengths and captured him at the peak of his art. Recording in Texas, Los Angeles, or Chicago, he concentrated on a band setting, reaching a seldom-rivalled level of persuasiveness. **Hung Down Head** contains a Dallas track made in 1954, *Reconsider Baby,* which is an archetypal classic slow blues. This evergreen is a memorable combination of passionate involvement and simple arrangement. Its directness and Fulson's perfectly conceived guitar solo have lent themselves to seemingly unending attempts at re-creation. *Trouble, Trouble* is an updated version of his first recording, though much more urgent and emotive. The performance also demonstrates his economy as a player and depth of feeling as a vocalist, and was covered by B.B. King. The instrumental *Low Society* is another scintillating remake, featuring Lloyd Glenn on piano and Billy Hadnott on bass. The CD also highlights the playing of alto saxophonist Earl "Good Rocking" Brown, whose Louis Jordan-based approach was a vital cog in the sound of the Lowell Fulson band. *It's Your Own Fault* is a slow-burning melody, which was central to Magic Sam's most popular and recurring slow blues motifs. *I Still Love You Baby, Hung Down Head,* and *Tollin' Bells* smolder with vitality and originality of lyrical and/or musical structure, though the tedious out-takes of the last might better have been replaced with some of the many other worthy Checker tracks. Fulson's tenure with the company lasted into the 1960s. The standard set by these recordings for slashing guitar, animated singing, unobtrusive but propulsive accompaniment, and outright expressiveness is in no danger of eclipse by the many peers who took heed of Fulson's style.

At an age long past that at which many artists have exhausted their inspiration and appeal, Fulson found new life with Kent in the mid-1960s with the R&B hits *Tramp* and *Black Nights*. He continued a thoroughly modern approach into the mid-1970s. Since then his albums have taken a more retrospective tone, but still show his vitality as a songwriter and performer.

By the mid-1980s, Texas blues guitar was well established as a renewed force. Albert Collins, who was born in 1932 and had left Houston in the 1960s for the West Coast, had been discovered by white audiences during the blues boom. He began recording for Alligator in 1978, and developed an international reputation with instant and profound impact on the blues-rock scene. His reverb-laden "cool sound" and high energy was perfect for the tastes of the times. A leaning towards funk gave his music another contemporary edge, and his stature was secure as the "King of the Texas Shuffle," exemplified by *Frosty*, a hit of the early 1960s. He was also one of blues' most visual showmen, with superb body language and entertainment techniques inspired by Guitar Slim, Gatemouth Brown, or Big Jay McNeely. Not the least of Collins' assets was the empathetic appeal of his lyrics, many of which concern domestic discord and financial travail.

Johnny Copeland, born in 1937, left Houston somewhat later and settled in New York. He emerged there in 1981 with a heralded Rounder LP *Copeland Special,* and became a top attraction with his fierce vocals and cutting guitar work. With Collins he brought belated recognition to such heroes of their tradition as T-Bone Walker and Gatemouth Brown. Once a strong disciple of Brown, in turn Collins became the most influential blues guitarist on the West Coast. One of those he inspired was Robert Cray, who heard him while in high school in Tacoma, Washington, and later backed him on tour in the mid-1970s.

The idea of a Texas guitar summit first flowered with the highly successful set by Copeland, Collins, and Brown that closed the Chicago Blues Festival of 1984. During planning for an LP, it became apparent that Cray would replace Brown; this solved some logistical problems and brought a more forward-looking dimension, with the added advantage of Cray's burgeoning popularity. The three joined forces in Chicago in September 1985, and with support from Collins' rhythm section cut **Showdown!** First Copeland coaxed Collins as close to his roots as he had been for a couple of decades: *Black Cat Bone* conjures reminiscences of Houston steel guitarist Hop Wilson (**156**), and there was an unadorned, blistering, updated version of *Albert's Alley*. Strong Copeland originals such as *Lion's Den* and the unrestrained and earthy *Bring Your Fine Self Home,* with raw harmonica by Collins, gave both artists well-focused outlets not only for their energy but for their empathy. As always, Copeland attacked his lyrics like the boxer he once was and played lean but punchy leads and solid rhythm lines. Collins dug deeply into his characteristic aggressiveness and "cool sound" on guitar between vocals.

While Copeland recuperated from stomach problems, Collins and Cray committed to tape some title exhibiting the passage of Cray from student to equal; indeed, with his soaring vocal delivery, fluid, inventive guitar, and strong sense of style, Cray proved the most complete artist of the three. *The Dream* is a well-arranged minor blues, while *She's Into Something* updates a Muddy Waters carioca often performed by the Cray band; both had stirring Collins solos. The three trade vocals on a version of *T-Bone Shuffle,* based mostly on Cray's bandstand arrangement (rooted in Buddy Guy's Atco recording), On the final track Collins sings a memorable rendition of *Blackjack,* with rousing solos by all. The band, which contributes the sound of the 1980s to *Black Cat Bone,* underscored the extent to which the "showdown" was an exemplary team effort. The album soared into the charts and won a Grammy Award. While it remains to be seen if it is as timeless as the Texas origins it commemorates, it certainly exemplifies 1980s guitar blues and the chemistry which can ensue when cohorts with mutual respect and common ground blend their skills and creativity.

444/5 The Complete Recordings Of T-Bone Walker 1940–1954
T-Bone Walker
Mosaic MD6-130—6 CD set
DISC ONE: *T-Bone Blues/I Got A Break Baby/Mean Old World/Low Down Dirty Shame Blues/Sail On Boogie/I'm Still In Love With You/You Don't Love Me Blues/T-Bone Boogie/Mean Old World Blues/Evening/My Baby Left Me/Come Back To Me Baby/I Can't Stand Being Without You/She Is Going To Ruin Me/No Worry Blues* (alternate take) *No Worry Blues/Don't Leave Me Baby* (alternate take)/*Don't Leave Me Baby/Bobby Sox Blues* (alternate take)/*Bobby Sox Blues/I'm Gonna Find My Baby/I'm In An Awful Mood/It's A Low Down Dirty Deal/Don't Give Me The Runaround*

DISC TWO: *Hard Pain Blues/I Know Your Wig Is Gone/T-Bone Jumps Again/Call It Stormy Monday* (alternate take)/*Call It Stormy Monday/She Had To Let Me Down* (alternate take)/*She Had To Let Me Down/She's My Old Time Used To Be/Dream Girl Blues* (alternate take)/*Dream Girl Blues/Midnight Blues* (alternate take)/*Midnight Blues/Long Lost Lover Blues* (alternate take)/*Long Lost Lover Blues/Triflin' Woman Blues* (alternate)/*Triflin' Woman Blues/Long Skirt Baby Blues* (alternate take)/*Long Skirt Baby Blues/Goodbye Blues/Too Much Trouble Blues* (alternate take)/*Too Much Trouble Blues/I'm Waiting For Your Call/Hypin' Woman Blues* (alternate take)/*Hypin' Woman Blues*

DISC THREE: *So Blue Blues/On Your Way Blues/The Natural Blues/That's Better For Me/First Love Blues* (alternate take)/*First Love Blues/Lonesome Woman Blues* (alternate take)/*Lonesome Woman Blues* (alternate take 2)/*Lonesome Woman Blues/Vacation Blues/Inspiration Blues* (alternate take)/*Inspiration*

Blues/Description Blues (alternate take)/*Description Blues/T-Bone Shuffle* (alternate take)/*T-Bone Shuffle/That Old Feeling Is Gone/The Time Seems So Long/Prison Blues/Home Town Blues/Wise Man Blues* (alternate take)/*Wise Man Blues/Misfortune Blues* (alternate take)/*Misfortune Blues*

DISC FOUR: *I Wish You Were Mine* (alternate take)/*I Wish You Were Mine/I'm Gonna Move You Out And Get Somebody Else/She's The No Sleepin'est Woman* (alternate take)/*She's The No Sleepin'est Woman/Plain Old Down Home Blues/Born To Be No Good/Go Back To The One You Love* (alternate take)/*Go Back To The One You Love/I Want A Little Girl/I'm Still In Love With You/You're My Best Poker Hand* (alternate take)/*You're My Best Poker Hand/West Side Baby/Glamour Girl/Strollin' With Bone/The Sun Went Down/You Don't Love Me/Travelin' Blues/The Hustle Is On* (78 take)/*The Hustle Is On* (LP take)/*Baby Broke My Heart* (78 take)/*Baby Broke My Heart* (LP take)

DISC FIVE: *Evil Hearted Woman/Evil Hearted Woman* (alternate take)/*I Walked Away/No Reason* (alternate take)/*No Reason/Look Me In The Eye* (LP take)/*Look Me In The Eye* (78 take)/*Too Lazy* (78 take)/*Too Lazy* (LP take) *Alimony Blues/Life Is Too Short/You Don't Understand/Welcome Blues/I Get So Weary/You Just Wanted To Use Me/Tell Me What's The Reason/I'm About To Lose My Mind/Cold, Cold Feeling/News For My Baby/Get These Blues Off Me/I Got The Blues Again/Through With Women/Street Walking Woman/Blues Is A Woman/I Got The Blues*

DISC SIX: *Here In The Dark/Blue Mood/Everytime/I Miss You Baby/Lollie Lou/Love Is A Gamble/High Society/Long Distance Blues/Got No Use For You/I'm Still In Love With You/Railroad Station Blues/Vida Lee/My Baby is Now On My Mind/Doin' Time/Bye, Bye, Baby/When The Sun Goes Down/Pony Tail/Wanderin' Heart/I'll Always Be In Love With You/I'll Understand/Hard Way/Teen Age Baby/Strugglin' Blues*

446 **Original Peacock Recordings**
Gatemouth Brown
Rounder CD 2039
Midnight Hour/Sad Hour/Ain't That Dandy/That's Your Daddy Yaddy Yo/Dirty Work At The Crossroads/Hurry Back Good News/Okie Dokie Stomp/Good Looking Woman/Gate's Salty Blues/Just Before Dawn/Depression Blues/For Now So Long

447 **Hung Down Head**
Lowell Fulson
MCA Chess CHD-9325
That's All Right/I Still Love You Baby/Reconsider Baby/I Want To Know/Low Society/Check Yourself/It's Your Own Fault/Do Me Right/Trouble, Trouble/Hung Down Head/Tollin' Bells

448 **Showdown!**
Albert Collins, Robert Cray and Johnny Copeland
Alligator CD 4743
T-Bone Shuffle/The Moon Is Full/Lion's Den/She's Into Something/Bring Your Fine Self Home/Black Cat Bone/The Dream/Albert's Alley/Blackjack

(iv) The Peak Of Duke-Peacock: Singer And Settings

Gatemouth Brown gave Don Robey and Peacock a solid entrée into the record business, but it is vocalist Bobby "Blue" Bland whose musical achievement was responsible for the peaks of popularity in Robey's entrepreneurial career. Bland was born in Rosemark, Tennessee, and worked around Memphis with his peers. These included B.B. King and Junior Parker, a subsequent touring partner and fellow star for Duke Records. His recording contract with Duke went to Robey when the label was sold. **I Pity The Fool/The Duke Recordings, Volume One** is the first of three two-CD sets to cover his Duke years, taking in 1952–60. He invariably drew on his gospel-based background, but did not always temper his approach. The forcefulness of his early Memphis tracks for Chess, Modern, and Duke, therefore, has seldom been equalled for overall effectiveness. When the maturing Bland began recording songs like *It's My Life Baby* in Houston in 1955, it was with small, guitar-based bands featuring Roy Gaines or Clarence Hollimon, even when the arrangers and leaders were horn players, such as the alto saxophonist Bill Harvey. By 1957 the resulting blues and shuffles like *Don't Want No Woman, I Smell Trouble* and *Farther Up The Road* were trend-setting, and Bland had risen to near the top rung of popularity, behind B.B. King. These two figures, and Parker, exemplify a type of blues that was regarded as more progressive and "cleaned up" than the raw, Delta blues of Muddy Waters. But Bland's potential and skills indicated that there was territory to conquer beyond blues. Great care was taken to select material for him and to orchestrate his recordings with soulful elegance. Trumpeter and arranger Joe Scott became Bland's band leader. By the 1960s the winning formula was set: a brassy horn section, in the tradition of the South-western big bands such as Count Basie's, provided the screaming answers to Bland's melismas, squalls, falsetto, and other pyrotechnics. A guitarist, usually Wayne Bennett (who had taken part in many Amos Milburn sessions), weaved light, jazzy, post-T-Bone shadings into the call-and-response dialog. Many hits and the model for popular gospel blues resulted. Ballads like *I'll Take Care Of You, Lead Me On* and *Cry, Cry, Cry* became as much a part of the Bland persona as the energetic *I Pity The Fool* and sanctified *Don't Cry No More.*

449 I Pity The Fool/The Duke Recordings, Volume One
Bobby Bland
MCA MCAD2 10665—2 CD set
DISC ONE: *I.O.U. Blues/Lovin' Blues/No Blow No Show/Wise Man's Blues/Army Blues/It's My Life Baby/Lost Lovers Blues/Honey Bee/Time Out/You Or None*

(alternate take)/*A Million Miles From Nowhere/You Or None/I Woke Up Screaming/I Can't Put You Down Baby/You've Got Bad Intentions/I Don't Believe/I Learned My Lesson/Don't Want No Woman/I Smell Trouble/Sometime Tomorrow/Farther Up The Road/Teach Me (How To Love You)*

DISC TWO: *Bobby's Blues/Loan Me A Helping Hand/You Got Me (Where You Want Me)/Last Night/Little Boy Blue/I Lost Sight Of The World* (LP version)/*You Did Me Wrong/I Lost Sight Of The World* (single version)/*I'm Not Ashamed/Wishing Well/Is It Real?/That's Why/Hold Me Tenderly/Someday/I'll Take Care of You/Cry, Cry, Cry/Lead Me On/I've Been Wrong So Long/I Pity The Fool/Close To You/Two Steps From The Blues/Don't Cry No More*

(v) West Coast Rhythm And Blues

Late in what had been a generally moribund decade for his musical career, R&B patriarch Johnny Otis was quick to recognize and seize upon the international renewal of interest in blues and R&B in the 1960s. He had fielded enough enquiries from discographers and collectors to sense a trend, and his son Shuggie was coming of age as a guitarist when the LP *Cold Shot!* was released by Kent in 1969. This reintroduced the Otis blues revue. Always a solid organizer and band leader, as well as a proven talent scout with a large number of artistic connections, he set about redirecting attention not only to himself but to those contemporaries whose place in blues history remained badly neglected. A documentary TV show with Charles Brown, T-Bone Walker, and others was one positive result; so was a contract with Epic. The high-water mark was an appearance at the Monterey Jazz Festival of 1970 that Epic chose to record.

It was quite an event, with crisply articulated and well-arranged band performances giving added confidence to the featured artists. The reed section was anchored by Preston Love, Clifford Solomon, and baritone saxophonist Big Jim Wynn, whose work underpinned countless illustrious recording sessions. Shuggie Otis' impeccable playing bore a noticeable debt in dry tonality and crisp phrasing to Johnny "Guitar" Watson. Esther Phillips paid her usual homage to Dinah Washington with a jazzy jump number and a slow medley which quoted T-Bone Walker and Billy Eckstine. Cleanhead Vinson performed his signature piece, with a "nasty" extended boppish introduction on alto saxophone and a rousing version of *Kidney Stew* over its classic riff. Joe Turner showed that he was still a vocal powerhouse in both boogie woogie and slow blues, with Shuggie Otis taking solo space on the latter. Ivory Joe Hunter performed his popular country-and-western-tinged exercise in gentle sentimentality. Roy Milton's jump hit *Baby You Don't Know* gave Preston Love and Johnny Otis (on vibraphone) a chance to shine, while *R.M. Blues,* his pioneering hit, featured a baritone solo. Gene "Mighty Flea" Connors, a mainstay in Otis' revue, played trombone solos behind Delmar Evans and Margie Evans, and took center stage long enough to dazzle the crowd with *Preacher's Blues*. The hugely influential singer Roy Brown proved that his high voice was in superb shape performing a tight, driving rendition of his first and biggest hit, *Good Rockin' Tonight,* with a stomping riff break. Shuggie Otis played an old-fashioned duet between slide guitar and harmonica and a stinging modern boogie with the full band, with a solo by Clifford Solomon and the archetypal T-Bone Walker stops. Singer and guitarist Pee Wee Crayton was unusually loose, flashy, and dynamic, as can be heard in his spoken introduction, yells, and asides. The guitar work showed equal gusto, especially the double-picked solo and typical ending of bent diminished chords. Of the two regular vocalists with the revue, Margie Evans shows an exuberance halfway between the smoothness of Esther Phillips and the rawness of Big Mama Thornton. Delmar Evans revealed his Chicago roots on some tough braggadocio recalling Muddy Waters' *I'm A Man,* even tossing in some howling along with his usual convincing street feel. Johnny Otis paced the band through a version of his biggest hit, *Willie And The Hand Jive,* from 1958, and joined Delmar Evans for the anthem *Goin' Back To L.A.,* which gave Shuggie a chance to "dust *his* broom."

Johnny Otis' accomplishment in presenting a line-up that reads like a page from someone's Hall of Fame and in providing immaculate, idiomatic backing was not only immense but timely. Little Esther Phillips, Cleanhead Vinson, Joe Turner, Ivory Joe Hunter, Roy Milton, Roy Brown, and Pee Wee Crayton have all since died. However belated the recognition, the lives of these artists were changed for the better by these recordings. Crayton signed a contract with Vanguard, Hunter was recorded by Epic; Otis himself produced albums by many of them over the next few years. The event he organized stands as a monument to the best of the blues revival and as a re-created but superbly encapsulated summary and affirmation of California rhythm and blues.

450 **Live At Monterey!**
The Johnny Otis Show
Epic/Legacy EK 53628
Johnny Otis, *Willie And The Hand Jive;* Little Esther Phillips, *Cry Me A River Blues;* Eddie Cleanhead Vinson, *Cleanhead's Blues;* Joe Turner, *I Got A Gal;* Ivory Joe Hunter, *Since I Met You Baby;* Roy Milton, *Baby You Don't Know;* Gene Connors, *Preacher's Blues;* Roy Brown, *Good Rockin' Tonight;* Shuggie Otis, *The Time Machine;* Margie Evans, *Margie's Boogie;* Little Esther Phillips, *Little Esther's Blues: Blowtop Blues/T-Bone Blues/Jelly Jelly;* Eddie Cleanhead

Vinson, *Kidney Stew;* Pee Wee Crayton, *The Things I Used To Do;* Roy Milton, *R.M. Blues;* Shuggie Otis, *Shuggie's Boogie;* Delmar Evans, *You Better Look Out;* Johnny Otis & Delmar Evans, *Goin' Back To L.A.;* Joe Turner, *Plastic Man;* Ensemble, *Boogie Woogie Bye Bye*

Basic Records

(i) Pianists

451 **The Birth Of A Legend 1949–1952**
Ray Charles
Ebony CD 8001/2—2 CD set
DISC ONE: *I Love You, I Love You/Confession Blues/Alone In This City/Can Anyone Ask For More?/Let's Have A Ball/Rockin' Chair Blues/If I Gave You My Love/Can't You See Darling?/This Love Of Mine/How Long Blues/Blues Before Sunrise/A Sentimental Blues/You'll Never Miss The Water/Ain't That Fine/Don't Put All Your Dreams In One Basket/Sittin' On Top Of The World/I've Had My Fun/See See Rider/What Have I Done?/Honey Honey/She's On The Ball*

DISC TWO: *The Ego Song/Late In The Evening Blues/Someday/I'll Do Anything But Work/I Wonder Who's Kissing Her Now/All To Myself/Lonely Boy/Baby Let Me Hold Your Hand/I'm Glad For Your Sake/Baby Won't You Please Come Home/Kissa Me Baby/Hey Now/The Snow Is Falling/Misery In My Heart/Let Me Hear You Call My Name/Why Did You Go?/I'm wondering And Wondering/Walkin' And Talkin'/Guitar Blues/Back Home*
Not quite as complete as advertised, this is nevertheless the best compendium of the young Ray Charles on the West Coast. His blend of Nat King Cole and Charles Brown is often cited as is the emerging secularized gospel fire. Echoes of Saunders King, T-Bone Walker, Floyd Dixon, and other blues precursors are obvious amid a broader repertoire. *Baby Let Me Hold Your Hand* mixes Brown and Walker motifs into a finely honed success; *Hey Now* was a fervid harbinger of the Atlantic years.

452 **Marshall, Texas Is My Home**
Floyd Dixon
Specialty SPCD 7011-2/Ace CDCHD 361 (UK)
Hard Living Alone/Please Don't Go/Old Memories/Hole In The Wall/Time Brings About A Change/Me Quieras/Call Operator 210/Ooh-Eee! Ooh-Eee!/Chicken Crowing/Carlos/Nose Trouble/Reap What You Sow/Judgement Day/Instrumental Shuffle/Ooh-Eee! Ooh-Eee! (alternate take)*/Hey Bartender/Never Can Tell When A Woman Changes Her Mind/Oh Baby/What Is Life Without A Home?/Rita/I'll Always Love You/Oooh Little Girl*
Another migrant from Texas to Los Angeles, Dixon was heavily influenced by Charles Brown, Amos Milburn, and Louis Jordan. He offered superior skills as a wry, exuberant, or lazy vocalist, solid pianist and songwriter, often with world class sidemen. Later than most of his hits, two Specialty sessions from 1953 feature guitarist Chuck Norris, alongside subsequent recordings for Cat, Ebb, and Cash.

453 One Room Country Shack
Mercy Dee Walton
Specialty SPCD 7036-2/Ace CDCHD 475 (UK)
One Room Country Shack/My Woman Knows The Score/Misery Blues/The Great Mistake/Save Me Some/Strugglin' With The Blues/Lonesome Cabin Blues/Rent Man Blues/Fall Guy/The Drifter/Hear Me Shout/Love Is A Mystery/Winter Blues/Pauline/Get To Gettin'/Dark Muddy Bottom/Whatcha Gonna Do/My Woman And The Devil/Big Minded Daddy/Perfect Health/Problem Child/Pull 'Em And Pop 'Em/8th Wonder Of The World/Rock And Roll Fever
A singing pianist from Waco, Texas, Mercy Dee spent much of his life on the West Coast in the rural settings evoked in *One Room Country Shack* and *Dark Muddy Bottom* (1952). Such masterpieces and wry, jaundiced battle-of-the-sexes compositions place him in the forefront of post-war blues songwriting.

454 Honky Tonk Train
Lloyd Glenn
Night Train International NTI CD 7002
Sunday Morning Boogie/Old Time Shuffle (alternate take)/*I Can't Stay Here* [Jesse Thomas, vocal]/*Honky Tonk Train/Blues Hangover/Alberta* [Joe Pullum, vocal]/*Century Room/It's You I'm Thinking Of* [Jesse Thomas, vocal]/*Good Times Back Home/My Woman* [Joe Pullum, vocal]/*Charlie Henry/I'm So Blue* [Jesse Thomas, vocal]/*Yancey Special/Now Is The Time* [Jesse Thomas, vocal]/*After Hours*
Glenn distinguished himself with greater-Texas territory bands before becoming a popular pianist and arranger in Los Angeles during the 1940s and early 1950s. His modified Jimmy Yancey left-hand approach, block chords and respect for tradition are integral to this Exclusive and Swingtime compilation, which includes uncredited vocalists, out-takes, and blues and boogie staples.

455 Why Do Everything Happen To Me
Roy Hawkins
Route 66 KIX-9 (Swe)—*LP*
Why Do Everything Happen To Me/On My Way/Where You Been/Wine Drinkin' Woman/My Temper Is Rising/I Walk Alone/Mean Little Girl/Blues All Around Me/The Thrill Is Gone/Trouble Makin' Woman/Would You/Highway 59/The Condition I'm In/Doin' All Right/If I Had Listened/The Thrill Hunt
Hawkins was an ill-fated Bay Area balladeer and bluesman. The title track, a hit in 1950, was written following a car crash that left him paralyzed on one side, and he died before establishing rights to *The Thrill Is Gone,* (1951), which B.B. King popularized. An inspired session with T-Bone Walker and Maxwell Davis in 1952 generated *Would You, Highway 59, The Thrill Hunt,* and *Doin' All Right.*

456 Roots Of Rhythm & Blues
Jimmy McCracklin & Paul Gayten
Roots RTS 33023 (Belg)
Jimmy McCracklin, *Minnie Lee/Everybody Rock [New Orleans Beat]/Suffer/The Wobble/I'm To Blame/The Walk/Later On/One Track Love/He Knows The Rules/Hurt Me/I Know/Take Care Of Yourself/I'll Take The Blame/Trottin'/Get Tough/Come On/Country Baby/I'm Through;* Paul Gayten, *Down Boy/Get It/*

Music Goes Round And Round/Windy/You Better Believe It/Mother Roux/Tickie Toe/Nervous Boogie/For You My Love/The Sweeper/Hot Cross Buns/The Hunch
McCracklin began playing piano in a rudimentary Walter Davis style and became a commercially sensitive, sophisticated, and prolific artist. His period with Chess (1957–62) began with *The Walk* (a hit) while *He Knows The Rules* represents one of his most ubiquitous song forms. Gayten was also a fine pianist, A&R man, and arranger in New Orleans (**319**) and then Los Angeles.

(ii) Down-Home Texas Blues

457 Jesse Thomas: Complete Recorded Works In Chronological Order:
1948–1958
Blues Documents BDCD 6044 (Au)
Same Old Stuff/D. Double Due Love You/Zetter Blues/Mountain Key Blues/Melody In C/You Are My Dreams/I Wonder Why/Another Friend Like Me/Guess I'll Walk Alone/Let's Have Some Fun/Gonna Write You A Letter/Meet Me Tonight Along The Avenue/Tomorrow I May Be Gone/Texas Blues/I Can't Stay Here/Xmas Celebration/Now's The Time/It's You I'm Thinking Of/It's You I'm Thinking Of (alternate take)/*I Am So Blue/Long Time/Cool Kind Lover/When I Say I Love You/Jack Of Diamonds/Another Fool Like Me/Gonna Move To California/Take Some And Leave Some/Blow My Baby Back Home*
Born in Louisiana, singer-guitarist Thomas was a living blues history who cut his first 78s in the 1920s (**149**). Remarkable for his longevity, eclecticism, and mastery of South-western blues, he died in 1995. This CD gathers all his vintage post-war couplings, from solo country blues to jazz and R&B, recorded mostly in Los Angeles.

(iii) The Guitar Legacy Of T-Bone Walker

458 Blues After Hours
Pee Wee Crayton
P-Vine PCD-3028 (Jap)
Texas Hop/Blues After Hours/I Love You So/Got A Letter From My Baby [Brand New Woman]/Central Avenue Blues/California Woman/Bounce Pee Wee/Change Your Way Of Lovin'/Jack And The Beanstalk [Huckle Boogie]/Please Come Back/Dedicating The Blues To You/Rockin' The Blues/Crayton's Blues/Pee Wee's Boogie/Some Rainy Day/Tired Of Travelin'/Mistreated Blues/Oh Yeah Boogie/Blues For My Baby
One of the T-Bone disciples who set the standard for modern blues guitar, Crayton blended power chords, lightning picking, and inspiration from Walker and Charlie Christian. His sessions in Los Angeles during the late 1940s for Modern produced his signature instrumentals *Blues After Hours* and *Texas Hop* as well as wistful vocals *(I Love You So, Central Avenue Blues)*.

459 Gonna Hit That Highway: The Complete RPM Recordings
Johnny "Guitar" Watson
P-Vine PCD-3026/7 (Jap)—*2 CD set*
DISC ONE: *Hot Little Mama/Hot Little Mama* No. 2 (take 1)/*I Love To Love*

You/I Love To Love You No. 2 (take 1)/*I Love To Love You* No. 4 (take 2)/*Too Tired/Too Tired* (alternate take)/*Don't Touch Me/Don't Touch Me (I'm Gonna Hit That Highway)* (take 1)/*Those Lonely Lonely Nights* (take 4)/*Someone Cares For Me/Oh Baby/Oh Baby* (take 2)/*Give A Little* (take 1)/*Give A Little* (take 3)/*Ruben/Three Hours Past Midnight/Three Hours Past Midnight* (take 2)/*Love Me Baby* (take 7)/*She Moves Me* (take 5)/*Lonely Girl/Ain't Gonna Hush/My Baby And Me/I'll Be Blue/Love Bandit [Gangster Of Love]/In The Middle Of The Night*

DISC TWO: *Those Lonely Lonely Nights* (takes 1, 2, 3, 5–10)/*Hot Little Mama* No. 1 (takes 2–6)/*Hot Little Mama* No. 2 (takes 2, 3, 5)/*Too Tired* No. 3 (takes 1–3)/*I Love To Love You* No. 4 (take 3–9)/*Ruben* (takes 1, 2, 4)/*Love Me Baby* (takes 4–6)/*She Moves Me* (takes 1–4)
Watson reached his peak as a blues guitarist in the mid-1950s, influences from Gatemouth Brown and Guitar Slim combing to affect his own wit and drawl. His complete RPM recordings demonstrate an unusually dynamic, sophisticated young talent framed by Maxwell Davis' fine arrangements.

460 Scratchin'
Various Artists
Charly CD Charly 268 (UK)
Jimmy Nolen, *Strollin' With Nolen* (alternate take); Pete "Guitar" Lewis, *Louisiana Hop;* Jimmy Nolen, *How Fine Can You Be;* Pete "Guitar" Lewis, *Scratchin';* Jimmy Nolen, *You've Been Goofing;* Pete "Guitar" Lewis, *Crying With The Rising Sun;* Jimmy Nolen, *The Way You Do;* Cal Green, *The Big Push;* Pete "Guitar" Lewis, *Raggedy Blues;* Jimmy Nolen, *I Can't Stand You No More* (alternate take)/*After Hours;* Pete "Guitar" Lewis, *Harmonica Boogie;* Jimmy Nolen, *Don't Leave Me No More;* Pete "Guitar" Lewis, *Chocolate Pork Chop Man;* Jimmy Nolen, *Wipe Your Tears;* Cal Green, *Green's Blues;* Jimmy Nolen, *It Hurts Me Too/Strollin' With Nolen;* Pete "Guitar" Lewis, *The Blast;* Jimmy Nolen, *Strawberry Jam;* Pete "Guitar" Lewis, *Ooh Midnight;* Jimmy Nolen, *Movin' On Down The Line*
Federal sides by three mainstay guitarists recorded in the 1950s, this disc will rock any house. Nolen's punchy Texas playing style accompanies vocals that sometimes mirror Fats Domino (1955–6). Lewis (succeeded by Nolen in the Johnny Otis band) had a similar, more aggressive approach on his tracks from 1952, with guitar, harp, and occasional vocals. Green performs two driving instrumentals made in 1958.

461 The Bottom Of The Top
Phillip Walker
Hightone HCD 8020/Demon FIEND CD 158 (UK)
I Can't Lose (With The Stuff I Use)/Tin Pan Alley/Hello Central/Hello My Darling/Laughing & Clowning/Crazy Girl/It's All In Your Mind/The Bottom Of The Top/Hey, Hey, Baby's Gone/Crying Time
A Texas veteran who moved to Los Angeles in the 1950s, Walker worked with producers Bruce Bromberg and Dennis Walker for approximately two decades. This CD reissue of his début LP represents five sessions recorded between 1969 and 1972. It features traditional Texas blues and R&B.

462 **Just Blues**
Sonny Rhodes and the Texas Twisters
Rhodes-Way RWR-4501
I Can't Lose/The Things I Used To Do/Please Love Me/House Without Love/Think/Cigarette Blues/Strange Things Happening/It Hurts Me Too/East Oakland Stomp
Rhodes went from Texas bassist to "The East Bay Sheik," a regular guitarist, a steel player in the mold of L.C. Robinson and a singer equally influenced by Jr Parker, ZZ Hill, and Percy Mayfield. This self-produced project of the mid-1980s holds its own alongside interesting contemporary work for established labels.

463 **The Touch**
Johnny Heartsman
Alligator ALCD 4800
Serpent's Touch/Paint My Mailbox Blue/You're So Fine/Tongue/Attitude/Got To Find My Baby/The Butler Did It/Please Don't Be Scared Of My Love/Oops/Walkin' Blues/Let Me Love You, Baby/Heartburn/Endless/Tongue (unexpurgated version)
One of the Bay Area's greatest blues studio musicians in the 1950s and 1960s, Heartsman is a spectacular guitarist, keyboard, bass, and flute player, as well as a distinctive vocalist, songwriter, and arranger. In his present city of residence, Sacramento, he cut this nearly all-original programme in 1991, demonstrating that he is still at the top of his game.

464 **Blue Soul**
Joe Louis Walker
Hightone HCD 8019/Demon FIEND CD 159 (UK)
Prove Your Love/Ain't Nothin' Goin' On/T.L.C./Personal Baby/Since You've Been Gone/Alligator/Dead Sea/City Of Angels/I'll Get To Heaven On My Own
Former house-band member at psychedelic Bay Area dance halls and roommate of Mike Bloomfield, Walker emerged as a major contemporary blues figure in the late 1980s. This third Hightone album (1989) illustrates the versatility and virtuosity of an increasingly personal, interesting musical force. The romping *Since You've Been Gone* and acoustic *I'll Get To Heaven On My Own* are equally striking.

465 **Rock This House**
Hollywood Fats
Black Top BT 1097
Rock This House/She's Dynamite/Okie Dokie Stomp/Suitcase Blues/Red Headed Woman/Lonesome/All Pretty Women/Prettiest Little Thing/Caldonia/Have A Good Time/Poor Boy/Too Many Drivers/I Got My Eyes On You/Little Girl/Kansas City/Shake Your Boogie/Read About My Baby
Hollywood Fats (Mike Mann), an influential West Coast guitarist died aged 32. His band's only LP, cut in 1979, used Al Blake's serviceable vocals and Chicago-styled harp. Riffs and licks on *She's Dynamite* and *Red Headed Woman* have become mandatory among similar guitarists. The CD includes six bonus tracks.

(iv) The Peak Of Duke-Peacock

466 **Junior's Blues/The Duke Recordings: Volume One**
Junior Parker
MCA MCAD 10669
I Wanna Ramble/Mother-In-Law Blues/Next Time You See Me/That's All Right/Sitting And Thinking/Sweet Home Chicago/Sometimes/Stand By Me/ Driving Wheel/Seven Days/In The Dark/Someone Somewhere/It's A Pity/ Yonder's Wall/Strange Things Happening/The Things I Used To Do/Jivin' Woman/Cryin' For My Baby
This collection from 1954–64 explores the repertoire of a pace-setting Roy Brown-influenced singer and top-rank harp player. *I Wanna Ramble* and his huge mid-1950s hits *Mother-In-Law Blues* and *Next Time You See Me* represent tough Memphis sounds, while, subsequent sides demonstrate broader and more up-town motifs. Horns and unamplified harmonica are blended judiciously in blues evergreens alongside ventures toward the pop market.

467 **Hound Dog/The Peacock Recordings**
Big Mama Thornton
MCA MCAD 10668
Hound Dog/My Man Called Me/I Smell A Rat/They Call Me Big Mama/You Don't Move Me No More/Let Your Tears Fall Baby/Rock-A-Bye Baby/Yes, Baby (duet with Johnny Ace)/*How Come/Nightmare/Stop A-Hoppin' On Me/ Just Like A Dog, Barking Up The Wrong Tree/Walking Blues/The Big Change/ Hard Times/Laugh, Laugh, Laugh/The Fish/I've Searched The Whole World Over.*
In addition to the notorious *Hound Dog,* there are plenty of growling, jumping blues, a duet, and novelties like *The Fish,* where Roy Gaines' guitar solo emphasizes the quality of Thornton's session musicians. These recordings of 1952–5 by one of blues' toughest singers were cut in Los Angeles and Houston (often with the Johnny Otis group).

468 **Best Of Duke-Peacock Blues**
Various Artists
MCA MCAD 10667
Gatemouth Brown, *My Time Is Expensive;* Elmore Nixon, *A Hepcat's Advice;* Big Mama Thornton, *Let Your Tears Fall Baby;* Earl Forest, *Whoopin' And Hollerin';* Johnny Ace, *How Can You Be So Mean;* Roscoe Gordon, *Keep On Doggin';* Andrew Tibbs, *Rock Savoy Rock;* Sonny Parker, *She Set My Soul On Fire;* Memphis Slim, *Living Like A King;* Little Richard, *Little Richard's Boogie;* Pete "Guitar" Lewis, *Goin' Crazy;* Junior Parker, *Drivin' Wheel;* Larry Davis, *Texas Flood;* Fenton Robinson, *Mississippi Steamboat;* James Davis, *Blue Monday;* Otis Rush, *Homework;* Bobby Bland, *Stormy Monday/Turn On Your Lovelight*
This program of recordings made all over the US between 1949 and 1963, represents the South-west (Brown and Thornton), Memphis transplants to Texas (Bland, Parker, Ace, Forest, and Gordon), and Chicago (Memphis Slim and Rush). A romping Little Richard work-out with the Johnny Otis band and James Davis' minor key perennial find themselves in worthy company.

(v) California Cross-Section

469 **The Swingtime Records Story**
Various Artists
Capricorn 9 42024-2—2 CD set
DISC ONE: Lowell Fulson, *Crying Blues [Street Walking Woman]/You're Gonna Miss Me When I'm Gone;* Floyd Dixon, *Mississippi Blues;* Eddie Williams & His Brown Buddies With Floyd Dixon, *Saturday Night Fish Fry;* Jimmy Witherspoon, *In The Evening When The Sun Goes Down/Wandering Gal/I Hate To See Christmas Come Around/Times Gettin' Tougher/Ain't Nobody's Business Part 1;* Joe Swift With The Johnny Otis Band, *Alligator Meat;* Charles Brown, *B & O Blues;* Nightengale Jubalaires, *Rough And Rocky Road;* Pete Johnson Orchestra, *Rocket Boogie 88* Part 2; Big Joe Turner, *Radar Blues/Wine-O-Baby Boogie;* Lowell Fulson, *Everyday I Have The Blues/Blue Shadows/Low Society Blues;* The Maxin [*sic*] Trio & Ray Charles, *I Love You, I Love You (I Will Never Let You Go);* Earl Jackson With The Johnny Otis Band, *Take Out The Squeal (If You Want A Meal)/A Woman Don't Want A Good Man No More;* Edgar Hayes & The Stardusters With Lloyd Glenn, *Backwater Blues* Stars Of Harmony, *Where Shall I Be;* Eddie Williams, *Broken Hearted;* The Maxim [*sic*] Trio & Ray Charles, *You'll Never Miss The Water (Until The Well's Gone Dry)*

DISC TWO: Percy Mayfield With The Monroe Tucker Band, *Two Years Of Torture/Baby You're Still A Square;* Ray Charles, *Someday* (alternate take)/*I'll Do Anything But Work* (alternate take); Clifford "Fat Man" Blivens With The Johnny Otis Band, *Korea Blues;* Lloyd Glenn's Combo, *Chica Boo;* Lloyd Glenn with the Fulson Unit, *Old Time Shuffle Blues* (alternate take); Lowell Fulson, *Sinner's Prayer* (alternate take); Jessie Thomas With Lloyd Glenn, *I Can't Stay Here;* Ray Charles, *Lonely Boy;* Jimmy McCracklin, *Rockin Man;* Lowell Fulson, *I'm A Night Owl* Part 1, Ray Charles, *Kissa Me Baby/The Snow Is Falling;* Lowell Fulson, *Let Me Ride In Your Automobile;* Joe Pullum With Lloyd Glenn, *My Woman;* Jimmy McCracklin, *Blues For The People* (alternate take); Lowell Fulson, *I Love My Baby;* Ray Charles, *I'm Wondering And Wondering;* Lloyd Glenn, *It Moves Me;* Earl Brown With The Red Calender Combo, *Lovin' A Married Woman;* Ray Charles, *Guitar Blues;* Three Muskateers, *Love Me Til Your Dying Day;* Playboy Thomas, *End Of The Road Baby;* The Hollywood Flames, *I Know*
Recordings from 1946–52 highlight this seminal Los Angeles label, run by African-American proprietor Jack Lauderdale, who also bought masters from Supreme and Exclusive and discovered Ray Charles in Seattle. Definitive landmarks on the road to prominence by Fulson, house arranger Glenn, Ray Charles, Brown, Witherspoon, Dixon, McCracklin, and the Otis ensemble, make this a welcome encapsulation of the burgeoning West Coast "cool blues" scene.

470 **Poet Of The Blues**
Percy Mayfield
Specialty SPCD-7001-2/Ace CDCHD 283 (UK)
Please Send Me Someone To Love/Prayin' For Your Return/Strange Things Happening/Life Is Suicide/What A Fool I Was/Lost Love/Nightless Lover/Advice (For Men Only)/Cry Baby/Lost Mind/I Dare You Baby/Hopeless/The Hunt Is

On/The River's Invitation/The Big Question/Wasted Dream/Louisiana/Bachelor Blues/Get Way Back/Memory Pain/Loose Lips/You Don't Exist No More/Nightmare/Baby You're Rich/My Heart Is Cryin'
Arguably modern blues' greatest songwriter and a sublime, individualistic blues and ballad vocalist, Mayfield made his mark on Specialty in 1950. This indispensable sampling from 1950–4 includes the enduring classics; contemporary cover recordings have made many other selections familiar. All are finely crafted, thanks in part to Maxwell Davis' arrangements and bands.

471 Roy Milton And His Solid Senders
Roy Milton
Specialty SPCD 7004-2/Ace CDCHD 308 (UK)
Milton's Boogie/R.M. Blues/True Blues/Camille's Boogie/Thrill Me/Big Fat Mama/Keep A Dollar In Your Pocket/Everything I Do Is Wrong/Hop, Skip & Jump/Porter's Love Song/The Hucklebuck/Information Blues/Where There Is No Love/Junior Jives/Bartender's Boogie/Oh Babe/Christmas Time Blues/It's Later Than You Think/The Numbers Blues/I Have News For You/T-Town Twist/Best Wishes/So Tired/Night And Day (I Miss You So)/Blue Turning Grey
Via *R.M. Blues,* cut in 1945, Milton was among the first to succeed with a stripped-down jump band. He was a singer/drummer, and his stalwarts included pianist Camille Howard, guitarist Junior Rogers, and saxophonists Buddy Floyd and Jackie Kelso. Many of the up-tempo tunes from 1945–52 will prompt a recognition that is testimony to the band's importance.

472 Joe Liggins And The Honeydrippers
Joe Liggins
Specialty SPCD 7006-2/Ace CDCHD 307 (UK)
Pink Champagne/Ramblin' Blues/Rag Mop/Rhythm In The Barnyard/Going Back To New Orleans/I've Got A Right To Cry/The Honeydripper/Don't Miss That Train/Frankie Lee/Brand New Deal In Mobile/Little Joe's Boogie/One Sweet Letter/Whiskey, Gin & Wine/Louisiana Woman/Trying To Lose The Blues/Shuffle Boogie Blues/Rain, Rain, Rain/The Flying Dutchman/Tanya/Blues For Tanya/Freight Train Blues/Whiskey, Women & Loaded Dice/The Big Dipper/Do You Love Me Pretty Baby?
The combo backing singer/pianist Liggins, with Little Willie Jackson on alto and baritone saxes, had a gentler sound than many. These tracks from 1950–4, however, show that it could keep a dance hall in high gear with blues and boogie hits like *Pink Champagne, I've Got A Right To Cry, The Honeydripper,* and *Tanya.*

473 Jimmy Liggins And His Drops Of Joy
Jimmy Liggins
Specialty SPCD 7005-2/Ace CDCHD 306 (UK)
I Can't Stop It/Troubles Goodbye/Teardrop Blues/Cadillac Boogie/Move Out Baby/Careful Love/Homecoming Blues/Baby I Can't Forget You/Don't Put Me Down/Nite Life Boogie/Mississippi Boogie/Come Back Baby/Answer To Teardrop Blues/That Song Is Gone/Saturday Night Boogie Woogie Man/Shuffle Shuck/The Washboard Special/That's What's Knockin' Me Out/Hep Cat Boogie/I Want My Baby For Christmas/Train Blues/Baby's Boogie/Drunk/Going Away/Come Back Home

Jimmy Liggins, a guitarist-vocalist, had a cruder sound, tilted more toward jump than his brother's though his group also had major impact. The influence of South-western styles, like those on this 1947–53 package, is exemplified by the subsequent transformation of *Cadillac Boogie* into Jackie Brenston's *Rocket 88* (**415**).

474 **Oakland Blues**
Various Artists
Arhoolie 2008—LP
K.C. Douglas, *Mercury Boogie;* Sidney Maiden, *Eclipse Of The Sun;* Willie B. Huff, *Beggar Man Blues;* Juke Boy Bonner, *Well Baby/Rock With Me Baby;* Mercy Dee, *Trailing My Baby;* L.C. Robinson, *Why Don't You Write To Me;* Johnny Fuller, *Train, Train Blues/First Stage Of The Blues;* Jimmy McCracklin, *When I'm Gone;* Jimmy Wilson, *Tin Pan Alley/A Woman Is To Blame/Blues At Sundown/Frisco Bay*
The atmospheric, laconic, and spare approach derived from Geddins is exemplified with powerful country blues by Douglas, Maiden, Huff, and Bonner (making his début in 1957). Mercy Dee's usual imaginative lyrics stand alongside Robinson's wailing vocals and steel guitar, Fuller's understated depth, a McCracklin slow blues, and spine-chilling vocals by Wilson, with pyrotechnic guitar by Lafayette Thomas.

475 **Mr. Fulbright's Blues**
Various Artists
P-Vine PCD-2008 (Jap)
Jimmy Nolen [Wilson], *Strangest Blues/I Used To Love A Woman;* Phillip Walker, *Louisiana Walk/I Want You For Myself/Playing In The Park/Hello My Darling;* Mac Willis, *Pretty Woman/Howling Woman;* Smokey Hogg, *Blue And Lonesome Blues/Misery In My Life;* Elmon Mickle, *Flat Foot Sam/I Got To Get Some Money;* Jesse Fuller, *Listen Here Mr. Fireman/San Francisco Bay Blues;* Big Son Tillis & D.C. Bender, *Zetela Blues/Rocks Is My Pillow/Ten Long Years/I Got A Letter;* Unknown Artist A, *Hard Luck Blues;* Jesse Thomas, *Another Fool Like Me;* George Smith, *West Helena Blues;* Unknown Artist B [Jesse Belvin], *Come Back Baby;* Unknown Artist C, *Strange Ol' Feeling;* J.D. Nicholson, *I Ain't Gonna Be Your Dog No More;* Jimmy Nolen, *Let's Try It Again;* Willie Egans, *It's A Shame/Willie's Boogie*
A quirky presentation of mostly down-home recordings by maverick J.R. Fulbright, based in Los Angeles. There are intense vocals by Wilson (as Nolen), a solid shuffle by the real Nolen, four rocking early Phillip Walker songs, country blues guitar, piano, and harp and rock 'n' roll by Egans.

476 **Blues From Dolphin's Of Hollywood**
Various Artists
Specialty SPCD 2172-2/Ace CDCHD 357 (UK)
Pee Wee Crayton, *The Darkest Hour/Forgive Me/Crying And Walking/Pappy's Blues/Baby, Pat The Floor/I'm Your Prisoner/Lovin' John* [James Wayne?]/ *Fillmore Street Blues/Boogie Bop;* Little Caesar, *You Can't Bring Me Down/ Cadillac Baby;* Percy Mayfield, *WDIA Station ID/Look The Whole World Over/The Monkey Song;* Memphis Slim, *Treat Me Like I Treat You/My Country Girl/Worried Life Blues/Pete's Boogie;* Jimmy Witherspoon, *Big*

Family Blues/Cain River Blues/Tennage Party/S.K. Blues; Floyd Dixon, *Never Know When A Woman Changes Her Mind/Oh Baby;* Peppermint Harris, *Cadillac Funeral/Treat Me Like I Treat You*
John Dolphin's record labels combine enjoyable blues and R&B from the early and mid-1950s. This disc includes Crayton's mood-setting guitar; Little Caesar's theatrical vocals; Mayfield's *WDIA Station ID* and two organ-driven swing tunes; the ubiquitous Witherspoon and Dixon; plus "outsiders" Memphis Slim and Peppermint Harris.

477 **Harmonica Ace**
Little George Smith
Flair/Virgin V2 86928/Ace CDCHD 337 (UK)
Rocking/Telephone Blues/Blues In The Dark/Blues Stay Away From Me/Have Myself A Ball/I Found My Baby (alternate take)/*Oopin' Doopin' Doopin'* (alternate take)/*California Blues* (alternate take)/*Hey Mr Porter* (alternate take)/*Early One Monday Morning* (take 1)/*Rocking* (alternate take)/*Love Life/Cross Eyed Suzie Lee/You Don't Love Me/I Found My Baby/Oopin' Doopin Doopin'/California Blues/Down In New Orleans [Hey Mr Porter]/Early One Monday Morning* (take 2)
An early master of amplified and chromatic harmonica, Smith worked with Muddy Waters during the 1950s and 1960s. *Telephone Blues,* from his classic Kansas City début session of 1955, mixes riveting harmonica with strong South-western guitar. The Los Angeles tracks of 1956 with Maxwell Davis are less distinctive.

478 **All Night Long They Play The Blues**
Various Artists
Specialty SPCD-7029-2/Ace CDCHD 440 (UK)
Little Johnny Taylor, *Part Time Love* (extended version); Saunders King, *S.K. Blues;* Big Mama Thornton, *Life Goes On;* Sonny Rhodes, *One Of These Days;* Clay Hammond, *There's Gonna Be Some Changes;* K.C. "Country Boy" Douglas, *The Things I Do For You;* Saunders King, *What's Your Story, Morning Glory?;* Charles Brown, *I'm Gonna Push On;* Phillip Walker, *Hey, Hey, Baby's Gone;* Clarence Smith [Sonny Rhodes], *All Night Long They Play The Blues;* K.C. Douglas, *Little Green House;* Little Johnny Taylor, *The Things That I Used To Do;* Big Mama Thornton, *Because It's Love;* J.J. Malone, *Danger Zone;* Sonny Rhodes, *Country Boy;* Phillip Walker, *Laughin' And Clownin';* Bill Coday, *You're Gonna Want Me;* Little Johnny Taylor, *Driving Wheel;* Charles Brown, *Cry No More;* Rodger Collins, *I'm Serving Time;* The Right Kind, *You Oughta Slow Dance, Baby;* Little Johnny Taylor, *Please Come Home For Christmas;* Merl Saunders, *Tighten Up*
These Los Angeles and Bay Area singles, recorded in 1962–71, were issued on Galaxy. Produced by Cliff Goldsmith or ace horn arranger Ray Shanklin, tracks such as Little Johnny Taylor's *Part Time Love* (1963) embody the post-B.B. King/Bobby Bland model of blues, with ornate horns and gospel-laced vocals supplementing keyboards and guitars.

479 **The Galaxy Years**
Little Johnny Taylor
Ace CHCHD 967 (UK)
You'll Need Another Favor/What You Need Is A Ball/Part Time Love/

Somewhere Down The Line/Since I Found A New Love/My Heart Is Filled With Pain/First Class Love/If You Love Me (Like You Say)/You Win, I Lose/Nightingale Melody/I Smell Trouble/True Love/For Your precious Love/I've Never Had A Woman Like You Before/Somebody's Got To Pay/Help Yourself/One More Chance/Please Come Home For Christmas/All I Want Is You/Zig Zag Lightning/The Things That I Used To Do/Big Blue Diamonds/I Know You Hear Me Calling/Driving Wheel/Sometimey Woman/Double Or Nothing.
Despite some overlap with the preceding, this collection of 1963–8 makes it clear why Taylor's Galaxy singles set a standard for intense, classy gospel blues. Shanklin's arrangements strengthened gems like *Part Time Love*; guitarist Arthur Wright stands tall on *You'll Need Another Favor* and many others; and George Smith's chromatic harmonica is an asset on *Help Yourself.*

480 **Evenin' Blues**
Jimmy Witherspoon
Original Blues Classics OBCCD 511-2
Money's Gettin' Cheaper/Grab Me A Freight/Don't Let Go!/I've Been Treated Wrong/Evenin'/Cane River/How Long Blues/Good Rockin' Tonight/Kansas City/Drinking Beer/Don't Let Go (alternate take)/*I've Been Treated Wrong* (alternate take)/*Evenin'* (alternate take)/*Cane River* (alternate take)
The mellow session of 1963 that resulted in this collection (including four outtakes) teamed master shouter Witherspoon with T-Bone Walker and a saxophone and organ combo led by Clifford Scott (tenor, alto, and flute). It yielded swinging and satisfying performances of slow and jump blues, plus *Evenin'* (a Walker ballad from the 1940s).

They Satisfy

JOHN BROVEN

13 New Orleans, Louisiana, and Zydeco

As you travel along Interstate 10 from New Orleans, via Baton Rouge to Lake Charles and beyond, you cannot help noticing numerous automobile plates bearing the legend "Sportsman's Paradise"—the Louisiana state motto. If there is any justice, those plates will be amended soon to "Music Paradise", because no other state can boast such mellifluous riches. Louisiana is one of the last bastions of living American roots music; and, through the gramophone record and personal appearances by musicians, the message is spreading worldwide.

Recordings of indigenous black music by Louisiana performers began in the 1920s. With the significant exception of the advent of creole jazz, however, few suggest the subsequent flowering of rhythm and blues in New Orleans, and swamp blues and zydeco in other areas of the state. These major musical styles are phenomena of the post-war years.

The particular sound of New Orleans R&B developed from a heritage of street marching bands in the "crecent city". Spurred by the national popularity of R&B, local performers forged a distinctive tradition, under the guiding influence of Dave Bartholomew and his most successful protégé, Fats Domino. Both men were fortunate in having the enlightened Cosimo Matassa as a studio owner and skillful recording engineer. A settled group of first-class players was used at his sessions during the 1950s. They included: Lee Allen (tenor saxophone), Alvin "Red" Tyler (tenor and baritone saxophone), Edward Frank (piano), Justin Adams and Edgar Blanchard (guitar), Frank Fields (bass), and Earl Palmer and Charles "Hungry" Williams (drums). It was these musicians who created the tight, funky, famous New Orleans R&B sound that became a bedrock of rock 'n' roll. Younger producers, including Harold Battiste, Allen Toussaint, and Wardell Quezergue, took over from Bartholomew and his circle in the late 1950s and early 1960s.

Louisiana did not have a regional blues scene of substance until 1954, when Jay Miller, based in Crowley, started recording Baton Rouge artists such as Lightnin' Slim, Slim Harpo, and Lazy Lester.

Accordion and Washboard players, New Iberia, Louisiana, 1938 (*Russell Lee/FSA/Library of Congress*)

With popular vocalists performing casually over a backdrop of wailing harmonicas, booming electric guitars, and wallowing backbeats, the music came to be known affectionately as "swamp blues". The door opened for Lonesome Sundown, Silas Hogan, Whispering Smith, and many other artists. This style is being kept alive in Baton Rouge (the state capital), by a younger generation of musicians.

Alongside commercial recordings of swamp blues, the folklorist Dr Harry Oster documented scattered rural blues traditions in historic field recordings made between 1956 and 1962. These led to significant discoveries such as Robert Pete Williams, James "Butch" Cage, Willie B. Thomas, and Smoky Babe (**78, 425, 426**).

Zydeco has become a potent force through the extraordinary talent of Clifton Chenier, who raised the international profile of this local style with records and striking personal performances. His interpretations followed the influence of old-time black French artists, such as Amédé Ardoin and Sidney Babineaux, and R&B of the 1950s—a compelling mix. There is now a host of young and old black musicians playing zydeco, making Chenier a prolific salesman for the piano accordion (his favored instrument).

Musicians in New Orleans and Louisiana evidently lay great store on the "hit" record. There is a danger that this commercial yardstick hides performances of artistic worth, but many local hits are of great musical merit and embedded engagingly in the state's folklore. The recording of all forms of Louisiana music continues apace. With multi-track techniques and hi-tech studio equipment, however, the sparky ambience of the best old recordings is lost and regional individuality is in danger of being eroded. Accordingly, there are few modern recordings among these selections, but Louisiana is still a paradise for live music.

Essential Records

(i) Classic New Orleans R&B

Little is known about blues in New Orleans before World War II. There were occasional blues recordings by the city's jazz musicians, and local renditions by singers such as Lela Bolden (1924), Willie Jackson (1926), Ann Cook, and Genevieve Davis (1927) (**7**). In the next decade a few sessions were made by vocalists, such as Blue Lu Barker (**278**), and singer-pianists, such as Jack Dupree (**248**). In 1938 the jazz composer and pianist Jelly Roll Morton recalled the local blues tradition in recordings for the Library of Congress (**56, 212**). Virtually all these sides, however, were cut in Northern cities rather than on location in the South.

In the late 1930s serious investigation began into the relationship between black New Orleans marching bands and their contribution to early jazz. Blues were featured occasionally in local recordings by these old-time musicians in the early 1940s. It was not until 1947, however, that a spectrum of contemporary black R&B performers made commercial recordings in the city for a company devoted to mass sales. This was Deluxe Records (of Linden New Jersey), whose success with sides by Roy Brown (**286**) and the team of Paul Gayten and Annie Laurie (**319**) was to spark the interest of similar organizations. Subsequent activity, by a variety of companies, established New Orleans as a leading center for recording Southern music.

Dave Bartholomew was another performer involved in recording for Deluxe (and Regal, their successors). A trumpet player and band leader, in 1949–50 he became involved in producing sides for Imperial Records. Run by Lew Chudd (in Hollywood, California), this label was to define the New Orleans sound throughout the 1950s. Bartholomew's association with Imperial was long-standing and lasted until the company was sold to Liberty Records in 1963. The **Spirit Of New Orleans: The Genius Of Dave Bartholomew** is a testament to this creative period and Bartholomew's role in producing R&B of the highest class, by all types of black performers. Three of the first sides he supervised for Chudd are in this two-CD set. Recorded in November 1949, by Jewel King and Tommy Ridgley, they follow the pattern of sophisticated soulful blues with brass and rhythm accompaniment. Four months later, however, a two-part performance of the blues ballad *Stack-A-Lee* harks back to a pre-war barrelhouse style both in lyrics and Archibald's piano playing. This mixture of contemporary and traditional themes was to be a hallmark of Bartholomew's productions, which was found to be commercially successful. He also maintained this approach in sides cut under his own name. Dave Bartholomew was responsible for supervising recordings by a roster of famous R&B performers, as can be discerned from the contents of this anthology. Some sessions, like those by the duo Shirley and Lee (Shirley Goodman and Leonard Lee), were for rival companies (in this instance, Aladdin) but, alongside occasional outside activities, he sustained loyalty to Lew Chudd and local artists. Bartholomew was also employed to produce records by visiting musicians, including sessions with Big Joe Turner, T-Bone Walker, Pee Wee Crayton, and other significant black R&B stars. The collection is a well-balanced expression of the styles that made-up New Orleans R&B in the 1950s and has been compiled with care to feature key performers from the period.

Cosmopolitan "good-time" attitudes may be responsible for lack of emotional depth in New Orleans blues recordings since 1947, even though most of the black population lives in shotgun shacks, project houses, and ghettos. There were, of course, isolated "country" performers such as Boogie Bill Webb and Babe Stovall. The local concept of recorded blues, however, is entwined with loud, rocking, urbanized music that become known as rhythm and blues. This evolved from a variety of black styles, notably big-band swing, boogie woogie, jazz, and gospel, with a less obvious contribution from other forms. Today, those considered blues singers in New Orleans are R&B shouters such Roy Brown, Joe "Mr Google Eyes" August, and Smiley Lewis.

Lewis was born Overton Amos Lemons in the small town of De Quincy in 1913. In his youth he moved to New Orleans and by the mid-1930s was playing one-night engagements with a small band for guarantees and tips. Uniform was a long frock tail coat and high beaver hat, in the troubadour tradition. His early accompanists included Thomas Jefferson on trumpet and Tuts Washington on piano.

Playing competent electric guitar, Smiley cut his first records during Deluxe's pioneering sessions in the city in 1947. His next recordings were made for Imperial in February 1950, at the behest of Dave Bartholomew. Although a mainstay of the "Classic New Orleans R&B" sound, and the label's catalog during the following decade, he never has a sizeable hit. *The Bells Are Ringing* (1952) and *I Hear You Knocking* (1955) appeared fleetingly near the top of the R&B charts, but did not reach the top 100 in the popular lists. Dave Bartholomew considered Lewis a "bad luck singer" because of his lack of commercial success. This was despite the benefit of musicians, songwriters, and production that had brought fame and fortune to others. Lewis even recorded out-and-out rock 'n' roll for teenage purchasers, but they probably considered his mellow shouting vocals as overpowering; he did not look the part either. Confirming this view (to Bunny Matthews), the veteran New Orleans record store owner Jim Russell recalled Smiley as follows:

> [He was] a sort of pudgy, old-looking black person to bring into a white teenage dance or a black teenage dance [. . .] at first they couldn't relate to him. They couldn't get stimulated with him when the band started to play—already they wondered if this was the same man who was going to do the singing. But when he jumped on the stage, they didn't ask any more questions because he captured them in the palm of his hand. He had them as long as he stayed there.*

*Quoted in sleeve notes to Stateside LP SSL6025 (*UK*).

The Best Of Smiley Lewis contains the cream of the singer's recordings for Imperial, including *Big Mamou, Real Gone Lover, One Night,* and *Shame, Shame, Shame. Tee-Nah-Nah,* his earliest side for Imperial, is a traditional theme, with a somber old-time verse referring to the state penitentiary at Angola. Mature big-voiced singing of the highest caliber and enlightened backing from Bartholomew's house band make this CD an epitome of the era.

Antoine "Fats" Domino was the most significant New Orleans personality in the Imperial catalog. A singer-pianist, Fats has been in the vanguard of the city's R&B since 10 December 1949, when he cut *The Fat Man,* accompanied by a band with considerable knowledge of local motifs. Fats was blazing a new trail with this first recording; the melody, however, was a traditional piano theme recorded by Jack Dupree as *Junker Blues* in 1941.

Domino started out as a New Orleans R&B performer but was also the principal artist from that city to achieve widespread success in the rock 'n' roll era. He has more than 20 gold records to his credit. For a black artist he sings in an unusually smooth manner, with a Creole-French inflection that, crucially, appealed to white audiences. The rolling piano, melodic saxophone solos, riffing horns, and insistent New Orleans street-parade rhythms were an added bonus. By happy chance, this technique was a seedcorn for rock 'n' roll and did not need alteration in the mid-1950s, when many R&B performers lost popularity to the new fashion. His music is closely associated with those heady times.

Domino's career can be measured against the success of his hit records. With some artists this is a suspect barometer, but his output was remarkably consistent, and is amply demonstrated by Bear Family's eight-CD compilation of his complete Imperial recordings, **Out Of New Orleans** (1949–62). An early chartmaker in the segregated R&B lists, he had hits with *The Fat Man, Goin' Home* and *Going To The River*. After a slow period in the mid-1950s he issued the classics *Ain't It A Shame, Blueberry Hill, Blue Monday,* and *I'm Walkin'*. By that time his records were played continuously on the radio, at high-school dances, on jukeboxes, at home; and he appeared in films on TV and in caravan shows. He was a rock 'n' roll star. For a time, every R&B aggregation in New Orleans, and the rest of the United States, played *exactly* like the Fats Domino band. Popular artists such as Clarence "Frogman" Henry and Chubby Checker also modeled their singing styles on his.

Domino's records maintained chart status in the late 1950s and early 1960s, some more successful than others—*Whole Lotta Loving, I Want To Walk You Home, I'm Gonna Be A Wheel Someday, Walking To*

New Orleans, and *My Girl Josephine.* Apart from the overdubbed strings in the version of *Walking To New Orleans* released in 1960, these recordings still represented the best of New Orleans R&B.

The first four CDs in Bear Family's comprehensive collection represent the cream of Domino's R&B recordings. They indicate the foundation for his music in local conventions, but also reflect the wider blues tradition. *Hey! La Bas Boogie* for example, relates directly to the repertoire of marching bands. There had been versions by Wooden Joe Nicholas (a research session for American Music, in 1945) and Papa Celestin (for Deluxe, in 1947). The latter band included Harrison Verrett, Fats' brother-in-law, in the compliment and was a mass-market release. *Careless Love* was also popular with marching bands, as was *Second Line Jump* (a boisterous musical component in wake ceremonies, following the solemnity of burial). "Second Line Jumping" can also take place in Carnival parades. Similarly, Domino's *Mardi Gras In New Orleans* celebrates the event; this, however, is a direct cover of a 1949 recording by Professor Longhair, a local contemporary. Other themes in his repertoire can be traced to earlier recordings. These include Big Bill Broonzy's *All By Myself* (1941) (**5**), *Swanee River Hop* (1946—based on *Swanee River Boogie* by Albert Ammons: (**235**); and *Helping Hand* (a version of *Waiting For A Train* popularized in 1928 by the old-time music star Jimmie Rodgers; **328**). Fats even recorded a local version of the black ballad *Stack-A-Lee,* under the title *Stack & Billy.* A proportion of the more popular tunes in his rock 'n' roll repertoire were also contemporary themes played by marching bands. A grounding in the local blues piano tradition is recognizable in his playing style. He has acknowledged listening to gramophone records and Harrison Verrett (banjo and guitar), but has otherwise not identified particular influences.

Black pianists are recalled in New Orleans sporting houses from the turn of the century, if not before, playing a musical repertoire broad enough to cater for every request. It is likely they incorporated blues into their music at these small clubs, brothels, and dives during the first two decades. Particular blues players rose to prominence during the 1920s and were also popular at parties and Saturday-night fish fries, where they performed for moonshine whiskey, home-brew, or rent money. Bumel or Burnell Santiago (the self-styled "King of Boogie"), Eileen Dufeau, Miss Isobel, and Stack-O-Lee—all unrecorded—are the best remembered pianists from this period. Their vitality was maintained by Fats Pichon, Jack Dupree, Archibald and Tuts Washington, before being taken up by Fats Domino, Edward Frank, Huey "Piano" Smith, James Booker, and Allen Toussaint.

Professor Longhair belonged to this great tradition, but introduced

Latin and rumba figures, full of polyrhythms, to his basic blues and boogie piano. His style is manifest in *Go To The Mardi Gras* (1959), a perennial New Orleans Carnival favorite; he recorded it twice in 1949 as *Mardi Gras In New Orleans*.

Born Henry Roeland Byrd in Bogalusa in 1918, he started to play professionally in New Orleans in the late 1940s. Longhair's first recordings were made for Star Talent (a Texas label) in 1949. They were followed by sessions for Atlantic later the same year and Mercury in February and June or July 1950. Despite having a small Southern hit with *Bald Head* (Mercury), however, he was unable to achieve significant popular success outside the city. He continued to record throughout the 1950s, for Federal, Atlantic, Ebb, and Ron for whom he made *Go To The Mardi Gras*. Further sessions for the local Rip and Watch labels followed, but his career came to an abrupt halt in the mid-1960s (as did those of many other New Orleans R&B artists). The times had changed. With a large family to support, he resorted to gambling and janitoring duties.

Once he had been rediscovered in 1969, Professor Longhair's music began to be appreciated by white audiences that were far bigger and more enthusiastic than any he had encountered previously. As his music spread throughout the USA and beyond, by way of records, TV, films, and personal appearances, he gradually assumed the role of "Father of New Orleans R&B". He even had a New Orleans club named after one of his popular tunes, *Tipitina*. Wisely managed by Quint Davis and Alison Kaslow, he headed the bill regularly at the annual New Orleans Jazz & Heritage Festival, and was expecting great things from a recording contract with the important Alligator label, when he died suddenly in 1980.

The Rhino collection, **'Fess: The Professor Longhair Anthology**, covers both periods of his career. Although it does not include any examples of his sides for Star Talent, there are early recordings of the same songs, such as *Bye Bye Baby* (remade for Atlantic as *Hey Now Baby* in 1949) and *She Ain't Got No Hair* (the Mercury rendering from 1950 as *Bald Head*). The four sides he recorded for Atlantic in 1954 are represented, including *Tipitina*, and there are four of his Ebb selections from 1957, with another remake of *She Ain't Got No Hair* as *Looka, No Hair*. In addition to *Go To The Mardi Gras* (the Ron version), *Big Chief* Part I (1964) is also a Carnival theme, with lyrics relating to Wild Indian masquerade bands. This piece represents his last session (for Watch) before the forced retirement. Except for the last two titles (made in 1978), the first CD is devoted to his original commercial recordings.

The second disc comprises a choice of his "rediscovery" sides and explores the depth of this repertoire in a modern setting. There are reworkings of old themes—some, like *Stag-O-Lee*, which he had not cut previously—and a number of new creations. All are performed with his customary exuberance and control. His *Rum & Coca-Cola* is based on an old black French-Caribbean melody, *L' Année Passée*, that traveled from Martinique to Trinidad and then to the USA. The final side is one of the most fascinating in the collection. Taken from a feature-length home video "Piano Players Rarely Ever Play Together", recorded soon before his death, it features his idol Tuts Washington, Allen Toussaint (a disciple), and himself sharing honors on *Boogie Woogie*, one of the pieces that define the piano blues tradition. The two-CD set is a fitting memorial to an original talent and a testament to the place of New Orleans R&B in the story of black music in the USA.

481 **Spirit Of New Orleans: The Genius Of Dave Bartholomew**
Various Artists
EMI 0777 7 80184–2 1—2 CD set
DISC ONE: Dave Bartholomew, *Ain't Gonna Do It*; Jewel King, *Don't Marry Too Soon*; Tommy Ridgely, *Shrewsbury Blues*; Archibald, *Stack-A-Lee* Part 1/ *Stack-A-Lee* Part 2; Joe Turner, *The Blues Jumped Over The Rabbit*; Rodney Harris & Dave Bartholomew, *Blow Your Top*; Jewel King, *3 ×7=21*; Dave Bartholomew, *Little Girl Sing Ding A Ling*; Shirley & Lee, *I'm Gone*; T-Bone Walker, *Pony Tail*; Smiley Lewis, *Blue Monday*; Little Sonny Jones, *I Got Booted*; The Hawks, *I-Yi*; Fats Domino, *Ain't It A Shame*; Little Booker, *Thinking About My Baby*; Pee Wee Crayton, *Every Dog Has Its Day*; Blanche Thomas, *You Ain't So Such A Much*; Bernie Williams, *Why Fool Yourself*; Billy Tate, *Single Life*; Shirley & Lee, *The Real Thing*; Al Reed, *Drops Of Rain*; Joan Scott, *Mighty Long Road*; T-Bone Walker, *Teen Age Baby*; Fats Domino, *Bo Weevil*; Pee Wee Crayton, *Runnin' Wild*

DISC TWO: Dave Bartholomew, *Jump Children*; The Hawks, Featuring Dave Bartholomew, *Can't See For Lookin'*; Little Booker, *Doin' The Hambone*; The Bees, *Toy Bell*; Smiley Lewis, *I Hear You Knocking*; The Spiders, *Witchcraft*; Bobby Mitchel & The Toppers, *Nothing Sweet As You*, Fats Domino, *Valley Of Tears*; Al Reed, *Hoo Doo* ; James "Sugar Boy" Crawford, *Morning Star*; Roy Brown, *Let The Four Winds Blow*; Chris Kenner, *Sick And Tired*; Dave Bartholomew, *Good News*; Bobby Mitchel, *I'm Gonna Be A Wheel Some Day*; Smiley Lewis, *One Night*; Fats Domino, *Young School Girl*; James "Sugar Boy" Crawford, *She Got A Wobble (When She Walks)*; Berna-Dean, *I Walk In My Sleep*; Earl King, *Come On* Part 1 /*Come On* Part 2; Al Robinson, *I Wanna Know*; Ford "Little Snook" Eaglin, *That Certain Door*; Fats Domino, *Walking To New Orleans* (undubbed); Berna-Dean, *Little Willie*; Earl King, *Trick Bag*; Al Robinson, *They Said It Couldn't Be Done*

482 **The Best Of Smiley Lewis—"Hear You Knocking"**
Smiley Lewis
Collectables COL 5630
Tee Nah Nah/Dirty People/Bee's Boogie/The Bells Are Ringing/Lillie Mae/

Gumbo Blues/Ain't Gonna Do It/Caldonia's Party/Big Mamou/Down The Road/ Blue Monday/Jailbird/Real Gone Lover/I Hear You Knocking/Bumpity Bump/ Queen Of Hearts/Come On/Nothing But The Blues/One Night/She Got Me Hook, Line & Sinker/Please Listen To Me/Rootin' And Tootin'/Down Yonder (We Go Ballin')/Shame, Shame, Shame!

3/4 **Out Of New Orleans**
Fats Domino
Bear Family BCD 15541 H1 (Ger)—*8 CD set*
DISC ONE: *Detroit City Blues/The Fat Man/Hide Away Blues/She's My Baby/ Brand New Baby/Little Bee/Boogie Woogie Baby/Hey! La Bas Boogie/Korea Blues/Every Night About This Time* (version 1)/*Careless Love/Hey! Fat Man/ Tired Of Crying* (master)/*Tired Of Crying* (alternate take)/*What's The Matter Baby/I've Got Eyes For You/Stay Away/Don't You Lie To Me/My Baby's Gone/Rockin' Chair/Sometimes I Wonder/Right From Wrong/You Know I Miss You/I'll Be Gone/No, No Baby/Reeling And Rocking/Goin' Home* (version 1)/ *The Fat Man's Hop/How long* (master)/*How Long* (alternate take)

DISC TWO: *Long Lonesome Journey* (master)/*Long Lonesome Journey* (alternate take)/*Poor Poor Me* (master)/*Poor Poor Me* (alternate take)/*Trust In Me/ Cheatin'/Mardi Gras In New Orleans/I Guess I'll Be On My Way/Nobody Loves Me/Dreaming/Going To The River/I Love Her/Second Line Jump/Good bye/ Swanee River Hop/Rose Mary* (version 1)/*Please Don't Leave Me/Domino Stomp/You Said You Love Me/Rose Mary* (version 2)/*Fats Domino Blues/Ain't It Good/The Girl I Love/Don't Leave Me This Way/Something's Wrong/Fat's Frenzy*

DISC THREE: *Goin' Back Home/You Left Me* (master)/*You Left Me* (alternate take)/*"44"/Barrel House/Little School Girl/If You Need Me/You Done Me Wrong/Thinking Of You/Baby Please/Where Did You Stay?/You Can Pack Your Suitcase/I Lived My Life/Little Mama/I Know/Love Me/Don't You Hear Me Calling You/Don't You Know/Helping Hand/Help Me/All By Myself/Ain't It A Shame/Oh Ba-a-by/La-La/Blue Monday/Troubles Of My Own/What's Wrong/ Poor Me*

DISC FOUR: *I Can't Go On/I'm In Love Again/Bo Weevil* (complete)/*Don't Blame It On Me/Howdy Podner/So Long/I Can't Go On This Way* (undubbed)/*My Blue Heaven/Don't Know What's Wrong/Ida Jane/When My Dreamboat Comes Home/What's The Reason I'm Not Pleasing You?/The Twist Set Me Free/ Blueberry Hill/Honey Chile/I'm Walkin'/What Will I Tell My Heart/I'm In The Mood For Love/Would You/My Happiness/Don't Deceive Me/The Rooster Song/Telling Lies/As Time Goes By/Town Talk/Twistin' The Spots/It's You I Love/Valley Of Tears* (master)/*Wait And See/True Confession*

DISC FIVE: *Sailor Boy/It Must Be Love/The Big Beat/Little Mary/Stack & Billy/ When I See You/Oh Whee/I Still Love You/My Love For Her/I Wan't you To Know/Yes, My Darling/Don't You Know I Love You/Sick And Tired/No, No/ Prisoner's Song/One Of These Days/I'll Be Glad When You're Dead You Rascal You/Young School Girl/I'm Gonna Be A Wheel Some Day/How Can I Be Happy/Lazy Woman/Isle Of Capri/Coquette/Once In A While/The Sheik Of Araby* (version 1)

DISC SIX: *Whole Lotta Loving/I Miss You So/Margie* (version 1)/*I'll Always Be In Love With You/If You Need Me/Hands Across The Table/So Glad/Darktown Strutters Ball/Margie* (version 2, master)/*The Shiek Of Araby* (version 2, master)/*My Heart Is Bleeding/I Hear You Knocking/Lil' Liza Jane/Every Night (About This Time)* (version 2)/*When The Saints Go Marching In/Country Boy/I'm Ready* (undubbed)/*I'm Ready* (master)/*I Want To Walk You Home/When I Was Young* (undubbed)/*When I Was Young* (master)/*Easter Parade/I've Been Around*

DISC SEVEN: *Be My Guest/Tell Me That You Love Me/Before I Grow T[o]o Old/Walking To New Orleans* (undubbed)/*Walking To New Orleans* (master)/*Don't Come Knockin'* (undubbed)/*Don't Come Knockin'* (master)/*La La/Put Your Arms Around Me Honey/Three Nights A Week/Shu Rah/Rising Sun/My Girl Josephine/You'll Always Hurt The One You Love* (complete)/*Magic Isles/Natural Born Lover* (complete)/*Am I Blue/It's The Talk Of The Town/It Keeps Rainin'/What A Price/Ain't That Just Like A Woman/Fell In Love On Monday* (undubbed)/*Fell In Love On Monday* (master)/*Trouble In Mind/Hold Hands/Bad Luck And Trouble/I've Been Calling/I Just Cry/Ain't Gonna Do It*

DISC EIGHT: *Won't You Come On Back/I Can't Give You Anything But Love/I'm Alone Because I Love You/Good Hearted Man/In A Shanty In Old Shanty Town/Along The Navajo Trail/One Night/Let The Four Winds Blow* (version 1)/*Trouble Blues/You Win Again/Your Cheatin' Heart/Let The Four Winds Blow* (version 2, master)/*Let The Four Winds Blow* (version 2, alternate)/*What A Party/Rockin' Bicycle/Did You Ever Seen A Dream Walking/Birds And Bees/Wishing Ring/Jambalaya [On The Bayou]/Do You Know What It Means To Miss New Orleans/South Of The Border/Teen Age Love/Stop The Clock/Goin' Home* (version 2)/*My Real Name/Hum Diddy Doo/Those Eyes/I Want To Go Home/Dance With Mr. Domino/Nothing New (Just The Same Old Thing)*

485 **'Fess: The Professor Longhair Anthology**
Professor Longhair
Rhino R2 71502—2 CD set
DISC ONE: Roy Byrd & His Blues Jumpers, *Bald Head/Hadacol Bounce;* [Professor Longhair], *Tipitina;* Professor Longhair & His Blues Scholars, *In The Night/Ball The Wall/Who's Been Fooling You;* [Professor Longhair], *Hey Now Baby;* Roland Byrd, *Hey Little Girl;* Professor Longhair & His Blues Scholars, *Walk Your Blues Away;* Roy "Baldhead" Byrd, *She Walks Right In;* Roland Byrd, *Willie Mae;* Professor Longhair & His Blues Scholars, *Professor Longhair Blues;* Professor Longhair [& Band], *Baby Let Me Hold Your Hand/No Buts—No Maybes/Misery/Looka, No Hair/Cuttin' Out/Go To The Mardi Gras/There is Something On Your Mind;* Professor Longhair [& The Clippers], *Big Chief* Part 2; Professor Longhair, *Hey Little Girl* (live)/*Hey Now Baby* (live)

DISC TWO: Roy Byrd [Professor Longhair], *Mardi Gras In New Orleans/Junco Partner/How Long Has That Train Been Gone/Stag-O-Lee/Meet Me Tomorrow Night/(They Call Me) Dr. Professor Longhair/Mess Around/Cry To Me/Whole Lotta Loving/Everyday (I Have The Blues)/Got My Mojo Working/Thank You Pretty Baby/Sick And Tired/Mean Old World/Tipitina* (live)/*Big Chief* (live)/*Rum & Coca-Cola* (version 2); Roy Byrd [Professor Longhair], Isidore "Tuts" Washington & Allen Toussaint, *Boogie Woogie*

(ii) Louisiana Swamp Blues and R&B

Before World War II black people in most Southern states developed identifiable regional rural blues styles. Despite a large black population, however, there were few parallels in Louisiana. This difference is partly a result of a French-Caribbean origin for some of the state's black inhabitants, allied to particular social conditions in New Orleans and parts of Louisiana. The back-porch sound of one man and his guitar was confined principally to the small farming communities around Shreveport and Baton Rouge. A handful of commercial recordings was made before 1942 by Shreveport artists such as Leadbelly or Oscar Woods and, following the war, by Country Jim, or Stick Horse Hammond (**128, 152, 429**). Jay Miller's release of sides by Lightnin' Slim (the Baton Rouge bluesman) in 1954, therefore, was significant in establishing the identity of a particular regional tradition—swamp blues. Slim Harpo and Lazy Lester also began traveling to Miller's studio, and it became clear that Baton Rouge had been harboring other talented performers.

The style is marked by unhurried vocals, lyrical harmonica, and lead-guitar lines, muffled drums, and cascading right-hand piano work (in the recording studio). This tradition of south Louisiana evolved from imitation of best-selling post-war blues recordings. Influential sides include those by Lightning Hopkins and John Lee Hooker (singer-guitarists), plus the Chicago harmonica players Sonny Boy (John Lee) Williamson, Little Walter, and, above all, Jimmy Reed.

By 1957 Slim Harpo and Lightnin' Slim had become the key swamp-blues figures. In that year Harpo cut *I'm A King Bee*. The recording was leased to Excello and, with the benefit of airplay over Radio WLAC Nashville, became a small Southern hit. In the early 1960s the song proved an important catalyst in the R&B boom in Britain.

At the outset Miller was not convinced by Slim Harpo's abilities and forced him to disguise his natural voice by adopting a nasal twang. The inspiration, at least for Miller, was Hank Williams. Harpo's attractive harmonica playing, however, was influenced by Reed and Walter. He began to assert himself in 1960 with the atmospheric *Blues Hang-Over,* a talking blues. Then came national success with *Rainin' In My Heart*, a spoken and sung ballad that was as much swamp pop as swamp blues. A royalty dispute with Miller ensued, which delayed the vital follow-up recording session and the impetus from the hit was lost. That should have been the end but, following an uneasy truce, Harpo cut *Baby Scratch My Back,* one of the biggest R&B recordings of 1966—a year dominated by Motown issues. After this the new Excello management spirited him away from Jay Miller forever.

I'm A King Bee, Blues Hang-Over, and *Rainin' In My Heart* are all included in Ace's exemplary collection of Harpo's early Excello sides; **I'm A King Bee**. The titles Jay Miller supplied for release between March 1957 and January 1964 are presented in sequence of their receipt by Excello and include several previously unissued items. The first six performances represent pairs of recordings from 1957 to 1959. From December 1959 (beginning with *Bobby Sox Baby*) Harpo used his own band at recording sessions, including the guitarists Rudolph Richard and James Johnson. Their professionalism is evident in accompaniments from this time; for example on slow titles such as *Dream Girl* or up-tempo performances like *Yeah Yeah Baby*. The lugubrious and compelling *Blues Hang-Over* is from this same session, in June 1960. On two previously unissued recordings, from November that year, Harpo is skillfully accompanied by Lazy Lester rather than his own harmonica—*My Home Is A Prison* and *Lover's Confession. Moody Blues* and *Snoopin' Around,* contemporary sides, are smooth Harpo instrumentals, demonstrating his considerable skills on the harmonica. *Rainin' In My Heart* also dates from this time. Following the hiatus over his contract, the next tapes were not sent to Excello until September 1963; these were the harmonica instrumental *Buzzin'* and lazy talking blues *I Love The Life I'm Living,* both of which show that he had lost none of his skills during the time lapse. Harpo plays his own guitar on the version of John Lee Hooker's *Boogie Chillun* (which dates from January 1964).

Slim Harpo scarcely made a bad recording, even in later years, and his artistic (and commercial) success refined the character of swamp blues. This enabled similar Jay Miller performers, such as Jimmy Anderson, Silas Hogan, Whispering Smith, and Tabby Thomas, to gain national exposure. Excello's reputation was consolidated by this famous musical sound and style from Miller's Crowley studio.

In south Louisiana, a largely rural area influenced by Cajun and hillbilly music and without a strong blues tradition, acceptance for R&B came more slowly than in other regions. In the early 1950s, however, visionary disc jockeys started playing the melodic "white" sounds of Fats Domino and tuneful R&B hits. These included *Lawdy Miss Clawdy* by Lloyd Price, *Pledging My Love* by Johnny Ace, *I Hear You Knocking* by Smiley Lewis, and *Those Lonely Lonely Nights* by Earl King. Naturally, it was the New Orleans brand of R&B that exerted the strongest influence. Another major figure was Guitar Slim (Eddie Jones). His one big hit, *The Things I Used To Do*, has a memorable melody that endeared it to music lovers in the region, where it is still performed.

At the same time, several good local R&B bands started playing the

Gulf Coast "chittlin circuit", a vital training ground of noisy juke joints, small theaters, and bar clubs that proliferated from Texas, through Louisiana, to Mississippi. The most prominent combos were those of Good Rockin' Bob, Guitar Gable, Bill Parker, and Huey Thierry (Cookie, of Cookie and the Cupcakes). Their bands helped formulate the swamp-pop sound, a likeable blend of New Orleans R&B, Cajun, and hillbilly music. This paved the way for "blue-eyed soul" aggregations such as Clint West and the Boogie Kings, and John Fred and the Playboys. The black tradition was carried into the soul era by Buckwheat and the Hitchikers, and "Lil" Bob and the Lollipops.

In the 1990s Kat and the Kittens are considered to be among the best soul and R&B artists, their entertaining revue being aimed at "all the blues lovers in the house". Kat's performance of *You Can Have My Husband But Don't Mess With My Man* (1989) is included in Flyright's broad-based anthology **More Louisiana Swamp Blues**. Beginning with sides recorded by Jay Miller in 1962, this enterprising collection features a variety of swamp-blues performances and a smattering of Louisiana R&B. Joe Johnson's moody *Dirty Woman Blues*, and the novelty *Shoo-Shoo Chicken* by Charles Sheffield are the earliest two titles. There are sides by familiar Miller artists (from his Excello productions) as well as others that he chose to issue himself, or have been selected by Flyright for first-time release. They exemplify the fertility of production ideas and quality of artists that have emanated from Miller's Crowley studios. In addition to expected singers, the CD includes the magnificent voice of Mr Calhoun—in *Change Your Ways*, or the smoldering Mr Mojo in *The World Loves A Lover*. Tabby Thomas performs an R&B version of *C.C. Rider* (a blues standard), and Carol Fran's recent *Runnin' And Hidin'* is in the same vein. Henry Gray, a pianist formerly based in Chicago, plays *Lucky Lucky Man*. The hallmark of Miller productions, a relaxed, melancholic, yet emotionally appealing sound, is evident throughout.

486 I'm A King Bee: The Early Swamp-Blues Classics

Slim Harpo

Ace CDCHD 510 (UK)

I'm A King Bee/I Got Love If You Want It/Wonderin' And Worryin'/Strange Love/You'll Be Sorry One Day/One More Day/Bobby Sox Baby/Late Last Night/Buzz Me Babe/Dream Girl/Yeah Yeah Baby/What A Dream/Don't Start Cryin' Now/Blues Hang-Over/Moody Blues/My Home Is A Prison/Please Don't Turn Me Down/Snoopin' Around/Rainin' In My Heart/That's Alright Baby/Lover's Confession/Buzzin'/I Love The Life I'm Living/Boogie Chillun

487 **More Louisiana Swamp Blues**
Various Artists
Flyright FLY CD 24 (UK)
Sylvester Buckley, *She Treats Me So Evil;* Boogie Jake, *I Don't Know Why;* Ramblin' High Harris, *Trying To Call My Baby;* Silas Hogan, *I'm A Free-Hearted Man*; Slim Harpo, *Got Love If You Want It*; Lightnin' Slim, *Stranger In Your Town;* Lonesome Sundown, *Mojo Man;* Lazy Lester, *Late Late In The Evening;* Mr Calhoun, *Change Your Ways*; Mr Mojo, *The World Loves A Lover;* Joe Mayfield, *Natural Born Man*; Joe Rich, *Dreaming Dreaming;* Jimmy Anderson, *Draft Board Blues*; Whispering Smith, *Crying Blues;* Joe Johnson, *Dirty Woman Blues;* Henry Gray, *Lucky Lucky Man;* Charles Sheffield, *Shoo-Shoo Chicken;* Tabby Thomas, *C.C. Rider;* Carol Fran, *Runnin' And Hidin';* Kat, *You Can Have My Husband But Don't Mess With My Man*

(iii) Cajun and Zydeco

Ancestors of the Cajuns were tough amiable farmers who sailed from western France in the 17th century to settle in the Canadian provinces now known as Nova Scotia and New Brunswick. The colony was orginally called "Acadie" after Arcadia, the pastoral region of ancient Greece considered a rural paradise; the word "Cajun" is a corruption of "Arcadian." Although Acadie fell to the British in 1710, the French farmers were allowed to remain as neutrals under the Treaty of Utrecht (1713). In 1755, preceding another war, the British demanded Acadians swear allegiance to the Crown; their refusal to do so resulted in mass expulsion. Migration of the French Canadians to Louisiana took place over 20 years. Congregating initially in the almost empty Attakapas Indian territory, west of New Orleans, the exiles settled gradually in small farming, fishing, and trapping communities throughout the bayous and prairies of Louisiana.

For almost two centuries the Cajuns remained a race apart, separated from the rest of the South by language, social structures, and traditions that underwent only minor changes. Often shunned by outsiders, the people toiled hard during the week, enjoyed themselves on weekends, went to Mass on Sunday, valued family ties, hunted, fished, played cards, raced horses, gambled, and gossiped. They relished their spicy food and sang and danced at every opportunity. Their music, which plays an important part in their lives, is a reflection of their individuality. From an early age a Cajun boy will hear the joyful whoop of a two-step or melancholy melody of a waltz played on the accordion, fiddle, or guitar to a repetitive beat. If so minded, he will start practicing music at home until he is ready to perform at house parties, *fais-do-dos,* country fairs, roadhouses, and clubs. Then, if he is good enough, he may be asked to record and broadcast, but even so he will have to take a regular job to support his wife and family.

Nathan Abshire is a prime case in point. Always resident in the heart of the Acadian prairies he saw the raw side of life, eking out a living at the Basile town dump and playing for his own people at weekends. Abshire's talent as an accordionist was unsurpassed in Cajun music. Quite simply, his music was drenched in the blues, reflecting the pain, sorrow, and hardship of the Acadian past. He recorded one session for Bluebird in 1935, in a period dominated by string bands. Encouraged by the success of his contemporary Iry Le June, however, in the immediate post-war years Nathan helped re-establish the accordion in Cajun music. In 1949 he recorded *Pine Grove Blues*. This, and similar historic performances from the early 1950s, is in the Arhoolie collection **French Blues**. In addition to Abshire, several vocalists feature in this cross-section of waltzes, two-steps, blues, and boogies. Unfortunately, he was unable to attain greater musical success, after making many of these sides for Khoury's Records of Lake Charles. Despite their variety and excellence in presentation, local styles were being shunned by the younger Cajuns, who wanted to be associated with modern America and not with the working-class poverty of the past. Old-time musicians such as Abshire kept working steadily at local dances because they knew nothing else. Everybody still had a good time dancing the furious two-steps and stately waltzes.

Abshire's luck began to change in 1960, when he was recorded by Jay Miller for his Kajun label. A few years later Floyd Soileau, of Swallow Records, Ville Platte, took over Abshire's contract. The accordionist embarked on a series of beautiful recordings, with instrumental backing from Dewey Balfa and the Balfa Brothers. With his death in 1980, Cajun music lost its most natural talent and a large repertoire of early folk tunes.

Zydeco is a black-French country dance style that evolved from Cajun and African-American traditions (including some from the Caribbean). It is sung in a Creole dialect to an insistent—often raw—bluesy accompaniment. To differentiate this indigenous music from R&B and soul it is sometimes called "zodico", "French" or "La-La" (referring to an earlier rural form). It is played throughout south Louisiana and east Texas. Surprisingly, and commensurate with the rise in popularity of Clifton Chenier, from the 1970s zydeco has become one of the better-known regional musical styles in the United States.

The word is thought to be a Creole contraction of *les haricots* (snap beans), inspired by the title of an old one-step tune, *L' Haricots Sont Pas Salé (The Snap Beans Are Not Salted)*. In a wider sense, like Cajun *fais do-do* a zydeco refers to a country party with plenty of eating, drinking, dancing, music, and fun. The spelling was formalized by the Houston folklorist Mack McCormick.

The musical roots of zydeco can be traced to the second half of the 18th century, both before and after the Haitian Revolution. During this period most of the French-speaking black and *mulâtre* people of Louisiana came to the state as the slaves of French planters, or *gens libres de couleur* (free men of colour). These new arrivals settled quickly among the close-knit Acadian family groups, easily adapting to their customs, language, music, and religion; and reciprocating elements of their own culture, including Creole folksongs. The descendants of these immigrants—known variously as black Cajuns, black French, Creoles or *noirs*—have evolved their own bluesy style of Cajun music within an African-Caribbean framework, giving rise to the fast, distinctive syncopation of zydeco (see also **257**).

The predecessor of zydeco was la-la or *la musique Creole*, which was played at country dances and house parties, like early Cajun music. The embryo zydeco developed rapidly during World War II, when many French-speaking black people took up jobs vacated by conscripted white workers in the Texas industrial towns of Houston, Galveston, and Port Arthur. For the first time, the rural music of the migrants came into contact with the rhythmic blues sounds of these urban centers. The shock waves of this fusion soon spread back to south-west Louisiana, by way of clubs, church dances, and barbecue picnics.

Zydeco has continued to develop. The repertoire is dominated by fast two-steps, blues, and more recently, soul numbers, together with a few melodic waltzes. The traditional Cajun instrumentation has also been modified to orientate the music strongly toward R&B. The principal instrument of most bands is the large piano accordion, which allows a wide choice of harmony; the Cajun diatonic accordion is smaller and less versatile. Another important zydeco instrument is the rub board or *frottier*, a relic from early black folk music that gives complex percussive figures when struck by the end of a fork or similar metallic implement. Currently, the saxophone is replacing the fiddle, while electric guitars and drums have become part of every group's equipment. As with Cajun music, however, dancing remains the primary function.

The Arhoolie collection **Zydeco: The Early Years (1961–1962)** is unsurpassed as the best introduction to the evolution of the music. Except for the final three tracks, all the recordings were made in the field by Chris Strachwitz. They range from [*Rayne*] *One Step & Zydeco Sont Pas Sale*, played by Sidney Babineaux (the old-timer who influenced Clifton Chenier), to the gutsy Houston sounds of Herbert Sam (father of the Sam Brothers) in *They Call Me Good Rockin'*. The final three tracks comprise Clifton Chenier's first recordings (from 1954) and Clarence Garlow's R&B hit of 1950, *Bon Ton Roulet (Let The*

Goods Times Roll) the title of which has become the slogan of zydeco. Interestingly, the first reference to zydeco on record is by the Houston bluesman Lightning Hopkins in his *Zolo Go*, made for Gold Star in 1949 (**129**).

In parallel with Nathan Abshire, Clifton Chenier was an accordion player of consummate natural talent. Unlike Abshire, however, he was fully aware of the trappings of stardom and reveled in the magisterial title of 'King of Zydeco', to the extent of wearing a mock crown and cape. Almost single-handedly, he was responsible for popularizing zydeco by blending old black French folk music with the latest R&B sounds.

After enjoying modest success as an R&B artist on the Southern chittlin' circuit in the 1950s, during which time he recorded some excellent sides for Specialty, Chenier lost direction. He was rescued from the small-time clubs of east Texas and Louisiana by Chris Strachwitz, who encouraged him as a zydeco artist with recordings for Arhoolie in 1964–65. Chenier's début album on Arhoolie was a sparse down-home production, supported by only washboard and drums, but the sessions yielded *Louisiana Blues*, a jukebox hit single issued on Bayou. From this time, Chenier never looked back and began to play all over the United States and tour Europe. Regrettably, managerial intransigence limited his European success.

Strachwitz sustained Chenier's cause by a steady flow of new albums, without flooding the market. R&B rather than zydeco numbers began to dominate his repertoire, and Clifton employed a large band that helped to project the electricity of club performances into his recordings. This "Red Hot Louisiana Band" more than justified its name. Musicians of the caliber of his brother Cleveland, on washboard, tenor saxophonist Blind John Hart, and guitarist Paul Senegal were driven by the relentless drumming of Robert Peters. The group was at its collective best in a session recorded in 1975 by Strachwitz at the Studio in the Country, Bogalusa, Louisiana,—as can be heard on the CD **Bogalusa Boogie**.

Like Nathan Abshire, Clifton Chenier hardly cut a poor recording. There are several CDs available on other labels, but those on Arhoolie capture him in his prime, before he suffered a debilitating kidney ailment in the years before his death in 1987. His early Specialty recordings have been collected in **Zodico Blues And Boogie (517)**. Chenier achieved legendary status in his lifetime, and his music has continued in the work of disciples, such as Rockin' Dopsie, Fernest Arceneaux, and Buckwheat. Others include the Sam Brothers, John Delafose, the Ardoin Brothers, and Clifton's son C.J. Chenier.

Somewhat ironically, zydeco was given an international boost in

1985 when Rockin' Sidney had a hit with *My Toot Toot*, using the accordion to effect. Many black Louisiana artists now feature this instrument on stage or in recordings.

488 **French Blues**
Nathan Abshire & The Pine Grove Boys
Arhoolie CD 373
Pine/Grove Blues/Kaplan Waltz/French Blues/New Orleans Waltz/Pine Grove Boogie [Roy Broussard, vocal]/*Hathaway Waltz/Step It Fast* [Ernest Thibodeaux, vocal]/*Jolie, Petite Juliette/Choupique Two Step/La Valse De Belezere* [Will Kegley, vocal]/*Pine Grove Blues* No. 2/*La Valse De Holly Beach/Iota Two Step/La Valse De Bayou Tech* [Kegley, vocal]/*Musical Five Special/Avalon Waltz/Tee Per Coine (Keep A Knocking But You Can't Come In)/The New Jolie Blon/Point De Lou Two Step/Texas Waltz/Lu Lu Boogie/Carolina Blues* [Dewey Balfa, vocal]/*Shamrock. Waltz* [unidentified, vocal]/*Mama Rosin* [Little Yvonne Le Blanc, vocal]/*L.S.U. French Waltz* [Balfa, vocal]/*Crying Pine Grove Blues* [Jack Miere, vocal]/*Red Rock Waltz/Cannon Ball Special*

489 **Zydeco: The Early Years (1961–1962)**
Various Artists
Arhoolie CD 307
Paul McZeil & Wallace Genger, *Allons A Lafayette/Tap Dance/French Waltz;* Sidney Babineaux, *[Rayne] One Step & Zydeco Sont Pas Sale [Original Zydeco];* Albert Chevalier, *Zydeco Sont Pas Sale [Les Haricot Sont Pas Sale]/ Moman Couche' [Mont Ma Coucher]/Ma Petite Fille/Bernadette, Cher;* George Alberts, *You Havin' A Good Time;* Peter King & Lester Herbert, *King's Zydeco/Lafayette Zydeco;* Willie Green's Zydeco Band, *Jole Blonde/Baby please Don't Go/Tell me, Pretty Baby/Announcement & Green's Zydeco;* Herbert "Good Rockin" Sam, *They Call Me Good Rockin';* Clifton Chenier, *Clifton's Blues/Louisiana Stomp;* Clarence Garlow, *Bon Ton Roulet*

490 **Bogalusa Boogie**
Clifton Chenier
Arhoolie CD 347
One Step At A Time/M' Appel Fou [They Call Me Crazy]/Quelque Chose Sur Mon Idée [There's Something On My Mind]/Ride 'Em Cowboy/Ma Mama Ma Dit [My Mama Told Me]/Je Me Reveillier Le Matin [I Woke Up This Morning]/I May Be Wrong/Take Off Your Dress/Allons A Grand Cocteau [Let's Go To Grand Cocteau]/Je Suis En Recolteur [I'm A Farmer]/Ti Na Na/ Come Go Along With Me/Bogalusa Boogie

Basic Records

(i) New Orleans R&B and Mardi Gras

491 **The Mercury New Orleans Sessions 1950**
Various Artists
Beat Family BFD 15308 (Ger)—*2 LP set*

RECORD ONE: Roy Byrd [Professor Longhair] & His Blues Jumpers, *Hey Now Baby/Bald Head/Her Mind Is Gone* (take 3)/*Oh Well/Hadacol Bounce/Longhair Stomp/Been Foolin'; Around/Between The Night And Day/Byrd's Blues;* Alma Mondy [Alma Lollipop], *Miss Lollipop's Confession* (take 3)/*Love Troubles* (take 4)/*Still My Angel Child/Baby Get Wise/Just As Soon As I Get [Go] Home* (take 1)/*No Stuff For Me/Street Walkin' Daddy/A Job For A Jockey*

RECORD TWO: Dwine Craven [Mr Brown], *Mercury Boogie/New Way Of Loving;* Little Joe Gaines, *She Won't Leave Me No More/Snuff Dipper;* Theard Johnson, *I Walk In My Sleep/Lost Love;* George Miller & His Mid Driffs, *Boogie The Thing/Bat-Lee Swing* (take 2)/*Bat-Lee Swing* (take 3); Alma Mondy [Alma Lollipop], *Miss Lollipop's Confession* (take 1)/*Love Troubles* (take 3)/*Just As Soon As I Get [Go] Home* (take 2); Roy Byrd [Professor Longhair] & His Blues Jumpers, *Her Mind Is Gone* (take 2)/*Hadacol Bounce* (alternate take)/ *Between The Night And Day* (alternate take)/*Longhair Stomp* (alternate take)
This double album contains recordings made in February and June or July 1950. The sides by Longhair are some of his finest and the lesser-known performers demonstrate under-represented aspects of the city's R&B repertoire.

492 **Creole Kings Of New Orleans [Volume 1]**
Various Artists
Specialty SPCD 2168–2/Ace CDCHD 393 (UK)
Joe Liggins & The Honeydrippers, *Going Back To New Orleans* (take 2, alternate); Percy Mayfield, *Louisiana/River's Invitation* (take 6, alternate); Lloyd Price, *Lawdy Miss Clawdy* (take 1, alternate)/*Where You At/Frogs Legs;* The Royal Kings, *Teachin' And Preachin;* Guitar Slim, *The Things I Used To Do;* The Kings, *Till I Say Well Done;* Clifton Chenier, *Ay-Tete Fee [Eh! Pettite Fille]* (alternate take); Albert Hall, *Oh! How I Need Your Love;* Leo Price, *Send Me Some Lovin';* Ernest Kador, *Do Baby Do;* Big Boy Miles & The Sha-Weez, *Who's Been Fooling You;* Li'l Millet & His Creoles, *Rich Woman;* Lloyd Lambert, featuring Joe Tillman on sax, *Whistlin' Joe;* Professor Longhair, *No Buts, No Maybes/Baby Let Me Hold Your Hand;* Roy Montrell, *(Every Time I Hear) That Mellow Saxophone;* Edgar Blanchard, *Bop Sit-In Blues*; Big Boy Miles, *Just To Hole My Hand;* Jerry Byrne, *Lights Out;* Art Neville, *Cha Dooky-Doo/I'm A Fool To Care;* Larry Williams, *Jockamo [Iko Iko]/Bad Boy [Junior Behave Yourself]* (alternate take)
The symbol of New Orleans as a center for good-time music is manifest in these recordings of the 1950s, culled from the Specialty archive. Some are by non-residents, but all display the vivacity associated with Creole-influenced R&B from the city.

493 **Gumbo Stew: Original "AFO" New Orleans R&B**
Various Artists
Ace CDCHD 450 (UK)
AFO Executives, *Olde Wine;* Barbara George, *I Know (You Don't Love Me No More);* Tami Lynn, *Mojo Hanna;* Prince La La, *Things Have Changed;* Eddie Bo, *Tee Na Na Na Na Nay;* Dr. John & Ronnie Barron, *My Key Don't Fit;* The Tick Tocks, *Mary;* Willie Tee, *All For One;* Wallace Johnson, *Private Eye;* Dr. John, *The Pot;* Pistol *Keep On Lovin' You;* Charles Carson, *Time Has Expired;* Nookie Boy, *I'll Make A Bet;* Robbie Lee, *True Love;* Willie Tee, *I Found Out (You Are My Cousin);* The Tick Tocks, *Is It Too Late;* The

Turquinettes, *Tell Me The Truth;* Alvin Robinson, *Turned In, Turned On;* Melvin Lastie & Harold Battiste With Cornell Dupree, *Ignant,* Alvin Robinson, *Empty Talk;* The Pastor, *I Shall Not Be Moved*
All For One—a musicians' label, founded by Harold Battiste in 1961—produced most of these classy recordings of the early 1960s. Imaginative songs are performed with verve and precision. The last five tracks were cut in California by a similar group in 1969–70.

494 **Lawdy!**
Lloyd Price
Specialty SPCD 7010-2/Ace CDCHD 360 (UK)
Lawdy Miss Clawdy/Mailman Blues/Chee Koo Baby/Oo-Ee Baby (take 3, alternate)/*So Long/Operator* (take 3, alternate)/*Laurelle* (take 4, alternate)/ *What's The Matter Now?/If Crying Was Murder/Walkin' The Track/Where You At?/Lord, Lord, Amen!/Carry Me Home/Froglegs* (alternate take)/*Froglegs/I Wish Your Picture Was You/Let Me Come Home Baby/Tryin' To Find Someone To Love/Night & Day Blues/All Alone/What A Fire/Rock 'N' Roll Dance/I'm Glad, Glad/Baby Please Come Home/Forgive Me, Clawdy*
Price had a hit in 1952 with his first Specialty recording, *Lawdy Miss Clawdy,* now an R&B classic. He met greater success in the late 1950s, recording pop-R&B for ABC Paramount. His Specialty sides have a more romping New Orleans tempo and this collection is the most consistent.

495 **The Legendary Masters, Volume 1: Shirley And Lee**
Collectables COL 5637
I'm Gone/Sweethearts/Baby/Why Did I/Confessin'/Keep On/Comin' Over/Takes Money/Feel So Good/Lee's Dream/Deed I Do/That's What I'll Do/Let The Good Times Roll/I Feel Good/When I Saw You/I Want To Dance/Rock All Night/ Don't You Know I Love You/I'll Thrill You/Everybody's Rockin'
The pioneering R&B duet of Shirley Goodman and Leonard Lee are acclaimed for *Let The Good Times Roll,* an anthem of the rock 'n' roll era (1956). Shirley's shrill voice and the teenage romance themes may be an acquired taste, but the rocking accompaniments pay generous tribute to Cosimo Matassa's studio musicians.

496 **Mardi Gras Rock 'n' Roll**
Art Neville
Ace CDCHD 188 (UK)
Zing Zing/Oooh-Whee Baby/Bella Mae/I'm Just A Fool To Care/Cha Dooky-Doo/Back Home To Me/What's Going On/That Old Time Rock 'N' Roll/ Rocking Pneumonia & The Boogie Woogie Flu (with Larry Williams)/*A Lover's Story/The Dummy/Oooh-Whee Baby* No. 1/*Let's Rock/Arabian Love Call/ Please Listen To My Song/The Whiffenpoof Song* (take 2)/*Zing Zing* (take 3)/ *Standing On The Highway/Let's Rock* (alternate take)
These Specialty recordings (produced by Harold Battiste in 1956–8) epitomize late 1950s New Orleans R&B. Neville contributes spirited, yet controlled, vocals to a typical rock-solid accompaniment. From a family with strong links to the city's traditions, he currently performs with the Neville Brothers (himself, Aaron, Cyril, Charles, and Ivan).

497 **The Things That I Used To Do**
Guitar Slim
Ace CDCHD 318 (UK)
Well I Done Got Over It/Trouble Don't Last/Guitar Slim/The Story Of My Life/A Letter To My Girl Friend/Reap What You Sow/Later For you Baby/The Things That I Used To Do/Quicksand/Bad Luck Blues/Think It Over/Our Only Child/I Got Sumpin' For You/Sufferin' Mind/Twenty Five Lies/Something To Remember You By/Certainly All/Going Down Slow/Stand By Me/You Give Me Nothing But The Blues/You're Gonna Miss Me/I Wanna Love-A You/I Got Sumpin' For You (alternate take)/*Reap What You Sow* (alternate take)
A New Orleans hero, Guitar Slim is famous for powerful electric guitar sounds, extravagant stage performances, and outrageous dress. His recording career is dominated by *The Things That I Used To Do,* a No. 1 R&B hit in 1954, with Ray Charles on piano. This collection features his best material for Specialty.

498 **Country Boy Down In New Orleans**
Snooks Eaglin [And Others]
Arhoolie CD 348
Country Boy Down In New Orelans/Mama Don't You Tear My Clothes/I've Had My Fun/Bottle Up And Go/Give Me The Good Old Boxcar/Walking Blues; [Lucius Bridges], *Possum Up A Simmon Tree*; Snooks Eaglin, *That's All Right*; [Percy Randolph], *Veal Chop And Pork Chop*; Snooks Eaglin, *Down By The Riverside;* [Percy Randolph], *Model T And The Train/Jack O'Diamonds*; Snooks Eaglin, *Death Valley/Rock Me Mama;* [Lucius Bridges], *John Henry;* [Percy Randolph], *Locomotive Train;* Snooks Eaglin, *I Had A Little Woman;* Lucius Bridges, *Rock Me Mama [Don't Leave Me Mama]*/Snooks Eaglin, *Mailman Passed/Going Back To New Orleans;* [Lucius Bridges & Snooks Eaglin], *Mardi Gras Mambo* [alternate take?]; Snooks Eaglin, *Bottle Up And Go* (alternate take); [Lucius Bridges & Snooks Eaglin], *This Train* (alternate take)
Solo recordings, accompanied by his own six- and 12-string acoustic guitar, plus sides with percussion and harmonica, confirm Eaglin as a performer of stature and diversity. His associates contribute several sides. At the time of these sessions of 1959–60 he was doubling as a commercial R&B artist for Imperial.

499 **Blues From The Gutter**
Champion Jack Dupree
Atlantic 7567-82434-2
Strollin'/T.B. Blues/Can't Kick The Habit/Evil Woman/Nasty Boogie/Junker's Blues/Bad Blood/Goin' Down Slow/Frankie & Johnny/Stack-O-Lee
Dupree reached a pinnacle in 1958, when he made these recordings, epitomizing the dark world of the drug addict. One of the first concept albums, the session is enhanced by a brilliant New York backing group, headed by alto saxophonist Pete Brown and guitarist Larry Dale.

500 **The Complete"Tousan" Sessions**
Allen Toussaint
Bear Family BCD 15641 AH (Ger)
Whirlaway/Happy Times/Up The Creek/Tim Tam/Me And You/Bono/Java/Wham Tousan/Nowhere To Go/Nashua/Po' Boy Walk/Pelican Parade/Chico/Back Home Again In Indiana/Second Liner/Cow Cow Blues/Moo Moo/Sweetie

Pie [Twenty Years Later]/You Didn't Know Did You?/Up Right/A Blue Mood/A Lazy Day (without organ)/*Naomi/Al's Theme/Real Churchy* (without organ)/*A Lazy Day* (with organ)/*Real Churchy* (with organ)
Although only in his early 20s at the time he cut these sides (1958–9), Toussaint shows precocious talent. He indulges in the styles of many great New Orleans pianists, with a potent selection of good-time blues and slow instrumentals.

501 **Check Mr. Popeye**
Eddie Bo
Rounder CD 2077
Check Mr. Popeye Part 1/*Now Let's Popeye* Part 2/*It Must Be Love/Dinky Doo/I'll Do Anything/Warm Daddy/Roamin-itis/Hey There Baby/I Need Someone/Tell It Like It Is/You Got Your Mojo Working/Ain't You Ashamed/ Baby I'm Every Dog Has Its Day*
Eddie Bo's *Mr. Popeye,* based on the cartoon character, inspired a local dance craze. Recorded for Ric in 1959–62, these sides feature the classic New Orleans R&B sound, with piping horns and brass over funky parade beat. He recorded prolifically throughout the R&B and soul eras.

502 **Soul Mine**
Lee Dorsey
Charly CDCD 1115 (UK)
Ya Ya/Do-Re-Me/Great Googa Mooga/Ride Your Pony/Can You Hear Me/Get Out Of My Life Woman/Confusion/Working In The Coal Mine/Holy Cow/My Old Car/Go Go Girl/Love Lots Of Lovin' [duet with Betty Harris]/*Everything I Do Gonna Be Funky (From Now On)/Give It Up/Sneakin' Sally Through The Alley/Freedom For The Stallion/Night People/Soul Mine*
With novelty songs such as *Ya Ya, Ride Your Pony,* and *Working In The Coal Mine,* Lee Dorsey was one of New Orleans' biggest hit makers in the 1960s. These recordings demonstrate the transition from R&B to soul in the city.

503 **I'm Back At Carnival Time**
Bo Dollis & The Wild Magnolias
Rounder CD 2094
Carnival Time/Bon Ton Roulet/Iko, Iko/Shallow Water Oh Mama/Golden Crown/Tipitina/I'm Back/Meet De Boys On The Battlefront/Big Chief/Coconut Milk/Jockomo, Jockomo [Mark Boudreaux, vocal]
This selection of Mardi Gras and New Orleans R&B themes is performed by a leader and members of various Wild Indian Carnival bands. Recorded in 1990, chants such as *Iko, Iko, Golden Crown, and Meet De Boys On The Battlefront* have been sung in Shrovetide parades for many years. Local musicians provide accompaniment.

504 **New Orleans Party Classics**
Various Artists
Rhino R2 70587
Professor Longhair, *Go To The Mardi Gras;* Huey Piano Smith & The Clowns, *Don't You Just Know It;* Fats Domino, *Jambalaya (On The Bayou);* A. Tousan [Allen Toussaint], *Whirlaway;* The Hawkettes, *Mardi Gras Mambo;* Al

Johnson, *Carnival Time*; "Lil" Bob & The Lollipops, *I Got Loaded;* Frankie Ford, *Sea Cruise;* Alvin "Red" Tyler & The Gyros, *Peanut Vendor;* Oliver Morgan, *Who Shot The LaLa;* Dr. John, *Iko Iko;*Professor Longhair, *Big Chief* Part 1; The Wild Tchoupitoulas, *Meet De Boys On The Battlefront;* Neville Brothers, *Hey Pocky Way;* The Dirty Dozen Brass Band, *Lil' Liza Jane;* Neville Brothers, *Dancin' Jones;* Stop Inc., *Second Line* Part 1; The Rebirth Brass Band, *Do Whatcha Wanna* Part 3
A feast of original music associated with the good-time philosophy of the crescent city. Recordings span more than three decades, from 1955 (*Mardi Gras Mambo*) to 1991 (*Do Whatcha Wanna*). There are piano stylists, R&B vocal groups, a saxophonist ("Red" Tyler), Carnival Wild Indians, and brass bands.

(ii) Louisiana Swamp Blues and R&B

505 Bayou Blues Blasters
Various Artists
Ace CDCHD 427 (UK)
Ivory Jackson, *I'm A Country Boy;* Clarence Garlow, *Purty Little Dolly [Doolie]*; Guitar Jr., *Going Crazy Baby*; Hop Wilson, *Broke & Hungry*; Little Bob, *Make Up My Mind*; Lazy Lester With Katie Webster & Ashton Savoy, *Need Shorter Hours*; Lonesome Sundown With Clarence Garlow, *It Ain't Right*; Juke Boy Bonner, *Just Got To (Take A) Ride*; Al Smith, *Wanna Do Me Wrong*; Jimmy Wilson, *Tin Pan Alley*; Charles "Mad Dog" Sheffield, *I Got Fever*; Tal Miller, *Life's Journey*; Left Hand Charlie, *Honey Bee*; Clarence Garlow, *Sunday Morning*; Jimmy Wilson, *Trouble In My Home*; Big Walter Price, *Oh Ramona*; Elton Anderson, *Highway Back Home*; Cookie & The Cupcakes, *I'm Going*; Carol Fran, *Please Stand By Me*; Elton Anderson, *Too Tired*; Big Chenier, *Let Me Hold Your Hand* Katie Webster, *What In The World Are You Gonna Do*; Rockin' Sidney, *Something Working Baby*; Marcel Dugas & Wild Bill's Washboard Band, *Pretty Little Red Dress*; Little Latour's Sulphur Playboys, *C-Key Blues*; Thaddus Declouet, *Catch That Morning Train*
Covering a time-span of almost 20 years (from 1956), these sides were made by Eddie Shuler for his Goldband Records. Based in Lake Charles, near the Louisiana border with Texas, he recorded blues, swamp blues, R&B and zydeco from both states. This imaginative anthology brings together vivid performances of these styles.

506 Authentic Excello R&B
Various Artists
Ace CDCHD 492 (UK)
Lightnin' Slim, *I'm Evil*; Lazy Lester, *You're Gonna Ruin Me Baby*; Slim Harpo, *I Got Love If You Want It*; Jimmy Anderson, *Going Through The Park*; Lightnin' Slim, *I'm Warning You Baby*; Lonesome Sundown, *Lonesome Lonely Blues*; Leroy Washington, *Wild Cherry*; Silas Hogan, *You're Too Late Baby*; Lazy Lester, *I'm A Lover Not A Fighter*; Slim Harpo, *I Love The Life I'm Living*; Jimmy Anderson, *Naggin'*; Silas Hogan, *I'm Gonna Quit You Pretty Baby*; Lonesome Sundown, *I'm Glad She's Mine*; Slim Harpo, *I'm A King Bee*; Whispering Smith, *Mean Woman Blues*; Lightnin' Slim, *Loving Around The Clock*; Lazy Lester, *Tell Me Pretty Baby*; Tabby Thomas, *Hoodoo Party*; Silas Hogan, *Lonesome La La*; Whispering Smith, *Wake Up Old Maid*; Lightnin'

Slim, *I'm Tired Waitin' Baby*; Lonesome Sundown, *Gonna Stick To You Baby*; Arthur Gunter, *No Naggin' No Draggin'*; Shy Guy Douglas, *I'm Doin' Alright*
This is an augmented version of the seminal album that introduced Louisiana swamp blues to Britain in the early 1960s. The collection revives availability of various hits including *I'm A King Bee* and *I'm A Lover Not A Fighter*, and endorses the popular appeal of these Excello performers.

507 **Louisiana R 'n' B**
Various Artists
Flyright FLY CD 42 (UK)
Guitar Gable/King Karl, *Walkin' In The Part*; Henry Clement, *So In Love With You*; Billy Tate, *Special Lesson No. 1;* The Gaynotes, *Plea Of Love*; Lester Robinson, *Ooh My Dear*; Lionel Torrence, *Rooty Tooty*; Carol Fran, *One Look At Your Daddy*; Classie Ballou, *Hey Ma Ma*; Wonder Boy Travis, *You Know Yeah*; Honey Boy Allen, *Ford V-8*; Leroy Washington, *Long Hair Knock Knees And Bow Legs*; Lightnin' Slim, *Hello Mary Lee*; Slim Harpo, *I Need Money*; Lonesome Sundown, *I'm A Samplin' Man*; Jay Nelson, *Rocka Me All Night Long*; Lil Bob, *I Wanna Be Your Man*; Wonder Boy Travis, *She's Got Eyes Like A Cat*; Charles Sheffield, *The Kangaroo*; Tabby Thomas, *Popeye Train*; Katie Webster, *Mama Don't Allow*
Like Eddie Shuler, in Lake Charles, Jay Miller recorded all types of Louisiana regional music. Made between 1957 and 1962, this sampling of his local R&B productions brings together rocking performances by stalwart swamp-blues artists as well as more urban-oriented singers.

508 **Rollin' Stone**
Lightning Slim
Flyright FLY CD 08 (UK)
Rock Me Mama/Bad Luck/New Orleans Bound/I Can't Live Happy/Bugger Bugger Boy/Ethel Mae/Mean Old Lonesome Train/I'm Grown/I'm A Rollin' Stone/Hoodoo Man/Long Leanie Mama/Tom Cat Blues/Rooster Blues/Nothing But The Devil/Wintertime Blues/Trip To Chicago/I Hate To Leave You/ Lightnin' Blues
Jay Miller once described the music of Lightnin' Slim as "low down gut-bucket blues". This CD has Slim's doom-ridden earliest sides (issued by Feature in 1954), plus alternative versions of some of his Excello hits. *Trip To Chicago* and *Lightnin' Blues,* both *cantes fables,* are among his most sublime recordings.

509 **I'm A Mojo Man**
Lonesome Sundown
Ace CDCHD 556 (UK)
Gonna Stick To You Baby/I'm A Mojo Man/I Stood By/Don't Go/Lonely Lonely Me/You Know I Love You/Learn To Treat Me Better/Lonesome Lonely Blues/ I'm Glad She's Mine/Sundown Blues/My Home Ain't Here/What You Wanna Do It For/I Woke Up Cryin (Oh What A Dream)/When I Had I Didn't Need (Now I Need, Don't Have A Dime)/I'm A Samplin' Man/Hoo Doo Woman Blues/I'm A Young Man/It's Easy When You Know How/I Got A Broken Heart/ Don't Say A Word/Lost Without Love/Leave My Money Alone/My Home Is A Prison/Lonesome Whistler

Sundown's Excello releases are explored in depth. His first sides were made in late 1956 and continued annually to 1964 (excluding 1962). His deep-voiced singing is accompanied by his effective guitar playing and regular instrumentalists from Jay Miller's Crowley studio. These tracks range from spirited uptempo pieces to performances of introspection.

510 I'm A Lover Not A Fighter

Lazy Lester

Ace CDCHD 518 (UK)

I'm A Lover Not A Fighter/Sugar Coated Love/Lester's Stomp/I Told My Little Woman/Tell Me Pretty Baby/Whoa Now/I Hear You Knockin'/Through The Goodness Of My Heart/I Love You, I Need You/Late, Late In The Evening/A Real Combination For Love/Bloodstains On The Wall/You Got Me Where You Want Me/I'm So Tired/Patrol Blues/I'm So Glad/Sad City Blues/If You Think I've Lost You/I Made Up My Mind/Lonesome Highway Blues/You're Gonna Ruin Me Baby/The Same Could Happen To You/Take Me In Your Arms/You Better Listen To What I Said

Lazy Lester is best known for his magical harmonica support to Lightnin' Slim. Influenced by Jimmy Reed (vocally and instrumentally), Lester recorded with strong Southern blues appeal; yet he never had a big hit. This representative disc includes his most enduring numbers, *Sugar Coated Love* and *I Hear You Knockin'*.

511 Katie Webster

Flyright FLY CD 12 (UK)

[Katie Webster & Ashton Conroy (Savoy)], *No Bread No Meat/I Want You To Love Me*; Katie Webster, *Baby Come On/I Wanna Know/Glory Of Love/The Katie Lee/Hoo Wee, Sweet Daddy/Sunny Side Of Love/I Feel So Low/Goodbye Baby I'm Still Leaving You* Parts 1 & 2/*Don't You Know/Mama Don't Allow/Close To My Heart/Hey Mr. Love/Open Arms/Sea Of Love/I Feel So Low* (alternate take)/*Sunny Side Of Love* (alternate take); [Katie Webster & Ashton Conroy (Savoy)], *Baby Baby*

Katie Webster is now a blues and boogie piano star, but in her early years was an anonymous studio accompanist for Jay Miller's blues, R&B, and swamp-pop artists. She made only a handful of singles, the best of which are in this set of Louisiana R&B.

512 So Long Blues

Silas Hogan

Ace CDCHD 523 (UK)

I'm Gonna Quit You Pretty Baby/Trouble At Home Blues/You're Too Late Baby/Airport Blues/Go On Pretty Baby/Here They Are Again/Lonesome La La/Roamin' Woman Blues/I'm Goin' In The Valley/Everybody Needs Somebody/Just Give Me A Chance/Dark Clouds Rollin'/Early One Morning/I'm In Love With You Baby/More Trouble At Home/Sittin' Here A Wondering/So Glad/Every Saturday Night/Baby Please Come Back To Me/If I Ever Needed You Baby/Out And Down Blues/So Long Blues

Older than Lightnin' Slim and Slim Harpo, the Baton Rouge artist Silas Hogan recorded a consistent series of swamp blues for Jay Miller in the 1960s that were released by Excello. His music has a relaxed feel, with good harmonica accompaniment from Sylvester Buckley and Whispering Smith.

513 **By Request**
Cookie And The Cupcakes
Jin 9037-2
Belinda [Cookie, vocal]/*Got You On My Mind* [Cookie & Shelton Dunaway, vocal]/*Mathilda* [Cookie, vocal]/*Walking Down The Aisle* [Little Alfred, vocal]/*Even Though* [Little Alfred, vocal]/*I Almost Lost My Mind* [Little Alfred, vocal]/*Just One Kiss* [Dunaway, vocal]/*Honey Hush* [Dunaway, vocal]/*Sea Of Love* [Cookie, vocal]/*Betty And Dupree* [Dunaway, vocal]/*Shake 'Em Up* [Dunaway, vocal]/*Breaking Up Is Hard To Do* [Cookie & Dunaway, vocal]/*I Cried* [Cookie, vocal]/*Long Time Ago* [Cookie, vocal]/*Trouble In My Life* [Cookie, vocal]/*Feel So Good* [Little Alfred, vocal]/*The Peanut* (instrumental)/*Charged With Cheating* [Little Alfred, vocal]/*I've Been So Lonely* [Cookie, vocal]/*The Duck* [Dunaway, vocal]
George Khoury recorded these classic swamp-pop and Louisiana R&B sides for his two labels Lyric and Khoury between 1958 and 1963. After being acquired by Floyd Solieau, many have remained in catalog. An old-time blues-ballad, *Betty And Dupree*, makes a surprising appearance.

514 **My Toot Toot**
Rockin' Sidney
Ace CDCH 160 (UK)
If I Could I Would/No Good Woman/You Ain't Nothing But Fine/Send Me Some Lovin'/Past Bedtime/No Good Man/You Don't Have To Go/It Really Is A Hurtin' Thing/Something's Wrong/My Little Girl/Wasted Days And Wasted Nights/Ya Ya/My Toot Toot/My Zydeco Shoes/Joy To The South/Jalapeno Lena/Alligator Waltz/Joe Pete Is In The Bed/If It's Good For The Gander/Twist To The Zydeco/Dance And Show Off/Let Me Take You To The Zydeco/Sweet Lil' Woman/Once Is Not Enough/Cochon De Lait
Sidney achieved international stardom in 1985 with *My Toot Toot*, but his early recordings for Jin are far more appealing. Dating from the 1960s, songs such as *If I Could I Would, No Good Woman*, and *You Ain't Nothing But Fine* combine a soft form of Excello-style blues and tuneful swamp pop.

(iii) Cajun and Zydeco

515 **Cajun's Greatest: The Definitive Iry Le June**
Ace CDCHD 428 (UK)
Grande Nuit Especial/Grande Bosco/Duraldo Waltz/I Went To The Dance/La Valse De Bayou Chene/I Made A Big Mistake/Come And Get Me/Donnes Moi Mon Chapeau/Waltz Of The Mulberry Limb/Church Point Breakdown/La Valse Du Grande Chemin/Jolie Catin/La Fitte La Vove/Bayou Pon Pon Special/La Valse De Cajin/Don't Get Married/Convict Waltz/It Happened To Me/Parting Waltz/Evangeline Special/Love Bridge Waltz/Teche Special/Calcasieu Waltz/Te Mone/Lacassine Special
The revival of Cajun accordion was sparked by Iry Le June, who made these recordings for Goldband between 1948 and 1955 (the year he died). Issued here for the first time in superlative sound, his brand of music was all sadness and loneliness, with blues echoing from every note.

516 "I'm Never Comin' Back": Amédé Ardoin—Pioneer of Louisiana French Blues; The Roots of Zydeco

Arhoolie-Folklyric CD 7007

Amadie Two Step/La Valse À Austin Ardoin [Austin Ardoin's Waltz]/Blues De Basile [Basile Blues]/La Valse À Thomas Ardoin [Thomas Ardoin's Waltz]/Two Step D' Elton [Elton Two Step]/La Valse De Gueydan [Gueydan Waltz]/Valse À Alice Poulard [Alice Poulard's Waltz]/One Step D' Oberlin [Oberlin One Step]/Valse De Opelousas [Opelousas Waltz]/One Step Des Chameaux [Chameaux One Step]/Les Blues De Voyage [Travel Blues]/La Valse De Amities [Love Waltz]/Les Blues De Crowley [Crowley Blues]/Oberlin/Tostape De Jennings [Jennings Two Step] [actually a waltz]/*Le Midland Two-Step [Midland Two-Step]/La Valse Des Chantiers Pétroli[p]ères [Waltz Of The Oil Fields]/Valse Brunette [The Brunette's Waltz]/Tortope D' Osrun [Osson Two Step]/La Valse Du Ballard [Ballard's Waltz]/La Turtape De Saroied [Savoy Two Step]* [actually a waltz]/*Valse De La Point[e] D[e] Eglise [Church Point Waltz]/Les Blues De La Prison [Jail House Blues]/[La] Valse De Mon Vieux Village [My Old Village/Home Town Waltz]/Si Dur D'Être Seul [So Hard To Be Alone]/Aimez-Mio [Ce] Soir/[Love Me Tonight]*

An accordion player, Amédé Ardoin was one of the first black-French artists from Louisiana to record (in 1929, 1930, and 1934). His influence was considerable. With Dennis McGee, a white fiddle player, he performed waltzes and two-steps at Cajun dances and, in the small hours, blues for his compatriots.

517 Zodico Blues And Boogie

Clifton Chenier

Specialty SPCD 7039-2/Ace CDCHD 389 (UK)

Boppin' The Rock/Ay-Te Te Fee (master)/*The Cat's Dreamin'/Squeeze Box Boogie/The Things I Did For You/Think It Over/Zodico Stomp/Yesterday (I Lost My Best Friend)/Chenier Boogie* (take 3)/*I'm On My Way (Back Home To You)* (take 2, with tenor sax)/*All Night Long* (take 8)/*Opelousas Hop* (take 3)/*I'm On My Way (Back Home To You)* (take 1—false start; take 2, without tenor sax)/*Wherever You Go I'll Go* (take 2)/*Opelousas Hop* (take 4)/*Clifton's Dreamin'/Chenier's Boogie* (take 4)/*Wherever You Go I'll Go* (take 6)/*Ay-Te Te Fee* (take 8)/*All Night Long* (take 7)

This represents virtually all existing takes for Clifton's Specialty recordings. Made at three sessions in Los Angeles in 1955, accompanied by a small band, they capture his exuberance in R&B and zydeco numbers. Several are instrumentals featuring his spirited accordion playing

518 Zodico: Louisiana Créole Music

Various Artists

Rounder 6009—Cassette

The Carrière Brothers, *La-La d'Un Pas [One Step La-La]/Tu M'as Quitté Dans La Porte [You Left Me Standing In The Door];* Fremont Fontenot, *Contradanse;* Inez Catalon, *Tites Toutes Rivières Faîtra Une Grand Rivière [Every Small River Makes A Big River]/Chaque Coronel [Each Colonel]/Marie Madeleine [Mary Magdeline]/Coosh-Coosh Après Brûler [The Coosh-Coosh Is Burning];* The Ardoin Family, *'Tite Fille [Little Girl]/Chant De Mardi Gras [Mardi Gras Chant]/Madame Edward (Petite Ou Grosse) [Madame Edward (Big Or Small)];* Mike & The Soul Accordion Band, *Lucille*; The Lawtell

Playboys, *Colinda/Les Flammes d'Enfer [The Flames Of Hell];* Sampy & The Bad Habits, *La Pistache A Tante Nana [Aunt Nana's Peanut]/Ma Coeur Cassé [My Broken Heart];* Wilfred Latour & His Travel Aces, *Bonsoir Two Step*
Zydeco is presented as a living tradition in this enterprising collection of field recordings, made in south-west Louisiana in 1976 by folklorist Nick Spitzer. The tape includes examples of the *cantique*, la-la, *contredanse*, Cajun waltz, Mardi Gras chant, and modern zydeco blues.

519 **Zydeco Blues**
Various Artists
Flyright FLY CD 36 (UK)
Fernest & The Thunders, *Little Woman* [Bobby Price, vocal]; Bobby Price With Marcel Dugas & The Entertainers, *Goin' Home/Teardrops On My Pillow*; Marcel Dugas & The Entertainers, *You Don't Have To Go* [Gene Morris, vocal]; Fernest & The Thunders, *Hey La Ba[s]* [Bobby Price, vocal]; Marcel Dugas & The Entertainers, *You Got Me Runnin'/Bald Headed Woman* [Gene Morris, vocal]; Fernest & The Thunders, *Lonely Lonely Nights* [Gene Morris, vocal]/*Lost Lover Blues* [Jerry Morris, vocal]/*Nobody Wants To Dance With Me* [Bobby Price, vocal]/*Irene* [Gene Morris, vocal]; Marcel Dugas & The Entertainers, *Going Back To Big Mamou* [Gene Morris, vocal]; Bobby Price With Fernest & The Thunders, *Mean Mean Woman/Send Me Some Lovin'*; Gene Morris With Marcel Dugas & The Entertainers, *La La/My Girl Josephine/Pork Chops Potatoes & Cheese*; Fernest & The Thunders, *Mother's Love* [Fernest Arceneaux, vocal]; Gene Morris With Marcel Dugas & The Entertainers, *My Baby Got Me Busted*; Bobby Price With Marcel Dugas & The Entertainers, *Jambalaya*
These well-produced sides were first issued by Jay Miller in the 1970s. A few reflect traditional themes, but most display the importation of R&B titles into the zydeco repertoire. Several are versions of Fats Domino hits, such *Goin' Home, La La,* and *My Girl Josephine.*

520 **Zydeco Party**
Various Artists
Ace CDCHD 430 (UK)
Lynn August, *Zydeco Groove*; Zydeco Force, *I'm On My Way*; Sam Brothers Five, *I'm Coming Home*; Clifton Chenier, *Johnny Can't Dance*; Boozoo Chavis, *Zydeco Hee Haw*; Rockin' Sidney, *Jalapeno Lena*; Lynn August, *Whatever Boils Your Crawfish*; Sam Brothers Five, *Leon's Zydeco*; Rockin' Dopsie, *Dopsie's Cajun Stomp*; Zydeco Brothers, *Down East*; John Delafose, *Loan Me Your Handkerchief*; Boozoo Chavis, *Do It All Night Long*; Morris Francis, *Fun In Acadiana*; Wilfred Chavis, *Eh Mon Allons Dancer Le Zydeco*; Clifton Chenier, *You Used To Call Me*; Rockin' Dopsie, *Shake Rattle And Roll*; Rockin' Sidney, *You Ain't Nothing But Fine*; Wilfred Chavis, *Keep On Dreaming*; Boozoo Chavis, *Deacon Jones*; Zydeco Brothers, *Reach Out (Touch A Hand, Make A Friend)*
This is an exciting cross-section of recordings from the 1980s, originally released by Floyd Solieau on his Maison de Soul label. Most vocals are in English, but a few remain in French Creole. The fusion of black musical styles is readily apparent, to the playing of the omnipresent piano accordion.

Louisiana-born Lazy Lester (Leslie Johnson) amplifies his harmonica, 1993 (*Brian Smith*)

ISIANA
YARD
DOG

MICHAEL HARALAMBOS AND MARK HARRIS

14 Modern Trends

Blues, it seems, have never been more popular. There are more blues CDs in shops than ever before and blues festivals across America and Europe attract ever-larger audiences. However, the future of blues is less assured than this suggests.

Most blues CDs are reissues. New recordings fall into two main categories: older blacks performing in a variety of dated styles; and younger blacks and whites whose material is usually derivative and similarly dated. There's nothing wrong with this: but where are the new sounds, new directions, freshness, and innovation which are essential to keep a musical genre alive?

Blues festivals have never been so numerous and well attended. Yet the artists who appear are often past their best and performing in styles which have changed little over the years. This may well be what today's audiences want. But again it does little for the future of blues. It merely preserves the past as artists re-create the performances of their youth.

Where does this leave a chapter on modern trends? Part of the answer is "in the past". Some of these trends are 20 to 30 years old, represented by artists such as B.B. King, Bobby Bland, and Little Milton who developed their current styles in the 1960s. For some commentators this is about as modern as blues gets.

Today's trendsetters are few and far between. This is not the fault of recording companies who trawl the USA for new, young talent. Much of what they have found, however, is second rate and derivative and would not have been recorded 20 years ago. There is a scattering of younger artists such as Willie Clayton, Robert Cray, and Larry McCray whose music shows evidence of originality and innovation. However, there is little to suggest that they are part of a developing style, of a new "modern" trend. In the past such companies as Duke, Chess, Hi, and Stax helped to establish new trends with their in-house songwriters, musicians, producers and arrangers. Such companies exist today, for example Evejim Records in Los Angeles, Malaco Records in Jackson, Mississippi, and Ace Records in Pearl, Mississippi, each with its own distinctive sound. It is probably companies such as these which offer the best future for blues.

There are problems, however. Malaco's top artists—Bobby Bland,

Albert King, playing his Y-body guitar (*Brian Smith*)

Little Milton, Denise LaSalle, Latimore—are in their 50s and 60s. So are many of their writers, musicians, producers, and arrangers. There is no sign of a younger generation coming through. The same is true for Evejim with the deaths of two of its top artists, Little Joe Blue (1990) and Buddy Ace (1994). Ace Records suggests a brighter future. Its artists are younger, for example Willie Clayton is in his 40s. It is cultivating its own sound, drawing partly on the expertise of Malaco musicians and arrangers such as Harrison Calloway; it is developing new artists such as Ronnie Lovejoy and directing them towards blues (**532**).

As this suggests, we have had to search hard for modern trends. Our criteria for selecting and recommending records in this category are first, that the trends represented are the most recent in blues (even if, in some cases, they date back some 20 or 30 years). Second, the trends must be new and innovative, which has nothing to do necessarily with the date of recording. For example, Otis Rush's Cobra records of the 1950s (**369**) are in many ways more modern than his recordings of the 1990s. Third, the records selected must be of high quality. This means that singers must be able to sing, songwriters to write, instrumentalists be more than competent and arrangers interesting. Too many blues records today fall short on all these counts.

Essential Records

(i) Modern blues: B.B. King, Bobby Bland, Little Milton, Albert King

Modern blues is a term used by many black Americans in the 1960s and 1970s to describe the style of blues exemplified by B.B. King, Bobby Bland, Little Milton, and Junior Parker. This style was seen as smoother, more sophisticated, and more up to date than other styles. Modern blues owed a lot to contemporary soul and gospel music, borrowing aspects of rhythm, harmony, and vocal technique. (For a fuller discussion of modern blues see Haralambos, 1994, pp.32–7.)

B.B. King is the best-known blues artist ever due to his tireless crusade as "Ambassador of the Blues" to over 50 countries. Billed across black America from the 1950s onwards as "King of the Blues", he had 73 entries in the R&B Top 100 from 1951 to 1985, including 24 in the top 10.* An expressive gospel-influenced vocalist, he has had an

*Unless otherwise stated the chart positions mentioned in this chapter are taken from *Billboard's* R&B charts of 1942–88 for singles and the *Cashbox* Black Contemporary Album Charts of 1975–87 for albums (see Whitburn, 1988 and Hoffmann and Albert, 1989).

enormous influence on both black and white blues artists. His guitar style—melodic, emotional, and economical—has served as a benchmark in blues and is still developing as he continues to study the instrument.

King Of The Blues is a boxed set of four CDs containing 77 tracks which trace his recording career from 1949 to 1991. It is a story of both continuity and change, of sticking to tried and trusted formulae and of innovation and experimentation. The first nine tracks cover his career up to his departure from Modern Records in 1961 to sign with ABC's Bluesway Records. They serve as a reminder of his early period (**287**). By comparison his later work is characterized by increasingly sophisticated production and arrangements and an ever-increasing diversity of material.

Until the late 1960s B.B. King's music was directed primarily towards his traditional black American audience. His recordings reflected this, particularly the classic *Live At The Regal,* recorded in 1965 at the now demolished Regal Theater on Chicago's south side. Two things changed this direction—his black audience was shrinking steadily and coincidentally his white audience was growing rapidly. Seeing the possibilities, B.B. and his new manager Sidney Seidenburg planned to break into new markets.

The breakthrough came in January 1970 when *The Thrill Is Gone* reached No. 3 in the *Billboard* R&B charts and No. 15 in the pop charts. For once artistic success met with commercial success in what many regard as the definitive modern blues. Produced by Bill Szymczyk with strings and horns arranged by Bert "Supercharts" DeCoteaux, this was a powerful and heartfelt rendition of the old Roy Hawkins hit of 1951 (**455**). The doors were now opened—to the supper clubs of Las Vegas, the largely white dance hall/theaters of the Fillmore East and West and nationally networked TV shows such as *The Tonight Show* and *The Ed Sullivan Show*.

B.B.'s music has changed over the years as he has tried to meet the expectations of both his old and new fans, developing himself as musician and artist while working with blues, soul, jazz, rock, folk, and classical musicians and a wide variety of producers and arrangers. A lesser artist would have been unable to do this with the minimum of compromise B.B. King has made. Admittedly *In London* (1971), the middle of the road pop of *Guess Who,* and the superstar-'n'-synth-swamped *King Of The Blues* (1989) are not in artistic terms among his more successful departures. However, his work with rock musician Leon Russell (which produced the haunting *Hummingbird*), with the Crusaders (notably on the laid-back funk of *Never Make A Move Too Soon*), and even with the Royal Philharmonic Orchestra (at the Royal Festival Hall, London, in 1981) have all shown his unnerving ability to push blues into areas which others wouldn't contemplate, let alone manage successfully. Later he moved into film soundtracks with the powerful *Into The Night* from the film of the same name and *Right Time, Wrong Place* with Bonnie Raitt from *Air America.*

Second only to B.B. King in terms of record sales to black American audiences (59 R&B Top 100 entries from 1957 to 1985), Bobby Bland is a singer of major importance. His use of a range of gospel techniques, combined with impeccable timing and control, generates an excitement that has women screaming and men testifying. His on-stage persona—sometimes helpless, naive, and childlike, other times assured, worldly and in control—gives him a sex appeal and presence which helps to account for the fact that women make up a large proportion of his fans.

In terms of chart entries, Bobby's years with Don Robey's Houston-based Duke Records were his most successful—41 out of 59 entries (**449**). Duke was sold in 1972 to ABC/Dunhill Records, where Bobby was placed with pop producer Steve Barri. This unlikely combination resulted in the excellent *Bobby Blue Bland: His California Album* (1973) and the even better *Dreamer* (1974), which included two of Bobby's finest recordings, *Ain't No Love In The Heart Of The City* and *I Wouldn't Treat A Dog (The Way You Treated Me),* both R&B top 10 entries. The band on both albums was arranged and conducted by Michael Omartian.

When ABC Records was sold to MCA in 1978, Bobby was placed with ICA Productions where he was produced by Al Bell (former head of Stax) and Monk Higgins with arrangements by Milton Bland. The result was a string of smooth, polished albums, sometimes reflecting the supper clubs, occasionally middle of the road and verging on the saccharine, but with Bobby in fine voice throughout.

In 1985, like so many blues and soul singers of his generation, Bobby Bland "came home" to Malaco Records in Jackson, Mississippi. Malaco put the South back into his recordings—there was more blues, more gospel, more Southern soul. The Malaco organization supported him with producers Tommy Couch and Wolf Stephenson; top arrangers such as Harrison Calloway; instrumentalists of the quality of trombonist Charles Rose, bassists Ray Griffin and David Hood, and guitarist Jimmy Johnson; and the finest group of blues and soul songwriters in the world today—Tommy Tate, George Jackson, Larry Addison, Frank Johnson, Sam Mosley, Robert A Johnson, John Ward, Johnny Barranco, and Frederick Knight. The result has been a series of high-quality albums which have sold steadily but unspectacularly in the lower reaches of the black album charts. Unlike B.B. King, Bobby has never really crossed over to a white or a world-wide audience, due maybe to his smoother, suaver style and the fact he does not play guitar. However, he retains a strong following in the black American South. We have chosen **Years Of Tears,** Bobby Bland's latest recording at time of writing, as our essential selection. After all these years the power, timbre and resonance in his voice is still there and the setting provided by the Malaco team for this classic set of modern blues could hardly be bettered.

While B.B. King's and Bobby Bland's influences are not immediately obvious, those of Little Milton are. Milton Campbell Jr cut his guitar playing skills in Willie Love's band (**418**) and went on to record for both Sun (**415**) and Meteor Records in the 1950s where influences ranging from T-Bone Walker to Fats Domino are apparent. From 1957 to 1962 he recorded for Bobbin in East St Louis under the direction of Love's son-in-law Oliver Sain, an arranger, band leader, and saxophonist. Apart from *I'm A Lonely Man,* a local hit, there was nothing really distinctive about these well-produced recordings. The first ten titles on **Welcome To The Club—The Essential Chess Recordings** are taken from Milton's last three sessions for Bobbin which were purchased by Chess Records. The influences of B.B. King on *Sneaking Around* and of Bobby Bland on *Never Too Old* are obvious; but it is on *I Need Somebody* that Milton really looks forward with the gospel inflexions of his rich powerful voice and his searing guitar style.

Little Milton recorded his first sessions with Chess in 1963. The quality of the production improved immediately. A powerful horn section mirrors his voice, something that was to characterize his career at Chess. By 1964 his vocal style had become sufficiently distinctive for him to make Bobby Bland's hit *Blind Man* his own. However, it is his work with producer Billy Davis and arranger Gene Barge which really moved things forward. *We're Gonna Make It,* co-written by Davis and Barge, had three weeks at the top of the R&B charts and reached No. 25 in the pop charts. *Who's Cheating Who,* his next release, was also a hit. Little Milton had reached artistic maturity and in commercial terms was at the peak of his career. For sheer driving power his *Grits Ain't Groceries* album, produced by Calvin Carter and arranged by Gene Barge, was unequaled. Both the title track and Milton's version of *Just A Little Bit* were top 20 R&B hits in 1969. The following year he successfully merged blues and soul in the swinging *Let's Get Together,* yet another of his 17 chart entries during 11 years with Chess.

Little Milton's style was established in the 1960s. Big-band blues and R&B were combined with contemporary soul stylings to produce something new and exciting. Throughout the 1970s this sound was maintained as Milton produced himself for his own Camil Productions. He joined Stax Records in 1971 but Stax producers such as Don Davis found it difficult to match the standards of Chess and Camil. In fact two Camil-produced albums were released on Stax. This policy continued after the collapse of Stax; Camil-produced albums were put out in 1976 and 1977 by Henry Stone's Miami-based TK Records. In 1984 Little Milton, like so many others in the later stages of their careers, joined Malaco Records. He was immediately at home—nothing new, no surprises, just album after album of quality blues and Southern soul.

"There's nothing too fancy or sophisticated about Albert King," to quote the sleeve notes on his first Stax album, released in 1967. He was born in 1923 in Indianola, Mississippi. Becoming a huge man (6 foot 4 inches, 250 pounds), he had a gruff but adequate voice and played guitar upside-down and left-handed. It was the sound built around his unique guitar style that set him apart. On most of Albert's pre-Stax recordings—for Parrott in Chicago, Bobbin and Coun-Tree in St Louis, and King in Cincinnati—the songs, rhythms, horn arrangements, and harmonies look back to the big-band blues and R&B of the early 1950s. However, his guitar stands out from these rather dated settings, as can be heard on his biggest hit *Don't Throw Your Love On Me So Strong,* which reached No. 14 in the R&B charts in 1961.

King Of The Blues Guitar contains Albert's first recording for Stax (1966–8). Blues met soul as Albert recorded with Booker T & the MGs and the Memphis Horns. State of the art soul rhythms provide a tightness and urgency not found on his earlier recordings; the horn arrangements are sharp and crisp with a mixture of blues and soul harmonies; the guitar is brought right up in the mix with Albert playing fewer notes with more sustain and obviously enjoying himself as he whoops and hollers during solos; the recordings quality has an immediate, almost live feel; the songs such as *Born Under A Bad Sign* written by Booker T. Jones and soul singer William Bell and *The Hunter* written by Booker T. and most of the MGs move beyond the traditional blues format, while standards such as *Kansas City* and *As The Years Go Passing By* are given a new lease of life.

Albert stayed with Stax until its collapse in the mid-1970s. His style continued to develop as Stax producers brought in the latest sounds as in the powerful blues funk of *That's What The Blues Is All About,* his second biggest R&B hit (No. 15 in 1974). Albert's Stax recordings are readily available and all, bar his Presley tribute album *Blues For Elvis,* are worth buying.

Albert excelled as a live performer. He had audiences in the palm of his hand with extended guitar solos, bending notes through half tones, full tones and beyond, with timing and dynamics that turned stomachs over and brought gasps of release and appreciation. It was this that influenced a generation of blues and rock guitarists, brought his records on to white radio stations and led to his booking at the Fillmore West in San Francisco and other largely white venues. Yet, unlike B.B. King, this cross-over did not lead to his development as an artist.

Albert's post-Stax recordings were at best workmanlike with little or no musical development. He needed the challenge, interplay, and support of producers, arrangers, musicians, and songwriters of the quality of Stax. This was the fusion that led to great music.

521 **King Of The Blues**
B.B. King
MCA MCAD4 10677—4 CD set
DISC ONE: *Miss Martha King/She's Dynamite/Three O'Clock Blues/Please Love Me/You Upset Me Baby/Everyday I Have The Blues/Rock Me Baby/Recession Blues/Don't Get Around Much Anymore* [with Duke Ellington Orchestra]/*I'm Gonna Sit In 'Til You Give In/Blues At Midnight/Sneakin' Around/My Baby's Comin' Home/Slowly Losing My Mind/How Blue Can You Get/Rockin' Awhile/Help The Poor/Stop Leadin' Me On/Never Trust A Woman/Sweet Little Angel* (live)/*All Over Again/Sloppy Drunk/Don't Answer The Door/I Done Got Wise/Think It Over/Gambler's Blues* (live)

DISC TWO: *Goin' Down Slow* (live)/*Tired Of Your Jive* (live)/*Sweet Sixteen* (live)/*Paying The Cost To Be The Boss/I'm Gonna Do What They Do To Me/Lucille/Watch Yourself/You Put It On Me/Get Myself Somebody/I Want You So Bad/Why I Sing The Blues/Get Off My Back Woman/Please Accept My Love* (live)/*Fools Get Wise/No Good/So Excited*

DISC THREE: *The Thrill Is Gone/Confessin' The Blues/Nobody Loves Me But My Mother/Hummingbird/Ask Me No Questions/Chains And Things/Eyesight To The Blind* (live)/*Niji Baby* (live)/*Blue Shadows/Ghetto Woman/Ain't Nobody Home/I Got Some Help I Don't Need* (single version)/*Five Long Years/To Know You Is To Love You/I Like To Live The Love/Don't Make Me Pay For His Mistakes*

DISC FOUR: *Let The Good Times Roll* (live) [with Bobby Bland]/*Don't You Lie To Me/Mother Fuyer/Never Make A Move Too Soon/When It All Comes Down (I'll Still Be Around)/Better Not Look Down/Caldonia* (live)/*There Must Be A Better World Somewhere/Play With Your Poodle* (solo)/*Darlin' You Know I Love You/Inflation Blues/Make Love To Me* (rehearsal with piano)/*Into The Night/Six Silver Strings/When Love Comes To Town* (7 inch version) [with U2]/*Right Time, Wrong Place* [with Bonnie Raitt]/*Many Miles Travelled/I'm Moving On/Since I Met You Baby* [with Gary Moore]

522 **Years Of Tears**
Bobby Bland
Malaco MCD 7469
Somewhere Between Right & Wrong/There's A Stranger In My House/Hole In The Wall/Years Of Tears To Go/Hurtin' Time Again/I Just Tripped On A Piece

Of Your Broken Heart/Sweet Lady Love/Love Of Mine/I've Got To Have Your Love Tonight/You Put The Hurt On A Hurtin' Man

523 **Welcome To The Club—The Essential Chess Recordings**
Little Milton
MCA Chess CHD2 9350—2 CD set
DISC ONE: *She Put A Spell On Me/Sneaking Around/I'm Coming Home/Lonely No More/Someone To Love/I Need Somebody/My Song/Never Too Old/I Wonder Why/So Mean To Me/Losing Hand/Ain't No Big Deal On You/Meddlin'/Blind Man/Stand By Me/Sacrifice/Blues In The Night/You're Welcome To The Club/Can't Hold Back The Tears/Country Style/We're Gonna Make It/Who's Cheating Who?/Without My Sweet Baby/Feel So Bad*

DISC TWO: *I'm Mighty Grateful/Give Me This Chance/Loving You/Man Loves Two [Man's Temptation]* (alternate take)*/Let Me Down Easy/My Baby's Something Else/Things Go Better With Coke* No. 1*/I/You Colored My Blues Bright/Moanin' For You Girl/You Mean Everything To Me/Things Go Better With Coke* No. 2*/Nothing Beats A Failure/More And More/Don't Talk Back/Twenty-Three Hours/Grits Ain't Groceries/Just A Little Bit/Steal Away/If Walls Could Talk/Spring/I'm Tired/Let's Get Together/I Play Dirty/Baby I Love You*

524 **King Of The Blues Guitar**
Albert King
Atlantic 8213–2 7567-82017-2 (UK)
Laundromat Blues/Overall Junction/Oh, Pretty Woman/Funk-Shun/Crosscut Saw/Down Don't Bother Me/Born Under A Bad Sign/Personal Manager/Kansas City/The Very Thought Of You/The Hunter/I Almost Lost My Mind/As The Years Go Passing By/Cold Feet/You Sure Drive A Hard Bargain/I Love Lucy/You're Gonna Need Me

(ii) Soul Blues: Ted Taylor, O.V. Wright, Z Z Hill

Soul blues describes a style on the borderline of blues and soul music. It combines elements of blues, soul, and gospel music. Ted Taylor is a classic example of this combination. He was born in Okmulgee, near Tulsa, Oklahoma, in 1937 and began recording as a solo artist in 1957. He recorded every year from 1957 to 1978, then less regularly until his death in 1987. The quality, range, and variety of his output make Ted Taylor an important artist, something of which can be judged by the number of top arrangers on his records. They include Carl Davis, Billy Sherrill, Teacho Wilshire, Gene Kent, Maxwell Davis, Miles Grayson, Bobby Patterson, John Stephens, and Wardell Quezerque. The attraction of working with Ted Taylor is obvious—a fine songwriter, an excellent guitarist and a unique voice. Ted Taylor began his singing career in his home town as a member of the Glory Bound Travellers, a gospel quartet. After moving to California he sang with the Mighty Clouds of Joy and the Santa Monica Soul Seekers. This background in gospel music has remained evident: he testifies and preaches; he makes frequent use of melisma (several notes for one syllable); and his backing singers often use gospel harmonies and call-and-response patterns. Ted Taylor is an original, a stylist whose voice is instantly recognizable. He moves effortlessly in and out of the falsetto range, his high, clear voice swooping and dipping as he embellishes a melody. He can sing with beauty and charm and with power and passion.

Ted Taylor's recorded output covers a wide range of styles—ballads, R&B, soul, and blues. In commercial terms his Ronn recordings of the late 1960s and early 1970s were his most successful, and artistically they are excellent (**537**). His Alarm album of 1976, arranged by Wardell Quezerque, deserves special mention. For the essential selection we've chosen his final LP originally released in 1987 as *Taylor Made For You* (SPG Records 1002) and re-released on CD as **Steal Away.** This contains new recordings of several of Taylor's better known compositions including *(I'm Just A) Crumb In Your Bread Box Of Love* and *Only The Lonely Knows.* It also contains new versions of several of his earlier records such as Jimmy Hughes' secular gospel song *Steal Away* and the soul ballad *Feed The Flame,* written by Dan Penn and Linden Oldham. The arrangements by John Stephens are always sympathetic and interesting. They range from the taut rhythms and punchy horns in *The Wolf,* a funk blues written by Ted Taylor, to the bluesy harmonies and crisp yet laid-back rhythm of Jimmy Lewis' song *Get Your Own Woman.* Ted's voice might not have the range and purity evident on his earlier records but there's a maturity and assurance which more than compensate.

Overton Vertis Wright, born in 1939 in Leno Tennessee, some 30 miles from Memphis, began his singing career in gospel music. He worked with a number of gospel groups, including the Spirit of Memphis Quartet and the Highway QCs and recorded with the Sunset Travellers for Don Robey's Peacock Records in Houston, Texas. Wright began recording secular songs for Robey's Back Beat label in the mid-1960s. His two biggest hits came from his period—*You're Gonna Make Me Cry* (No. 6 in 1965) and *Eight Men, Four Women* (No. 4 in 1967). From 1967 until his death in 1980 O. V. worked closely with producer and arranger Willie Mitchell. *Heartaches, Heartaches,* written and produced by Willie, was his third chart success. In 1976 Wright signed for Mitchell's Hi label. Their collaboration produced recordings of consistently high quality. O. V. never left his gospel roots. He was reportedly turned down by Stax Records because his gospel style was felt to be uncommercial. But it is this very style which gives Wright's voice its power, intensity, and validity. He is able to make the most banal lyric sound poignant and heartfelt and to give depth and significance to the most naive sentiment.

The Soul Of OV Wright contains 18 of Wright's Back Beat recordings, including his best-selling singles. The disc is worth buying just for his and Willie Mitchell's finest moment—*A Nickel And A Nail* (released 1971). This stunning performance is a story of hard luck and trouble framed in rich powerful harmonies from the horns and backing singers. O.V. admits his failure yet affirms his existence by testifying to anyone who will listen that he has nothing left in life except a nickel and a nail. As on all his recordings from the early 1970s, Wright's voice combines the purity and clarity of his youth with the power and authority of his later years. The CD provides a cross-section of Wright's recordings from 1965 to 1974. It contains the secular gospel of his early work in songs like *You're Gonna Make Me Cry,* the swinging R&B of his own composition *Gonna Forget About You* and a thrilling version of *Drowning On Dry Land,* its controlled passion providing a definitive example of soul blues. Wright fitted easily into the emerging Hi/Stax sounds of Memphis in the early 1970s. The chugging rhythms of *Don't Let My Baby Ride* and *I'd Rather Be Blind, Crippled And Crazy* are provided by what was to become the Hi rhythm section. Mitchell's arrangements broke new ground yet Wright was able to develop his style without compromise. They come full circle with a return to gospel at the close of the album in *I'm Going Home (To Live With God).*

Wright's recordings for Hi continue from where he left off with Back Beat. From 1976 to 1979 he recorded a series of albums which maintained the power and intensity of his earlier work. Something of his standing in the black community can be seen from the OV Wright Band, a tribute band which toured for several years after his death in 1980.

The story of "Z Z" Hill's recording career is of a series of producers and arrangers trying to package an excellent singer in the hope of hitting the big time. In the early 1980s, it worked. Three of Hill's LPs for the Malaco label lasted longer and reached higher positions in the black album charts than those of any other blues singer at the time. In 1982 *Down Home* spent 43 weeks in the charts, reaching No. 20; *The Rhythm And The Blues* 51 weeks in 1982–3, reaching No. 16; and *I'm A Blues Man* 46 weeks in 1983–4, reaching 30. Malaco had found a market that other labels had overlooked. Similarly, London Records' album of Southern soul by Marvin Sease became a best seller in 1987–8 when everybody thought that market was dead and gone. And like Marvin Sease, Z Z Hill was no newcomer.

Born in Naples, Texas, in 1935 Z Z Hill made his first record for MH Records (a label run by his brother Matt) in 1963. Its success led to a contract with Kent Records in 1964. Over the next four years he recorded a series of bluesy soul ballads and mid-tempo R&B songs for Kent. Despite working with the talented producer and arranger

Maxwell Davis, Hill had little commercial success. In 1971 he returned to his brother's labels (Hill Records and Audrey Records) for two of his finest singles, both co-written and arranged by Miles Grayson, *Don't Make Me Pay For His Mistakes* (one of his biggest hits) and *You Better Take Time.* Both are superbly arranged soul blues sung by a singer with power and maturity. That same year he recorded an excellent album entitled *The Brand New Z Z Hill,* produced by Swamp Dog (Jerry Williams Jr). A mixture of contemporary blues and soul, the album produced three chart singles. Hill's career should have gone from strength to strength. He signed with two major labels—United Artists, then Columbia—but the best he could manage, despite the efforts of producers and arrangers of the caliber of Lamont Dozier and Allen Toussaint, was a few minor successes in the black singles charts. Then, at last, his career took off as songs from his Malaco album *Down Home* were broadcast by black radio stations across the USA. And then, two years later in 1984 Z Z Hill was dead.

The CD of Z Z Hill's **Greatest Hits** contains 11 of his Malaco recordings and includes his biggest single for the label, *Cheatin In The Next Room.* This song exemplifies the final phase of his career. It is a bluesy soul ballad with a strong melody and narrative, sympathetically arranged. Hill sounds confident and in control, his vocals restrained yet powerful. He was well served at Malaco with fine writers like George Jackson and Frank Johnson and excellent arrangers such as Harrison Calloway. And no attempt was made to fit him to the latest trends—there was no repeat of Columbia's effort to turn him into a disco singer. Malaco simply took him as he was and showcased his talent. The disc (a cross-section from several albums) is a mixture of blues, soul, and R&B, all of high quality.

525 **Steal Away**
Ted Taylor
Paula PCD 345
My Key Jumpback In My Hand/Home At Last/The Wolf/Feed The Flame/I Can't Take No More/Crumb In Your Bread Box Of Love/Steal Away/Get Your Own Woman/Only The Lonely Knows/Torch of Love

526 **The Soul Of OV Wright**
O.V. Wright
MCA MCAD 10670
You're Gonna Make Me Cry/I'd Rather Be Blind, Crippled And Crazy/When You Took Your Love From Me/Gonna Forget About You/Everybody Knows (The River Song)/Don't Let My Baby Ride/I Don't Want To Sit Down/Born All Over/Ace Of Spades/Eight Men, Four Women/A Nickel And A Nail/Heartaches, Heartaches/Drowning On Dry Land/Monkey Dog/He's My Son (Just The Same)/I've Been Searching/Motherless Child/I'm Going Home (To Live With God)

527 **Greatest Hits**
Z Z Hill
Malaco MAL 7437 CD
Cheatin In The Next Room/Down Home Blues/Please Don't Let Our Good Thing End/Right Arm For Your Love/Open House At My House/Someone Else Is Steppin' In/Get A Little, Give A Little/Shade Tree Mechanic/Three Into Two Won't Go/Stop You From Givin' Me The Blues/Friday Is My Day

(iii) New sounds: Clay Hammond, Willie Clayton, Walter Wolfman Washington

In 1989 Evejim Records released an album by Clay Hammond. Evejim Records, based in Los Angeles, is owned and operated by Leon Haywood—and operated is the operative word. Leon produces, arranges, mixes, writes songs, designs covers, sings background vocals, plays keyboards, and even answers the phone. He draws on years of experience as a singer and songwriter with hit records from the mid-1960s to the mid-1980s. Evejim is not, however, a one-man-band. Arrangers include John Stephens and Shuggie Otis; instrumentalists include guitarist Roy Gaines and drummer James Gadson.

Evejim is a very important label. It has a "sound." It can make a good singer sound great, it can make an old song sound fresh, it can give a tired career a new lease of life. The reasons are quality and originality—good songs, top quality musicians, first-class arrangements and that something special that can't be put into words.

Like Leon Haywood, Clay Hammond has a long track record. As a songwriter he is well known for *Part Time Love,* a No. 1 hit for Little Johnny Taylor in 1963. He recorded sporadically from the 1960s to the 1980s for various labels including Kent and Galaxy. **Streets Will Love You** was released by Evejim in 1989. The title track, written and first recorded by Haywood, is the outstanding song. Clay's voice has tremendous power, the horn arrangement is instantly memorable, the guitar solo should be learned by every budding blues guitarist, and the bass, drums, and keyboard are an object lesson in rhythm. The songs range from straight blues—*Part Time Love*—to bluesy soul—*License To Steal*—to blues ballads—*I Know What Love Is.* The link is quality.

Evejim has also produced albums by Little Joe Blue, Jimmy McCracklin, Buddy Ace (**539**), and Ronnie Lovejoy.

Willie Clayton might well be the voice of the 1990s. And Johnny Vincent's Ace Records based in Pearl, Mississippi, would definitely be included in any list of a top ten labels for the same decade; it rivals Malaco as the font of modern blues. Ace has many of the qualities of Evejim—high standards, a roster of excellent singers (Frank-O Johnson, Lee Fields, Robert "the Duke" Tillman, Ronnie Lovejoy, Chuck

Strong), quality songwriters (Frank Johnson), excellent arrangers (Harrison Calloway), and first-class musicians (bassist Willie James Hatten). Most of Ace's output can be classified as Southern soul. However Willie Clayton's album **Let's Get Together** (1993) is sufficiently blues based to review here. It contains possibly the finest version of Miles Grayson's classic *Don't Make Me Pay (For His Mistakes)*, a showcase for the power, timbre, and sheer quality of Willie's voice. Willie has written several of the songs; he shares the arranging with Harrison Calloway; and both play keyboards on the album. The four-piece horn section is clean and sharp, the rhythm section tight and the finest instrument in the band—Willie's voice—soars over the top. Songs range from blues to Southern soul, from ballads to up-tempo numbers of the Tyrone Davis type.

Clayton has served a long apprenticeship. In the early 1970s he recorded a series of Southern soul songs produced by Willie Mitchell and released on Pawn, a subsidiary of Hi Records. Throughout the 1980s he recorded for a number of small labels, including his own Kirstee Records, with a couple of minor hits in 1984. This album for Ace is the nearest he's come to blues. And his voice is getting better and better.

Clay Hammond and Willie Clayton have been selected as much for the sound of the label as the caliber of the individual. Walter Wolfman Washington has been chosen for himself. He sounds exactly what he is—a top working musician, a professional band leader used to playing live.

Born and bred in New Orleans, Walter worked as a guitarist and band leader with, among others, Lee Dorsey, Irma Thomas, and Johnny Adams. He has clearly been influenced by Johnny Guitar Watson, Tyrone Davis, Bobby Bland, and James Brown. But Walter is instantly recognizable as himself. His work is steeped in blues, overlaid with funk, and tinged with jazz. And the fusion works. His own compositions, included on all his albums, have strong melodies and interesting chord structures. When he covers other people's songs, he makes them his own. His guitar style, a rhythmic fusion of jazz and blues, is a feature of all his work.

Walter is a musician first and a singer second. His voice is rough and emotional, part of the overall sound of the band rather than a virtuoso performance. The band drives and swings with a variety of rhythms, usually played by his regular drummer Wilbert "Junkyard Dog" Arnold and bass player Jack Cruz. Walter takes credit for the rhythm arrangements while the horn arrangements are by Sam Henry Jr (*Get On Up*, 1981), Bill Samuel on Walter's three Rounder albums (*Wolf Tracks*, 1986; *Out Of The Dark*, 1987; and *Wolf At The Door*, 1990), and Craig Wroten (*Sada*, 1991). The arrangements are often novel, always interesting. **Sada** contains Walter's best funk track to date—

Skin Tight, and the driving *Girl I Wanna Dance With You*. Both songs have excellent arrangements and guitar solos and are worth the price of the album on their own. However, there's little point in recommending just one album. Each has its own character. If you like Walter then buy them all!

528 **Streets Will Love You**
Clay Hammond
Evejim EJR 4014 CD
Streets Will Love You/License To Steal/Too Many Irons In The Fire/I Know What Love Is/They Don't Makeum No More/Ask Me For What You Want/Part Time Love/Monkey

529 **Let's Get Together**
Willie Clayton
Ace Records Ace 2052
Three People (Sleeping In My Bed)/Don't Make Me Pay/Back Street Love Affair/Let's Get Together/Does Your Mama Know/Walk Away/Welcome Home/Party Down/I Love Stealing It/How Do You Love 2/Let Me Love You/Feels Like Love

530 **Sada**
Walter Wolfman Washington
Pointblank VPBCD 4 (UK)
I'll Be Good/Skin Tight/Ain't No Love In The Heart Of The City/Girl I Wanna Dance With You/Share Your Love/Chokin' Kind/Southern Comfort/I Got A Woman/Sada/Nothing Left To Be Desired/What's It Gonna Take

Basic Records

531 **The Blues Is In The House**
Harvey Scales
Kash Gold CD 0001
That Thang That U Got/Slow Roll Me/Bad News Travels Fast/Giving U What U Want/Front Door, Back Door/Who You Gonna Believe?/The Blues Is In The House/That Thang That You Got Rap/I'd Do It With You/I Can Take A Hint/Party Til U Sweat/Somebody Else's Somebody I'm In Love/Too Much Is Not Enough
Beginning as lead singer with the Esquires in the early 1960s, Harvey helped to found funk, wrote Johnnie Taylor's million selling *Disco Lady*, and has recorded for a variety of labels. He co-wrote all but one of the strong and distinctive songs on this disc (1994), which contains hard-edged blues, uptempo funk, and powerful Southern soul.

532 **My Baby's Cheating On Me**
Ronnie Lovejoy
Ace Records 2057
Cheating On Me/Party All Night Long/Rock My Cradle/You Got To Know/

Can't Leave Love Alone/You Can't Run Away From Love/Set The World On Fire/In Need Of A Good Woman/It's Alright/Until You Get Enough Of Me/Starting All Over/Evil Eye Of Love

While there is a touch of Bobby Bland, Tyrone Davis, and Z Z Hill, Ronnie Lovejoy is his own man. A musician, songwriter, arranger, and producer with a rich, powerful voice, he offers a real future for modern blues. Production of this disc, released in 1994, is shared with Willie Clayton and Xavier Parker and arrangements with Clayton and Harrison Calloway.

533 **Too Hip To Be Happy**

Cicero Blake

Valley Vue V2-72920

Dip My Dipper/Don't Throw Your Love On Me So Strong/Too Hip To Be Happy/I Saw It Coming/School Of Life/She's Cheatin' On You/Oh Pretty Woman/I've Got To Use My Imagination

Blake has sung styles from doo-wop to soul to blues over the past 30 years. Recorded in Chicago in 1988, this disc features an excellent-band with clean, crisp horn arrangements by Bill McFarland and Rico McFarland's ringing guitar. Cicero uses his clear, gospel-tinged voice with expert timing and control. The songs range from blues to soul to R&B.

534 **Is It Because I'm Black?**

Syl Johnson

Charly CPCD 8011 (UK)

Dresses Too Short/I Can Take Care Of Business/Different Strokes/Going To The Shack/I Resign/Get Ready/I Take Care Of Homework/I'll Take Those Skinny Legs/Come On Sock It To Me/Is It Because I'm Black?/Concrete Reservations/One Way Ticket To Nowhere/Thank You Baby/I Feel An Urge/Right On/Walk A Mile In My Shoes/I'm Talkin' Bout Freedom/Kiss By Kiss/Same Kind Of Thing

Syl has recorded bluesier material but this represents his most exciting and original work. Taken from Twilight/Twinight recordings of the late 1960s and early 1970s it encompasses his characteristics—a unique voice, an urgency and tension never far from the surface, and a blend of funk, blues, and soul that only a few of his Mississippi-born, Chicago-based peers have approached.

535 **A Man Can Give It But He Can't Take It**

Bobby Rush

LaJam LJ 0005—LP

A Man Can Give It (But He Can't Take It)/Ain't That Good Lovin'/Bad Mother For Ya/I Am Tired/Hurt Me So Bad/Nine Below Zero/Hoy Hoy/Playin' Me Crazy

In 1971 Bobby's *Chicken Heads* reached No. 34 in the R&B charts. It was a unique combination of blues and funk which set the style for subsequent, recordings, including five albums of his songs for James Bennett's LaJam Records, based in Jackson, Mississippi. A dry voice matches the sardonic humor often found in Rush's cautionary tales about love, sex, and infidelity. The band is sparse, tight, and funky.

536 **Sad Shades Of Blue**
Geater Davis
Charly R&B CRB 1132 (UK)—*LP*
Ain't Worried About Jody Part 1 /*Your Heart Is So Cold/I Know My Baby Loves Me/I'll Meet You/Why Does It Hurt So Bad/A Whole Lot Of Man/A Sad Shade Of Blue/Will It Be Me Or Him* Part 1/*Will It Be Me Or Him* Part 2/ *Long Cold Winter/I've Got To Pay The Price/I'm Gonna Change/Two That Sticks Together/I'm So In Love With You*
Davis' first release, *Sweet Woman's Love* on the House of Orange label, reached No. 45 on the R&B charts in 1970. Standing on the borderline between blues and soul, it identified his strengths—a powerful gravelly voice, controlled gospel passion, and a style that out-"Blands" Bobby Bland. This selection from the early to mid-1970s is drawn from John Richbourg's Nashville-based Sound Stage 7 Records.

537 **Taylor Made**
Ted Taylor
Paula PCD 337
It's A Funky Situation/Something Strange Is Going On In My House/Houston Town/Who's Doing It To Who/Call The House Doctor/(This Is A) Troubled World/Papa's Gonna Make Love/How's Your Love Life Baby/Only The Lonely Knows/Sweet Lovin' Pair/Can't Take No More/I Feel A Chill
Featuring Ronn material from the early 1970s, this disc has hard-edged blues and soul, cutting guitars and horns, funky bass and drums, with Ted's crystal-clear, high-pitched voice soaring and dipping over tight, taut arrangements. Taylor's Ronn recordings account for four of his six entries in the R&B charts.

538 **Southern Country Boy**
Little Joe Blue
Jewel LPS 5008—LP
Encourage Me Baby/If You'd Only Let Me Love You/Southern Country Boy/ Little Joe Blue/Sometime Tomorrow/Just Love Won't Do/I'm Not Your First Love/Right There Where You Left It/Only A Fool/Gonna Walk On
Born in 1934 in Mississippi and raised in Louisiana, Little Joe was a straight down the line modern blues singer-guitarist. These recordings for Stan Lewis from the early 1970s are among his best. They are no frills modern blues, with Joe's fluent guitar and warm rich voice, a fine band, and top producers such as Maxwell Davis.

539 **Don't Hurt No More**
Buddy Ace
Evejim EJ 2018 CD
Root Doctor/I Kicked The Habit/Love Of Mine/Don't Hurt No More/Chokin' Kind/Pouring Water On A Drowning Man/Your Time To Cry/She Ain't Givin' Up No Love
After two minor hits in 1966 and 1967 Ace's career stalled until he made two albums for Evejim. This selection was released in 1990. His powerful yet controlled vocals are framed by arrangements by Leon Haywood and John Stephens. The material is varied—slow blues, up-tempo R&B, bluesy versions of soul classics, and blues funk. Sadly Buddy's comeback ended with his untimely death in 1994.

540 **Raw Blues/Little Bluebird**
Johnnie Taylor
Stax CDSXD 051 (UK)
Where There's Smoke There's Fire/Hello Sundown/Pardon Me Lady/Where Can A Man Go From Here/That Bone/That's Where It's At/Part Time Love/If I Had It To Do All Over/You're Good For Me/You Can't Keep A Good Man Down/You Can't Win With A Losing Hand/Little Bluebird/Toe Hold/I've Got To Love Somebody's Baby/Just The One (I've Been Looking For)/Outside Love/You Can't Get Away From It/I Had A Dream/Somebody's Sleeping In My Bed/I Ain't Particular/Steal Away (live)/*Stop Dogging Me* (live)/*Jody's Got Your Girl And Gone* (live)
Throughout a long career as a soul singer Taylor has made excellent blues records. This blues and soul fusion comes from the late 1960s, when Stax was bursting with freshness and creativity. Quality is assured by producers and arrangers such as Don Davis and Al Bell and writers and musicians such as Isaac Hayes and Booker T. Jones. Johnnie's rich and soulful voice is immediately recognizable.

541 **Love Me Right**
Denise LaSalle
Malaco MCD 7464
Don't Jump My Pony/Long Dong Silver/You Can't Get Nothin' Straight Between Us/Love Me Right/When We're Making Love/I'm Not That Kind Of Girl/Too Many Hungry Mouths Around The Table/One More Wrong Step/Fast Hands And A Dirty Mind/Another One Bites The Dust/Don't Pick It Up
LaSalle had a string of hits during the 1970s and repeated this success with albums on joining Malaco in 1983. Released in 1992, this CD exemplifies her present style—gospel-tinged soul, blues, and R&B. She is an accomplished writer and powerful singer; her songs revolve around the joys of good loving, women's hopes, and men's failure to live up to them. She is supported by high-class instrumentalists and arrangers.

542 **Like It Is**
Junior Parker
Mercury SR 61101—LP
Country Girl/You Can Make It If You Try/Wish Me Well/Hey Lawdy Mama/Sometimes I Wonder/(Ooh Wee Baby) That's The Way You Make Me Feel/Come Back Baby/Just Like A Fish/Baby Please/You Ain't Got No Heart/Cracked Up Over You
After leaving Duke in the late 1960s (**466**), Parker recorded for a variety of labels. This album represents some of the best of these later recordings. It was produced by Bobby Robinson and has tasteful arrangements by Gene Miller for a fine band; Junior's rich mellow voice glides powerfully through a selection of old and new material.

543 **Joy & Pain**
Shirley Brown
Malaco MCD 7467
Joy And Pain/Hearts Are Made To Be Loved/Take It Like A Woman/It's A Pleasure Easin' Your Pain/You're Gonna Make Me Cry/A Two-Way Thang/

'Bout To Make Me Leave Home/You Know What You're Gettin' At Home/It Don't Hurt Like It Used To/Long On Lovin'
Shirley's first and biggest hit, the Southern soul classic *Woman To Woman,* sold a million in 1974. Since joining Malaco in the late 1980s she has moved steadily towards gospel and blues. This disc of 1993, featuring Muscle Shoals musicians, exemplifies a vocal depth and intensity not found on her earlier recordings as she draws on and fuses blues, soul, and gospel traditions.

544 **Watch Me Now**
Otis Clay
Waylo WAY 269510 2 (Neth)
Two Wrongs (Don't Make A Right)/Soap Opera Blues/I Don't Understand It/ Feeling Single Seeing Double/I Know I'm Over You/I Do Don't You/You Are My Life/All I Wanna Do/Nobody's On The Phone
Too many producers try to re-create the past when they record blues and soul greats. Willie Mitchell however, always produces contemporary discs, as he did with Clay for his Waylo label in 1989. Otis has never sounded more modern, yet the new songs and arrangements complement traditional strengths—his gospel blues voice and Southern soul feeling.

545 **Room With A View Of The Blues**
Johnny Adams
Rounder CD 2059/Demon FIEND CD 111 (UK)
Room With A View/I Don't Want To Do Wrong/Not Trustworthy (A Lyin' Woman)/Neither One of Us (Wants To Be The First To Say Goodbye)/Body And Fender Man/I Owe You/Wish I'd Never Loved You At All/The Hunt Is On/ A World I Never Made
Adams is a professional who sings gospel, country soul, R&B, jazz, and blues with equal integrity. Recorded in 1987, this CD presents his blues side. He is backed by an all-star band including guitarists Walter Wolfman Washington and Duke Robillard, Dr John on keyboards, and saxophonist Bill Samuel. A stylist, he makes a song his own yet remains true to the genre.

546 **Sweet Vibrations—The Best Of Latimore**
Latimore
Sequel NEX CD 166 (UK)
(They Call It) Stormy Monday/Ain't Nothing You Can Do/Snap Your Fingers/ Let's Straighten It Out/Keep The Home Fires Burnin'/There's A Red-Neck In The Soul Band/Qualified Man/It Ain't Where You Been/Something 'Bout 'Cha/ Sweet Vibrations/I Get Lifted/Dig A Little Deeper/Long Distance Love
With a rich, powerful gospel-influenced voice and impressive keyboard and songwriting skills, Latimore provides music that defies classification. Drawing on blues, gospel, jazz, soul, and funk he had a string of hits between 1973 and 1978, his most creative period. This collection (from Glades) includes his two biggest, the landmark soul blues *Let's Straighten It Out* (No. 1 in 1974) and the memorable *Something 'Bout 'Cha,* with its strong melody and distinctive arrangement.

547 **Catchin Up**
Latimore
Malaco MCD 7468
Lay Another Log On The Fire/Meet Me In The Middle Of The Bed/Skinny Little White Girl/Your Sweetness Is My Weakness/Snatchin' It Back/Catches Up On Love/I Smell A Rat/Shake The Sheets/If I Had Loved You More/Something 'Bout 'Cha/Feed Your Hungry Man/Deal Down And Dirty
Since joining Malaco in the early 1980s, Latimore has lacked some of the excitement and originality of his Glades recordings. This CD from 1993 is his best for years. The songwriting is back on form with the funky and amusing *Skinny Little White Girl;* he rivals the power and commitment of C.L. Blast's *Lay Another Log On The Fire;* and he almost outdoes himself with a remake of *Something 'Bout 'Cha.*

548 **Louisiana Soul Man**
Dalton Reed
Bullseye Blues BB9517
Read Me My Rights/Blues Of The Month Club/Keep On Loving Me/Last To Understand/Heavy Love/Full Moon/Keep The Spirit/I'm Only Guilty Of Loving You/Party On The Farm/Chained And Bound
Released in 1992, this is Reed's first CD, produced by Scott Billington and Lee Allan Zeno; most songs are Southern soul with a touch of blues. Dalton's rich, powerful gospel-trained voice is complemented by a band of south Louisiana musicians with horns arranged by Zeno and Bill Samuel. *Blues Of The Month Club* is classic modern blues.

549 **Everybody Knows About My Good Thing**
Little Johnny Taylor
Mojo 2916-015 (UK)—*LP*
Baby Get Hip To Yourself/How Are You Fixed For Love/How Can A Broke Man Survive/Keep On Keeping On/Everybody Knows About My Good Thing Part 1/*Everybody Knows About My Good Thing* Part 2/*There's Something On Your Mind/You've Got The Love I Need/It's My Fault Darling/Make Love To Me Baby/Sweet Soul Woman*
Like many of his contemporaries, Taylor brought gospel music into blues combining a mellow voice with a fervor and intensity which echoed his teenage years with the Mighty Clouds of Joy. He hit the big time twice—on Galaxy with *Part Time Love* in 1963 (**479**) and on Ronn in 1971 with *Everybody Knows About My Good Thing,* included here.

550 **Different Shades Of Blue**
Artie Blues Boy White
Waldoxy WCD 2803
I'm Gonna Marry My Mother-In-Law/Hot Wired My Heart/There's Nothing I Wouldn't Do/When You Took Your Love From Me/Willie Mae Don't Play/I've Been Shackin'/Did Alright By Myself/Ain't Nothing You Can Do/I'd Rather Be Blind, Crippled and Crazy/All In The Open Now
Often producing and arranging his own records, White is an experienced modern blues singer. This disc, produced by Tommy Couch Jr and Paul 'Heavy' Lee, with horn arrangements by Charles Rose, contains straight blues

and bluesy Southern soul. Malaco writers, singers, and instrumentalists provide the setting and support for a fine, underrated blues singer.

551 **Ambition**
Larry McCray
Virgin 86178-2/Pointblank VPBCD 1 (UK)
Ambition/Count On Me For Love/Me And My Baby/One More Lonely Night/ Frustrated Baby/Keep On Walking/Sally's Got A Friend In New York City/I Don't Mind/Nobody Never Hurt Nobody With The Blues/Country Girl/Secret Lover/The Sun Rises In The East
Coming like a whirlwind out of Detroit, McCray made his recording début with this CD in 1990, kicking hard against the boundaries of the blues with vitality, directness, and honesty. Playing virtuoso guitar and with a voice as big as his physical stature, he generates high energy levels seldom heard. He produced this disc in his spare time while working at General Motors.

552 **Listen/I Don't Want To Be Alone, Stranger**
Johnny Guitar Watson
Ace CDCHD 408 (UK)
If I Had The Power/You've Got A Hard Head/Lovin' You/It's All About You/ You're The Sweetest Thing I've Ever Had/I Get A Feeling/Like I'm Not Your Man/You Bring Love/You Stole My Heart/I Don't Want To Be A Lone Ranger/ Your New Love Is A Player/Tripping/Lonely Man's Prayer/You Make My Heart Want To Sing/It's Way Too Late/Love Is Sweet Misery/You Can Stay But The Noise Must Go/Strong Vibrations
With a percussive blues/jazz guitar style, a distinctive voice, and arrangements and songs all his own, Johnny trod a lone path, adapting his music to fit the times. This CD contains his Fantasy albums of 1973 and 1975. The first is a cool, hip, understated set of songs with echoes of contemporary stylings. The second moves on to the disco floor but remains vintage.

553 **Beyond Cool**
Lucky Peterson
Verve 521 147-2 (UK)
I'm Talking To You/Count On Me/Compared To What/Up From The Skies/ Your Love Is Amazing/That's The Way It Ought To Be/Pouring Water On A Drowning Love Affair/Beyond Cool/You Haven't Done Nothin'/Your Good Thing Is About To Run Out/You Can't Fool Me/Drivin' Wheel
Peterson sings and plays keyboards and guitar. He made his first recording aged five and served his apprenticeship in the bands of Little Milton and Bobby Bland. Recorded locally with the Memphis Horns, in 1993 when he was in his late 20s, the sound is hard-edged and funky with a live feel. His varied influences are evident but he is never far from the blues.

554 **It's Party Time**
Ernie Johnson
Paula PCD 9004
It's Party Time/Honey I Love You/That Thang/Congratulations/Broke Man Can't Win/Dreams To Remember/Hard Times/Am I Losing You/Crying Out The Blues/Final Notice/I'm Doing Alright/Jesus Is A Way Maker

Stan Lewis continues his policy of promoting the latest and best. Drawing on gospel influences, Johnson's vocals recall Bobby Bland and fellow Dallas resident Z Z Hill. This thoroughly modern production reflects the programming abilities of Ernie's collaborator Naren Hingorain. As Ernie tells us on *Crying Out The Blues,* "I got the 1990 blues."

555 **Raw Blues**
Jessie Tolbert
Tolbert TOL 101—LP
Back Out In The Rain/Baby We Can't Get Married (But We Can Always Shack)/She Gave Me The Blues/Sold On You/Jessie's Rock/Partee/I've Got A Long Way To Go/No Snatching It Back
Substituting synthesizers for session musicians allows artists like Tolbert to produce their own material. Possessing a frail yet endearing voice, he extends traditional themes to new limits on this album (released in 1990, vinyl only). The jack-hammer snare and growling bass sounds on *Back Out In The Rain* make it one of the most stunning blues of the decade. The repertoire spans funk to sophisticated blues.

556 **Stickin' To My Guns**
Etta James
Island 842 926-2/Island CID 9955/IMCD 191 (UK)
Whatever Gets You Through The Night/Love To Burn/The Blues Don't Care/ Your Good Thing (Is About To End)/Get Funky/Beware/Out Of The Rain/ Stolen Affection/A Fool In Love/I've Got Dreams To Remember
Produced by Barry Beckett, Etta explores the full gamut of R&B. Supported by musicians from Nashville and Los Angeles, this session has an edge not found on her other recordings from the 1990s. Her voice has matured into a powerful and expressive instrument as she reworks classics such as *Beware* and new material such as her own *The Blues Don't Care.*

557 **Bad Influence**
The Robert Cray Band
Hightone HCD 8001/Mercury 830 245-2 (UK)
Phone Booth/Bad Influence/The Grinder/Got To Make A Comeback/So Many Women, So Little Time/Where Do I Go From Here/Waiting For The Tide To Turn/March On/Don't Touch Me/No Big Deal/Share What You Got, Keep What You Need/I Got Loaded
Cray's first production for Hightone (the second album in his career) has clarity and directness. Supervised by Bruce Bromberg and Dennis Walker, it defines the young singer-guitarist's light, soulful voice; and instantly recognizable guitar style; and his ability to write strong melodies.

558 **Funny Stuff**
Larry Davis
Rooster Blues R 2616 (UK)—*LP*
Funny Stuff/Teardrops/Next Time You See Me/Worried Dream/Totsy/Since I Been Loving You/That Will Never Do/Walk Out Like A Lady/Find 'Em, Fool 'Em & Forget 'Em/Got To Be Some Changes Made
After successful 45s for Duke in the 1950s, Davis recorded sporadically before

cutting this album in 1981. His startling voice and guitar combine with the understated playing of Johnnie Johnson on piano and drummer Billy Gayles. A refreshing set of modern blues, the innovative blues funk of Oliver Sain's *Funny Stuff* and *Since I Been Loving You* is particular interesting.

559 **It Don't Have To Be This Way**

R L Griffin

Black Grape BGCD 103 (UK)

There Is Something On Your Mind/I Don't Think I'm Gonna Make It/It Don't Have To Be This Way/Are You Lonely For Me Baby/I Smell Trouble/Baby Work Out/A Woman, A Lover, A Friend/Just The One I've Been Looking For/Bringing My Love Down/Cry Cry Cry/You Gotta Be Foolin' You/Heaven Help The Blind Man/I Wanna Be Rich/Can I Talk to You/Playin' Me Crazy/Just A Little Bit/Got To Go On

Griffin is proprietor of R L's Blues Palace in South Dallas. His admiration for Bobby Bland is readily apparent in recordings made between 1979 and 1992. Dubbed The "Right Reverend of the Blues" by a local DJ, his gospel blues styling is framed by a powerful band. Productions are by Al TNT Braggs, Andrew Jones, and himself. This is an excellent reflection of music enjoyed by regulars at his club.

560 **A Good Woman Is Hard To Find**

Percy Strother

Blue Moon Records BMR-012

A Good Woman Is Hard To Find/Your Fool Done Woke Up/If You Don't Love Me When I Want It, Somebody Else Will/I'm Falling In Love With You Baby/Someday I Will Be Over You/Will You Be My Part-Time Lady?/I Made A Good Woman Go Bad/Love Is Growing Cold/She Keeps Me Satisfied/Can't Let You Go

Mississippi born, Strother has a powerful voice and confident guitar style. Another asset is his songwriting; which shows him to be unafraid to step out of the usual blues or soul formats; his songs have strong melodies and relevant lyrics. Recorded in Minneapolis in 1992, this disc includes driving numbers built around strong guitar figures, slow blues and Southern soul.

Walter 'Wolfman' Washington plays in concert, London, 1996 (*Mick Huggins*)

List of Discs, Cassettes, and Long-Playing Records by Label

The numbers in bold refer to the discographical references in this *Guide*; the label numbers refer to CDs unless otherwise stated.

Texan pianist Katie Webster (*Brian Smith*)

Extra information for ordering Folkways and Library of Congress cassettes

Current Smithsonian-Folkways CDs and cassettes are available from usual suppliers. Those designated simply Folkways or RBF in this *Guide* are specially prepared from master tapes of former Folkways LPs and are available only from:

Smithsonian-Folkways Recordings
Office of Folklife Programs
955 l'Enfant Plaza, Suite 2600
Smithsonian Institution
Washington, DC 20560
USA

All Library of Congress long-playing records are out of print. Specially prepared cassettes of these LPs are available only from:

Moton Picture, Broadcasting and Recorded Sound Division
The Library of Congress
Washington, DC 20540
USA

We advise writing to the institution concerned before placing an order to ascertain availability and current price details.

Recommended Reading

The following list of books for further reading brings together the recommendations of the contributors to this volume. Where possible, books that are currently available have been cited, though in some instances they may be temporarily out of print. As the subjects covered by these works do not necessarily directly correspond with those of the chapter in this *Guide*, they have been grouped under more general headings. A fuller bibliography may be found in *The New Grove Gospel, Blues and Jazz* by Paul Oliver, Max Harrison, and William Bolcom (London: Macmillan, 1986), pp. 178–88.

Background

Epstein, Dena J., *Sinful Tunes and Spirituals: black folk music to the civil war* (Urbana: University of Illinois Press, 1977).

Jackson, Bruce, *Wake Up Dead Man: Afro-American worksongs from Texas prisons* (Cambridge, Mass.: Harvard University Press, 1972).

Levine, Lawrence, *Black Culture and Black Consciousness* (New York: Oxford University Press, 1977) [Cultural contexts of black song].

Lomax, Alan, *The Land Where the Blues Began* (London: Methuen, 1993) [Field recording in the South].

Nathan, Hans, *Dan Emmett and the Rise of Early Negro Minstrelsy* (Norman: University of Oklahoma Press, 1962).

Oliver, Paul, *Savannah Syncopators: African retentions in the blues* (London: Studio Vista, 1970).

—, *Songsters and Saints: vocal traditions on race records* (Cambridge, UK: Cambridge University Press, 1984).

Ramsey, Frederic, Jr, *Been Here and Gone* (New Brunswick: Rutgers University Press, 1960) [Black music in the Deep South in the 1950s].

Southern, Eileen, *The Music of Black Americans: a history*, (New York: W.W. Norton, 1971, 2nd edn, 1983).

General blues histories

Charters, Samuel B. *The Blues Makers* (New York: Da Capo, 1991).

Cohn, Lawrence (ed.). *Nothing But the Blues: the music and musicians* (New York and London: Abbeville Press, 1993).

Oakley, Giles, *The Devil's Music: a history of the blues* (London: British Broadcasting Corporation, 1976).

Oliver, Paul, *The Story of the Blues* (London: Barrie and Jenkins, 1969; Philadelphia: Chilton, 1970).

—, "Blues" in Paul Oliver, Max Harrison, and William Bolcom, *The New Groove Gospel, Blues and Jazz* (London: Macmillan, 1986), pp. 36–188.

Regional and other studies

Allen, Bob, *The Blackwell Guide to Recorded Country Music* (Oxford and Cambridge, Mass.: Blackwell Reference, 1994).

Bastin, Bruce, *Crying for the Carolines* (London: Studio Vista, 1971) [Blues in the eastern states].

—, *Red River Blues: the blues tradition in the Southeast* (Urbana: University of Illinois Press, 1986).

Broven, John, *South to Louisiana: the music of the Cajun bayous* (Gretna, LA: Pelican, 1988).

—, *Walking to New Orleans: the story of New Orleans rhythm and blues* (Bexhill-on-Sea: Blues Unlimited, 1974; republished as *Rhythm & Blues in New Orleans*, 1978).

Demetre, Jacques, and Marcel Chauvard, *Voyage au Pays du Blues/Land of the Blues*) (Paris: CLARB, 25 rue Trezel, 92300 Levallois-Perrett, 1994) [1959 blues research trip. French and English text].

Evans, David, *Big Road Blues: tradition and creativity in the folk blues* (Berkeley: University of California Press, 1982) [Mississippi and the life and influence of Tommy Johnson].

Ferris, William, *Blues From the Delta* (Garden City, NY: Doubleday, 1978) [Blues performance in the field].

George, Nelson, *The Death of Rhythm and Blues* (New York: Pantheon, 1988).

Govenar, Alan, *Meeting the blues* (Dallas: Taylor Publishing Company, 1985) [Outline of blues in Texas].

Groom, Bob, *The Blues Revival* (London: Studio Vista, 1971).

Hannusch, Jeff, *I Hear You Knockin': the sound of New Orleans rhythm and blues* (Ville Platte, LA: Swallow, 1985).

Haralambos, Michael, *Right On: from blues to soul in black America* (Ormskirk: Causeway Press, 1994).

Harrison, Daphne Duval, *Black Pearls: blues queens of the 1920s* (New Brunswick: Rutgers University Press, 1988) ["Classic" blues singers].

Olsson, Bengt, *Memphis Blues and Jug Bands* (London: Studio Vista, 1970).

Oster, Harry, *Living Country Blues* (Detroit: Folklore Associates, 1969) [Fieldwork in Louisiana].

Palmer, Robert, *Deep Blues* (New York: Viking, 1981) [Mississippi tradition].

Rowe, Mike, *Chicago Breakdown* (London: Eddison Press, 1973; retitled as *Chicago Blues: the city and the music,* New York: Da Capo, 1981) [Development of modern Chicago blues].

Russell, Tony, *Blacks, Whites and Blues* (London: Studio Vista, 1972) [cross-overs in the blues].

Tracy, Steven C., *Going to Cincinnati: a history of the blues in the Queen City* (Urbana: University of Illinois Press, 1993).

Shaw, Arnold, *Honkers and Shouters: the golden years of rhythm and blues* (New York: Macmillan, 1978).

Blues biographies

Albertson, Chris, *Bessie* (New York: Stein and Day, 1972) [Bessie Smith].

Bruynoghe, Yannick and Broonzy, Big Bill, *Big Bill Blues* (London: Cassell and Company, 1955) [Big Bill Broonzy's reminiscences].

Burton, Thomas G. (ed.), *Tom Ashley, Sam McGee, Bukka White* (Knoxville: University of Tennessee Press, 1981).
Calt, Stephen, *I'd Rather Be The Devil: the blues of Skip James* (New York: Da Capo, 1994)
Calt, Stephen, and Wardlow, Gayle, *King of the Delta Blues: the life and music of Charlie Patton* (New Jersey: Rock Chapel Press, 1988).
Chilton, John, *Let The Good Times Roll: the story of Louis Jordan and his music* (London: Quartet, 1992).
Collins, Tony, *Rock Mr. Blues: the life and music of Wynonie Harris* (Milford, NH, 1995).
Dance, Helen Oakley, *Stormy Monday: the T-Bone Walker story* (Baton Rouge: Louisiana State University Press, 1987).
Dixon, Willie, *I Am the Blues* (London: Quartet, 1989).
Evans, David, *Tommy Johnson* (London: Studio Vista, 1971).
Fahey, John, *Charley Patton* (London: Studio Vista, 1970).
Garon, Paul, *The Devil's Son-in-Law: the story of Peetie Wheatstraw and his songs* (London: Studio Vista, 1971).
Garon, Paul, and Garon, Beth, *Woman with Guitar: Memphis Minnie's blues* (New York: Da Capo, 1992) [In-depth study of her repertoire].
Greenberg, Alan, *Love in Vain: the life and legend of Robert Johnson* (Garden City, NY: Doubleday, 1983).
Guralnick, Peter, *Searching for Robert Johnson* (New York: E.P. Dutton, 1989).
Harris, Sheldon, *Blues Who's Who* (New Rochelle, NY: Arlington House, 1979).
Hodes, A., and Hansen, C. (eds.), *Selections from the Gutter: jazz portraits from "The Jazz Record"* (Berkeley, CA: University of California Press, 1977).
Joseph, Pleasant "Cousin Joe", and Ottenheimer, Harriet J., *Cousin Joe: blues from New Orleans* (Chicago: University of Chicago Press, 1987).
Lieb, Sandra, *Mother of the Blues: a study of Ma Rainey* (Amherst: University of Massachusetts, 1981).
Lipscomb, Mance, *I Say Me For a Parable: the oral autobiography of Mance Lipscomb, Texas bluesman,* ed. Glen Alyn (New York and London: W.W. Norton, 1993).
Otis, Johnny, *Upside Your Head!: rhythm and blues on Central Avenue* (Hanover: Wesleyan University Press, 1993).
Pearson, Barry Lee, *Virginia Piedmont Blues: the lives and art of two Virginia bluesmen* (Philadelphia: University of Pennsylvania Press, 1990) [Archie Edwards and John Cephas].
Sacre, Robert (ed.), *The Voice of the Delta* (Liège: Presses Universitaires de Liège, 1987) [Charley Patton].
Sawyer, Charles, *The Arrival of B.B. King* (New York: Doubleday, 1980).
Tilling, Robert (ed.), *"Oh What A Beautiful City": a tribute to Rev. Gary Davis 1896–1972* (Jersey, CI: Paul Mill Press, 1992).
Wolfe, Charles, and Lornell, Kip, *The Life and Legend of Leadbelly* (New York: Harper Collins, 1992).

Content and analysis

Garon, Paul, *Blues and the Poetic Spirit* (London: Eddison, 1975).
Keil, Charles, *Urban Blues* (Chicago: University of Chicago Press, 1966).
Lomax, Alan, *Hard Hitting Songs for Hard-Hit People* (New York: Oak Publications, 1967).

Macleod, R.R., *Yazoo 1–20; Yazoo 21–83; Document Blues—1; Document Blues—2* (Edinburgh: PAT Publications, 1988–1996) [Series of blues lyric transcriptions].
Oliver, Paul, *Blues Fell This Morning: the meaning of the blues* (London: Cassell and Company, 1960) (revised edition, Cambridge: Cambridge University Press, 1990).
—, *Screening the Blues: aspects of the blues tradition* (London: Cassell and Company, 1968; New York: Da Capo, 1988).
van Rijn, Guido, *Roosevelt's Blues: African-American blues and gospel artists on President Franklin D. Roosevelt* (Oxford: University of Mississippi Press, 1996).
Titon, Jeff Todd, *Early Downhome Blues: a musical and cultural analysis* (Urbana: University of Illinois Press, 1977); (reprinted, with afterword, Chapel Hill: University of North Carolina Press, 1994) [1925–30].

Discographies

Gart, Galen, and Ames, Roy C., *Duke-Peacock records: an illustrated history with discography* (Milford, NH: Big Nickel Publications, 1990).
Dixon, R.M.W., Godrich, John and Rye, Howard, *Blues and Gospel Records 1890–1943* (Oxford: Oxford University Press, 1996).
Hoffmann, Frank, and Albert, George, *The Cashbox Contemporary Album Charts 1975–1987* (Metuchen, NJ, and London: Scarecrow Press, 1989).
Leadbitter, Mike, and Slaven, Neil, *Blues Records, 1944–1970 Vol. One, A–K* (London: Record Information Services, 1987).
Leadbitter, Mike, Fancourt, Les, and Pelletier, Paul, *Blues Records 1943–1970 Vol. 2, L–Z.* (London, Record Information Services, 1995)
Whitburn, Joel, *Top R & B Singles 1942–1988* (Menomonee Falls: Record Research, 1988).

Journals

Blues magazines are published in many countries, including France, Finland, Germany, Italy, Japan, and Sweden. The following are among the best-known British and American journals:

Blues Access: Editor Gary Wolfson
Dept BRQ, 1514 North Street, Boulder, CO 80304-3514, USA [Contemporary blues news].
Blues and Rhythm: Editor Tony Burke
82 Quenby Way, Bromham, Bedfordshire, MK43 8QP, England [Monthly].
Blues Revue: Editor Bob Vorel
Rt 2, Box 118, West Union, WV 26456, USA [Quarterly, traditional blues].
Blue Suede News: Editor Marc Bristol
Box 25, Duvall, WA 98019, USA [Covers all 'roots' music].
Juke Blues: Editor Cilla Huggins
PO Box 148, London W9 1DY, England [Quarterly].
Living Blues: Editor Peter Lee
Center for the Study of Southern Culture, University, MS 38677, USA [Quarterly].
78 Quarterly: Editor/Publisher, Pete Whelan
P.O. Box 283, Key West, FL 33041, USA [Intermittent].

Canray Fontenot, Zydeco fiddle player (*Brian Smith*)

Index of Names

Note: numbers in **bold** refer to disc numbers, and are listed separately after the page numbers.

Johnny Heartsman, Alligator Recording artist (*Kent Lacin/Alligator/Juke Blues*)